Principles of
Accounting

THIRD EDITION

Vic D'Amico, BBA, MEd

Executive Director
NECTAR Foundation

Ted Palmer, HBA, MEd

Executive Director
Business Education Council
  of Niagara

**Tom D'Amico, BPE, BE,
MPE (admin)**

Principal–Continuing
  & Community Education
Ottawa Carleton Catholic
  School Board

PEARSON
Prentice
Hall

Toronto

The publisher has taken every care to meet or exceed industry specifications for the manufacturing of textbooks. The spine and the endpapers of this sewn book have been reinforced with special fabric for extra binding strength. The cover is a premium, polymer-reinforced material designed to provide long life and withstand rugged use. Mylar gloss lamination has been applied for further durability.

ISBN: 0-13-034090-1

Publisher Reid McAlpine
Editor Marg Bukta
Production Coordinator Helen Luxton, Sandra Magill
Cover Design Alex Li
Interior Design Dave Murphy/Artplus Limited
Page Layout Artplus Limited

Printed and bound in Canada

6 7 8 TCP 10 09 08

Disclaimer

An honest attempt has been made to secure permission for and acknowledge contributions of all material used. If there are errors or omissions, these are wholly unintentional and the publisher will be grateful to learn of them.

ACKNOWLEDGMENTS

To the many people who completed or participated in the review survey and focus groups for *Principles of Accounting, 3rd Edition*, the authors and publisher would like to extend their sincere appreciation.

REVIEWERS/CONSULTANTS

The authors and publisher would like to sincerely thank the following reviewers, content contributors, and consultants.

Patricia Gerard, Pitt Meadows Secondary School, Pitt Meadows, BC
Dale Green, John Fraser Secondary School, Mississauga, ON
Debbie Macdonald, Jarvis Collegiate Institute, Toronto, ON
Judith McCutcheon, Markville Secondary School, Markham, ON
Marlene Patterson, Centennial Secondary School, Belleville, ON
Bob Shurge, Bishop Redding High School, Milton, ON

Shahe Avedissian, Owner and President, Laurier Office-Mart Inc., Ottawa, ON
Sandie Bender, SANNE Educational Consulting, Nepean, ON
Beryl Bingham, Education Consultant, Winnipeg, MB
Scott Carmichael, Owner, A Cut Above Lawn Care, Brantford, ON
Chris Chapman, NECTAR Foundation, Ottawa, ON
Keith Corkam, D.E. Systems Ltd., Ottawa, ON
Margo Crawford, Director of Human Resources, Edgeflow, Stittsville, ON
David Galotta, Assistant Professor, Algoma University College, Sault Ste. Marie, ON
John Galotta, Pembina Resources, Wainwright, AB
Mary Galotta, Galco Holding Co., Fonthill, ON
Rob Hideg, Independent Contractor, Ottawa, ON
Marjorie Hutlet, Education Consultant, Winnipeg, MB
Martin Lavergne, Operations Manager, Canada Care Medical, Ottawa, ON
Jim Leclaire, Heron Road Canadian Tire Store, Ottawa, ON
Anne Marie Lever, Human Resources Adviser, Nortel Networks, Ottawa, ON
Brian Lever, Mother Teresa High School, Ottawa, ON
Ken MacEachern, Owner, Heron Road Canadian Tire Store, Ottawa, ON
Jim Moore, Manager, Scotiabank, Merivale Road, Ottawa, ON
Mary Lou Mulvey, CGA, Accountant, Greeley, ON
Elaine Pitcher, Lawyer, Sault Ste. Marie, ON
Liset Stanton, CA, Accounting Consultant, Ottawa, ON
Mark Thiessen, President, Growerflowers.com, Leamington, ON
Karen Power, CA, Canada Customs and Revenue Agency

Accounting Consultant: Jeff Buckstein, CGA, Kanata, ON

SPECIAL THANKS

The authors are especially grateful for the encouragement, friendship, assistance, and advice received from Marg Bukta, Reid McAlpine, Helen Luxton, Theresa Thomas, and Susan Cox, who have contributed so much in so many ways to this publication.

Finally, the authors would like to express their sincere appreciation for the encouragement, support, and understanding of their families.

TABLE OF CONTENTS

Welcome to Principles of Accounting, 3rd Edition!

Principles of Accounting, 3rd Edition, is written and structured so that you can study accounting with your teacher in a classroom setting or on your own as an independent learner. This introduction explains how the textbook chapters are organized and shows how they link to the student Study Guide and Working Papers.

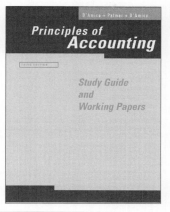

THE UNIT STRUCTURE

Each chapter is divided into units, which are numbered consecutively throughout the textbook.

At the beginning of each unit, the learning objectives are summarized under the heading **What Learning You Will Demonstrate**.

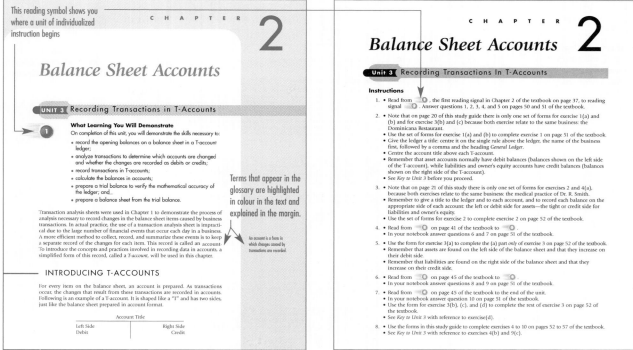

A unit will usually contain several reading symbols that break up units into lessons for independent learners. Those who wish to follow the individualized learning program are strongly advised to use the Study Guide and Working Papers designed specifically for *Principles of Accounting, 3rd Edition*.

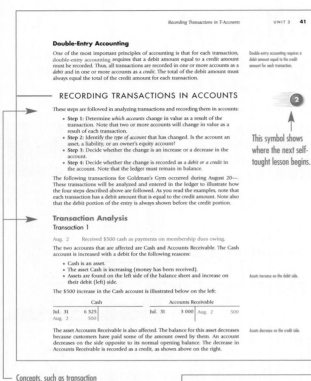

Double-Entry Accounting

One of the most important principles of accounting is that for each transaction, double-entry accounting requires that a debit amount equal to a credit amount must be recorded. Thus, all transactions are recorded in one or more accounts as a *debit* and in one or more accounts as a *credit*. The total of the debit amount must always equal the total of the credit amount for each transaction.

Double-entry accounting requires a debit amount equal to the credit amount for each transaction.

RECORDING TRANSACTIONS IN ACCOUNTS

These steps are followed in analyzing transactions and recording them in accounts:

• **Step 1:** Determine *which accounts* change in value as a result of the transaction. Note that two or more accounts will change in value as a result of each transaction.
• **Step 2:** Identify the *type of account* that has changed. Is the account an asset, a liability, or an owner's equity account?
• **Step 3:** Decide whether the change is an increase or a decrease in the account.
• **Step 4:** Decide whether the change is recorded as a *debit or a credit* in the account. Note that the ledger must remain in balance.

The following transactions for Goldman's Gym occurred during August 20—. These transactions will be analyzed and entered in the ledger to illustrate how the four steps described above are followed. As you read the examples, note that each transaction has a debit amount that is equal to the credit amount. Note also that the debit portion of the entry is always shown before the credit portion.

This symbol shows where the next self-taught lesson begins.

Transaction Analysis
Transaction 1

Aug. 2   Received $500 cash as payments on membership dues owing.

The two accounts that are affected are Cash and Accounts Receivable. The Cash account is increased with a debit for the following reasons:

• Cash is an asset.
• The asset Cash is increasing (money has been received).
• Assets are found on the left side of the balance sheet and increase on their debit (left) side.

Assets increase on the debit side.

The $500 increase in the Cash account is illustrated below on the left:

Cash		Accounts Receivable		
Jul. 31	6 325	Jul. 31	3 000	Aug. 2	500
Aug. 2	500			

The asset Accounts Receivable is also affected. The balance for this asset decreases because customers have paid some of the amount owed by them. An account decreases on the side opposite to its normal opening balance. The decrease in Accounts Receivable is recorded as a credit, as shown above on the right.

Assets decrease on the credit side.

Concepts, such as transaction analysis, are first described in general terms, then illustrated with easy-to-follow examples.

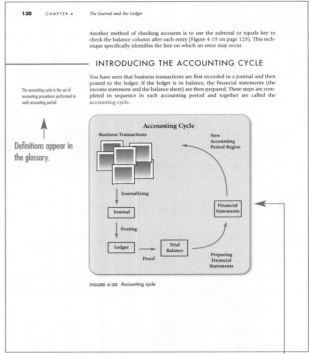

Another method of checking accounts is to use the subtotal or equals key to check the balance column after each entry (Figure 4-19 on page 129). This technique specifically identifies the line on which an error may occur.

INTRODUCING THE ACCOUNTING CYCLE

You have seen that business transactions are first recorded in a journal and then posted to the ledger. If the ledger is in balance, the financial statements (the income statement and the balance sheet) are then prepared. These steps are completed in sequence in each accounting period and together are called the accounting cycle.

The accounting cycle is the set of accounting procedures performed in each accounting period.

Definitions appear in the glossary.

FIGURE 4-20 Accounting cycle

Often, illustrations are used to visually reinforce and summarize the concepts learned in the text.

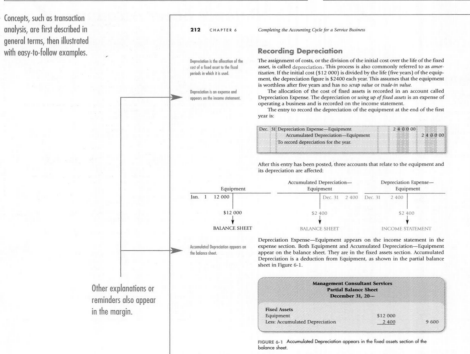

Recording Depreciation

Depreciation is the allocation of the cost of a fixed asset to the fiscal periods in which it is used.

The assignment of costs, or the division of the initial cost over the life of the fixed asset, is called depreciation. This process is also commonly referred to as *amortization*. If the initial cost ($12 000) is divided by the life (five years) of the equipment, the depreciation figure is $2400 each year. This assumes that the equipment is worthless after five years and has no *scrap value* or *trade-in value*.

Depreciation is an expense and appears on the income statement.

The allocation of the cost of fixed assets is recorded in an account called Depreciation Expense. The depreciation or *using up of fixed assets* is an expense of operating a business and is recorded on the income statement.

The entry to record the depreciation of the equipment at the end of the first year is:

Dec.	31	Depreciation Expense—Equipment	2 4 0 0 00	
		Accumulated Depreciation—Equipment		2 4 0 0 00
		To record depreciation for the year.		

After this entry has been posted, three accounts that relate to the equipment and its depreciation are affected:

Equipment		Accumulated Depreciation—Equipment		Depreciation Expense—Equipment	
Jan. 1	12 000		Dec. 31 2 400	Dec. 31 2 400	

$12 000 → BALANCE SHEET $2 400 → BALANCE SHEET $2 400 → INCOME STATEMENT

Accumulated Depreciation appears on the balance sheet.

Depreciation Expense—Equipment appears on the income statement in the expense section. Both Equipment and Accumulated Depreciation—Equipment appear on the balance sheet. They are in the fixed assets section. Accumulated Depreciation is a deduction from Equipment, as shown in the partial balance sheet in Figure 6-1.

Management Consultant Services
Partial Balance Sheet
December 31, 20—

Fixed Assets		
Equipment	$12 000	
Less: Accumulated Depreciation	2 400	9 600

FIGURE 6-1 Accumulated Depreciation appears in the fixed assets section of the balance sheet.

Other explanations or reminders also appear in the margin.

Each unit presents the theory to be covered, followed by review questions and practical exercises.

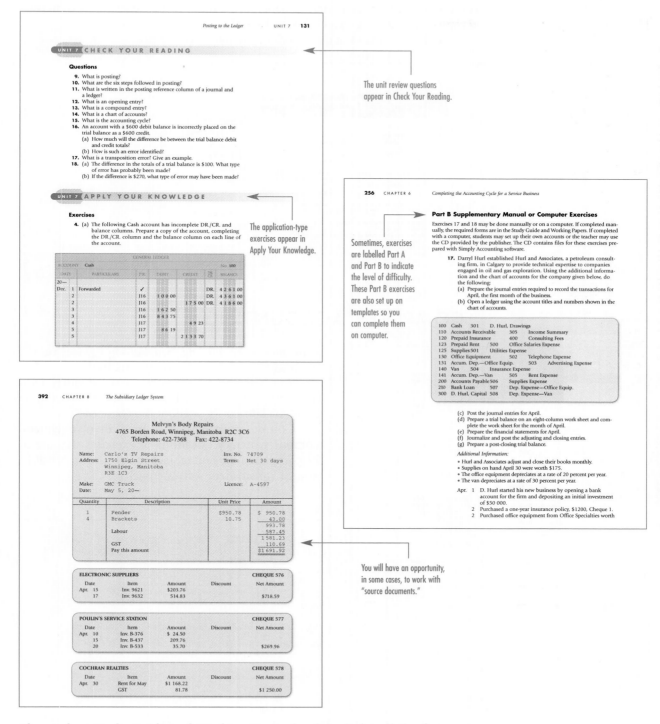

The unit review questions appear in Check Your Reading.

The application-type exercises appear in Apply Your Knowledge.

Sometimes, exercises are labelled Part A and Part B to indicate the level of difficulty. These Part B exercises are also set up on templates so you can complete them on computer.

You will have an opportunity, in some cases, to work with "source documents."

The student Study Guide and Working Papers book includes all the forms you need to complete these exercises in a single volume.

SUMMARY OF THEORY

The theory part of each chapter concludes with a useful chart titled **Generally Accepted Accounting Principles and Key Ideas**.

Use these charts for a quick review and reference.

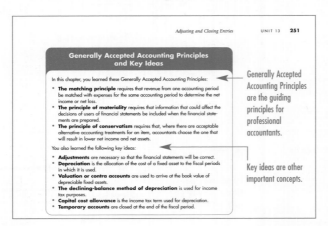

COMPUTER ACCOUNTING

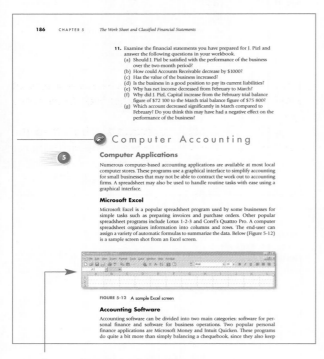

Principles of Accounting, 3rd Edition focuses on the computer as a principal accounting tool.

You will find descriptions of such widely used accounting software packages as Simply Accounting and QuickBooks throughout the textbook.

Computer assignments may involve general computer literacy questions or exercises that are to be completed on general ledger, accounts receivable, and/or spreadsheet software packages.

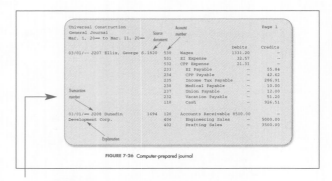

You see actual computer screens for many of the most popular accounting packages used by businesses today.

You see actual output from computer accounting software.

COMPUTER ASSIGNMENTS AND WEB EXTENSIONS

Exercise-type assignments that involve "doing" accounting are completed both manually and on the computer, so it is possible for you to compare the two methods.

All computer exercises can be completed on whatever software packages are available.

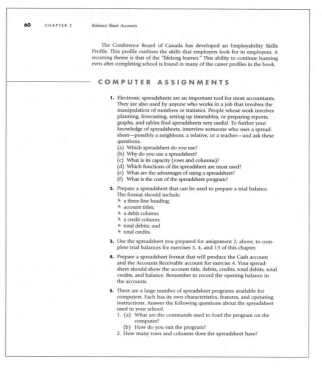

60   CHAPTER 2   *Balance Sheet Accounts*

The Conference Board of Canada has developed an Employability Skills Profile. This profile outlines the skills that employers look for in employees. A recurring theme is that of the "lifelong learner." This ability to continue learning even after completing school is found in many of the career profiles in the book.

COMPUTER ASSIGNMENTS

1. Electronic spreadsheets are an important tool for most accountants. They are also used by anyone who works in a job that involves the manipulation of numbers or statistics. People whose work involves planning, forecasting, setting up timetables, or preparing reports, graphs, and tables find spreadsheets very useful. To further your knowledge of spreadsheets, interview someone who uses a spreadsheet—possibly a neighbour, a relative, or a teacher—and ask these questions.
   (a) Which spreadsheet do you use?
   (b) Why do you use a spreadsheet?
   (c) What is its capacity (rows and columns)?
   (d) Which functions of the spreadsheet are most used?
   (e) What are the advantages of using a spreadsheet?
   (f) What is the cost of the spreadsheet program?

2. Prepare a spreadsheet that can be used to prepare a trial balance. The format should include:
   ▸ a three-line heading;
   ▸ account titles;
   ▸ a debit column;
   ▸ a credit column;
   ▸ total debits; and
   ▸ total credits.

3. Use the spreadsheet you prepared for assignment 2, above, to complete trial balances for exercises 3, 4, and 13 of this chapter.

4. Prepare a spreadsheet format that will produce the Cash account and the Accounts Receivable account for exercise 4. Your spreadsheet should show the account title, debits, credits, total debits, total credits, and balance. Remember to record the opening balance in the accounts.

5. There are a large number of spreadsheet programs available for computers. Each has its own characteristics, features, and operating instructions. Answer the following questions about the spreadsheet used in your school.
   1. (a) What are the commands used to load the program on the computer?
      (b) How do you exit the program?
   2. How many rows and columns does the spreadsheet have?

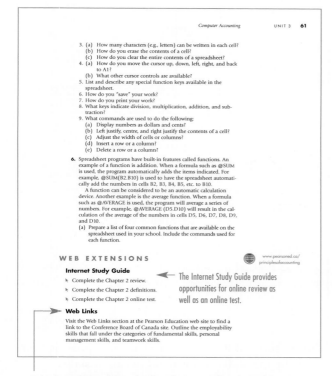

Computer Accounting   UNIT 3   **61**

3. (a) How many characters (e.g., letters) can be written in each cell?
   (b) How do you erase the contents of a cell?
   (c) How do you clear the entire contents of a spreadsheet?
4. (a) How do you move the cursor up, down, left, right, and back to A1?
   (b) What other cursor controls are available?
5. List and describe any special function keys available in the spreadsheet.
6. How do you "save" your work?
7. How do you print your work?
8. What keys indicate division, multiplication, addition, and subtraction?
9. What commands are used to do the following:
   (a) Display numbers as dollars and cents?
   (b) Left justify, centre, and right justify the contents of a cell?
   (c) Adjust the width of cells or columns?
   (d) Insert a row or a column?
   (e) Delete a row or a column?

6. Spreadsheet programs have built-in features called functions. An example of a function is addition. When a formula such as @SUM is used, the program automatically adds the items indicated. For example, @SUM(B2.B10) is used to have the spreadsheet automatically add the numbers in cells B2, B3, B4, B5, etc. to B10.
   A function can be considered to be an automatic calculation device. Another example is the average function. When a formula such as @AVERAGE is used, the program will average a series of numbers. For example, @AVERAGE (D5.D10) will result in the calculation of the average of the numbers in cells D5, D6, D7, D8, D9, and D10.
   (a) Prepare a list of four common functions that are available on the spreadsheet used in your school. Include the commands used for each function.

WEB EXTENSIONS   www.pearsoned.ca/ principlesofaccounting

Internet Study Guide   ◀—— The Internet Study Guide provides
▸ Complete the Chapter 2 review.   opportunities for online review as
▸ Complete the Chapter 2 definitions.   well as an online test.
▸ Complete the Chapter 2 online test.

Web Links
Visit the Web Links section at the Pearson Education web site to find a link to the Conference Board of Canada site. Outline the employability skills that fall under the categories of fundamental skills, personal management skills, and teamwork skills.

Web Links provides direct links to selected sites of interest to students of accounting.

The power of the Internet and its many sources of information are accessed through the **Web Extensions** in each chapter.

The **Web Extensions** activities are linked to the web site integrated with this text: www.pearsoned.ca/ principlesofaccounting

CASE STUDIES CAREER EDUCATION ACTIVITIES

Each chapter contains realistic **Case Studies** of both large and small companies. These will help you develop critical-thinking and decision-making skills.

You will be asked to apply the theory learned in each chapter and make judgments and decisions. You will have to determine a range of possible alternatives and decide which one best fits the situation at hand.

Case Studies can form the basis for vigorous class discussion, because often there is no one correct answer to a problem.

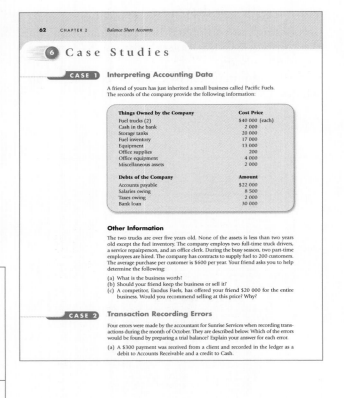

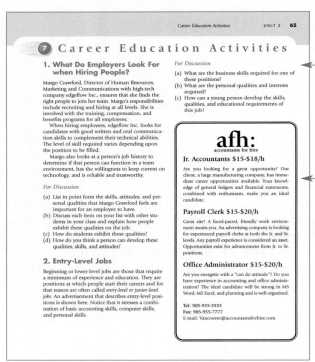

Advertisements that provide real-world information form the basis for thoughtful classroom discussions.

To be successful in a career, you must possess both specific job skills and general personal skills.

The **Career Education Activities** help you look at your interests, your aptitudes, and what is available to you in the way of future employment.

CAREER PROFILES

Career Profiles of people in accounting and other business careers provide realistic job descriptions and suggest possible career options.

Each profile outlines the education, experience, and personal requirements for a type of job.

Most people profiled have had a number of different jobs; some have even changed their careers dramatically.

For individuals who want to succeed, education is an ongoing process.

For Discussion allows you to exchange ideas on the reading with your classmates.

Career Profile

It has been said that education is lifelong—that we will continue to learn and be re-educated throughout our lives. This statement seems to apply to David Galotta, who has mixed permanent and part-time work with education programs since graduation from high school.

Dave grew up in Niagara Falls where he attended Niagara Falls Collegiate and Vocational Institute. While taking accounting courses at high school and working part-time in his family's business, Dave developed an interest in a business career. He enjoyed working at the Cascade Inn, a hotel operated by his parents in Niagara Falls. During the summers and on weekends, Dave worked in the hotel candy shop and pizza parlour, did routine maintenance work, was a bus boy, and worked as the desk clerk. After working as an assistant manager at the hotel for a short period of time, Dave left home to attend Queen's University.

The Bachelor of Commerce program at Queen's University was Dave's choice for professional training. Among the courses that Dave enjoyed at Queen's were accounting, marketing, industrial relations, computer studies, and law. During the summer, Dave had a variety of jobs, including a position as a marketing research assistant at the School of Business at Queen's.

After graduating from Queen's with an honours Bachelor of Commerce degree, Dave was hired as a management trainee by the Bank of Nova Scotia. His first position was at a Scotiabank in Kingston. After a year in the Kingston branch, Dave was transferred to Ottawa where he was promoted to the position of credit officer. Next came another promotion and a move to Nepean, Ontario, where Dave became an assistant manager at the Bell's Corners branch of the Scotiabank. Within a year, Dave was again promoted and moved to the Westboro Branch, where he became the assistant manager of commercial credit. In four years, Dave had worked in four different bank branches and received three promotions.

Dave's experience in the family business, in the banking system, and in the Bachelor of Commerce program at Queen's University convinced him that he would like to pursue a career in finance in a large corporation. Having set this as his long-term goal, he decided that additional education was required. He considered two educational programs: a master's degree in business administration and the chartered accountant designation. He decided to return to Queen's University and to enrol in the Master of Business Administration (M.B.A.) program.

The M.B.A. program at Queen's is a demanding two-year course. Entrance requirements include an honours degree with good marks, suitable work experience, and acceptable marks on the GMAT. The GMAT—Graduate Management Admission Test—is widely used as an entry requirement to post-graduate business programs.

Dave met the entrance requirements and returned to Queen's University. Because of his practical experience, he could see the relevance of the material he was studying and was able to understand the theory being taught. He completed the two-year M.B.A. program and obtained a Master of Business Administration degree from Queen's.

Dave was successful in obtaining a position with the Bank of Nova Scotia, finance division, in the bank's corporate headquarters in Toronto. His job title was Financial Analyst and the position involved studying the advantages, disadvantages, costs, and benefits of purchasing buildings and

---

equipment for the bank. After working for the Bank of Nova Scotia for three years, Dave moved to Sault Ste. Marie where he married.

Dave is now an Assistant Professor in the Department of Administration at Algoma University College. He teaches finance and administration courses and is the Head of the Department.

Dave has been very systematic in planning his career. He has developed short- and long-term goals, obtained work experience in his chosen fields, and obtained the education required for a career in finance. He has worked very hard but finds time to enjoy life as well. He has travelled widely in North America and Europe. He relaxes by enjoying tennis, golf, cooking, and skiing, and by spending time at two other hobbies, photography and genealogy.

Dave's career profile illustrates several points:
- the need to set short- and long-term goals;
- the value of work experience in helping to make career decisions;
- the fact that formal education does not necessarily end with a high school diploma or university degree; and
- the fact that it may be necessary to relocate a number of times during a business career.

For Discussion

(a) Have you set both short- and long-term goals for yourself?
(b) What are your short-term goals?
(c) What are your long-term goals?
(d) Are you learning about your interests and abilities through part-time work experience programs?
(e) Would you be willing to move and relocate yourself and your family for career reasons?

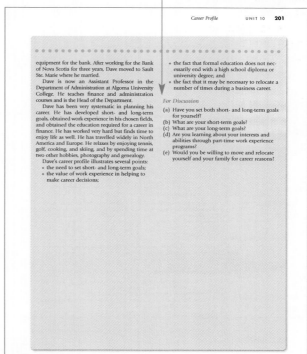

PERFORMANCE TASKS

Performance Tasks appear after Chapters 5, 6, 10, 11, 12, 13, and 14. They have been provided to reinforce your knowledge of the accounting process. The tasks sometimes require both group and individual work, and they encourage the development of organizational skills, leadership qualities, and social interaction skills.

As is the case with the units, each performance task begins with **What Learning You Will Demonstrate**, a list of expectations applicable to the material at hand.

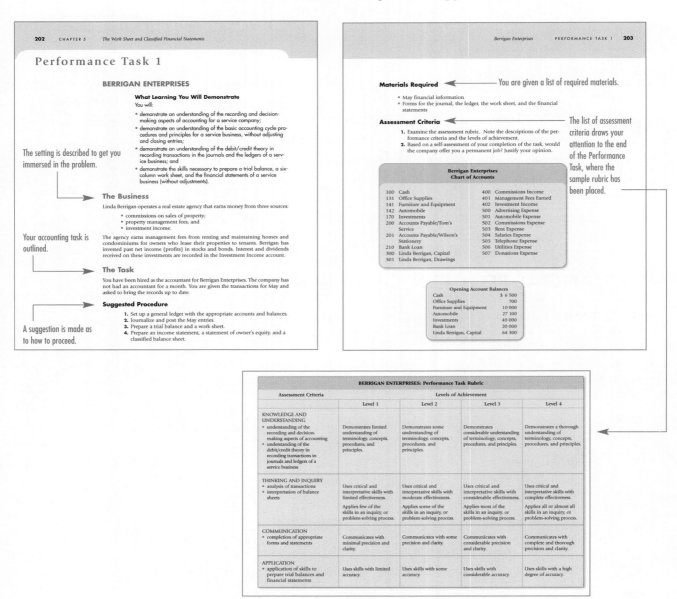

Each **Performance Task** is accompanied by a sample **Rubric** to make you aware of relevant assessment criteria before you begin work.

The Balance Sheet

UNIT 1 Financial Position

What Learning You Will Demonstrate

On completion of this unit, you will demonstrate the skills necessary to:

- determine the financial position of a business;
- classify items as assets, liabilities, or owner's equity;
- calculate owner's equity;
- prepare a balance sheet; and
- use correct recording procedures.

FINANCIAL POSITION OF AN INDIVIDUAL

Anna Szabo is an assistant manager in a community branch of the Regional Bank of Canada. As part of her duties, she authorizes loans to individuals and to businesses that wish to borrow money.

Recently, Lara Chari visited Anna to apply for a loan. Lara is a graduate of her local college's horticulture program and has been working for a landscaper for the past year.

Lara has the entrepreneurial spirit—that is, she would like to own and operate a business. Although quite young, Lara feels that her college training, combined with the practical experience gained over the past year, will enable her to successfully start her own landscaping business.

Lara needs $10 000 to start the business and is applying to Anna's bank for a loan. In deciding whether to grant a loan, Anna needs to examine the financial position of the applicant. This is what she does. First, she lists the items owned by Lara:

Items Owned by Lara Chari	
Cash	$ 4 000
Government Bonds	5 000
Clothing	3 000
Furniture	15 000
Equipment	10 000
Automobile	20 000
	$57 000

A creditor is a person or business that has extended credit or loaned money.

Next, Anna lists what Lara owes to creditors. Creditors are people or businesses that extended credit when goods or services were purchased or who loaned money used to purchase possessions. These creditors must be paid before an individual has complete title to his or her possessions.

Debts Owed to Creditors by Lara Chari	
Credit Card Debt	$ 2 000
Bank Loan	10 000
	$12 000

Now Anna determines Lara's financial position.

Calculation of Financial Position

Lara's financial position is determined by making the following calculation:

Total Value of Items Owned		Total Owed to Creditors		Personal Net Worth
	−		=	
$57 000	−	$12 000	=	$45 000

By calculating the cost of the items owned by an individual and subtracting the debts owed, it is possible to determine someone's personal net worth at any given time. The net worth represents the difference between the total cost of items owned and the debts owed. Thus, Anna has determined that Lara Chari's net worth is $45 000.

> Personal net worth is the difference between the cost of items owned and the debts owed.

Accounting Terminology

The subject *accounting* is often called *the language of business*. An understanding of accounting terminology will help you in both your personal life and in your business career. Starting with the items owned by Lara, let's translate Lara's financial position into the language of accounting.

Assets

In accounting, items of value owned by a business or a person are called assets. The total cost of Lara's assets is $57 000. Now let's look at the accounting terminology for debts.

> Assets are items of value owned by a business or a person.

Liabilities

Debts or amounts owed to others by a business or a person are called liabilities. Lara's liabilities total $12 000. The last part of determining the financial position is the net worth.

> Liabilities are the debts of a business or a person.

Personal Equity

Personal equity is a term that represents a person's net worth. Lara's personal equity or net worth is $45 000. Because there is a substantial difference between Lara's assets and liabilities, the bank gave her the loan. Lara's very positive net worth indicated to the bank that she would be able to repay the loan.

> Personal equity is a person's net worth.

Balance Sheet Equation

The financial position of a person or a business can be stated in the form of an equation called the balance sheet equation, as follows:

> The balance sheet equation is the basic equation that underlies double-entry accounting.
> $A = L + OE$

$$\text{Assets} \quad = \quad \text{Liabilities} \quad + \quad \text{Owner's Equity}$$

In Lara's case, the balance sheet equation is:

	$57 000	=	$12 000 + $45 000
or	$57 000	=	$57 000

This fundamental balance sheet equation is the basic equation underlying double-entry accounting and is the basis for much of the accounting theory you will learn.

Balance Sheet

Lara's financial position is illustrated in Figure 1-1 in the form of a balance sheet. This is a financial statement that lists her assets, liabilities, and personal equity (net worth) at a specific date.

Lara Chari
Personal Balance Sheet
September 30, 20—

Assets		Liabilities	
Cash	$ 4 000	Credit Card Debt	$ 2 000
Government Bonds	5 000	Bank Loan	10 000
Clothing	3 000	Total Liabilities	12 000
Furniture	15 000		
Equipment	10 000	**Personal Equity**	
Automobile	20 000	L. Chari, Net Worth	45 000
		Total Liabilities	
Total Assets	$57 000	and Personal Equity	$57 000

FIGURE 1-1 Personal balance sheet

FINANCIAL POSITION OF A BUSINESS

The financial position of a business is determined in the same way as that described for Lara Chari. In the next few pages, we will examine the financial position and the balance sheet for a small business. Goldman's Gym will be used in this text to demonstrate a variety of accounting procedures. We will follow this business from its formation through its first year of operation, thereby having an opportunity to examine both accounting and non-accounting procedures, problems, and decision making faced by all business proprietors.

Background Information

Rick Millar and his family opened Goldman's Gym in St. Catharines, Ontario. Many factors influenced Rick's decision to become an entrepreneur and open his own business.

Rick's background and continued interest in athletics, combined with his formal education, provided the expertise necessary to operate this type of business. His athletic background included playing tennis on the Windsor Junior Tennis Team and racquet ball for the Windsor A Team. Rick capitalized on his interest in athletics by completing a degree in physical education with a minor in business.

Rick felt his unique background and interests, combined with a capacity for hard work and a desire to succeed, qualified him to become a successful entrepreneur. He decided to investigate the potential in the Niagara Region for opening a gym for men and women of all ages. Through his tennis playing, he had become familiar with Goldman's Gym, a chain that had started in California and spread across the United States and Europe, but had only begun to enter the Canadian market. Rick felt the use of the Goldman's name and promotional material would assist him in building a clientele for his gym, so he applied to become a licensee. A licensee pays a monthly rate to Goldman's Gyms International for the use of Goldman's name in a particular region of the country but operates the business as his or her own. Because of Rick's background, he was approved as the licensee for the Niagara Region.

As with any business, starting this business required the owner to take risks in the hope of being successful. Rick collected all of his available cash and applied for a loan and mortgage from the bank to start his gym.

Introducing Accounting

The Millar family had to make many decisions in developing their gym into a successful business. A method of keeping accurate records was needed to provide the information required to make these decisions. This fact serves to introduce the subject of accounting.

Purpose of Accounting

The *purpose of accounting* is to provide financial information for decision making. To fill this need, a professional accounting firm was hired to develop an accounting system for Goldman's. An accounting system involves an organized method of recording and reporting financial data. Every accounting system must:

The purpose of accounting is to provide financial information for decision making.

- record the day-to-day financial activities of the business; and
- summarize and report information in financial statements for analysis and decision making.

Business Entity Principle

In this chapter, the study of accounting will begin with a look at the balance sheet, which is one of the financial statements for Goldman's Gym. It should be pointed out at this time that to prepare accurate financial statements, the financial data for the business must be kept *separate* from Rick's personal financial data. Furthermore, each business should be considered as a separate unit or *entity* for the purpose of keeping accounting records. This is known as the business entity principle.

The business entity principle requires that each business be considered a separate entity, and that the financial data for the business be kept separate from the owner's personal financial data.

COMPANY BALANCE SHEET

A balance sheet is a financial statement that lists the assets, liabilities, and owner's equity at a specific date.

Owner's equity is the owner's claim against the assets of the company.

The financial position of Goldman's Gym on June 30th is shown in Figure 1-2, a balance sheet. As with the personal balance sheet for Lara Chari, the company's balance sheet is a formal report or statement that shows the financial position of the business at a certain date. It lists assets, liabilities, and owner's equity, which is an accounting term for the owner's claim against the assets of the company.

Goldman's Gym
Balance Sheet
June 30, 20—

Assets		Liabilities	
Cash	$ 5 000	Accounts Payable	$ 4 000
Accounts Receivable	6 000	Bank Loan	65 000
Office Supplies	500	Mortgage Payable	80 000
Land	25 000	Total Liabilities	149 000
Building	110 000		
Training Equipment	94 500	**Owner's Equity**	
		R. Millar, Capital	92 000
		Total Liabilities	
Total Assets	$241 000	and Owner's Equity	$241 000

FIGURE 1-2 Company balance sheet

The company's financial position can also be described in terms of the balance sheet equation, as follows:

	Assets	=	Liabilities	+	Owner's Equity
	$241 000	=	$149 000	+	$92 000
or					
	$241 000	=	$241 000		

In this equation, the two sides balance. The left side ($241 000) equals the right side ($241 000).

Notice that the balance sheet also balances. The total of the left side equals the total of the right side. This is why it is called a *balance sheet*. Notice also that accounting terminology is used for all of the items on the balance sheet. The amount owed by customers for memberships, $6000, is called *Accounts Receivable*. The amount owed as debts to creditors, $4000, is called *Accounts Payable*. The loan (mortgage) owed on the building, $80 000, is called *Mortgage Payable*.

Balance Sheet Preparation

The opening balance sheet for Goldman's Gym will be used as an example to discuss the correct format and procedures to follow when you prepare a balance sheet. This is a *formal report,* since it is prepared according to a specific set of rules outlined in the following steps.

Step 1: Prepare Statement Heading

The three-line heading is centred at the top of the page and is designed to provide information in this sequence:

Line 1: Who?	—	Goldman's Gym	—	business name
Line 2: What?	—	Balance Sheet	—	statement name
Line 3: When?	—	June 30, 20—	—	statement date

Step 2: List Assets

The assets are listed on the left side of the page. Before the assets are totalled, the liabilities must be listed and totalled. Then, if required, the necessary number of blank lines must be inserted before the owner's equity section or before the assets total so that the final totals on both sides of the statement will be on the same line.

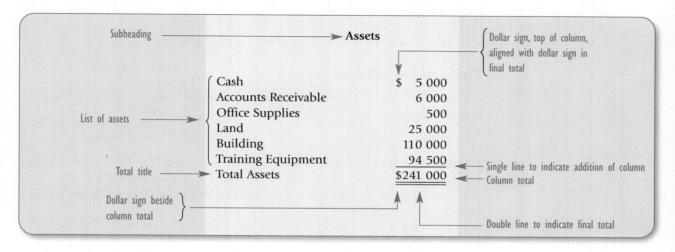

Step 3: List Liabilities

The liabilities are listed and totalled on the right side of the page:

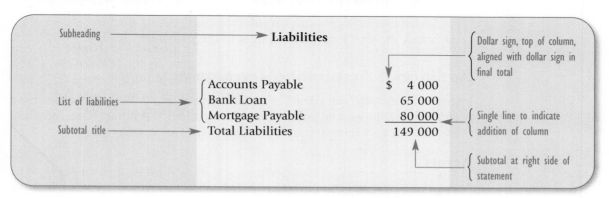

Step 4: Show Owner's Equity

The owner's equity section, showing the owner's investment, is also on the right side of the page after the liabilities section. As explained previously, the final totals of both the left and right sides must be on the same line. This allows for a more attractive presentation of the information and emphasizes the fact that the left side of the balance sheet equals the right side, that is, $A = L + OE$.

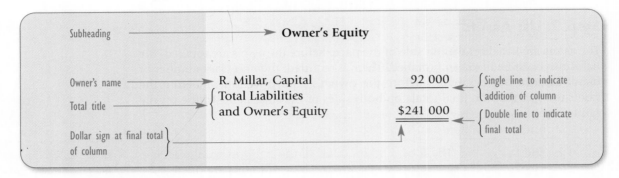

Facts to Remember

The total assets and the total liabilities and owner's equity are written on the same line:

Total Assets $ 241 000	Total Liabilities and Owner's Equity $ 241 000

The appearance of the balance sheet is very important, since the statement may be viewed by a variety of people inside and outside the business. Statements such as this create an impression regarding the business and should be prepared as attractively and accurately as possible. In addition to the specifications for balance sheet preparation given in the examples, the following requirements should be considered:

1. No abbreviations should be used in the statement.
2. The statement should contain no corrections.
3. Dollar signs should be aligned with one another and placed as follows:

- beside the first figure in each column; and
- beside the *final* total on both sides of the statement.

Additional Accounting Terminology

Earlier in the chapter, you started to build your accounting vocabulary by learning what assets, liabilities, and equity were. Here is additional information regarding these terms as they relate to the balance sheet for Goldman's Gym.

Assets

Assets are resources or items of value owned by a business. They include the following:

- **Cash:** Currency (bills and coins), bank deposits, cheques, money orders, and credit card receipts.

- **Accounts Receivable:** The total amount due from debtors (customers). Debtors are persons or businesses that owe a business money as a result of purchasing goods or services on credit. The amount is often due within 30 days.
- **Office Supplies:** Items purchased for use within the business office.

Liabilities

Liabilities are the debts of the business. The creditors who are owed these amounts are said to have a claim against the assets of the business. This claim by the creditors is the right to be paid the amount owed to them before the owner of the business can benefit from the sale of assets. For example, Goldman's Gym lists a building bought at $110 000 as an asset. A mortgage is included in the liabilities at $80 000. If the building were sold, the creditor would have to be paid in full before the owner could obtain the balance.

Liabilities include items such as:

- **Accounts Payable:** The total amount owed to the creditors for the purchase of goods or services by the business. These amounts are often due in 30 days.
- **Bank Loan:** The amount of loans owing to the bank. These loans vary in length of time (typically 1–5 years for most loans). Some bank loans are "demand" loans and are due whenever payment is demanded by the bank.
- **Mortgage Payable:** The amount borrowed from financial institutions, usually to purchase buildings or land. The lender has the right to obtain control of the property in the event that the borrower fails to repay the debt. Since this liability is normally large in amount, the time to repay is longer than for other liabilities (many, for example, run 25 years).

Equities

The assets are listed on the left side of the balance sheet. On the right side are the *claims against the assets, called* equities.

The *liabilities* section lists the claims of the creditors. The *owner's equity* section lists the owner's claim to the remaining value, or net value, of the company's assets after deducting the liabilities. The owner's claim is what the company is "worth to the owner," or the net worth. It is listed on the balance sheet using the word "Capital" beside the owner's name (see *R. Millar, Capital* on page 6). The owner's equity is the difference between the assets and the liabilities ($OE = A - L$).

Order of Items on the Balance Sheet

Generally, assets and liabilities are listed on the balance sheet in a particular order.

Assets

There are two types of assets: those that last a long time and those that last a short time. Assets that *last a short time* are listed in order of their liquidity. The liquidity order is the order in which the assets would likely be converted to cash. Using the balance sheet for Goldman's Gym as an example, the liquidity order

Accounts receivable refers to the total amount due from debtors (customers).

Accounts payable refers to the total amount owed to creditors for the purchase of goods or services by the business.

Equities are claims against the assets of a company.

Liquidity order is the order in which assets would likely be converted to cash.

would be Cash, Accounts Receivable, and Office Supplies. Next come assets that *last a long time* and are used for a long time to operate the business. Examples include Land, Building, and Training Equipment. They are listed in order of their useful life to the business, with the longest lasting listed first.

Order of Assets		Reasons
Cash	$ 5 000	Most liquid asset
Accounts Receivable	6 000	Received within 30 days
Office Supplies	500	May be easily converted to cash
Land	25 000	Assets listed in order of length of
Building	110 000	useful life in the business; longest
Training Equipment	94 500	life listed first and shortest life last

Liabilities

Liabilities are listed according to when they must be paid in full, from shortest to longest term. The payment due date is known as the maturity date.

Liabilities are listed according to the date they are due to be paid, that is, their maturity date.

Order of Liabilities		Reasons
Accounts Payable	$ 4 000	Payable within 30 days
Bank Loan	65 000	Payable usually within 1–5 years
Mortgage Payable	80 000	Payable within 25 years

Valuation of Items on the Balance Sheet

All of the items on the balance sheet have a dollar value. There are accounting rules that govern the methods used to assign dollar values. One of them is the cost principle.

Cost Principle

Assets are shown on the balance sheet at the cost of their acquisition or construction.

Assets are valued according to the cost principle. When an asset is obtained, its value is recorded at the actual cost to the business. This figure is *never* increased even though the owner might think that the value of the asset has risen.

Users of the Balance Sheet

A number of people and organizations could be interested in the financial position of a business. The following chart provides a brief introduction to the users of a balance sheet and indicates reasons for their interest. When you consider the potential number of users of this financial information and the importance of the decisions they make, it is easy to see why it is essential to use the most objective, accurate data available in preparing the balance sheet.

Users	Reasons for Interest in Balance Sheet
Owner	The balance sheet indicates the owner's claim on the business assets. Comparing balance sheets at different points in time will show whether or not the financial position is improving.
Creditors	Companies that consider extending credit or lending money are interested in the liquid assets available to meet payments as well as the claims on assets.
Investors	The financial position of a business is one of the factors investors consider when deciding whether or not to invest in a business. They want to protect their investment and are interested in much the same information as are creditors.
Government	Government departments need information for policy decision making, statistical reports, and taxation.

COMMON RECORDING PRACTICES

There are several common recording practices followed by most accountants. They are described and illustrated below:

1. When ruled accounting paper is used, dollar signs, commas, spaces, and decimals are not used.
2. A single line indicates addition or subtraction.
3. A double line indicates final totals.

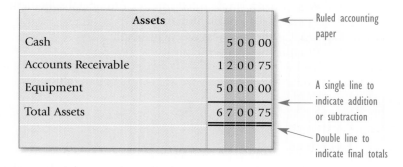

Assets	
Cash	5 0 0 00
Accounts Receivable	1 2 0 0 75
Equipment	5 0 0 0 00
Total Assets	6 7 0 0 75

Ruled accounting paper

A single line to indicate addition or subtraction

Double line to indicate final totals

4. When ruled accounting forms are not used, dollar signs, spaces or commas, and decimals are used.
5. Dollar signs are placed in alignment before the first figure in a column and beside final column totals when accounting forms are not used.

Assets	
Cash	$ 500.00
Accounts Receivable	1 200.75
Equipment	5 000.00
Total Assets	$6 700.75

6. Abbreviations are not used on financial statements unless the official name of the company contains an abbreviation. For example, Lumonics Inc. does contain a short form (Inc.) in its official name and should be written as *Lumonics Inc*. Goldcorp Investments Limited should *not* be written in short form since the company uses *Limited*, not Ltd., as part of its official name.

7. Accounting records must be neat and legible. They are used by many people and are kept for a long period of time. They are either printed, keyed, or written in ink. Care must be taken to write numbers and words clearly and legibly.

UNIT 1 CHECK YOUR READING

Questions

1. What is meant by *financial position*?
2. Define *asset* and give an example.
3. (a) Define *liability* and give an example.
(b) Define *owner's equity*.
4. What is the balance sheet equation?
5. What is a balance sheet?
6. Why did Rick Millar decide to go into business for himself? What risks did he take?
7. How is the owner's equity calculated?
8. In what order are assets listed on the balance sheet?
9. In what order are liabilities listed on the balance sheet?
10. What does a single ruled line on a financial statement indicate? What does a double line mean?
11. What is the business entity principle?
12. What is the cost principle?

UNIT 1 APPLY YOUR KNOWLEDGE

Exercises

1. Diane Kirchner is a student at Glendale Secondary School. She works part-time as a secretary at a local real estate office. The following is a list of items Diane has prepared to calculate her personal financial position on April 30, 20—.

Cash in Bank	$ 200
Portable Stereo System	300
Clothes	2 000
Tape Collection	230
Jewellery	500
Loan from Father for Stereo	200

(a) Determine Diane's financial position by calculating her net worth.

(b) Determine your own net worth.

2. Complete the following equations in your study guide or notebook.

A =	L +	OE
$ 75 000	$25 000	$50 000
?	80 000	45 000
110 000	49 000	?
50 000	40 000	?
80 000	49 000	?

3. Classify the following items as assets, liabilities, or owner's equity.

Cash
Bank Loan
Equipment
Land
Mortgage
Furniture
Owner's Investment in the Business

4. The balance sheet items for Crispo Company are listed in random order below.

(a) Prepare lists of the assets, the liabilities, and the owner's equity.

(b) Complete the balance sheet equation for Crispo Company in your study guide or notebook, following the format shown below.

Assets $_____ = Liabilities $_____ + Owner's Equity $_____

Cash	$11 500
Building	60 000
Land	35 000
Bank Loan	9 500
Mortgage	40 000
Equipment	20 000
J. Crispo, Capital	77 000

5. Prepare balance sheets using the format in Figure 1-1 (page 4) and Figure 1-2 (page 6) for the following:

(a) Diane Kirchner (refer to exercise 1)

(b) Crispo Company (refer to exercise 4)

6. The balance sheet items for Chihaya Real Estate are listed below. Prepare a balance sheet dated September 15, 20—.

Cash	$ 2 500
Accounts Receivable	?
Office Equipment	5 000
Bank Loan	3 500
Accounts Payable	2 000
Building	55 000
M. Chihaya, Capital	45 000
Land	25 000
Mortgage Payable	40 000
Supplies	600

7. The assets and liabilities of Doreen Simpson, a lawyer, on March 31, 20—, are as follows:

Cash	$11 000
Due from Clients	28 000
Office Supplies	1 700
Office Equipment	19 000
Bank Loan	7 500
Owed to Creditors	5 000

(a) Classify each item as an asset or a liability.
(b) Calculate Doreen's equity.
(c) Prepare a balance sheet.

8. Chez Moi is a restaurant owned by Michel Artois. The restaurant's assets and liabilities on September 30, 20—, are as follows:

Cash	$ 17 000
Food Supplies	3 000
Restaurant Supplies	4 000
Equipment and Fixtures	50 000
Land and Building	190 000
Payable to Suppliers	12 000
Mortgage Payable	85 000
Bank Loan	20 000

(a) Calculate Michel's equity.
(b) Prepare a balance sheet.

UNIT 2 Business Transactions

3

What Learning You Will Demonstrate

On completion of this unit, you will demonstrate the skills necessary to:

- record transactions that affect assets, liabilities, and owner's equity on a transaction analysis sheet;
- prove the mathematical accuracy of a transaction analysis sheet; and
- prepare a balance sheet from a completed transaction analysis sheet.

The balance sheet for Goldman's Gym was prepared on June 30, 20—. Events will occur in the business after this date and will change the value of the balance sheet items. For example, customers will pay the remainder owing on their memberships, equipment will be purchased for the business, and payments will be made to creditors. All of these events are examples of transactions.

INTRODUCING TRANSACTIONS

A *transaction* is an event that occurs during the operation of a business and results in a financial change. A **business transaction** always is an exchange of things of value.

A business transaction is an exchange of things of value.

Transaction

Something of value   Something of value
is given.   is received.

The balance sheet provides a detailed picture of the financial position of a business on a certain date. This same information is presented in summary form by the balance sheet equation:

Assets   =   Liabilities   +   Owner's Equity

A *transaction analysis sheet* will be used to assist in the examination of transactions and their effects on the balance sheet. This places the balance sheet items in equation form to more easily examine the effect of transactions on these items as well as on the balance sheet equation. Transaction analysis sheets are not used in business, but the technique of analysis developed by their use will be helpful throughout your career.

A number of common transactions will be analyzed and recorded for Goldman's Gym. This example will begin with the information found on the June 30, 20—, balance sheet; it will analyze and record a series of sample transactions for one month; and it will conclude with the preparation of a new balance sheet at the end of this accounting period. The term **accounting period** refers to the length of time between the preparation of financial reports. This period can vary, often from one month to one year, depending on many factors such as business size and current need for the data contained in the reports.

The accounting period is the period of time covered by financial statements.

USING A TRANSACTION ANALYSIS SHEET

The first step in preparing a transaction analysis sheet is to restate the balance sheet in balance sheet equation form on a transaction analysis sheet. Figure 1-3 shows the June 30 balance sheet for Goldman's Gym.

Goldman's Gym
Balance Sheet
June 30, 20—

Assets		Liabilities	
Cash	$ 5 000	Accounts Payable	$ 4 000
Accounts Receivable	6 000	Bank Loan	65 000
Office Supplies	500	Mortgage Payable	80 000
Land	25 000	Total Liabilities	149 000
Building	110 000		
Training Equipment	94 500	**Owner's Equity**	
		R. Millar, Capital	92 000
		Total Liabilities	
Total Assets	$241 000	and Owner's Equity	$241 000

FIGURE 1-3 June 30 balance sheet

Figure 1-4 is a transaction analysis sheet that contains the June 30 balance sheet information. Notice that the left side contains the assets and the right side the liabilities plus owner's equity.

			ASSETS				=		LIABILITIES		+	OWNER'S EQUITY
	Cash	Accts. Rec.	Off. Supps.	Land	Bldg.	Train. Equip.		Accts. Pay.	Bank Loan	Mtge. Pay.		R. Millar, Capital
Bal.	$5 000 +	$6 000 +	$500 +	$25 000 +	$110 000 +	$94 500	=	$4 000 +	$65 000 +	$80 000 +		$92 000

FIGURE 1-4 Transaction analysis sheet—opening balances

The following transactions will cause changes in items on the balance sheet:

Jul. 1   Purchased new training equipment for $500 cash.
   5   Bought office supplies for $55, on credit, from Central Supply Co.
   10   Received $3000 cash from customers (various accounts receivable) who owed money.

These transactions must now be analyzed to determine the changes caused to the items on the balance sheet. The changes will then be recorded on the transaction analysis sheet.

Transaction Analysis

Transaction 1: Asset Purchased for Cash

Jul.   1   Purchased new training equipment for $500 cash.

The following questions are asked to assist in analyzing a transaction:

(a) Which items change in value as a result of the transaction?
     (At least two must change in value to keep the equation
     in balance.)
(b) How much do the items change?
(c) Do the items increase or decrease in value?
(d) After the change is recorded, is the equation still in balance?

In the first transaction, *Training Equipment* and *Cash* will change. Training Equipment will *increase* by $500 since the company now owns more equipment. Cash will *decrease* by $500 since the company has spent money. Notice how these changes are shown on the transaction analysis sheet in Figure 1-5. After the transaction is recorded, the total assets ($241 000) still equal the total liabilities plus owner's equity ($241 000).

			ASSETS				=	LIABILITIES			OWNER'S + EQUITY
	Cash	Accts. Rec.	Off. Supps.	Land	Bldg.	Train. Equip.		Accts. Pay.	Bank Loan	Mtge. Pay.	R. Millar, Capital
Bal.	$5 000 +	$6 000 +	$500 +	$25 000 +	$110 000 +	$94 500 =		$4 000 +	$65 000 +	$80 000 +	$92 000
Jul. 1	−500					+500					
New Bal.	4 500 +	6 000 +	500 +	25 000 +	110 000 +	95 000 =		4 000 +	65 000 +	80 000 +	92 000

FIGURE 1-5 Transaction analysis sheet—July 1 transaction

Transaction 2: Asset Purchased on Credit

Jul.   5   Bought office supplies for $55, on credit, from Central Supply Co.

Which items on the balance sheet change? Do they increase or decrease? If you said the asset *Office Supplies increases* by $55 and the liability *Accounts Payable* also *increases* by $55, you were correct. Look at how this transaction is recorded on the transaction analysis sheet in Figure 1-6. Is the equation still in balance? If you add up the asset balances after the second transaction, you will get a total of $241 055. The liabilities and owner's equity now total $241 055. The equation is still in balance.

		ASSETS					=	LIABILITIES			+	OWNER'S EQUITY
	Cash	Accts. Rec.	Off. Supps.	Land	Bldg.	Train. Equip.		Accts. Pay.	Bank Loan	Mtge. Pay.		R. Millar, Capital
Bal.	$5 000 +	$6 000 +	$500 +	$25 000 +	$110 000 +	$94 500 =		$4 000 +	$65 000 +	$80 000 +		$92 000
Jul. 1	−500					+500						
New Bal.	4 500 +	6 000 +	500 +	25 000 +	110 000 +	95 000 =		4 000 +	65 000 +	80 000 +		92 000
Jul. 5			+55					+55				
New Bal.	4 500 +	6 000 +	555 +	25 000 +	110 000 +	95 000 =		4 055 +	65 000 +	80 000 +		92 000

FIGURE 1-6 Transaction analysis sheet—July 5 transaction

Transaction 3: Cash Received from Customers

Jul. 10   Received $3000 cash from customers (various accounts receivable) who owed money.

Which items change? Do they increase or decrease? Look at Figure 1-7 to see how this transaction is recorded. Is the equation still in balance?

		ASSETS					=	LIABILITIES			+	OWNER'S EQUITY
	Cash	Accts. Rec.	Off. Supps.	Land	Bldg.	Train. Equip.		Accts. Pay.	Bank Loan	Mtge. Pay.		R. Millar, Capital
Bal.	$5 000 +	$6 000 +	$500 +	$25 000 +	$110 000 +	$94 500 =		$4 000 +	$65 000 +	$80 000 +		$92 000
Jul. 1	−500					+500						
New Bal.	4 500 +	6 000 +	500 +	25 000 +	110 000 +	95 000 =		4 000 +	65 000 +	80 000 +		92 000
Jul. 5			+55					+55				
New Bal.	4 500 +	6 000 +	555 +	25 000 +	110 000 +	95 000 =		4 055 +	65 000 +	80 000 +		92 000
Jul. 10	+3 000	−3 000										
New Bal.	7 500 +	3 000 +	555 +	25 000 +	110 000 +	95 000 =		4 055 +	65 000 +	80 000 +		92 000

FIGURE 1-7 Transaction analysis sheet—July 10 transaction

Additional Transactions

Look at the four transactions below. For each of them, ask yourself which items change. Do they increase or decrease?

Jul. 15   Sold some unused equipment for $400 cash.
     18   Paid $375 cash to Central Supply Co. for an account payable that had become due.
     21   Owner invested an additional $800 cash in the business.
     25   Purchased equipment from Niagara Sport Ltd. for $3000; $2000 was paid in cash and $1000 will be paid in 30 days.

Now look at Figure 1-8 and follow the recording of each of these transactions. Note that the final transaction involves changes to three items.

		ASSETS					=	LIABILITIES			+	OWNER'S EQUITY
	Cash	Accts. Rec.	Off. Supps.	Land	Bldg.	Train. Equip.		Accts. Pay.	Bank Loan	Mtge. Pay.		R. Millar, Capital
Bal.	$5 000 +	$6 000 +	$500 +	$25 000 +	$110 000 +	$94 500 =		$4 000 +	$65 000 +	$80 000 +		$92 000
Jul. 1	−500					+500						
New Bal.	4 500 +	6 000 +	500 +	25 000 +	110 000 +	95 000 =		4 000 +	65 000 +	80 000 +		92 000
Jul. 5			+55					+55				
New Bal.	4 500 +	6 000 +	555 +	25 000 +	110 000 +	95 000 =		4 055 +	65 000 +	80 000 +		92 000
Jul. 10	+3 000	−3 000										
New Bal.	7 500 +	3 000 +	555 +	25 000 +	110 000 +	95 000 =		4 055 +	65 000 +	80 000 +		92 000
Jul. 15	+400					−400						
New Bal.	7 900 +	3 000 +	555 +	25 000 +	110 000 +	94 600 =		4 055 +	65 000 +	80 000 +		92 000
Jul. 18	−375							−375				
New Bal.	7 525 +	3 000 +	555 +	25 000 +	110 000 +	94 600 =		3 680 +	65 000 +	80 000 +		92 000
Jul. 21	+800											+800
New Bal.	8 325 +	3 000 +	555 +	25 000 +	110 000 +	94 600 =		3 680 +	65 000 +	80 000 +		92 800
Jul. 25	−2 000					+3 000		+1 000				
New Bal.	$6 325 +	$3 000 +	$555 +	$25 000 +	$110 000 +	$97 600 =		$4 680 +	$65 000 +	$80 000 +		$92 800
			$242 480				=		$149 680		+	$92 800
			$242 480				=		$242 480			

FIGURE 1-8 Transaction analysis sheet—July 15–25 transactions

PREPARING A NEW BALANCE SHEET

The completed transaction analysis sheet now contains the changes caused by the July transactions. The equation is still in balance; that is, the total of the left side equals the total of the right side. The new balances are used when the new balance sheet is prepared on July 31, 20—. Figure 1-9 shows the July 31 balance sheet.

Goldman's Gym
Balance Sheet
July 31, 20—

Assets		Liabilities	
Cash	$ 6 325	Accounts Payable	$ 4 680
Accounts Receivable	3 000	Bank Loan	65 000
Office Supplies	555	Mortgage Payable	80 000
Land	25 000	Total Liabilities	149 680
Building	110 000		
Training Equipment	97 600	**Owner's Equity**	
		R. Millar, Capital	92 800
		Total Liabilities	
Total Assets	$242 480	and Owner's Equity	$242 480

FIGURE 1-9 July 31 balance sheet

INTRODUCING GENERALLY ACCEPTED ACCOUNTING PRINCIPLES

It is very important to the users of accounting information, whether they are owners, creditors, bankers, or investors, that the information presented to them be prepared according to a common set of rules.

Only in this way can users compare the data of various businesses to make decisions. Generally Accepted Accounting Principles (GAAPs) and their underlying concepts provide a set of consistent rules used by all accountants to prepare financial statements such as the balance sheet. In Canada, the Canadian Institute of Chartered Accountants (CICA) publishes the *CICA Handbook*, which outlines these principles. Where appropriate throughout this text, GAAPs and other key ideas will be discussed as part of the development of accounting theory. In addition, GAAPs and key ideas you have learned in the current chapter will be highlighted, as in the following section.

Generally Accepted Accounting Principles are standard accounting rules and guidelines.

Generally Accepted Accounting Principles and Key Ideas

In this chapter, you learned the following Generally Accepted Accounting Principles:

- **The Business Entity Principle:** Each business is considered a separate unit or entity. For the purpose of accounting, the financial data for a business must be kept separate from the owner's personal data.
- **The Cost Principle:** Assets are shown on the balance sheet at the cost of their acquisition or construction.

You also learned the following key ideas:

- The **purpose of accounting** is to provide financial information for decision making.
- The **liquidity order** is the order in which assets that last a short time are listed on the balance sheet. It is the order in which those assets can be converted to cash.
- The **maturity date** governs the order in which liabilities are listed on the balance sheet. Liabilities are listed according to the order they are to be repaid, with the soonest repayments listed first.

UNIT 2 CHECK YOUR READING

Questions

13. Define the term *transaction*.
14. What four questions are asked when analyzing a business transaction?
15. Define the term *accounting period*.
16. What is meant by *Generally Accepted Accounting Principles*?

UNIT 2 **APPLY YOUR KNOWLEDGE**

Exercises

9. The September 30 balance sheet for Ngon Lam Bookkeeping Service is shown here.

Ngon Lam Bookkeeping Service
Balance Sheet
September 30, 20—

Assets		Liabilities	
Cash	$ 3 000	Accounts Payable	$ 2 000
Accounts Receivable	4 000	Mortgage Payable	45 000
Office Supplies	6 000	Total Liabilities	47 000
Building	195 000	**Owner's Equity**	
		N. Lam, Capital	161 000
		Total Liabilities	
Total Assets	$208 000	and Owner's Equity	$208 000

The following transactions occurred in October:

Oct.   4   Paid $500 cash on some accounts payable.
       15   Received $900 cash from an account receivable.
       20   Purchased office supplies for $750 on credit (payment is due in 30 days).
       29   The owner, N. Lam, invested an additional $2000 in the business.

(a) Place the September 30 balances on a transaction analysis sheet.
(b) Record the transactions on the transaction analysis sheet. Follow the format of the transaction analysis sheet in Figure 1-8 on page 19. Be sure that the total assets equal the total liabilities and owner's equity after each transaction.
(c) In your study guide, complete the balance sheet equation on October 31 following this format:

Assets $_____ = Liabilities $_____ + Owner's Equity $_____

(d) Prepare a new balance sheet for October 31.

10. The balance sheet for Cesario's Body Repairs as of June 30 is shown on the next page.

Cesario's Body Repairs
Balance Sheet
June 30, 20—

Assets		Liabilities	
Cash	$ 7 500	Accounts Payable	$ 3 400
Accounts Receivable	15 300	Bank Loan	1 500
Equipment	55 000	Total Liabilities	4 900
		Owner's Equity	
		F. Cesario, Capital	72 900
		Total Liabilities	
Total Assets	$77 800	and Owner's Equity	$77 800

The following transactions took place during July:

Jul.   3   Received $450 cash from K. Bell, a customer.
       4   Purchased a new $1500 air compressor from K. D.
           Manufacturers on credit.
       5   Borrowed $2000 cash from the bank.
       8   Paid $600 to General Auto Parts, a supplier, to pay
           off some of the balance owing to them.
      15   Made a $500 cash payment on the bank loan.
      20   The owner, F. Cesario, invested a further $3000 in
           the business.

(a) Prepare a transaction analysis sheet for Cesario's Body Repairs and
    record the transactions.
(b) After the last transaction has been recorded, prepare the balance
    sheet equation to prove the accuracy of your work.

11. Mail-O-Matic Printing produces a variety of advertising materials, such
as brochures and flyers, and distributes them door-to-door for retail
stores. The February 28 balance sheet for Mail-O-Matic Printing and
several transactions that occurred during March follow.
(a) Complete a transaction analysis sheet for Mail-O-Matic.
(b) After the last transaction, prove the arithmetical accuracy of your
    work by preparing the balance sheet equation.

Mail-O-Matic Printing
Balance Sheet
February 28, 20—

Assets		Liabilities	
Cash	$ 14 000	Accounts Payable	$ 6 500
Accounts Receivable	23 000		
Printing Supplies	8 900	**Owner's Equity**	
Equipment	97 000	S. Zimic, Capital	136 400
		Total Liabilities	
Total Assets	$142 900	and Owner's Equity	$142 900

Mar. 1 Purchased $950 worth of printing supplies from Cooper Products on credit.

      5 Some of the printing supplies bought on March 1 were damaged. Returned $200 worth of supplies to Cooper.

      9 Paid $700 to Clear Chemicals Ltd., a supplier, to reduce balance owing.

    10 Purchased a new $15 000 copier from Conway Manufacturers. Made a down payment of $3000 cash, and the balance of $12 000 is to be paid later.

12. At first glance, the following balance sheet for Dart Company may appear to be correct but it has several major and minor errors.
(a) List the errors.
(b) Prepare a correct balance sheet.

Dart Company			
December 31, 20—			
Cash	$ 2 500	Bank Loan	$ 44 400
Truck	10 600	Accounts Payable	3 600
Building	152 000		
Less Mortgage	76 000		
Land	42 300		
Equipment	5 100	Dart Co. Capital	88 500
	$136 500		$136 500

13. Maria Lopez presented the following list to her accountant to have a balance sheet prepared for Lopez Latin Dance Studio. Maria included all items she felt were important.

Cash in Business Bank Account	$ 1 800
Personal Bank Account	2 500
Accounts Receivable	1 500
Accounts Payable	500
Personal Car Loan	5 000
House and Lot	245 000
Dance Studio Building (Cost)	130 000
Dance Studio Building (Current Market Price)	235 000
Land	80 000
Personal Car	25 000
Mortgage on Dance Studio	138 000
Mortgage on House	132 000
Studio Equipment	3 100
Bank Loan on Studio Equipment	6 000
Personal Property	6 600

(a) Prepare a balance sheet for Lopez Latin Dance Studio on December 31, 20—.

(b) Explain why you did not include all the listed items in the balance sheet you just prepared. Refer to the GAAP that influenced your decision.

(c) Which GAAP was applied to determine the value of the dance studio building on the balance sheet?

(d) Use the data and concepts from (a), (b), and (c) to prepare a personal balance sheet for Maria on the same date.

14. The following is a completed transaction analysis sheet for Metro Cleaners. For (b) to (f), describe the transactions that must have occurred in the business to produce the changes shown on the transaction sheet. Part (a) has been done for you.

Example

(a) Cash increased by $500 as a result of the collection of $500 from a customer (an account receivable).

	Cash		Accts. Rec.		Clean. Equip.		Bldg.		Land	=	Accts. Pay.		Mtge. Pay.	+	Q. Kitt, Capital
					ASSETS					**=**	**LIABILITIES**			**+**	**OWNER'S EQUITY**
Bal.	$5 000	+	$2 000	+	$7 500	+	$42 000	+	$18 000	=	$ 750	+	$38 000	+	$35 750
(a)	+500		−500												
New Bal.	5 500	+	1 500	+	7 500	+	42 000	+	18 000	=	750	+	38 000	+	35 750
(b)	−700				+1 500						+800				
New Bal.	4 800	+	1 500	+	9 000	+	42 000	+	18 000	=	1 550	+	38 000	+	35 750
(c)	+2 000														+2 000
New Bal.	6 800	+	1 500	+	9 000	+	42 000	+	18 000	=	1 550	+	38 000	+	37 750
(d)	−800										−800				
New Bal.	6 000	+	1 500	+	9 000	+	42 000	+	18 000	=	750	+	38 000	+	37 750
(e)	+300		+700		−1 000										
New Bal.	6 300	+	2 200	+	8 000	+	42 000	+	18 000	=	750	+	38 000	+	37 750
(f)	−100	+													−100
	$6 200	+	$2 200	+	$8 000	+	$42 000	+	$18 000	=	$ 750	+	$38 000	+	$37 650

Computer Accounting

Throughout this course, you will learn the theory of accounting—the general principles and rules that make up the subject of accounting. As you learn each part of the theory of accounting, you will apply that theory by completing problems and exercises.

Up to this point, you have been doing problems and exercises manually, that is, handwriting the solutions to assignments. As you will see, many tasks in accounting are repeated over and over. For example, sales are made and recorded every day and balance sheets are prepared every month. Such repetitive tasks are ideal for a computer. Consequently, accountants view the computer as a very helpful tool.

Computers can do the following tasks very quickly:

- ‣ perform mathematical calculations;
- ‣ store large amounts of information;
- ‣ retrieve stored information; and
- ‣ classify, sort, summarize, move, and compare information.

These tasks are all routinely performed by accountants, so it makes sense for them to make use of the power and speed of computers. When a computer is combined with other equipment, such as printers, additional terminals, projection devices, Internet connections, and other communication devices, the resulting computer system becomes a very powerful tool indeed.

INTRODUCING THE ELECTRONIC SPREADSHEET

A spreadsheet is an *electronic calculation tool*. It is a computer tool that can do things that people generally do with pencils, paper, and calculators. It does many of these things automatically and offers the capability of storing, displaying, and printing the results. It is a software application that combines the capabilities of a calculator and a word processor.

A spreadsheet can be used in accounting to perform tasks such as totalling and balancing journals; calculating GST, sales tax, and discounts; and estimating profits and prices. In today's business world, it is common to find spreadsheets being used by all levels of workers—from beginning clerical employees to high-level managers.

In its simplest form, a spreadsheet consists of columns and rows. Figure 1-10 illustrates a basic spreadsheet. The columns are labelled A, B, C, etc., and the rows are numbered 1, 2, 3, etc. The size of the spreadsheet, that is, the number of columns and rows, is determined by the user, depending upon his or her needs. Any location on a spreadsheet can be identified by describing its column and row position. For example, can you locate B2 in Figure 1-10? Locations such as B2 on a spreadsheet are sometimes called *cells*.

	A	B	C	D
1				
2				
3				
4				
5				
6		Cell B2		
7				
8				
9				
10				

FIGURE 1-10 Electronic spreadsheet with the cursor located at cell B2

Both numbers and words can be entered on a spreadsheet. The power of a spreadsheet is in its ability to be programmed or formatted to perform specific tasks automatically and to print or display the results.

Formatting a Spreadsheet

Preparing a spreadsheet is called *formatting*. This involves adding instructions and formulas to the basic spreadsheet. The instructions and formulas are then executed (carried out) automatically by the spreadsheet.

The spreadsheet in Figure 1-11 has been formatted to calculate the GST on invoices.

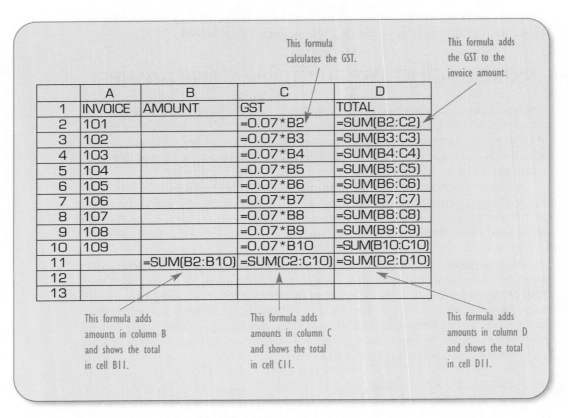

FIGURE 1-11 Spreadsheet formulas

(a) At cell B11, a formula has been prepared to add the dollar amount in cells B2 to B10. The formula is =SUM(B2:B10). This instruction results in an automatic totalling of the amounts in cells B2 to B10. The sum will appear in cell B11.

(b) Another formula has been entered in cells C2 to C10 to automatically calculate the GST for each invoice amount and display the tax in cells C2 to C10.

(c) A formula similar to that in (a) adds cells C2 to C10 and displays the total in cell C11.

(d) Another formula has been entered in cells D2 to D10 to add the GST to the invoice amount and display the total amount for each invoice in column D.

(e) Cell D11 contains a formula that adds the amounts in D2 cells to D10 and presents the total in cell D11.

Note: The wording (syntax) of a formula will vary depending on the software you are using; for example, other spreadsheet software might use @SUM(B2.B10) instead of =SUM(B2:B10). Check your software documentation for the syntax for formulas.

	A	B	C	D
1	Invoice	Amount	GST	Total
2	101	$ 100.00	$ 7.00	$ 107.00
3	102	249.75	17.48	267.23
4	103	1820.00	127.40	1947.40
5	104	320.00	22.40	342.40
6	105	795.50	55.69	851.19
7	106	4388.21	307.17	4695.38
8	107	29.95	2.10	32.05
9	108	51620.00	3613.40	55233.40
10	109	321.66	22.52	344.18
11	Totals	$59645.07	$4175.16	$63820.23

FIGURE 1-12 Formatted spreadsheet

Once a spreadsheet format has been prepared, the calculations are automatically made and appear on the screen (see Figure 1-12). Thus, the formatted spreadsheet in Figure 1-11 will do the following:

- show invoice numbers in column A;
- show the amounts of the invoices in column B;
- calculate the GST on the sales at 7 percent in column C;
- add the tax to the amounts of the sales and show the totals in column D; and
- calculate totals for all columns.

The only thing the computer user has to do is to enter the invoice numbers and amounts (columns A and B). The amounts and totals in columns C and D are calculated and appear almost instantly. The spreadsheet results can then be saved and printed.

Note: All spreadsheets operate in the basic way described here. However, the commands used, the structure of the formulas, the size of the spreadsheet, and other characteristics vary from spreadsheet to spreadsheet.

COMPUTER ASSIGNMENTS

1. Ask your teacher to provide you with a formatted spreadsheet like the one shown in Figure 1-11 on page 26. Record the invoices listed below on the computer. Save your data and then print the results. Compare your answers with Figure 1-12.

Invoice	Amount
101	$ 100.00
102	249.75
103	1 820.00
104	320.00
105	795.50
106	4 388.21
107	29.95
108	51 620.00
109	321.66

2. In this assignment, you will be required to do the spreadsheet formatting as well as the data entry.
   (a) Prepare a spreadsheet format that will do the following:

   ➤ List and total a company's assets
   ➤ List and total a company's liabilities
   ➤ Subtract the liabilities from the assets
   ➤ Print the balance sheet equation:

   Assets $_____ = Liabilities $_____ + Owner's Equity $_____

   (b) Enter the data for each of the companies below and print the balance sheet equation for each.

Company A: True Blue Ltd.

Assets		Liabilities	
Cash	$ 9 000	Accounts Payable	$4 000
Accounts Receivable	20 000	Bank Loan	7 000
Supplies	2 000		
Equipment	30 000		

Company B: J.M. Smart Inc.

Assets		Liabilities	
Cash	$ 8 000	Accounts Payable	$10 000
Accounts Receivable	17 000	Bank Loan	6 000
Office Supplies	500		
Office Equipment	13 400		

Company C: E.Z. Street Ltd.

Assets		Liabilities	
Cash	$ 2 900	Accounts Payable	$11 000
Accounts Receivable	7 100	Bank Loan	2 000
Delivery Equipment	17 000		
Furniture	8 000		
Office Equipment	12 000		

Company D: C.U. Soon Inc.

Assets		Liabilities	
Cash	$ 4 322.95	Accounts Payable	$14 920.00
Accounts Receivable	19 620.33	Bank Loan	11 200.00
Office Supplies	900.00	Mortgage Payable	90 000.00
Office Equipment	21 895.50		
Delivery Equipment	42 000.00		
Building	245 000.00		

WEB EXTENSIONS

Internet Study Guide

 www.pearsoned.ca/
principlesofaccounting

▸ Complete the Chapter 1 review.

▸ Complete the Chapter 1 definitions.

▸ Complete the Chapter 1 online test.

Web Links

Visit the Web Links section at the Pearson Education web site to find a link to an accounting site. Indicate the benefits of this site to someone considering a career in accounting.

6 Case Studies

CASE 1   Use of Business Funds

You are the accountant for Lily Shen, who owns and operates Superior Personnel. This firm specializes in supplying temporary office employees to firms that need short-term assistance during peak work periods. Lily has just signed a contract to purchase a car and instructs you to prepare a cheque payable to Ed Learn Motors for the down payment and to send the monthly payments to the local credit union. She requests you to draw these cheques on the company account and to list the car as an asset on Superior Personnel's balance sheet. When you ask why she would like the transaction handled in this manner, she informs you that she assumes the owner of a business can use the business funds however she wishes.

(a) Is Lily correct in her assumption?
(b) Which accounting principle should you use to support your answer?

CASE 2   Evaluation of Assets

Diovanny Diaz owns a small courier service. He asks you, his accountant, to prepare a balance sheet for him to present to the bank for evaluation in order to obtain a loan. A friend of his who works in the real estate business has indicated that Diovanny's building would probably be worth $400 000 if offered for sale. The current records of the business show the building has a value of $250 000, which is what Diovanny paid five years ago when he moved to this location. Diovanny feels the higher amount should be used on the balance sheet because it better reflects to the bank manager the current value of his business.

(a) Should you follow Diovanny's instructions when you prepare the balance sheet? Include any GAAP and accounting concepts that you have considered in your answer.
(b) Would the bank be interested in the current market price of the building? Why?

CASE 3   Errors on a Balance Sheet

There are several mistakes in the setup and content of the balance sheet at the top of the next page. Can you locate them?

M. Mancini & Company
Balance Sheet
August 31, 20—

Assets		Liabilities	
Cash	1 000	Accounts Receivable	3 000
Accounts Payable	2 000	Equipment	5 000
Supplies	1 000	Bank Loan	30 000
Building	100 000	Total Liabilities	38 000
		Owner's Equity	
		M. Mancini, Capital	78 000
		Total Liabilities	
Total Assets	104 000	and Owner's Equity	106 000

Owner's Claim on Assets

CASE 4

Josie Clarke, the owner of a retail store, has come to you for advice. She shows you her latest balance sheet. The assets total $200 000, the liabilities are $130 000, and the owner's equity is $70 000. Included in the assets are old equipment and merchandise at a book value of $120 000. Realistically, these assets are now worth $40 000.

Josie is considering selling all of the assets. She feels she could get about $120 000 cash if all the assets were sold. She would then take her investment (equity of $70 000) and close down the business. The remaining $50 000 from the sale of the assets would be available to satisfy the creditors' claims against the assets.

What advice would you give Josie concerning her proposal?

Value of a Business

CASE 5

George Harris, a friend of yours, owns his own business. He offers to sell you half of the business for $40 000. George suggests that this is an excellent price since the assets of the business total $235 000. The balance sheet of the company is shown on the next page.

(a) Based only on the facts presented above and on the balance sheet, what do you think of the deal offered to you? Give an explanation for your response.

George Harris & Company
Balance Sheet
September 30, 20—

Assets		Liabilities	
Cash	$ 1 500	Accounts Payable	$ 10 000
Accounts Receivable	2 000	Bank Loan	30 000
Supplies	500	Mortgage Payable	190 000
Equipment	9 000	Total Liabilities	230 000
Land and Building	222 000		
		Owner's Equity	
		G. Harris, Capital	5 000
		Total Liabilities	
Total Assets	$235 000	and Owner's Equity	$235 000

(b) Assume that the following actions occur:
  • A real estate agent estimates the current value of the land and building to be $350 000 and predicts they will increase in value in the future.
  • George agrees to pay off the company's $30 000 bank loan using personal funds. This will increase his capital in the company to $35 000.
  • In return for your $40 000 cash, the company will create a capital account in your name with a balance of $40 000 in it and you will become an equal partner.

Taking these facts into consideration and applying the cost principle, prepare a new balance sheet. Would you pay the $40 000? Give reasons for your response.

7 Career Education Activities

1. Self-Knowledge: A Starting Point

Most people will end up working for a rather large part of their lives. A job or a career is important to all of us. It gives us security, a chance to use our skills and abilities, and an opportunity to reach our personal potential. As you think ahead, plan, and prepare yourself for the world of work, consider the following:

• You will probably have a number of different jobs.
• You will be trained and re-educated several times. (It's true—education never really ends!)

Even though permanent employment may be some time away for you, it is wise to start thinking and planning now for the future. The starting point is to find out what you are like. Think about what you like doing and what you feel is important as you mentally answer the following questions.

1. What are your favourite subjects at school? Why?

2. What are your hobbies?

3. Outside of school, on what activities do you spend a great deal of time?

4. Do you do any volunteer work?

5. What part-time work have you done that you enjoyed?

6. Name one personal strength that you have.

7. Name a personal weakness.

8. What experiences have you had that will help you in the future?

9. How do you evaluate yourself?

   (a) Are you a leader or a follower?
   (b) Do you like physical work or mental work?
   (c) Do you prefer to work alone or with people?
   (d) Are you organized or disorganized?
   (e) Do you like to be told what to do or to determine what to do yourself?
   (f) Are you a creative or structured person?
   (g) Are you a good or poor manager of time?
   (h) Are you a good or poor planner?
   (i) Do you enjoy quiet or bustling situations?

The questions you have just answered were designed to get you *started* to think about yourself. Your school's guidance department can provide you with formal and more comprehensive exercises to help you discover your personal interests and skills. Why not pay a visit to your counsellor?

Your school probably has access to computer programs that will help you to examine a variety of careers and to discover your interests. CHOICES is one such program, and SGIS, Student Guidance Information Service, is another. Has your school got either of these or similar programs?

2. Volunteer Work

One way to gain worthwhile learning and life experiences is to engage in volunteer work. By giving yourself volunteer experience you may find out that you:

• like working with small children;
• enjoy working with senior citizens;
• have recreational skills;
• would like to work with teenagers;
• have the ability to work with the disabled; or
• have an interest in health services.

In short, you will learn a lot about yourself.

A record of having been involved in volunteer work will also be a valuable addition to your personal résumé when you apply for jobs.

For Discussion

(a) Is there a central volunteer bureau in your location?
(b) What opportunities for volunteer work are there locally?
(c) Can you do volunteer work in your school?
(d) Have you done any volunteer work?
(e) Discuss the opportunities for volunteer work in your community with other students.

3. Full-Time Employment

All businesses and organizations must keep financial records. This means that there are many jobs available for those with knowledge, background, and experience in accounting. Refer to the accompanying advertisement and discuss the points that follow.

For Discussion

(a) What are the responsibilities for each of these positions?
(b) What accounting skills are required?
(c) What personal skills are required?
(d) What experience is required for each position?

Payroll Clerk

Responsible for processing payroll, record keeping, employee inquiries, reconciliation, and additional benefit administration. To be successful, the ideal candidate is detailed-oriented, has general accounting experience, and is proficient in the use of spreadsheet and word-processing applications.

Accounts Payable Clerk

Responsible for processing invoices, client inquiries, account reconciliation, and special projects. To be successful, the ideal candidate has good accounting skills, has a minimum of 3 years accounting experience, is a good team player, and is proficient with Excel.

If interested, please e-mail your résumé to:

Mrs. Betty Poaps

bpoaps@accounting.com

111 Main Street, 5th Floor
Edmonton, Alberta

Career Profile

Mark Thiessen grew up on the family farm in Leamington, Ontario. For over 30 years, the Thiessen family has grown a variety of cash crops, including flowers in greenhouses and orchards on their farm.

Mark attended Leamington High School and, after he graduated, he decided to pursue his interest in farming and business at the University of Guelph. As he studied horticulture and business courses, he developed skills in accounting and computer applications. These in turn led him to an interest in using computer technology in the family business. After graduation, Mark returned to work on the family farm with his father Pete and brother Andrew.

Seeing the business potential of e-commerce, Mark created Expressroses.com in 1994 to take advantage of the potentially vast Internet-based consumer market. His idea was to eliminate the costs of the "middlemen," by selling flowers over the Internet and shipping them directly to customers from the greenhouses in Leamington. Mark's idea seems to be working. Customers place orders from among some 40 products on the company web site (www.growerflowers.com) using an electronic order form. To reduce the recording of accounting transactions, all customer purchases are paid by credit card. This eliminates the accounts receivable function. The orders are shipped by courier and received by the customer within one day of placing the order. In effect, the flowers are cut one day and received by the customer the next—now that's fresh!

The Thiessens grow about 800 000 roses a year in their two acres of plastic-covered greenhouses. The company has a regular staff of about 20 people who grow, package, and market the flowers. This staff increases temporarily for Valentine's Day and Mother's Day, when the business does about 35 percent of its annual business. Mark runs the business and marketing side of the operation and his brother Andrew is director of greenhouse growing and production. The farm uses sophisticated growing techniques and a state-of-the-art computer network in its growing operations.

The company is now expanding by working with other growers and companies with high-traffic web sites. Partner companies can offer flowers supplied by the Thiessens for sale on their own web sites. Orders are automatically sent to Expressroses.com and filled from Leamington (or by one of its partner growers). An example is the NHL website. You can go to this site, click on the NHL store, select flowers, and place an order. You order from the NHL web site, but the flowers are shipped by courier from Leamington.

For Discussion

1. What skills did Mark develop at university that assisted him to set up his business?
2. How does Mark have customers pay for their purchases, and what are the advantages of this system?
3. How do the systems used by the company ensure that flowers ordered by customers are received fresh?
4. Would you order flowers using the Internet? Give reasons for your answer.
5. Go to the company's Internet site, www.growerflowers.com, then explain how the "affiliate program" works.

Balance Sheet Accounts

UNIT 3 Recording Transactions in T-Accounts

What Learning You Will Demonstrate

On completion of this unit, you will demonstrate the skills necessary to:

- record the opening balances on a balance sheet in a T-account ledger;
- analyze transactions to determine which accounts are changed and whether the changes are recorded as debits or credits;
- record transactions in T-accounts;
- calculate the balances in accounts;
- prepare a trial balance to verify the mathematical accuracy of the ledger; and
- prepare a balance sheet from the trial balance.

Transaction analysis sheets were used in Chapter 1 to demonstrate the process of analysis necessary to record changes in the balance sheet items caused by business transactions. In actual practice, the use of a transaction analysis sheet is impractical due to the large number of financial events that occur each day in a business. A more efficient method to collect, record, and summarize these events is to keep a separate record of the changes for each item. This record is called an **account**. To introduce the concepts and practices involved in recording data in accounts, a simplified form of this record, called a *T-account*, will be used in this chapter.

> An account is a form in which changes caused by transactions are recorded.

INTRODUCING T-ACCOUNTS

For every item on the balance sheet, an account is prepared. As transactions occur, the changes that result from these transactions are recorded in accounts. Following is an example of a T-account. It is shaped like a "T" and has two sides, just like the balance sheet prepared in account format.

Account Title	
Left Side Debit	Right Side Credit

Debit refers to the left side of an account.

Credit refers to the right side of an account.

Debit is the accounting term used for the *left side* of the account. **Credit** is the accounting term used for the *right side* of the account. Following is an account used to record transactions that involve cash. It has a debit (left) side and a credit (right) side. One side is used to record increases in cash, that is, money received, and the other side is used to record decreases in cash, that is, money paid out.

Cash	
Debit	Credit

T-accounts are not needed in business but are often used by accountants for their rough work when they analyze transactions. T-accounts are used at this time to introduce a number of basic accounting procedures and concepts.

On the next few pages, we will examine the use of accounts by recording transactions for Goldman's Gym. As a first step, look again at the July 31 balance sheet for Goldman's Gym shown in Figure 2-1.

Goldman's Gym
Balance Sheet
July 31, 20—

Assets		Liabilities	
Cash	$ 6 325	Accounts Payable	$ 4 680
Accounts Receivable	3 000	Bank Loan	65 000
Office Supplies	555	Mortgage Payable	80 000
Land	25 000	Total Liabilities	149 680
Building	110 000		
Training Equipment	97 600	**Owner's Equity**	
		R. Millar, Capital	92 800
		Total Liabilities	
Total Assets	$242 480	and Owner's Equity	$242 480

FIGURE 2-1   July 31 balance sheet

Recording Balances in Accounts

A separate account is required for each asset, for each liability, and for the owner's equity on the balance sheet. For Goldman's Gym, ten accounts are required because there are six assets, three liabilities, and one equity account. These ten accounts are shown in Figure 2-2 on page 40. The beginning, or opening, amounts on the balance sheet are called *balances*. For each item on the balance sheet, the opening balance is recorded in a T-account. The Cash account is shown at the top of the next page after the opening balance has been recorded. Since Cash appears on the left side of the balance sheet, the opening balance for cash is recorded on the left side of the Cash account. This rule applies to all asset accounts.

There is a separate account for each asset and liability and for the owner's equity.

Asset balances are recorded on the left side of asset accounts.

Since assets are located on the left side of the balance sheet, the opening balance of an asset is recorded on the left or debit side of its account.

```
                            Cash
   _____
   Jul. 31            6 325  |
```

Since liabilities are located on the right side of the balance sheet, the opening balance of a liability account is placed on the credit (right) side of the liability account. For the same reason, the opening balance for the owner's equity account is placed on the credit side of its account. This rule applies to all liability and owner's equity accounts.

> Since liabilities and owner's equity are located on the right side of the balance sheet, their opening balances are recorded on the credit or right side of their accounts.

Liability balances are recorded on the right side of the liability accounts.

INTRODUCING LEDGERS

A ledger is a group of accounts. It may be kept in the form of a binder that contains pages for each account in a manual accounting system, or it may be stored on disk or tape in a computerized accounting system. The accounts in the ledger are designed to collect the data concerning changes in the value of each item on the balance sheet on an individual basis.

A ledger is a group of accounts.

Opening the Ledger

The balance sheet shown below can be visualized as a large "T," with the assets on the left and the liabilities and owner's equity on the right. This will help you remember that asset accounts normally have debit balances (balances shown on the left side of the T-account), while liability and owner's equity accounts have credit balances (balances shown on the right side of the T-account).

Left Side		Right Side	
Assets		**Liabilities**	
Cash	$ 6 325	Accounts Payable	$ 4 680
Accounts Receivable	3 000	Bank Loan	65 000
Office Supplies	555	Mortgage Payable	80 000
Land	25 000	Total Liabilities	149 680
Building	110 000		
Training Equipment	97 600	**Owner's Equity**	
		R. Millar, Capital	92 800
		Total Liabilities	
Total Assets	$242 480	and Owner's Equity	$242 480

To open accounts in the ledger, these steps should be followed:

- Place the account name in the middle of each account.
- Record the date and opening balance from the balance sheet on the appropriate side in the account.

The ledger for Goldman's Gym is shown in Figure 2-2. A separate account has been opened for each item on the balance sheet.

Cash		Accounts Payable	
Jul. 31 6 325			Jul. 31 4 680

Accounts Receivable		Bank Loan	
Jul. 31 3 000			Jul. 31 65 000

Office Supplies		Mortgage Payable	
Jul. 31 555			Jul. 31 80 000

Land		R. Millar, Capital	
Jul. 31 25 000			Jul. 31 92 800

Building	
Jul. 31 110 000	

Training Equipment	
Jul. 31 97 600	

FIGURE 2-2   Ledger for Goldman's Gym showing balances in each account

Now let's analyze Figure 2-2. Since *assets* are found on the left side of the balance sheet, the value of each asset account has been recorded on the *left or debit side* of the account. Since *liabilities* are found on the right side of the balance sheet, the value of each liability account has been recorded on the *right or credit side* of the account. Since *owner's equity* is found on the right side of the balance sheet, the value of the owner's equity account has been recorded on the *right or credit side* of the account.

Note that if the debit balances are added together they will equal the total of the credit balances:

Debits:
$6325 + $3000 + $555 + $25 000 + $110 000 + $97 600 = $242 480

Credits:
$4680 + $65 000 + $80 000 + $92 800 = $242 480

This is known as having the ledger in balance. This relationship must continue as transactions are recorded, in keeping with the important principle of *double-entry accounting.*

Total debit balances must equal total credit balances.

Double-Entry Accounting

One of the most important principles of accounting is that for each transaction, double-entry accounting requires that a debit amount equal to a credit amount must be recorded. Thus, all transactions are recorded in one or more accounts as a *debit* and in one or more accounts as a *credit*. The total of the debit amount must always equal the total of the credit amount for each transaction.

Double-entry accounting requires a debit amount equal to the credit amount for each transaction.

RECORDING TRANSACTIONS IN ACCOUNTS

These steps are followed in analyzing transactions and recording them in accounts:

- **Step 1:** Determine *which accounts* change in value as a result of the transaction. Note that two or more accounts will change in value as a result of each transaction.
- **Step 2:** Identify the *type of account* that has changed. Is the account an asset, a liability, or an owner's equity account?
- **Step 3:** Decide whether the change is an increase or a decrease in the account.
- **Step 4:** Decide whether the change is recorded as a *debit or a credit* in the account. Note that the ledger must remain in balance.

The following transactions for Goldman's Gym occurred during August 20—. These transactions will be analyzed and entered in the ledger to illustrate how the four steps described above are followed. As you read the examples, note that each transaction has a debit amount that is equal to the credit amount. Note also that the debit portion of the entry is always shown before the credit portion.

Transaction Analysis

Transaction 1

Aug. 2   Received $500 cash as payments on membership dues owing.

The two accounts that are affected are Cash and Accounts Receivable. The Cash account is increased with a debit for the following reasons:

- Cash is an asset.
- The asset Cash is increasing (money has been received).
- Assets are found on the left side of the balance sheet and increase on their debit (left) side.

Assets increase on the debit side.

The $500 increase in the Cash account is illustrated below on the left:

Cash				Accounts Receivable		
Jul. 31	6 325			Jul. 31	3 000	Aug. 2 500
Aug. 2	500					

The asset Accounts Receivable is also affected. The balance for this asset decreases because customers have paid some of the amount owed by them. An account decreases on the side opposite to its normal opening balance. The decrease in Accounts Receivable is recorded as a credit, as shown above on the right.

Assets decrease on the credit side.

Here is a summary of how this transaction was recorded:

Account Affected	Type of Account	Increase/ Decrease	Debit/ Credit	Amount
Cash	Asset	Increase	Debit	$500
Accounts Receivable	Asset	Decrease	Credit	500

Notice that in recording the transaction, there is a debit of $500 and a credit of $500. A general rule for recording transactions can now be stated:

> Accounts increase on the same side as they appear on the balance sheet and they decrease on the opposite side.

Following are four specific statements based on this general rule:

1. If *assets increase,* the amount is recorded on the *debit side.*
2. If *assets decrease,* the amount is recorded on the *credit side.*
3. If *liabilities or owner's equity increase,* the amount is recorded on the *credit side.*
4. If *liabilities or owner's equity decrease,* the amount is recorded on the *debit side.*

Transaction 2

Aug. 5   Purchased $25 worth of office supplies from Central Supply Co., with 30 days to pay.

Which accounts are changed by this transaction? What type of accounts are they? Do they increase or decrease and are they debited or credited to record the changes? The answers to these questions will help you to understand how this transaction is recorded.

The *asset account Office Supplies increases* because the company now has more supplies. Assets are found on the *left* side of the balance sheet; therefore, the *increase* in supplies is recorded on the *debit* (left) side of the Office Supplies account.

Liabilities increase on the credit side.

The company now owes more money on an account payable. Therefore, the *liability account Accounts Payable increases.* Since liabilities are found on the right side of the balance sheet, the liability Accounts Payable *increases* on the *credit* (right) side. The transaction is shown recorded in the accounts below:

Office Supplies		Accounts Payable	
Jul. 31 555		Jul. 31 4 680	
Aug. 5 25		Aug. 5 25	

Here is a summary of how this transaction was recorded:

Account Affected	Type of Account	Increase/ Decrease	Debit/ Credit	Amount
Office Supplies	Asset	Increase	Debit	$25
Accounts Payable	Liability	Increase	Credit	25

An asset increased by $25 and was debited. A liability increased by $25 and was credited. There was a debit of $25 and an equal credit of $25. The ledger remains in balance.

Transaction 3

Aug. 5   Paid $705 now due to Equipment Unlimited for goods previously purchased but not paid for.

Can you determine which account is debited? Which account is credited? The *asset Cash decreases* because money was paid out. Assets decrease on the credit side; therefore, Cash is credited.

The *liability Accounts Payable* also *decreases* because less money is now owed to the creditor. Liabilities decrease on the debit side; therefore, Accounts Payable is debited. This transaction is shown in the accounts below.

> Liabilities decrease on the debit side.

Accounts Payable				Cash			
Aug. 5	705	Jul. 31	4 680	Jul. 31	6 325	Aug. 5	705
		Aug. 5	25	Aug. 2	500		

Here is a summary of how this transaction was recorded:

Account Affected	Type of Account	Increase/ Decrease	Debit/ Credit	Amount
Accounts Payable	Liability	Decrease	Debit	$705
Cash	Asset	Decrease	Credit	705

An *asset decreased* by $705 and was *credited*. A *liability decreased* by $705 and was *debited*. Therefore, the ledger remains in balance. The total of the debits will still equal the total of the credits.

Transaction 4

Aug. 7   Purchased three new tennis trainers for $545 each (total $1635). A cash down payment of $535 was made. The remaining amount ($1100) is to be paid at a later date.

This transaction involves changes in *three accounts*. They are the assets Cash and Training Equipment, and the liability Accounts Payable. Can you determine the debits and credits?

Training Equipment increases by $1635. Cash decreases by $535. Accounts Payable increases by the amount still owing, $1100. This is how the transactions are recorded in the accounts:

Training Equipment			Cash				Accounts Payable			
Jul. 31	97 600		Jul. 31	6 325	Aug. 5	705	Aug. 5	705	Jul. 31	4 680
Aug. 7	1 635		Aug. 2	500	7	535			Aug. 5	25
									7	1 100

Here is a summary of how this transaction was recorded:

Account Affected	Type of Account	Increase/ Decrease	Debit/ Credit	Amount
Training Equipment	Asset	Increase	Debit	$1 635
Cash	Asset	Decrease	Credit	535
Accounts Payable	Liability	Increase	Credit	1 100

Remember: assets are recorded at their cost price whether or not they are fully paid for at the time of purchase. The asset increase of $1635 (debit) is balanced by an asset decrease of $535 (credit) and a liability increase of $1100 (credit). Therefore, the ledger remains balanced. The total debits are equal to the total credits.

Transaction 5

Aug. 7   Owner invested an additional $5000 in the business.

This transaction causes the *company's cash to increase*. It also causes the *owner's equity to increase* because the business is now worth more. The two accounts that change, Cash and R. Millar, Capital, are shown below:

Cash					R. Millar, Capital		
Jul. 31	6 325	Aug. 5	705			Jul. 31	92 800
Aug. 2	500	7	535			Aug. 7	5 000
7	5 000						

Here is a summary of how this transaction was recorded:

Owner's equity increases on the credit side.

Account Affected	Type of Account	Increase/ Decrease	Debit/ Credit	Amount
Cash	Asset	Increase	Debit	$5 000
R. Millar, Capital	Owner's Equity	Increase	Credit	5 000

Note that the proprietor's investment of additional cash increases the owner's equity. The company's Cash account increases by $5000 (debit) and this is balanced by the owner's equity account increase of $5000 (credit). Therefore, the ledger remains in balance.

CALCULATING NEW BALANCES IN THE ACCOUNTS

The accounts in the ledger of Goldman's Gym now contain the opening balances from the July 31, 20—, balance sheet plus the entries to record the changes in value of these accounts up to August 7, 20—. To determine the new *account balance*, the following calculations are made for each account:

1. Add up the debit side of the account.
2. Add up the credit side of the account.
3. Subtract the smaller amount from the larger and place the answer on the larger side of the account. This is the new balance for the account.

Two examples are provided below:

The difference between the totals of the two sides of an account is called the account balance.

The account balance is placed on the side of the account with the highest total.

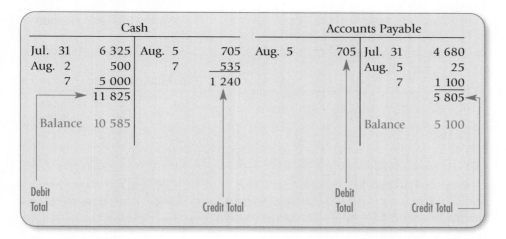

Note that the final Cash balance was placed on the debit side and the final Accounts Payable balance was placed on the credit side. The account balances are always placed on the side of the account that has the larger total. For assets, this is usually the debit side; for liabilities and owner's equity, this is usually the credit side. The ledger for Goldman's Gym would appear as shown in Figure 2-3 on page 46 after the August 7 balances have been calculated for all the accounts.

PREPARING A TRIAL BALANCE

A trial balance is prepared to verify that the total debits are still equal to the total credits in the ledger. The **trial balance** is a list of all the accounts with their current balances. They are listed in the order that they appear in the ledger. Two columns are required to prepare the trial balance. The first column is used to record the debit balances and the second column is used to record the credit balances. Since the trial balance is used within the business, it is an informal statement compared to the balance sheet, which is considered to be a formal financial statement. Because the trial balance is an informal statement, it is possible to use abbreviations. However, the statement should still be prepared as neatly as possible.

A trial balance is a list of the ledger account balances. The total of the debit balances should equal the total of the credit balances. The trial balance indicates the mathematical accuracy of the ledger.

Cash					Accounts Payable				
Jul. 31	6 325	Aug. 5	705	Aug. 5	705	Jul. 31	4 680
Aug. 2	500	7	535			Aug. 5	25
7	5 000		1 240			7	1 100
	11 825						5 805
Balance	10 585					Balance	5 100

Accounts Receivable					Bank Loan		
Jul. 31	3 000	Aug. 2	500			Jul. 31	65 000
Balance	2 500					Balance	65 000

Office Supplies				Mortgage Payable		
Jul. 31	555				Jul. 31	80 000
Aug. 5	25					
Balance	580				Balance	80 000

Land				R. Millar, Capital		
Jul. 31	25 000				Jul. 31	92 800
					Aug. 7	5 000
Balance	25 000				Balance	97 800

Building	
Jul. 31	110 000
Balance	110 000

Training Equipment	
Jul. 31	97 600
Aug. 7	1 635
Balance	99 235

FIGURE 2-3 Ledger for Goldman's Gym with balances calculated in each account

The trial balance for Goldman's Gym, dated August 7, 20—, is shown in Figure 2-4 on the next page. The format for the trial balance is as follows:

Heading

Line 1: Who?	—	Goldman's Gym
Line 2: What?	—	Trial Balance
Line 3: When?	—	August 7, 20—

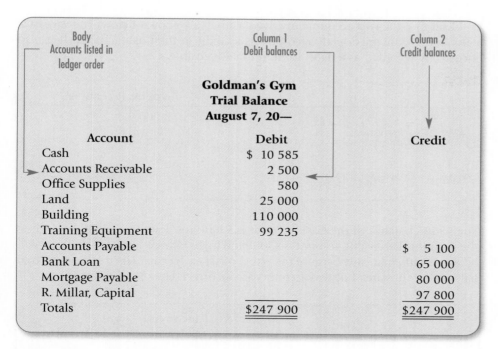

FIGURE 2-4   Trial balance for Goldman's Gym

Limitations of the Trial Balance

The trial balance simply indicates the mathematical accuracy of the ledger. It shows that the total debits equal the total credits. It verifies that a debit amount was recorded for each credit amount; that is, that the principle of double-entry accounting was followed. However, the trial balance does not indicate if the wrong accounts were used to record a transaction.

If, for example, the first transaction for Goldman's Gym was recorded incorrectly by reversing the debit and credit, the error would not be discovered on a trial balance. In that first transaction, $500 cash was received from members who owed payments on their memberships. The transaction was *analyzed* correctly as:

Cash	Debit	$500
Accounts Receivable	Credit	500

If this was mistakenly *recorded* as:

Accounts Receivable	Debit	$500
Cash	Credit	500

the error would not be discovered on a trial balance.

Examine the two accounts involved as they are shown below. The August 2 entry for $500 is incorrectly recorded as a credit in the Cash account. It is also incorrectly recorded as a debit in Accounts Receivable.

Cash				Accounts Receivable			
Jul. 31	6 325	Aug. 2	500*	Jul. 31	3 000		
Aug. 7	5 000	5	705	Aug. 2	500*		
	11 325	7	535	Balance	3 500		
			1 740				
Balance	9 585					*Incorrect entry	

The $9585 balance of the Cash account is $1000 too low. The $3500 balance of the Accounts Receivable account is $1000 too high. However, the trial balance will balance mathematically because the errors offset each other. The totals on the trial balance are the same but two accounts are incorrect. Here is a summary:

Reference	Correct Balance	Incorrect Balance	Difference
Cash account	$ 10 585	$ 9 585	−$1 000
Accounts Receivable account	2 500	3 500	+$1 000
Trial balance	247 900	247 900	No change

Note that when the amount is placed on the opposite side of the account, the error is double the original amount. Remembering this will help you locate errors, as discussed in Chapter 4. It is sufficient to remember at this time that the trial balance only indicates that equal debit and credit entries have been made for each transaction and that no errors have been made in calculating the account balances. Limitations of the trial balance and the topic of error location will be covered more fully in Chapter 4.

Preparing a New Balance Sheet

To provide a formal statement of financial position on August 7, 20—, a new balance sheet, as prepared from the information contained on the trial balance, is shown in Figure 2-5.

Goldman's Gym
Balance Sheet
August 7, 20—

Assets		Liabilities	
Cash	$ 10 585	Accounts Payable	$ 5 100
Accounts Receivable	2 500	Bank Loan	65 000
Office Supplies	580	Mortgage Payable	80 000
Land	25 000	Total Liabilities	150 100
Building	110 000		
Training Equipment	99 235	**Owner's Equity**	
		R. Millar, Capital	97 800
		Total Liabilities	
Total Assets	$247 900	and Owner's Equity	$247 900

FIGURE 2-5   August 7 balance sheet

Generally Accepted Accounting Principles and Key Ideas

In this chapter, you learned the following four key ideas:

- **Double-entry accounting** requires that, in recording transactions, the total of the debit amounts must always equal the total of the credit amounts.
- **Assets** are located on the left side of the balance sheet. Asset accounts increase on the debit (left) side and decrease on the credit (right) side.
- **Liabilities and owner's equity** are located on the right side of the balance sheet. Liability and owner's equity accounts increase on the credit (right) side and decrease on the debit (left) side. These concepts, known as the rules of debit and credit, are summarized in the chart below.
- A **trial balance** proves the mathematical accuracy of the ledger. It does not indicate that transactions were all correctly recorded as debits and credits.

Assets		=	Liabilities		+	Owner's Equity	
Debit	Credit		Debit	Credit		Debit	Credit
Increase	Decrease		Decrease	Increase		Decrease	Increase

SUMMARY OF ACCOUNTING PROCEDURES

Figure 2-6 summarizes, in chart form, the important accounting procedures and concepts that have been covered in this chapter.

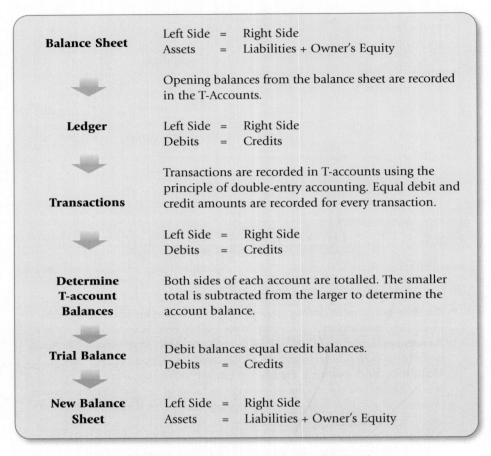

Balance Sheet	Left Side = Right Side Assets = Liabilities + Owner's Equity
⬇	Opening balances from the balance sheet are recorded in the T-Accounts.
Ledger	Left Side = Right Side Debits = Credits
⬇	
Transactions	Transactions are recorded in T-accounts using the principle of double-entry accounting. Equal debit and credit amounts are recorded for every transaction.
⬇	Left Side = Right Side Debits = Credits
Determine T-account Balances	Both sides of each account are totalled. The smaller total is subtracted from the larger to determine the account balance.
⬇	
Trial Balance	Debit balances equal credit balances. Debits = Credits
⬇	
New Balance Sheet	Left Side = Right Side Assets = Liabilities + Owner's Equity

FIGURE 2-6 Summary of accounting procedures discussed in this chapter

UNIT 3 CHECK YOUR READING

Questions

1. What is the meaning of each of the following?
   (a) Account   (c) Credit
   (b) Debit   (d) Ledger
2. On which side of the account is the balance of an asset recorded? Why?
3. On which side of the account is the balance of a liability recorded? Why?
4. On which side of the account is the balance of the owner's equity recorded? Why?

5. On which side of the account would the opening balance for each of the following accounts be recorded?
   (a) Cash
   (b) Supplies
   (c) Mortgage Payable
   (d) Accounts Payable
   (e) Computer Equipment
   (f) Bank Loan
   (g) Land
   (h) Building
   (i) Delivery Truck
   (j) Owner, Capital
6. List the increase and decrease side for each of the following:
   (a) Asset account
   (b) Liability account
   (c) Owner's equity account
7. Explain the principle of double-entry accounting.
8. How many accounts are there in a ledger?
9. What three steps are followed in determining the balance for an account?
10. (a) What is a trial balance?
    (b) What does a trial balance indicate?

UNIT 3 APPLY YOUR KNOWLEDGE

Exercises Part A

1. The May 31 balance sheet for Dominicana Restaurant is shown below.
   (a) Open accounts in a ledger for each of the assets and liabilities and for the owner's equity.
   (b) Record the May 31 balances in the accounts.

Dominicana Restaurant
Balance Sheet
May 31, 20—

Assets		Liabilities	
Cash	$ 5 000	Accounts Payable	$ 16 000
Supplies	10 000	Mortgage Payable	84 000
Land	40 000	Total Liabilities	100 000
Building	200 000		
Equipment	50 000		
		Owner's Equity	
		X. Diaz, Capital	205 000
		Total Liabilities	
Total Assets	$305 000	and Owner's Equity	$305 000

2. Open a ledger for Dr. R. Smith and record the following January 31 balances in the accounts: Cash $6000; Accounts Receivable $19 000; Supplies $6000; Equipment $35 000; Accounts Payable $5000; Bank Loan $13 000; R. Smith, Capital $48 000.

3. (a) Dominicana Restaurant, first seen in exercise 1, had the following transactions to record during the first week of June. Analyze each transaction using the format indicated below. List the debit portion of the entry before the credit portion. The June 1 transaction is done for you as an example.

   Jun.   1   Purchased a new oven from Restaurant Supplies Co. for $780 on credit.
          2   Made the regular monthly payment of $880 on the mortgage.
          3   Paid $1300 to reduce the balance owing to Wholesale Foods Limited.
          5   Purchased a new table and four chairs from Owen Furniture for a $280 cash down payment and $320 due in 30 days.
          6   Owner, X. Diaz, invested an additional $3000 cash in the business.

   Example:

Transaction	Account Affected	Type of Account	Increase/ Decrease	Debit/ Credit	Amount
Jun.1	Equipment	Asset	Increase	Debit	$780
	Accounts Payable	Liability	Increase	Credit	780

   (b) Now record the June 1–6 transactions in the ledger accounts prepared for exercise 1.
   (c) Calculate the new balances for each of the accounts.
   (d) Prepare a trial balance.

4. (a) Use the accounts set up for Dr. R. Smith in exercise 2 to record the transactions shown below for the doctor's practice.
   (b) Calculate the balances for the accounts and prepare a trial balance.

   Feb.   1   Received $100 from a patient as payment for services.
          3   Paid $3000 cash for computer equipment (use the Equipment account).
          5   Bought medical supplies for $250 on credit. The bill is to be paid in 30 days.
          6   Paid $600 on the bank loan.
          7   Paid $500 to reduce the balance owing to an account payable.

5. Claire's Beauty Salon has been in operation for a number of years. The September 30 balance sheet for the business follows on the next page.
   (a) Prepare T-accounts for Claire's Beauty Salon using the accounts and balances given in the September 30 balance sheet.

(b) Record the October transactions in the accounts.
(c) Calculate the account balances and prepare a trial balance on October 7, 20—.

Claire's Beauty Salon
Balance Sheet
September 30, 20—

Assets		Liabilities	
Cash	$ 4 800	Accounts Payable	$ 800
Accounts Receivable	3 600	Bank Loan	2 700
Supplies	2 400	Mortgage Payable	88 000
Land	30 000	Total Liabilities	91 500
Building	90 000		
Equipment	40 000	**Owner's Equity**	
		C. Williams, Capital	79 300
		Total Liabilities	
Total Assets	$170 800	and Owner's Equity	$170 800

Oct. 2 Purchased shampoo, hair spray, etc., from Beauty Products, $250 on credit.

3 Returned some of the supplies purchased yesterday for a credit of $75 since they were not what had been ordered.

4 Received $2200 cash from customers who paid their accounts.

4 Made the regular $700 payment on the mortgage.

5 Bought four hair dryers worth $12 000 from Beauty Products. The business made a $3000 cash deposit on the dryers and the balance was to be paid later.

6 Obtained a bank loan of $10 000, part of which will be used to pay for the hair dryers.

7 Paid Beauty Products $9975; payment in full of the amount owing to them.

6. On June 1, Mei Lin Chan started M.L. Chan Real Estate. Enter the following transactions in appropriate accounts.

Jun. 1 Mei Lin Chan opened a bank account in the name of her new business by depositing $50 000 cash.

1 Bought a building to use as an office. The price was $200 000. (The land is worth $60 000.) Paid $20 000 cash and obtained a mortgage for remainder.

2 Bought furniture for $7800. A down payment of $5000 was made, with the remaining balance due in 30 days.

3 Office equipment was purchased for $5600 on credit.

3 Paid the outstanding balance on the June 2 furniture purchase.

5 The owner, Mei Lin Chan, invested an additional $5000 in the business.

7. Bradley Air Service provides aviator training and leases or rents aircraft. The transactions shown below occurred during the first week of September. Analyze each transaction using the format indicated in the example. List the debit part of the entry before the credit part.

Example:

Transaction	Account Affected	Type of Account	Increase/ Decrease	Debit/ Credit	Amount
Sep.1	Bank Loan	Liability	Decrease	Debit	$500
	Cash	Asset	Decrease	Credit	500

Sep. 1   Made the regular monthly payment of $500 on the bank loan.
   2   Purchased a new air pump from Cadence Industries for $1700; payment to be made later.
   4   Secured a further bank loan of $15 000 to pay for a future aircraft purchase.
   5   Purchased a new aircraft for $24 000 from Airways Manufacturing. Made a $14 000 down payment, with the $10 000 balance to be paid later.
   7   Received $2500 cash on account from L. Rosewood, a customer.

8. The accounts at the top of page 55 contain a series of transactions for Disk Jockeys Unlimited. For each of the entries labelled (a) to (e), indicate how accounts have changed and describe the transaction that must have occurred to cause the entry. Use a chart similar to the one below, where transaction (a) has been done for you as an example.

Example:

Transaction	Account Affected	Type of Account	Increase/ Decrease	Debit/ Credit	Amount
(a)	Accounts Payable	Liability	Decrease	Debit	$150
	Cash	Asset	Decrease	Credit	150
Paid an account payable.					

	Cash				Truck	
Balance	1 500	(a)	150	Balance	7 500	
(b)	250	(d)	100			
		(e)	250			

	Accounts Receivable				Accounts Payable		
Balance	1 000	(b)	250	(a)	150	Balance	500
				(e)	250	(c)	500
						(d)	200

	CDs				Bank Loan		
Balance	2 000					Balance	2 500
(d)	300						

	Equipment				M. Potter, Capital		
Balance	5 500					Balance	14 500
(c)	500						

9. Ben Irving, CA, operates a single proprietorship that provides a wide range of accounting services to his clients. The balance sheet for this firm on April 30 is shown below.

(a) Open a T-account ledger for Ben Irving, CA, using the accounts and balances provided in the April 30 balance sheet.

(b) Record the May transactions listed on page 56 in the ledger.

(c) Calculate the account balances and prepare a trial balance on May 7, 20—.

Ben Irving, CA
Balance Sheet
April 30, 20—

Assets		Liabilities	
Cash	$ 5 200	Accounts Payable	$ 3 750
Accounts Receivable	6 500	Taxes Payable	830
Office Supplies	1 700	Bank Loan	8 520
Land	25 500	Mortgage Payable	44 000
Building	75 000	Total Liabilities	57 100
Office Equipment	42 100	**Owner's Equity**	
		B. Irving, Capital	98 900
		Total Liabilities	
Total Assets	$156 000	and Owner's Equity	$156 000

May 1 Received cheques from clients totalling $500 in the mail today in payment of amounts previously billed.

1 Made the regular monthly payment of $220 on the bank loan.

2 Purchased a new computer system for the office from Computer Accounts Co. for $9250. A down payment of $2000 was made today and the balance will be due in 30 days.

3 The owner, B. Irving, invested an additional $1500 in the business.

4 Paid $750 to various creditors to reduce balances owing to them.

5 Purchased additional supplies for the computer system for $500 cash.

5 Returned $60 worth of supplies for a cash refund since they were defective.

6 The owner had recently purchased a laser printer for personal use. Since the firm required a similar piece of equipment, the owner decided to place this printer in the business on a permanent basis instead of buying another one for the business after incurring the expense of the computer system. The printer cost B. Irving $1800. (*Note:* This transaction represents an additional investment by the owner in the business.)

10. The T-accounts on page 57 contain a number of transactions for Action Auction Sales. For each of the entries labelled (a) to (f), indicate how the accounts have changed and the transaction that must have taken place to generate the entry. The chart below, with transaction (a) done as an example, will assist you in describing the transactions correctly.

Example:

Transaction	Account Affected	Type of Account	Increase/ Decrease	Debit/ Credit	Amount
(a)	Cash	Asset	Increase	Debit	$10 000
	V. Henry, Capital	Owner's Equity	Increase	Credit	10 000

Since the Cash and Capital accounts both increased, the owner must have invested cash in the business.

Cash				Accounts Payable			
(a)	10 000	(b)	500	(d)	250	(c)	2 000
(f)	5 500	(c)	1 000			(e)	5 000
		(d)	250				

Supplies				Bank Loan			
(b)	500					(f)	5 500

Furniture				V. Henry, Capital			
(c)	3 000					(a)	10 000

Equipment		
(e)	5 000	

Exercises Part B

11. The following is the ledger, in T-account form, for General Delivery Co. Note that dates of entries have been omitted for this exercise.
   (a) Calculate the balance in each account.
   (b) Prepare a trial balance to verify the accuracy of the ledger.
   (c) One account has an exceptional (different from normal) balance. How could this occur?

Cash		Truck	
11 000	300	13 500	
500	200		
3 500	55		
	230		
	100		

Accounts Receivable		Accounts Payable	
1 000	1 600	300	2 500
500		200	190

Supplies		Bank Loan	
55		230	3 500
190			

Equipment		D. Kim, Capital	
15 000		100	37 400

12. Dr. E. King has the following account balances on August 31, 20—. The balances have been listed in no particular order: Cash $35 000; due to suppliers $4000; Equipment $130 000; due from patients $6000; Bank Loan $7000; due from Provincial Health Plan $14 000; Dr. E. King, Capital $176 000; Medical Supplies $2000.

(a) Open a T-account ledger in the correct order from the balances listed above.

(b) Record the following September transactions in the ledger.

(c) Prepare a trial balance.

(d) Prepare a balance sheet on September 13, 20—.

Sep. 2   Dr. King invested an additional $50 000 cash in the business to assist in financing a new office.

3   C. Patten, a patient, paid $55 (an amount owed).

4   Bought surgical bandages and other medical supplies from Medical Suppliers, $78 on credit.

5   Returned $43 worth of supplies to Medical Suppliers because they were not the type ordered.

6   Paid $90 to Pharmaceutical Products, a creditor, to reduce the amount owing to them.

7   Made the regular $200 payment on the bank loan.

8   Received a cheque from the Provincial Health Plan for $11 500.

9   Dr. King located a satisfactory office building for his practice. The property cost $292 000, with the land worth $150 000 and the building worth the remainder ($142 000). A mortgage was secured from TD Canada Trust for $200 000 and the balance was paid in cash.

10   Purchased a new computer and printer from Ace Computers for $4000 cash.

12   Purchased the software necessary for the computer from the same supplier for $2500, on credit.

13   Sold an old printer for $300 cash.

13. Mouradian Realty has been in business for several years. Here, in random order, are the balances in the accounts on September 30: Cash ?; Accounts Payable $5250; Land $183 200; Bank Loan $9570; Accounts Receivable $6325; Building $182 100; Mortgage $105 500; Equipment $9375; T. Mouradian, Capital $267 500; Supplies $1150.

(a) Calculate the correct balance in the Cash account.

(b) Open a T-account ledger in correct order using the balances shown above.

(c) Record the following October transactions in the ledger.

(d) Prepare a trial balance and a balance sheet on October 14, 20—.

Oct. 1   Received $1000 due from a client since last month.

2   Purchased $25 worth of office supplies for cash.

4   Obtained an additional bank loan for $18 000 to purchase a company car.

5   Purchased a car from Cullen Motors for $18 250 cash.

7   Made the regular $500 monthly mortgage payment.

9   An office chair purchased on credit last month was returned to the supplier since it was defective. The chair originally cost $175.

10   Sold an unused portion of the land beside the office for $80 000 cash. This amount was equal to the original cost of the land.

11   Purchased a new telephone system for the office for $3500. A down payment of $1000 was required, with the balance due on receipt of the invoice.

12   T. Mouradian purchased $75 worth of postage stamps for the business from his own funds.

14   Paid $250 to a creditor.

 # Computer Accounting

Business Computers

Computers are used extensively in business offices to perform a wide range of tasks, including word processing, data management (spreadsheets and databases), accounting, and time management.

One Typical Business Application

Vancouver Condominium Services employs about 20 people. Its main activity is to provide management services to condominium owners. The services provided include overseeing building maintenance, repairs, and landscaping, promoting rentals, and preparing a variety of accounting and financial reports for the directors and owners of the condominiums. Computers are used to provide some of these services to clients.

On a regular basis, reports and financial information are prepared and mailed to about 10 000 different unit owners. Can you imagine addressing envelopes to that many people time after time? A computer is used to help in this repetitive task. A mailing list is maintained on the computer and software automatically prints mail labels when needed.

A large number of reports, letters, notices, and newsletters are prepared using the word processing capabilities of the company's computers. Computers are capable of producing different styles of print. This makes the printed material more attractive and easy to read, and creates a favourable image of the company in the view of its clients. The company can also use its computers to run a number of business and accounting programs, such as spreadsheets.

Skill Development

Employers place a high value on employees who can adapt to new equipment and who can learn new systems and procedures on their own. Such employees have the self-confidence, ability, and self-discipline to learn on their own, to teach themselves, to read instruction manuals, and to build on their previous experience and education.

The Conference Board of Canada has developed an Employability Skills Profile. This profile outlines the skills that employers look for in employees. A recurring theme is that of the "lifelong learner." This ability to continue learning even after completing school is found in many of the career profiles in the book.

COMPUTER ASSIGNMENTS

1. Electronic spreadsheets are an important tool for most accountants. They are also used by anyone who works in a job that involves the manipulation of numbers or statistics. People whose work involves planning, forecasting, setting up timetables, or preparing reports, graphs, and tables find spreadsheets very useful. To further your knowledge of spreadsheets, interview someone who uses a spreadsheet—possibly a neighbour, a relative, or a teacher—and ask these questions.
   (a) Which spreadsheet do you use?
   (b) Why do you use a spreadsheet?
   (c) What is its capacity (rows and columns)?
   (d) Which functions of the spreadsheet are most used?
   (e) What are the advantages of using a spreadsheet?
   (f) What is the cost of the spreadsheet program?

2. Prepare a spreadsheet that can be used to prepare a trial balance. The format should include:
   ➤ a three-line heading;
   ➤ account titles;
   ➤ a debit column;
   ➤ a credit column;
   ➤ total debits; and
   ➤ total credits.

3. Use the spreadsheet you prepared for assignment 2, above, to complete trial balances for exercises 3, 4, and 13 of this chapter.

4. Prepare a spreadsheet format that will produce the Cash account and the Accounts Receivable account for exercise 4. Your spreadsheet should show the account title, debits, credits, total debits, total credits, and balance. Remember to record the opening balance in the accounts.

5. There are a large number of spreadsheet programs available for computers. Each has its own characteristics, features, and operating instructions. Answer the following questions about the spreadsheet used in your school.
   1. (a) What are the commands used to load the program on the computer?
      (b) How do you exit the program?
   2. How many rows and columns does the spreadsheet have?

3. (a) How many characters (e.g., letters) can be written in each cell?
   (b) How do you erase the contents of a cell?
   (c) How do you clear the entire contents of a spreadsheet?
4. (a) How do you move the cursor up, down, left, right, and back to A1?
   (b) What other cursor controls are available?
5. List and describe any special function keys available in the spreadsheet.
6. How do you "save" your work?
7. How do you print your work?
8. What keys indicate division, multiplication, addition, and subtraction?
9. What commands are used to do the following:
   (a) Display numbers as dollars and cents?
   (b) Left justify, centre, and right justify the contents of a cell?
   (c) Adjust the width of cells or columns?
   (d) Insert a row or a column?
   (e) Delete a row or a column?

6. Spreadsheet programs have built-in features called functions. An example of a function is addition. When a formula such as @SUM is used, the program automatically adds the items indicated. For example, @SUM(B2.B10) is used to have the spreadsheet automatically add the numbers in cells B2, B3, B4, B5, etc. to B10.

   A function can be considered to be an automatic calculation device. Another example is the average function. When a formula such as @AVERAGE is used, the program will average a series of numbers. For example, @AVERAGE (D5.D10) will result in the calculation of the average of the numbers in cells D5, D6, D7, D8, D9, and D10.

   (a) Prepare a list of four common functions that are available on the spreadsheet used in your school. Include the commands used for each function.

WEB EXTENSIONS

www.pearsoned.ca/
principlesofaccounting

Internet Study Guide

➤ Complete the Chapter 2 review.

➤ Complete the Chapter 2 definitions.

➤ Complete the Chapter 2 online test.

Web Links

Visit the Web Links section at the Pearson Education web site to find a link to the Conference Board of Canada site. Outline the employability skills that fall under the categories of fundamental skills, personal management skills, and teamwork skills.

6 Case Studies

CASE 1 Interpreting Accounting Data

A friend of yours has just inherited a small business called Pacific Fuels. The records of the company provide the following information:

Things Owned by the Company	Cost Price
Fuel trucks (2)	$40 000 (each)
Cash in the bank	2 000
Storage tanks	20 000
Fuel inventory	17 000
Equipment	13 000
Office supplies	200
Office equipment	4 000
Miscellaneous assets	2 000

Debts of the Company	Amount
Accounts payable	$22 000
Salaries owing	8 500
Taxes owing	2 000
Bank loan	30 000

Other Information

The two trucks are over five years old. None of the assets is less than two years old except the fuel inventory. The company employs two full-time truck drivers, a service repairperson, and an office clerk. During the busy season, two part-time employees are hired. The company has contracts to supply fuel to 200 customers. The average purchase per customer is $600 per year. Your friend asks you to help determine the following:

(a) What is the business worth?
(b) Should your friend keep the business or sell it?
(c) A competitor, Exodus Fuels, has offered your friend $20 000 for the entire business. Would you recommend selling at this price? Why?

CASE 2 Transaction Recording Errors

Four errors were made by the accountant for Sunrise Services when recording transactions during the month of October. They are described below. Which of the errors would be found by preparing a trial balance? Explain your answer for each error.

(a) A $300 payment was received from a client and recorded in the ledger as a debit to Accounts Receivable and a credit to Cash.

(b) A payment was made by Sunrise Services on an account payable in the amount of $100. It was recorded as a debit to Accounts Payable for $10 and a credit to Cash for $10.

(c) Equipment was purchased for $500 on credit. It was recorded as a debit to Equipment for $500 and a debit to Accounts Payable for $500.

(d) The owner invested an additional $1000 cash in the company. The transaction was recorded as a debit to Cash for $1000 and a credit to Capital for $100.

Unbalanced Trial Balance

CASE 3

When Grimwood Printers prepared a trial balance on October 30, it did not balance. As a result of checking through the record of transactions, an error was discovered; namely, $250 received from a customer was recorded as a debit to Cash of $5 and a credit to Accounts Receivable of $250. The total of the credit side of the trial balance was $52 225. Answer the following questions regarding the preceding trial balance information. Explain each of your answers fully.

(a) Was Accounts Receivable too high, too low, or correct?
(b) Was Cash too high, too low, or correct?
(c) Was the trial balance credit total of $52 225 too high, too low, or correct?
(d) What was the amount of the debit total on the unbalanced trial balance?
(e) Was this debit total too high, too low, or correct?

Trial Balance Errors

CASE 4

The trial balance for J. Singhal Co. is shown on page 64. It does not balance. The following errors were made during the month.

- A $300 payment was received from a client and recorded in the ledger as a debit to Accounts Receivable and a credit to Cash.
- A payment was made by J. Singhal Co. on an account payable in the amount of $100. It was recorded as a debit to Accounts Payable for $10 and a credit to Cash for $10.
- Equipment was purchased for $500 on credit. It was recorded as a debit to Equipment for $500 and a debit to Accounts Payable for $500.
- The owner invested an additional $1000 cash in the company. The transaction was recorded as a debit to Cash for $1000 and credit to Capital for $100.
- A $1200 payment on the mortgage was recorded as a $2100 debit to Mortgage Payable and a $1200 credit to Cash.
- A $100 purchase of office supplies for cash was not recorded.

(a) For each of the errors, indicate the accounts affected, the amount, and whether the account balances are too high or too low.
(b) Prepare a new, corrected trial balance.

<table>
<thead>
<tr><th colspan="3">J. Singhal Co.
Trial Balance
June 30, 20—</th></tr>
<tr><th>Account</th><th>Debit</th><th>Credit</th></tr>
</thead>
<tbody>
<tr><td>Cash</td><td>$ 2 610</td><td></td></tr>
<tr><td>Accounts Receivable</td><td>4 150</td><td></td></tr>
<tr><td>Office Supplies</td><td>1 800</td><td></td></tr>
<tr><td>Building</td><td>200 000</td><td></td></tr>
<tr><td>Equipment</td><td>40 000</td><td></td></tr>
<tr><td>Furniture</td><td>4 000</td><td></td></tr>
<tr><td>Accounts Payable</td><td></td><td>$ 3 910</td></tr>
<tr><td>Bank Loan</td><td></td><td>12 000</td></tr>
<tr><td>Mortgage Payable</td><td></td><td>124 900</td></tr>
<tr><td>J. Singhal, Capital</td><td></td><td>108 950</td></tr>
<tr><td></td><td>$252 560</td><td>$249 760</td></tr>
</tbody>
</table>

CASE 5   Double-Entry Accounting

A student has learned the double-entry method of accounting. The student states that it is based on the idea that *items owned equal claims against items owned.* Further, because of this relationship, debits must always equal credits if the balance sheet equation, $A = L + OE$, is to remain in balance. The student then draws this false conclusion: "In recording a transaction, an asset must change and either a liability or the owner's equity must also change."

Using your knowledge of double-entry accounting, explain the fallacy in the student's thinking.

⑦ Career Education Activities

1. What Do Employers Look For when Hiring People?

Margo Crawford, Director of Human Resources, Marketing and Communications with high-tech company edgeflow Inc., ensures that she finds the right people to join her team. Margo's responsibilities include recruiting and hiring at all levels. She is involved with the training, compensation, and benefits programs for all employees.

When hiring employees, edgeflow Inc. looks for candidates with good written and oral communication skills to complement their technical abilities. The level of skill required varies depending upon the position to be filled.

Margo also looks at a person's job history to determine if that person can function in a team environment, has the willingness to keep current on technology, and is reliable and trustworthy.

For Discussion

(a) List in point form the skills, attitudes, and personal qualities that Margo Crawford feels are important for an employee to have.
(b) Discuss each item on your list with other students in your class and explain how people exhibit these qualities on the job.
(c) How do students exhibit these qualities?
(d) How do you think a person can develop these qualities, skills, and attitudes?

2. Entry-Level Jobs

Beginning or lower-level jobs are those that require a minimum of experience and education. They are positions at which people start their careers and for that reason are often called *entry-level or junior-level jobs*. An advertisement that describes entry-level positions is shown here. Notice that it stresses a combination of basic accounting skills, computer skills, and personal skills.

For Discussion

(a) What are the business skills required for one of these positions?
(b) What are the personal qualities and interests required?
(c) How can a young person develop the skills, qualities, and educational requirements of this job?

accountants for hire

Jr. Accountants $15-$18/h

Are you looking for a great opportunity? Our client, a large manufacturing company, has immediate career opportunities available. Your knowledge of general ledgers and financial statements, combined with enthusiasm, make you an ideal candidate.

Payroll Clerk $15-$20/h

Great site! A faced-paced, friendly work environment awaits you. An advertising company is looking for experienced payroll clerks at both the Jr. and Sr. levels. Any payroll experience is considered an asset. Opportunities exist for advancement from Jr. to Sr. positions.

Office Administrator $15-$20/h

Are you energetic with a "can do attitude"? Do you have experience in accounting and office administration? The ideal candidate will be strong in MS Word, MS Excel, and planning and is well organized.

Tel: 905-955-5555
Fax: 905-955-7777
E-mail: Vancouver@accountantsforhire.com

Career Profile •

How does a person get to be a bank manager? We asked Anna Hembroff, a bank manager, that question and she provided this career information.

Anna attended Pauline Johnson Collegiate and after receiving her Grade 12 diploma she went directly into the world of business. She was able to obtain an entry-level job as a clerk-typist and receptionist because of the business skills she developed while in school. At Pauline Johnson Collegiate, her program included keyboarding, accounting, business machines, computer studies, secretarial subjects, and the required academic courses.

Her first employer was a finance company. She stayed with this firm for a number of years and progressed from receptionist to a number of more responsible positions, including manager of the branch office.

Her financial and management experience qualified her for a position with a major full-service bank as a loan officer. Anna applied her personal skills to the new position and progressed from loan officer to manager of consumer loans and services—and eventually to bank manager.

As manager of consumer loans and services, she approved all loans—including mortgage loans to people buying homes—and provided financial counselling to customers.

Anna was asked to describe the skills and education required for her current job. She feels that the ability to get along with people, to cope with stressful situations, to make intelligent decisions, and to use good judgment are the required personal characteristics and skills.

This managerial level of a job in a bank now requires community college or university levels of education. As well, the banks offer on-the-job training programs for persons wishing to further

their careers. These training programs require self-discipline and the ability to learn independently and the sacrifice of some personal time.

Anna's future goals and plans are to gain banking experience in a larger branch bank, and to move to branches that will broaden her background and lead to possibilities for more responsible positions. She also intends to obtain post-secondary education as a part-time student.

For Discussion

(a) What are the business skills and experience that qualified Anna for her current job?
(b) What personal skills does Anna feel are important?
(c) What are the present educational qualifications for Anna's current position?

The Income Statement

What Learning You Will Demonstrate

On completion of this unit, you will demonstrate the skills necessary to:

- classify items as revenue or expense;
- prepare an income statement;
- explain the time-period principle;
- explain the matching principle;
- use the accrual basis of accounting for revenue and expenses; and
- explain the cash basis of accounting.

REVIEWING THE PURPOSE OF ACCOUNTING

In Chapter 1, the purpose of accounting was expressed as a system designed *to provide the financial information that is used to make decisions.* This involves two types of accounting activity:

- recording daily transactions; and
- preparing reports that summarize those daily transactions.

In Chapters 1 and 2, you learned how daily business transactions were recorded and how a statement called a balance sheet was prepared. The balance sheet presented the assets, liabilities, and owner's equity at a specific date. In this chapter, you will expand your knowledge of business transactions and learn how and why a second financial statement, called an *income statement,* is prepared.

PROFIT AND LOSS

People go into business for themselves for a variety of reasons. Rick Millar, the owner of Goldman's Gym, started his business to:

- use his personal talents and abilities to the fullest;
- achieve pride of ownership of his own business;
- gain the satisfaction of building a successful business; and
- earn a profit on his investment of money and labour.

Once the gym was established, it grew and became successful as a result of the hard work and business knowledge of the owner. One of the major criteria for the success of a business is its profitability. A business cannot survive for very long unless it earns a profit.

Defining Profit and Loss

Profit is the increase in owner's equity that results from the successful operation of a business. In this chapter, we will determine how to calculate whether a business is profitable. When the business is not successful, a loss occurs and owner's equity decreases.

A business sells *goods*, such as cameras, automobiles, clothes, and furniture, or it sells *services*, such as television repairs, transportation, Internet access, and hair styling. The money, or the promise of money, received from the sale of goods or services is called revenue.

To sell goods and services, money is spent to operate the business. Costs such as salaries, advertising, delivery, and many other things required to run a business are called expenses.

Take the case of a television set that has a selling price of $500, and the seller has to spend $400 to sell the TV. When the TV is sold, does the seller make a profit or is there a loss? In this case, there is a profit of $100.

As the television example illustrates, when total revenue is greater than total expenses there is a *profit*. *Net income* is the preferred accounting term for profit. Net income occurs when total revenue is greater than total expenses.

Revenue	–	Expenses	=	Profit or Net Income
$500	–	$400	=	$100

However, sometimes total expenses may be greater than total revenue and then the result is called a loss or net loss.

Revenue	–	Expenses	=	Loss or Net Loss
$500	–	$550	=	$(50)

Notice that the $50 loss is shown in brackets. The use of brackets to indicate a loss is a commonly accepted practice in accounting.

Profit is the increase in owner's equity that results from the successful operation of a business.

A business sells goods or services.

Revenue is amounts earned from the sale of goods or services during the routine operation of the business.

Expenses are the costs of items or services used up in the routine operation of the business.

Net income is the difference between revenue and expenses when revenue is greater than expenses.

Net loss is the difference between revenue and expenses when expenses are greater than revenue.

THE INCOME STATEMENT

In Chapter 1, we prepared a financial statement called a balance sheet to show the financial position of Goldman's Gym at a certain date. The second major financial statement that every business prepares is an *income statement*. The income statement summarizes the items of revenue and expense and determines the net income or net loss for a stated period of time, called an **accounting period**. The accounting period may be a week, a month, a quarter, a year, or any other regular period of time.

A synonym for accounting period is *fiscal period*. Businesses prepare statements on a yearly basis for tax purposes. The statements prepared for this purpose are said to be prepared for the fiscal year. This fiscal year may or may not coincide with a calendar year. For example, a company's fiscal year may extend from July 1, Year 1, to June 30, Year 2, while the calendar year starts January 1, Year 1, and ends December 31, Year 1.

The income statement presents the revenue, expenses, and net income/loss for a specific period of time.

The accounting period is the period of time covered by the financial statements.

INCOME STATEMENT PREPARATION

An income statement prepared for Goldman's Gym for the month of September 20— will be used to discuss the correct format and procedures followed to prepare a formal financial statement. This income statement is shown in Figure 3-1.

Goldman's Gym Income Statement For the month ended September 30, 20—		
Revenue		
Members' Fees	$11 500	
Tanning Bed Rental	650	
Towel Rental	150	
Total Revenue		$12 300
Expenses		
Salaries	3 850	
Advertising	2 450	
Telephone	190	
Maintenance	720	
Licence*	1 100	
Interest	1 500	
Laundry	95	
Total Expenses		9 905
Net Income		$ 2 395

* Licence Expense is the amount paid to the parent company for the exclusive rights to the Goldman's Gym name in the Niagara Region.

FIGURE 3-1 September income statement

Step 1: Prepare Statement Heading

The four steps followed in preparing an income statement are described on the following pages.

The three-line heading is centred at the top of the page and is designed to provide information in this sequence:

Line 1: Who?	—	Goldman's Gym
Line 2: What?	—	Income Statement
Line 3: When?	—	For the month ended September 30, 20—

Note: The income statement provides data for a given time period (a week, a month, a year), while the balance sheet provides data on a specific date. The income statement loses its usefulness if the accounting period is not specified. Thus, if Line 3 were omitted from our example, we would have no way of knowing whether the net income of $2395 was for a week, a month, or a year. The owner would have a very different reaction when reading the statement if the income shown was for a week versus a year.

Step 2: Prepare Revenue Section

The revenue received from the business operations is listed under the subheading Revenue. The largest revenue item is usually listed first. The revenue is totalled and the total is placed in the right column as follows:

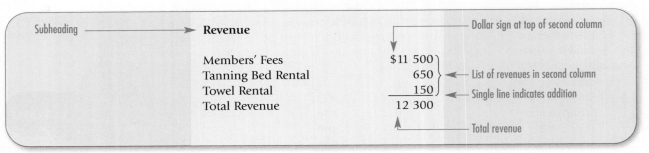

Step 3: Prepare Expenses Section

The expense items are listed in the order in which they appear in the ledger.

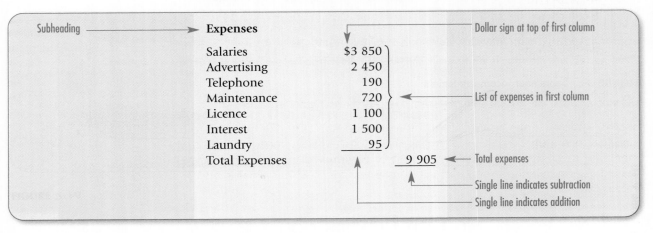

Step 4: Determine Net Income or Net Loss

The difference between total revenue and total expenses is the *net income or net loss*. There is a net income (profit) when total revenue is greater than total expenses. There is a net loss when total expenses are greater than total revenue.

In Figure 3-1 there is a net income of $2395. This is determined by subtracting the expenses from the revenue ($12 300 – $9905 = $2395). Notice in Figure 3-1 that there is a dollar sign beside the net income and the net income is ruled with a double line. Double lines are *ruled below* the net income or net loss. They indicate the final total.

Facts to Remember

For the income statement, dollar signs should be placed:

- beside the first figure in each column; and
- beside the net income or net loss figure at the bottom of the statement.

Time-Period Principle

The time-period principle requires the definition and use of the same period of time for the accounting period. For comparison reasons, *it is important that the accounting period consistently cover the same period of time.*

Each business sets up and defines its accounting period. This allows the owners and other users of the financial statements to analyze and compare data for similar periods of time. For example, the owner can determine if the business is as profitable this year as in previous years if one year is the accounting period.

The time-period principle is followed by accountants to produce accurate and consistent financial statements. Another principle that is followed is the matching principle.

> The time-period principle requires the definition and use of the same period of time for the accounting period.

Matching Principle

The matching principle says that costs recorded as expenses should be matched with the revenue they help to generate during the same accounting period. This results in an accurate net income for that accounting period.

When you determine the net income for an accounting period, it is important to include *only revenue earned during that period* and *only expenses incurred during that period* to produce the revenue. The net income or loss calculated will then accurately reflect only the business activities that took place during that period. For the introductory chapters of this text, a simple rule will assist you in applying the matching principle: *Expenses are recorded when the cost is incurred, whether paid in cash or on credit.* In normal practice, the receipt of a bill provides evidence that the expense was incurred and should be recorded.

> According to the matching principle, expenses should be recorded and matched with the revenue they help to generate during the same accounting period.

Effect of an Error in Applying the Matching Principle

The chart below shows abbreviated sample income statements for June and July. The statements on the left were prepared with correct information. The statements on the right demonstrate the result of making an error in applying the matching principle. An expense of $2000 that was incurred in June was mistakenly recorded in July.

	Correct			Incorrect	
	June	July		June	July
Revenue	$5 000	$6 000	Revenue	$5 000	$ 6 000
Expenses	4 000	5 000	Expenses	2 000	7 000
Net Income	$1 000	$1 000	Net Income (Loss)	$3 000	$(1 000)

What is the effect of the error? Both the June and July statements are incorrect. When the owner or people outside the business examine the statements, they will believe that the business had a very good month in June and a very poor month in July. In fact, both months exhibit relatively consistent performance when the statements are prepared correctly.

The accrual basis of accounting is a system of accounting related to the matching principle.

Accrual Basis of Accounting

The accrual basis of accounting matches revenue earned with expenses incurred to produce the revenue during the accounting period.

A business that records revenue when earned and expenses when incurred is using the accrual basis of accounting. This method produces an accurate picture of profitability for an accounting period *because it matches revenue earned with the expenses necessary to produce the revenue during the accounting period*. The accrual basis of accounting will be used throughout this book.

Recording Revenue

When a business follows the accrual basis of accounting, revenue is recognized *as it is earned*. It is recorded when the service is performed or when goods are shipped to a customer *even if cash has not been received*. For demonstration purposes, we will consider the accounting methods in a legal firm.

During the first week in June, lawyer Carmen Piccolo performed a variety of services for clients. Some of the clients paid cash for services totalling $2000. The remainder of the clients were billed $2500 for the services. The total revenue recorded for June was $4500 even though only $2000 cash was received.

Services Performed and Paid for in Cash	+	Services Performed on Credit	=	Total Revenue
$2000		$2500		$4500

What effect does earning this revenue have on the balance sheet equation for Carmen Piccolo's law firm? The assets increase by a total of $4500, there is no change in the liabilities, and the owner's equity increases by $4500.

A	=	L	+	OE
Cash: $2000		No Change	+	$4500
A/R: +$2500				

Revenue increases owner's equity.

When revenue is earned, it increases owner's equity.

Recording Expenses

Expenses are the costs incurred to generate the revenue. A separate account is kept in the ledger for each of the expenses. The transactions are recorded in the expense accounts *whether they are cash transactions or credit transactions*. Remember, expenses are recorded as they are incurred.

Cash Basis of Accounting

The **cash basis of accounting** recognizes revenue and expenses on a cash basis, not on an accrual basis. Expenses are recorded only *when cash is paid for an expense*. Revenue is recorded only *when cash is received for sales or other revenue.*

The cash basis of accounting does not compare all the revenue for an accounting period with all the expenses for the same period. It does not conform to *the matching principle.* For that reason, the cash basis of accounting is not used by accountants for a business.

The cash basis of accounting recognizes revenue and expenses on a cash basis.

UNIT 4 CHECK YOUR READING

Questions

1. Name two financial statements.
2. Write definitions for each of the following:
   (a) Revenue   (c) Net income
   (b) Expense   (d) Net loss
3. What is the purpose of the income statement?
4. What are the three parts of the heading of an income statement?
5. What are the two main sections of the body of the income statement?
6. How is net income determined?
7. When is there a net loss?
8. Write definitions for:
   (a) Income statement
   (b) Accounting period
   (c) Balance sheet
9. List the four steps followed to prepare an income statement.
10. What is the time-period principle?
11. Explain the matching principle.
12. (a) Explain the accrual basis of accounting.
    (b) Explain the cash basis of accounting.

UNIT 4 APPLY YOUR KNOWLEDGE

Exercises Part A

1. Classify the following accounts as asset, liability, owner's equity, revenue, or expense. Part (a) has been done for you as an example.
   (a) Cash   (f) Y. Aunger, Capital
   (b) Accounts Payable   (g) Accounts Receivable
   (c) Building   (h) Salaries Expense
   (d) Fees Earned   (i) Commissions Earned
   (e) Advertising Expense   (j) Bank Loan
   Example:
   (a) Cash—asset

2. Calculate the net income or net loss for each of the following; then identify the accounting period.

   (a) Revenue for the year: $500 000
       Expenses for the year: 375 000
   (b) Revenue for September: 90 000
       Expenses for September: 86 000
   (c) Revenue for 6 months: 329 000
       Expenses for 6 months: 362 000
   (d) Revenue for January 1–March 31:   290 000
       Expenses for January 1–March 31:   230 000
   (e) Revenue for October: 68 350
       Expenses for October: 79 800

3. Prepare an income statement for Dr. Julie Summers for the year ended December 31, 20—, using the following accounts from the ledger: Income from Fees $225 000; Investment Income $9500; Automobile Expense $3800; Supplies Expense $4600; Rent Expense $24 000; Salaries Expense $47 000; Donations Expense $4500; Utilities Expense $8000; Insurance Expense $6500; Miscellaneous Expense $7000.

4. Prepare an income statement for Mountainview Cleaners for the month ended September 30, 20—, using the ledger accounts given here in random order: Salaries Expense $4000; Advertising Expense $1000; Telephone Expense $600; Delivery Expense $2000; Cleaning Revenue $12 000; Office Expense $2000; Repairs Revenue $1000; Rent Expense $4000.

Exercises Part B

5. The following transactions occurred during October. Indicate each time whether the transaction represents revenue to the legal firm in October. Explain your answers.

   Oct. 1   Received payment of $500 on an account receivable from a customer.
         4   Prepared a will for a client today and was paid $250.
        10   Obtained a bank loan of $3500 to purchase a new computer system.
        11   Owner invested an additional $2500 in the business.
        15   Completed the legal work started last week on a house sale and billed the client $1000.

6. The following transactions occurred in October. Indicate each time whether the transaction is an October expense for the legal firm.

   Oct. 8   Paid the weekly office salaries of $2400.
        10   Paid $250 to Office Supply Co. to reduce the balance owing.
        11   Purchased a new computer system for $5500 cash.
        14   Received a $75 bill from the *Tribune* for advertising placed last week.

Rules of Debit and Credit for Revenue and Expense Accounts

In Chapter 2, the procedure for entering transactions in the balance sheet accounts was explained. It is summarized in Figure 3-2.

Assets		=	Liabilities		+	Owner's Equity	
Debit	Credit		Debit	Credit		Debit	Credit
Increase	Decrease		Decrease	Increase		Decrease	Increase

Assets are shown on the left side of the balance sheet equation. Because they are on the left side, they increase on the left (debit) side of accounts and decrease on the right (credit) side of accounts.

Liabilities and owner's equity are shown on the right side of the balance sheet equation. Because they are on the right side, they increase on the right (credit) side of accounts and decrease on the left (debit) side of accounts.

FIGURE 3-2 Theory summary for recording debits and credits in balance sheet accounts

The procedure for recording transactions that affect revenue and expense accounts will now be demonstrated.

Before a transaction can be recorded in the accounts, it is necessary to determine whether the account will be debited or credited. As was shown earlier, net income and revenue increase owner's equity. Owner's equity is increased on the credit side. Therefore, when revenue occurs, it is recorded on the credit side of the revenue account.

Revenue increases owner's equity.

Revenue is recorded on the credit side.

Owner's Equity	
Debit	Credit
Decrease	Increase
	Revenue increases owner's equity.

Expenses decrease owner's equity. Owner's equity is decreased on the debit side. Therefore, when expenses occur, they are recorded on the debit side of the expense accounts.

Expenses decrease owner's equity. Expenses are recorded on the debit side.

Owner's Equity	
Debit	Credit
Decrease	Increase
Expenses decrease owner's equity.	

Debits and credits to revenue and expense accounts are determined by the effect of each transaction on owner's equity. *Revenue increases equity and is recorded as a credit. Expenses decrease equity and are recorded as debits.* These points are illustrated in Figures 3-3 and Figure 3-4.

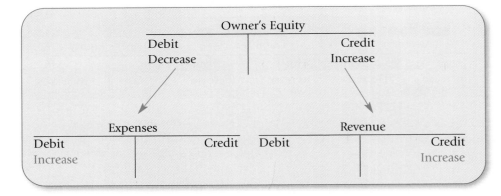

FIGURE 3-3 Determining debits and credits in revenue and expense accounts

Expense Accounts		Revenue Accounts	
Debit	Credit	Debit	Credit
Increase	Decrease	Decrease	Increase
Expenses are recorded as debits because expenses decrease equity.		Revenue is recorded as a credit because revenue increases equity.	

FIGURE 3-4 Theory summary for recording debits and credits in income statement accounts

Reason for Revenue and Expense Accounts

If revenue increases equity, expenses decrease equity, and net income/loss is eventually added to the owner's equity on the balance sheet, *why are revenue and expense accounts necessary? Why not enter transactions directly into the equity account?*

The answer is that one of the main purposes of accounting is to provide information to management about the operations of the business. Separate accounts for revenues and expenses show at a glance which sources are contributing most to the company's total revenue and which expenses are increasing too rapidly. Individual accounts for revenue and expenses provide managers with detailed information that helps them make decisions about the business they are running and control expenses, increase revenue, and operate the business effectively.

Transaction Analysis

As you have already learned, at least two accounts are involved in recording every business transaction and total debits must equal total credits for each transaction. In this chapter, you will see that the same principles of double-entry accounting

apply when you record transactions that involve revenue and expense accounts. Total debits must equal total credits for each transaction. The transactions in this chapter will involve five types of accounts: asset, liability, owner's equity, revenue, and expense.

Following are six transactions for lawyer, C. Piccolo. Examine carefully how each transaction is analyzed and the position of the debit and the credit in the T-accounts.

Transaction 1: Asset and Revenue Transaction

Jul.   1   Received $175 cash from a client for drawing up a new will.

The accounts affected are Cash and Fees Earned. Cash is an asset that increases, so the account should be debited. By completing the performance of a service, the firm earned revenue in the form of fees. Since revenue increases owner's equity, the revenue account, Fees Earned, would be credited.

Cash			Fees Earned	
Jul. 1 175			Jul. 1	175

Account Affected	Type of Account	Increase/ Decrease	Debit/ Credit	Amount
Cash	Asset	Increase	Debit	$175
Fees Earned	Revenue	Increase	Credit	175

Transaction 2: Asset and Revenue Transaction

Jul.   2   Billed client $1200 for legal services to close purchase of home.

The accounts affected are Accounts Receivable and Fees Earned. Accounts Receivable is an asset that increases, so the account is debited. By performing a service, the firm earned revenue. Revenue should be recorded when the service is completed whether the bill is paid or not. Since revenue increases owner's equity, it is credited on July 2.

Accounts Receivable			Fees Earned	
Jul. 2 1 200			Jul. 1	175
			2	1 200

Account Affected	Type of Account	Increase/ Decrease	Debit/ Credit	Amount
Accounts Receivable	Asset	Increase	Debit	$1 200
Fees Earned	Revenue	Increase	Credit	1 200

Transaction 3: Asset and Asset Transaction

Jul. 3 Received $600 from the client as partial payment of $1200 billed on July 2.

The accounts affected are Cash and Accounts Receivable. This transaction does not involve revenue because the revenue was previously recorded in Fees Earned on July 2. The asset Cash increases and is debited. The asset Accounts Receivable decreases and is credited.

Cash				Accounts Receivable			
Jul.	1	175		Jul.	2	1 200	Jul. 3	600
	3	600					

Account Affected	Type of Account	Increase/ Decrease	Debit/ Credit	Amount
Cash	Asset	Increase	Debit	$600
Accounts Receivable	Asset	Decrease	Credit	600

Transaction 4: Expense and Asset Transaction

Jul. 4 Paid $95 to Telus for telephone bill received today.

The accounts affected are Telephone Expense and Cash. The telephone cost is incurred to produce revenue and should be recognized as an expense when the bill is received. The expense decreases owner's equity and should be debited. Cash is an asset that decreases and should be credited.

Telephone Expense			Cash				
Jul. 4	95		Jul.	1	175	Jul. 4	95
				3	600		

Account Affected	Type of Account	Increase/ Decrease	Debit/ Credit	Amount
Telephone Expense	Expense	Increase	Debit	$95
Cash	Asset	Decrease	Credit	95

Transaction 5: Expense and Liability Transaction

Jul. 5 Received a bill from the *Calgary Herald* for $150 for advertising the new location of the practice. The terms of payment allow 30 days to pay. The bill will be paid later.

The accounts affected are Advertising Expense and Accounts Payable. Advertising was done to produce revenue so its cost is an expense. It should be recorded upon receipt of the bill even though the bill is not paid immediately. Since an expense decreases owner's equity, it should be debited. Accounts Payable is credited since it is a liability that increases.

Advertising Expense			Accounts Payable	
Jul. 5 150				Jul. 5 150

Account Affected	Type of Account	Increase/ Decrease	Debit/ Credit	Amount
Advertising Expense	Expense	Increase	Debit	$150
Accounts Payable	Liability	Increase	Credit	150

Transaction 6: Liability and Asset Transaction

Jul. 6   Paid $100 to the *Calgary Herald* as partial payment of their bill for $150 received on July 5.

The accounts affected are Accounts Payable and Cash. *Notice that even though a bill is paid, an expense does not result. The expense was recorded when the bill was received on July 5.* This is a simple payment on account. Accounts Payable is a liability that decreases and is debited. Cash is an asset that decreases and is credited.

Accounts Payable		Cash		
Jul. 6 100	Jul. 5 150	Jul. 1 175	Jul. 4 95	
		3 600	6 100	

Account Affected	Type of Account	Increase/ Decrease	Debit/ Credit	Amount
Accounts Payable	Liability	Decrease	Debit	$100
Cash	Asset	Decrease	Credit	100

The six transactions described above were analyzed and recorded in a systematic fashion. The answers to the following four questions helped to correctly record the transactions:

- What accounts were affected?
- Were they asset, liability, owner's equity, revenue, or expense accounts?
- Did the accounts increase or decrease?
- Were the accounts debited or credited?

SUMMARY OF DEBIT AND CREDIT THEORY

Accurate recording of transactions is based on the rules of debit and credit. The basis for recording transactions in balance sheet and income statement accounts is shown on page 82.

Balance Sheet Accounts

The debits and credits for balance sheet accounts are determined by the balance sheet equation:

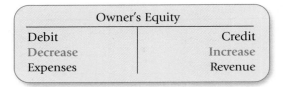

Assets		=	Liabilities		+	Owner's Equity	
Debit	Credit		Debit	Credit		Debit	Credit
Increase	Decrease		Decrease	Increase		Decrease	Increase

The following rules are based on the balance sheet equation:

1. Assets are on the left side of the balance sheet equation.
2. Asset accounts increase on the left or debit side.
3. Asset accounts decrease on the right or credit side.
4. Liabilities and owner's equity are on the right side of the balance sheet equation.
5. Liability and owner's equity accounts increase on the right or credit side.
6. Liability and owner's equity accounts decrease on the left or debit side.

Income Statement Accounts

The income statement accounts (revenue and expenses) have debits and credits determined by their effect on owner's equity.

Owner's Equity	
Debit	Credit
Decrease	Increase
Expenses	Revenue

The following rules relate to the owner's equity account:

1. Owner's equity increases on the right or credit side.
2. Revenue increases owner's equity.
3. Revenue is recorded on the credit side of revenue accounts.
4. Owner's equity decreases on the left or debit side.
5. Expenses decrease owner's equity.
6. Expenses are recorded on the debit side of expense accounts.

FURTHER STUDY OF OWNER'S EQUITY

Introducing the Owner's Drawings Account

At the beginning of the chapter, it was indicated that one of the reasons people start their own business is to earn a profit and increase the value of their equity. The owner of a business may make a regular practice of withdrawing money or other assets for personal use. This withdrawal of assets decreases the value of the owner's equity. (*This event is similar to an expense transaction since owner's equity is reduced. However, as you know, expenses are recognized only if the cost was incurred to produce revenue. Therefore, the withdrawal of assets by the owner is not an expense.*)

A withdrawal of assets is recorded in an account called Drawings. Since the withdrawal of assets affects the owner's investment, the Drawings account is an equity account. This account appears in the owner's equity section of the general ledger and decreases the owner's equity on the balance sheet. The Drawings account normally has a debit balance since withdrawals decrease owner's equity.

The Drawings account records the withdrawal of assets from the business by the owner.

The owner's Drawings account is debited whenever assets are withdrawn by the owner for personal use. Examples of this are:

- withdrawing cash;
- removing merchandise for personal use;
- taking equipment from the business for personal use; and
- using company funds for personal expenses of the owner or the owner's family.

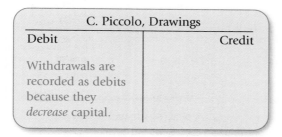

On October 15, for example, C. Piccolo, the owner, withdrew $1000 cash from the business for personal use. The effect of this withdrawal is illustrated by these T-accounts:

C. Piccolo, Drawings		Cash	
Oct. 15 1 000			Oct. 15 1 000

Owner's Salary

A salary may be paid by a business to the owner of that business. However, for income tax purposes, the business may not record the payment in an expense account such as Salaries Expense. Therefore, the payment of wages or salaries to an owner must be recorded in the Drawings account.

Drawings Account in the General Ledger

The study of the general ledger can now be summarized. You have learned that a ledger is a group of accounts. In the general ledger, there is one account for each asset, for each liability, and for the owner's equity. There is also an account for each type of revenue, for each type of expense, and for Drawings. As transactions occur, the changes caused by them are recorded in these accounts.

At the end of the accounting or fiscal period, a trial balance is prepared. The revenue and expense accounts are used to prepare the income statement. The assets, liabilities, and owner's equity accounts (including Drawings) are used to prepare the balance sheet. A complete summary of some typical general ledger accounts, the account classifications, and the financial statements prepared from these accounts is shown in Figure 3-5 on page 84.

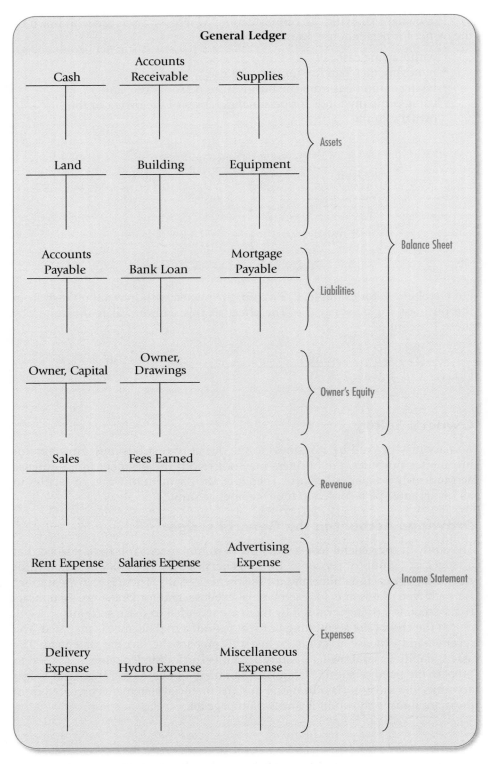

FIGURE 3-5 General ledger containing asset, liability, owner's equity, revenue, and expense accounts

Equity Accounts on the Balance Sheet

The income statement is prepared first because the result, the net income or net loss, affects the balance sheet.

The owner's Capital account and Drawings account appear in the owner's equity section of the balance sheet. The Capital account is a record of the owner's investment in the business. It is the owner's claim against the assets. The Capital account increases if there is a net income earned or if the owner increases the assets of the business by further investment in it. The Capital account decreases if there is a net loss or if the owner withdraws assets from the business for personal use. The owner's Drawings account is used to record all withdrawals. The results of increases or decreases in the Capital account are shown in the equity section of the balance sheet.

Figures 3-6, 3-7, and 3-8 show the owner's equity section of three balance sheets. In the October balance sheet shown in Figure 3-6, the business had a net income of $3000; the owner, C. Piccolo, withdrew $1000 for personal use; and the Capital account increased by $2000 to $22 000. Notice how three money columns are used to record this information.

Owner's Equity

C. Piccolo, Capital October 1		$20 000
Add: Net Income for October	$3 000	
Less: C. Piccolo, Drawings	1 000	
Increase in Capital		2 000
C. Piccolo, Capital October 31		$22 000

FIGURE 3-6 Capital increases when withdrawals are less than net income.

In the November balance sheet shown in Figure 3-7, the Capital account decreased because the owner withdrew $1500 while the net income was only $1000. The result was a decrease in the Capital account of $500. Again, three money columns are used to show the changes.

Owner's Equity

C. Piccolo, Capital November 1		$22 000
Add: Net Income for November	$1 000	
Less: C. Piccolo, Drawings	1 500	
Decrease in Capital		500
C. Piccolo, Capital November 30		$21 500

Figure 3-7 Capital decreases when withdrawals are greater than net income.

In the December balance sheet shown in Figure 3-8, the Capital account decreases because of a net loss of $500 and drawings of $800. The total decrease is $1300. Therefore, the Capital account decreases from $21 500 to $20 200.

Owner's Equity

C. Piccolo, Capital December 1		$21 500
Less: Net Loss for December	$500	
Less: C. Piccolo, Drawings	800	
Decrease in Capital		1 300
C. Piccolo, Capital December 31		$20 200

FIGURE 3-8 Capital decreases when there is a loss and the owner has withdrawn assets.

REPORT FORM OF BALANCE SHEET

The account form balance sheet lists the assets on the left side and the liabilities and owner's equity on the right side.

Up to this point, the *account form* of balance sheet has been used. The **account form balance sheet** lists the assets on the left side and the liabilities and owner's equity on the right side. The account form balance sheet was essential to establishing the concept:

$$\text{Left Side} \quad = \quad \text{Right Side}$$

From this concept, the balance sheet equation was derived:

$$\text{Assets} \quad = \quad \text{Liabilities} \quad + \quad \text{Owner's Equity}$$

The balance sheet equation is an inflexible rule and forms the basis of the double-entry accounting system.

The balance sheet does not always appear in the account form, however. Another form of balance sheet is the report form, shown in Figure 3-9. In the **report form balance sheet**, the assets, liabilities, and owner's equity are listed vertically.

The report form balance sheet lists the assets, liabilities, and owner's equity vertically.

In Figure 3-9, of course, the balance sheet concept Left Side = Right Side no longer applies, since the balance sheet is written *vertically* and there is no left side and right side. Remember, though, that the balance sheet equation still applies:

$$\begin{array}{ccccc} \text{Assets} & = & \text{Liabilities} & + & \text{Owner's Equity} \\ \$244\ 285 & & \$157\ 630 & & \$86\ 655 \end{array}$$

Facts to Remember

A slight modification of the rule given in Chapter 1 for the placement of dollar signs on the balance sheet is now required. For the report form balance sheet, dollar signs should be placed as follows:

- beside the first figure in each column in both sections of the statement; and
- beside the final total in both sections of the statement.

Goldman's Gym
Balance Sheet
September 30, 20—

Assets

Cash	$ 7 325	
Accounts Receivable	2 000	
Office Supplies	725	
Land	225 000	
Building	110 000	
Training Equipment	99 235	
Total Assets		$244 285

Liabilities and Owner's Equity

Liabilities

Accounts Payable	$12 630	
Bank Loan	65 000	
Mortgage Payable	80 000	
Total Liabilities		$157 630

Owner's Equity

R. Millar, Capital September 1		85 260	
Add: Net Income for September	$2 395		
Less: R. Millar, Drawings	1 000		
Increase in Capital		1 395	
R. Millar, Capital September 30			86 655
Total Liabilities and Owner's Equity			$244 285

FIGURE 3-9 Report form balance sheet

PREPARING FINANCIAL STATEMENTS FROM THE TRIAL BALANCE

Figures 3-10, 3-11, and 3-12 on pages 88 and 89 illustrate that the financial statements are prepared from the trial balance in this order:

Trial Balance → Income Statement → Balance Sheet

First, Figure 3-10 shows all of the accounts on the trial balance.

Goldman's Gym
Trial Balance
October 31, 20—

Balance Sheet Accounts			
	Cash	$ 7 650	
	Accounts Receivable	2 700	
	Office Supplies	695	
	Land	225 000	
	Building	110 000	
	Training Equipment	99 235	
	Accounts Payable		$ 11 600
	Bank Loan		63 000
	Mortgage Payable		80 000
	R. Millar, Capital		86 655
	R. Millar, Drawings	1 200	
	Members' Fees		14 600
	Tanning Bed Rental		725
	Towel Rental		160
	Salaries Expense	3 850	
	Advertising Expense	2 880	
	Telephone Expense	190	
	Maintenance Expense	650	
	Licence Expense	1 100	
	Interest Expense	1 500	
	Laundry Expense	90	
		$256 740	$256 740

FIGURE 3-10 Trial balance containing all ledger accounts

Remember that the trial balance is a list of the accounts and balances from the general ledger in ledger order. The accounts are arranged with the balance sheet accounts preceding the income statement accounts. However, since you must calculate the net income/loss for the accounting period to complete the equity section of the balance sheet, *the income statement is prepared before the balance sheet.*

The income statement is prepared before the balance sheet.

Figure 3-11 is the income statement that is prepared using the revenue and expense accounts shown in Figure 3-10.

Remember that even though Drawings has a debit balance, it is not an expense account and is not included on the income statement. Drawings will be used along with the net income ($5225) in the equity section of the balance sheet.

Figure 3-12 is the balance sheet. It contains asset, liability, and owner's equity accounts. It is prepared in the *report form.*

Goldman's Gym
Income Statement
For the month ended October 31, 20—

Revenue		
Members' Fees	$14 600	
Tanning Bed Rental	725	
Towel Rental	160	$15 485
Expenses		
Salaries	3 850	
Advertising	2 880	
Telephone	190	
Maintenance	650	
Licence	1 100	
Interest	1 500	
Laundry	90	10 260
Net Income		$ 5 225

FIGURE 3-11 Income statement

Goldman's Gym
Balance Sheet
October 31, 20—

Assets		
Cash	$ 7 650	
Accounts Receivable	2 700	
Office Supplies	695	
Land	225 000	
Building	110 000	
Training Equipment	99 235	
Total Assets		$245 280

Liabilities and Owner's Equity

Liabilities		
Accounts Payable	$11 600	
Bank Loan	63 000	
Mortgage Payable	80 000	
Total Liabilities		$154 600
Owner's Equity		
R. Millar, Capital October 1		86 655
Add: Net Income for October	$5 225	
Less: R. Millar, Drawings	1 200	
Increase in Capital		4 025
R. Millar, Capital October 31		90 680
Total Liabilities and Owner's Equity		$245 280

FIGURE 3-12 Balance sheet

Generally Accepted Accounting Principles and Key Ideas

In this chapter, you learned the following Generally Accepted Accounting Principles:

- **The Time-Period Principle:** Each company sets and defines an accounting period. The period may be a month, three months, a year, etc. The company consistently uses the same time period when it prepares its financial statements.
- **The Matching Principle:** The costs recorded in the expense accounts should be matched with the revenue of the same accounting period to determine net income.

You also learned the following key ideas:

- The **accrual basis of accounting** records *revenue* when it is *earned*, whether that revenue is in the form of cash or credit granted. *Expenses* are recorded when *incurred*, whether those expenses are paid for in cash or credit granted by the supplier.

UNIT 5 CHECK YOUR READING

Questions

13. (a) Does revenue increase or decrease owner's equity?
    (b) Do expenses increase or decrease owner's equity?
14. (a) What is the increase side for revenue accounts? Why?
    (b) What is the increase side for expense accounts? Why?
15. (a) Give an example of a transaction that is recorded in the owner's Drawings account.
    (b) On which financial statement does the owner's Drawings account appear?
16. In which account is the payment of a salary to the owner recorded?
17. What is a report form balance sheet?
18. Which financial statement is prepared first? Why?

UNIT 5 APPLY YOUR KNOWLEDGE

Exercises Part A

8. The following accounts are found in the general ledger of Almond Nursery School: Cash; Accounts Receivable; Playground Equipment; Accounts Payable; L. Almond, Drawings; Fees Earned; Advertising Expense; Automobile Expense; Salaries Expense. Referring to these accounts, analyze the transactions shown on the next page for this business. Use the format demonstrated in the example to assist you. List the debit portion of the entry before the credit portion. Transaction (a) has been done for you.

(a) Received $155 cash from a client for the weekly nursery school fees.

(b) Paid $35 cash for gas for the station wagon used to transport the children to school.

(c) Received a bill for $100 from the *Standard* for advertising.

(d) Purchased a new swing set for the playground from School Supply for $350 on credit.

(e) Paid the weekly salary of $3000 to the staff.

(f) The owner, L. Almond, withdrew $500 for personal use.

(g) Paid the $100 bill received previously from the *Standard*.

Example:

Transaction	Account Affected	Type of Account	Increase/ Decrease	Debit/ Credit	Amount
(a)	Cash	Asset	Increase	Debit	$155
	Fees Earned	Revenue	Increase	Credit	155

9. Gibson's Service Centre repairs automobiles on a cash or credit basis. Accounts in the general ledger include: Cash $10 000; Accounts Receivable $3500; Tools $5500; Equipment $25 500; Accounts Payable $2200; P. Gibson, Drawings; P. Gibson, Capital $42 300; Repair Service Revenue; Advertising Expense; Rent Expense; Telephone Expense. Transactions that occurred during October are given below.

(a) Set up a T-account ledger, then record the balances and the following transactions.

(b) Prepare a trial balance.

Oct. 2 Paid the monthly rent of $4000 to Deneer Co.

3 Repaired Jim Jones' car and billed him $535.

4 Purchased a new set of tools for $1275 on credit from Tool Supply.

6 Received a bill for $475 from the *Gazette* for advertising.

6 Paid Auto Supply $750 for amounts owing to them.

7 Paid the telephone bill received today, $85.

10 The owner, P. Gibson, withdrew $500 for his own use.

11 Received $215 cash from a customer for a tune-up and oil change done today.

11 Received $175 cash on account from a customer who was sent a bill last month.

10. Record the following transactions for Stokes Driving School in these accounts: Cash; Accounts Receivable/L. Starr; Equipment; Automobiles; Accounts Payable/Grant's Esso; R. Stokes, Capital; Revenue from Lessons; Salaries Expense; Advertising Expense; Automobile Expense; Utilities Expense.

Aug. 1 R. Stokes invested $35 000 cash.
       2 Purchased equipment for $2000 cash.
       4 Purchased two cars from Dardick Motors for $30 000 cash.
       5 Received $700 cash from customers' driving lessons.
       7 Paid $700 cash for instructor's salary for the first week.
       9 Paid $45 cash to the telephone company.
     10 Received $800 cash from customers taking driving lessons.
     11 Issued a bill of $100 to L. Starr, who is taking lessons but will pay at a later date.
     11 Received a bill for $75 from Grant's Esso for gas and oil used by the cars.
     12 Paid $95 cash for hydro and electricity.
     13 Sent a $290 cheque to the *Daily Star* for advertising space.
     14 Received $100 cash from L. Starr in payment of a bill sent previously.

(a) Balance the accounts and prepare a trial balance.
(b) Prepare an income statement for the two weeks ended August 14.

11. The T-accounts shown on the next page contain a series of transactions for Tancredi Realty. For each of the labelled entries, indicate how the accounts have changed and the transaction that must have occurred to generate the entry. The chart below, with transaction (a) done as an example, will assist you in completing the question.

Example:

Transaction	Account Affected	Type of Account	Increase/ Decrease	Debit/ Credit	Amount
(a)	Cash	Asset	Increase	Debit	$500
	Accounts Receivable	Asset	Decrease	Credit	500

Cash increased and Accounts Receivable decreased. Therefore, an account receivable was collected.

12. Complete the following chart by indicating the amount of the increase or decrease in Capital and the ending amount in Capital.

Beginning Capital	Net Income	Net Loss	Drawings	Inc. or Dec. in Capital	Ending Capital
(a) $10 000	$1 000	—	$ 500	?	?
(b) 25 000	1 000	—	1 500	?	?
(c) 18 000	—	$2 000	600	?	?
(d) 12 000	3 000	—	1 000	?	?

General Ledger

Cash

Balance	2 500	(b)	100
(a)	500	(d)	650
(f)	3 500	(g)	1 200
(i)	1 000	(h)	90
		(j)	175

J. Tancredi, Drawings

| (b) | 100 | | |

Accounts Receivable

| Balance | 3 500 | (a) | 500 |
| (c) | 1 000 | | |

Commissions Earned

| | | (c) | 1 000 |
| | | (f) | 3 500 |

Office Furniture

| Balance | 8 000 | | |

Office Salaries Expense

| (d) | 650 | | |

Office Equipment

| Balance | 12 000 | | |

Advertising Expense

| (e) | 400 | | |

Accounts Payable

| | | Balance | 1 700 |
| | | (e) | 400 |

Rent Expense

| (g) | 1 200 | | |

Bank Loan

| | | Balance | 9 000 |

Telephone Expense

| (h) | 90 | | |

J. Tancredi, Capital

| | | Balance | 15 300 |
| | | (i) | 1 000 |

Utilities Expense

| (j) | 175 | | |

13. Prepare the owner's equity section of the balance sheet for each of the following three months for Dr. W. Lucey, who has just begun a medical practice.

(a) Capital Balance January 1 — $36 000
Net Loss for January — 4 000
Drawings for January — 6 000
(b) Capital Balance February 1 — ?
Net Income for February — 1 000
Drawings for February — 5 000
(c) Capital Balance March 1 — ?
Net Income for March — 5 000
Drawings for March — 4 500

Exercises Part B

14. On April 1, Ted's Golfing School had the following accounts, some with balances and some without: Cash $3000; Accounts Receivable/P. Moores $150; Accounts Receivable/L. Troop; Equipment $4700; Accounts Payable/Jack's Repair Shop $750; T. Craig, Capital $7100; Fees Income; Advertising Expense; Rent Expense; Equipment Repairs Expense; Utilities Expense.
   (a) Set up the general ledger for Ted's Golfing School on April 1 and record the transactions listed below.
   (b) On April 12, balance the accounts and prepare a trial balance, an income statement for the two weeks, and a balance sheet.

Apr.	2	Received $300 cash from customers for golf lessons.
	2	Issued a bill for $95 to L. Troop for lessons that will be paid for later.
	3	Paid $1400 cash to United Realty for the monthly rent.
	4	Received $50 cash from P. Moores to be applied to amount outstanding.
	5	Received a $175 bill from Jack's Repair Shop for repairing equipment.
	8	Received $2000 cash from customers for lessons.
	8	Issued another $45 bill to L. Troop for lessons.
	9	Received $100 cash from P. Moores to pay balance owed.
	10	Received a $500 bill for equipment bought from Jack's Repair Shop.
	12	Paid $90 cash for electricity and water.
	12	Paid $300 to Jack's Repair Shop to reduce the balance owing.
	12	Paid $355 cash to the *Gazette* for advertising.

15. On October 1, the Courtland Cougars Hockey Team, owned by J. Lambert, had the following accounts, some with balances and some without: Cash $12 000; Accounts Receivable/Stokes Dept. Stores; Equipment $4000; Bus $15 000; Accounts Payable/Klaman Motors $5300; J. Lambert, Capital $25 700; Ticket Sales; Players' Salaries Expense; Bus Maintenance Expense; Arena Rental Expense; Advertising Expense.
   (a) Set up the general ledger for the hockey team on October 1, and record the transactions given below for the month of October.
   (b) On October 31, balance the accounts and prepare a trial balance, an income statement for the month, and a balance sheet.

Oct.	2	Received $120 000 cash from sales of season tickets.
	4	Purchased equipment for $3000 cash.
	8	Received a $250 bill from Klaman Motors for repairs to the team bus.
	9	Issued a bill for $2100 to Stokes Department Stores, which bought 500 tickets for the team's opening home game. (The tickets will be used for promotional purposes.)
	10	Paid a $350 rental fee for use of the arena for the last two weeks' practice.

14   Issued cheques for $10 400 to pay the players' salaries for the past two weeks.

16   Paid $350 cash to KCV TV for advertising the first home game on October 26.

17   Paid $470 to the *Daily Reporter* for advertising.

20   The week's sale of tickets for the opening game brought in $3500 in cash.

24   Paid $50 cash for gas and oil for the bus on the first away-from-home game.

26   Received a further $8700 cash for ticket sales on the opening game.

28   Paid $2100 cash to the arena for the last two week's rent.

29   Issued cheques for $9800 to pay the players' salaries for the rest of the month.

16. The Foothills Flyers are a minor league professional baseball team owned by Dawn French. A partial list of the accounts used by the team are as follows: Cash $10 000; Equipment; Accounts Payable; Bank Loan $10 000; D. French, Capital; D. French, Drawings; Gate Receipts; Parking Revenue; Concession Revenue; Advertising Expense; Players' Salaries Expense; Interest Expense; Rent Expense; Transportation Expense.

(a) Set up the general ledger for Foothills Flyers Baseball Club Inc. Record the following transactions and calculate the account balances.

Jun.   1   D. French, the owner, invested an additional $25 000 in the team.

1   Received a bill for $750 from the *Gazette* for advertising. The amount is due in 30 days.

2   Purchased a new speaker system for the field from Electronics Inc. Paid $500 cash and the remaining $1500 is to be paid in 30 days.

2   Paid the players' salaries for the week, $22 500.

3   The game today produced gate receipts $4500, parking revenue $490, and concession revenue $1375.

4   Signed a new player to a standard player's contract calling for a payment of $750 per week for the remainder of the season. The player will join the club for tomorrow's game.

4   Made the regular monthly payment of $1000 on the bank loan. The payment consisted of $100 in interest and $900 that reduced the amount of the loan.

4   Today's game generated gate receipts of $3900, parking revenue of $425, and concession revenue of $1100.

4   Paid the stadium rent to the city for the last two games. The rent was 10 percent of gate receipts.

5   The owner, D. French, withdrew $700 to make the monthly payment to GMAC on her personal car loan.

5   Received a bill from Buckley's Transit for the bus used on the last road trips, $2200. Sent a cheque in full payment.

17. A random-order list of accounts and balances for a one-month accounting period is shown below for TAC Plumbing. Prepare the financial statements for the company on February 28.

General Expense	$ 500	Cash	$6 500
Accounts Receivable	1 600	Salaries Expense	7 000
Rent Expense	1 100	Plumbing Supplies	6 000
Equipment	26 000	Advertising Expense	900
Truck	8 000	Sales	9 000
Accounts Payable	2 600	C. Bell, Drawings	1 700
C. Bell, Capital	43 200	Bank Loan	4 500

Computer Accounting

Canadian Tire Stores

Canadian Tire stores are found in most communities in Canada. There are about 444 Canadian Tire retail outlets located across all ten provinces.

In the following case profile, we will examine how this Canadian Tire store uses computers to complete some of its accounting tasks. The store is located on Heron Road in Ottawa and is owned by Ken MacEachern. There are approximately 160 employees involved in running the store and an automotive repair centre.

Accounting System

Outside of management, there are five people involved in accounting in this business. As well, several major accounting functions are contracted from outside companies. A breakdown of the accounting system follows. The office manager coordinates the payroll, financial statements, and general ledger functions.

Payroll Services

The payroll is prepared in-house using a computerized payroll system and distributed by the Canadian Imperial Bank of Commerce. Employee work information is sent to the bank and the bank calculates gross pay, deductions, and net earnings and provides a pay statement for each employee. The bank provides a payroll summary to the company for its records.

Inventory Control

These functions are performed by the inventory manager, Gerry Brisson, and the computer operator, Denise Rhéaume, using an "in-house" computer system.

Cash Control

The daily balancing of the cash register terminals, credit card accounting, and banking is performed by three accounting employees.

Financial Statements and General Ledger

A public accounting firm, Sharp, Edmunds Sharp LLP, of Don Mills, Ontario, provides this service on a monthly basis.

Financial Management

Financial decisions of a management nature are made by the store's Associate Dealer, Ken MacEachern, and the operations manager, Lawson MacEachern, using information generated by the accounting system. The computer system is an important part of this accounting system.

Computer System

The computer system processes data and provides reports which are used to make effective business decisions. The hardware part of the system includes an IBM AS 400 system (see photograph below). The AS 400 is a general purpose business mini-computer system. It uses six IBM exclusive processors which each access the main server which has a large storage capacity. The server and a printer are located in the office area of the store. Over thirty separate computer terminals and seven printers are connected to the host server in the main office. Seventeen terminals are used by the cashiers as cash register terminals in the customer check-out area of the store. Three terminals are used for administrative and accounting purposes and twelve are located in various parts of the store for the use of sales personnel. One computer is set aside in the office area to handle cash balancing. A stand-alone computer (not attached to the main system) is used to create store signs. This computer is attached to a Hewlett-Packard Laser printer. The many software programs needed to run this system were developed by a team consisting of computer consultants, IBM programmers, and Canadian Tire representatives.

Inventory Control

Up to 100 000 different products are sold in Canadian Tire stores. Each item has its own computer code number. A master inventory file contains complete inventory information about each product such as:

- Balance on hand
- Price
- Quantity on order
- Order date
- Expected delivery date
- Sales, previous year
- Sales, to date this year

This large data bank of inventory information can be accessed by a number of different software programs to provide a variety of information and reports. Let's examine how the computer uses its bank of inventory information to assist the store employees to carry out their duties effectively.

Cash Register Terminals

When a customer hands an item to the cashier, the inventory code is scanned into the cash register terminal. The terminal is connected to the computer's inventory data bank. Immediately, the price of the item is drawn out of the data bank and shown on the screen along with a description of the product. It is not necessary for the terminal operator to enter the price or any other information except the amount of money given by the customer. The amount of change owed to the customer is automatically calculated and shown on the screen.

The details of the sale are retained in the computer's inventory file. This information is used by the computer to produce a new balance on hand for each item. At the end of the day, the computer also produces a tape summary for each cash register terminal which shows:

- Cash sales
- Credit card sales
- Returns
- Coupons received
- Coupons issued

This information is used to "balance the cash" for each cash register terminal.

Sales Floor Terminals

Several computer terminals are located in the sales area of the store. When a customer requests an item which cannot be found on the shelves, a salesperson can enter the product code using the terminal and in a second the information about the product appears on the screen. The computer indicates if there is a supply of the product in the inventory storeroom. If so, the salesperson can get the product for the customer. If there is no stock on hand, the computer indicates when the delivery date of the new stock is expected. Again, this only takes a very brief time and the result is better service to the customer.

Inventory Reports

Computers have powerful retrieval, sorting, and classifying capabilities. They can store and access large amounts of data and manipulate it to produce reports, information, and summaries in a very short time. The Canadian Tire inventory records are updated automatically every twenty minutes. The updated information is available in visual form on the computer terminals or can be provided in the form of the printed reports described below.

Sales History Report

This report is available for all items or for selected items. It shows the sales for the item(s) for each quarter (three months) for each of the past three years.

Order Audit Report

The computer is programmed to forecast which items need to be ordered. This report indicates, for each item, last year's sales and the sales to date this year, and recommends a quantity to be ordered. The inventory manager analyses this report and decides, using judgment and experience, which items and quantities to order. The information provided by the computer is very helpful in making these decisions.

Discontinued Merchandise Report

Occasionally items are purchased which do not sell very well. Such merchandise is not reordered and is removed from the company's product list. The discontinued merchandise report indicates the balance on hand for each discontinued item. Decisions concerning special sales can be made by referring to this report.

Other Computer Functions

The computer provides a number of other functions to this store. The system is directly linked to the Canadian Tire distribution centres in Brampton and Montreal and to the financial services office in Welland (Canadian Tire Acceptance Ltd.). This direct link provides:

- Electronic merchandise order process
- E-mail
- Delivery information
- Price tickets (if required)
- Credit sale information

Electronic Merchandise Order Process

Each day, the inventory manager analyses the daily inventory report. Decisions are made concerning which items should be ordered. The computer operator then sends a list of products and quantities to the Brampton distribution centre using SpacePak, a satellite system which connects all Canadian Tire stores through their Parts depots. The next day, the Brampton distribution centre confirms the orders. It indicates, using the computer to communicate, that the orders have been received and when delivery will be made.

Delivery Information

The computer in the Brampton distribution centre is used to send messages concerning the delivery of merchandise to the regional stores. A message indicating the contents of each truckload of merchandise is sent by computer. The message is printed in Ottawa in the form of a list of merchandise being delivered.

The receiving computer then updates its inventory file. The price information is on bar codes affixed to products by the manufacturer.

Credit Sales Information

Prior to the installation of the present computer system at Canadian Tire, all charge sales were updated manually at the regional store and then the paperwork was forwarded by courier to the head office in Welland. The Heron Road Canadian Tire store utilizes a custom software program called Draft Capture which electronically forwards all customer charges directly to the financial services office in Welland via the computer terminal. The paperwork and courier service have been eliminated.

Summary

The foregoing description illustrates the effective use of computer power as part of an accounting system. Computer systems can do the following:

- Store large amounts of information
- Sort, classify, and produce information almost instantly
- Print data at high speeds
- Do mathematical calculations accurately and quickly
- Produce information quickly in visual and print formats
- Transmit information quickly over long distances
- Communicate with other electronic equipment

Canadian Tire stores use the power of the computer to make their accounting systems effective.

The computerized inventory system described in this case profile is a perpetual inventory system. It is a continuous record of the 100 000 items of merchandise sold by the store. In a manual perpetual inventory system, a stock card is kept for each item of stock. In the case of the Canadian Tire store, this would mean 100 000 stock cards that would have to be maintained by hand. Every sale and every delivery of new stock would have to be manually recorded on the stock cards — an almost impossible task.

Questions

1. Approximately how many Canadian Tire stores are there in Canada?
2. How many people are employed by the Canadian store mentioned in your textbook? How many are involved in the accounting function?
3. Why would this Canadian Tire store choose to contract out the payroll service?
4. Who provided the hardware part of the Canadian Tire computer accounting system? Who developed the software programs?

5. Explain the various functions provided by the cash register terminals.
6. What are the sales floor terminals used for?
7. What are the advantages and disadvantages of a computerized perpetual inventory system compared to a manual system?
8. Briefly explain the types of information provided by the following reports:
   a) Daily inventory report
   b) Sales history report
   c) Order audit report
   d) Discontinued merchandise report
9. What other functions does the computer perform for the Canadian Tire store?
10. Visit a local department, hardware, or similar type of retail store that uses a computerized accounting system. Describe the store's system by writing your own case study similar to the Canadian Tire Case Study.

COMPUTER ASSIGNMENTS

1. (a) Format a spreadsheet to be used to determine the net income or net loss for exercise 2 on page 74.
   (b) Print your answers for exercise 2.
2. (a) Format a spreadsheet that can be used to prepare an income statement.
   (b) Use the spreadsheet to print an income statement for exercise 3 on page 74.
   (c) Print an income statement for exercise 4.
3. (a) Format a spreadsheet for exercise 13 on page 93.
   (b) Print your answers for this exercise.

4. Laser Inc. is a multinational corporation that produces a variety of lasers for marking, scientific, and medical applications. Laser Inc. sells its products in four geographic areas, including Canada, Japan, the United States, and Europe. The president of the company has asked for some specific information about each geographic area. The period of interest is the last five years. As a financial manager of the company, provide this information by doing the following tasks:
   (a) Design your spreadsheet on paper and then format a spreadsheet that will print the following:

   ▶ Total sales for each year
   ▶ Percentage of total sales for each area for each year

   (b) Load your spreadsheet program and enter the data shown in the table below. Print your spreadsheet.

Laser Inc.
Sales for the Last Five Years
(in thousands of dollars)

	Year 1	Year 2	Year 3	Year 4	Year 5
Japan	$ 368	$ 450	$ 380	$ 495	$ 820
Europe	456	507	1 030	1 980	3 760
Canada	924	1 095	1 445	1 665	1 740
United States	2 052	3 648	4 445	4 860	6 260

(c) Write a summary for the president, highlighting the financial data by geographic area.

5. The operating results for five years for the M. Sampath Consulting are shown below.

M. Sampath Consulting
Operating Results
(in thousands of dollars)

	Year 1	Year 2	Year 3	Year 4	Year 5
Revenue					
Fees Earned	$250	$274	$298	$300	$345
Investment Income	12	9	9	7	6
TOTAL REVENUE					
Expenses					
Automobile	10	11	13	14	15
Advertising	9	12	15	17	18
Promotion	4	5	6	7	8
Office	20	24	26	28	30
Salaries	80	85	90	110	130
Other	30	45	55	70	86
Total Expenses					
Net Income/(Loss)					

(a) Format a spreadsheet that will do the following:
  ‣ Calculate the total revenue, total expenses, and net income or loss each year.
  ‣ Calculate the percentage that each expense item is of the Fees Earned.
(b) Prepare suggestions for the owner of the business.

WEB EXTENSIONS

www.pearsoned.ca/
principlesofaccounting

Internet Study Guide

- Complete the Chapter 3 review.
- Complete the Chapter 3 definitions.
- Complete the Chapter 3 online test.

Web Links

Visit the Web Links section at the Pearson Education web site to find a link to the Canadian Tire site. Outline the benefits and potential revenue sources that an e-business site provides to Canadian Tire.

8 Case Studies

CASE 1 Income Statement Analysis

You are the loan manager for a bank. A customer, Wireless Network Devices, has applied for a loan to expand its business. In support of the loan application, the company has supplied an income statement for the last six months that shows a net income of $12 000.

The following factors were not considered in the preparation of the income statement:

- Salaries of $3000 are owed to workers for last month but have not been paid or recorded as an expense.
- Interest of $1000 is owed to another bank.

(a) What effect does the omission of these two items have on the firm's net income?
(b) What is the correct net income?
(c) What Generally Accepted Accounting Principle (GAAP) has not been followed?

CASE 2 Recording Transactions

National Products is a very large manufacturer of household products. It has several factories that produce items sold by 45 branch offices located throughout the country. As an incentive for the branch managers, a bonus is offered if yearly budgeted net income figures are exceeded.

You are the accountant for a branch office of National Products. The branch manager is Suzanne Dorelle. You are aware that Suzanne has obtained a new position and plans to leave National Products early in January. Late in December she instructs you to omit from your records several large expenses, including insurance, overtime pay for December, and fuel and hydro costs. She tells you to pay these expenses as usual in December but to delay recording the items until some time in the new year.

(a) What will be the effect of not recording the expenses in December?
(b) What would you do? What are your alternatives? What are the consequences of each alternative?
(c) What GAAP is involved in this case?

CASE 3 Income Statement Errors

(a) There are several errors in the following income statement. Prepare a list of the errors.
(b) What is the correct net income or net loss?

Income Statement
Berlin and Associates
April 30, 20—

Revenue

Sales		$50 000
Investment Income		2 000
Cash		7 000
		59 000

Expenses

Advertising	$ 2 000	
Salaries	40 000	
Accounts Payable	5 000	
Rent	8 000	
General	1 000	56 000
Net Income		$ 3 000

Charge Accounts

CASE 4

We are all familiar with bank credit cards such as MasterCard and Visa. Many large department stores such as The Bay and Sears issue their own credit cards to their customers. Here is how one store, *Z Department Store,** decides whether a person will receive the privilege of using its credit card.

1. Have the applicant complete a standard application form. Call the credit references supplied on the form. Call the employer to verify employment. If these steps indicate that the person has a job and has a good payment record for the last six months, *approve* the application at once. If this information is not available, proceed to step two.

2. Call the Credit Bureau. If the person receives a favourable credit check, *approve* the application at once. If there is no file on the person, proceed to step three.

3. Confirm the person's employment. If working full time, *approve* the application at once. If unemployed, *reject*.

If a charge account is granted to a customer, then a credit limit is set. This is the maximum amount that may be outstanding in the customer's account. The limit is set by completion of this guide:

* *The name has been changed.*

A Marital Status	Married	Single	Widowed	Other
Points	+2	+1	+4	0
B Years Married	0–2	2–5	5–10	10 or more
Points	0	+2	+3	+5
C Residence	Own	Mobile home	Rent	Live at home
Points	+5	+3	0	+2
D Years at Address	Up to 2	2–5	5 or more	
Points	0	+2	+3	
E Spouse's Age	Up to 30	30–36	36–45	45 or more
Points	0	+2	+3	+5
F Telephone	Yes	No		
Points	+4	0		

Points are allocated to the answers to A to F. If a person obtains fewer than 12 points, a charge account is not issued. If a person obtains 13 to 18 points, a credit limit of $2000 is established with a monthly minimum payment of $100. If a person obtains a total over 19 points, a limit of $5000 is established with a monthly payment of $300.

(a) What is your opinion of the advantages and disadvantages of this system of granting charge accounts?

(b) Can you suggest a better method?

9 Career Education Activities

1. Personal Résumé

A résumé is a device used to communicate your talents, education, qualifications, and experience to potential employers. A résumé is like a personal fact sheet—it tells the reader the facts about you that will help in a decision concerning employment. It can be considered to be a personal advertisement.

Some of the things that impress potential employers include:
- good grades at school;
- leadership activities;
- athletic accomplishments;
- volunteer and charitable work;
- hobbies; and
- interests outside of school.

You might consider creating a portfolio in which to accumulate data about yourself that will be useful when you prepare a résumé in the future.

For Discussion and Follow-Up

(a) What would you include in a personal résumé if you prepared one today?

(b) Go to your library, or use the Internet, and obtain samples of the format to use in a résumé.

(c) Start a résumé for yourself today and then continue to update it as you proceed through school.

2. Experience—Who's Got Experience?

The following advertisement for an accounts receivable/payable clerk describes accounting tasks that you will be able to perform after you complete this course. Applicants must have accounting work experience. How does a young person leaving school obtain experience? Most jobs require experience, yet you cannot get experience without a job! Quite a dilemma.

For Discussion

(a) Can you suggest ways of getting experience now that will help you in the future? The career profile that follows describes one method.

(b) In small groups, prepare a list of experiences that group members have had and that will help them in the future.

ACCOUNTS RECEIVABLE/PAYABLE CLERK

Part-time/Full-time
This position requires two years' accounting experience handling both accounts receivable and accounts payable. The successful candidate will have a desire to learn and a willingness to do administrative tasks. Good computer and communication skills are a requirement. Completion of accounting courses would be considered an asset.

ADMINISTRATIVE CLERK

Our dynamic environment requires a sharp administrative clerk to do filing and miscellaneous administrative functions. Must have professional attire, possess good communication and computer skills, and be willing to complete a 3-week training program.

If interested contact:
Anderson Inc.
100 Ellington Ave. East, Suite 100
Toronto, ON M3C 1H9
(416) 444-3838, Fax: (416) 444-3939
E-mail: jobs@andersoninc.com

Career Profile

Trevor Yeung is a senior student at Laura Secord Secondary School. Trevor's ultimate goal is to obtain a university degree and the CA (chartered accountant) designation. He enjoys courses in computers, mathematics, and accounting.

After graduation, Trevor wants to work full-time or part-time to support himself and to attend Brock University in the co-operative accounting program. Trevor has learned that realistic, on-the-job experience is required by most employers. To obtain this much-needed experience, Trevor enrolled in a co-operative education program offered by the Lincoln County Board of Education during the summer. A co-operative education is one that has an academic (in-school) component and a work experience (out-of-school) component.

During the school year, Trevor took academic and business courses. During the summer, he applied the theory learned in school while he worked as a student-learner at the St. Catherines Hydro Utility Company. He was assigned to a training supervisor in the accounting department.

Trevor was trained to process sales invoices and to record them in a sales journal, and to record payments in a cash payments journal, using a computer. He also learned to do banking and to prepare a bank reconciliation statement after checking the bank statement for accuracy and determining outstanding cheques. Another task Trevor had was to balance the cash received each day. He did this by checking to see if the summary sheets prepared by cashiers agreed with amounts on a computer printout.

Trevor also worked on a special task that involved designing a summary form to record employee payroll information on a computer spreadsheet. The spreadsheet form had to record and calculate totals for hours worked, overtime, vacation time accrued, and sick leave earned.

Trevor enjoyed the co-operative education method of learning very much. He obtained much-needed experience using real systems and computers. He was being taught on the job by highly trained people and received instruction on a one-to-one basis.

To obtain the co-operative education position at the hydro company, Trevor had to have some background in high school accounting. Being organized, willing to learn, and patient were other requirements.

Trevor has set long-term goals for himself and has planned the steps leading to the achievement of his goals. He realizes that it is necessary to have a balanced life and spends time relaxing and pursuing personal interests, including swimming, biking, reading, and music.

For Discussion and Follow-Up

(a) What would you say are the main benefits to Trevor of the co-operative education program?

(b) What educational and personal qualifications did Trevor bring to his job?

(c) Do you think you would benefit from and enjoy a co-operative education program?

(d) In what career area would you choose a co-operative education experience?

(e) Co-operative education programs provide students with the real work experience that is a requirement for many jobs. What other sources of real work experience are available to students in your area?

(f) Visit your guidance department to determine which colleges and universities in your area offer co-operative education programs.

The Journal and the Ledger

UNIT 6 The Journal

What Learning You Will Demonstrate

On completion of this unit, you will be able to:

- explain the purpose of a journal; and
- demonstrate the skills necessary to record transactions in a journal for a service company.

Imagine a business, such as a major department store, that has a very large number of accounts in its ledger. Imagine also that a $50 error was made in recording one of the transactions. The debit of $50 was placed in the wrong account. How would the $50 error be traced? The accountant would have to go through all of the accounts until the incorrect entry was located. The debit and credit parts of the transaction could be in widely separated parts of the ledger and it could take a long time to locate the error. This difficulty is eliminated by the use of a journal.

> A journal is a record of transactions recorded in chronological order (order of date).

INTRODUCING THE JOURNAL

The journal *records all parts of a transaction in one place*. The date, the debit, the credit, and an explanation for each transaction are recorded together. Transactions can be conveniently located because they are recorded *chronologically*, that is, in the order in which they take place. The main journal of a business is often the general journal. Other types of journals will be discussed in later chapters.

A journal is sometimes called a book of original entry because it is where transactions are first recorded. Transactions may be written in a journal manually or they may be prepared using a computer. A journal prepared by computer is described in the Computer Accounting section of this chapter.

> The general journal is often the main journal of a business.

Journal Entries

Each transaction recorded in a journal is called an entry. The process of recording transactions in a journal is called journalizing. Each journal entry has four parts, as shown in Figure 4-1.

- the date of the transaction;
- the account debited and the amount;
- the account credited (indented) and the amount; and
- an explanation giving details of the transaction.

Sample Transactions

Figure 4-1 illustrates how the following three transactions appear when they are recorded in the general journal:

Oct. 1   Sold services to R. Heino for $900 cash, Sales Slip 1.
    3   Paid $400 to the *Gazette* for a newspaper ad, Cheque 1.
    5   Paid secretary's salary, $700, Cheque 2.

In T-account form the first transaction would be recorded as follows:

Cash		Sales	
Oct. 1 900			Oct. 1 900

In Figure 4-1, the same transaction is shown in the general journal. In the journal, Cash is debited $900 and Sales is credited $900, just as in the T-accounts.

GENERAL JOURNAL				PAGE 3
DATE	PARTICULARS	P.R.	DEBIT	CREDIT
20—				
Oct. 1	Cash		9 0 0 00	
	Sales			9 0 0 00
	Sold services to R. Heino for cash, Sales Slip 1.			
3	Advertising Expense		4 0 0 00	
	Cash			4 0 0 00
	Paid the *Gazette* for a newspaper ad, Cheque 1.			
5	Salaries Expense		7 0 0 00	
	Cash			7 0 0 00
	Paid secretary's salary, Cheque 2.			

FIGURE 4-1 Transactions recorded in a general journal

Debits and credits are determined according to the same rules you learned in previous chapters. Note also that there is a consistent procedure for recording debits and credits in the general journal.

JOURNAL RECORDING PROCEDURES

There are four steps for recording transactions in a journal. All of them are shown in Figure 4-1.

Step 1: Record the Date

In a journal, the first entry on each page must show the year, the month, and the day. Only the day of the month needs to be recorded for other entries on the page unless the month changes before a page is completed. In that event, the new month is shown in the date column.

The year and month are shown on each journal page.

Step 2: Record the Debit

The name of the account to be debited is written next to the date. The name should be written exactly as it appears in the general ledger. For example, if cash is received, the appropriate account title would be Cash, not Cash Received. The dollar amount of the debit is written in the debit column.

The debit is shown first.

Step 3: Record the Credit

The credit is recorded on the next line. The account name is indented about a paragraph indent to distinguish it visually from the debit entry. The dollar amount is written in the credit column.

The credit is indented.

Step 4: Record the Explanation

On the next line, starting at the margin, an explanation of the transaction is written. The invoice or cheque number is included.

The explanation includes an invoice or cheque number.

Advantages of the Journal

Although transactions may be recorded directly into ledger accounts, many businesses prefer to record transactions in a journal first for the following reasons:

- The complete transaction is recorded in one place.
- The use of a journal reduces errors. When entries are recorded directly into ledger accounts, it is easy to make a mistake such as recording two debits and no credits or recording only the debit or only the credit. Such errors are less likely to occur in a journal; but, if they do, they are easy to spot. A quick check of each page in a journal will reveal any entry that does not show an equal debit and credit.
- A journal represents a chronological history of all of the business transactions.
- A journal makes it possible to determine the daily, weekly, or monthly volume of business and to identify busy periods more easily.
- A journal provides a convenient picture of each day's business.

A journal presents a chronological history of all the company's transactions.

Double-Entry Accounting

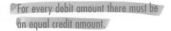
For every debit amount there must be an equal credit amount.

You have already learned that when you record a transaction *the debit amount(s) recorded must always equal the credit amount(s)*. This principle applies even if more than two accounts are used to record the transaction. You will continue to apply the principle of double-entry accounting as you learn to use a journal. Look again at the journal entries in Figure 4-1 on page 110. Notice that for every entry, the debit (left side) equals the credit (right side).

UNIT 6 CHECK YOUR READING

Questions

1. What is a journal?
2. Why is a journal sometimes called a book of original entry?
3. What is a journal entry?
4. What is journalizing?
5. Name the four parts of a journal entry.
6. Which part of a journal entry is indented?
7. (a) Describe four advantages of using a journal.
   (b) In what order do entries appear in a journal?
8. Explain the principle of double-entry accounting.

UNIT 6 APPLY YOUR KNOWLEDGE

Exercises

1. Journalize the following transactions for Mirabeau Theatre, using these accounts: Cash; A. Mirabeau, Capital; Ticket Sales; Refreshment Sales; Salaries Expense; Film Rental Expense; Hydro Expense; Advertising Expense.

   Oct. 1 A. Mirabeau invested an additional $20 000 cash.
       4 Ticket sales for the week, $16 000.
       4 Refreshment sales for the week, $2400.
       7 Paid for film rental, $5000, Cheque 241.
       7 Paid salaries, $1900, Cheque 242.
      10 Paid the *Citizen* for newspaper advertising, $700, Cheque 243.
      11 Paid the hydro bill, $250, Cheque 244.

2. Journalize the following transactions on page 299 for Northern Driving School, using these accounts: Cash; Accounts Receivable/ L. Starr; Equipment; Automobiles; Accounts Payable/Grant's Esso; R. Liley, Capital; Revenue from Lessons; Salaries Expense; Advertising Expense; Automobile Expense; Utilities Expense.

   Aug. 1 R. Liley invested an additional $40 000 cash.
       2 Purchased equipment for $2000, Cheque 107.

4   Purchased two cars from Dardick Motors for $36 000, Cheque 108.
5   Received $1700 from customers taking driving lessons, Sales Slips 293–296.
7   Paid $1300 for instructors' salaries for the week, Cheque 109.
9   Paid $275 to Bell Canada, Cheque 110.
10   Received $1800 from customers taking driving lessons, Sales Slips 297–300.
11   Issued Sales Invoice 192 for $400 to L. Starr, who is taking lessons but will pay at a later date.
11   Received a bill for $290 from Grant's Esso for gas and oil used by the cars.
12   Paid $190 for hydro, Cheque 111.
13   Sent $170 to the *Daily Star* for advertising, Cheque 112.
14   Received $400 from L. Starr to pay off amount owing for lessons, Cash Receipt 427.

3. Journalize the following transactions on page 417 for G. Sloan Small Business Services. Select appropriate accounts for each transaction. *Note:* This firm keeps a separate account for each account receivable and each account payable.

Feb.   1   G. Sloan invested $9000 more cash in the business.
2   Sold services to D. Ferris, $600, Sales Slip 472.
3   Sold services to W. Anderson, $250 on credit, Sales Invoice 872.
4   Sold services to T. Tidey, $700 on credit, Sales Invoice 873.
5   Received $100 from W. Anderson as part payment of amount owing, Cash Receipt 741.
8   Received $700 from T. Tidey in full payment of amount owing, Cash Receipt 742.
8   The owner, G. Sloan, paid the office rent for the month, $1500, out of a personal bank account (not the company account).
9   Purchased a new computer from Office Systems for $2500. They required a 10 percent down payment today and the remainder within 30 days; Purchase Invoice 4692 and Cheque 791.
10   Received the hydro bill, $357, to be paid in 10 days.

UNIT 7 Posting to the Ledger

3

What Learning You Will Demonstrate

On completion of this unit, you will be able to:

- demonstrate the skills necessary to enter data and calculate balances using the balance-column form of ledger account;
- post journal transactions to ledger accounts;
- journalize and post an opening entry;
- prepare trial balances in three formats:
  - formal trial balance,
  - informal list of debits and credits, and
  - calculator tape lists;
- locate and correct errors;
- define *posting, journal, chart of accounts,* and *ledger;* and
- outline the steps in the accounting cycle learned to this point.

The general journal is a chronological record of all transactions. It shows the accounts debited and credited for every transaction in the order in which the transactions occur. However, it does not provide the balance for each account. It does not tell the accountant how much cash is on hand, and it also does not record the balance of each of the accounts that will appear on the financial statements. This type of information is found in the accounts in the general ledger. The information in the general journal (as well as the other journals to be discussed later in the book) is transferred to the general ledger by a process called posting.

> Posting is the transfer of information from a journal to the general ledger.

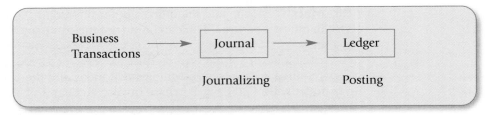

FIGURE 4-2 Posting is the transfer of information from a journal to the accounts in the ledger.

INTRODUCING THE BALANCE-COLUMN FORM OF LEDGER ACCOUNT

The T-account was introduced in Chapter 2 as a simple way to record transactions in ledger accounts. It is an ideal form for learning the rules of debit and credit, but a T-account is not very practical for use in business. The most widely used form of account is the balance-column ledger account, which is sometimes called a three-column account.

> The balance-column ledger account provides a running balance on each line.

In Figure 4-3, a number of transactions are recorded in a Cash T-account.

```
                    Cash
Nov.  1    2 000 | Nov.  3        150
      3       75 |       6        200
      5      100 |                350
           2 175 |
Balance    1 825 |
```

FIGURE 4-3 Transactions recorded in a Cash T-account

Exactly the same transactions appear in Figure 4-4 in balance-column ledger account format. *Why is it called a balance-column account?*

	GENERAL LEDGER						
ACCOUNT Cash							No. 100

DATE		PARTICULARS	P.R.	DEBIT	CREDIT	DR. CR.	BALANCE
20—							
Nov.	1		J1	2 0 0 0 00		DR.	2 0 0 0 00
	3		J1	7 5 00		DR.	2 0 7 5 00
	3		J1		1 5 0 00	DR.	1 9 2 5 00
	5		J2	1 0 0 00		DR.	2 0 2 5 00
	6		J3		2 0 0 00	DR.	1 8 2 5 00

FIGURE 4-4 Transactions shown in Figure 4-3 recorded in a balance-column ledger account

Compare the information in the T-account in Figure 4-3 with the same information shown in the balance-column account in Figure 4-4. Notice that in the balance-column account a running balance is provided on each line. The accountant can see at a glance how much cash the company has at the close of each transaction. The DR./CR. (debit/credit) column indicates that the balance in the example is a debit balance; that is, the debits are larger than the credits. Although entries in the account on November 3 and 6 are credits, the DR./CR. column on these dates indicates that there is still a debit balance. The DR./CR. column also indicates the column of the trial balance in which the account balance will appear. Since the $1825 balance in the Cash account in Figure 4-4 is a DR. (debit), the Cash account balance will be listed in the debit column of the trial balance.

Notice that each account is numbered. In Figure 4-4, the Cash account is number 100. The accounts are filed numerically in the general ledger.

The DR./CR. column indicates whether the account balance is a debit or a credit.

CHART OF ACCOUNTS

A chart of accounts is a list of the names and account numbers of all of the accounts in a ledger.

Each account in a ledger has a title and a number. Accounts are placed in a ledger in numerical sequence so they may be located quickly. A list of the ledger account names and numbers, called a chart of accounts, is used by accounting employees. The chart of accounts is an aid in deciding which accounts may be used when transactions are journalized and in locating accounts when posting to the ledger.

The accounts in the ledger are numbered in the same order as they appear on the balance sheet and income statement. Notice that in the chart of accounts for Rainbow Painting Contractors (Figure 4-5) a series of numbers is assigned to each type of account.

Rainbow Painting Contractors
Chart of Accounts

Assets
100	Cash
101	Accounts Receivable/A. Baker
102	Accounts Receivable/L. Carter
131	Painting Supplies
141	Equipment
142	Truck

Liabilities
200	Accounts Payable/International Paints
201	Accounts Payable/Hardware Supply Corp.
221	Bank Loan

Owner's Equity
300	K. Schmidt, Capital
301	K. Schmidt, Drawings

Revenue
400	Sales

Expenses
500	Advertising Expense
501	Rent Expense
502	Salaries Expense
503	Utilities Expense

FIGURE 4-5 Chart of accounts for Rainbow Painting Contractors

A sample outline for an account numbering system is:

100–199	Asset accounts
200–299	Liability accounts
300–399	Owner's equity accounts
400–499	Revenue accounts
500–599	Expense accounts

In large companies with a large number of accounts, a four-digit series of numbers may be required to cover all of the accounts. For example, asset accounts might be numbered 1000–1999 and liability accounts might be numbered 2000–2999. In computer accounting, the account number becomes a numeric code and is used in place of the account title when you journalize transactions. Only the number is entered on the keyboard. The account name then automatically appears on the screen.

POSTING TO A BALANCE-COLUMN FORM OF LEDGER ACCOUNT

Figure 4-6 shows how a $900 general journal entry is posted to the Cash account in the balance-column form of ledger account.

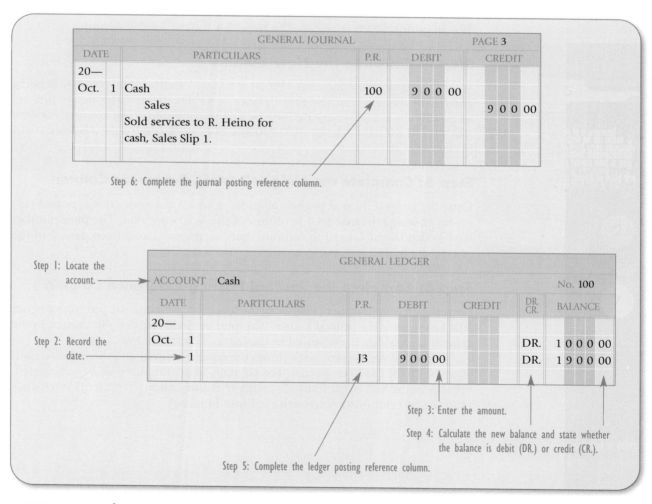

FIGURE 4-6 Steps for posting the journal to the ledger

Steps in Posting

To avoid mechanical errors in the posting procedure, follow these steps which are illustrated in Figure 4-6.

Step 1: Locate the Account

Look at the name of the account to be posted to and locate that account in the ledger. On October 1 in Figure 4-6, that account is Cash.

Step 2: Record the Date

The transaction date is recorded in the account. The month and year need not be repeated if they are already recorded on that page of the account.

Step 3: Enter the Amount

The amount of $900 is recorded in the debit column of the account.

Step 4: Calculate the New Balance

Since the previous balance was $1000 (debit) and another debit of $900 is being entered in the account, the new balance is $1900 (debit). The two debits are *added* ($1000 + $900) because they are on the same side of the account, *the debit side*. Record the new balance of $1900 and indicate that it is a *debit balance* (DR.) in the DR./CR. column.

Step 5: Complete the Ledger Posting Reference Column

Enter the general journal page number from which the amount was posted (J3) in the posting reference (P.R.) column of the ledger account. The page number is preceded by the letter J to indicate that the amount came from page 3 of the general journal.

Step 6: Complete the Journal Posting Reference Column

Copy the account number (100) from the ledger account into the posting reference (P.R.) column of the general journal. This number indicates that the amount in the general journal has been posted to the ledger in account 100.

Figure 4-7 on the next page shows the general journal and the Sales account after the credit has been posted. The six steps in posting have all been repeated. What does the 400 in the journal posting reference column represent? What does J3 in the account posting reference column indicate?

| GENERAL JOURNAL | | | | PAGE 3 | |
DATE	PARTICULARS	P.R.	DEBIT		CREDIT
20—					
Oct. 1	Cash	100	9 0 0 00		
	Sales	400			9 0 0 00
	Sold services to R. Heino for cash,				
	Sales Slip 1.				

| GENERAL LEDGER | | | | | | |
| ACCOUNT Sales | | | | | | No. 400 |
DATE	PARTICULARS	P.R.	DEBIT	CREDIT	DR. CR.	BALANCE
20—						
Oct. 1		J3		9 0 0 00	CR.	9 0 0 00

FIGURE 4-7 Posting to the Sales account

POSTING REFERENCES

Numbers in the posting reference columns serve an important purpose. They are cross references that link particular journal entries to corresponding postings to the ledger accounts.

A journal page number in the ledger account posting reference column indicates where more information about the transaction can be found. For instance, the information explaining the transaction with R. Heino (Figure 4-7) can be located by referring to page 3 of the general journal.

The ledger account number in a journal posting reference column indicates that the amount has been posted. It tells the accounting clerk where he or she left off in posting to the ledger.

Periodically, all companies have their records audited. An **audit** is a systematic check of accounting records and procedures by an accountant. The cross-reference provided by posting reference numbers helps the auditor to check the accuracy of the journalizing and posting of transactions. The posting reference numbers allow the transactions to be traced from a journal to the ledger and also from the ledger to a journal.

Figure 4-8 on page 120 represents page 12 of the general journal used by Rainbow Painting Contractors. Figure 4-9 on pages 120 and 121 is a portion of the company's ledger to which the transactions recorded in Figure 4-8 have been posted. Trace the transactions from the general journal to the ledger. The posting reference column will help you.

An audit is a systematic check of accounting records and procedures by an accountant.

GENERAL JOURNAL				PAGE 12	
DATE	PARTICULARS	P.R.	DEBIT	CREDIT	
20—					
Nov. 1	Cash	100	1 3 0 0 00		
	Sales	400		1 3 0 0 00	
	Sold services to W. Mason, Sales Slip 49.				
3	Advertising Expense	500	2 7 5 00		
	Cash	100		2 7 5 00	
	Paid *Ottawa Journal* for a newspaper advertisement, Cheque 15.				
5	Salaries Expense	502	2 5 0 00		
	Cash	100		2 5 0 00	
	Paid secretary's salary, Cheque 16.				
6	Cash	100	7 0 0 00		
	Sales	400		7 0 0 00	
	Painted house for M. Blais, Sales Slip 50.				

FIGURE 4-8 Page 12 of the general journal for Rainbow Painting Contractors

GENERAL LEDGER						
ACCOUNT Cash						No. 100
DATE	PARTICULARS	P.R.	DEBIT	CREDIT	DR. CR.	BALANCE
20—						
Nov. 1	Forwarded	✓			DR.	4 0 0 0 00
1		J12	1 3 0 0 00		DR.	5 3 0 0 00
3		J12		2 7 5 00	DR.	5 0 2 5 00
5		J12		2 5 0 00	DR.	4 7 7 5 00
6		J12	7 0 0 00		DR.	5 4 7 5 00

ACCOUNT Sales						No. 400
DATE	PARTICULARS	P.R.	DEBIT	CREDIT	DR. CR.	BALANCE
20—						
Nov. 1		J12		1 3 0 0 00	CR.	1 3 0 0 00
6		J12		7 0 0 00	CR.	2 0 0 0 00

ACCOUNT	Advertising Expense						No. 500	
DATE	PARTICULARS	P.R.	DEBIT	CREDIT	DR. CR.	BALANCE		
20—								
Nov. 3		J12	2 7 5 00		DR.	2 7 5 00		

ACCOUNT	Salaries Expense						No. 502	
DATE	PARTICULARS	P.R.	DEBIT	CREDIT	DR. CR.	BALANCE		
20—								
Nov. 5		J12	2 50 00		DR.	2 50 00		

FIGURE 4-9 Portion of the ledger for Rainbow Painting Contractors affected by the transactions in Figure 4-8

OPENING THE BOOKS

Figures 4-8 and 4-9 illustrated how routine transactions are recorded in the general journal and then posted to ledger accounts. The special procedures followed when a business first begins operations will now be examined.

The Opening Entry

A special entry, called an *opening entry,* is prepared when a business first begins operations.

On September 1, K. Schmidt invested money of his own and borrowed $15 000 from a bank to purchase assets and start a painting business. The assets of the new business are:

Cash	$ 4 000
Equipment	5 000
Truck	20 000
Total	$29 000

The business has one liability:

Bank Loan	$15 000

Schmidt's equity is calculated by applying the balance sheet equation:

$$\begin{array}{ccccc} A & = & L & + & OE \\ \$29\ 000 & = & \$15\ 000 & + & \$14\ 000 \end{array}$$

Schmidt's equity is $14 000.

To open the books, the general journal is set up and the business' assets, liability, and owner's equity are recorded. This first entry, illustrated in Figure 4-10, is called the **opening entry**.

The opening entry records the assets, liabilities, and owner's equity when a business first begins operations.

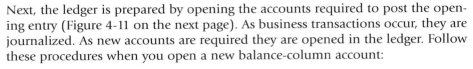

GENERAL JOURNAL				PAGE 1	
DATE	PARTICULARS	P.R.	DEBIT	CREDIT	
20—					
Sep. 1	Cash		4 0 0 0 00		
	Equipment		5 0 0 0 00		
	Truck		20 0 0 0 00		
	Bank Loan			15 0 0 0 00	
	K. Schmidt, Capital			14 0 0 0 00	
	Started a painting business with the above				
	assets, liability, and owner's equity.				

FIGURE 4-10 Opening entry in the general journal for Rainbow Painting Contractors

Notice that the opening entry shows three debits and two credits, with the three debit amounts ($29 000) equal to the two credit amounts ($29 000). This entry, which shows more than one debit or credit, is called a compound entry. All entries, including compound ones, must have equal debit and credit amounts. After the opening entry is journalized, the daily entries of the business can be recorded.

A compound entry has more than one debit or more than one credit.

OPENING LEDGER ACCOUNTS

Next, the ledger is prepared by opening the accounts required to post the opening entry (Figure 4-11 on the next page). As business transactions occur, they are journalized. As new accounts are required they are opened in the ledger. Follow these procedures when you open a new balance-column account:

1. Write the name of the account to the right of the word "Account."
2. Write the account number at the far right on the top line.
3. Write the date in the date column.
4. Write "Opening Entry" on the first line in the particulars column. This will help distinguish the opening entry from the changes that occur to the account as business transactions take place.
5. Write J1 for general journal page 1 in the posting reference column.
6. Record the amount in the correct debit or credit column.
7. Enter the balance in the balance column.
8. Depending on the balance, write DR. or CR. in the DR./CR. column.
9. Enter the ledger account number in the posting reference column of the general journal.
10. Insert the account in numerical sequence in the ledger.

Figure 4-11 shows the posting of the opening entry to the ledger accounts. For each item in the opening entry, an account has been prepared. Notice that "Opening Entry" has been written in the particulars column and that the six steps in posting have been followed.

GENERAL LEDGER							
ACCOUNT　Cash							No. 100
DATE	PARTICULARS	P.R.	DEBIT	CREDIT	DR. CR.	BALANCE	
20—							
Sep.　1	Opening Entry	J1	4 0 0 0 00		DR.	4 0 0 0 00	

ACCOUNT　Equipment							No. 141
DATE	PARTICULARS	P.R.	DEBIT	CREDIT	DR. CR.	BALANCE	
20—							
Sep.　1	Opening Entry	J1	5 0 0 0 00		DR.	5 0 0 0 00	

ACCOUNT　Truck							No. 142
DATE	PARTICULARS	P.R.	DEBIT	CREDIT	DR. CR.	BALANCE	
20—							
Sep.　1	Opening Entry	J1	20 0 0 0 00		DR.	20 0 0 0 00	

ACCOUNT　Bank Loan							No. 221
DATE	PARTICULARS	P.R.	DEBIT	CREDIT	DR. CR.	BALANCE	
20—							
Sep.　1	Opening Entry	J1		15 0 0 0 00	CR.	15 0 0 0 00	

ACCOUNT　K. Schmidt, Capital							No. 300
DATE	PARTICULARS	P.R.	DEBIT	CREDIT	DR. CR.	BALANCE	
20—							
Sep.　1	Opening Entry	J1		14 0 0 0 00	CR.	14 0 0 0 00	

FIGURE 4-11 Ledger after posting the opening entry

FORWARDING PROCEDURE

The active accounts of a business show many transactions recorded on the pages of the ledger. When an account page is filled, a new page is opened according to the following procedure:

1. Head up a new page with the same account name and number (Figures 4-12 and 4-13 on page 124).

2. Write "Forwarded" on the last line of the old page in the particulars column (Figure 4-12).

	GENERAL LEDGER						
ACCOUNT	Accounts Receivable/L. Carter						No. 102
DATE	PARTICULARS	P.R.	DEBIT	CREDIT	DR. CR.	BALANCE	
20—							
Nov. 3		J19	1 2 0 0 00		DR.	1 2 0 0 00	
3		J19	5 0 0 00		DR.	1 7 0 0 00	
4		J19		1 0 0 0 00	DR.	7 0 0 00	
5		J20	1 0 0 00		DR.	8 0 0 00	
5		J20		3 0 0 00	DR.	5 0 0 00	
6		J21	4 0 0 00		DR.	9 0 0 00	
7		J21	2 3 0 0 00		DR.	3 2 0 0 00	
7	Forwarded	J21		3 0 5 0 00	DR.	1 5 0 00	

FIGURE 4-12 Ledger page that has been filled and forwarded

3. On the first line of the new page, write the date (year, month, day), "Forwarded" in the particulars column, and the balance in the balance column. Indicate the type of balance. Place a check mark in the posting reference column as shown in Figure 4-13.

ACCOUNT	Accounts Receivable/L. Carter						No. 102
DATE	PARTICULARS	P.R.	DEBIT	CREDIT	DR. CR.	BALANCE	
20—							
Nov. 7	Forwarded	✓			DR.	1 5 0 00	

FIGURE 4-13 New ledger page

Note that aside from the Opening Entry and Forwarded notations, the particulars column is seldom used. If further information is required about a transaction, use the posting reference numbers to trace the entry back to the general journal where more detailed information can be found.

REVIEWING THE TRIAL BALANCE

A trial balance is proof of the mathematical accuracy of the ledger.

At regular intervals, usually monthly, a trial balance is prepared. A **trial balance** is proof of the mathematical accuracy of the ledger. As you learned in Chapter 2, a trial balance is a list of the debit and credit account balances. The total of the debit balances should equal the total of the credit balances. A formal trial balance for Rainbow Painting Contractors is illustrated in Figure 4-14.

Rainbow Painting Contractors
Trial Balance
November 30, 20—

Account	Acc. No.	Debit	Credit
Cash	100	$ 3 515	
Accounts Receivable/A. Baker	101	295	
Accounts Receivable/L. Carter	102	1 200	
Equipment	141	5 000	
Truck	142	20 000	
Accts. Pay./International Paints	200		$ 695
Accts. Pay./Hardware Supply Corp.	201		315
Bank Loan	221		15 000
K. Schmidt, Capital	300		14 000
		$30 010	$30 010

FIGURE 4-14 Formal trial balance

Forms of the Trial Balance

The trial balance may take several forms:

- Formal trial balance (Figure 4-14).
- List form of trial balance, in which the total of the list of debits equals the total of the list of credits (Figure 4-15).
- Machine tape form of trial balance, in which the debit balances minus the credit balances equal zero (Figure 4-16).

Rainbow Painting
Contractors
Trial Balance
November 30, 20—

DEBIT	CREDIT
$ 3 515	$ 695
295	315
1 200	15 000
5 000	14 000
20 000	
$30 010	$30 010

FIGURE 4-15 List form of trial balance—total debits equal total credits

Rainbow Painting
Contractors
Trial Balance
November 30, 20—

```
        0
   3 515+
     295+
   1 200+
   5 000+
  20 000+
     695−
     315−
  15 000−
  14 000−
        0 *
```

FIGURE 4-16 Machine tape form of trial balance—debits minus credits equal zero

DEALING WITH ERRORS

Avoiding Posting Errors

The types of errors listed below can be avoided if the six steps in posting given previously are followed:

- not posting an entire transaction;
- not posting either the debit or credit part of a transaction;
- posting to the correct side but to the wrong account;
- posting to the wrong side of an account;
- calculating the balance incorrectly; and
- transposing figures (posting 96 instead of 69).

Locating Trial Balance Errors

The trial balance is a test, or trial, to prove that the ledger is mathematically in balance. If the totals of the debit and credit columns of the trial balance are not the same, the error must be located before the financial statements are prepared.

Locating errors can be very discouraging and time-consuming. The suggestions that follow represent procedures for identifying the type of error that has occurred and methods for tracking it down. They are useful when only one error has been made.

1. Determine the difference between the debit and credit totals.
2. If the difference is 1, 10, 100, etc., there may be an addition or subtraction error on the trial balance or in the ledger accounts.
3. Check to see if an account in the ledger with the same balance as the difference (Step 1) has been omitted from the trial balance.
4. Divide the difference (Step 1) by 2. That amount may have been placed in the wrong column of the trial balance.
5. If the difference is divisible evenly by 9, the error may be due to a transposition of numbers (for example 97 written as 79).
6. If a difference is divisible by 9 and the difference is 2, e.g., 18/9 = 2, then the numbers that have been transposed have a difference of 2, e.g., 57 should be changed to 75.
7. Check to see if the amount of the difference was overlooked when it should have been posted from a journal to the ledger.
8. If the error still escapes you:
   (a) Check each balance in each account in the ledger.
   (b) Check the posting reference column of each journal to locate unposted items.
   (c) Recheck each posting.
9. If you still have not found the error—relax! Go on with something else, then return later with a clear frame of mind and try again.

Example of a Transposition Error

Below is a list of debits and credits from a trial balance. The totals do not balance because an error has been made. The debit total is $2075 and the credit total is $2165.

Debit	Credit
$ 150	
400	
560	
200	
765	
	$ 495
	1 670
$2 075	$2 165

In order to find the error, the following is done:

1. *Re-add the columns to ascertain if an addition error has been made.*
2. *Determine the difference.* The difference between the debit total ($2075) and the credit total ($2165) is $90.
3. *Is the difference evenly divisible by 9?* Since the difference is evenly divisible by 9 (90 ÷ 9 = 10), there may be a transposition error. That is, numbers may be reversed and they have a difference of 1.
4. *Check each number for a reversal.* A check of each ledger account balance indicates that an account balance of $560 was incorrectly written. It should be $650. The 5 and 6 have been transposed, that is, reversed in order. Notice that 6 minus 5 is 1.

The correct trial balance follows:

Debit	Credit
$ 150	
400	
650	
200	
765	
	$ 495
	1 670
$2 165	$2 165

Correcting Errors

The accepted method of correcting errors is to rule out the mistake and to rewrite the correction:

~~256~~   *265*

Some businesses insist that all corrections be initialled:

~~195~~   *259 C.D.*

Correcting Journal Entries

Suppose the following entry has been made in the journal and posted to the ledger accounts.

Jun.	2	Equipment	143	5 0 00	
		Cash	100		5 0 00
		Cheque 141, purchase of equipment.			

The amount of the entry should have been $500. The accepted method of correcting this error is to cancel the entry and re-enter the transaction. This is done as illustrated below.

Cancel the entry:

Jun.	3	Cash	100	5 0 00	
		Equipment	143		5 0 00
		To cancel the June 2 entry for Cheque 141,			
		incorrect amount.			

Re-enter the transaction:

Jun.	2	Equipment	143	5 0 0 00	
		Cash	100		5 0 0 00
		Cheque 141, purchase of equipment.			

Checking for Accuracy

When using a printing calculator to check calculations, follow the procedures illustrated in Figure 4-17 and outlined at the top of the next page.

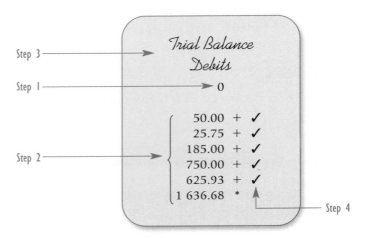

FIGURE 4-17 Checking debit column of trial balance using machine tape method

1. Clear the calculator.
2. Enter and total the data.
3. Label the tape.
4. If the totals do not balance, audit the tape by checking the numbers on the tape against the source. This will locate keying errors.
5. Staple the labelled tape to the material being checked.

Checking Accounts

The balance of an account may be checked on a printing calculator by entering each debit with the plus (+) key and each credit with the minus (−) key. Take the total after the last entry. Figure 4-18 illustrates this procedure.

			GENERAL LEDGER				

ACCOUNT Cash No. 100

DATE		PARTICULARS	P.R.	DEBIT	CREDIT	DR. CR.	BALANCE
20—							
Nov.	1	Forwarded	✓			DR.	2 1 9 0 00
	2		J16	2 5 00		DR.	2 2 1 5 00
	3		J16		3 9 5 00	DR.	1 8 2 0 00
	5		J16		6 2 0 00	DR.	1 2 0 0 00
	5		J17	8 9 5 60		DR.	2 0 9 5 60
	5		J17		8 70	DR.	2 0 8 6 90
	5		J18	6 9 9 20		DR.	2 7 8 6 10

Cash account

```
           0
    2 190.00
+     25.00
−    395.00
−    620.00
+    895.60
−      8.70
+    699.20
=  2 786.10
```

FIGURE 4-18 Checking accounts by calculator

Cash account

```
           0
    2 190.00
+     25.00
=  2 215.00
−    395.00
=  1 820.00
−    620.00
=  1 200.00
+    895.60
=  2 095.60
−      8.70
=  2 086.90
+    699.20
=  2 786.10
```

FIGURE 4-19 Checking accounts by calculator using subtotal method

Another method of checking accounts is to use the subtotal or equals key to check the balance column after each entry (Figure 4-19 on page 129). This technique specifically identifies the line on which an error may occur.

INTRODUCING THE ACCOUNTING CYCLE

You have seen that business transactions are first recorded in a journal and then posted to the ledger. If the ledger is in balance, the financial statements (the income statement and the balance sheet) are then prepared. These steps are completed in sequence in each accounting period and together are called the accounting cycle.

The accounting cycle is the set of accounting procedures performed in each accounting period.

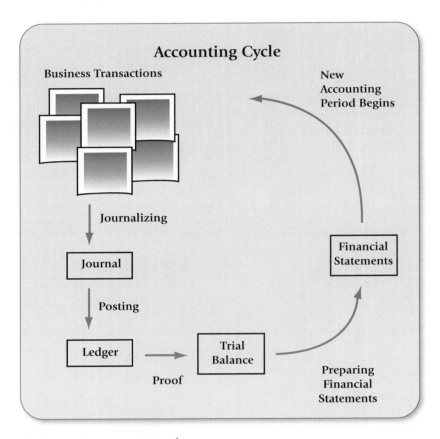

FIGURE 4-20 Accounting cycle

UNIT 7 CHECK YOUR READING

Questions

9. What is posting?

10. What are the six steps followed in posting?

11. What is written in the posting reference column of a journal and a ledger?

12. What is an opening entry?

13. What is a compound entry?

14. What is a chart of accounts?

15. What is the accounting cycle?

16. An account with a $600 debit balance is incorrectly placed on the trial balance as a $600 credit.
  (a) How much will the difference be between the trial balance debit and credit totals?
  (b) How is such an error identified?

17. What is a transposition error? Give an example.

18. (a) The difference in the totals of a trial balance is $100. What type of error has probably been made?
  (b) If the difference is $270, what type of error may have been made?

UNIT 7 APPLY YOUR KNOWLEDGE

Exercises

4. (a) The following Cash account has incomplete DR./CR. and balance columns. Prepare a copy of the account, completing the DR./CR. column and the balance column on each line of the account.

GENERAL LEDGER							
ACCOUNT Cash							No. 100
DATE	PARTICULARS	P.R.	DEBIT	CREDIT	DR. CR.	BALANCE	
20—							
Dec. 1	Forwarded	✓			DR.	4 2 6 1 00	
2		J16	1 0 0 00		DR.	4 3 6 1 00	
2		J16		1 7 5 00	DR.	4 1 8 6 00	
3		J16	1 6 2 50				
3		J16	8 4 3 75				
4		J17		4 9 23			
5		J17	8 6 19				
5		J17		2 1 3 3 70			

(b) Assume that the account page for Cash is filled. Apply the forwarding procedure and forward the balance to a new account page for Cash.

(c) Prepare a chart of accounts for Goldman's Gym. Number each of the accounts using the numbering system on page 116. In random order, the accounts found in the ledger are listed below. Complete this exercise in your notebook.

Cash	Mortgage Payable
Accounts Receivable	Members' Fees
Towel Rental	Salaries Expense
Accounts Payable	Advertising Expense
Bank Loan	Office Supplies
R. Millar, Capital	Telephone Expense
Training Equipment	Building
Licence Expense	Interest Expense
Land	R. Millar, Drawings
Sports Equipment Rental	Laundry Expense
Maintenance Expense	

5. On February 1, M. Conway, an architect, opened a business. A chart of accounts for the business is given below.
   (a) Journalize the February transactions using accounts from the chart of accounts.
   (b) Open ledger accounts using account titles and numbers from the chart of accounts.
   (c) Post the general journal entries.
   (d) Prepare a trial balance.

100	Cash	300	M. Conway, Capital
101	Accounts Receivable/Bak Contractors	400	Fees Earned
141	Office Equipment	507	Rent Expense
142	Automobile	508	Salaries Expense
200	Accounts Payable/Ajax Motors	510	Telephone Expense

Feb. 1 M. Conway invested $40 000 cash in an architectural consulting business.
      2 Bought office equipment, $3000, Cheque 1.
      3 Bought an automobile for the business from Ajax Motors Ltd. on credit. The price of the car was $21 000, Invoice 7469.
      4 Received $1500 for services provided to a customer, Sales Slip 1.

    5   Sent Invoice 1 for $1000 to Bak Contractors for services
         provided.
    5   Paid the February rent, $1600, Cheque 2.
    5   Paid office salaries, $1450, Cheque 3.
    5   Paid $150 for the installation of a telephone, Cheque 4.

6. An accounting clerk has prepared three *mini* trial balances that do
not balance. Calculate the difference in the debit and credit totals
and indicate the probable type of error made in each case.

(a)

Debit	Credit
$3 000	
1 000	
700	
420	
	$2 950
2 170	
$5 120	$5 020

(b)

Debit	Credit
$200	
300	
50	
	$ 75
	25
	300
	200
$550	$600

(c)

Debit	Credit
$3 000	
1 000	
700	
240	
	$2 950
	2 170
$4 940	$5 120

7. The Supplies account shown below contains a number of errors.
    (a) List the errors.
    (b) Prepare a corrected Supplies account.

GENERAL LEDGER

ACCOUNT   Supplies   No. 103

DATE		PARTICULARS	P.R.	DEBIT	CREDIT	DR. CR.	BALANCE
20—							
Nov.	1	Forwarded	✓			DR.	2 2 0 0 00
	2		J3		2 0 0 00	CR.	2 0 0 0 00
	3		J3	4 0 0 00		DR.	2 4 0 0 00
	4		J3	1 5 0 00		DR.	2 5 5 0 00
	5		J3	5 0 00		DR.	2 5 0 0 00

8. Ahmad Nauman opened an insurance agency on October 1 with
the following assets and liabilities: Cash $2500; Equipment
$5500; Building $175 000; Land $75 000; Bank Loan $3000;
Mortgage $70 000.
    (a) Record the opening entry for the business in a general journal.
        (Remember that your entry must balance.)

9. Vanita Khanna opened an office services business on September 1
with the following assets and liabilities: Cash $2200; Equipment
$4300; Bank Loan $3500.
    (a) Prepare an opening entry in a general journal.

(b) The following events occurred during September. Journalize the items that must be entered in the books of the company. Revenue should be recorded in the Fees from Clients account.

(c) Explain your reasons for omitting any events.

Sep. 1   Paid the first month's rent on the office, $1500, Cheque 1.

1   Completed keying a report for a client, J. Jamison, and mailed the bill for $250, Invoice 1.

2   Received Invoice 6789 from the *Express* for advertising, $175.

3   Purchased office supplies from Beattie's Stationery, $115 on credit, Invoice 2694.

4   Received $85 from a client for work completed today, Sales Slip 1.

5   Mailed a cheque for $825 drawn on the company bank account to pay Ms. Khanna's apartment rent, Cheque 2.

6   Signed a contract with Continental Inc. to provide overload keying services. It is anticipated this will result in $1000 worth of business each month.

8   J. Jamison paid the bill issued September 1 in full.

9   Returned a $50 box of envelopes purchased September 3 to Beattie's Stationery; incorrect size. Beattie's gave a credit for the amount. (This means the firm now owes Beattie's $50 less as a result of the transaction.)

10   Paid the *Express* bill of September 2, Cheque 3.

11   Paid Beattie's in full, Cheque 4.

UNIT 8   Source Documents

What Learning You Will Demonstrate

On completion of this unit, you will:

- be able to identify and record source documents;
- understand that a source document is prepared for every transaction;
- be able to outline the principle of objectivity; and
- understand that source documents are prenumbered and that all source documents must be accounted for.

As business transactions occur, information about the transactions is recorded on some form of business document. For example, when a cash sale is made a sales slip is prepared. A copy is given to the customer and a copy is kept by the seller. The accountant for the seller uses the sales slip as the source of information that a sale has been made. The accountant for the buyer uses the copy of the same document as a source of information that a purchase has been made. This is where the term *source document* comes from. A source document is any business form that serves as the original source of information that a transaction has occurred. The most commonly used source documents will be described in this chapter.

A source document is a concrete object that proves that a business transaction did, in fact, occur. It is generally prepared with at least two copies, so that the two parties to a transaction, generally the seller and the buyer, each receive an exact copy.

CASH SALES SLIPS

A cash sales slip is prepared for all cash sales by a business. The cash sales slip in Figure 4-21 on page 136 indicates that a painter (International Painting) has provided painting services for cash. While this cash sales slip shows both GST (Goods and Services Tax) and PST (Provincial Sales Tax), you will not be journalizing and posting tax amounts until later in this book.

Three copies of the cash sales slip are prepared when a cash sale is made. These are distributed as follows:

- **Copy 1:** Given to the customer.
- **Copy 2:** Used by the accounting department of the seller to record the transaction.
- **Copy 3:** Kept in a numerical file that serves as a record of all cash sales. Every sales slip must be accounted for in this file.

This entry is made by the seller's accountant from copy 2:

May	21	Cash		4 6 0 00	
		Sales			4 6 0 00
		Sales Slip 43785.			

It should be noted that in actual practice, groups of sales slips would be combined and an entry similar to the preceding one would be made to record the total of the group of slips.

The buyer's accountant uses copy 1 as the source of information to record this entry:

May	21	Maintenance Expense		4 6 0 00	
		Cash			4 6 0 00
		Paid for painting services.			

160 SPRUCE STREET   OTTAWA, ONT. K1R 6P2   TEL (613) 236-0716
                                                          FAX (613) 236-1874

CASH SALE
VENTE AU COMPTANT
International Painting

DATE *May 21*, 20 ——

NAME
NOM *Warrendon Sports Ltd.*

ADDRESS
ADRESSE *2579 Base Line Rd., Ottawa, Ont. K2H 7B3*

DESCRIPTION		UNIT PRICE PRIX L'UNITE	AMOUNT MONTANT	
Painting Services			$400	00
			GST (7%) TPS	28	00
CASH ✓	CHX.	REF.	CHEQUE	PROV. TAX (8%) TAXE PROV.	32	00
SALESPERSON VENDEUR/EUSE				TOTAL	$460	00

43785

CUSTOMER'S COPY
COPIE DU CLIENT

GST Registration No. R711382977

FIGURE 4-21 Cash sales slip

Figure 4-22 illustrates how both the buyer and the seller use copies of the same source document, the cash sales slip in Figure 4-21, to record the transaction.

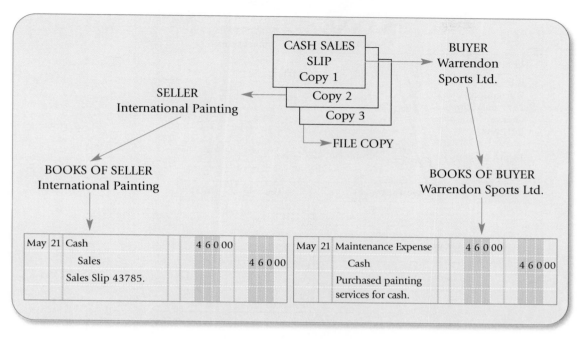

FIGURE 4-22 Both the seller and the buyer use the same source document to record a transaction.

SALES INVOICES

Sanne Consultants provides business consulting and training services to businesses. Sanne Consultants has been training the Warrendon Sports staff and is now charging Warrendon for the services.

Figure 4-23 on page 138 is an example of another source document called a *sales invoice*. The sales invoice is the bill of sale, or simply the bill, completed by the seller (Sanne Consultants) and given to the buyer (Warrendon Sports) as a record of a credit sale. A *credit sale* is one for which the customer agrees to pay at a later date. Other terms used to describe a credit sale are *charge sale* or *sale on account*.

The selling company makes several copies of the sales invoice and distributes them as follows:

- **Copies 1 & 2:** Sent to the customer.
- **Copy 3:** Used by the accounting department of the seller as the source of information to record the transaction.
- **Copy 4:** Kept by the sales department as a record of the sale.

A sales invoice is the bill completed by the seller and given to the buyer as a record of a credit sale.

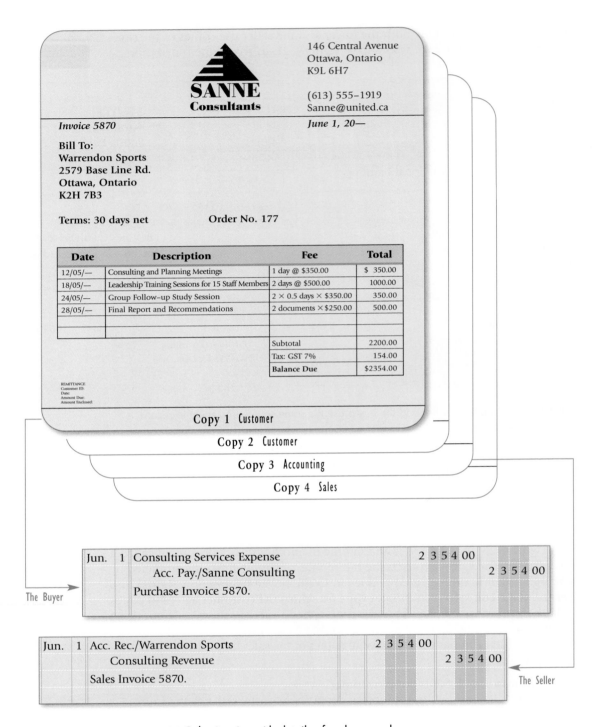

FIGURE 4-23 Sales invoice with details of a charge sale

This entry is made by the accounting department of the seller from copy 3:

Jun.	1	Accounts Receivable/Warrendon Sports	2 3 5 4 00	
		Consulting Revenue		2 3 5 4 00
		Invoice 5870, consulting services, net 30 days.		

PURCHASE INVOICES

Look again at Figure 4-23. What is the name of the seller? The buyer? To the seller, Sanne Consultants, this is a *sales invoice* and copy 3 of this sales invoice is used to prepare the entry shown above. To the buyer, Warrendon Sports Ltd., this is a purchase invoice. Copies 1 and 2 are records of what Warrendon has purchased and indicate how much is owed to the seller.

> A purchase invoice is the bill received by the purchaser as proof of a purchase on account.

When must Warrendon Sports Ltd. pay the $2354? What happens if the invoice is not paid on time? The buyer, Warrendon Sports, would make this journal entry to record the purchase invoice:

Jun.	3	Training Expense	2 3 5 4 00	
		Accounts Payable/Sanne Consultants		2 3 5 4 00
		Purchased consulting services, Invoice 5870,		
		net 30 days.		

You can see that the same document is used to record the sale by the seller and the purchase by the customer. As has been stated, the sellers call their document a *sales invoice* and the buyers call their copy a *purchase invoice*.

CHEQUES

Cheques Issued

On June 1, Warrendon Sports owed $2354 for training services to Sanne Consultants. The terms of payment were net 30 days. This means that the $2354 must be paid within 30 days from the date of the invoice. On June 30, Warrendon Sports prepared Cheque 1624, illustrated in Figure 4-24 on page 140, to pay Invoice 5870 in full.

> Cheques are issued to make cash purchases and to pay bills.

WARRENDON SPORTS LTD.	NO. 1624
2579 Base Line Rd.	
Ottawa, Ontario K2H 7B3	Jun. 30, 20 —

PAY TO THE
ORDER OF   Sanne Consultants $2354.00

SUM OF   Two thousand three hundred and fifty-four------00/100 DOLLARS

THE REGIONAL BANK OF CANADA
2573 Bond St.
Ottawa, Ontario K2B 7C3

W. Creighton
WARRENDON SPORTS LTD.

⑆1624 ⑆41872 033 291 4286⑆

- -

(Detach and retain this statement)

WARRENDON SPORTS LTD.   NO. 1624

THE ATTACHED CHEQUE IS IN PAYMENT OF ITEMS LISTED BELOW

DATE	ITEM	AMOUNT	DISCOUNT	NET AMOUNT
June 30	Inv. 5870	$2354.00		$2354.00

Copy to Accounting

FIGURE 4-24 Cheque issued by Warrendon Sports

The cheque form consists of two parts, the cheque itself and an attached portion that provides the details to explain why the cheque was written. The original cheque form is sent to Sanne Consultants. The copy of the cheque is kept by Warrendon Sports and is the source document for this transaction. The cheque copy is used by Warrendon's accountant to record this entry:

Jun.	30	Accounts Payable/Sanne Consultants		2 3 5 4 00	
		Cash			2 3 5 4 00
		Issued Cheque 1624 to pay Invoice 5870.			

Cheques Received

Cheque 1624 is mailed to Sanne Consultants. When it is received by Sanne Consultants, the cheque is separated from the record portion (bottom half). The cheque is endorsed with a restrictive endorsement (Deposit only to the account of Sanne Consultants) and immediately deposited in Sanne Consultants' bank account.

Cheques are received as payments for amounts owed or when customers buy something for cash.

An *endorsement* is the signature placed on the back of a cheque by the person or company depositing the cheque. A *restrictive endorsement* is used to control what will happen to the funds from the cheque. The record portion of the cheque is used to prepare the following entry:

Jul.	2	Cash		2 3 5 4 00	
		Accounts Receivable/Warrendon Sports			2 3 5 4 00
		Received Cheque 1624 for Invoice 5870.			

List of Cheques Received

Companies that receive a large number of cheques each day prepare a list of those cheques. The cheques are then immediately deposited in the bank. The list is used by the accountant to prepare the journal entries to record the money received and to lower the amounts owing on the customer accounts.

BANK SOURCE DOCUMENTS

Banks prepare source documents when changes are made to bank accounts. For example, a bank credit memo is used as the basis for increasing a customer's account. This happens when interest or other amounts are added to the account.

A bank debit memo is used as the basis for decreasing a customer's account. An example would be interest on a loan deducted from a company's account.

These source documents and journal entries for them are illustrated in Chapter 11.

A bank credit memo gives notice of a increase in a customer's bank account.

A bank debit memo gives notice of a decrease in a customer's bank account.

FURTHER FACTS ABOUT SOURCE DOCUMENTS

Prenumbered Source Documents

Source documents are prenumbered, and every document must be accounted for. The numbering of documents is a control procedure designed to prevent errors and losses due to theft or to the use of false documents. Source documents are kept on file and must be made available to persons who have the authority to check a company's records. These include:

- owners and managers of the business;
- outside accountants hired to check the records;
- federal income tax and GST personnel (Canada Customs and Revenue Agency);

- provincial sales tax and Ministry of Labour personnel; and
- officials of the courts.

Source documents are an important part of a company's accounting system. Every business should take care to produce neat, legible documents that are numbered and filed in a well-organized manner.

Source Documents as Evidence for Transactions

Source documents provide evidence that a transaction has actually occurred. If a check is made of a company's accounting records, the company must be able to prove that the transactions did happen. Source documents such as cash sales slips, sales invoices, and purchase invoices provide the necessary proof.

Further checks on the accuracy of the company's records can be made by comparing the source document copies of both the buyer and the seller. The information on the documents should be the same.

The Principle of Objectivity

The principle of objectivity requires objective evidence to support the value used to record transactions.

Source documents assist the accountant in satisfying the principle of objectivity, which requires that there should be objective evidence to support the value used to record transactions. The dollar values used in transactions should be determined in a very objective way. Source documents provide objective, verifiable evidence to support the value placed on transactions.

A company could overstate the value of its assets by recording them at a high value. This would make the company appear to be more valuable than it really is. To avoid such situations, accountants follow the principle of objectivity.

Summary

Remember that it is important in accounting for a source document to be prepared for every business transaction. The chart below summarizes the source documents used in this chapter.

Source Document	Business Transaction
Cash sales slip	Cash sale to a customer
Bank debit memo	Deduction from a company's bank account
Bank credit memo	Increase in a company's bank account
Sales invoice	Sale on account to a customer
Purchase invoice	Purchase on account by the business
Cheque issued	Payment made to a creditor (account payable) or for a cash purchase
Cheque received	Payment received from a customer (account receivable)

Generally Accepted Accounting Principles and Key Ideas

In this chapter, you learned the following Generally Accepted Accounting Principle:

- The **principle of objectivity** requires that accounting records be based on *objective evidence*. Source documents provide objective evidence to support the value used to record transactions.

You also learned the following key ideas:

- A **source document** is prepared for every business transaction.
- **Source documents** are prenumbered and all source documents must be accounted for.

UNIT 8 CHECK YOUR READING

Questions

19. (a) What is a source document?
   (b) Give four examples of source documents.
   (c) Why are source documents prenumbered?
   (d) Name a source document for each of the following:
      (i)   Cash sale
      (ii) Sale on account
      (iii) Purchase on account
      (iv) Payment by cheque

20. For the Sanne Consultants invoice shown on the next page, answer the following:
   (a) Who is the seller?
   (b) Who is the buyer?
   (c) What is the invoice number? Invoice date? Invoice total?

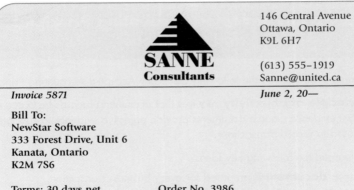

Exercises Part A

10. Following is the opening balance sheet on November 30 for the Ridgeview Motel, owned by Bruna Fenato.

Ridgeview Motel
Balance Sheet
November 30, 20—

Assets		Liabilities	
Cash	$ 3 000	Accounts Payable/	
Supplies	2 000	Acme Supply	$ 3 000
Office Equipment	2 000	Bank Loan	25 000
Building	150 000	Mortgage Payable	60 000
Furniture	20 000	Total Liabilities	88 000
Automobile	6 000		
		Owner's Equity	
		B. Fenato, Capital	95 000
		Total Liabilities and	
Total Assets	$183 000	Owner's Equity	$183 000

The chart of accounts contains the accounts shown on the balance sheet plus the following:

301	B. Fenato, Drawings	502	Salaries Expense
400	Room Rentals	503	Telephone Expense
500	Advertising Expense	505	Utilities Expense
501	General Expense	506	Automobile Expense

(a) Journalize the opening entry.

(b) Journalize the December transactions using account titles found in the balance sheet and in the chart of accounts.

(c) Open the ledger accounts. Refer to page 116 for sample numbers for the asset, liability, and equity accounts.

(d) Post the opening entry and the December general journal entries.

(e) Prepare a trial balance.

(f) Prepare the December financial statements.

Dec. 1 Paid $50 for automobile repairs, Cheque 125.

2 B. Fenato withdrew $150 cash for personal use, Cheque 126.

3 Paid $1000 to Acme Supply to reduce the amount owing, Cheque 127.

4 Paid $175 to Bell Canada for the telephone bill received today, Cheque 128.

5 Received $900 cash for room rentals for the week, Sales Slips 246–269.

8 Purchased cleaning supplies from Acme Supply, $120, Invoice 742.

10 Paid $125 for repairs to Fenato's personal car, Cheque 129.

11 Bought an electronic printing calculator for the office, $200, Cheque 130.

12 Received $1100 cash for room rentals for the week, Sales Slips 270–289.

12 Paid $12 for postage stamps (General Expense), Cheque 131.

12 Paid the hydro bill, $290, and the water bill, $175, received today, Cheques 132 and 133.

15 Paid $75 to Ace Printing for an advertising brochure, Cheque 134.

15 Paid $45 for a small advertisement in *The Bugle* newspaper, Cheque 135.

16 B. Fenato withdraw $250 for her own use, Cheque 136.

16 Paid salaries for the first half of the month, $750, Cheque 137.

18 The bank sent a memo informing B. Fenato that $350 had been taken out of the business bank account to pay for interest on the bank loan. (Open a new account numbered 507 for Interest Expense.)

19 Received $1750 cash for room rentals for the week, Sales Slips 290–317.

22 Received a $225 bill from Acme Supply for new linen and towels, Invoice 3264.

23 Received an $85 bill from Kelly Motors for gasoline and oil used in the business car, Invoice 684. (A new account will have to be opened for Kelly Motors.)

25 Paid $350 on account to Acme Supply, Cheque 138.

26 Received $1525 cash for room rentals for the week, Sales Slips 318–340.

31 Paid salaries for the rest of the month, $1365, Cheque 139.

11. Should B. Fenato be satisfied with the performance of her business in December? What information would you like to have to better answer this question?

12. The following general journal contains a number of errors.

DATE		PARTICULARS	P.R.	DEBIT	CREDIT
		GENERAL JOURNAL			PAGE 27
20—					
Oct. 1	Cash			1 0 0 0 00	
		W. Wakelin, Capital			1 0 0 0 00
	Owner investment in business.				
2	Cash			5 2 5 00	
		Sales			5 2 5 00
	Sold merchandise on account and mailed invoice.				
3		Accounts Payable			1 1 0 00
	Office Supplies			1 1 0 00	
	Purchased supplies on account.				
3	Telephone Expense			5 3 00	
		Cash			5 3 00
	Paid phone bill.				
4	W. Wakelin, Drawings			2 5 0 00	
		Cash			2 5 0 00
5	Accounts Receivable			8 9 00	
		Cash			9 8 00
	Received $89 on account.				
6	Advertising Expense				7 5 00
		Cash			7 5 00	
	Paid for advertising.				

(a) List the errors you discover.

(b) What effect, if any, would each error have on the trial balance totals and account balances?

(c) When would the error made on October 2 be discovered?

(d) When would the error made on October 5 be discovered?

13. The working papers contain a copy of the chart on page 148. Analyze the errors that were made in recording transactions and indicate the immediate effect of the errors on the value of the financial statement elements shown in the chart. The errors could result in a higher value than it should be ($\uparrow$), a lower value than it should be ($\downarrow$), or no effect (–). Error (a) has been completed for you.

14. List the source documents commonly used to provide evidence for the following transactions:

(a) Cash sale

(b) Sale on account

(c) Cash purchase

(d) Purchase on account

(e) Payment by cheque

(f) Collection of an account receivable

Complete this exercise in your workbook.

15. Refer to the purchase invoices shown on pages 150 and 151. Notice that the invoice from Electronic Suppliers was dated November 12 and the invoice from Poulin's Service Station was dated November 13. Both invoices were received by Carlo's TV Repairs on November 15.

(a) Why would the invoices be recorded in the journal on November 15? What GAAP is involved in this procedure?

(b) When did the suppliers journalize these invoices? What GAAP was involved in this procedure?

Part B Supplementary Manual or Computer Exercise

Exercise 16 may be done manually or on a computer. If completed manually, the required forms are in the Study Guide and Working Papers. If completed with a computer, students may set up their own accounts or the teacher may use the CD provided by the publisher. The CD contains files for this exercise prepared with Simply Accounting software.

16. (a) Using the trial balance shown on page 149, open the accounts in the ledger for Carlo's TV Repairs.

(b) At the end of each day, C. Amato does his accounting from the source documents that he received or issued that day. Record the source documents for November 15 on page 26 of a general journal. The source documents are shown on pages 149–152.

Error	Total Revenue	Total Expense	Net Income	Total Assets	Total Liabilities	Owner's Equity
(a) Omitted recording the sale of services to a customer.	↓	–	↓	↓	–	↓
(b) Omitted recording the receipt of a payment on account by a customer.						
(c) Recorded a sale on account as a cash sale.						
(d) Recorded purchase of a new truck as a debit to Truck Repair Expense and a credit to Cash.						
(e) A withdrawal by the owner was debited to Bank Loan and credited to Cash.						
(f) The collection of an account receivable was debited to Cash and credited to Revenue.						
(g) An invoice received for advertising was debited to Telephone Expense and credited to Accounts Payable.						
(h) The payment of the owner's personal car loan was debited to Car Expense and credited to Cash.						
(i) Omitted recording the investment of additional funds by the owner.						
(j) Recorded a cash sale of $525 as $252.						

Carlo's TV Repairs
Trial Balance
November 15, 20—

Account	Acc. No.	Debit	Credit
Cash	100	$ 4 500.00	
Accts. Rec./B. Dover	101	147.43	
Accts. Rec./Drive-Inn Motor Hotel	102	398.76	
Accts. Rec./L. Mansfield	103	225.50	
Equipment	141	25 000.00	
Truck	142	8 000.00	
Accts. Pay./Electronic Suppliers	200		$ 2 047.50
Accts. Pay./Poulin's Service Station	201		276.89
C. Amato, Capital	300		35 947.30
Sales	400		0
Hydro Expense	504	0	
Truck Expense	506	0	
Equipment Repairs Expense	507	0	
		$38 271.69	$38 271.69

Sales invoices:

INVOICE
Carlo's TV Repairs

1750 Elgin Street, Winnipeg, Manitoba   R3E 1C3
Tel: (204) 941-8232   Fax: (204) 941-3987

DATE: Nov. 15, 20—
INV. NO: 1501
TERMS: Net 30 days

SOLD TO:
B. Dover
141 Dynes Road
Winnipeg, Manitoba   R2J 0Z8

RE: R.C.A. Colour TV

Labour	$160.00
Parts	89.85
	$249.85

AMOUNT OF THIS INVOICE: $249.85

INVOICE
Carlo's TV Repairs

1750 Elgin Street, Winnipeg, Manitoba   R3E 1C3

Tel: (204) 941-8232   Fax: (204) 941-3987

DATE: Nov. 15, 20—
INV. NO: 1502
TERMS: Net 30 days

SOLD TO:
Drive-Inn Motor Hotel
1460 River Road
Winnipeg, Manitoba   R2M 3Z8

RE: TVs in rooms 117, 119, and 212

Labour	$356.00
Parts	137.50
	$493.50

AMOUNT OF THIS INVOICE: $493.50

Purchase invoices:

ELECTRONIC SUPPLIERS

Montreal
Toronto
Winnipeg
Vancouver

147 Industrial Blvd., Winnipeg, Manitoba   R2W 0J7

Tel. (204) 475-6643
Fax (204) 475-2843

Terms: Net 15 days

SOLD TO   SHIP TO

Carlo's TV Repairs   SAME
1750 Elgin Street
Winnipeg, Manitoba   R3E 1C3

GST Registration No.	Prov. Sales Tax No.	Date Invoiced	Invoice No.
S473542119	435 70913	11/12/—	7463

Quantity	Description	Unit Price	Amount
1	Equipment	$453.90	$453.90
	Pay this amount		$453.90

INVOICE
POULIN'S SERVICE STATION

1553 Park Drive, Winnipeg, Manitoba R3P 0H2

Tel: (204) 321-1154   Fax: (204) 321-2139

Date: Nov. 13/—   Terms: Net 15 days   Inv. No. B-151

Part No.	Part Name	Total		
X340	Oil filter	$ 8.50	Make	GMC Truck
	4 L oil	10.50	Licence:	A-4597
316-092	Spark plugs	15.90	Name	Carlo's TV Repairs
			Address	1750 Elgin Street
				Winnipeg, Manitoba
				R3E 1C3

	WORK COMPLETED	AMOUNT
	Oil Change	
	Tune-up	$63.00
	TOTAL LABOUR	63.00
TOTAL PARTS FORWARD $34.90	PARTS	34.90
	PAY THIS AMOUNT	$97.90

Cheques issued:

Carlo's TV Repairs   NO. 347
1750 Elgin Street
Winnipeg, Manitoba R3E 1C3   Nov. 15, 20 —

PAY TO THE
ORDER OF   Electronic Suppliers -------------------------$ 2047.50

SUM OF Two thousand and forty-seven ---------------------50/100 DOLLARS

THE REGIONAL BANK OF CANADA
3017 Lelland Road
Winnipeg, Manitoba R2K 0J7

Carlo Amato
Carlo's TV Repairs

⑈⑈⑈ ⑈⑈⑈⑈ ⑈⑈⑈ ⑈⑈⑈ ⑈⑈⑈⑈

348 21639 033 416 2859

(Detach and retain this statement)

Carlo's TV Repairs   NO. 347

THE ATTACHED CHEQUE IS IN PAYMENT OF ITEMS LISTED BELOW

DATE	ITEM	AMOUNT	DISCOUNT	NET AMOUNT
Oct. 28	Inv. 7393	$2047.50		$2047.50

Carlo's TV Repairs
1750 Elgin Street
Winnipeg, Manitoba R3E 1C3

NO. 348

Nov. 15,   20 –

PAY TO THE
ORDER OF   Winnipeg Hydro --------------------------------$79.50

SUM OF   Seventy-nine ---50/100 DOLLARS

THE REGIONAL BANK OF CANADA
3017 Lelland Road
Winnipeg, Manitoba R2K 0J7

Carlo Amato
Carlo's TV Repairs

⑈⑈⑈ ⑈⑈⑈⑈ ⑈⑈⑈ ⑈⑈⑈ ⑈⑈⑈
348 21639 033 416 2859

(Detach and retain this statement)

Carlo's TV Repairs

NO. 348

THE ATTACHED CHEQUE IS IN PAYMENT OF ITEMS LISTED BELOW

DATE	ITEM	AMOUNT	DISCOUNT	NET AMOUNT
Nov. 15	Inv. B-741	$79.50		$79.50

**Cash Receipts List
November 15, 20—**

Customer	Invoice	Amount
L. Mansfield	1370	$ 225.50
Drive-Inn Motor Hotel	1269	398.76
Cash sales		1 156.63
		$1 780.89

(c) In the general journal, record the following November 16 source documents.

(d) Post the general journal to the ledger and prepare a trial balance.

Nov. 16   Sales invoices issued:
No. 1503 to L. Mansfield for $477.
No. 1504 to Drive-Inn Motor Hotel for $573.60.

Purchase invoice received:
No. 7533 from Electronic Suppliers, $550.80 for servicing the equipment.

Cheques issued:
No. 349 to Poulin's Service Station, $276.89 on account.
No. 350 to Electronic Suppliers, $453.90 on account.

Cash received from:
B. Dover, $147.43.
Drive-Inn Motor Hotel, $293.50.
Cash sales, $1453.70.

Computer Accounting

Computer Accounting Software

An accounting student should know the advantages and disadvantages of using accounting programs, as well as their structure and terminology. Most businesses, even the smallest, use a computer to assist with their record keeping. They use a spreadsheet to some extent and many use comprehensive accounting software.

There are a number of computer accounting programs available, including QuickBooks, NewViews, Peachtree Accounting, Great Plains Accounting, AccPac, and Simply Accounting. In the following chapters, several widely used software packages will be described.

Simply Accounting

In this section, the Simply Accounting program will be described. Simply Accounting is produced, marketed, and supported by AccPac International, a division of Computer Associates, a large software company with revenues of over $1 billion a year. Computer Associates sells several computer accounting programs, including Simply Accounting, AccPac, and AccPac Plus Accounting.

Simply Accounting is entry-level software for small businesses. It is an easy-to-use program that provides journalizing, automatic posting, payroll, inventory, job costing, and automatic preparation of financial reports. The program is available in Windows and Macintosh versions.

Simply Accounting offers the choice of setting up a company using either accounting or non-accounting terminology. All computer screens shown in this text and all files provided for student use will be set up using the accounting terminology option.

Program Characteristics

Simply Accounting is designed as a computer database program. Transaction data are entered into the computer as journal entries. The entries are then posted automatically to ledger accounts. The program sorts and classifies data, calculates account balances, and produces a variety of reports automatically. These functions are illustrated in Figure 4-25.

Journal Entries	Entered by the accountant
Posting to Ledger Accounts	Done by the computer
Preparation and Printing of Reports	Done by the computer
Trial Balance	Done by the computer
Income Statement	Done by the computer
Balance Sheet	Done by the computer
Chart of Accounts	Done by the computer
Journals	Done by the computer
Ledgers	Done by the computer
Special Reports	Done by the computer

FIGURE 4-25 Simply Accounting program functions

Simply Accounting greatly reduces the manual work for the accountant. After the accounts and report formats have been set up, most of the writing, the arithmetic, and the printing of reports and statements is done by the computer. Once the accountant has entered the transaction in the journal, all the remaining steps (i.e., the posting and preparation of financial reports) are done by the software. In addition, because of the database structure of the program, it can automatically provide other reports and documents from the information it stores in memory. The following types of reports and documents can be produced:

- lists of customers and creditors;
- cheques;
- invoices and statements;
- payroll summaries; and
- mailing labels.

Simply Accounting is an integrated software package. It consists of six accounting *modules*: General, Payables, Receivables, Payroll, Inventory and Services, and Project. The modules, illustrated in the main menu in Figure 4-26 are *integrated*, which means they are linked together.

FIGURE 4-26 The Simply Accounting Home Window (main menu)

Using Simply Accounting to Record Journal Entries

In the following section an example of journalizing using Simply Accounting is presented. This example uses the general journal. A sample general journal entry for M. Conway, Architect, is shown below both in manual-accounting format and in computer-accounting format. The manual-accounting entry is as follows:

		GENERAL JOURNAL		PAGE 1	
DATE		PARTICULARS	P.R.	DEBIT	CREDIT
20—					
Feb.	1	Cash		15 0 0 0 00	
		M. Conway, Capital			15 0 0 0 00
		Investment, personal cheque P-156.			

Using Simply Accounting, the journal entry would appear as follows when printed by the computer:

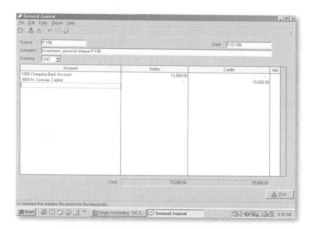

Notice that the explanation is printed first in the computer entry; the date, February 1, 2000, is shown as 02/01/00; and the journal entry number is transaction number J1. Simply Accounting assigns a sequential journal number to every transaction beginning with J1. This number enables the accountant, the auditor, or the owner to find and track each transaction through the accounting system. The account names and numbers are shown as well as the debit and credit amounts. The total of the debits and credits is shown to indicate that the entry balances. Now let's examine how journal entries are made using Simply Accounting.

Simply Accounting Journal Entry Instructions

Suppose you want to record transactions in a general journal. You select the **GENERAL** icon from the main menu and the computer presents you with the general journal input form, Figure 4-27. Enter the transaction as follows:

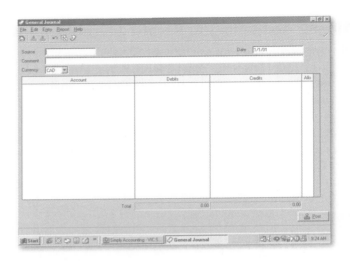

FIGURE 4-27 The general journal input form

1. Enter the source document number (**P-156**) in the **Source** field and press TAB.
2. Enter the date, February 1, 2000, as **02/01/00** (month, day, year) and press TAB.
3. Enter the Comment (explanation), **Investment in a new business**, then press TAB.
4. With the cursor now in the **Account** field, press ENTER. This will provide you with a list of accounts. Select the one you want to debit, **1080, Cash**, then click **Select**. The program will show the account title and number on the screen. Press TAB.
5. The cursor will now be in the **Debit** field. Enter the amount, **15000**, and press TAB.
6. Enter the credit by pressing ENTER to see the list of accounts. Then select the account to be credited, **3100, M. Conway, Capital**. The account title and number will appear on the screen.
7. Enter the credit amount, **15000**. Press TAB.
8. You cannot post the entry unless the debit amount equals the credit amount. The **Post** button will remain dim (remain inactive) until the debits equal the credits.
9. A check of your accuracy can be made by choosing **Display general journal entry** from the Report menu. This will show the entry you have just made.
10. If you feel the entry is correct, select **Post** and the computer will post the entry for you. Simply Accounting automatically saves your work each time you post.
11. You can correct or change an entry *before* posting it by returning to the field and making the change. You can do this using the mouse or by pressing SHIFT and TAB.
12. Corrections discovered *after* posting are made by reversing the original entry and then making the correct entry.

Some Recording Hints

When you use Simply Accounting remember the following:

- ➤ Enter the date in this format: MM/DD/YY, that is, month, day, and year, using two digits for each and a slash as a separator, e.g., 02/01/00.
- ➤ Review every transaction before you post it to the ledger. This is done by ensuring that the journal screen shows equal debits and credits and that the accounts selected are the correct ones. A second check can be made by selecting the Report menu and choosing Display general journal entry. This will show you the entry in journal format.
- ➤ Once an entry is posted it becomes a permanent part of the accounting records. It cannot be removed. Corrections are made by reversing the original entry and then making the correct entry.

Simply Accounting Account Numbers

Companies that use Simply Accounting must adhere to the account numbering system that is built into the program. The following numbering system is used by the Windows and Macintosh versions of the program:

Asset Accounts	1000–1999
Liability Accounts	2000–2999
Equity Accounts	3000–3999
Revenue Accounts	4000–4999
Expense Accounts	5000–5999

Using Simply Accounting for Computer Assignments

You will use Simply Accounting in one of two ways as you complete the computer assignments in this text.

1. Your teacher will supply a data file that contains the ledger accounts for the textbook exercises. You will use Simply Accounting to:

- ➤ retrieve the exercise data file;
- ➤ journalize transactions; and
- ➤ print reports.

OR

2. You will set up the chart of accounts yourself and then complete the exercises as indicated in 1 above.

For both methods, your teacher may have you prepare your data beforehand using a computer data entry sheet.

Computer Data Entry Sheet

Many companies feel it is more efficient to separate the accounting analysis tasks from the computer entry tasks. One person, with an accounting background, is assigned the job of analyzing and checking source documents. The information to be entered into the computerized accounting system is recorded on a data entry sheet. This includes the accounts to be debited and credited, the amount, and the explanation of the transaction. Another person, who is a data entry specialist,

A data entry sheet is used to organize the information to be entered into a computerized accounting system. This includes accounts to be debited and credited, the amount, and the explanation of the transaction.

enters the information onto the computer from the data entry sheet that has been prepared by the accountant. It is felt that this division of duties is efficient because it allows each person to specialize in what he or she does best. An example of a data entry sheet is shown in Figure 4-28.

		DATA ENTRY SHEET				
SOURCE DOC.	DATE	EXPLANATION	ACCT. DEBIT	AMOUNT DEBIT	ACCT. CREDIT	AMOUNT CREDIT
P-156	02-01-00	Conway's investment	1080	$15 000	3100	$15 000

FIGURE 4-28 A data entry sheet

General Ledger Computer Application Software

The computer assignments in this chapter can be done using a general ledger computer accounting package such as Simply Accounting, QuickBooks, or Peachtree. In completing these assignments you will be using only the general journal. The other journals available with the software will not be used.

COMPUTER ASSIGNMENTS

1. Marion Conway, an architect, provides design services to the commercial and residential construction industry. As her accountant you are responsible for the following tasks: analyzing transactions, determining the computer coding, completing data entry sheets, and recording transactions from the data entry sheet using a program such as Simply Accounting.

   (a) Analyze each of the following transactions.
   (b) Enter the transactions on a data entry sheet. Use appropriate explanations. Select account numbers from the chart of accounts in Figure 4-29. The first transaction is completed for you in Figure 4-28.
   (c) Launch the Simply Accounting program from your computer or school computer network.
   (d) Select Simply Accounting Data Files.
   (e) Select M. Conway.
   (f) Select General Journal.
   (g) Enter the transactions from your data entry sheet into the general journal.
   (h) Print a journal, a ledger, and a trial balance.

   Feb. 1 M. Conway invested $15 000 in the business, Cheque P-156.
   2 Bought office equipment for $5000 cash, Cheque 1.
   3 Bought an automobile for the business from Bytown Motors on credit, Invoice B-3609. The car cost $15 000.

    4   Received $500 cash for services provided to a customer, Cash Receipt 1.

    5   Sent an invoice for $1500 to Foothills Construction for services provided on account, Invoice 1.

    5   Paid the February rent, $950, Cheque 2.

    5   Paid office salaries for the week, $800, Cheque 3.

    5   Paid $1600 for a telephone system, Cheque 4.

Marion Conway, Architect
Chart of Accounts

Account Title	Account Number
Cash	1080
Accounts Receivable/Foothills Construction	1220
Office Equipment	1350
Automobile	1400
Accounts Payable/Bytown Motors	2200
M. Conway, Capital	3100
Fees Earned	4100
General Expense	5100
Rent Expense	5120
Salaries Expense	5130
Telephone Expense	5140

FIGURE 4-29 Chart of accounts

  2. Use your computer accounting program to complete exercises 9, 10, and 16 of this chapter.

WEB EXTENSIONS

www.pearsoned.ca/
principlesofaccounting

Internet Study Guide

 Complete the Chapter 4 review.

 Complete the Chapter 4 definitions.

 Complete the Chapter 4 online test.

Web Links

Visit the Web Links section at the Pearson Education web site to find a link to the SkillNet.ca web site. Outline the skill requirements for an accounting job posted on the site.

12 Case Studies

CASE 1 Source Documents

Erin Liley is the owner of Grocery Express. While glancing through the company's ledger, Erin notices a December 12 credit of $398 in the Sales account. Suspecting that the $398 amount should be $39.80, Erin decides to check the original source document to determine the correct amount.

(a) How can Erin trace the entry back to the original source document to check the amount?
(b) What type of source document(s) could have been prepared for the December 12 transaction?
(c) What is the quickest way to locate the source document?

CASE 2 Accrual Method of Accounting

The following data were collected for Reid Cleaners for the month of November.

1. Payments received on previous accounts receivable, $2400.

2. Cash received for cleaning services performed this month, $6000.

3. Cleaning services performed for credit customers this month, $3500.

4. Payments made on previous accounts payable, $3000.

5. Expenses of this month paid in cash, $4000.

6. Expenses incurred this month that remain unpaid at month-end, $3200.

Reid Cleaners follows the accrual system of accounting for revenue and expense. State the amount of revenue, expense, and net income for the month of November.

CASE 3 General Journal Errors

There are several errors in the following general journal.

(a) Prepare a list of the errors.
(b) Prepare a corrected general journal.

GENERAL JOURNAL					PAGE 17	
DATE	PARTICULARS	P.R.	DEBIT		CREDIT	
20—						
Nov. 2	Cash		5 0 0 00			
	Sales				5 0 0 00	
	Sold goods for cash.					
3	Supplies		1 0 0 00			
	Cash				1 0 0 00	
3	Cash				2 0 0 00	
	Delivery Expense		2 0 0 00			
	Cheque 81 to Central Cartage.					
Nov.	Accounts Receivable		5 0 0 00			
	Sales				5 0 0 00	
	Inv. 871.					
5	Supplies		1 2 0 00			
	Accounts Payable				1 2 0 00	
	Inv. B-120, Grand & Toy.					

Locating Ledger Errors

CASE 4

The accountant for Mary Catherine's Boutique has made several errors in posting from the journal to the ledger.

(a) Which of the following errors will cause the trial balance totals to be out of balance?

(b) Which of the following errors will *not* be indicated by the trial balance?

   (i)   Both a $1000 debit and a $1000 credit were posted as $100.

   (ii)   A debit of $75 to General Expense was incorrectly posted to Delivery Expense.

   (iii) A debit of $35 to General Expense was posted as a credit to General Expense.

   (iv) A debit of $98.50 to W. Davis was posted in error to M. Davis's account.

   (v)   A debit and a credit of $875 were both posted as $785.

CASE 5 Journal Entries

Sally Tse is a civil engineer who specializes in designing commercial and industrial projects. After working for eight years for a large consulting engineering firm, she decided to go into business for herself. Her experience included consulting on the design and construction of apartment buildings, schools, shopping plazas, and several manufacturing facilities. She enjoyed an excellent reputation in her field. Clients often asked to have her assigned to their projects because of her talent and experience.

At the beginning of this year Sally formed The Structural Design Co. She rented offices and hired a small staff. The company is just completing its first year of business. It has been a very busy year for Sally. She has worked very hard and has found that although she has the technical skills required to operate a consulting firm, she needs help with administrative matters.

Sally has not set up an accounting system. She has hired you to do that. As an accounting consultant, your task is to sort out her records and to report on her financial position. On December 31, you are provided with the following information concerning the first year of operations:

- Sally invested $70 000 cash in the business.
- The company leased space in a strip mall at $3200 per month. The rent is paid at the end of each month. The December rent has not yet been paid.
- The company purchased furniture worth $6000 on credit from Valley Furniture.
- Computer and other office equipment was purchased for $8000 cash.
- Office supplies were purchased for $900 cash.
- The company paid the debt owing to Valley Furniture.
- The company had sales of $250 000. These were cash ($30 000) and credit ($220 000). At the end of the year, the amount still receivable from customers was $95 000.
- Salaries of $120 000 had been paid during the year. On December 31, $2000 in salaries was still owed to employees.
- Other operating expenses paid for during the year totalled $18 000.
- The company owes $4000 to the federal government for income taxes deducted from employees (debit Salaries Expense and credit Income Tax Payable).

1. Prepare journal entries to record the first year's transactions. Include entries to record the rent payable, the salary owing to Sally and to the employees, and the amount owing to the federal government for employee income tax deductions.

2. Prepare an income statement and a balance sheet.

3. Prepare a report for Sally that indicates the following:
   - the company's cash position;
   - the net income for the year; and
   - any other relevant financial advice you can provide.

4. What other information do you feel you need to advise Sally properly?

Transposition Errors

You have learned that a transposition of figures is the reversing of the numbers of an amount. For example, $75 written as $57 is a transposition error. A transposition error may be indicated if the difference in a trial balance is exactly divisible by 9. If the difference in the two totals of a trial balance is $81, the difference may have been caused by a transposition, since 81 is divisible evenly by 9.

Once a transposition error is suspected, it may be located by the following rule: *The number of times the amount of the difference is divisible by 9 is the difference between the two digits transposed.*

Suppose the difference is 81. The difference is divisible by 9 (81 divided by 9 is 9). Therefore, the difference between the two numbers transposed is 9. The only two numbers with a difference of 9 are 0 and 9. Therefore, the amounts transposed must have been 90 written as 9, or 9 written as 90. By looking for 9 or 90 on the trial balance, you will locate the error.

Suppose the error is 63. Since 63 divided by 9 is 7, the difference between the transposed numbers is 7. Therefore, the numbers transposed must be 7 and 0, or 2 and 9, or 8 and 1.

As the accountant for Joanne's Dressmaking Service, you examine four sets of trial balance totals that have differences as follows:
- Difference of 72
- Difference of 27
- Difference of 36
- Difference of 54

1. For each of these trial balance differences, state:
    (a) The number of times the difference is divisible by 9
    (b) The combination of numbers that might be transposed

⑬ Career Education Activities

1. Employee Characteristics

To be a life-long learner one must know one's own strengths and weaknesses. Which characteristics do you possess that would make you an asset to an employer? Your teacher will provide you with a checklist similar to the one that appears below. Using the form provided by your teacher, for each characteristic place a check mark in the appropriate column.

(a) If you indicated that you could never develop a specific skill, explain why not.
(b) Indicate how you can develop the skills check marked in the Need to Develop column.

Characteristic	Yes	Need to Develop	Could Never Develop
Self-confidence			
Ability to learn on my own			
Ability to teach others			
Problem-solving skills			
Written communication skills			
Oral communication skills			
Hobbies and/or extracurricular interests			
Interpersonal skills			
Organization skills			
Time-management skills			
Leadership skills			
Self-starter (shows initiative)			
Team player			
Technical skills			

2. Online Career Postings

The Internet has become a convenient location for employers to post their job advertisements. An Ontario government site lists advertisements similar to the one in Figure 4-30.

(a) Read the advertisement in Figure 4-30 and list the accounting duties involved in the position.

(b) What personal characteristics are required?

(c) Explain the meaning of the following:
   • Experience with relevant information technology
   • Working experience with start up organizations

(d) What are the advantages to the employer of posting job advertisements on the Internet?

(e) What are the advantages to the job seeker of looking for jobs on the Internet?

ONTARIO **GOjobs**
Government of Ontario Job Opportunities
| central site | feedback | search | site map | français |

| Home | Search jobs | List jobs | Government Overview | Eligibility | How to apply | After you apply | Job archive |

Location: Management Board Secretariat > GOjobs > Search Gojobs

ACCOUNTING & FINANCIAL REPORTING ADVISER
Ministry of Finance

$60951.00 - $76107.00 / year

Location: Toronto
Area of Search:

The Ministry of Finance, Ontario Financing Authority, capital markets treasury division, has a challenging opportunity for you to provide policy/technical advice for the province's investment/debt activities and financial reporting. You will: research policy changes/effect on government financial statements; negotiate with external parties; prepare reports; manage staff; co-ordinate research/reporting with ministry/external auditors.

Qualifications: expert knowledge of financial/accounting theories, principles, practices; excellent knowledge of government policies, procedures, financial reporting, budgeting; good understanding of financial instruments, associated current accounting issues; demonstrated success delivering service, managing projects, negotiating, managing staff; excellent analytical, writing, presentation, consulting skills; experience with relevant information technology; sound judgment; working experience with start up organizations.

FIGURE 4-30   Online advertisement

Career Profile • • • • • • • • • • • • • • • • • •

Very often, a high school student isn't really sure of his or her lifetime career goal. When Elaine Pitcher was growing up in Sault Ste. Marie, she couldn't decide if she wanted a career in law or in business. She decided to obtain experience in both areas and then to select a career based on which area she found more satisfying.

Elaine's career plan included taking courses and gaining work experience in business and law. While attending Sir James Dunn Collegiate and Vocational School in Sault Ste. Marie, Elaine took courses in both areas as planned. Her summer jobs included working at Algoma Steel Corporation, in a dental office, and as a librarian's assistant.

After graduating from Sir James Dunn, Elaine enrolled in the honours bachelor of commerce program at Queen's University. She majored in finance and took a variety of courses in accounting, business law, marketing, and computer studies.

During one summer, she worked for the City of Sault Ste. Marie in the legal department as a student assistant doing research, drafting bylaws, and working on contracts. Another summer she worked for the city's police department as the manager of the summer student program. In this job, she was involved in crime prevention programs such as Operation Identification and Neighourhood Watch. Elaine also took an income tax preparation course from H & R Block, and worked part-time for Beneficial Income Tax Service in Sault Ste. Marie preparing personal income tax returns.

Elaine's summer work and the courses she took at Queen's confirmed that she was interested in both business and the legal world. After graduating from Queen's with a Bachelor of Commerce degree, Elaine decided to try out the world of business. Her first full-time job was with the Canadian Imperial Bank of Commerce as a branch officer in training. She was assigned to a branch in Nepean, Ontario. Although she enjoyed working in banking, Elaine realized that she would like to combine a business career with law. This led her to decide to return to university to pursue a degree in law.

For the next three years, she studied at the Faculty of Law at Queen's University, where she graduated and received an LL.B., Bachelor of Laws degree.

Elaine then did required *articling* for one year with the law firm Wishart Noble in Sault Ste. Marie. The next step was to enroll in the Bar Admission Program operated by the Law Society of Upper Canada. Elaine moved to Ottawa to take this program. Finally, after passing the Bar Admission exams, Elaine was *called to the Bar* and became a full-fledged lawyer.

Elaine was hired by the firm with which she had articled, Wishart Noble, and began her professional career as a lawyer. Her specialty is working in the areas of real estate and corporate and commercial law. After three successful years of practice, Elaine became the first female partner in the firm, now called Wishart and Partners. At the same time she married.

Elaine continues to work and live in Sault Ste. Marie. She feels it is important to combine outside interests, hobbies, and family life with hard work to succeed. She enjoys tennis, sailing, reading, sewing, cooking, and playing the piano. In addition, Elaine contributes to her community by being active in several associations, including being on the Board of Governors of Sault College.

For Discussion

(a) If you have interests in different career areas, are you leaving your options open by choosing an appropriate variety of courses?

(b) Are you trying to obtain work experience in all of the areas that interest you?

(c) Give examples of where work experience benefited Elaine or was required by her career.

(d) Why are leisure activities an important part of any serious student's life?

5

The Work Sheet and Classified Financial Statements

What Learning You Will Demonstrate

On completion of this unit, you will demonstrate the skills necessary to:

- complete a six-column work sheet, the trial balance, and the financial statements of a service business;
- prepare an income statement from a work sheet; and
- prepare a balance sheet from a work sheet.

Figure 5-1 illustrates the steps in the manual accounting cycle as they have been described up to this point.

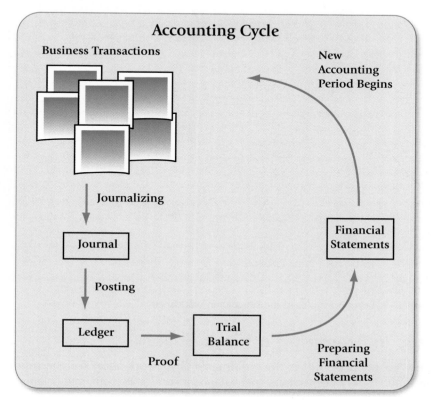

FIGURE 5-1 Steps in the manual accounting cycle covered to this point

A work sheet is a device that organizes the accounting data required for the preparation of financial statements.

The end of the fiscal period is a particularly busy time for accountants. They must prove the mathematical accuracy of the general ledger by preparing a trial balance, and then they must prepare the income statement and the balance sheet. As an aid in avoiding errors and to help organize their work, accountants may use a device called a work sheet.

INTRODUCING THE WORK SHEET

A work sheet is a large sheet of accounting paper used to organize data in the preparation of financial statements. It is one of the few forms that may be completed in pencil since it is not part of permanent accounting records. It is designed to discover and to eliminate errors before they become part of permanent records, and to provide an overall picture of the accounting process to assist in the preparation of financial statements. The work sheet constitutes part of what accountants traditionally refer to as their *working papers.* It is not a formal statement provided for management, or for the owners, or for persons interested in the financial position of the business.

Figure 5-2 illustrates the basic principles of the six-column work sheet. All of the account titles and balances are taken from the general ledger and written on the work sheet in the trial balance section. The account balances are then transferred to either the income statement section or the balance sheet section of the work sheet.

			Work Sheet					
	ACC.	TRIAL BALANCE		INCOME STATEMENT		BALANCE SHEET	
ACCOUNT TITLE	NO.	DEBIT	CREDIT	DEBIT	CREDIT	DEBIT	CREDIT
Assets		X X X				X X X	
		X X X				X X X	
		X X X				X X X	
Liabilities			X X X				X X X
			X X X				X X X
			X X X				X X X
Owner's Equity			X X X				X X X
			X X X				X X X
Revenue			X X X		X X X		
			X X X		X X X		
Expenses		X X X		X X X			
		X X X		X X X			

FIGURE 5-2 Basic principles of the six-column work sheet

Steps in Preparing a Work Sheet

Figure 5-3 on page 170 is the Goldman's Gym work sheet for the month of November. It has three sections: trial balance, income statement, and balance sheet.

Each section has a debit column and a credit column. See if you can follow the steps required to complete the work sheet shown in Figure 5-3 on page 170.

Step 1: Write the Heading

Write the main heading showing *Who? What?* and *When?* across the top of the work sheet. Notice that *the date line indicates the length of time covered by the accounting period*—one month in this example.

Step 2: Record the Trial Balance

Record the titles and balances from all of the general ledger accounts on the work sheet. Add the debit column balances and the credit column balances. The debit and credit columns should show the same totals.

Step 3: Transfer the Balance Sheet Items

The first accounts on the trial balance relate to assets, liabilities, and owner's equity. These amounts are transferred to the balance sheet section of the work sheet. For example, the Cash debit of $7800 is extended to the debit column of the balance sheet section since Cash is an asset. Extend the remaining asset, liability, and equity amounts to the appropriate debit or credit column of the balance sheet section.

Step 4: Transfer the Income Statement Items

The revenue and expense accounts on the trial balance are now transferred. For example, Members' Fees is a revenue account with a credit balance of $12 530. This amount is transferred to the credit column of the income statement section. The remaining revenue accounts are transferred as well. The expense accounts have debit balances and are transferred to the debit column.

Step 5: Complete the Income Statement Section

The net income or net loss is now determined by doing the following:

- Rule a single line below the income statement debit and credit columns and add each column.
- Write the totals below the single line. In Figure 5-3, the debit total is $10 790 and the credit total is $13 240.
- Determine the difference between the two columns. In Figure 5-3, the debit total (expenses) of $10 790 is subtracted from the credit total (revenue) of $13 240.
- Write the difference on the smaller side (see the $2450 amount in Figure 5-3).

In Figure 5-3 is there a profit or a loss? If the credit column exceeds the debit column, revenues exceed expenses and a net income has been made during the accounting period. The amount of this net income is entered below the total of the debit column, so that when these two amounts are added, the two columns are equal. *Net income* is written in the account titles section opposite the amount of the net income. If the debit column exceeds the credit column, expenses

Goldman's Gym
Work Sheet
For the month ended November 30, 20—

		ACCOUNT TITLE	ACC. NO.	TRIAL BALANCE		INCOME STATEMENT		BALANCE SHEET	
				DEBIT	CREDIT	DEBIT	CREDIT	DEBIT	CREDIT
Step 1: Write the heading.		Cash	100	7 8 0 0 00				7 8 0 0 00	
		Accounts Receivable	101	2 6 0 0 00				2 6 0 0 00	
Step 2: Record the trial balance.		Office Supplies	110	6 9 5 00				6 9 5 00	
		Land	120	25 0 0 0 00				25 0 0 0 00	
Step 3: Transfer the balance sheet items.		Building	121	110 0 0 0 00				110 0 0 0 00	
		Training Equipment	122	99 2 3 5 00				99 2 3 5 00	
		Accounts Payable	200		10 7 0 0 00				10 7 0 0 00
		Bank Loan	221		63 0 0 0 00				63 0 0 0 00
		Mortgage Payable	231		80 0 0 0 00				80 0 0 0 00
		R. Millar, Capital	300		90 6 8 0 00				90 6 8 0 00
Step 4: Transfer the income statement items.		R. Millar, Drawings	301	1 5 0 0 00				1 5 0 0 00	
		Members' Fees	400		12 5 3 0 00		12 5 3 0 00		
		Sports Equipment Rental	401		5 6 0 00		5 6 0 00		
		Towel Rental	402		1 5 0 00		1 5 0 00		
Step 5: Complete the income statement section.		Salaries Expense	500	4 6 5 0 00		4 6 5 0 00			
		Advertising Expense	501	2 7 0 0 00		2 7 0 0 00			
		Telephone Expense	502	1 9 0 00		1 9 0 00			
		Maintenance Expense	503	6 0 0 00		6 0 0 00			
Step 6: Complete the balance sheet section.		Licence Expense	504	1 1 0 0 00		1 1 0 0 00			
		Interest Expense	505	1 5 0 0 00		1 5 0 0 00			
		Laundry Expense	506	5 0 00		5 0 00			
Step 7: Rule the work sheet.				257 6 2 0 00	257 6 2 0 00	10 7 9 0 00	13 2 4 0 00	246 8 3 0 00	244 3 8 0 00
		Net Income				2 4 5 0 00			2 4 5 0 00
						13 2 4 0 00	13 2 4 0 00	246 8 3 0 00	246 8 3 0 00

FIGURE 5-3 Steps in preparing a work sheet

exceed revenues and a net loss has occurred. The difference between the two columns is written in the credit column opposite the words *net loss*.

Step 6: Complete the Balance Sheet Section

Rule a single line and total the columns in the balance sheet section. Enter the *net income* amount below the total of the *credit* column of the balance sheet section. The **net income** represents the *increase to the owner's equity* for the period. If there has been a net loss, enter the amount of the *loss* below the *debit* column total. The **net loss** represents the decrease to the owner's equity for the period. If the amount of the net income or net loss added to the column total makes it equal to the other column total in the balance sheet section, the work sheet is mathematically correct.

Net income increases owner's equity.

Net loss decreases owner's equity.

Step 7: Rule the Work Sheet

Rule double lines below the totals to indicate completion and proof that the work is mathematically correct.

Recording a Net Loss on a Work Sheet

Figure 5-4 illustrates a work sheet that has a net loss. (Only part of the work sheet is shown.) The following is a description of how a loss is handled.

- Obtain the amount of the loss by subtracting the smaller total, revenue ($75 000), from the larger, expenses ($83 000). The difference, or net loss ($8000), is written under the credit (revenue) total.
- Write "net loss" in the account title section on the same line as the loss ($8000).
- Enter the loss in the balance sheet section debit column.
- Check that the debit and credit totals in the balance sheet section are identical.
- Rule double lines.

ACCOUNT TITLE	ACC. NO.	TRIAL BALANCE DEBIT	TRIAL BALANCE CREDIT	INCOME STATEMENT DEBIT	INCOME STATEMENT CREDIT	BALANCE SHEET DEBIT	BALANCE SHEET CREDIT
Cash	100	5 0 0 0 00				5 0 0 0 00	
Accounts Receivable	101	10 0 0 0 00				10 0 0 0 00	
Maintenance Expense	510	2 0 0 0 00		2 0 0 0 00			
		250 0 0 0 00	250 0 0 0 00	83 0 0 0 00	75 0 0 0 00	176 0 0 0 00	184 0 0 0 00
Net Loss					8 0 0 0 00	8 0 0 0 00	
				83 0 0 0 00	83 0 0 0 00	184 0 0 0 00	184 0 0 0 00

Brulé Services
Work Sheet
For the month ended October 31, 20—

FIGURE 5-4 Recording a net loss on a work sheet

USING THE WORK SHEET

2

The completed work sheet is used to prepare the financial statements at the end of the fiscal period.

When the work sheet is complete, it contains, in an organized, systematic, and convenient form, all of the information that the accountant needs to prepare formal financial statements.

Preparing the Income Statement

The information from the income statement section of the work sheet is used to prepare the formal income statement. When the credit column of this section shows a greater total than the debit column, the amount of the difference is the *net income*. When the debit column total exceeds the credit column total, the difference is called *net loss*. When the formal income statement is complete, the conclusion (net income or net loss) should be the same as the matching conclusion on the work sheet.

The income statement shows the operating results for a business *over a period of time*. Figure 5-5 is the income statement of Goldman's Gym for the month of November. Notice that the heading clearly shows the period of time covered by the statement.

The information for the body of the income statement is taken from the income statement section of the work sheet. The *revenue* information is found in the credit column of that section. The *expense* data are found in the debit column. The net income of $2450 appears both on the work sheet (Figure 5-3) and on the income statement (Figure 5-5).

Goldman's Gym		
Income Statement		
For the month ended November 30, 20—		
Revenues		
Members' Fees	$12 530	
Sports Equipment Rental	560	
Towel Rental	150	$13 240
Expenses		
Salaries	4 650	
Advertising	2 700	
Telephone	190	
Maintenance	600	
Licence	1 100	
Interest	1 500	
Laundry	50	10 790
Net Income		$ 2 450

FIGURE 5-5 Income statement

Preparing the Balance Sheet

A balance sheet presents the financial position of a business *at a specific date*. Figure 5-6 is the balance sheet of Goldman's Gym prepared on November 30. It shows the assets, liabilities, and owner's equity at that specific date.

Just as the information for the income statement originated on the work sheet, so does the information for the balance sheet. Notice that in Figure 5-6 all of the data used on the balance sheet came from the balance sheet section of the work sheet in Figure 5-3 on page 170. Notice also that the net income of $2450 increases the Capital in the owner's equity section of the balance sheet. The balance sheet in Figure 5-6 is a *report form balance sheet*, which has a vertical format. (It has also been prepared as a "classified" balance sheet. The preparation of a classified balance sheet is described in the next unit.)

A report form balance sheet is prepared in vertical format.

Goldman's Gym
Balance Sheet
November 30, 20—

Assets

Current Assets		
Cash	$ 7 800	
Accounts Receivable	2 600	
Office Supplies	695	
Total Current Assets		$ 11 095
Fixed Assets		
Land	25 000	
Building	110 000	
Training Equipment	99 235	
Total Fixed Assets		234 235
Total Assets		$245 330

Liabilities and Owner's Equity

Current Liabilities		
Accounts Payable		$ 10 700
Long-Term Liabilities		
Bank Loan	$ 63 000	
Mortgage Payable	80 000	
Total Long-Term Liabilities		143 000
Total Liabilities		153 700
Owner's Equity		
R. Millar, Capital November 1		90 680
Add: Net Income for November	$2 450	
Less: R. Millar, Drawings	1 500	
Increase in Capital		950
R. Millar, Capital November 30		91 630
Total Liabilities and Owner's Equity		$245 330

FIGURE 5-6 Balance sheet

UNIT 9 CHECK YOUR READING

Questions

1. What is a work sheet?
2. What three items of information are included in the work sheet heading?
3. What fiscal period (accounting period) is covered by the November work sheet for Goldman's Gym, Figure 5-3?
4. What are the three major sections in the body of a work sheet?
5. Which accounts from the trial balance are extended to the balance sheet section of the work sheet?
6. Which accounts from the trial balance are extended to the income statement section of the work sheet?
7. When the debit column total of the income statement section of the work sheet is greater than the credit column total, what is the difference called?
8. When the credit column total of the income statement section is greater than the debit column total, what is the difference called?
9. When is a work sheet considered to be mathematically correct?
10. Why is the net income from the income statement section of the work sheet transferred to the credit column of the balance sheet section of the work sheet?
11. What is the difference between the report form and the account form of the balance sheet?
12. Prepare a diagram that illustrates the steps in the accounting cycle.

UNIT 9 APPLY YOUR KNOWLEDGE

Exercises

1. On the following page is a list of account titles. Your working papers contain a chart like the one in the example. Indicate on which statement section and in which column of the work sheet each account would appear. The first one, Cash, is done for you.

ACCOUNT TITLE	INCOME STATEMENT		BALANCE SHEET	
	DEBIT	CREDIT	DEBIT	CREDIT
Cash			✓	
Supplies				
Rent Expense				
C. Tran, Capital				
Office Equipment				
Accounts Payable				
Advertising Expense				
Light, Heat, Water Expenses				
Bank Loan				
Sales				
Accounts Receivable				
Investment Income				
Land				
C. Tran, Drawings				

2. Prepare a work sheet for the month of April from the following trial balance.

M. Odawo
Trial Balance
April 30, 20—

Account	Acc. No.	Debit	Credit
Cash		$ 2 000	
Accounts Receivable		4 300	
Equipment		6 200	
Accounts Payable			$ 2 500
M. Odawo, Capital			5 000
Sales			8 000
Salaries Expense		1 200	
General Expense		800	
Advertising Expense		1 000	
		$15 500	$15 500

3. Prepare a work sheet for the month of July from the following trial balance.

I. Gereluk
Trial Balance
July 31, 20—

Account	Acc. No.	Debit	Credit
Cash		$ 1 400	
Accounts Receivable		2 035	
Supplies		960	
Equipment		1 500	
Delivery Truck		7 800	
Accounts Payable			$ 1 245
Loan Payable			1 400
I. Gereluk, Capital			10 500
I. Gereluk, Drawings		1 000	
Sales			8 970
Salaries Expense		6 000	
Rent Expense		500	
Miscellaneous Expense		540	
Office Expense		255	
Telephone Expense		125	
		$22 115	$22 115

UNIT 10 Classified Financial Statements

What Learning You Will Demonstrate

On completion of this unit, you will:

- demonstrate the skills necessary to prepare a classified balance sheet;
- define *current and fixed assets* and *current and long-term liabilities*;
- explain the importance of current assets when interpreting the balance sheet;
- prepare supporting schedules, including a statement of owner's equity and a schedule of accounts receivable; and
- demonstrate an understanding of liquidity order and the cost principle.

The purpose of financial statements is to provide financial information about a company to owners, investors, management, creditors, and government. By classifying items on the statements into special categories, it is possible to provide more information and to provide it in a way that is more easily interpreted.

CLASSIFIED BALANCE SHEET

In Figure 5-6 on page 173 of the previous unit, information was provided in the classified balance sheet to answer the following questions:

- *Which debts must be paid within a year?*
- *Is there sufficient cash (or assets) on hand to pay debts?*
- *Which debts must be paid in future years?*

Look at Figure 5-6 and answer the preceding questions.

Assets and Liabilities

The balance sheet of Goldman's Gym, illustrated in Figure 5-6, is a classified balance sheet that includes some of the standard classifications. In this example, the assets are divided into two main groups: *current* and *fixed*. The liabilities are divided into two groups: *current* and *long-term*.

> A classified balance sheet lists items in special categories such as current and fixed assets, and current and long-term liabilities.

Current Assets

Cash and other assets that will be converted into cash or sold or consumed in the ordinary course of business (usually within one year) are called current assets. The list that follows provides some examples and the order in which current assets usually appear. They are listed in *order of liquidity*, that is, the order in which those assets may be converted into cash.

> A current asset is cash or some other asset that, in the normal course of operations, will be converted to cash or sold or consumed within the year.
>
> Current assets are listed in order of liquidity.
>
> Liquidity order is the order in which assets that last a short while may be converted into cash.

> **Current Assets**
> Cash
> Government Bonds
> Marketable Securities
> Accounts Receivable
> Prepaid Expenses

Government bonds and marketable securities often are easily converted into cash. Accounts receivable represent debts that are often due within 30 days.

Prepaid expenses are expense payments made in advance. They are items such as *prepaid insurance* and *prepaid rent*. They represent the value of the unused portions of insurance policies owned by the company and rental leases for which payment has been made in advance.

> Prepaid expenses are expense payments made in advance.

Fixed Assets

Fixed assets are assets such as land, buildings, equipment, and trucks that are used in operating the business and have a *long life*, in excess of one year. This section of the balance sheet may also be titled "plant and equipment" or "capital assets." The fixed assets that have the longest life are generally listed first. Here are some examples of accounts that may fall within this grouping.

> Fixed assets are assets that have a long life (over one year).

> **Fixed Assets**
> Land
> Building
> Equipment
> Delivery Trucks

Fixed assets are recorded using the price at which they were purchased (cost principle). This is a standard principle used by all accountants.

Current Liabilities

Current liabilities are liabilities due to be paid within a year.

The term current liabilities generally refers to liabilities that must be paid within a year or less. If possible, current liabilities are listed in the order that they are to be paid. Examples of current liabilities include the following:

> **Current Liabilities**
> Accounts Payable
> Taxes Payable
> Salaries Payable
> Loans Payable

Long-Term Liabilities

Long-term liabilities are liabilities that are not due to be paid for more than one year.

Long-term liabilities are liabilities that are not due to be paid for more than one year. A loan payable in two years and a mortgage payable in 25 years are examples of long-term liabilities.

Owner's Equity Section of the Balance Sheet

The owner's equity in a business increases when the business operates profitably. Owner's equity decreases when there has been a net loss and when the owner withdraws assets from the business.

The owner's equity section of the balance sheet in Figure 5-6 on page 173 is an example of equity increasing as a result of Goldman's Gym earning a net income that is greater than the owner's withdrawals from the business. Figure 5-7 shows how the owner's equity section of a balance sheet is set up to record a net loss.

> **Owner's Equity**
> | R. Millar, Capital May 1 | | $99 245 | |
> | Less: Net loss for May | $1 200 | | |
> | Less: R. Millar, Drawings | 1 800 | | |
> | Decrease in Capital | | 3 000 | |
> | R. Millar, Capital May 31 | | | $96 245 |

FIGURE 5-7 Net loss

It is possible for a business to earn a net income yet still have a decrease in owner's equity. This happens when the owner's withdrawals are greater than the net income. Figure 5-8 illustrates the setup of the owner's equity section when withdrawals are greater than net income.

Owner's Equity

R. Millar, Capital May 1		$99 245
Add: Net income for May	$1 000	
Less: R. Millar, Drawings	1 800	
Decrease in Capital		800
R. Millar, Capital May 31		$98 445

FIGURE 5-8 Withdrawals greater than net income

SUPPORTING STATEMENTS AND SCHEDULES

In addition to the basic income statement and balance sheet, a number of additional statements or schedules may be used to provide financial information.

Statement of Owner's Equity

The statement of owner's equity provides the owner of a business with data regarding the change in value of his or her equity for an accounting period. It is a *supporting statement* that is prepared separately from the balance sheet. The owner's equity balance at the end of the period is shown on the balance sheet instead of the full calculation. Figure 5-9 illustrates a statement of owner's equity.

The statement of owner's equity describes the changes in owner's equity for the accounting period.

Goldman's Gym
Statement of Owner's Equity
For the month ended November 30, 20—

R. Millar, Capital November 1		$90 680
Add: Net Income	$2 450	
Less: R. Millar, Drawings	1 500	
Increase in Capital		950
R. Millar, Capital November 30		$91 630

FIGURE 5-9 Statement of owner's equity

The balance sheet for Goldman's Gym in Figure 5-6 on page 173 could have been presented with the separate statement of owner's equity shown in Figure 5-9. In such a case, the final balance of the R. Millar, Capital account, $91 630, would be shown on the balance sheet in place of the complete equity calculation. This is illustrated in the balance sheet in Figure 5-10.

Goldman's Gym
Balance Sheet
November 30, 20—

Assets

Current Assets

Cash	$ 7 800	
Accounts Receivable	2 600	
Office Supplies	695	
Total Current Assets		$ 11 095

Fixed Assets

Land	25 000	
Building	110 000	
Training Equipment	99 235	
Total Fixed Assets		234 235
Total Assets		$245 330

Liabilities and Owner's Equity

Current Liabilities

Accounts Payable		$ 10 700

Long-Term Liabilities

Bank Loan	$ 63 000	
Mortgage Payable	80 000	
Total Long-Term Liabilities		143 000
Total Liabilities		153 700

Owner's Equity

R. Millar, Capital November 30		91 630
Total Liabilities and Owner's Equity		$245 330

FIGURE 5-10 Balance sheet

Schedule of Accounts Receivable

A supporting schedule provides details about an item on a main statement.

Supporting schedules are used to provide details about an item on a main statement. An example of a supporting schedule is the *schedule of accounts receivable*, shown in Figure 5-11 on the next page. It provides a list of the individual accounts receivable and the amounts owed. This provides the details regarding the Accounts Receivable total on the balance sheet. In Figure 5-10, the Accounts Receivable total is $2600. Further information about the amount owed by each customer is found on the schedule (Figure 5-11). Notice that the total on the schedule, $2600, is the same as the Accounts Receivable total on the balance sheet (Figure 5-10).

Goldman's Gym
Schedule of Accounts Receivable
November 30, 20—

B. Adamo	$ 250
C. Beck	250
L. Fantovic	200
W. Lanetti	200
D. McIsaac	300
K. Otte	100
R. Roarke	200
G. Schmidt	250
B. Taylor	250
H. Van de Slyke	300
K. Wier	100
A. Winetraub	200
Total Accounts Receivable	$2 600

FIGURE 5-11 Schedule of accounts receivable

Supporting schedules and statements may be prepared whenever the accountant feels they would provide additional useful information for the readers of the financial statements.

Generally Accepted Accounting Principles and Key Ideas

In this chapter, you learned the following four key ideas:

- A **work sheet** is not a formal accounting statement. It is a device that organizes the accounting data required for the preparation of financial statements.
- **Current assets** are listed on the classified balance sheet in order of liquidity.
- **Assets with the longest life** are listed first in the fixed assets section of the balance sheet.
- **Fixed assets** are recorded using the cost principle.

UNIT 10 CHECK YOUR READING

Questions

13. What is a classified financial statement?

14. Explain the following terms:
(a) Current asset
(b) Fixed asset
(c) Liquidity order
(d) Current liability
(e) Long-term liability

15. Explain the cost principle as it is applied to fixed assets on the balance sheet.

16. What effect does a withdrawal of assets from the business by the owner have on the owner's equity?

17. (a) What effect does a net loss have on the owner's equity?
(b) What effect does a net income have on the owner's equity?

UNIT 10 APPLY YOUR KNOWLEDGE

Exercises Part A

4. Classify each of the following as a current asset, a fixed asset, a current liability, or a long-term liability:
(a) Accounts Receivable
(b) Land
(c) Bank Loan (6 months)
(d) Office Supplies
(e) Delivery Truck
(f) Prepaid Rent
(g) Automobile
(h) Mortgage Payable
(i) Taxes Owing
(j) Government Bonds
(k) Accounts Payable

5. (a) List the current assets in exercise 4 in order of liquidity.
(b) List the fixed assets in exercise 4 in proper order.

6. The completed work sheet for the month of January for D. Lo, a lawyer, is shown on the next page. Prepare the income statement and classified balance sheet.

D. Lo
Work Sheet
For the month ended January 31, 20—

ACCOUNT TITLE	ACC. NO.	TRIAL BALANCE DEBIT	TRIAL BALANCE CREDIT	INCOME STATEMENT DEBIT	INCOME STATEMENT CREDIT	BALANCE SHEET DEBIT	BALANCE SHEET CREDIT
Cash		3 0 0 0 00				3 0 0 0 00	
Accounts Receivable		5 0 0 00				5 0 0 00	
Office Equipment		6 0 0 0 00				6 0 0 0 00	
Automobile		8 0 0 0 00				8 0 0 0 00	
Accts. Pay./Willson Supply Ltd.			2 0 0 00				2 0 0 00
D. Lo, Capital			15 7 0 0 00				15 7 0 0 00
Fees Income			4 0 0 0 00		4 0 0 0 00		
Automobile Expense		1 0 0 00		1 0 0 00			
Rent Expense		8 0 0 00		8 0 0 00			
Salaries Expense		1 0 0 0 00		1 0 0 0 00			
General Expense		5 0 0 00		5 0 0 00			
		19 9 0 0 00	19 9 0 0 00	2 4 0 0 00	4 0 0 0 00	17 5 0 0 00	15 9 0 0 00
Net Income				1 6 0 0 00			1 6 0 0 00
				4 0 0 0 00	4 0 0 0 00	17 5 0 0 00	17 5 0 0 00

7. (a) Using the trial balance below, prepare a work sheet for the three months ended September 30, 20—, for the Spruce Ridge Golf Club.

(b) Prepare an income statement, a statement of owner's equity, and a classified balance sheet.

Spruce Ridge Golf Club
Trial Balance
September 30, 20—

Account	Acc. No.	Debit	Credit
Cash		$ 3 000	
Supplies		9 000	
Land		200 000	
Equipment		30 000	
Accounts Payable			$ 2 000
Bank Loan (5 years)			95 000
J. Strathearn, Capital			98 000
J. Strathearn, Drawings		2 000	
Membership Fees			110 000
Salaries Expense		50 000	
Maintenance Expense		2 000	
Utilities Expense		7 000	
Office Expense		2 000	
		$305 000	$305 000

8. The following is the December 31 trial balance for the Spruce Ridge Golf Club.
   (a) Prepare a work sheet for the three months ended December 31, 20—.
   (b) Prepare an income statement.
   (c) Why do you think the operating results for this three-month period are different from the three-month period in exercise 7?

Spruce Ridge Golf Club
Trial Balance
December 31, 20—

Account	Acc. No.	Debit	Credit
Cash		$ 3 500	
Supplies		2 000	
Land		200 000	
Equipment		30 000	
Accounts Payable			$ 1 000
Bank Loan (5 years)			91 000
J. Strathearn, Capital			145 000
J. Strathearn, Drawings		1 000	
Membership Fees			19 500
Salaries Expense		12 000	
Maintenance Expense		5 000	
Insurance Expense		1 500	
Utilities Expense		1 000	
Office Expense		500	
		$256 500	$256 500

Exercises Part B

9. The work sheet on page 185 contains several errors.
   (a) List the errors.
   (b) Prepare a correct work sheet.
   (c) What is the correct net income?
   (d) If these errors were not discovered, what would the effect be on the net income and the final balance in the owner's Capital account?

10. Trial balance figures for February and March for a business owned by J. Pizl are shown at the bottom of page 185.
    (a) Prepare a work sheet, an income statement, a statement of owner's equity, and a balance sheet for February.
    (b) Prepare a work sheet and financial statements for March (including a statement of owner's equity).

Worksheet for exercise 9

ACCOUNT TITLE	ACC. NO.	TRIAL BALANCE DEBIT	CREDIT	INCOME STATEMENT DEBIT	CREDIT	BALANCE SHEET DEBIT	CREDIT
			A. Littleton Co. Work Sheet For the month of May 20—				
Cash		3 0 0 0 00				3 0 0 0 00	
Accounts Receivable		8 0 0 0 00					8 0 0 0 00
Equipment		20 0 0 0 00				20 0 0 0 00	
Accounts Payable			5 0 0 00				5 0 0 00
Bank Loan (5 years)			2 0 0 0 00				2 0 0 0 00
A. Littleton, Capital			21 0 0 0 00				21 0 0 0 00
A. Littleton, Drawings		7 0 0 0 00		7 0 0 0 00			
Sales			80 0 0 0 00		80 0 0 0 00		
Rent Expense		3 0 0 0 00		3 0 0 0 00			
Salaries Expense		60 0 0 0 00		60 0 0 0 00			
Office Expense		1 9 0 0 00		1 9 0 0 00			
General Expense		6 0 0 00		6 0 0 00			
		103 5 0 0 00	103 5 0 0 00	72 5 0 0 00	80 0 0 0 00	23 5 0 0 00	31 0 0 0 00
Net Income				7 5 0 0 00		7 5 0 0 00	
				80 0 0 0 00	80 0 0 0 00	31 0 0 0 00	31 0 0 0 00

	FEBRUARY DEBIT	CREDIT	MARCH DEBIT	CREDIT
Cash	3 0 0 0 00		2 0 0 0 00	
Accounts Receivable	7 0 0 0 00		6 0 0 0 00	
Prepaid Insurance	8 0 0 00		6 0 0 00	
Land	30 0 0 0 00		30 0 0 0 00	
Building	90 0 0 0 00		90 0 0 0 00	
Furniture	5 0 0 0 00		5 0 0 0 00	
Accounts Payable		4 0 0 0 00		5 0 0 0 00
Taxes Owing		1 0 0 0 00		1 0 0 0 00
Bank Loan (2 years)		15 0 0 0 00		16 9 0 0 00
Mortgage Payable		40 0 0 0 00		38 0 0 0 00
J. Pizl, Capital		72 1 0 0 00		75 8 0 0 00
J. Pizl, Drawings	1 0 0 0 00		2 0 0 0 00	
Sales		20 0 0 0 00		14 0 0 0 00
Salaries Expense	12 0 0 0 00		13 0 0 0 00	
Delivery Expense	1 2 0 0 00		9 0 0 00	
Utilities Expense	7 0 0 00		7 0 0 00	
Advertising Expense	9 0 0 00		1 0 0 00	
Miscellaneous Expense	3 0 0 00		2 0 0 00	
Insurance Expense	2 0 0 00		2 0 0 00	
	152 1 0 0 00	152 1 0 0 00	150 7 0 0 00	150 7 0 0 00

Trial balance figures for exercise 10

11. Examine the financial statements you have prepared for J. Pizl and answer the following questions in your workbook.

(a) Should J. Pizl be satisfied with the performance of the business over the two-month period?

(b) How could Accounts Receivable decrease by $1000?

(c) Has the value of the business increased?

(d) Is the business in a good position to pay its current liabilities?

(e) Why has net income decreased from February to March?

(f) Why did J. Pizl, Capital increase from the February trial balance figure of $72 100 to the March trial balance figure of $75 800?

(g) Which account decreased significantly in March compared to February? Do you think this may have had a negative effect on the performance of the business?

Computer Accounting

Computer Applications

Numerous computer-based accounting applications are available at most local computer stores. These programs use a graphical interface to simplify accounting for small businesses that may not be able to contract the work out to accounting firms. A spreadsheet may also be used to handle routine tasks with ease using a graphical interface.

Microsoft Excel

Microsoft Excel is a popular spreadsheet program used by some businesses for simple tasks such as preparing invoices and purchase orders. Other popular spreadsheet programs include Lotus 1-2-3 and Corel's Quattro Pro. A computer spreadsheet organizes information into columns and rows. The end-user can assign a variety of automatic formulas to summarize the data. Below (Figure 5-12) is a sample screen shot from an Excel screen.

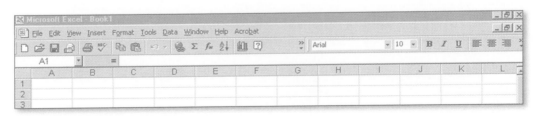

FIGURE 5-12   A sample Excel screen

Accounting Software

Accounting software can be divided into two main categories: software for personal finance and software for business operations. Two popular personal finance applications are Microsoft Money and Intuit Quicken. These programs do quite a bit more than simply balancing a chequebook, since they also keep

track of personal accounts, investments, retirement planning, loans and mortgages, insurance, and even risk assessments. Below (Figure 5-13) is a screen shot
from the Microsoft Money 2000 Home Page.

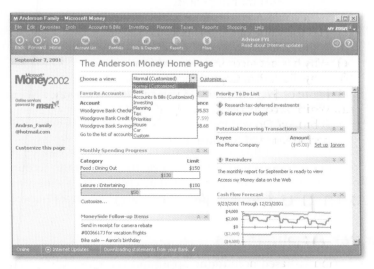

FIGURE 5-13 The Microsoft Money 2000 Home Page

Peachtree Complete Accounting, MYOB Premier Accounting, QuickBooks, and
Simply Accounting are examples of some of the accounting software packages
designed to automate accounting functions. Below (Figure 5-14) is a screen
shot from Peachtree Complete Accounting.

FIGURE 5-14 The Peachtree Complete Accounting home screen

Outsourcing

Some small businesses may elect to outsource the accounting functions rather than purchase and learn accounting software packages. Web-based solutions allow customers to access their accounts to track all kinds of transactions, including invoices and payments. These outsourcing companies use Internet-based solutions to provide accounting support to small businesses by handling a number of items, such as accounts receivable, accounts payable, and payroll on their secure web sites.

Comparing Manual and Computer Accounting

In the last chapter, you used general ledger software to record transactions. You saw that once transactions had been recorded, the computer was able to print journals, ledgers, trial balances, and financial statements. It was not necessary for you to re-enter information for the computer to complete the steps in the accounting cycle.

The software was able to use the initial data entered for a variety of purposes. Let's examine how this was done, and look at the differences between manual and computer accounting.

Manual Accounting Characteristics

Figure 5-15 illustrates what is involved in completing the steps of the accounting cycle. The steps are shown in the order that they are performed when accounting is done by hand, that is, manually. Each step requires that the data be rewritten.

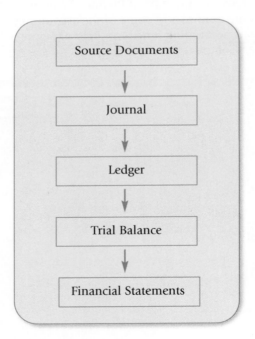

FIGURE 5-15 Steps in a manual accounting system

Computer Accounting Characteristics

Computers have the ability to quickly process large amounts of data. A 1-GHz processor is capable of executing one billion cycles per second. This speed allows for complex mathematical tasks to be completed by the computer.

When accounting data have been input, the computer processes the data and then provides a variety of user-friendly outputs (reports). The nature of both the processing and the output is determined by the speed of the CPU (central processing unit) and by the software application being used.

Figure 5-16 shows the same accounting cycle steps as outlined in Figure 5-15, but they are listed in the order in which they are completed in a computerized accounting system.

In a computerized accounting system, the accounting cycle is reduced to just three basic steps:

1. inputting data;
2. processing data; and
3. outputting data.

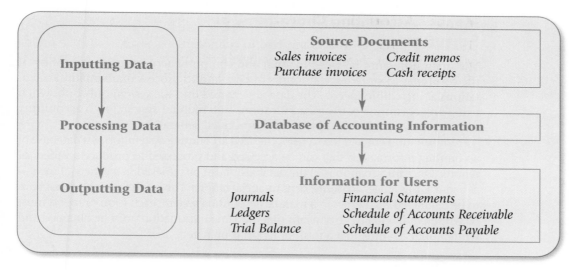

FIGURE 5-16 Steps in a computerized accounting system

Step 1: Inputting Data

Source documents are the source of information for the computer operator. A source document is prepared for every transaction and the information is entered into the computer system from the source document. Some companies, however, prefer to list the source documents on a data entry sheet prior to computer entry (see page 157).

Step 2: Processing Data

All of the information concerning transactions is stored in the computer or on an external storage device. Here it forms a database (or data bank) of accounting information. This database of information can be manipulated (processed) in a variety of ways. The software determines what processing will actually occur. The result of the processing can be printed as "output." It can be recalled from memory and used in a variety of ways depending on the type of output desired. The information does not have to be re-entered each time it is to be used for a report or form. Even though it has been used, it is still stored in memory and can be used again for different output purposes.

Step 3: Outputting Data

Output refers to the information produced by the software application. Information can be produced in a variety of ways, including printed reports, visual reports on the computer screen, electronic reports for later access, and Internet display for controlled access.

Let's examine the variety of accounting reports that can be printed by the software application. As illustrated in Figure 5-16, the output can be a journal, a trial balance, ledger account information, or financial statements and supporting schedules. The actual type and format of the report is determined by the needs of the company and the capabilities of the software being used.

Summary

The main difference between manual and computer accounting is the ability of the computer to store large amounts of data and to process mathematical calculations at incredible speeds. The data are entered into the system only once when using an accounting software application. In a manual system, each accounting step requires that data be written and processed separately.

Information entered into a computerized accounting system forms a database of accounting information that can be accessed and processed to produce a variety of reports. Once information is in the database, it can be retrieved in a variety of ways— as a journal, as ledger accounts, or as financial reports. The information does not have to be re-entered each time. In a manual accounting system, each form or report must be written individually. This means that the same information must be obtained and written out each time that a form or report is prepared.

Questions

1. Explain the differences between the two main categories of accounting software.
2. Describe the three steps involved in computer accounting.
3. What are the main differences between computerized accounting systems and manual accounting systems?
4. Outline the advantages of a small business storing its financial data in an electronic database.

Computer-Prepared Supporting Schedules

Figure 5-11, on page 181, shows a *manually* prepared schedule of accounts receivable. It provides the amount owed by each customer. The total amount, $2600, is shown as the asset, Accounts Receivable, on the balance sheet in Figure 5-10 on page 180.

Because of the processing ability of a computer, a more detailed schedule of accounts receivable can be produced *automatically*. Once accounting information has been input, it becomes a database of information. Most accounting programs are capable of producing a schedule such as the one in Figure 5-17. Notice that it indicates *how old* each customer's debt is. For example, the $2400 owed by Ashmore Reinforcing has been owed for between 61 to 90 days. It should have been paid within 30 days. This is valuable information and has been produced automatically by the computer. The same information can be produced manually—but it would take considerable time and effort.

Questions

1. Use the information on computer-prepared supporting schedules to discuss the following statements:
   - ▶ One of the purposes of accounting is "to provide information for decision making."
   - ▶ The computer has been described as "a tool of the accountant."
2. If you were the manager of Lippett Construction, how would you use the information in Figure 5-17?

NO.	CUSTOMER	TOTAL	CURRENT	31–60	61–90	91+
724	Alberta Trust Limited	$ 19 400.00	$ 19 400.00			
231	Ashmore Reinforcing	2 400.00			$ 2 400.00	
42	Atkins Mall	139 472.43	7 928.74	$ 16 966.83	114 576.86	
189	Bay Hospital	53 312.75	53 312.75			
746	Bell Morgan Ltd.	10 500.00	10 000.00		500.00	
123	Clare Holdings Ltd.	467.50	467.50			
113	Davison & Co.	1 599.50	1 599.50			
233	Drapeau & Wong	2 650.00		2 650.00		
121	Dunn, Shaw & Levin Development	3 881.32	2 138.73		1 742.59	
118	Eaglecrest Hotel	16 800.00			16 800.00	
45	Flag Motors	8 880.00	6 080.00		2 800.00	
85	Forge Motel	4 800.00		4 800.00		
		$264 163.50	$100 927.22	$ 24 416.83	$138 819.45	

Lippett Construction Ltd.
Customer Summary, March 30, 20—

FIGURE 5-17 Computer-prepared schedule of accounts receivable

COMPUTER ASSIGNMENTS

1. Format a spreadsheet (Excel, Lotus 1-2-3, Quattro Pro, Works, etc.) that can be used to prepare a work sheet. Your formatted spreadsheet should:
   - contain standard work sheet headings;
   - prepare totals for all columns;
   - determine the net income or net loss;
   - add a net income to the balance sheet section credit column; and
   - add a net loss to the balance sheet section debit column.

2. Use your formatted spreadsheet to print the answers to exercises 2, 3, 7(a), and 8(a) of this chapter.

 www.pearsoned.ca/ principlesofaccounting

WEB EXTENSIONS

Internet Study Guide

- Complete the Chapter 5 review.
- Complete the Chapter 5 definitions.
- Complete the Chapter 5 online test.

Web Links

Visit the Web Links section at the Pearson Education web site to find links to one of the accounting software packages mentioned in this chapter. Outline the benefits of the software package as listed at the site.

7 Case Studies

Comparative Balance Sheets

The June 30 and November 30 balance sheets for LeCroix Enterprises are shown below and on the next page. Compare the two balance sheets and answer these questions. Give reasons for all of your answers.

CASE 1

(a) Has the financial position of the business improved, weakened, or stayed approximately the same during these five months of operation?
(b) What additional information would you want to see to determine whether or not LeCroix has been successful in this venture up to now?
(c) Does the current balance sheet indicate any potential problems for LeCroix?
(d) Why has the value of the mortgage stayed approximately the same even though LeCroix has made regular monthly payments?
(e) LeCroix's Capital has decreased. Does this mean the business has a total net loss for the five months of operation?

LeCroix Enterprises
Balance Sheet
June 30, 20—

Assets

Current Assets

Cash	$ 50 000	
Accounts Receivable	60 000	
Office Supplies	5 500	
Total Current Assets		$115 500

Fixed Assets

Land	50 000	
Building	150 000	
Training Equipment	94 500	
Total Fixed Assets		294 500
Total Assets		$410 000

Liabilities and Owner's Equity

Current Liabilities

Accounts Payable		$ 40 000

Long-Term Liabilities

Bank Loan	$ 65 000	
Mortgage Payable	80 000	
Total Long-Term Liabilities		145 000
Total Liabilities		185 000

Owner's Equity

H. LeCroix, Capital June 30		225 000
Total Liabilities and Owner's Equity		$410 000

LeCroix Enterprises
Balance Sheet
November 30, 20—

Assets

Current Assets

Cash	$ 68 000	
Accounts Receivable	40 000	
Office Supplies	7 000	
Total Current Assets		$115 000

Fixed Assets

Land	50 000	
Building	150 000	
Training Equipment	99 235	
Total Fixed Assets		299 235
Total Assets		$414 235

Liabilities and Owner's Equity

Current Liabilities

Accounts Payable		$ 57 000

Long-Term Liabilities

Bank Loan	$ 63 000	
Mortgage Payable	80 000	
Total Long-Term Liabilities		143 000
Total Liabilities		200 000

Owner's Equity

H. LeCroix, Capital November 30		214 235
Total Liabilities and Owner's Equity		$414 235

CASE 2   Work Sheet and Financial Statements

Jenna is a student who has just completed a work sheet and financial statements. She notes the following about her work:

- The net income obtained on the income statement is exactly the same as the net income obtained on the work sheet.
- The totals of the revenue and expenses on the income statement are the same as the corresponding totals on the work sheet.
- The total of the balance sheet section debit column on the work sheet is higher than the total of the assets on the balance sheet.

Jenna does not understand why the asset total on the balance sheet is not the same as the debit column of the balance sheet section of the work sheet. Can you give her an explanation?

Financial Condition

Following are the current assets and current liabilities of a business:

Current Assets		Current Liabilities	
Cash	$ 500	Accounts Payable	$3 000
Accounts Receivable	2 000	Taxes Payable	700
Supplies	500	Salaries Payable	2 000
	$3 000		$5 700

(a) How would you describe the financial condition of this business?
(b) What advice might you give the management of the business?
(c) The owner of this business has applied to you for a short-term loan, explaining that the business makes a profit of $2000 per month and therefore would have enough cash to pay loan payments. In your opinion, would this business be a good risk for a short-term loan?

Income Tax

B. Joanisse owns the Hillside Distributing Company. The company is organized as a sole proprietorship; that is, one person, B. Joanisse, owns it. Hillside Distributing is very successful and Joanisse receives a monthly salary of $6000 for managing the business. For the last fiscal year, the company's operating results were:

Revenue	–	Expenses	=	Net Income
$470 000	–	$410 000	=	$60 000

Included in the expense total is $72 000 paid to Joanisse as a salary for managing the business. Joanisse feels justified in paying personal income tax only on this income or salary of $72 000.

Read the following income tax and accounting rules and then answer the questions.

1. A sole proprietorship does not pay income tax on its net income. However, the net income is considered to be the income of the owner.

2. For tax purposes, a proprietorship must record salary payments to its owner in the owner's Drawings account.
  (a) Applying the preceding principles, correctly complete this equation:

Revenue	–	Expenses	=	Net Income
$470 000	–	?	=	?

  (b) For personal income tax purposes, what is Joanisse's income for the year?
  (c) In the company ledger, what is the year-end balance in the Drawings account? Assume there were no other withdrawals than those mentioned.

CASE 5 ## Financial Position

The Cascade Inn incurs a relatively large amount of debt at the beginning of each tourist season. Supplies to operate the Inn are bought in large quantities. Repairs are made to television sets and to the plumbing. Painting and landscaping are done to spruce up the property. These debts are then paid off as money is received throughout the tourist season. Arrangements are made with creditors so that payments may be spread out over the summer.

(a) How would you assess the financial position of the business after examining the statements shown below and on the next page? Give reasons for your comments.

The Cascade Inn
Income Statement
For the month ended June 30, 20—

Revenue		
Room Rentals	$250 000	
Restaurant Income	6 000	$256 000
Expenses		
Salaries	100 000	
Advertising	10 000	
Telephone	2 000	
Laundry	36 000	
Maintenance	60 000	
Interest	20 000	228 000
Net Income		$ 28 000

(b) If you operated a television repair business, would you do $2000 worth of repair work for the Cascade on credit? What other information might you require to make this decision?

The Cascade Inn
Balance Sheet
June 30, 20—

Assets

Current Assets

Cash	$ 38 000	
Supplies	17 000	
Total Current Assets		$ 55 000

Fixed Assets

Land	250 000	
Building	750 000	
Room Furniture	225 000	
Office Equipment	25 000	
Total Fixed Assets		1 250 000
Total Assets		$1 305 000

Liabilities and Owner's Equity

Current Liabilities

Accounts Payable		$ 50 000

Long-Term Liabilities

Bank Loan	$ 70 000	
Mortgage Payable	280 000	
Total Long-Term Liabilities		350 000
Total Liabilities		400 000

Owner's Equity

B. Galotta, Capital June 1		879 000
Add: Net Income for June	$28 000	
Less: B. Galotta, Drawings	2 000	
Increase in Capital		26 000
B. Galotta, Capital June 30		905 000
Total Liabilities and Owner's Equity		$1 305 000

⑦ Career Education Activities

1. Career Decisions and Change

Very few adults have a career that involves only one job until retirement. For most people, the path shown in Figure 5-18 is not realistic.

FIGURE 5-18 Unrealistic career path

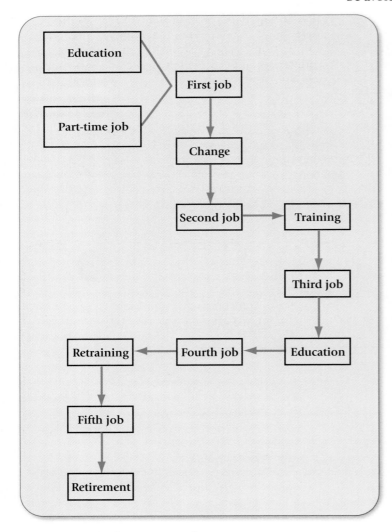

FIGURE 5-19 Realistic career path

Jobs and circumstances change. Companies close down. New companies, products, and opportunities appear. People and their values and needs change. Most people will hold several jobs, be trained, and return to educational programs several times before retirement. Therefore, the path shown in Figure 5-19 represents reality for most people.

Figure 5-19 represents several changes in a person's lifetime. How do you feel about change? For many people, change is stressful and causes anxiety. It makes them feel uncomfortable. It is something to be avoided. It is unacceptable.

For other people, change is a fact of life. It is something that cannot be avoided, so it must be managed. Change might mean opportunity.

How do you feel about change? Here are some changes that students make:

- change of courses at school;
- decision to leave school;
- decision to continue at school;
- change of educational program or institution;
- decision to go/not to go to university or college;
- decision to enter/not to enter a training program; and
- decision to work part-time.

As adults, people are also affected by change in their personal business lives. We should all expect changes of a variety of types to affect us as students and as adults. If we expect to encounter change, we are more likely to handle it effectively and in beneficial ways. Just knowing that change will occur will reduce the stress and anxiety in our lives and should make us more productive.

It is important to realize that there will be many opportunities in our careers. There will be chances to go on to further education, as adults, if we wish. There will be chances to attend mini-courses that will improve our qualifications.

Opportunities for retraining will occur. What can we do to prepare for these opportunities? Here are some suggestions:

- Be realistic about your career.
- Be prepared for change.
- Learn to accept and handle change.
- Maintain a positive outlook about future opportunities.
- Realize that you learn from all experiences.

For Discussion and Follow-Up

(a) Speak to three friends or relatives who have been out of school for several years. Ask them the following questions:
  (i) How many different jobs have you had?
  (ii) For how many different organizations have you worked?
  (iii) Since leaving high school, how many different educational programs, mini-courses, seminars, or training courses have you attended?
  (iv) How has change affected your life?

(b) Visit the Web Extensions web site (www.pearsoned.ca/principlesofaccounting)

and select Student Resources. Visit one of the career sites and outline the qualifications needed for an entry-level job in accounting.

2. The Corporate Controller

One of the higher-level jobs in accounting is that of controller. (A slightly different name for the same position is comptroller.) The controller is responsible for the major financial decisions made by a company. The controller is responsible for the work of others and must have the ability to work with people at all levels in the company. As the advertisement below indicates, companies that have such a position are often large international corporations with divisions in many different countries—an ideal type of employer for people who like to travel.

For Discussion

(a) What are the educational qualifications for the position in the advertisement?
(b) What personal qualities and characteristics are required?

Head Office
Corporate Controller

An international corporation requires a senior controller. The controller will be responsible for a staff of twenty, including four division heads. The computerized ledgers cover both Canadian and international operations. An excellent opportunity for advancement exists as the company is expanding to other countries. You will be responsible for the company's largest multi-million dollar project that will commence in the next quarter.

Reporting to the President, the candidate should be a CA, CMA, or CGA with a minimum 10 years' experience. An M.B.A. would be considered an asset.

The ability to communicate well with other executives and contribute to a team environment is essential. Salary will be negotiated.

Call: Job Search at 1-899-800-8000

Career Profile ●

It has been said that education is lifelong—that we will continue to learn and be re-educated throughout our lives. This statement seems to apply to David Galotta, who has mixed permanent and part-time work with education programs since graduation from high school.

Dave grew up in Niagara Falls where he attended Niagara Falls Collegiate and Vocational Institute. While taking accounting courses at high school and working part-time in his family's business, Dave developed an interest in a business career. He enjoyed working at the Cascade Inn, a hotel operated by his parents in Niagara Falls. During the summers and on weekends, Dave worked in the hotel candy shop and pizza parlour, did routine maintenance work, was a bus boy, and worked as the desk clerk. After working as an assistant manager at the hotel for a short period of time, Dave left home to attend Queen's University.

The Bachelor of Commerce program at Queen's University was Dave's choice for professional training. Among the courses that Dave enjoyed at Queen's were accounting, marketing, industrial relations, computer studies, and law. During the summer, Dave had a variety of jobs, including a position as a marketing research assistant at the School of Business at Queen's.

After graduating from Queen's with an honours Bachelor of Commerce degree, Dave was hired as a management trainee by the Bank of Nova Scotia. His first position was at a Scotiabank in Kingston. After a year in the Kingston branch, Dave was transferred to Ottawa where he was promoted to the position of credit officer. Next came another promotion and a move to Nepean, Ontario, where Dave became an assistant manager at the Bell's Corners branch of the Scotiabank. Within a year, Dave was again promoted and moved to the Westboro Branch, where he became the assistant manager of commercial credit. In four years, Dave had worked in four different bank branches and received three promotions.

Dave's experience in the family business, in the banking system, and in the Bachelor of Commerce program at Queen's University convinced him that he would like to pursue a career in finance in a

large corporation. Having set this as his long-term goal, he decided that additional education was required. He considered two educational programs: a master's degree in business administration and the chartered accountant designation. He decided to return to Queen's University and to enrol in the Master of Business Administration (M.B.A.) program.

The M.B.A. program at Queen's is a demanding two-year course. Entrance requirements include an honours degree with good marks, suitable work experience, and acceptable marks on the GMAT. The GMAT—Graduate Management Admission Test—is widely used as an entry requirement to post-graduate business programs.

Dave met the entrance requirements and returned to Queen's University. Because of his practical experience, he could see the relevance of the material he was studying and was able to understand the theory being taught. He completed the two-year M.B.A. program and obtained a Master of Business Administration degree from Queen's.

Dave was successful in obtaining a position with the Bank of Nova Scotia, finance division, in the bank's corporate headquarters in Toronto. His job title was Financial Analyst and the position involved studying the advantages, disadvantages, costs, and benefits of purchasing buildings and equipment for the bank. After working for the Bank of Nova Scotia for three years, Dave moved to Sault Ste. Marie where he married.

Dave is now an Assistant Professor in the Department of Administration at Algoma University College. He teaches finance and administration courses and is the Head of the Department.

Dave has been very systematic in planning his career. He has developed short- and long-term goals, obtained work experience in his chosen fields, and obtained the education required for a career in finance. He has worked very hard but finds time to enjoy life as well. He has travelled widely in North America and Europe. He relaxes by enjoying tennis, golf, cooking, and skiing, and by spending time at two other hobbies, photography and genealogy.

Dave's career profile illustrates several points:
- the need to set short- and long-term goals;
- the value of work experience in helping to make career decisions;
- the fact that formal education does not necessarily end with a high school diploma or university degree; and
- the fact that it may be necessary to relocate a number of times during a business career.

For Discussion

(a) Have you set both short- and long-term goals for yourself?
(b) What are your short-term goals?
(c) What are your long-term goals?
(d) Are you learning about your interests and abilities through part-time work experience programs?
(e) Would you be willing to move and relocate yourself and your family for career reasons?

Performance Task 1

BERRIGAN ENTERPRISES

What Learning You Will Demonstrate

You will:

- demonstrate an understanding of the recording and decision-making aspects of accounting for a service company;
- demonstrate an understanding of the basic accounting cycle procedures and principles for a service business, without adjusting and closing entries;
- demonstrate an understanding of the debit/credit theory in recording transactions in the journals and the ledgers of a service business; and
- demonstrate the skills necessary to prepare a trial balance, a six-column work sheet, and the financial statements of a service business (without adjustments).

The Business

Linda Berrigan operates a real estate agency that earns money from three sources:

- commissions on sales of property;
- property management fees; and
- investment income.

The agency earns management fees from renting and maintaining homes and condominiums for owners who lease their properties to tenants. Berrigan has invested past net income (profits) in stocks and bonds. Interest and dividends received on these investments are recorded in the Investment Income account.

The Task

You have been hired as the accountant for Berrigan Enterprises. The company has not had an accountant for a month. You are given the transactions for May and asked to bring the records up to date.

Suggested Procedure

1. Set up a general ledger with the appropriate accounts and balances.
2. Journalize and post the May entries.
3. Prepare a trial balance and a work sheet.
4. Prepare an income statement, a statement of owner's equity, and a classified balance sheet.

Materials Required

- May financial information
- Forms for the journal, the ledger, the work sheet, and the financial statements

Assessment Criteria

1. Examine the assessment rubric. Note the descriptions of the performance criteria and the levels of achievement.
2. Based on a self-assessment of your completion of the task, would the company offer you a permanent job? Justify your opinion.

Berrigan Enterprises
Chart of Accounts

100 Cash	400 Commissions Income
131 Office Supplies	401 Management Fees Earned
141 Furniture and Equipment	402 Investment Income
142 Automobile	500 Advertising Expense
170 Investments	501 Automobile Expense
200 Accounts Payable/Tom's Service	502 Commissions Expense
	503 Rent Expense
201 Accounts Payable/Wilson's Stationery	504 Salaries Expense
	505 Telephone Expense
220 Bank Loan	506 Utilities Expense
300 Linda Berrigan, Capital	507 Donations Expense
301 Linda Berrigan, Drawings	

Opening Account Balances

Cash	$ 6 500
Office Supplies	700
Furniture and Equipment	10 000
Automobile	27 100
Investments	40 000
Bank Loan	20 000
Linda Berrigan, Capital	64 300

May Transactions

May 2 Received $4000 commission for the sale of property, Contract 79.

2 Paid $1700 for the month's rent for the office, Cheque 631.

3 Received a bill from Tom's Service Centre for $295 for gas, oil, and repairs to the company automobile. Invoice 241 is to be paid on May 15.

4 Received $5000 commission for the sale of property, Contract 80.

5 Received a bill for $450 for printing letterhead, envelopes, and sales contract forms from Wilson's Stationery. Invoice 1469 is to be paid on May 15.

6 Paid $350 for a new filing cabinet for the office, Cheque 632.

8 Received $8000 commission for the sale of property, Contract 81.

8 Paid office salaries, $900, Cheque 633.

11 Paid $690 to the *Spectator* for newspaper advertising, Cheque 634.

12 Received a $300 fee for renting a home, client's Cheque 102.

13 L. Berrigan, the owner, withdrew $1000 for personal use, Cheque 635.

14 Received commissions totalling $15 500 from the sale of properties, Contracts 82, 83, and 84.

14 Paid Bell Canada $175 for the telephone bill, Cheque 636.

15 Paid Tom's Service Centre for the invoice of May 3, Cheque 637.

15 Paid Wilson's Stationery for the invoice of May 5, Cheque 638.

15 Paid $350 for the hydro bill, Cheque 639.

15 Donated $100 to charity, Cheque 640.

15 Received $400 in dividends from investments owned.

15 Purchased $5000 worth of Government of Canada bonds, Cheque 641.

15 Paid $5000 to Dell Computers for a new computer system, Cheque 642.

15 Paid office salaries, $900, Cheque 643.

15 Paid $5000 in commissions to Berrigan Enterprises' salespeople, Cheques 643 to 647.

BERRIGAN ENTERPRISES: Performance Task Rubric

Assessment Criteria	Level 1	Level 2	Level 3	Level 4
		Levels of Achievement		
KNOWLEDGE AND UNDERSTANDING • understanding of the recording and decision-making aspects of accounting • understanding of the debit/credit theory in recording transactions in journals and ledgers of a service business	Demonstrates limited understanding of terminology, concepts, procedures, and principles.	Demonstrates some understanding of terminology, concepts, procedures, and principles.	Demonstrates considerable understanding of terminology, concepts, procedures, and principles.	Demonstrates a thorough understanding of terminology, concepts, procedures, and principles.
THINKING AND INQUIRY • analysis of transactions • interpretation of balance sheets	Uses critical and interpretative skills with limited effectiveness. Applies few of the skills in an inquiry, or problem-solving process.	Uses critical and interpretative skills with moderate effectiveness. Applies some of the skills in an inquiry, or problem-solving process.	Uses critical and interpretative skills with considerable effectiveness. Applies most of the skills in an inquiry, or problem-solving process.	Uses critical and interpretative skills with complete effectiveness. Applies all or almost all skills in an inquiry, or problem-solving process.
COMMUNICATION • completion of appropriate forms and statements	Communicates with minimal precision and clarity.	Communicates with some precision and clarity.	Communicates with considerable precision and clarity.	Communicates with complete and thorough precision and clarity.
APPLICATION • application of skills to prepare trial balances and financial statements	Uses skills with limited accuracy.	Uses skills with some accuracy.	Uses skills with considerable accuracy.	Uses skills with a high degree of accuracy.

6

Completing the Accounting Cycle for a Service Business

UNIT 11 Adjusting the Books

What Learning You Will Demonstrate

On completion of this unit, you will be able to:

- explain why adjustments are necessary;
- prepare adjusting entries for prepaid expenses;
- prepare adjusting entries to record depreciation;
- calculate depreciation using the declining-balance method;
- describe the principle of materiality; and
- describe the principle of conservatism.

The basic accounting cycle was introduced in the first five chapters of this text. In this chapter, the accounting procedures performed at the end of the accounting cycle will be introduced. These procedures include adjustments, financial statements, and closing the books.

One of the main purposes of accounting is *to provide information for decision making*. The information is presented in the form of financial statements. If decisions are to be made based on data in the financial statements, it is essential that the statements be as accurate as possible.

INTRODUCING ADJUSTMENTS

It is not enough that the debits equal the credits and that the statements be mathematically correct. They must also be *accurate*.

Many transactions are begun in one accounting period but have an effect for several accounting periods. The matching principle, discussed in Chapter 3, requires that the revenue of a particular accounting period be matched with the expenses of the same accounting period to produce an accurate picture of profitability. All asset, liability, and equity account balances must be correct.

Revenue and expenses from the same period are matched together to determine net income or net loss.

Adjustments are accounting changes recorded to ensure that all account balances are correct.

The books are adjusted to make sure the financial statements are accurate.

Adjustments are accounting changes recorded to ensure that all account balances are correct. *The purpose of adjusting the books is to ensure that the financial statements are accurate.*

The balance sheet must show, as accurately as possible, the value of all of the assets, liabilities, and equity accounts at the end of the fiscal period. The income statement must accurately present the revenue and expenses for the fiscal period it covers.

Adjusting the Books

Suppose that employees work overtime or earn bonuses that have not been recorded by the end of the fiscal period. What will be wrong with the financial statements? Both the income statement and the balance sheet will be incorrect.

The expenses will be too low because Salaries Expense does not include the overtime. This failure to accurately match the expenses of this accounting period with the revenue earned will result in the income statement understating expenses and overstating net income.

The liabilities will be incorrect because the debt owing to the workers, called Salaries Payable, will not be shown on the balance sheet. This will result in the total liabilities of the company being understated.

It is necessary to adjust the books to ensure that all accounts have correct balances. In this chapter, some of the accounts of Management Consultant Services will be examined and the adjustments to the accounts that are required before the financial statements are prepared will be described. J. Turner is the owner of Management Consultant Services. This business provides management advice to other companies and is located in a rented office.

PREPAID EXPENSES

Prepaid expenses are expense payments made in advance.

Prepaid expenses are current assets.

In Chapter 3, expenses were defined as the costs of items used up in operating a business. Payments made in advance for items such as rent, insurance, and supplies are called prepaid expenses. Often, the payments are made in advance for more than one fiscal period. Prepaid expenses are items of value. *They are current assets.*

Prepaid expenses are considered to be assets—items of value owned—*until they are used up* or no longer have value. For example, office supplies are assets as long as they are owned by a business and are unused. Once they have been used, they no longer have value and therefore *are no longer assets. They have changed to expenses.*

When prepaid expenses such as office supplies are purchased, they are recorded as assets. When they are *used,* the value of the assets has changed by the amount used and the asset accounts should be decreased. Since they have changed to expenses, the amount used should be recorded in an appropriate expense account. This change from prepaid asset to expense may occur on a regular basis; however, the change is normally recorded when financial statements are prepared to ensure their accuracy. At the end of the accounting period, entries are made to record the conversion of prepaid assets to expenses, to correct the account balances for the balance sheet, and to record the appropriate expense for the period on the income statement. These entries are called *adjusting entries,* and typically involve a change in both an income statement account (revenue or expense) and a balance sheet account (asset or liability).

Prepaid Rent

The office lease of Management Consultant Services requires that rent of $1700 per month be paid in advance for three months. Therefore, on April 1, a cheque for $5100 is issued for the April, May, and June rents. *Because the rent is being paid in advance* for three months, Rent Expense is not debited. Instead, an account called *Prepaid Rent* is debited.

At the end of April, Management Consultant Services prepares financial statements that cover one month. *Should Prepaid Rent be shown as a current asset with a value of $5100?* The answer is "no." After one month, one-third of the asset Prepaid Rent has been used. The business has used up $1700 of the prepaid rent. The account balance must be reduced by $1700 if the asset Prepaid Rent is to be correct. It is now worth $3400, not $5100.

Furthermore, since $1700 of the rent has been used, an expense of $1700 must be recorded. The following *adjusting entry* is made:

Apr.	30	Rent Expense	1 7 0 0 00	
		Prepaid Rent		1 7 0 0 00
		To record rent expense for April.		

This adjusting entry has two effects:

- It records Rent Expense of $1700 for April.
- It decreases Prepaid Rent by $1700.

The entry in T-account form is:

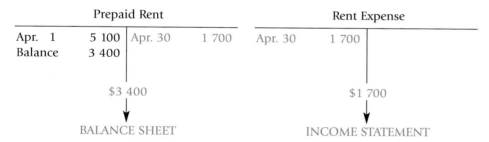

When the financial statements for the month ended April 30 are prepared, Rent Expense of $1700 will be shown on the income statement. Prepaid Rent of $3400 will appear on the balance sheet. If this adjusting entry were not made, expenses would be too low and, as a result, net income would be too high. Also, the assets would be too high.

Supplies

The Supplies account is another prepaid expense. By the end of April, supplies worth $700 have been purchased by Management Consultant Services. These supplies will last for several fiscal periods.

Each working day, small amounts of supplies are used up. The Supplies account is not decreased each time an item is used because it would be time-consuming and inconvenient. Thus, the Supplies account is deliberately allowed to become incorrect. However, at the end of April when financial statements are prepared, the Supplies account must be adjusted. This is how it is done.

First, a count of all supplies *left* on April 30 is made. The value of the unused supplies is $600. Then, the amount of supplies *used* is determined by this calculation:

Total supplies *purchased*	$700
Less: Supplies *left*	600
Supplies *used*	$100

Supplies Expense is the value of supplies used.

The value of supplies used is transferred to Supplies Expense. The asset Supplies should be decreased by the amount used. The following adjusting entry is made:

Apr.	30	Supplies Expense	1 0 0 00	
		Supplies		1 0 0 00
		To adjust the Supplies account and to		
		record the supplies expense for the month.		

The effect of this adjusting entry is shown in the T-accounts below.

When the April 30 financial statements are prepared, the asset Supplies, with a value of $600, appears on the balance sheet. Supplies Expense and a cost of $100 appears on the income statement.

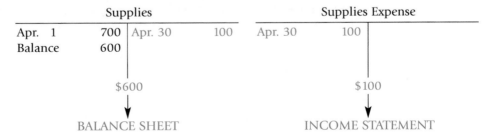

Prepaid Insurance

On April 1, a comprehensive insurance policy that covers fire, theft, and accidental damage to all office furniture and equipment is purchased. The cost of the insurance for one year is $720.

At the end of April, one month's insurance has been used and must be recorded as an expense. The cost of one month's insurance is 1/12 of $720, or $60. This adjusting entry is made:

Apr.	30	Insurance Expense		6 0 00	
		Prepaid Insurance			6 0 00
		To record one month's insurance expense.			

The effect of this adjusting entry is shown in these T-accounts:

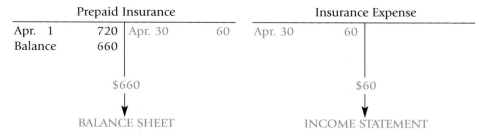

On the April financial statements, Prepaid Insurance with a value of $660 appears in the asset section of the balance sheet. Insurance Expense at a cost of $60 appears on the income statement.

INTRODUCING DEPRECIATION

Management Consultant Services purchases office equipment for $12 000 on January 1. This purchase is recorded by decreasing the Cash account and increasing the fixed asset account, Equipment.

The equipment will be used to help operate the business. Fax machines, calculators, and computers are only some of the types of equipment used by companies.

Early in this text, you learned a simple definition of an expense: money spent on things used to produce revenue for a business. Since the equipment is *used up* in operating the business, its cost becomes an expense of the business. For example, Management Consultant Services may estimate that the equipment purchased will probably last five years. After that time, it will be worthless. The $12 000 spent on the equipment will have been used up.

However, the equipment does not suddenly become worthless—it loses some of its value each year. A portion of the cost of the equipment should be assigned, or allocated, as an expense to each year's operation.

This allocation of the cost of the fixed asset as an expense during the accounting period when the asset is used to produce revenue is consistent with the matching principle. There is a cost of using fixed assets during an accounting period to produce the revenue for that period. This cost should therefore be shown as an expense on the income statement for that period.

An expense is the cost of items used to produce revenue for a business.

Recording Depreciation

Depreciation is the allocation of the cost of a fixed asset to the fiscal periods in which it is used.

The assignment of costs, or the division of the initial cost over the life of the fixed asset, is called depreciation. This process is also commonly referred to as *amortization*. If the initial cost ($12 000) is divided by the life (five years) of the equipment, the depreciation figure is $2400 each year. This assumes that the equipment is worthless after five years and has no *scrap value* or *trade-in value*.

Depreciation is an expense and appears on the income statement.

The allocation of the cost of fixed assets is recorded in an account called Depreciation Expense. The depreciation or *using up of fixed assets* is an expense of operating a business and is recorded on the income statement.

The entry to record the depreciation of the equipment at the end of the first year is:

Dec.	31	Depreciation Expense—Equipment	2 4 0 0 00	
		Accumulated Depreciation—Equipment		2 4 0 0 00
		To record depreciation for the year.		

After this entry has been posted, three accounts that relate to the equipment and its depreciation are affected:

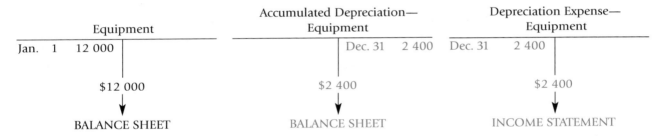

Accumulated Depreciation appears on the balance sheet.

Depreciation Expense—Equipment appears on the income statement in the expense section. Both Equipment and Accumulated Depreciation—Equipment appear on the balance sheet. They are in the fixed assets section. Accumulated Depreciation is a deduction from Equipment, as shown in the partial balance sheet in Figure 6-1.

Management Consultant Services
Partial Balance Sheet
December 31, 20—

Fixed Assets		
Equipment	$12 000	
Less: Accumulated Depreciation	2 400	9 600

FIGURE 6-1 Accumulated Depreciation appears in the fixed assets section of the balance sheet.

Depreciation is a method of spreading the cost of a fixed asset over the life of that asset. It is a process of converting the cost of a fixed asset into an expense over the time the asset will make a contribution to the business. There is a separate Depreciation Expense account and a separate Accumulated Depreciation account for each group of fixed assets, such as Buildings, Equipment, Delivery Trucks, and Machinery. Once an asset has been depreciated 100 percent, no further depreciation is allowed. Suppose an asset costs $10 000 and, over the years, 20 percent is deducted each year. When the Accumulated Depreciation account reaches $10 000, no further depreciation is available.

You might ask why it is necessary to use an Accumulated Depreciation account. *Why not simply credit Equipment to show the decrease in its value?* The use of the Accumulated Depreciation account as well as the Equipment account provides two types of information. One is the *original cost* of the equipment, found in the Equipment account. The other is *the total amount of depreciation* recorded over the years. Accounts such as Accumulated Depreciation are set up to record *subtractions* from related accounts. These contra accounts, or *valuation accounts*, reduce the value of assets on a balance sheet.

> A contra account offsets the value of another account.

Valuation or Contra Accounts

Accumulated Depreciation is sometimes called a *valuation account* because it is used to arrive at the value of an asset. It is also known as a *contra asset account* because it has a credit balance rather than the normal debit balance found in most asset accounts. It has a credit balance because it is subtracted from the cost of an asset to show the correct net balance sheet value or book value.

> Book value is the cost of an asset minus the accumulated depreciation.

When an asset is purchased, it is recorded at its cost price. Each year, depreciation builds up in the Accumulated Depreciation account. The book value of the asset is the cost minus the accumulated depreciation. This value is the value according to the books of the company. It is not the *actual* value, which is the amount received if the asset is sold.

Look again at Figure 6-1. In the fixed asset section of the balance sheet, Equipment is shown at its cost price of $12 000. Accumulated Depreciation of $2400 is subtracted to arrive at a book value of $9600. However, *depreciation is not valuation*. The fact that in Figure 6-1 a current value of $9600 is shown for the equipment does *not* mean the equipment is worth $9600. It does *not* mean the equipment can be sold for $9600. The figures simply mean that:

- the equipment *cost* $12 000;
- depreciation of $2400 has been recorded; and
- $9600 remains to be depreciated.

The term *book value* is used to describe the $9600 undepreciated cost.

Contra accounts provide information to the reader of the financial report. It is clear that the equipment cost was $12 000, that the depreciation charged to date is $2400, and that additional depreciation charges are available in the future. The net, or book, value of Equipment shown on the balance sheet is $9600. The $9600 represents the undepreciated value of this fixed asset at the end of the fiscal period.

METHODS OF CALCULATING DEPRECIATION

There are several methods for calculating depreciation. The two methods that will be discussed in this chapter are:

- straight-line method; and
- declining-balance method, fixed percentage.

Straight-Line Method

Straight-line depreciation allocates the same amount of depreciation to each fiscal period.

A widely used method of calculating depreciation expense is the *straight-line method.* As shown in Figure 6-1, the equipment depreciated 20 percent or $2400 per year. After five years, a total of $12 000 depreciation will have been recorded (5 × $2400 = $12 000). Following the straight-line method of depreciation, for each fiscal period the same amount of depreciation is recorded. The table in Figure 6-2 summarizes the calculation of annual depreciation by the straight-line method. In the example, the equipment has no salvage value at the end of five years. The salvage value must be deducted from the original cost to get the total writeoff over the period the item is used.

		Depreciation Schedule—Equipment **Straight-Line Method**		
Year	Calculation		Depreciation Expense	Accumulated Depreciation
1	0.20 ×	$12 000	$ 2 400	$ 2 400
2	0.20 ×	12 000	2 400	4 800
3	0.20 ×	12 000	2 400	7 200
4	0.20 ×	12 000	2 400	9 600
5	0.20 ×	12 000	2 400	12 000
			$12 000	

Original cost − Salvage value = Total writeoff over the period the item is used.

FIGURE 6-2 Depreciation by the straight-line method

Declining-Balance Method, Fixed Percentage

Declining-balance depreciation allocates a greater amount of depreciation to the first years of an asset's life.

The straight-line method of depreciation allocates an equal amount of depreciation expense to each fiscal period. It can be argued that this is not accurate because the rate of depreciation is often greatest in the first few years of an asset's life. For example, an automobile's depreciation is greatest in its first year.

A greater amount of depreciation expense is allocated to the first years when the declining-balance method of depreciation is used. Suppose that equipment worth $12 000 is depreciated using the *declining-balance* method. Each year a fixed percent, for example 20 percent of the declining balance, is charged. The table in Figure 6-3 shows the calculation of depreciation expense using the declining-balance method.

Depreciation Schedule—Equipment
Declining-Balance Method

Year	Undepreciated Cost	Amount of Depreciation at 20%	Declining Balance, End of Year
1	$12 000.00	$2 400.00	$9 600.00
2	9 600.00	1 920.00	7 680.00
3	7 680.00	1 536.00	6 144.00
4	6 144.00	1 228.80	4 915.20
5	4 915.20	983.04	3 932.16

FIGURE 6-3 Depreciation by the declining-balance method

Notice that each year, as the asset grows older, the depreciation amount is smaller. The cost of the fixed asset is never completely written off as long as the asset is being used. However, each year's depreciation is progressively smaller.

Journal Entries for the Declining-Balance Method

The adjusting entry used for the declining-balance method of depreciation must show a different amount each year:

Year	1	Depreciation Expense—Equipment	2 4 0 0 00	
		Accumulated Depreciation—Equipment		2 4 0 0 00
		To record the first year's depreciation.		
Year	2	Depreciation Expense—Equipment	1 9 2 0 00	
		Accumulated Depreciation—Equipment		1 9 2 0 00
		To record the second year's depreciation.		

Depreciation and Income Taxes

Two methods of calculating depreciation have been described. However, for income tax purposes in Canada, the declining-balance method must generally be used. This method is called capital cost allowance under the *Income Tax Act*.

The maximum rate of depreciation (capital cost allowance), as well as the method used, is controlled by the government. Assets are grouped into classes and a maximum rate of depreciation is set for each class. A few of the classes are shown in Figure 6-4.

For income tax purposes, depreciation is called capital cost allowance.

Class	Capital Cost Allowance Description of Asset	Maximum Rate
3	Buildings of brick, stone, cement	5%
6	Buildings of frame, log, stucco, galvanized or corrugated iron	10%
8	Machinery and equipment	20%
10	Trucks, tractors, automobiles, trailers, buses, wagons	30%

FIGURE 6-4 Depreciation for income tax purposes

Figure 6-4 describes only a few assets and their maximum rates of capital cost allowance. The income tax regulations provide a list of all types of assets and the classes to which they belong. The rates vary from 4 percent per year for Class 1 to 100 percent for Classes 12, 23, and 25. Class 1 includes items such as bridges and airplane runways. Class 12 includes tools and dental instruments that cost less than $200.

It is important to note that land is not depreciable. Land has an unlimited life—it does not wear out or deteriorate. Unlike a building or equipment, it does not eventually have to be replaced. Because land is so permanent, it is not an asset for which depreciation is recorded. For income tax purposes, a business may not claim capital cost allowance on land.

It is also important to remember that, except for a few isolated items such as fishing and farming assets acquired prior to 1972, the straight-line method may not be used for income tax purposes. The declining-balance method, called capital cost allowance in the *Income Tax Act*, must generally be used for any depreciation expense used as an income tax expense.

The capital cost allowance regulations under the *Income Tax Act* set out the *maximum* amount of depreciation expense that may be deducted for income tax purposes. However, a company may decide to use no depreciation in a particular year. *Can you think of a situation in which a business might decide to use no depreciation expense?*

Suppose a business is having a poor year. The accountant knows that a loss will be suffered even without including depreciation as an expense. The accountant may decide to save the year's depreciation expense and use it in future years. If the company suffers a loss during the year, no income tax will be payable for that year. In future years, when the business operates profitably, the depreciation expense will be available to decrease the net income and thus to reduce income taxes.

A company may use any amount of depreciation *up to the allowable amount* for each class of asset (Figure 6-4). The amount of depreciation used in a particular year is often determined by the estimated profits or losses and the estimated income tax.

Two Sets of Books!

Business people are often sarcastically accused of keeping two sets of books— one for themselves and one for the government. But it is legal to have separate records of the same business results. Here is an example.

Land is not depreciable.

For income tax purposes, a business does not have to use depreciation expense (capital cost allowance) in a particular year.

An accountant feels that the straight-line method of calculating depreciation is the best. It allots the same amount of depreciation to each fiscal period. The straight-line method, therefore, is used on the company's books. For income tax purposes, the accountant must use the capital cost allowance (declining-balance) method. This means that the net income reported to the government is different from the net income on the company's books. The difference is caused by the use of the two methods of calculating depreciation.

So you see, it is possible to have two sets of books—legally!

The Principle of Materiality

In this unit, you learned that adjustments are necessary for the financial statements to be accurate. For example, if an adjustment for supplies expense is not made, expenses will be understated on the income statement and the resulting net profit will be too great or the net loss will be too small.

The principle of materiality requires that information that could affect the decisions of the users of financial statements be included when the financial statements are prepared. For example, if a balance sheet includes an account receivable of $5000 that the accountant knows the customer will never be able to pay, that information is *material*. That is, it is important information that must be disclosed to the users or readers of the balance sheet. *Information is material if it will affect the decisions of the users of the financial statements.*

> The principle of materiality requires that information that could affect the decisions of the users of financial statements be included when the financial statements are prepared.

The Principle of Conservatism

Another principle related to the accuracy of financial reports is the principle of conservatism, which requires that, where there are acceptable alternative accounting treatments for an item, accountants choose the one that will result in lower net income and net assets. This is known as *applying a conservative philosophy to the accounting process*.

> The principle of conservatism requires that, where there are acceptable alternative accounting treatments for an item, accountants choose the one that will result in lower net income and net assets.

UNIT 11 CHECK YOUR READING

Questions

1. (a) What is meant by *adjusting the books*?
   (b) Why are adjustments necessary?
   (c) List three parties that would be interested in studying accurate financial statements for a company.
2. (a) What type of accounts are prepaid expenses?
   (b) On which financial statement do they appear?
3. (a) Why is the Supplies account allowed to become incorrect?
   (b) Why is it not credited each time supplies are used?
   (c) On which financial statement does the Supplies account appear? On which statement is Supplies Expense found?
4. (a) What type of account is Prepaid Insurance?
   (b) What type of account is Insurance Expense?
5. Define *depreciation*.
6. Which types of assets depreciate?

7. On which financial statement do Depreciation Expense and Accumulated Depreciation appear?
8. "Depreciation is not valuation." What does this mean?
9. Two methods of calculating depreciation are the straight-line method and the declining-balance method. Explain each of them.
10. What is capital cost allowance?
11. For income tax purposes, which method of depreciation must be used?
12. What is a contra, or valuation, account? Give an example.
13. Explain the principles of materiality and conservatism.

UNIT 11 APPLY YOUR KNOWLEDGE

Exercises

1. The Supplies account had a balance of $700 at the beginning of the fiscal period. At the end of the fiscal period, an inventory shows supplies worth $100 on hand.
   (a) What was the value of supplies used during the fiscal period?
   (b) What is the supplies expense for the fiscal period?
   (c) What should the balance in the Supplies account be at the end of the fiscal period?
   (d) Prepare the adjusting entry to record the supplies used.
   (e) What is the amount in Supplies Expense, which will appear on the income statement?
   (f) What is the value of the asset Supplies, which will appear on the balance sheet?

2. Prepare adjusting entries for the month of January for the following:
   (a) Balance of Supplies account on January 1: $700. Supplies on hand on January 31: $250.
   (b) Rent was paid for three months on January 1, $2400.
   (c) A 12-month insurance policy was purchased on January 15, $1200.

3. Three accounts related to the fixed asset account Automobile (which was established one year ago) follow:

Automobile	Accumulated Depreciation—Automobile	Depreciation Expense—Automobile
Jan. 1 25 000		

   (a) Prepare the general journal adjusting entry for December 31 to depreciate the automobile for one year at the rate of 30 percent.
   (b) Post the entry to T-accounts.
   (c) Give the accounts and balances that appear in the balance sheet and the income statement.

4. It has been estimated that equipment bought for $24 000 will have a useful life of six years, at which time it will be thrown away.
   (a) Using the straight-line method of depreciation, what will be the amount of depreciation each year?
   (b) Complete the working papers copy of the chart on the following page for a period of six years.
   (c) How would the equipment appear in the fixed asset section of the balance sheet at the end of year five? Year six?

Year	Value at Beginning of Year	Depreciation for the Year	Accumulated Depreciation	Book Value at End of Year
1	$24 000	$4 000	$4 000	$20 000
2				
3				
4				
5				
6				

5. (a) In your working papers, complete the chart for equipment purchased for $55 000, which depreciates at the rate of 20 percent per year on the declining balance.
   (b) Show the journal entries required to record the depreciation expenses in the first four years.

Year	Value at Beginning of Year	Depreciation for the Year	Accumulated Depreciation	Book Value at End of Year
1	$55 000	$	$	$
2				
3				
4				

6. Newton Electric prepares monthly financial statements. Fixed assets owned by the company include equipment valued at $14 000 and a service truck worth $30 000. Accumulated depreciation on the equipment is $7170. Accumulated depreciation on the truck is $6500. Prepare adjusting entries to record one month's depreciation, using the declining-balance method. The rate of depreciation for one year for the equipment is 20 percent, and for the truck 30 percent.

UNIT 12 Work Sheet, Adjustments, Financial Statements

What Learning You Will Demonstrate

On completion of this unit, you will be able to:

- prepare adjustments on a work sheet for prepaid expenses and depreciation of fixed assets;
- complete an eight-column work sheet;
- complete a ten-column work sheet; and
- prepare financial statements from a work sheet.

So far in this chapter, you have learned:

- that adjustments are necessary if financial statements are to be correct;
- how to adjust prepaid expenses such as supplies, rent, and insurance; and
- how to adjust the book value of fixed assets by recording depreciation expense.

Adjustments are first prepared on the work sheet.

In this part of the chapter, you will learn how the adjustments are entered on the work sheet and how the financial statements are prepared.

EIGHT-COLUMN WORK SHEET

The trial balance for Management Consultant Services is shown in Figure 6-5 on an eight-column work sheet. In Chapter 5, you learned how a six-column work sheet is used to help organize the financial statements. The trial balance is written on a work sheet. The amounts on the trial balance are then transferred to either the income statement section or the balance sheet section of the work sheet. The difference in the totals of the income statement section is the net income or the net loss for the accounting period. The difference in the totals of the balance sheet section is also the net income or the net loss. This difference in the balance sheet section should, of course, be the same as that obtained in the income statement section.

The eight-column work sheet serves the same purpose. It is prepared in the same way as a six-column work sheet, but an *adjustments* section is added. It is also used by the accountant to *rough out* or plan the necessary adjustments so that the financial statements will be correct. There are four sections on an eight-column work sheet, as shown in Figure 6-5.

- Trial balance
- Adjustments
- Income statement
- Balance sheet

Management Consultant Services
Work Sheet
For the month ended January 31, 20—

	ACCOUNT TITLE	ACC. NO.	TRIAL BALANCE		ADJUSTMENTS		INCOME STATEMENT		BALANCE SHEET		
			DEBIT	CREDIT	DEBIT	CREDIT	DEBIT	CREDIT	DEBIT	CREDIT	
1	Cash	100	13 0 0 0 00								1
2	Accounts Receivable	102	7 0 0 0 00								2
3	Supplies	131	1 0 0 0 00								3
4	Prepaid Insurance	132	7 2 0 00								4
5	Prepaid Rent	133	5 1 0 0 00								5
6	Equipment	141	12 0 0 0 00								6
7	Accumulated Depreciation—Equipment	142		2 4 0 0 00							7
8	Accounts Payable	200		1 0 0 0 00							8
9	Bank Loan	221		3 0 0 0 00							9
10	J. Turner, Capital	300		29 6 0 0 00							10
11	J. Turner, Drawings	301	1 5 0 0 00								11
12	Fees Earned	400		12 0 0 0 00							12
13	Salaries Expense	500	7 5 0 0 00								13
14	Utilities Expense	501	1 2 0 00								14
15	Miscellaneous Expense	502	6 0 00								15
16			48 0 0 0 00	48 0 0 0 00							16
17											17
18											18
19											19
20											20
21											21
22											22
23											23
24											24
25											25
26											26
27											27
28											28

FIGURE 6-5 Eight-column work sheet

In the next few pages, the work sheet will be completed for Management Consultant Services. The period of time covered by this work sheet will be one month. The first step in preparing the work sheet is to gather the information required to complete the adjustments. This information includes:

- A count made of all supplies on hand shows $900 worth left on January 31.
- On January 1, a three-year insurance policy was purchased. One month of the policy is now expired.
- The balance in the Prepaid Rent account represents a payment on January 1 for the January, February, and March rents.
- The equipment depreciates 20 percent per year. The declining-balance method is used.

Using this information, the adjustments are prepared on the work sheet.

PREPARING ADJUSTMENTS

In this example, four accounts need to be adjusted:

- Supplies
- Prepaid Insurance
- Prepaid Rent
- Equipment

Supplies

Supplies has a $1000 balance. However, the inventory taken at the end of the fiscal period indicates only $900 worth of supplies are left. This means that $100 worth of supplies have been used and should be recorded as an expense.

Total supplies purchased	$1 000
Supplies left	900
Supplies Expense	$ 100

It is necessary to record Supplies Expense of $100 and to decrease Supplies by $100. To do this, you debit Supplies Expense and credit Supplies. Figure 6-6 shows how this adjustment is prepared on the work sheet. In preparing the adjustment, it is necessary to add the Supplies Expense account to the bottom of the list of accounts because it does not appear on the trial balance. Supplies Expense is debited $100 in the adjustments debit column. Supplies is credited $100 in the adjustments credit column. The effect of this adjustment, in T-account form, is:

Supplies				Supplies Expense		
Jan. 31	1 000	Jan. 31	100	Jan. 31	100	
Balance	900					

This adjustment decreases the asset Supplies by $100 to the correct balance of $900. It also records the amount of supplies used ($100) in the Supplies Expense account.

Management Consultant Services
Work Sheet
For the month ended January 31, 20—

ACCOUNT TITLE	ACC. NO.	TRIAL BALANCE DEBIT	TRIAL BALANCE CREDIT	ADJUSTMENTS DEBIT	ADJUSTMENTS CREDIT	INCOME STATEMENT DEBIT	INCOME STATEMENT CREDIT	BALANCE SHEET DEBIT	BALANCE SHEET CREDIT	
Cash	100	13 000 00								1
Accounts Receivable	102	7 000 00								2
Supplies	131	1 000 00			1 0 0 0 00 [a]					3
Prepaid Insurance	132	720 00								4
Prepaid Rent	133	5 100 00								5
Equipment	141	12 000 00								6
Accumulated Depreciation—Equipment	142		2 400 00							7
Accounts Payable	200		1 000 00							8
Bank Loan	221		3 000 00							9
J. Turner, Capital	300		29 600 00							10
J. Turner, Drawings	301	1 500 00								11
Fees Earned	400		12 000 00							12
Salaries Expense	500	7 500 00								13
Utilities Expense	501	120 00								14
Miscellaneous Expense	502	60 00								15
		48 000 00	48 000 00							16
Supplies Expense	503			1 0 0 0 00 [a]						17
										18
										19
										20
										21
										22
										23
										24
										25
										26
										27
										28

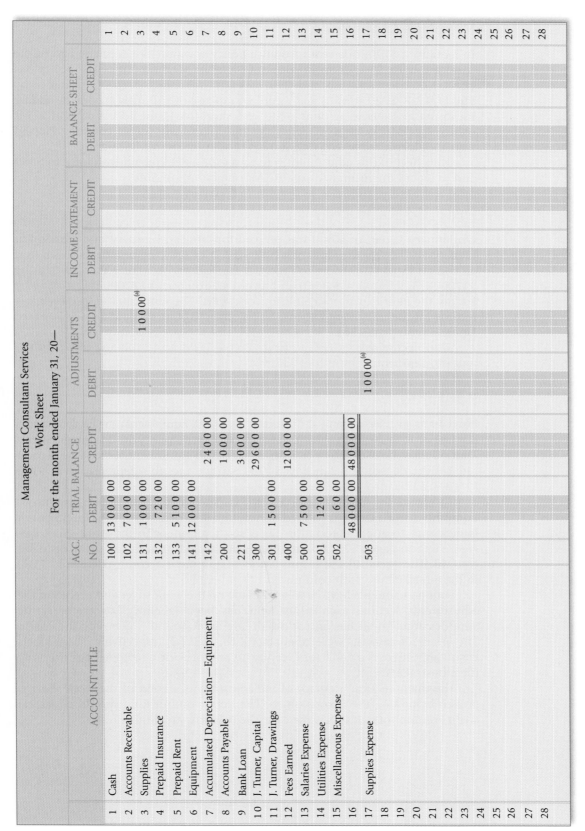

FIGURE 6-6 The adjustment for Supplies is shown on lines 3 and 17.

Prepaid Insurance

In January, a $720, one-year insurance policy was purchased. At the end of the current month, 11 months of insurance remain. One month of the policy has expired or been used up and it is necessary to reduce Prepaid Insurance by $60 (1/12 × $720 = $60) and record an expense of $60. This is done by adding the Insurance Expense account to the work sheet (see Figure 6-7). A debit of $25 is written beside Insurance Expense in the adjustments debit column. Prepaid Insurance is reduced by entering $60 in the adjustments credit column.

The effect of this adjustment is to lower the asset Prepaid Insurance to $660 and to record the insurance expense for one month of $60.

Prepaid Rent

On January 1, rent of $5100 was prepaid for January, February, and March. On January 31, the rent for January is no longer prepaid. One month has been *used up* and an expense must be recorded. It is necessary to reduce Prepaid Rent by $1700 (1/3 × $5100 = $1700) and record an expense of $1700. This is done by adding the Rent Expense account to work sheet. The rent expense for January is recorded by debiting Rent Expense $1700 and crediting Prepaid Rent $1700 (see Figure 6-8 on page 226).

The effect of this entry is to lower Prepaid Rent to $3400 and to record the rent expense for one month of $1700.

Equipment

Fixed assets such as equipment depreciate each year. Equipment may be depreciated at a rate of up to 20 percent per year. For income tax purposes, the declining-balance method must be used. The year's depreciation on equipment, using a 20 percent rate on the declining balance, is $1920, so one month's depreciation is $160 (1/12 × $1920 = $160).

To record the depreciation, a debit is entered in Depreciation Expense—Equipment and a credit is entered in Accumulated Depreciation—Equipment. It is necessary to add Depreciation Expense—Equipment to the work sheet (see Figure 6-9 on page 227). This account is debited $160 in the adjustments debit column. The Accumulated Depreciation—Equipment account is credited $160 in the adjustments credit column.

Four adjustments have now been made on the work sheet and placed in the adjustments section; each adjustment has been labelled. For example, the Supplies adjustment has an (a) beside the debit and an (a) beside the credit. The other adjustments were labelled (b), (c), and (d) respectively. These labels ensure that there is a debit for every credit and provide a reference for checking the adjustments.

The mathematical accuracy of the adjustments section of the work sheet is proven by adding the two columns. The debit column total should equal the credit column total. If this is the case, the columns are double-ruled.

Management Consultant Services
Work Sheet
For the month ended January 31, 20—

	ACCOUNT TITLE	ACC. NO.	TRIAL BALANCE		ADJUSTMENTS		INCOME STATEMENT		BALANCE SHEET	
			DEBIT	CREDIT	DEBIT	CREDIT	DEBIT	CREDIT	DEBIT	CREDIT
1	Cash	100	13 000 00							
2	Accounts Receivable	102	7 000 00							
3	Supplies	131	1 000 00			1 0 0 0 00 (a)				
4	Prepaid Insurance	132	720 00			6 0 0 00 (b)				
5	Prepaid Rent	133	5 100 00							
6	Equipment	141	12 000 00							
7	Accumulated Depreciation—Equipment	142		2 400 00						
8	Accounts Payable	200		1 000 00						
9	Bank Loan	221		3 000 00						
10	J. Turner, Capital	300		29 600 00						
11	J. Turner, Drawings	301	1 500 00							
12	Fees Earned	400		12 000 00						
13	Salaries Expense	500	7 500 00							
14	Utilities Expense	501	120 00							
15	Miscellaneous Expense	502	60 00							
16			48 000 00	48 000 00						
17	Supplies Expense	503			1 0 0 0 00 (a)					
18	Insurance Expense	504			6 0 0 00 (b)					
19										
20										
21										
22										
23										
24										
25										
26										
27										
28										

FIGURE 6-7 The adjustment for Prepaid Insurance is shown on lines 4 and 18.

Management Consultant Services
Work Sheet
For the month ended January 31, 20—

	ACC.	TRIAL BALANCE		ADJUSTMENTS		INCOME STATEMENT		BALANCE SHEET		
ACCOUNT TITLE	NO.	DEBIT	CREDIT	DEBIT	CREDIT	DEBIT	CREDIT	DEBIT	CREDIT	
1 Cash	100	13 0 0 0 00								1
2 Accounts Receivable	102	7 0 0 0 00								2
3 Supplies	131	1 0 0 0 00			1 0 0 0 00[a]					3
4 Prepaid Insurance	132	7 2 0 00			6 0 0 00[b]					4
5 Prepaid Rent	133	5 1 0 0 00			1 7 0 0 00[c]					5
6 Equipment	141	12 0 0 0 00								6
7 Accumulated Depreciation—Equipment	142		2 4 0 0 00							7
8 Accounts Payable	200		1 0 0 0 00							8
9 Bank Loan	221		3 0 0 0 00							9
10 J. Turner, Capital	300		29 6 0 0 00							10
11 J. Turner, Drawings	301	1 5 0 0 00								11
12 Fees Earned	400		12 0 0 0 00							12
13 Salaries Expense	500	7 5 0 0 00								13
14 Utilities Expense	501	1 2 0 00								14
15 Miscellaneous Expense	502	6 0 00								15
16		48 0 0 0 00	48 0 0 0 00							16
17 Supplies Expense	503			1 0 0 0 00[a]						17
18 Insurance Expense	504			6 0 0 00[b]						18
19 Rent Expense	505			1 7 0 0 00[c]						19
20										20
21										21
22										22
23										23
24										24
25										25
26										26
27										27
28										28

FIGURE 6-8 The adjustment for Prepaid Rent is shown on lines 5 and 19.

Management Consultant Services
Work Sheet
For the month ended January 31, 20—

ACCOUNT TITLE	ACC. NO.	TRIAL BALANCE DEBIT	CREDIT	ADJUSTMENTS DEBIT	CREDIT	INCOME STATEMENT DEBIT	CREDIT	BALANCE SHEET DEBIT	CREDIT	
Cash	100	13 000 00						13 000 00		1
Accounts Receivable	102	7 000 00						7 000 00		2
Supplies	131	1 000 00			100 00 (a)			900 00		3
Prepaid Insurance	132	720 00			60 00 (b)			660 00		4
Prepaid Rent	133	5 100 00			1 700 00 (c)			3 400 00		5
Equipment	141	12 000 00						12 000 00		6
Accumulated Depreciation—Equipment	142		2 400 00		160 00 (d)				2 560 00	7
Accounts Payable	200		1 000 00						1 000 00	8
Bank Loan	221		3 000 00						3 000 00	9
J. Turner, Capital	300		29 600 00						29 600 00	10
J. Turner, Drawings	301	1 500 00						1 500 00		11
Fees Earned	400		12 000 00				12 000 00			12
Salaries Expense	500	7 500 00				7 500 00				13
Utilities Expense	501	120 00				120 00				14
Miscellaneous Expense	502	60 00				60 00				15
		48 000 00	48 000 00							16
Supplies Expense	503			100 00 (a)		100 00				17
Insurance Expense	504			60 00 (b)		60 00				18
Rent Expense	505			1 700 00 (c)		1 700 00				19
Depreciation Expense	506			160 00 (d)		160 00				20
				2 020 00	2 020 00	9 700 00	12 000 00	38 460 00	36 160 00	21
Net Income						2 300 00			2 300 00	22
						12 000 00	12 000 00	38 460 00	38 460 00	23

FIGURE 6-9 Completed work sheet

COMPLETING THE WORK SHEET

After the adjustments have been completed and the adjustments columns totalled, the amounts are transferred to either the income statement or balance sheet sections of the work sheet. The income and expenses are transferred to the income statement section. The asset, liability, and equity accounts are transferred to the balance sheet section.

For example, Figure 6-9 on page 227 shows that Cash, $13 000, is transferred to the balance sheet *debit* column (line 1). Accounts Receivable, $7000, is also transferred to the balance sheet debit column (line 2). However, there is a complication on line 3 of the work sheet. Supplies has a debit of $1000 on the trial balance and a credit of $100 in the adjustments section. The difference between a debit of $1000 and a credit of $100 is $900. Because Supplies is an asset account, the $900 balance is transferred to the balance sheet debit column.

Prepaid Insurance is handled in the same way as Supplies. The difference between the $720 debit and the $60 credit is $660. This amount ($660) is transferred to the balance sheet debit column (line 4). On line 5, the difference in the Prepaid Rent account is $3400. There is no change in the Equipment account. Thus $12 000 is transferred to the balance sheet debit column (line 6). On line 7, there are two credits for Accumulated Depreciation—Equipment. These are added and the balance, $2560, is transferred to the balance sheet credit column. Accounts Payable, Bank Loan, and J. Turner, Capital are all transferred to the balance sheet credit column. J. Turner, Drawings is transferred to the balance sheet debit column.

Fees Earned, on line 12, is the revenue of Management Consultant Services and is transferred to the income statement dedit column.

Salaries Expense, Utilities Expense, and Miscellaneous Expense did not require adjustment and are transferred to the income statement debit column. At the bottom of the work sheet are found Supplies Expense, Insurance Expense, Rent Expense, and Depreciation Expense—Equipment, which required adjustments. These expenses are transferred to the income statement debit column.

Determining the Net Income or Net Loss

After all of the amounts have been transferred to either the balance sheet or income statement sections, it is quite simple to determine the net income or net loss. First, add the income statement debit and credit columns and then find the difference between them. This difference is the net income or the net loss. *There is a net income if the credit column total is greater than the debit column total. Conversely, there is a net loss if the debit column total is greater than the credit column total.* Looking at Figure 6-9, it can be seen that the credit column total of the income statement section is greater and thus shows a net income ($2300).

Next, add the balance sheet debit and credit columns and determine the difference between them. The difference is the net income or net loss. There is a net income if the debit column total is greater than the credit column total, and a net loss if the credit column total is the larger of the two. Notice that the debit column total in Figure 6-9 is greater and the difference is the same as the difference in the income statement columns—both differences are $2300. This should come as no surprise since both differences are measuring the same thing—net income.

Balancing the Work Sheet

After the net income (or net loss) has been determined, the amount (in this example $2300) is added to the smaller column total of both the income statement and the balance sheet sections of the work sheet. *The net income figure is added to both the debit side of the income statement section and to the credit side of the balance sheet. A net loss would be added to the credit side of the income statement section and to the debit side of the balance sheet section.* The columns are then double-ruled, as shown in Figure 6-9.

Steps in Preparing the Eight-Column Work Sheet

To summarize, these are the steps followed when you prepare an eight-column work sheet:

1. Write the heading on the work sheet.
2. Write the trial balance on the work sheet.
3. Gather the data needed to prepare the adjustments.
4. Prepare the adjustments and total, balance, and rule the adjustments columns.
5. Transfer all amounts to either the income statement or balance sheet columns.
6. Total the income statement and balance sheet columns and determine the net income or net loss.
7. Balance and rule the work sheet.

TEN-COLUMN WORK SHEET

Many businesses use a ten-column work sheet instead of the eight-column work sheet. The extra two columns are used to prepare an "adjusted trial balance." This trial balance is prepared on the work sheet after the adjustments have been completed. It is prepared to ensure that the ledger accounts are still in balance; that is, to ensure that the *debit balances* equal the *credit balances*. If the ledger is still in balance, then the accountant proceeds to complete the work sheet. The ten-column work sheet for Management Consultant Services is shown in Figure 6-10 on page 230. Notice that the adjusted trial balance section comes after the adjustments section and before the financial statement sections.

Management Consultant Services
Work Sheet
For the month ended January 31, 20—

ACCOUNT TITLE	ACC. NO.	TRIAL BALANCE DEBIT	TRIAL BALANCE CREDIT	ADJUSTMENTS DEBIT	ADJUSTMENTS CREDIT	ADJUSTED TRIAL BALANCE DEBIT	ADJUSTED TRIAL BALANCE CREDIT	INCOME STATEMENT DEBIT	INCOME STATEMENT CREDIT	BALANCE SHEET DEBIT	BALANCE SHEET CREDIT	
Cash	100	13 000 00				13 000 00				13 000 00		1
Accounts Receivable	102	7 000 00				7 000 00				7 000 00		2
Supplies	131	1 000 00			1 0 0 00 (a)	900 00				900 00		3
Prepaid Insurance	132	720 00			60 00 (b)	660 00				660 00		4
Prepaid Rent	133	5 100 00			1 700 00 (c)	3 400 00				3 400 00		5
Equipment	141	12 000 00				12 000 00				12 000 00		6
Acc. Dep.—Equipment	142		2 400 00		1 600 00 (d)		2 560 00				2 560 00	7
Accounts Payable	200		1 000 00				1 000 00				1 000 00	8
Bank Loan	221		3 000 00				3 000 00				3 000 00	9
J. Turner, Capital	300		29 600 00				29 600 00				29 600 00	10
J. Turner, Drawings	301	1 500 00				1 500 00				1 500 00		11
Fees Earned	400		12 000 00				12 000 00		12 000 00			12
Salaries Expense	500	7 500 00				7 500 00		7 500 00				13
Utilities Expense	501	120 00				120 00		120 00				14
Miscellaneous Expense	502	60 00				60 00		60 00				15
		48 000 00	48 000 00									16
Supplies Expense	503			1 0 0 00 (a)		100 00		100 00				17
Insurance Expense	504			60 00 (b)		60 00		60 00				18
Rent Expense	505			1 700 00 (c)		1 700 00		1 700 00				19
Dep. Exp.—Equipment	506			1 600 00 (d)		160 00		160 00				20
				2 020 00	2 020 00	48 160 00	48 160 00	9 700 00	12 000 00	38 460 00	36 160 00	21
								2 300 00			2 300 00	22
								12 000 00	12 000 00	38 460 00	38 460 00	23
												24
												25
												26
												27
												28

FIGURE 6-10 Ten-column work sheet

Steps in Preparing the Ten-Column Work Sheet

These steps are followed when you complete a ten-column work sheet:

1. Write the heading on the work sheet.
2. Write the trial balance on the work sheet.
3. Gather the data needed to prepare the adjustments.
4. Prepare the adjustments and total, balance, and rule the adjustments columns.
5. Transfer *all* amounts to the adjusted trial balance columns and recalculate the balances where necessary. Total, balance, and rule the adjusted trial balance columns.
6. Transfer *all* amounts from the adjusted trial balance to either the income statement or the balance sheet columns.
7. Total the income statement and balance sheet columns and determine the net income or net loss.
8. Balance and rule the work sheet.

PREPARING THE FINANCIAL STATEMENTS

When the work sheet has been completed, the formal financial statements are prepared. All of the information necessary for the preparation of the income statement is found on the work sheet in the income statement columns. Similarly, all of the necessary data for the balance sheet are found on the work sheet in the balance sheet columns.

Financial statements are prepared from the work sheet.

Figures 6-11 and 6-12 illustrate the financial statements prepared from the completed work sheet. Note the following about the two statements:

- The new expenses that result from the adjustments are included on the income statement. These are Supplies Expense, Insurance Expense, Rent Expense, and Depreciation Expense—Equipment.
- Accumulated Depreciation is shown as a subtraction from Equipment in the fixed asset section of the balance sheet.

Management Consultant Services
Income Statement
For the month ended January 31, 20—

Revenue		
Fees Earned		$12 000
Expenses		
Salaries	$7 500	
Utilities	120	
Miscellaneous	60	
Supplies	100	
Insurance	60	
Rent	1 700	
Depreciation—Equipment	160	9700
Net Income		$ 2 300

FIGURE 6-11 Income statement prepared from the work sheet

Management Consultant Services
Balance Sheet
January 31, 20—

Assets

Current Assets

Cash	$ 13 000	
Accounts Receivable	7 000	
Supplies	900	
Prepaid Insurance	660	
Prepaid Rent	3 400	
Total Current Assets		$24 960

Fixed Assets

Equipment	12 000	
Less: Accumulated Depreciation	2 560	
Total Fixed Assets		9 440
Total Assets		$34 400

Liabilities and Owner's Equity

Current Liabilities

Accounts Payable	$ 1 000	
Bank Loan	3 000	
Total Current Liabilities		$ 4 000

Owner's Equity

J. Turner, Capital January 1		29 600	
Add: Net Income for the month	$2 300		
Less: J. Turner, Drawings	1 500		
Increase in Capital		800	
J. Turner, Capital January 31			30 400
Total Liabilities and Owner's Equity			$34 400

FIGURE 6-12 Balance sheet prepared from the work sheet

Book Value of Assets

The concept of "book value" is an important one in accounting. In Unit 11, you learned that the amount remaining after the accumulated depreciation has been subtracted from the cost price of a fixed asset is its book value.

The book value of equipment owned by Management Consultant Services is $9440. This is the net value of the asset. It is determined by subtracting the accumulated depreciation from the cost of the asset. The book value should not be confused with the market value or the cost of the asset. It is simply the remaining value of the asset that has not yet been converted to expense (that is, it is the undepreciated value).

UNIT 12 CHECK YOUR READING

Questions

14. (a) What two new columns are added to an eight-column work sheet?
(b) For what are the two new columns used?

15. How is the net income or net loss determined on the work sheet?

16. When there is a net loss, which column total of the income statement section of the work sheet is greater? Which column total of the balance sheet section is greater?

17. When there is a net income, to which columns on the work sheet is the amount of the net income added?

18. List the seven steps in preparing an eight-column work sheet.

19. How is the book value of a fixed asset determined? Give an example.

UNIT 12 APPLY YOUR KNOWLEDGE

Exercises

7. The trial balance for Latin Beat Disco follows. Prepare an eight-column work sheet for the year ended December 31, 20—, using the following additional information:

- Supplies on hand on December 31 are valued at $200.
- The declining-balance method of depreciation is used, and equipment depreciates at the rate of 20 percent per year.

Latin Beat Disco
Trial Balance
December 31, 20—

Account	Acc. No.	Debit	Credit
Cash	100	$ 12 000	
Accounts Receivable	102	4 000	
Supplies	131	700	
Equipment	141	45 000	
Accumulated Depreciation—Equipment	142		$ 15 400
Accounts Payable	200		7 000
S. Acevedo, Capital	300		29 600
S. Acevedo, Drawings	301	18 000	
Sales	400		90 000
Salaries Expense	500	42 000	
Rent Expense	501	14 000	
Telephone Expense	502	1 400	
Miscellaneous Expense	503	1 900	
Office Expense	504	3 000	
		$142 000	$142 000

8. Prepare a ten-column work sheet for Health Care Consultants using the trial balance and additional information given below. The fiscal period is one year.

- Supplies on hand on December 31 are valued at $700.
- The three-year insurance policy was purchased on January 1 for $2400.
- The declining-balance method of depreciation is used to record depreciation for office equipment (20 percent per year) and automobiles (30 percent per year).

Health Care Consultants
Trial Balance
December 31, 20—

Account	Acc. No.	Debit	Credit
Cash	100	$ 4 500	
Accounts Receivable	102	17 000	
Supplies	131	2 000	
Prepaid Insurance	132	2 400	
Office Equipment	141	11 000	
Acc. Depreciation—Office Equip.	142		$ 3 760
Automobiles	143	42 000	
Acc. Depreciation—Automobiles	144		15 760
Accounts Payable	200		1 500
S. Chari, Capital	300		47 980
S. Chari, Drawings	301	18 000	
Fees Income	400		120 000
Salaries Expense	500	80 000	
Rent Expense	501	7 200	
Automobile Expense	502	800	
Utilities Expense	503	1 100	
Office Expense	504	3 000	
		$189 000	$189 000

9. Prepare a work sheet for Timmins Travel, for the year, using the trial balance on the next page and the additional information given here.

- Timmins Travel prepares a ten-column work sheet for the year.
- Supplies on hand at the end of January cost $600.
- The declining-balance method of depreciation is used to record depreciation for office equipment (20 percent per year) and automobile (30 percent per year).

Timmins Travel
Trial Balance
January 31, 20—

Account	Acc. No.	Debit	Credit
Cash	100	$ 9 000	
Accounts Receivable	102	22 000	
Supplies	131	2 000	
Office Equipment	141	15 000	
Acc. Depreciation—Office Equip.	142		$ 5 000
Automobile	143	29 000	
Acc. Depreciation—Automobile	144		8 700
Accounts Payable	200		2 000
Bank Loan	220		3 000
M. Pollon, Capital	300		31 500
M. Pollon, Drawings	301	23 000	
Sales	400		140 100
Advertising Expense	500	6 500	
Salaries Expense	501	57 000	
Rent Expense	502	17 800	
Office Expense	503	9 000	
		$190 300	$190 300

UNIT 13 Adjusting and Closing Entries

What Learning You Will Demonstrate

On completion of this unit, you will be able to:

- prepare adjusting entries from a work sheet;
- explain how closing entries update the Capital account;
- describe how closing entries prepare the revenue and expense accounts for the entries of the next accounting period;
- prepare entries to close the revenue, expense, Drawings, and Income Summary accounts;
- explain why asset, liability, and Capital accounts are not closed; and
- prepare a post-closing trial balance.

The books of a company consist of the various journals and ledgers it uses. The work sheet is not part of a company's permanent records. It is used by the accountant as an aid in organizing data used to prepare the financial statements.

In the example used in this chapter, the asset accounts Supplies, Prepaid Insurance, Prepaid Rent, and Accumulated Depreciation—Equipment were adjusted.

Four expense accounts were added: Insurance Expense, Supplies Expense, Rent Expense, and Depreciation Expense—Equipment. All of these adjustments were made on the work sheet. The ledger accounts have not as yet been changed. They are incorrect and must be changed to reflect the adjustments made on the work sheet. *Adjusting entries* are used to record the adjustments in the ledger accounts.

ADJUSTING ENTRIES

The ledger accounts must be updated to agree with the adjustments on the work sheet.

Adjusting entries are used to update the ledger accounts.

The recording of adjusting entries is quite simple because the adjustments have already been figured out on the work sheet. It is only necessary to record the adjustments in journal form and to post them to the ledger.

When the adjustments were made on the work sheet, they were coded (a), (b), (c), and (d). The debit and credit for the Supplies adjustment were coded (a). By referring to the work sheet and finding the (a) adjustment (Figure 6-9 on page 227), this entry is journalized:

Jan.	31	Supplies Expense	1 0 0 00	
		Supplies		1 0 0 00
		To record supplies used in January.		

Similar entries are recorded in the general journal for each of the adjustments. All of the adjustments are shown in Figure 6-13.

GENERAL JOURNAL				PAGE 21	
DATE	PARTICULARS	P.R.	DEBIT	CREDIT	
20—					
Jan. 31	Supplies Expense		1 0 0 00		
	Supplies			1 0 0 00	
	To record supplies used in January.				
31	Insurance Expense		6 0 00		
	Prepaid Insurance			6 0 00	
	To record insurance for the month.				
31	Rent Expense		1 7 0 0 00		
	Prepaid Rent			1 7 0 0 00	
	To record rent for one month.				
31	Depreciation Expense—Equipment		1 6 0 00		
	Acc. Depreciation—Equipment			1 6 0 00	
	To record one month's depreciation, declining-balance method.				

FIGURE 6-13 General journal entries to record the adjustments

Posting the Adjusting Entries

After the adjusting entries have been journalized, they are posted to the general ledger. Some of the ledger accounts of Management Consultant Services are shown in Figure 6-14. These T-accounts contain the end-of-the-fiscal-period balances found on the trial balance *before* adjustments have been made.

Several expense accounts in Figure 6-14 have no balance. If the adjustments were not journalized and posted, Supplies Expense, Insurance Expense, Rent Expense, and Depreciation Expense—Equipment would all have *nil* balances at the end of the fiscal period. That would be wrong, since supplies were used, insurance did expire, the office was used for the month, and there was wear on the equipment.

Figure 6-15 on page 238 shows the accounts after the adjusting entries have been posted. *Can you trace the entries from the general journal in Figure 6-13 to this ledger?*

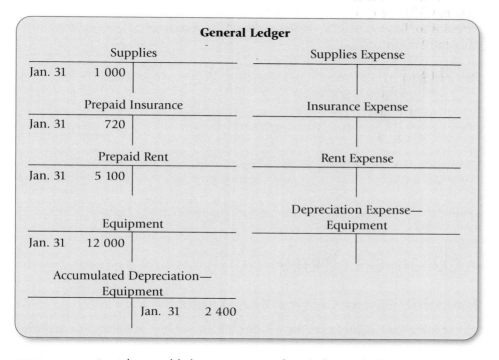

FIGURE 6-14 Partial general ledger in T-account form before end-of-month adjustments have been posted

Adjusted Trial Balance

After posting the adjusting entries, the accountant may prepare an adjusted trial balance to verify that the ledger still balances before preparing the financial statements.

The account balances shown in Figure 6-15 are the adjusted balances. They appear on the financial statements in Figures 6-11 and 6-12 on pages 231 and 232. *Can you find each of them? What would be wrong with the income statement if adjustments had not been made? What would be wrong with the balance sheet if adjustments had not been made?*

General Ledger

Supplies				Supplies Expense	
Jan. 31	1 000	Jan. 31	100	Jan. 31	100
Balance	900				

Prepaid Insurance				Insurance Expense	
Jan. 31	720	Jan. 31	60	Jan. 31	60
Balance	660				

Prepaid Rent				Rent Expense	
Jan. 31	5 100	Jan. 31	1 700	Jan. 31	1 700
Balance	3 400				

			Depreciation Expense— Equipment	
Equipment				
Jan. 31	12 000		Jan. 31	160

Accumulated Depreciation— Equipment			
	Jan. 31	2 400	
	31	160	
	Balance	2 560	

FIGURE 6-15 Partial general ledger in T-account form after end-of-month adjustments have been posted

CLOSING ENTRIES

Introduction to Closing the Books

The income statement shows the net income, or net loss, for a specific accounting period. The data required to determine the net income or net loss are found in the revenue and expense accounts.

When a new accounting period begins, the revenue and expense accounts should show *zero* balances so that they contain only data that refer to the new period. This allows the calculation of net income according to the *matching principle*, which states:

> Revenue for each accounting period is matched with expenses for that accounting period to determine the net income or net loss.

The revenue and expense accounts are reduced to zero by a process called closing the books. At the end of each accounting period, the balances of the revenue and expense accounts are reduced to zero so that they are ready to accumulate data for the next accounting period. For this reason, they are known as temporary accounts. They contain information for the current accounting period only. They do not carry their balances forward to the next accounting period.

Closing the books is the process by which revenue and expense accounts are reduced to zero at the end of each accounting period.

Revenue and expense accounts are known as temporary accounts.

Asset, liability, and owner's equity accounts are known as permanent accounts. Their balances are carried forward from accounting period to accounting period. They are not closed (reduced to zero) at the end of each accounting period.

Purpose of Closing the Books

As has been stated, the process of reducing revenue and expense accounts to a zero balance is known as *closing the books.* Generally, the accounts are closed once a year, although some businesses perform this procedure more frequently. Closing the books serves two purposes:

1. to prepare the revenue and expense accounts for the next accounting period by reducing them to zero; and
2. to update the owner's equity account.

Updating the Owner's Equity Account

Before closing entries are prepared, the owner's Capital account does *not* include the net income or net loss and withdrawals by the owner (Drawings account). When the balance sheet is prepared, *the owner's Capital account is adjusted* by the amount of the net income or net loss and withdrawals. A net income is added to the Capital account. A net loss and withdrawals are subtracted from the Capital account.

The closing entries *update the Capital account in the ledger.* They increase or decrease the Capital balance by the amount of the net income or net loss. Closing entries also decrease Capital by the amount the owner has withdrawn from the business for personal use (Drawings). The closing entries bring the Capital account into agreement with the balance sheet. The Capital account has now been updated.

Income Summary Account

Revenue and expense accounts are closed by *transferring* their balances to an account called Income Summary. This procedure is illustrated in Figure 6-16. The credit balance in Income Summary indicates a net income was earned.

When the revenue and expense account balances have been transferred to Income Summary, the balance of this account is the net income or net loss. The balance in Income Summary should match the net income (or net loss) shown on the work sheet.

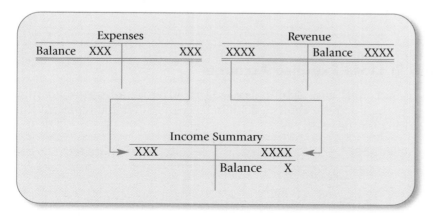

FIGURE 6-16 Closing the revenue and expense accounts to the Income Summary account

Steps in Closing the Books

The closing of revenue and expense accounts is first recorded in the general journal. These journal entries are called *closing entries*. After journalizing, the closing entries are posted to the general ledger accounts. The four steps required to close the books follow.

Step 1: Close Revenue Accounts

Revenue accounts have credit balances. The following Sales account shows a credit balance of $20 000 that represents the total sales for the year:

Sales		
	Dec. 31	20 000

When an account is closed, its balance is reduced to zero.

To close Sales means to reduce its balance to zero by transfering the balance to Income Summary. This procedure is illustrated by the following journal entry:

Dec.	31	Sales	20 0 0 0 00	
		Income Summary		20 0 0 0 00
		To close the Sales account.		

The following T-accounts illustrate the effect of this entry on the two accounts:

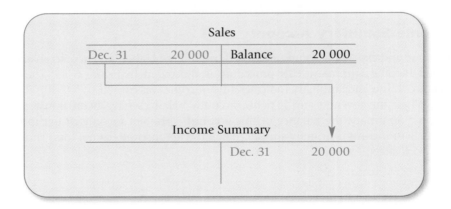

Step 2: Close Expense Accounts

Expense accounts have debit balances. The Advertising Expense account illustrated in the T-account shows a debit balance of $3000 that represents the total advertising for the year:

Advertising Expense		
Dec. 31	3 000	

The following entry and T-accounts illustrate the closing of an expense account:

Dec.	31	Income Summary		3 0 0 0 00	
		Advertising Expense			3 0 0 0 00
		To close Advertising Expense.			

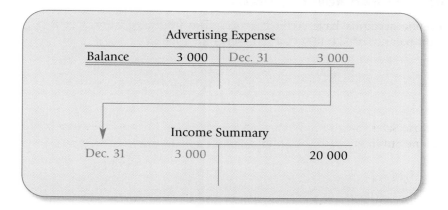

Advertising Expense

Balance	3 000	Dec. 31	3 000

Income Summary

Dec. 31	3 000		20 000

Each expense account in the ledger is closed in the same way. If a business has four expense accounts, they can be closed with four individual entries similar to the one closing Advertising Expense. However, it is much simpler to make one compound entry such as the following:

Dec.	31	Income Summary		14 0 0 0 00	
		Advertising Expense			3 0 0 0 00
		Salaries Expense			10 0 0 0 00
		Telephone Expense			5 0 0 00
		General Expense			5 0 0 00
		To close the expense accounts.			

Step 3: Close the Income Summary Account

After the entries to close the revenue and expenses have been posted, Income Summary contains the revenue for the period on the credit side and the expenses on the debit side. Since the credit side is larger, the $6000 balance represents the net income for the period.

Income Summary

Dec. 31	14 000	Dec. 31	20 000
		Balance	6 000

The net income of $6000 increases the owner's equity, or, in other words, the net income belongs to the owner. The balance of the Income Summary account is therefore transferred to the owner's Capital account by this closing entry:

Dec.	31	Income Summary			6 0 0 0 00		
		D. Adams, Capital				6 0 0 0 00
		To close Income Summary and transfer				
		the net income to Capital.				

The following T-accounts illustrate the effect of this entry on the two accounts:

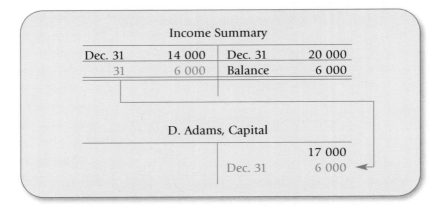

This entry increases the balance of the owner's Capital account by $6000, the amount of the profit (net income) for the accounting period.

Step 4: Close the Drawing Account

During the accounting period, withdrawals of cash and other assets by the owner are recorded in the Drawings account. Since withdrawals by the owner affect the owner's investment, Drawings is closed with the following entry:

Dec.	31	D. Adams, Capital			2 0 0 0 00		
		D. Adams, Drawings				2 0 0 0 00
		To close the Drawings account.				

The following T-accounts illustrate the effects of this entry:

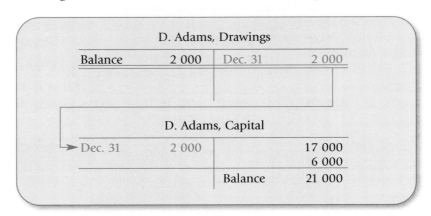

This entry reduces the owner's Capital account by $2000, the amount withdrawn from the business by the owner. Since the owner has withdrawn assets from the business, the owner's equity is decreased. The effect of this entry is to decrease the Capital account.

After these last two entries have been posted, Income Summary has been closed (reduced to zero), Drawings has been closed, and Capital has been updated so that it agrees with the balance for Capital shown on the balance sheet.

Summary

In summary, there are four steps involved in closing the books:

1. Close the revenue accounts into Income Summary.
2. Close the expense accounts into Income Summary.
3. Close Income Summary into Capital.
4. Close Drawings into Capital.

See if you can follow the four steps in Figure 6-17.

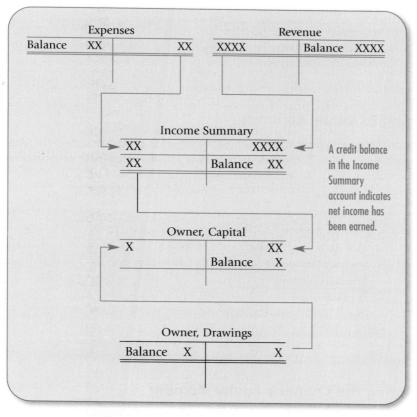

FIGURE 6-17 Closing the books

Closing the Books from the Work Sheet

The completed work sheet for Management Consultant Services on December 31, 20—, is found in Figure 6-18. The revenue and expense accounts are found in the income statement columns of the work sheet. As we journalize and post the closing entries, remember the purposes served by these entries.

Reviewing the Purpose of Closing Entries

Two main purposes are served by closing entries:

1. Revenue and expense accounts are prepared for the next accounting period.
2. The Capital account is updated.

Closing Revenue Accounts

On the work sheet (Figure 6-18), the revenue account Fees Earned has a credit balance of $154 000. To reduce it to zero, Fees Earned is debited $154 000. This closing entry is journalized:

Dec. 31	Fees Earned	154 0 0 0 00	
	Income Summary		154 0 0 0 00
	To close the revenue account.		

Closing Expense Accounts

There are seven expenses in the debit column of the income statement section of the work sheet. Each is credited to reduce it to zero. This entry is journalized:

Dec. 31	Income Summary	123 5 2 0 00	
	Salaries Expense		95 8 8 0 00
	Utilities Expense		3 3 0 0 00
	Miscellaneous Expense		7 0 0 00
	Supplies Expense		6 0 0 00
	Insurance Expense		7 2 0 00
	Rent Expense		20 4 0 0 00
	Depreciation Expense—Equipment		1 9 2 0 00
	To close the expense accounts.		

Updating the Owner's Equity Account

Two entries are required to update the owner's equity account. The first is to transfer the net income or net loss to Capital from Income Summary. The net income of $30 480 earned during the year increases the owner's Capital account. In very simple terms, *the net income belongs to the owner.* For this reason, the net income is credited to the owner's Capital account. This increases the owner's equity. If there was a net loss, Capital would be decreased. This entry is journalized:

Management Consultant Services
Work Sheet
For the year ended December 31, 20—

	ACC. NO.	ACCOUNT TITLE	TRIAL BALANCE DEBIT	TRIAL BALANCE CREDIT	ADJUSTMENTS DEBIT	ADJUSTMENTS CREDIT	INCOME STATEMENT DEBIT	INCOME STATEMENT CREDIT	BALANCE SHEET DEBIT	BALANCE SHEET CREDIT	
1	100	Cash	18 000 00						18 000 00		1
2	102	Accounts Receivable	19 000 00						19 000 00		2
3	131	Supplies	1 450 00			5 0 00 [a]			1 400 00		3
4	132	Prepaid Insurance	6 0 00			6 0 00 [b]			0 00		4
5	133	Prepaid Rent	1 700 00			1 700 00 [c]			0 00		5
6	141	Equipment	12 000 00						12 000 00		6
7	142	Accumulated Depreciation—Equipment		4 160 00		1 60 00 [d]				4 320 00	7
8	200	Accounts Payable		1 000 00						1 000 00	8
9	221	Bank Loan		3 000 00						3 000 00	9
10	300	J. Turner, Capital		29 600 00						29 600 00	10
11	301	J. Turner, Drawings	18 000 00						18 000 00		11
12	400	Fees Earned		154 000 00				154 000 00			12
13	500	Salaries Expense	95 880 00				95 880 00				13
14	501	Utilities Expense	3 300 00				3 300 00				14
15	502	Miscellaneous Expense	7 00 00				7 00 00				15
16	503	Supplies Expense	5 50 00		5 0 00 [a]		6 00 00				16
17	504	Insurance Expense	6 60 00		6 0 00 [b]		7 20 00				17
18	505	Rent Expense	18 700 00		1 700 00 [c]		20 400 00				18
19	506	Depreciation Expense—Equipment	1 7 60 00		1 60 00 [d]		1 9 20 00				19
20			191 760 00	191 760 00	1 9 70 00	1 9 70 00	123 520 00	154 000 00	68 400 00	37 920 00	20
21							30 480 00			30 480 00	21
22							154 000 00	154 000 00	68 400 00	68 400 00	22
23											23
24											24
25											25
26											26
27											27
28											28

FIGURE 6-18 Completed work sheet for the year

Dec. 31	Income Summary		30 4 8 0 00	
	J. Turner, Capital			30 4 8 0 00
	To transfer net income to the owner's			
	Capital account.			

A second entry that involves owner's equity is needed to close Drawings into Capital. This entry is journalized:

Dec. 31	J. Turner, Capital		18 0 0 0 00	
	J. Turner, Drawings			18 0 0 0 00
	To close the Drawings account into the			
	Capital account.			

The closing entries just described are all recorded in the general journal. The source of information is the income statement columns of the work sheet except for the Drawings account, which is found in the balance sheet columns of the work sheet.

After the closing entries have been journalized, they are posted to the general ledger. Selected ledger accounts are shown in Figure 6-19, which begins below. This ledger contains the adjusting and closing entries that have been posted from the general journal. All of the revenue and expense accounts have a zero balance. They are double-ruled and are now ready to receive data for the new fiscal period. Notice that Drawings and Income Summary are also closed. The asset, liability, and owner's Capital accounts are *not* closed. Their balances continue into the next fiscal period.

Asset, liability, and owner's Capital accounts are not closed at the end of a fiscal period.

GENERAL LEDGER							
ACCOUNT **Cash**							No. **100**
DATE	PARTICULARS	P.R.	DEBIT	CREDIT	DR. CR.	BALANCE	
20—							
Dec. 31		✓			DR.	18 0 0 0 00	

GENERAL LEDGER							
ACCOUNT **Supplies**							No. **131**
DATE	PARTICULARS	P.R.	DEBIT	CREDIT	DR. CR.	BALANCE	
20—							
Dec. 31		✓			DR.	1 4 5 0 00	
31	Adjusting Entry	J34		5 0 00	DR.	1 4 0 0 00	

ACCOUNT	Prepaid Insurance						No. 132
DATE		PARTICULARS	P.R.	DEBIT	CREDIT	DR. CR.	BALANCE
20—							
Dec.	31		✓			DR.	6 0 00
	31	Adjusting Entry	J34		6 0 00	DR.	0 00

ACCOUNT	Equipment						No. 141
DATE		PARTICULARS	P.R.	DEBIT	CREDIT	DR. CR.	BALANCE
20—							
Dec.	31		✓			DR.	12 0 0 0 00

ACCOUNT	Accumulated Depreciation—Equipment						No. 142
DATE		PARTICULARS	P.R.	DEBIT	CREDIT	DR. CR.	BALANCE
20—							
Dec.	31		✓			CR.	4 1 6 0 00
	31	Adjusting Entry	J34		1 6 0 00	CR.	4 3 2 0 00

ACCOUNT	Accounts Payable						No. 200
DATE		PARTICULARS	P.R.	DEBIT	CREDIT	DR. CR.	BALANCE
20—							
Dec.	31		✓			CR.	1 0 0 0 00

ACCOUNT	J. Turner, Capital						No. 300
DATE		PARTICULARS	P.R.	DEBIT	CREDIT	DR. CR.	BALANCE
20—							
Dec.	31		✓			CR.	29 6 0 0 00
	31	Net Income for Year	J35		30 4 8 0 00	CR.	60 0 8 0 00
	31	Drawings	J35	18 0 0 0 00		CR.	42 0 8 0 00

ACCOUNT	J. Turner, Drawings						No. 301
DATE		PARTICULARS	P.R.	DEBIT	CREDIT	DR. CR.	BALANCE
20—							
Dec.	31		✓			DR.	18 0 0 0 00
	31	Closing Entry	J35		18 0 0 0 00		0 00

ACCOUNT	Income Summary						No. 302
DATE	PARTICULARS	P.R.	DEBIT	CREDIT	DR. CR.	BALANCE
20—						
Dec. 31	To Close Fees Earned	J35		154 0 0 0 00	CR.	154 0 0 0 00
31	To Close Expenses	J35	123 5 2 0 00		CR.	30 4 8 0 00
31	To Close Income Summary	J35	30 4 8 0 00		CR.	0 00

ACCOUNT	Supplies Expense						No. 504
DATE	PARTICULARS	P.R.	DEBIT	CREDIT	DR. CR.	BALANCE
20—						
Dec. 31		✓			DR.	6 0 0 00
31	Closing Entry	J35		6 0 0 00		0 00

ACCOUNT	Insurance Expense						No. 505
DATE	PARTICULARS	P.R.	DEBIT	CREDIT	DR. CR.	BALANCE
20—						
Dec. 31		✓			DR.	7 2 0 00
31	Closing Entry	J35		7 2 0 00		0 00

ACCOUNT	Depreciation Expense—Equipment						No. 506
DATE	PARTICULARS	P.R.	DEBIT	CREDIT	DR. CR.	BALANCE
20—						
Dec. 31		✓			DR.	1 9 2 0 00
31	Closing Entry	J35		1 9 2 0 00		0 00

FIGURE 6-19 Partial general ledger for Management Consultant Services after adjusting and closing entries have been posted

POST-CLOSING TRIAL BALANCE

After the adjusting and closing entries have been posted to the general ledger, a **post-closing trial balance** is prepared (Figure 6-20). Its purpose is to prove the mathematical accuracy of the general ledger. If the debit total equals the credit total, the ledger is assumed to be *in balance*. It is ready for the next fiscal period. The post-closing trial balance is quite a bit shorter than other general ledger trial balances. This is because it contains only asset, liability, and Capital accounts, which have balances. The revenue, expense, and Drawings accounts have been reduced to zero and do not appear on this final trial balance.

The post-closing trial balance is prepared after the closing entries have been posted to the general ledger.

The post-closing trial balance contains only asset, liability, and Capital accounts.

Management Consultant Services
Post-Closing Trial Balance
December 31, 20—

Account	Acc. No.	Debit	Credit
Cash	100	$18 000	
Accounts Receivable	102	19 000	
Supplies	131	1 400	
Equipment	141	12 000	
Accumulated Depreciation—Equipment	142		$ 4 320
Accounts Payable	200		1 000
Bank Loan	221		3 000
J. Turner, Capital	300		42 080
		$50 400	$50 400

FIGURE 6-20 Post-closing trial balance prepared after the closing of the books

Effect of a Net Loss

How is the closing process affected when a business has a net loss? Revenue and expense accounts are closed as already described in this chapter. However, because there is a loss, the owner's Capital account will *decrease*. Look at this example:

Expenses	Revenue	Owner, Capital
Dec. 31 50 000	Dec. 31 47 200	Dec.1 100 000

As you can see, the expenses are greater than the revenue. The first two entries are shown below.

Dec.	31	Revenue	47 2 0 0 00	
		Income Summary		47 2 0 0 00
		To close the revenue accounts.		
	31	Income Summary	50 0 0 0 00	
		Expenses		50 0 0 0 00
		To close the expense accounts.		

After these entries have been posted, Income Summary has a debit balance of $2800—this is a net loss. What effect will this loss have on the owner's Capital account?

Expenses				Revenue			
Dec. 31	50 000	Dec. 31	50 000	Dec. 31	47 200	Dec 31	47 200

Income Summary				Owner, Capital			
Dec. 31	50 000	Dec. 31	47 200			Dec. 1	100 000
Balance	2 800						

The entry to close Income Summary and to transfer the loss to Capital is:

Dec.	31	Owner, Capital	2 8 0 0 00	
		Income Summary		2 8 0 0 00
		To close Income Summary to Capital.		

The owner's Capital account is now updated.

Income Summary				Owner, Capital			
Dec. 31	50 000	Dec. 31	47 200	Dec. 31	2 800	Dec. 1	100 000
		31	2 800			Balance	97 200

Capital has *decreased* from $100 000 to $97 200 because of the net loss.

Additions to the Accounting Cycle

Figure 6-21 illustrates the accounting cycle with the addition of the adjusting and closing entries and the post-closing trial balance.

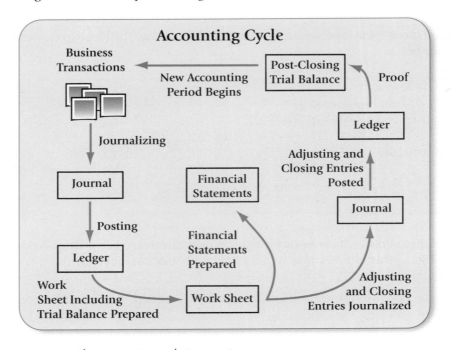

FIGURE 6-21 The accounting cycle is a continuous process.

Generally Accepted Accounting Principles and Key Ideas

In this chapter, you learned these Generally Accepted Accounting Principles:

- **The matching principle** requires that revenue from one accounting period be matched with expenses for the same accounting period to determine the net income or net loss.
- **The principle of materiality** requires that information that could affect the decisions of users of financial statements be included when the financial statements are prepared.
- **The principle of conservatism** requires that, where there are acceptable alternative accounting treatments for an item, accountants choose the one that will result in lower net income and net assets.

You also learned the following key ideas:

- **Adjustments** are necessary so that the financial statements will be correct.
- **Depreciation** is the allocation of the cost of a fixed asset to the fiscal periods in which it is used.
- **Valuation or contra accounts** are used to arrive at the book value of depreciable fixed assets.
- **The declining-balance method of depreciation** is used for income tax purposes.
- **Capital cost allowance** is the income tax term used for depreciation.
- **Temporary accounts** are closed at the end of the fiscal period.

UNIT 13 CHECK YOUR READING

Questions

20. Why is it necessary to record adjusting entries in the journal?
21. What two purposes are served by closing the books?
22. What type of accounts are closed?
23. (a) Which accounts are permanent accounts?
    (b) Which accounts are temporary accounts?
24. Is a revenue account debited or credited when it is closed?
25. To close an expense account, is a debit or a credit necessary in the account?
26. Into which account are revenue and expenses closed?
27. Into which account are Income Summary and Drawings closed? Why?
28. What is the purpose of the post-closing trial balance?
29. Which types of accounts appear on the post-closing trial balance?

Exercises

10. Refer to the work sheet completed in exercise 7 on page 233 for Latin Beat Disco. Prepare the adjusting entries in a general journal.

11. Use the T-account ledger below.
   (a) Prepare January 31 closing entries in a journal and post them to the ledger.
   (b) Calculate the final balance on January 31 in the A. Holmes, Capital account.

A. Holmes, Capital	300		Auto Expense	501
	Jan. 31 60 000	Jan. 31 1 000		

A. Holmes, Drawings	301		General Expense	502
Jan. 31 3 000		Jan. 31 3 000		

Income Summary	302		Rent Expense	503
		Jan. 31 5 000		

Sales	400		Salaries Expense	504
	Jan. 31 45 000	Jan. 31 24 000		

Advertising Expense	500
Jan. 31 2 000	

12. The completed six-column work sheet for J. Fioravanti is shown on the following page.
   (a) Open a ledger for the company and include account 302, Income Summary.
   (b) Prepare closing entries in a general journal.
   (c) Post the closing entries to the ledger.
   (d) Prepare a post-closing trial balance.

13. The trial balance for I. Gereluk is shown on the next page.
   (a) Open a ledger using the accounts and balances on the trial balance and account 302, Income Summary.
   (b) Journalize the closing entries for the month of December.
   (c) Post the closing entries.
   (d) Prepare a post-closing trial balance.
   (e) Prepare a statement of owner's equity.
   (f) Does the final balance in the Capital account in the ledger agree with the statement of owner's equity?

J. Fioravanti
Work Sheet
For the month ended April 30, 20—

	ACCOUNT TITLE	ACC. NO.	TRIAL BALANCE DEBIT	TRIAL BALANCE CREDIT	INCOME STATEMENT DEBIT	INCOME STATEMENT CREDIT	BALANCE SHEET DEBIT	BALANCE SHEET CREDIT	
1	Cash	100	2 000 00				2 000 00		1
2	Accounts Receivable	101	4 300 00				4 300 00		2
3	Equipment	110	6 200 00				6 200 00		3
4	Accounts Payable	200		2 500 00				2 500 00	4
5	J. Fioravanti, Capital	300		5 000 00				5 000 00	5
6	Sales	400		8 000 00		8 000 00			6
7	Salaries Expense	500	1 200 00		1 200 00				7
8	General Expense	501	800 00		800 00				8
9	Advertising Expense	502	1 000 00		1 000 00				9
10			15 500 00	15 500 00	3 000 00	8 000 00	12 500 00	7 500 00	10
11	Net Income				5 000 00			5 000 00	11
12					8 000 00	8 000 00	12 500 00	12 500 00	12
13									13
14									14

I. Gereluk
Trial Balance
December 31, 20—

Account	Acc. No.	Debit	Credit
Cash	100	$ 1 400	
Accounts Receivable	101	2 035	
Supplies	102	960	
Equipment	110	1 500	
Delivery Truck	112	7 800	
Accounts Payable	200		$ 1 245
Bank Loan	210		1 400
I. Gereluk, Capital	300		10 500
I. Gereluk, Drawings	301	1 000	
Sales	400		8 970
Salaries Expense	500	6 000	
Rent Expense	501	500	
Miscellaneous Expense	502	540	
Office Expense	503	255	
Telephone Expense	504	125	
		$22 115	$22 115

14. Complete the following procedures using the completed work sheet for C. Hall, Electric on the next page.
   (a) Prepare the financial statements including a statement of owner's equity.
   (b) Journalize the adjusting entries.
   (c) Post the adjusting entries.
   (d) Journalize and post the closing entries.
   (e) Prepare the post-closing trial balance.

15. Refer to exercise 7 on page 233, Latin Beat Disco, and to exercise 10 on page 252 where the adjusting entries were prepared.
   (a) Prepare the closing entries in a journal.
   (b) Open ledger accounts and post the adjusting and closing entries.
   (c) What should the balance in Income Summary be after closing the revenue and expense accounts?
   (d) Prepare a post-closing trial balance.
   (e) Prepare the financial statements.

16. Refer to exercise 9 on page 234, Timmins Travel, and do the following:
   (a) Prepare closing entries.
   (b) Open accounts for Drawings, Capital, and Income Summary. Post the closing entries.

C. Hall, Electric
Work Sheet
For the month ended October 31, 20—

	ACCOUNT TITLE	ACC. NO.	TRIAL BALANCE		ADJUSTMENTS		INCOME STATEMENT		BALANCE SHEET	
			DEBIT	CREDIT	DEBIT	CREDIT	DEBIT	CREDIT	DEBIT	CREDIT
1	Cash	100	3 5 0 0 00						3 5 0 0 00	
2	Accounts Receivable	102	2 3 0 0 00						2 3 0 0 00	
3	Supplies	131	7 2 0 0 00			5 0 0 00(a)			6 7 0 0 00	
4	Prepaid Rent	132	1 8 0 0 00			6 0 0 00(b)			1 2 0 0 00	
5	Equipment	143	21 0 0 0 00						21 0 0 0 00	
6	Accumulated Depreciation—Equipment	144		7 5 6 0 00		2 2 4 00(c)				7 7 8 4 00
7	Accounts Payable	200		3 5 0 0 00						3 5 0 0 00
8	C. Hall, Capital	300		24 6 4 0 00						24 6 4 0 00
9	C. Hall, Drawings	301	9 0 0 00						9 0 0 00	
10	Service Income	400		5 7 0 0 00				5 7 0 0 00		
11	Salaries Expense	500	4 2 0 0 00				4 2 0 0 00			
12	Equipment Repairs Expense	501	2 0 0 00				2 0 0 00			
13	Miscellaneous Expense	502	3 0 0 00				3 0 0 00			
14			41 4 0 0 00	41 4 0 0 00						
15	Supplies Expense	510			5 0 0 00(a)		5 0 0 00			
16	Rent Expense	511			6 0 0 00(b)		6 0 0 00			
17	Depreciation Expense—Equipment	512			2 2 4 00(c)		2 2 4 00			
18					1 3 2 4 00	1 3 2 4 00	6 0 2 4 00	5 7 0 0 00	35 6 0 0 00	35 9 2 4 00
19	Net Loss							3 2 4 00	3 2 4 00	
20							6 0 2 4 00	6 0 2 4 00	35 9 2 4 00	35 9 2 4 00
21										
22										
23										
24										
25										
26										
27										
28										

Part B Supplementary Manual or Computer Exercises

Exercises 17 and 18 may be done manually or on a computer. If completed manually, the required forms are in the Study Guide and Working Papers. If completed with a computer, students may set up their own accounts or the teacher may use the CD provided by the publisher. The CD contains files for these exercises prepared with Simply Accounting software.

17. Darryl Hurl established Hurl and Associates, a petroleum consulting firm, in Calgary to provide technical expertise to companies engaged in oil and gas exploration. Using the additional information and the chart of accounts for the company given below, do the following:
   (a) Prepare the journal entries required to record the transactions for April, the first month of the business.
   (b) Open a ledger using the account titles and numbers shown in the chart of accounts.

100 Cash	301 D. Hurl, Drawings
110 Accounts Receivable	305 Income Summary
120 Prepaid Insurance	400 Consulting Fees
123 Prepaid Rent	500 Office Salaries Expense
125 Supplies	501 Utilities Expense
130 Office Furniture and Equipment	502 Telephone Expense
131 Accum. Dep.—Office Equip.	503 Advertising Expense
140 Van	504 Insurance Expense
141 Accum. Dep.—Van	505 Rent Expense
200 Accounts Payable	506 Supplies Expense
210 Bank Loan	507 Dep. Expense—Office Equip.
300 D. Hurl, Capital	508 Dep. Expense—Van

   (c) Post the journal entries for April.
   (d) Prepare a trial balance on an eight-column work sheet and complete the work sheet for the month of April.
   (e) Prepare the financial statements for April.
   (f) Journalize and post the adjusting and closing entries.
   (g) Prepare a post-closing trial balance.

Additional Information:
   • Hurl and Associates adjust and close their books monthly.
   • Supplies on hand April 30 were worth $175.
   • The office equipment depreciates at a rate of 20 percent per year.
   • The van depreciates at a rate of 30 percent per year.

   Apr. 1 D. Hurl started his new business by opening a bank account for the firm and depositing an initial investment of $50 000.
        2 Purchased a one-year insurance policy, $1200, Cheque 1.
        2 Purchased office equipment from Office Specialties worth

$8300, Invoice 3274. Paid 20 percent in cash (Cheque 2) and the remainder was due in two equal payments on the 15th and 30th of April.

2 Hurl and Associates were engaged by Northwind Petroleum as consultants on a drilling project at a fixed consulting fee of $3000 per month for a one-year period, Invoice 1. The first month's fee was received today.

3 Paid the rent for April, May, and June, $3300, Cheque 3.

5 Purchased office supplies, $320, Cheque 4.

7 Purchased a van for use in the business, $24 800. A down payment of $4800 was made today, Cheque 5. A three-year bank loan was obtained to finance the remainder.

12 Submitted Invoice 2 to Kilty Exploration for consulting services performed during the last week, $5000.

15 Received Invoice P4823 for advertising from *Petroleum Weekly*, $325.

15 Paid the first instalment due to Office Specialties as a result of the April 2 purchase of office equipment, Cheque 6.

15 Paid the office salaries for the first two weeks of operation, $720, Cheque 7.

19 D. Hurl withdrew $1000 for personal use, Cheque 8.

20 Received $1500 from a client for consulting services completed today, their Cheque 2285.

25 Purchased additional office supplies, $125, Cheque 9.

27 Received Cheque 6649 from Kilty Exploration to pay one-half of their account.

30 Paid the monthly utility bills, $620, Cheque 10.

30 Paid the monthly telephone bill, $315, Cheque 11.

30 Paid the final instalment due to Office Specialties for the equipment purchase of April 2, Cheque 12.

30 Returned $25 worth of office supplies and received Credit Memo 666 for that amount.

18. Connie Rosenblatt, M.D., recently graduated from medical school and decided to establish her practice in Vancouver, British Columbia. Using the additional information and the chart of accounts given on the next page, do the following:

(a) Prepare the journal entries necessary to record the transactions for June, the first month of the practice.

(b) Open the general ledger using the account titles and numbers in the chart of accounts.

(c) Post the June entries to the ledger.

(d) Prepare a trial balance using a ten-column work sheet.

(e) Prepare the financial statements, including a statement of owner's equity.

(f) Journalize and post the adjusting entries.

(g) Journalize and post the closing entries.

(h) Prepare a post-closing trial balance.

Additional Information:

- C. Rosenblatt, M.D., adjusts and closes her books monthly.
- The office supplies on hand June 30 were worth $140.
- The medical supplies on hand June 30 were worth $275.
- Depreciation is calculated using the declining-balance method. Office equipment and medical equipment depreciate at a rate of 20 percent per year.

100	Cash	305	Income Summary
110	Rec.—Prov. Health Plan	400	Patient Fees
120	Prepaid Insurance	401	Emergency Fees
123	Prepaid Rent	500	Office Salaries Expense
125	Office Supplies	501	Utilities Expense
127	Medical Supplies	502	Telephone Expense
130	Office Equipment	503	Advertising Expense
131	Acc. Dep.—Office Equip.	504	Insurance Expense
140	Medical Equipment	505	Rent Expense
141	Acc. Dep.—Medical Equip.	506	Office Supplies Expense
200	Accounts Payable	507	Medical Supplies Expense
210	Bank Loan	508	Dep. Exp.—Office Equip.
300	C. Rosenblatt, Capital	509	Dep. Exp.—Medical Equip.
301	C. Rosenblatt, Drawings		

Jun. 1 C. Rosenblatt opened a bank account in the name of her business and deposited $15 000, which represented her initial investment in the practice.

1 Paid three months' rent in advance to Sure Realty, $3000 for office space, Cheque 1.

1 Borrowed $10 000 from the bank to purchase the necessary equipment for the office. The term of the loan was 30 months.

2 Paid $2000 for a six-month insurance policy, Cheque 2.

2 Sent $800, Cheque 3, to Newport Realty to pay this month's rent on C. Rosenblatt's apartment (her home).

3 Signed an agreement with Medical Services Inc. to provide emergency medical service for $1800 per month. The June fee was collected today.

4 Purchased medical supplies for the office, $625, Cheque 4.

5 Purchased furniture for the office at a cost of $10 000, Invoice 2973. Paid $1000, Cheque 5, and the remainder was due in 30 days to The Office People.

6 Purchased medical instruments worth $15 000 from James Medical Supplies, Invoice J2888. A down payment of $3000 was made today by Cheque 6 and the remainder was due in four equal monthly payments payable at the end of the month.

14 Patient fees submitted to the Provincial Health Insurance Plan for two weeks were $2875.

14 Received Invoice 8942 from the *Vancouver Sun* for advertising the opening of the practice, $325.

16 Paid office salaries for the first two weeks, $1500, Cheque 7.

19 Purchased office supplies on account from The Office People, $310, Invoice 3873.

21 Received Cheque 746892 from the Provincial Health Insurance Plan in payment of fees submitted June 14.

24 C. Rosenblatt withdrew $1000 for personal use, Cheque 8.

27 Paid the *Vancouver Sun* in full for the invoice received June 14, Cheque 9.

28 Submitted patient fees for the two-week period ended today to the Provincial Health Insurance Plan, $3875.

30 Paid the utility bills for the month, $516, Cheque 10.

30 Paid the monthly payment to James Medical Supplies, Cheque 11.

30 Paid the telephone bill for the month, $294, Cheque 12.

30 Paid the office salaries, $1500, Cheque 13.

 # Computer Accounting

Avoiding Disaster: Backup Systems

L. Stewart is an accountant for Digby Supply Co., which is located in Digby, Nova Scotia. Stewart uses the KIS computerized accounting system produced by KIS Information Systems of Vancouver.

One Tuesday morning, Stewart entered the office and discovered that a burglary had occurred. Some equipment and a small amount of cash had been stolen. Included among the missing items were several boxes of computer diskettes on which were recorded the company's accounting records. The computer itself was not stolen because it was fixed to a desk with a security device.

In some cases, this type of theft could have been a disaster. All accounting records for three years were recorded on the missing diskettes. To re-enter the transactions for three years would be an almost impossible task!

Computer Data Backup

Stewart had prepared for unexpected disasters, such as thefts or fire, by making a *backup copy* of all accounting records every week. The backup records were stored on diskettes that were kept *at a separate location*—not in the same office as the computer system. Since the most recent backup had been done the previous Friday, only the transactions entered on Monday were really missing.

It was not too difficult for Stewart to reconstruct the accounting records and to re-enter all of the source documents that had been recorded since the last backup had been prepared. Here is what was done to reconstruct the accounting records:

1. A copy was made of all of the missing accounting records using the backup diskettes.

2. Stewart printed a copy of the last journal entries made on the backup diskettes.
3. The printout of the journal entries provided the source document numbers and dates for the transactions that had been recorded up to the last backup date, which was Friday. It was not too difficult to compare the source document numbers in the last journal entries with the source document copies on file to identify all of the source documents that had been recorded on Monday and that were now missing from the records because of the theft.
4. The source document copies for the Monday transactions were pulled from the file system and re-entered on the computer.

In effect, Stewart had reconstructed the accounting system using the backup copy of the records and the copy of the source documents kept on file for every transaction. As you can see, a potential disaster—the loss of the accounting records—was averted. Rather than losing a great deal of accounting data, only a small amount was lost. The time taken on a regular basis to prepare backup diskettes had paid off.

Questions

1. What is meant by "backing up" data?
2. Explain the importance of the location of backup data or diskettes.
3. How did Stewart determine which data needed to be re-entered?
4. Explain the significance of having a source document copy on file for every transaction.
5. Many companies now use online data backup systems either via the Internet or a direct dial up connection to an offsite computer. What are the advantages of having a daily backup of data occur over an Internet connection instead of saving to a local disk or tape backup?

End of the Accounting Period Procedures

When you use a computer program, the adjusting entries must be entered into the computer before the financial statements are prepared for the accounting period. This is done to ensure that the financial statements will be accurate.

Simply Accounting automatically closes the revenue and expense accounts when the date is advanced to the new fiscal period.

The Simply Accounting software automatically prepares the ledger accounts for the new fiscal year by reducing them to zero. This means that all of the year's financial information disappears from the computer files. Can you imagine what would happen if the computer program did this and the adjustments and the financial statements had not been prepared? The company would have to re-enter the entire year's transactions to prepare the income statement and balance sheet. To prevent such a disaster, Simply Accounting displays the following warning on the screen (Figure 6-22):

> **CAUTION:**   This date is in a new fiscal year. If you proceed, the program will close the revenue and expense accounts into retained earnings and reset the start and finish dates for the new fiscal year. You should make a backup before proceeding.
>
> ***press RETURN to proceed or ESCAPE to reconsider***

FIGURE 6-22 New fiscal year warning

When company records are set up in the Simply Accounting program, the new fiscal period starting date, e.g., June 1, 20—, and the current period ending date, e.g., May 31, 20—, are identified. One month before the new fiscal period begins, Simply Accounting advises the user to make preparations for the year end. These preparations include gathering information for the adjusting entries and making backup files of the accounting records.

The following end-of-accounting-period procedures are completed when using an accounting program such as Simply Accounting:

1. A backup copy (at least one) is made of the company's computer accounting files for the fiscal period that is ending.
2. Adjustments are prepared, journalized, and posted.
3. T-4 slips are printed for all employees. A T-4 slip is a record of the employee's earnings and payroll deductions for the year and is required by each employee for income tax purposes.
4. The trial balance is printed. It is also saved in the computer system.
5. The income statement and balance sheet for the fiscal period are printed. The statements are saved on the computer file for the year.
6. The computer is then instructed to proceed. It automatically prepares a compound closing entry to close the income and expense accounts and to reduce their balances to zero.

At this point the company will have two sets of records: (1) a new set of books with zero balances in the income and expense accounts and ongoing balances in the asset, liability, and owner's equity accounts; and (2) a computer file that contains the entire set of records for the previous accounting period.

In actual practice, the adjusting entries and the preparation of the financial statements are not done until some time after the accounting period ends. This is because all of the information needed to do the adjustments is not known. For example, the value of the ending inventory is not known until a physical count of all items in stock is completed after the close of business on the last day of the fiscal year. There will also be a delay in recording all invoices for goods purchased until invoices are received from suppliers. For these reasons, two sets of records are kept.

Accounting information for the new fiscal period is recorded in the new set of books. Information for the previous period, such as the adjusting entries, is recorded in the old books. When all adjustments for the previous period have been made, this set of books is closed and the procedures described above in items 2, 3, 4, 5, and 6 are performed. An example involving The Caravelle Gift Shop follows.

The Caravelle Gift Shop

Mary Galotta owns and operates The Caravelle Gift Shop. Located in the heart of the tourist area in Niagara Falls, the shop serves a large number of visitors each year. Mary does her own accounting using a combination of the Lotus 1-2-3 spreadsheet and Simply Accounting. The fiscal year for the business is June 1 to May 31. At the end of the fiscal year, adjustments are made and financial statements and closing entries are prepared. In detail, here are the tasks completed by Mary.

> May 31   The fiscal year ends. All sales and other transactions for the day are journalized using Simply Accounting.

Two backup copies of all of the Simply Accounting files for the year are made.

The command *proceed to the next fiscal period* is entered on the Simply Accounting program. This reduces the revenue and expense account balances to zero and prepares them for the next fiscal period, which begins the next day, June 1. All other account balances are carried forward. In effect, a new set of books is created.

Jun. 1 The next fiscal period begins. Records are kept on the new set of books. From June 1, each day's business transactions (for example, sales, purchases, payments, etc.) that apply to the new fiscal period are recorded on the new set of Simply Accounting files.

1 to 20 All information that involves adjustments for the previous fiscal period is gathered. This includes counting all merchandise in the store after closing on May 31, determining supplies on hand, preparing information on salaries owing as of May 31, and gathering information for the insurance adjustment and invoices for items purchased before May 31 but not received until after May 31.

20 Using all of the relevant information, adjustments are prepared for items that belong to the previous fiscal period. This is recorded on the backup Simply Accounting file prepared at the end of the business day on May 31. The adjusting entries are posted. The result is that the accounting records on the backup set of information for the previous fiscal period are now up to date.

20 Using the backup file of records, which now have been updated to include all of the accounting information for the period, including the adjustments, a trial balance, an income statement, and a balance sheet are prepared for the previous fiscal period. These reports will now be accurate, since they contain all of the information that pertains to the previous fiscal period.

20 Adjustments are prepared so that the current year's balance sheet accounts can be updated to match the balance sheet accounts for the previous year.

20 Printed copies of the financial statements are prepared and the backup disk that contains the accounting records for the previous year is stored in a safe place.

Lotus 1-2-3 Spreadsheet

Mary uses Lotus 1-2-3 each day to balance the cash. She has a format that is used to compare the cash taken in each day with the actual cash in the cash register. The result is that the cash balances, or is short or over, each day. If it does not balance, the shortage or overage is recorded as a journal entry using Simply Accounting.

In addition, at the end of the fiscal period, Lotus is used to prepare a work sheet. The adjustments are planned on the work sheet. When they are completed, the adjusting entries are then prepared from the work sheet and entered into the Simply Accounting program.

COMPUTER ASSIGNMENTS

1. Use a computer spreadsheet program or depreciation software to determine the yearly depreciation of $20 000 worth of equipment over a five-year period. Use a 20 percent rate and the straight-line depreciation method. The data should be recorded in the following format:

Year	Value at Beginning of Year	Depreciation for the Year	Accumulated Depreciation	Book Value at End of Year
1	$20 000			
2				
3				
4				
5				

2. Use a computer spreadsheet program or depreciation software to determine the yearly depreciation of $20 000 worth of equipment over a five-year period. Use a 20 percent rate and the declining-balance depreciation method. The data should be recorded in the format shown below:

Year	Value at Beginning of Year	Depreciation for the Year	Accumulated Depreciation	Book Value at End of Year
1	$20 000			
2				
3				
4				
5				

Note: Computer assignments 3, 4, and 5 will be completed using the general journal available with your software. The other journals will not be used in this chapter.

3. Use general ledger software to do the following:
(a) Prepare a ledger for Hurl and Associates, exercise 17 on page 256.
(b) Record the April transactions.
(c) Print the journal, ledger, and trial balance.

4. Refer to exercise 18 on page 257, Connie Rosenblatt, M.D., and use general ledger software to do the following:
   (a) Open ledger accounts.
   (b) Journalize the June transactions.
   (c) Print the trial balance.
   (d) Journalize adjusting entries.
   (e) Print a new (adjusted) trial balance.
   (f) Print the financial statements.
   (g) Journalize the closing entries.
   (h) Print the ledger.
   (i) Print the post-closing trial balance.

www.pearsoned.ca/
principlesofaccounting

WEB EXTENSIONS

Internet Study Guide

➤ Complete the Chapter 6 review.

➤ Complete the Chapter 6 definitions.

➤ Complete the Chapter 6 online test.

Web Links

Visit the Web Links section at the Pearson Education web site to find links to the CMA, CA, and CGA Canadian associations. Visit each site and give examples of jobs being performed by accountants with each professional designation.

10 Case Studies

Comparative Financial Positions

CASE 1

Company A has current assets totalling $55 000. One of the current assets is Cash, $2000. The company has recently paid its rent for three months in advance. Prepaid Rent, $4500, is one of the current assets. Company B has current assets totalling $55 000. It has cash of $2500. Rent of $1500 is paid monthly. This month's payment has been made. Both companies have current liabilities of $12 000.

Considering only the facts given, which company is in the better financial position, Company A or B? Give reasons.

Overstating Net Income

CASE 2

At the end of the year, the accountant for A-Cut-Above Lawn Care prepares financial statements but neglects to prepare the adjustment for the Supplies account. The balance in the Supplies account at the end of the year is $1500. An actual count shows that the value of supplies on hand is $200.

The net income for the year as calculated by the accountant is $22 000 and the total assets are $110 000. However, these figures are incorrect because Supplies has not been adjusted.

(a) By how much is the net income overstated?
(b) By how much are the assets overstated?
(c) What are the correct figures for the net income and the total assets?

Value of a Business

CASE 3

Jeremy Cheung owns Great Sounds D.J. He wishes to sell his business and approaches you with this offer: he will sell you his business, including all of its assets and liabilities, for $15 000. Jeremy states that the business has earned a net income every year for the last eight years. He provides this balance sheet information:

Assets		
Cash	$ 2 000	
Accounts Receivable	500	
Supplies	1 000	
Equipment	20 000	
Accumulated Depreciation—Equipment		$14 750
Van	9 000	
Accumulated Depreciation—Van		7 562
Liabilities		
Bank Loan		2 000

Jeremy states that the business is well worth $15 000 since the van and equipment cost a total of $29 000.

(a) What is the owner's equity in this business?
(b) What is the book value of the van and equipment?
(c) Approximately how many years have the equipment and van been owned by the business?
(d) What do you think is a fair selling price based only on the figures provided?
(e) What other factors might affect the setting of a fair price for this business?

CASE 4 The Accrual Method of Accounting

Goldman's Gym normally signs up members for a one- or two-year period and collects the full membership fee for the complete period when the contract is signed or within 30 days. If you were the accountant for Goldman's Gym and were using the accrual basis of accounting:

(a) Would you record the membership fees as revenue when the contract was signed?
(b) What GAAP influences your decision?
(c) Can you devise an account that would more accurately record these data? (It will be similar to a prepaid expense.)
(d) What type of account is the one you used to record the memberships?
(e) Would an adjusting entry be necessary at the end of the fiscal period to correct the revenue?

CASE 5 Recording Depreciation

Alex Nguyen is the owner of a furniture moving business. The business has a van worth $29 000 and equipment worth $14 000. Depreciation has not been recorded on these fixed assets.

(a) What effect has the omission of depreciation got on the operating results of the business?
(b) How is income tax affected?
(c) Why might depreciation have been deliberately not recorded?
(d) What method should have been used?
(e) What GAAP is involved?

CASE 6 Looking Beyond the Figures

The revenue and expense accounts of Yoshii Enterprises are shown below.

Revenue		Expenses	
Year 1	100 000	Year 1	75 000

Financial statements were prepared at the end of the fiscal period. The net income was $25 000. The accountant quit after preparing the statements and a new accountant began work in the new year. At the end of the second year, the accounts appear as summarized below.

Revenue		
Year 1	100 000
Year 2	130 000
Total	230 000

Expenses		
Year 1	75 000
Year 2	90 000
Total	165 000

Financial statements prepared at the end of the second year indicated a net income of $65 000. The owner thought this was too good to be true. The owner was right!

(a) Why is the $65 000 net income figure incorrect?
(b) What is the correct net income for the second year?

Closing Entry Errors

CASE 7

Look at the general journal shown below.

	GENERAL JOURNAL			PAGE 89
DATE	PARTICULARS	P.R.	DEBIT	CREDIT
20—				
Dec. 31	Sales		24 0 0 0 00	
	Advertising Expense		1 0 0 0 00	
	Income Summary			25 0 0 0 00
31	Income Summary		16 9 0 0 00	
	Rent Expense			5 0 0 00
	Salaries Expense			13 0 0 0 00
	Office Expense			4 0 0 00
	General Expense			1 0 0 0 00
	Selling Expense			2 0 0 0 00
31	Income Summary		2 0 0 0 00	
	Owner, Drawings			2 0 0 0 00
31	Owner, Capital		8 1 0 0 00	
	Income Summary			8 1 0 0 00

(a) There are several errors in this general journal. Can you locate them?
(b) Prepare a corrected journal.
(c) What is the correct net income or net loss?
(d) If the balance in the Capital account was $33 000 at the beginning of the period, what is the new balance at December 31?

⑪ Career Education Activities

1. Professional Careers in Accounting

The traditional role of the accountant has changed in recent years. Gone are the days of simply "crunching" numbers in the back office of a company. Today, accountants are active in advising company executives, forensic accounting, strategic planning, management and consulting services, information technology, environmental accounting, and traditional roles such as taxation and auditing.

There are three professional accounting designations in Canada:
• Certified Management Accountant (CMA)
• Certified General Accountant (CGA)
• Chartered Accountant (CA)

Certified Management Accountant

A CMA combines accounting experience with business management skills to help with the strategic planning for an organization. Prior to obtaining CMA status, a university degree is required. Other requirements include completion of a two-part National Entrance Examination. Part one is a four-hour multiple choice and case study exam. Part two consists of a four-hour detailed business case study. Students must also take part in a Strategic Leadership Program over a two-year period while they gain practical experience in the field. The final evaluation component consists of a Report to the Board, where reports are graded on a national basis. Currently, CMA Canada represents more than 31 000 Certified Management Accountants and 10 000 applicants and students.

Certified General Accountant

To become a CGA, a university degree is required along with completion of the CGA program of professional studies. There are exceptions for entering the program without a university degree. Students may also elect to earn their professional designation and a university degree concurrently by completing a Bachelor of Accounting Science (BAccS). The program of professional studies consists of 14 courses and four Professional Admission Comprehensive Examinations (PACE).The Professional Applications (PA1) Examination is the final examination taken after the applicant has completed all the course requirements. The final requirement is two to three years of practical work experience. To allow students to obtain their CGA designation while working, many of the CGA courses are offered over the Internet and using CD-ROM delivery methods. CGA Canada is a national association of 55 000 Certified General Accountants and students in CGA programs.

Chartered Accountant

Chartered accountants specialize in analyzing and interpreting financial information. CAs can be found on business management teams, running their own businesses, in government, and in all areas of the public sector. To become a CA, students must complete a university degree followed by professional courses and practical work experience. The process for becoming a CA is slightly different depending upon one's province of study. In Ontario the steps are:
• a university degree (although there are exceptions) that includes 51 credit hours of courses specified by the Canadian Institute of Chartered Accountants;
• 30 months' employment in an office approved to train CA students;
• a one-week staff training program;
• a four-week School of Accountancy; and
• the national Uniform Final Examination.

Regardless of their province, all students must pass the Uniform Final Exam (UFE) before they become a CA. The Canadian Institute of Chartered Accountants has a membership of over 68 000 accountants and 8500 students.

2. Position of Controller

Look at the following two advertisements for the position of controller.

(a) What types of accounting designation are required in each advertisement for the position of controller?
(b) What "people" skills are required to fulfill the roler of controller?
(c) Explain what is meant by the title "controller."

Controller

Toronto Research Park Company, the developer and manager of a high-technology business park in the Toronto area, is seeking a Controller. You must have a CA designation with a minimum five years' experience. Your experience should include an emphasis in the real estate development and property management sector. You are an entrepreneurial self-starter with strong organizational skills and a team player.

Please reply in confidence to
Toronto Research Park Company
Suite 200, 111 Leggo Drive,
Toronto, Ontario

Attention: President

Controller
Public Relations
$100,000

Bring your 10 years' experience in a billing environment to one of Canada's most dynamic and successful "people firms." Duties include financials, budgeting, tax reporting, and supervising a department of 16 staff. You will be responsible for the preparation of year-end financial reports.

You will have a CGA designation, a positive attitude, and a desire to develop new programs.

You desire working with a dynamic group of people and excel in a fast-paced environment.

We offer a comprehensive benefit and vacation plan.

Email: ThomasDuggan@Consultants.com
Fax: 519-966-3223
Duggan
Management Consultants
111 Hazel Avenue, London, Ontario
Phone: 519-966-3233

Career Profile •

When Mary Lou Mulvey attended Hillcrest High School she knew that she enjoyed math and business, but she wasn't sure what she wanted to do for the rest of her life. Like many graduating high school students she attended university to pursue her education, not just to pursue a particular career. She enrolled in the Bachelor of Commerce program at the University of Ottawa and completed a four-year degree.

After she graduated, Mary Lou entered the technology field, working for Mitel and Cognos. Mary Lou discovered that her education did not end once she entered the workforce. She continued to challenge herself by enrolling in the CGA program. After she obtained her CGA designation she continued to work for Cognos, specializing in a financial application software package.

Mary Lou left Cognos when a new company, Multiview, took over the financial application software. She worked as the company controller until she left the workforce to start a family.

Work–home balance became an important priority for Mary Lou. She returned to Multiview, working three days in the office and a half-day a week teleworking from home. Her responsibilities included assisting the controller, quality assurance, and technical writing. The extra time at home provided Mary Lou with more time to spend with her young children and time to explore her interests in children's education, writing, running, and exercise.

Mary Lou is now moving toward applying her overall knowledge and experience in accounting by starting her own public practice. She assists clients

with all aspects of the accounting process. She attributes her successful career in accounting to good organization, planning, and time management skills.

For Discussion

(a) Prepare a chart that outlines Mary Lou's career path.
(b) What is meant by *teleworking*?
(c) Explain the advantages and disadvantages that come with working part-time.
(d) To what skills does Mary Lou attribute her successful career?

Performance Task 2

Community Theatre

What Learning You Will Demonstrate
You will:

- demonstrate an understanding of the recording and decision-making aspects of accounting;
- demonstrate an understanding of the basic accounting cycle procedures and principles for a service business;
- demonstrate an understanding of the debit/credit theory in recording transactions in the journals and ledgers of a service business;
- describe the effects that transactions have on the accounts of a service business;
- demonstrate the skills necessary to prepare trial balances and financial statements for a service business; and
- explain the importance of current assets when you interpret the balance sheet.

The Task

Community Theatre has recently terminated a contract with their accountant due to incompetence. They have offered you a trial contract. Your future as their permanent accountant depends on your timely, thorough, and accurate completion of certain tasks.

Parameters of Your Trial Contract

A. Complete the work sheet and financial statements for the month of January, prepare and post adjusting and closing entries, and prepare a post-closing trial balance.

B. Journalize the February transactions, post them to the ledger accounts, and prepare a trial balance.

C. Complete the work sheet, financial statements, adjusting and closing entries, and post-closing trial balance for February.

D. Examine the financial results for the theatre for two months and make recommendations to the owners by way of a written report and presentation.

Materials Required

- January financial information
- February source documents
- Additional information for February
- Appropriate work sheets, forms, and statements

Suggested Procedure

A. January Financial Statements
1. Complete an eight-column work sheet.
2. Prepare the monthly financial statements.
3. Set up a general ledger with the appropriate accounts and balances.
4. Journalize and post the adjusting and closing entries.
5. Prepare a post-closing trial balance.

B. February Source Documents
1. Journalize the source documents and post to the general ledger.
2. Prepare a trial balance.

C. February Financial Statements
1. Complete an eight-column work sheet.
2. Prepare the financial statements.
3. Journalize and post the adjusting and closing entries.
4. Prepare a post-closing trial balance.

D. Analysis
1. Prepare a written report to analyze current profitability, possibilities to finance expansion, and strategies to increase future profitability.
2. Present your report to the owners of the business.

Assessment Criteria

Examine the assessment rubric. Note the descriptions of the performance criteria and the levels of achievement.

Evaluation

Based on a self-assessment of your completion of the task, would Community Theatre offer you a permanent contract? Justify your opinion.

PART A

January Financial Information

Community Theatre rents its premises from the Community Shopping Centre. The theatre has been open for a month and management wants to find out if the business has made a profit or a loss. Using the additional information, follow the suggested procedure to complete the task.

Additional Information:
- The straight-line depreciation method is used by Community Theatre. The equipment depreciates by 20 percent of the original value per year and will have no residual value. *Note*: Calculate the depreciation to the nearest dollar value.
- Rent was prepaid for three months on January 1.

- Insurance was prepaid for three months on January 1.
- Supplies on hand on January 31 were valued at $260.

Community Theatre
Trial Balance
January 31, 20—

Account	Acc. No.	Debit	Credit
Cash	100	$ 5 653	
Prepaid Rent	115	6 000	
Prepaid Insurance	116	1 800	
Supplies	117	520	
Equipment	120	89 563	
Accounts Payable	200		$ 890
Bank Loan	201		10 387
J. Singh, Capital	300		94 212
J. Singh, Drawings	301	1 600	
Ticket Sales	400		15 493
Confectionery Income	401		2 407
Salaries Expense	500	6 801	
Advertising Expense	501	2 563	
Film Rental Expense	502	3 563	
Cleaning Expense	503	850	
Telephone Expense	504	95	
Equipment Repairs & Maintenance Expense	505	2 293	
Film Transportation Expense	506	248	
Heating Expense	507	858	
Electricity and Water Expense	508	632	
General Expense	509	350	
		$123 389	$123 389

Additional Accounts:

Accumulated Depreciation—Equipment	121
Income Summary	302
Depreciation Expense—Equipment	510
Rent Expense	511
Insurance Expense	512
Supplies Expense	513

PART B

February Source Documents

Feb. 7   Cash register tapes from the box office for the week show transactions No. 5345 to No. 6253 for total sales of $2858. The money was deposited in the bank account.

Weekly sales report for the confectionery shows a net income of $225. The money was deposited in the bank account.

Purchase invoices received:
No. 3817 from Electronics Canada Ltd., $256 for final adjustments to the projector.
No. 5112 from *The Daily Sentinel*, $750 for newspaper advertisements.

Cheques issued:
No. 375 to City Utility, $350 for electricity and water.
No. 376 to Bell Canada, $45.

14   Cash register tapes from the box office for the week show transactions No. 6254 to No. 8871 for total sales of $7534.

Weekly sales report for the confectionery shows a net income of $612.

Purchase invoices received:
No. 5528 from International Film Distributors, $1289 for rental of the film shown from February 1 to 7.
No. T581 from Commercial Cleaners Ltd., $420 for cleaning the premises in the first half of the month.

Cheques issued:
No. 377 to Craig Stationers, $35 for supplies.
No. 378 to International Film Distributors, $890 on account.
No. 379 to J. Singh, the owner, $350 for personal drawings.
No. 380, $2890 for salaries from February 1–14.

21   Cash register tapes from the box office for the week show transactions No. 8872 to No. 11 608 for total sales of $8132.

Weekly sales report for the confectionery shows a net income of $657.

Purchase invoices received:
No. 571985 from Air Canada, $178 for transportation of film.
No. DC475 from CCHH Radio and TV, $371 for spot advertising.

No. 329F from Stinson Fuels, $356 for heating oil.

Cheques issued:
No. 381 to Electronics Canada Ltd., $256 on account.
No. 382 to *The Daily Sentinel*, $750 on account.
No. 383 to Triangle Office Supply, $445 for supplies.

28   Cash register tapes from the box office for the week show transactions No. 11 609 to 14 142 for total sales of $7483.

Weekly sales report for the confectionery shows a net income of $589.

Purchase invoices received:
No. 6315 from International Film Distributors, $2658 for rental of film from February 8 to 28.
No. T699 from Commercial Cleaners Ltd., $435 for cleaning of premises.

Cheques issued:
No. 384 to Commercial Cleaners Ltd., $420 on account.
No. 385 to J. Singh, the owner, $350 for personal drawings.
No. 386, $2635 for salaries from February 15–28.

Additional Information for February:

Supplies on hand, February 28, were valued at $300.

Community Theatre: Performance Task Rubric

Assessment Criteria	Levels of Achievement			
	Level 1	Level 2	Level 3	Level 4
KNOWLEDGE AND UNDERSTANDING • understanding of recording and decision-making aspects of accounting • understanding of the debit/credit theory in recording transactions in the journals and ledgers of a service business	Demonstrates limited understanding of terminology, concepts, procedures, and principles.	Demonstrates some understanding of terminology, concepts, procedures, and principles.	Demonstrates considerable understanding of terminology, concepts, procedures, and principles.	Demonstrates a thorough understanding of terminology, concepts, procedures, and principles.
THINKING AND INQUIRY • analysis of transactions • interpretation of the balance sheets • assessment of financial status • forming conclusions regarding profitability	Uses critical and interpretative skills with limited effectiveness. Applies few of the skills in an inquiry, or problem-solving process.	Uses critical and interpretative skills with moderate effectiveness. Applies some of the skills in an inquiry, or problem-solving process.	Uses critical and interpretative skills with considerable effectiveness. Applies most of the skills in an inquiry, or problem-solving process.	Uses critical and interpretative skills with a high degree of effectiveness. Applies all or almost all skills in an inquiry, or problem-solving process.
COMMUNICATION • completion of appropriate forms and statements • formation of a written report using appropriate procedures and principles • presentation to owners	Communicates with minimal precision and clarity.	Communicates with some precision and clarity.	Communicates with considerable precision and clarity.	Communicates with complete and thorough precision and clarity.
APPLICATION • application of skills to preparetrial balances and financial statements	Uses skills with limited accuracy.	Uses skills with some accuracy.	Uses skills with considerable accuracy.	Uses skills with a high degree of accuracy.

The Merchandising Company

UNIT 14 Merchandising Accounts

What Learning You Will Demonstrate

On completion of this unit, you will be able to:

- describe three types of business operations;
- prepare a schedule of cost of goods sold;
- record merchandise purchased for resale under the periodic inventory system;
- record transactions for merchandising accounts under the periodic inventory method using the following accounts: Sales Returns and Allowances, Sales Discounts, Purchases, Purchases Returns and Allowances, Purchases Discounts, Transportation-in, and Delivery Expense;
- record transactions for merchandise inventory under the perpetual inventory method using the following accounts: Merchandise Inventory and Cost of Goods Sold; and
- define *contra revenue* and *contra cost* accounts.

— TYPES OF BUSINESS OPERATIONS

The three basic types of business operations and their interrelationships are shown in Figure 7-1.

Service Companies

Up to this point, accounting procedures have been illustrated mainly by reference to businesses such as a gym, a motel, a cinema, a contractor, a doctor, etc. All of these businesses offer services to their customers. They do not sell products, e.g., mouthwash or tires; they sell services and are called service companies.

A service company sells services.

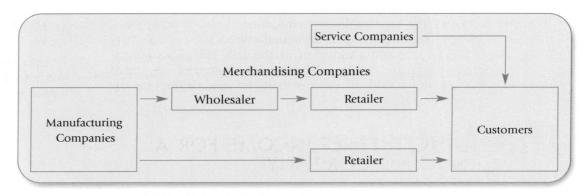

FIGURE 7-1 The three basic types of business operations—service, merchandising, and manufacturing companies

Merchandising Companies

A merchandising company sells products.

Businesses that sell products, not services, are known as merchandising companies. Both wholesalers and retailers are included in this group. Retailers usually buy merchandise from wholesalers or manufacturers and sell it to their customers at a price that covers their costs and provides a net income.

Manufacturing Companies

A manufacturing company makes products.

A firm that converts raw materials into saleable products is called a manufacturing company. Usually, a manufacturer sells products to merchandising companies such as retailers and wholesalers.

Warrendon Sports: A Merchandising Company

The accounting procedures of a merchandising company are a little different from those of a service company. The difference can be illustrated by examining Warrendon Sports, a retail store located in Ottawa.

FIGURE 7-2 Warrendon Sports—a merchandising company

Warrendon Sports buys bicycles, hockey equipment, baseball equipment, and hundreds of other sporting goods from manufacturers such as Spalding, Schwinn, Winwell, Slazenger, and a variety of wholesalers. The goods bought from these manufacturers and sold to Warrendon's customers are called merchandise. The total dollar value of goods on hand for resale is found in the Merchandise Inventory account.

DETERMINING THE NET INCOME FOR A MERCHANDISING COMPANY

In Chapter 3, you learned that expenses are the cost of the goods or services used in the operation of a business. To calculate the net income for a service business, expenses are subtracted from the revenue. This calculation is illustrated by the equation:

$$\text{Revenue} \quad - \quad \text{Expenses} \quad = \quad \text{Net Income}$$

A merchandising company must buy and pay for the merchandise it sells as well as pay the expenses of operating the business. The following two equations illustrate how net income is calculated for a merchandising company:

$$\text{Revenue} \quad - \quad \text{Cost of Goods Sold} \quad = \quad \text{Gross Profit}$$

$$\text{Gross Profit} \quad - \quad \text{Expenses} \quad = \quad \text{Net Income}$$

Net income occurs when revenue from sales exceeds *both the cost of goods sold and the operating expenses.*

The preparation of the income statement for a merchandising enterprise is a little more complicated than for a service business. Figure 7-3 on page 280 shows an income statement for a merchandising company. Notice that there are three sections in the body of the statement—revenue, cost of goods sold, and operating expenses. Can you locate the following equations on the income statement?

Revenue		Cost of Goods Sold		Gross Profit
$56 000	−	$34 000	=	$22 000

Gross Profit		Expenses		Net Income
$22 000	−	$12 600	=	$9 400

One of the major expenses for a merchandising company is the *cost of the goods that it buys for resale.* Since the cost of goods sold is a major expense, it receives special attention on the income statement or *in a separate schedule.*

SCHEDULE OF COST OF GOODS SOLD

A schedule is a supporting statement that provides details of an item on a main statement.

In the income statement format used by Warrendon Sports, a single total, $34 000, appears in the cost of goods sold section. This total includes all of the costs involved in purchasing the merchandise to be sold. It is arrived at by the completion of the *schedule of cost of goods sold*, illustrated in Figure 7-4. The use of this schedule simplifies the presentation of the income statement.

Warrendon Sports
Income Statement
For the month ended May 31, 20—

Revenue		
Sales		$56 000
Cost of Goods Sold		
Cost of Goods Sold (per schedule)		34 000
Gross Profit		22 000
Operating Expenses		
Advertising	$2 400	
Delivery	700	
Office	400	
Miscellaneous	500	
Rent	2 600	
Salaries	5 400	
Utilities	600	
Total Expenses		12 600
Net Income		$ 9 400

FIGURE 7-3   Income statement for Warrendon Sports

Warrendon Sports
Schedule of Cost of Goods Sold
For the month ended May 31, 20—

Merchandise Inventory, May 1	$16 000
Add: Purchases	36 000
Total Cost of Merchandise	52 000
Less: Merchandise Inventory, May 31	18 000
Cost of Goods Sold	$34 000

FIGURE 7-4   Schedule of cost of goods sold for Warrendon Sports

Preparing a Schedule of Cost of Goods Sold

The steps followed in preparing a schedule of cost of goods sold can be illustrated as follows:

Beginning Merchandise Inventory	+	Purchases of Merchandise	=	Cost of Merchandise Available for Sale	−	Ending Merchandise Inventory	=	Cost of Goods Sold

However, there are several other items that affect the cost of goods sold. These include:

- purchases returns and allowances;
- purchases discounts; and
- transportation on purchases.

How do each of these items affect the total cost of merchandise? Figure 7-5, the expanded schedule of cost of goods sold, contains each of these additional items.

Warrendon Sports
Schedule of Cost of Goods Sold
For the month ended June 30, 20—

Merchandise Inventory, June 1			$18 000
Add: Purchases		$42 400	
Less: Purchases Returns			
and Allowances	$8 000		
Purchases Discounts	400	8 400	
Net Purchase Cost		34 000	
Add: Transportation-in		2 000	
Total Cost of Merchandise Purchased			36 000
Cost of Merchandise Available for Sale			54 000
Less: Merchandise Inventory, June 30			20 000
Cost of Goods Sold			$34 000

FIGURE 7-5 Expanded schedule of cost of goods sold, including net purchases calculation and transportation cost

Purchases Returns and Allowances

If goods that have been purchased and recorded in the Purchases account are *returned*, the cost of purchases decreases. The *Purchases Returns and Allowances account is used to record such returns*. On the schedule of cost of goods sold (Figure 7-5), the amount shown for the Purchases Returns and Allowances account is a *subtraction*.

Purchases Discounts

When a cash discount off the invoice price is received, the discount is recorded in the *Purchases Discounts account*. The cost of the merchandise decreases because of the discount received. Therefore, on the schedule in Figure 7-5, the amount shown for the Purchases Discounts account is *subtracted* from the amount in the Purchases account.

Net Purchase Cost

The Purchases figure less the Purchases Returns and Allowances figure and the Purchases Discounts figure equals the net purchase cost. The calculation follows:

Calculation of Net Purchases		
Purchases		$42 400
Less: Purchases Returns and Allowances	$8 000	
Purchases Discounts	400	8 400
Net Purchase Cost		$34 000

Transportation on Purchases

Transportation-in is the account used to record the transportation charges on merchandise pruchased.

The cost of merchandise purchased for resale is increased by the cost of transporting the merchandise to the retailer's place of business. **Transportation-in**, *Transportation on Purchases*, or *Freight-in* is the account used to record this cost. Figure 7-5 shows how the transportation cost is added to the net purchases total. The $2000 transportation cost is added to the $34 000 net purchase cost to arrive at a total of $36 000, called *total cost of merchandise purchased*.

MERCHANDISE INVENTORY

The Merchandise Inventory account contains the total dollar value of *goods on hand for resale (merchandise)*. The schedule of cost of goods sold contains the inventory value at the beginning of the accounting period (beginning inventory), and at the end of the accounting period (ending inventory). The dollar value of inventory may be determined in one of two ways: *the perpetual inventory method* or *the periodic inventory method*.

Perpetual Inventory Method

The perpetual inventory method is a continuous record of all merchandise on hand.

The **perpetual inventory method** is commonly used by retailers who need to know exactly how much of each item of merchandise is on hand. Under this system, records are kept for each individual item the company sells. The record, often called a *stock card*, is updated each time the item is purchased or sold. This type of retailer normally sells a low number of "high-priced" items, such as cars or major appliances.

However, the system is also used by many retailers who have computerized point-of-sale terminals. When a customer takes an item to a computerized cash register, the clerk uses a scanner to record the sale on the cash register tape. At the same time, the computer deducts the item purchased from the stock, or inventory, so that a continuously updated record of items of merchandise is available. For more information on point-of-sale terminals, see page 571. The accounting system used for the perpetual inventory method is fully explained later in this unit.

Periodic Inventory Method

The periodic inventory method is used by retailers who do not feel it is necessary to keep a *continuously updated record of items of merchandise*. We will discuss in detail the accounting procedures and entries required for this method throughout this text unless the perpetual method is specifically identified.

If a business sells a large quantity of relatively low-priced merchandise, such as candy or potato chips in a variety store, it is not practical to record the number of each item bought and sold during the accounting period. These retailers usually determine the amount of each item on hand and the cost of merchandise only at the end of the fiscal period, when the cost is needed to prepare financial statements.

Businesses that use the periodic inventory method determine the value of the ending inventory by taking a *physical inventory*. A physical inventory *simply means counting all of the various types of merchandise on hand*. The value of this inventory is then determined by multiplying the quantity of each item by its cost price and adding the costs of all the various units together.

The total value of the merchandise on hand is recorded in the Merchandise Inventory account. The value of the inventory is used on both the schedule of cost of goods sold (Figure 7-5) and the balance sheet (Figure 7-6).

The Merchandise Inventory balance appears in the current assets section of the balance sheet, as shown in Figure 7-6.

The periodic inventory method requires that a count be made of all inventory at the end of the fiscal period for valuation purposes.

A physical inventory is a count of all goods on hand.

Warrendon Sports
Partial Balance Sheet
June 30, 20—

Assets

Current Assets		
Cash	$ 8 000	
Accounts Receivable	54 000	
Merchandise Inventory	20 000	
Office Supplies	2 000	
Total Current Assets		$84 000

FIGURE 7-6 The Merchandise Inventory balance is shown in the current assets section of the balance sheet.

CHART OF ACCOUNTS FOR A MERCHANDISING BUSINESS

As you have learned, the income statement for a merchandising company contains a new expense section—the cost of goods sold. For each item in this section, there is an account in the general ledger. Figure 7-7 lists the accounts usually found in the general ledger of a merchandising company. Those accounts that are particular to a merchandising company have been highlighted.

Merchandising Company Chart of Accounts

Section	No.	Title
(1) Assets	101	Cash
	110	Accounts Receivable
	120	Merchandise Inventory
	125	Office Supplies
	126	Store Supplies
	150	Land
	151	Building
	160	Equipment
(2) Liabilities	200	Accounts Payable
	205	PST Payable
	206	GST/HST Payable
	207	GST/HST Refundable
	210	Bank Loan
	250	Mortgage Payable
(3) Owner's Equity	300	Owner, Capital
	301	Owner, Drawings
	302	Income Summary
(4) Revenue	400	Sales
	401	Sales Returns and Allowances
	402	Sales Discounts
(5) Cost of Goods Sold	500	Purchases
	501	Purchases Returns and Allowances
	502	Purchases Discounts
	503	Transportation-in
	550	Cost of Goods Sold
(6) Expenses	600	Advertising Expense
	601	Delivery Expense
	602	Miscellaneous Expense
	603	Office Expense
	604	Salaries Expense
	605	Utilities Expense

FIGURE 7-7 Chart of accounts for a merchandising company with new merchandising accounts highlighted

Notice that there are six sections in the general ledger of a merchandising company. They are: assets, liabilities, owner's equity, revenue, cost of goods sold, and expenses. The general ledger of a service business has only five sections. It does not have a cost of goods sold section. Most, but not all, of the new merchandising accounts are found in the new cost of goods sold section.

DEBIT AND CREDIT RULES FOR MERCHANDISING ACCOUNTS

In this chapter, you will learn additional debit and credit rules for the accounts of a merchandising company. The rules are based on the balance sheet equation:

Assets   =   Liabilities   +   Owner's Equity

You will remember that income statement accounts are related to the owner's equity account. The two basic principles that determine the debit and credit rules for the new accounts are:

- Revenue increases owner's equity.
- Expenses decrease owner's equity.

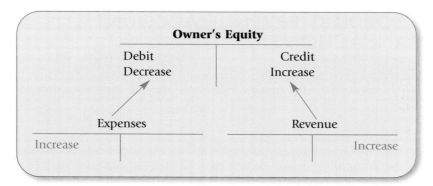

Expenses decrease owner's equity and are recorded as debits. Expense accounts increase on the debit side and decrease on the credit side.

Revenue increases owner's equity and is recorded as a credit. Revenue accounts increase on the credit side and decrease on the debit side.

INCOME STATEMENT ACCOUNTS

The income statement in Figure 7-3 on page 280 demonstrates the three sections of the statement for a merchandising enterprise and the calculations necessary to determine net income. This section of the unit will discuss the new accounts necessary to record the sale and purchase of merchandise for a merchandising company.

Revenue Section of the Income Statement

For a business to record a net income (have a net profit), the *revenue* from sales *must exceed the cost of goods sold and the operating expenses* (rent, advertising, light, heat, salaries, etc.). Figure 7-8 on the next page is the revenue section of the income statement for Warrendon Sports for June.

Warrendon Sports Partial Income Statement For the month ended June 30, 20—		
Revenue		
Sales		$62 000
Less: Sales Returns and Allowances	$1 500	
Sales Discounts	500	2 000
Net Sales		$60 000

FIGURE 7-8 Revenue section of the income statement

RECORDING REVENUE ACCOUNT TRANSACTIONS

Sample transactions that involve Warrendon Sports' revenue accounts follow. To keep things simple, all transactions are considered to be tax-exempt.

Sales

"Sales" means the amount of cash sales and credit sales made by the business during the accounting period. When merchandise is sold to a customer, it is recorded in the Sales account.

Transaction 1: Cash Sale

Jun.   1   Cash register total for the day, $4250.

A point-of-sale terminal is an electronic cash register linked to a computer.

Cash sales are entered into the cash register or computerized **point-of-sale terminal** at the time of the sale. At the end of the day, a total is obtained and is recorded by the following journal entry:

Jun.	1	Cash		4 2 5 0 00	
		Sales			4 2 5 0 00
		To record cash sales summary for Jun. 1.			

Transaction 2: Credit Sale

Revenue accounts increase on the credit side.

Jun.   2   G. Giles purchased a pair of skates and three hockey sticks, $150 on account, Invoice 386.

This transaction is recorded as follows:

Jun.	2	Accounts Receivable/G. Giles		1 5 0 00	
		Sales			1 5 0 00
		Sold merchandise on account, Invoice 386.			

The first two transactions are shown in the T-accounts below:

Cash		Accounts Receivable/G. Giles		Sales	
Jun. 1 4 250		Jun. 2 150		Jun. 1 4 250	
				2 150	

Sales Returns and Allowances

There is always a chance that a buyer of merchandise may not be satisfied with the goods received. The goods may be the wrong size or colour; they may be defective; or they may be unsatisfactory for other reasons. Such goods are either returned to the seller for a full refund, or the seller gives the customer an allowance, or rebate, on the selling price. Normally, a customer is given a cash refund if the merchandise was paid for in cash, and a credit to his or her account if the merchandise was purchased on account and the bill is unpaid.

The Sales Returns and Allowances account is used to record a return of merchandise by a customer. Since this, in effect, cancels all or a portion of a previous sale, this transaction *reduces sales revenue*. Sales Returns and Allowances is often called a *contra revenue account* because its debit balance is the *opposite* of the credit balance of the revenue account, Sales. The Sales account could be debited to record these transactions, but most retailers use Sales Returns and Allowances to have separate information in this important area. It is important since an increase in sales returns and allowances results in a decrease in revenue for the period. Continued increases in returns may indicate a number of problems, such as poor handling of merchandise, shipping problems, or problems with merchandise quality.

The Sales Returns and Allowances account is used by the seller to record merchandise returned by a customer.

Transaction 3: Sales Return on a Credit Sale

Jun. 3   G. Giles returned one defective hockey stick, priced at $15, from merchandise purchased on June 2, Invoice 896.

This transaction represents a sales return from a credit customer, so the customer's account balance must be reduced (credit). Sales Returns and Allowances is debited to record a reduction in revenue (contra revenue) as a result of a return.

Jun.	3	Sales Returns and Allowances	1 5 00	
		Accounts Receivable/G. Giles		1 5 00
		Goods returned by G. Giles, Invoice 896.		

This transaction is shown in the T-accounts that follow:

Sales Returns and Allowances		Accounts Receivable/G. Giles	
Jun. 3 15		Jun. 2 150	Jun. 3 15

Transaction 4: Sales Return on a Cash Sale

Jun. 4   Customer returned merchandise worth $25 together with Cash Sales Slip 10942 for a refund. The goods were bought for cash on June 1.

Since the customer originally paid for the merchandise, a cash refund is given. The journal entry would be as follows:

Jun.	4	Sales Returns and Allowances		2 5 00	
		Cash			2 5 00
		Goods returned for cash refund,			
		Cash Sales Slip 10942.			

This transaction is shown in the T-accounts that follow:

Sales Returns and Allowances			Cash			
Jun. 3	15		Jun. 1	4 250	Jun. 4	25
4	25					

A sales return represents a decrease in revenue and is recorded as a debit. Since revenue accounts like Sales increase on the credit side, they decrease on the debit side. The Sales Returns and Allowances amount is subtracted from the Sales figure in the revenue section on the income statement (see Figure 7-8 on page 286).

Credit Invoices

A credit invoice is a source document issued by the seller to indicate the amount of credit allowed to a customer for returned or defective goods.

All business transactions must be supported by an original source document. The source document that is completed when goods are returned is the credit invoice, as shown in Figure 7-9. The credit invoice is prepared by the seller, in this case Warrendon Sports, and sent to the customer, G. Giles. A copy is kept by the seller and used as the basis for the entry to reduce the customer's account and to record the sales return in the Sales Returns and Allowances account. A credit invoice provides the details about a reduction in a customer's account, the amount, the reason, and the original invoice number.

The credit invoice and its copy are used by both the seller and the buyer to prepare an entry to record the return. The seller records a sales return, and the buyer records a purchase return. Another term used for credit invoice is *credit memorandum* or *credit note*.

Sales Discounts

Sales discounts are offered to encourage early payment of customer account balances.

The second item that results in a reduction in sales is a discount given for prompt payment. A discount given to a customer for early payment is called a sales discount. Such discounts are indicated in the *terms of sale* agreed upon between the seller and the customer.

WARRENDON SPORTS

2579 Base Line Road
Ottawa, ON K2H 7B3
Tel: 684-1287   Fax: 684-5381

CREDIT INVOICE

Sold To
G. Giles
32 Cleary Ave.
Ottawa, ON K2A 4A1

No.   149
Date   June 3, 20—

Quantity	Description	Unit Price	Amount
1	Re: Our Invoice 896—defective hockey stick	$15	$15
	CREDIT		

FIGURE 7-9 Credit invoice recording goods returned by G. Giles

Terms of Sale

The invoice sent by the supplier to the buyer contains the agreed-upon terms for payment of the items purchased. If payment is to be made immediately, the terms are *cash* or *cash on receipt of invoice*. If the buyer is allowed a period of time for payment, the terms are said to be *on account*, or *on credit*, and the sale is called a *credit sale*. Some firms offer the same terms to all customers. Other firms offer a variety of terms. Here is a list of some commonly used terms of sale:

- **C.O.D.:** Payment must be made when the goods are delivered (cash on delivery).
- **Receipt of invoice:** Payment is to be made when the invoice is received.
- **Net 30:** The full amount of the invoice is due 30 days from the invoice date.
- **EOM:** Payment is due at the end of the month.
- **10th following:** Payment is due on the tenth day of the following month.
- **2/10, n/30:** The buyer may deduct a 2 percent discount from the invoice amount *if payment is made within 10 days* from the date of the invoice. The full amount (net) is due in 30 days if the buyer does not pay within 10 days.
- **1/10, n/30, EOM:** A 1 percent discount may be taken if payment is made within 10 days. The full amount must be paid within 30 days after the end of the month.

It is common practice for firms to negotiate the terms of sale with their customers. Favourable terms, for example 60 days, may be offered to a valued customer. Less favourable terms may be offered to customers who buy small amounts of goods or services or who have a very poor record of paying amounts owed.

Transactions 5 and 6 are examples of a sale to a customer that involves a discount for early payment of an invoice.

Transaction 5: Credit Sale Offering Sales Discount

Jun. 5   Sold merchandise to W.P. Mulvihill, Invoice 907, terms 3/10, n/30, $620 on account.

To encourage early payment, terms of 3/10, n/30 were offered to Mulvihill. On June 5, Warrendon's accounts appeared as follows, in T-account form:

Acounts Receivable/W.P. Mulvihill		Sales	
Jun. 5 620			Jun. 5 620

Transaction 6: Recording the Sales Discount

Jun. 15   Received a cheque for $601.40 from W.P. Mulvihill in payment of Invoice 907.

Mulvihill decided that it was worth paying within 10 days because it meant a saving of $18.60 ($0.03 \times \$620 = \$18.60$). Therefore, on June 15, exactly 10 days from the date of the invoice (June 5), payment of $601.40 was made to Warrendon. Warrendon received the cheque and recorded it in their accounts as follows, in T-account form:

Cash		Sales Discounts		Acc. Rec./W.P. Mulvihill	
Jun. 15 601.40		Jun. 15 18.60		Jun. 5 620.00	Jun. 15 620.00

Sales discounts decrease owner's equity and are recorded as debits.

Note that the Sales Discounts account is *debited*. The debit represents a decrease in revenue; therefore, Sales Discounts is a contra revenue account like Sales Returns and Allowances. The company has lost or given away $18.60 to encourage early payment. Note also that Mulvihill's account is credited *for the full amount owing*, $620, even though only $601.40 was received. The $601.40 cancels the full amount owing of $620.

In general journal form these entries would appear as follows:

Jun.	5	Accounts Receivable/W.P. Mulvihill	6 2 0 00	
		Sales		6 2 0 00
		Invoice 907, terms 3/10, n/30.		
	15	Cash	6 0 1 40	
		Sales Discounts	1 8 60	
		Accounts Receivable/W.P. Mulvihill		6 2 0 00
		Payment received for Invoice 907.		

After these two entries are posted, there is a zero balance in Accounts Receivable/W.P. Mulvihill.

Sales discounts reduce the total revenue that will be received from sales. Since a reduction in revenue decreases Capital, discounts given to customers are recorded as debits in the Sales Discounts account. The Sales Discounts amount is subtracted from the Sales figure on the income statement, as shown in Figure 7-10.

For the month of June, Warrendon's total sales were $62 000. However, since some customers returned merchandise (sales returns of $1500), the amount of sales for the month must be decreased by $1500. Also, since sales discounts of $500 were given to customers for early payment, sales must be decreased by $500.

On the income statement, the total of Sales Returns and Allowances and Sales Discounts, $2000 ($1500 + $500), is subtracted from Sales in the revenue section. The result, $60 000, is called *net sales*.

Warrendon Sports
Partial Income Statement
For the month ended June 30, 20—

Revenue		
Sales		$62 000
Less: Sales Returns and Allowances	$1 500	
Sales Discounts	500	2 000
Net Sales		$60 000

FIGURE 7-10 The total of Sales Returns and Allowances and Sales Discounts is subtracted from Sales.

Relationship Between Sales Discounts and Sales Returns

When merchandise is returned to a supplier as unsuitable, a credit invoice is issued to the customer. The discount period for that original sales invoice is calculated from the date of the credit invoice. Following is an example that illustrates this type of situation.

On June 5, Warrendon Sports sold $500 worth of sports equipment to the Parks and Recreation Commission with terms of 2/10, n/30. When the goods were received by Parks and Recreation, it was discovered that part of the order was merchandise that was not ordered and the incorrect merchandise was returned. A credit invoice for $100 was issued by Warrendon on June 10. By which date must the original invoice be paid to take advantage of the discount?

The discount period begins from the date of the credit invoice, which is June 10. If the invoice is paid 10 days from June 10, the discount may be taken by the customer.

Disallowance of Sales Discounts

If a payment is received after the discount period, but with the discount subtracted, it is necessary to inform the customer that the discount is disallowed. The amount of the discount is still owed and remains as a balance on the customer's account.

RECORDING COST OF GOODS SOLD ACCOUNT TRANSACTIONS

In the next part of this unit, the rules of debit and credit for the cost of goods sold accounts will be described. Some sample transactions for Warrendon Sports follow. It is assumed that Warrendon uses the periodic inventory system.

Purchases

The cost of merchandise purchased for resale is recorded in the Purchases account.

The Purchases account is used to record *the cost of merchandise bought for resale.* Goods purchased for resale are one of the major costs of operating a merchandising business. Because costs (like expenses) decrease net income and ultimately decrease owner's equity, Purchases is debited when merchandise is purchased for resale.

Transaction 7: Cash Purchase of Merchandise

Jun. 8   Purchased sports equipment from Schwinn, $500, Cheque 86.

For this transaction, Warrendon Sports has issued a cheque. The two accounts involved are Cash and Purchases. Cash, an asset, decreases and is credited. Purchases, a cost account, is debited because it reduces owner's equity. In general journal format, the entry is:

Jun.	8	Purchases	5 0 0 00	
		Cash		5 0 0 00
		Purchased sports equipment from Schwinn,		
		Cheque 86.		

This transaction is shown in the T-accounts below.

Purchases		Cash	
Jun. 8 500			Jun. 8 500

Transaction 8: Credit Purchase of Merchandise

Jun. 9   Purchased tennis equipment from Spalding Ltd., Invoice 2974, net 30, $200 on account.

The two accounts involved are Purchases and Accounts Payable/Spalding Ltd. Accounts Payable Spalding Ltd. is a liability account; it increases and is credited. Purchases is a cost account and is debited because it reduces owner's equity. Following is the journal entry to record the transaction:

Jun.	9	Purchases	2 0 0 00	
		Accounts Payable/Spalding Ltd.		2 0 0 00
		Purchased tennis equipment, terms		
		net 30 days, Invoice 2974.		

This transaction is shown in the T-accounts below.

	Purchases			Accounts Payable/Spalding Ltd.	
Jun. 8	500			Jun. 9	200
9	200				

Recognition of Costs

As indicated earlier in this text, costs or expenses are recorded *when incurred, not when paid*. Therefore, cash and credit purchases are both recorded in the Purchases account to obtain the correct balance for merchandise purchases for the accounting period.

Purchases Returns and Allowances

If the merchandise purchased from suppliers is unsuitable for resale, it is returned. The accounting entries and procedures for purchases returns are similar to those for sales returns. When the purchaser returns merchandise, a cash refund is given for items previously paid for, and a credit is given for unpaid invoice items. The Purchases Returns and Allowances account, which is often called a *contra cost account* because it reduces the cost of a purchase, is used to record the returns on the books of the purchaser.

The Purchases Returns and Allowances account is used by the buyer to record the return of goods.

Transaction 9: Goods Returned for Cash Refund

Jun. 10   Returned merchandise worth $100, purchased for cash. Received refund cheque for $100 from Schwinn.

To record this transaction, Cash, an asset, is increased with a debit of $100. Purchases Returns and Allowances, because it is a contra cost account, is credited $100. This transaction results in an increase in equity, therefore Purchases Returns and Allowances is credited. The journal entry is as follows:

Jun.	10	Cash	1 0 0 00	
		Purchases Returns and Allowances		1 0 0 00
		To record cash refund received from Schwinn.		

T-accounts for this transaction are shown below.

	Cash			Purchases Returns and Allowances	
Jun. 10	100			Jun. 10	100

Transaction 10: Goods Returned for Credit

Jun. 11 Returned defective tennis equipment purchased for $200, on account, on June 9. Received Credit Invoice 981 for $200 from Spalding Ltd.

Accounts Payable/Spalding Ltd. decreases and is debited. Purchases Returns and Allowances is credited because it decreases Purchases. Following are the journal entry and the T-accounts:

Jun.	11	Accounts Payable/Spalding Ltd.	2 0 0 00	
		Purchases Returns and Allowances		2 0 0 00
		To record Credit Invoice 981 for the return of		
		defective merchandise.		

Accounts Payable/Spalding Ltd.			
Jun. 11	200	Jun. 9	200

Purchases Returns and Allowances	
Jun. 10	100
11	200

Credit Invoice

As mentioned already, the source document that is completed when goods are returned is the credit invoice. It is prepared by the seller and sent to the purchaser. The seller keeps a copy and uses it to enter the amount by which the customer's account is reduced. As well, the seller uses the credit invoice to record the return of merchandise in Sales Returns and Allowances. The purchaser, on the other hand, uses the credit invoice to record the purchase return in its books.

Purchase Discounts

Just as Warrendon offers discounts to its customers for early payment of bills, it receives discounts for the same reason from its creditors. When Warrendon receives such a discount, it is called a *purchase discount*. The next two transactions illustrate how purchase discounts are recorded.

Transaction 11: Credit Purchase with Purchase Discount Available

Jun. 12 Received Invoice 4918 for $500 from Spalding Ltd., terms 2/15, n/30.

Warrendon Ltd. checked the invoice for accuracy and, since the merchandise was received in good condition, the invoice was approved for payment. Warrendon's accounts that record the invoice appeared as follows, in T-account form:

Purchases			
Jun. 12	500		

Accounts Payable/Spalding Ltd.			
		Jun. 12	500

Transaction 12: Recording the Purchase Discount

Jun. 27   Cheque 4822 for $490 to Spalding Ltd. in payment of Invoice 4918.

When Invoice 4918 was received, it was placed in a date file in a folder dated June 27. Then, on June 27, when the payment for $490 was due to Spalding Ltd., it was recorded in Warrendon's accounts as follows, in T-account form:

Accounts Payable/ Spalding Ltd.		Cash	Purchases Discounts
Jun. 27 500	Jun. 12 500	Jun. 27 490	Jun. 27 10

In general journal form, these two entries would be made as follows:

Jun.	12	Purchases	5 0 0 00	
		Accounts Payable/Spalding Ltd.		5 0 0 00
		Invoice 4918, terms 2/15, n/30.		
	27	Accounts Payable/Spalding Ltd.	5 0 0 00	
		Cash		4 9 0 00
		Purchases Discounts		1 0 00
		Paid Invoice 4918, less 2 percent discount.		
		Cheque 4822.		

Purchase discounts reduce the total cost of goods purchased and are recorded as credits in the Purchases Discounts account. Purchases Discounts, like Purchases Returns and Allowances, is often called a contra cost account because it reduces the cost of a purchase.

Purchases Discounts appears in the schedule of cost of goods sold, where it is subtracted from the cost of purchases. This is illustrated in Figure 7-11 on the next page.

Purchase discounts increase owner's equity and are recorded as credits.

Transportation on Purchases

The cost of merchandise purchased for resale is increased by the cost of transporting the merchandise to the retailer's place of business. Transportation-in or Transportation on Purchases is the account used to record this cost. Figure 7-11 shows how transportation adds to the final cost of goods purchased during the accounting period.

5

The Transportation-in account records the transportation charges on merchandise purchased.

Warrendon Sports
Schedule of Cost of Goods Sold
For the month ended June 30, 20—

Merchandise Inventory, June 1			$18 000
Add: Purchases		$42 400	
Less: Purchases Returns			
and Allowances	$8 000		
Purchases Discounts	400	8 400	
Net Purchase Cost		34 000	
Add: Transportation-in		2 000	
Total Cost of Merchandise Purchased			36 000
Cost of Merchandise Available for Sale			54 000
Less: Merchandise Inventory, June 30			20 000
Cost of Goods Sold			$34 000

FIGURE 7-11 Expanded schedule of cost of goods sold, including net purchases calculation and transportation cost

Transaction 13: Transportation-in

Jun. 14   Received Invoice 4685 for $55 from CN Express for transportation of merchandise purchased, net 30.

The invoice received from CN Express is to cover the cost of transporting merchandise from a manufacturer to Warrendon's store. Since this transaction adds to the costs of operating the business, owner's equity is reduced and therefore the Transportation-in account is debited. The liability account Accounts Payable/CN Express increases and is credited. The company has incurred more costs and has another debt. The transaction is shown below in general journal and T-account form:

Jun.	14	Transportation-in	5 5 00	
		Accounts Payable/CN Express		5 5 00
		Invoice 4685 from CN Express for the		
		transportation of merchandise purchased.		

Transportation-in		Accounts Payable/CN Express	
Jun. 14 55			Jun. 14 55

Delivery Expense

The Delivery Expense account is used to record the cost of delivering merchandise to customers.

The cost of delivering merchandise to customers is recorded in Delivery Expense. This account appears in the expenses section of the income statement, as shown in Figure 7-12.

Warrendon Sports
Income Statement
For the month ended June 30, 20—

Revenue
Sales		$62 000	
Less: Sales Returns and Allowances	$1 500		
Sales Discounts	500	2 000	
Net Sales			$60 000

Cost of Goods Sold
Cost of Goods Sold (per schedule)	34 000
Gross Profit	26 000

Operating Expenses
Delivery	2 400
Office	800
Miscellaneous	600
Rent	400
Salaries	2 600
Utilities	400
Total Expenses	7 200
Net Income	$18 800

FIGURE 7-12 Income statement for a merchandising company

Transaction 14: Delivery Expense

Jun. 18   Paid $75 to a local cartage firm for delivering merchandise sold to customers, Cheque 387.

Delivery Expense reduces owner's equity and is debited. Cash decreases and is credited. This transaction is shown below in general journal and T-account form:

Jun.	18	Delivery Expense	7 5 00	
		Cash		7 5 00
		Paid for the delivery of goods to customers, Cheque 387.		

Delivery Expense		Cash	
Jun. 18 75			Jun. 18 75

The 14 sample transactions described in this unit involved the new accounts used by merchandising companies. Look at Figure 7-11, the schedule of cost of goods sold, and Figure 7-12, the income statement. Can you locate the new accounts? What effect do they have on the statements?

DEBIT AND CREDIT SUMMARY

Several new income statement accounts have been introduced in this chapter. Figure 7-13 summarizes the recording of debits and credits in these new accounts.

Transactions that involve five of the new accounts normally cause a decrease in owner's equity. These accounts are Delivery Expense, Purchases, Transportation-in, Sales Returns and Allowances, and Sales Discounts. These five accounts usually have a debit balance.

In previous chapters, you learned that transactions involving the Sales account increase owner's equity and are recorded as credits. Transactions for two other accounts—Purchases Returns and Allowances and Purchases Discounts—also increase owner's equity and are recorded as credits.

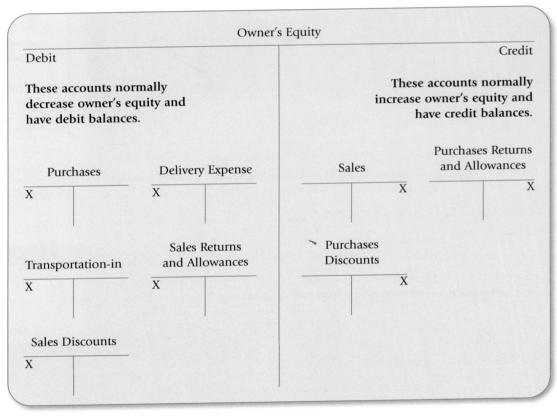

FIGURE 7-13 Summary of debits and credits for the new accounts introduced in this chapter

ALTERNATIVE METHOD OF RECORDING INVENTORIES

Perpetual Inventory Procedures

In this unit, you have learned about the accounting system for firms that use the periodic inventory method. It requires that:

- the purchase of merchandise be recorded as a debit in the Purchases account;
- the value of the Merchandise Inventory account be updated periodically after taking a physical inventory; and
- the cost of goods sold be calculated when this information is required.

A perpetual inventory system requires the establishment of Merchandise Inventory and Cost of Goods Sold accounts.

An increasing number of firms use a perpetual inventory system to account for merchandise inventory. Traditionally, this method was used mainly by retailers who sold high-value articles such as cars or computer equipment. The number of units sold was relatively small when compared to a supermarket or variety store, where there are a great many sales transactions of smaller unit price. Firms that use the perpetual inventory method continually (rather than periodically) update the Merchandise Inventory account. The advantage of this method (over the periodic inventory method) is that the inventory value is current at all times. The disadvantage for many small businesses is that the accounting system is more complex and expensive to operate. The increased use of computer accounting systems in small business permits more firms to enjoy the advantage of timely information for decision making at an affordable cost.

How do the accounting procedures used for the perpetual inventory method differ from the periodic inventory system? Continually updating Merchandise Inventory under a perpetual inventory system requires that:

- the purchase of merchandise be recorded as a debit *directly* in the Merchandise Inventory account;
- a Cost of Goods Sold account be established in the general ledger; and
- when merchandise is sold, the cost of goods sold be determined and recorded by a debit to Cost of Goods Sold and a credit to Merchandise Inventory.

How do the journal entries differ between the two inventory systems? The following examples compare the journal entries for a periodic inventory system with those required to record the same transactions using a perpetual inventory system.

Comparison of Journal Entries

Purchase of Merchandise

Transaction 1: Cash Purchase of Merchandise

Jun. 8 Purchased sports equipment from Schwinn, $500, Cheque 86.

Periodic Inventory System

Jun.	8	Purchases	5 0 0	
		Cash		5 0 0
		Purchased sports equipment from Schwinn, Cheque 86.		

Perpetual Inventory System

Jun.	8	Merchandise Inventory	5 0 0	
		Cash		5 0 0
		Purchased sports equipment from Schwinn, Cheque 86.		

Transaction 2: Credit Purchase of Merchandise

Jun. 9 Purchased tennis equipment from Spalding Ltd., Invoice 2974, net 30, $200 on account.

Periodic Inventory System

Jun.	9	Purchases	2 0 0	
		A/P Spalding Ltd.		2 0 0
		Purchased tennis equipment, terms net 30 days, Invoice 2974.		

Perpetual Inventory System

Jun.	9	Merchandise Inventory	2 0 0	
		A/P Spalding Ltd.		2 0 0
		Purchased tennis equipment, terms net 30 days, Invoice 2974.		

Transaction 3: Goods Returned for Cash Refund

Jun. 10 Received refund cheque for $100 from Schwinn for goods returned.

Periodic Inventory System

Jun.	10	Cash	1 0 0	
		Purch. Ret & Allow.		1 0 0
		To record cash refund received from Schwinn.		

Perpetual Inventory System

Jun.	10	Cash	1 0 0	
		Merchandise Inventory		1 0 0
		To record cash refund received from Schwinn.		

Transaction 4: Goods Returned for Credit

Jun. 11   Received Credit Invoice 981 for $200 from Spalding Ltd. for
             returned tennis equipment.

Periodic Inventory System

Jun.	11	A/P Spalding Ltd.	2 0 0	
		Purch. Ret. & Allow.		2 0 0
		To record Credit Invoice 981		
		for return of defective		
		merchandise.		

Perpetual Inventory System

Jun.	11	A/P Spalding Ltd.	2 0 0	
		Merchandise Inventory		2 0 0
		To record Credit Invoice 981		
		for return of defective		
		merchandise.		

Transaction 5: Credit Purchase with Purchase Discount Available

Jun. 12   Received Invoice 4918 for $500 from Spalding Ltd., terms 2/15, n/30.

Periodic Inventory System

Jun.	12	Purchases	5 0 0	
		A/P Spalding Ltd.		5 0 0
		Invoice 4918, 2/15, n/30.		

Perpetual Inventory System

Jun.	12	Merchandise Inventory	5 0 0	
		A/P Spalding Ltd.		5 0 0
		Invoice 4918, 2/15, n/30.		

Transaction 6: Recording the Purchase Discount

Jun. 27   Sent cheque for $490 to Spalding Ltd. in payment of Invoice 4918.

Periodic Inventory System

Jun.	27	A/P Spalding Ltd.	5 0 0	
		Cash		4 9 0
		Purchases Discounts		1 0
		Paid Invoice 4918, less		
		2 percent discount.		

Perpetual Inventory System

Jun.	27	A/P Spalding Ltd.	5 0 0	
		Cash		4 9 0
		Merchandise Inventory		1 0
		Paid Invoice 4918, less		
		2 percent discount.		

Summary

The periodic inventory system uses Purchases, Purchases Returns and Allowances,
and Purchases Discounts accounts to record the value of merchandise inventory
acquired during the accounting period. The perpetual inventory system immediately
records changes in inventory value directly in the Merchandise Inventory account.

Sale of Merchandise

Transaction 7: Cash Sale

Jun. 2 Sold merchandise costing $750 for $1000, Cash Sales Slips 482–496.

Periodic Inventory System

Jun.	2	Cash	1 0 0 0	
		Sales		1 0 0 0
		To record Cash Sales		
		Slips 482–496.		

Perpetual Inventory System

Jun.	2	Cash	1 0 0 0	
		Sales		1 0 0 0
		To record Cash Sales Slips		
		482–496.		
	2	Cost of Goods Sold	7 5 0	
		Merchandise Inventory		7 5 0
		To record cost of merchandise		
		sold for cash June 2.		

You will notice in the above transaction that two entries are required to record the sale of merchandise in the perpetual inventory system. In the first entry, the sale is recorded at retail price in the Sales account. This entry is exactly the same as under the periodic inventory system and increases the Cash and Sales accounts by the selling price of the merchandise. What accounts have not been brought up to date? Remember that in the perpetual inventory system the Merchandise Inventory and Cost of Goods Sold accounts are maintained perpetually. In the second entry, the merchandise sold is recorded at cost price in the Cost of Goods Sold and Merchandise Inventory accounts. The cost price is recorded as an addition (debit) to Cost of Goods Sold and a subtraction (credit) to Merchandise Inventory.

A similar procedure is used to record sales returns and discounts.

Transaction 8: Credit Sale Offering Sales Discount

Jun. 5 Sold $1000 worth of merchandise on account to Bjorn Huot, Invoice 910, terms 1/10, n/30. The cost of the merchandise is $600.

Periodic Inventory System

Jun.	5	A/R B. Huot	1 0 0 0	
		Sales		1 0 0 0
		Invoice 910, terms 1/10,		
		n/30.		

Perpetual Inventory System

Jun.	5	A/R B. Huot	1 0 0 0	
		Sales		1 0 0 0
		Invoice 910, terms 1/10,		
		n/30.		
	5	Cost of Goods Sold	6 0 0	
		Merchandise Inventory		6 0 0
		To record cost of merchandise		
		sold, Invoice 910.		

Transaction 9: Sales Return on Credit Sale

Jun. 10   B. Huot returned $100 of merchandise from June 5 sale on credit. Cost price of the merchandise is $60, Credit Invoice 76.

Periodic Inventory System

Jun.	10	Sales Ret. & Allow.	1 0 0	
		A/R B. Huot		1 0 0
		Sales return, Credit		
		Invoice 76.		

Perpetual Inventory System

Jun.	10	Sales Ret. & Allow.	1 0 0	
		A/R B. Huot		1 0 0
		Sales return, Credit		
		Invoice 76.		
	10	Merchandise Inventory	6 0	
		Costs of Goods Sold		6 0
		To record cost price of goods		
		returned, Credit Invoice 76.		

Transaction 10: Recording a Sales Discount

Jun. 15   B. Huot forwarded Cheque 1012 for $891 in full payment of Invoice 910, less the return and sales discount.

Periodic Inventory System

Jun.	15	Cash	8 9 1	
		Sales Discounts	9	
		A/R B. Huot		9 0 0
		Received Cheque 1012 in		
		payment of Invoice 910,		
		less return and sales		
		discount.		

Perpetual Inventory System

Jun.	15	Cash	8 9 1	
		Sales Discounts	9	
		A/R B. Huot		9 0 0
		Received Cheque 1012 in		
		payment of Invoice 910,		
		less return and sales		
		discount.		

Note: This entry has no effect on the Merchandise Inventory account.

Inventory Shortages

Using a perpetual inventory system does not guarantee the accuracy of the Merchandise Inventory account. The inventory is still counted at least once a year to discover any discrepancies between the ledger account balance and the actual value of inventory on hand. Differences could arise as a result of theft, spoilage, or recording errors. At this time, an entry is made to adjust the value of Merchandise Inventory under the perpetual inventory system.

Merchandise Inventory (ledger balance)	$24 000
Physical merchandise inventory count	23 700
Merchandise Inventory shortage	$ 300

Transaction 11: Recording an Inventory Shortage

Jun. 30   The ledger balance in Merchandise Inventory indicates $24 000, while a physical inventory totals $23 700.

Perpetual Inventory System

Jun.	10	Inventory Shortage	3 0 0	
		Merchandise Inventory		3 0 0
		To record difference between		
		Merchandise Inventory		
		account and physical		
		inventory.		

The inventory shortage would be charged as an expense of the business, thereby reducing both the company's net income and, ultimately, the owner's equity on the balance sheet.

Summary

The perpetual inventory system uses Sales, Sales Returns Allowances, and Sales Discounts accounts to record the retail value of merchandise inventory sold during the accounting period. This is the same process as the periodic inventory system.

In addition, however, the perpetual inventory system requires the Merchandise Inventory and Cost of Goods Sold accounts to be adjusted by the cost of the merchandise sold. This method of updating when sales occur provides current data on the value of Cost of Goods Sold and Merchandise Inventory throughout the accounting period. Merchandise Inventory always contains the current value of merchandise that is in inventory.

Source Documents for a Perpetual Inventory System

A stock record is used for each type of merchandise on hand.

You have discovered in the previous comparison of inventory systems' journal entries that an additional piece of information is required under a perpetual inventory system: the cost of inventory purchased and sold. The source of this information is a stock record (see Figure 7-14), which may be maintained manually or by computer.

A separate stock record is used for each type of merchandise. It provides a perpetual record of the cost and quantity on hand of each item. Since the expenditure on merchandise inventory is very significant for most merchandising firms, it is very important to minimize the amount of company funds invested in this item. The maximum and minimum quantities listed on the record help to ensure merchandise inventory costs are monitored or controlled and that inventory is neither overstocked, which results in an unnecessary cost to the firm, nor understocked, which could result in lost sales.

Warrendon Sports
Stock Record

Item: Tennis Racket Pro 100 Stock Item XL-2001
Supplier: Sporting Equipment
Address: 347 Tacherson Blvd.
             Montreal, PQ
             H2C 3B3
Telephone: (514) 911-2000
Supplier: Code Number: 922   Usual Terms: Net 30
Min. Quantity: 2   Max. Quantity: 8

DATE	ON ORDER Purchase Req. #	Amount	STOCK RECEIVED Purchase Order #	Units	Unit Cost	Total	STOCK ISSUED Stock Req. #	Units	Unit Cost	Total	BALANCE Units	Unit Cost	Balance
20—													
June 1											4	$65	$260
10							719	1	$65	$65	3	$65	$195
15			4298	3	$70	$210					3	$65	
											3	$70	$405
30							824	1	$65	$65	2	$65	
											3	$70	$340

FIGURE 7-14 Stock record

Questions

1. A business may be classified according to what it does. A company that sells services to customers is called a service business. Name two other types of businesses and describe what they do.
2. Prepare a list of firms in your area, including the names of five companies in each of the three classifications identified in question 1.
3. When you use the periodic inventory method:
   (a) Which account is debited when merchandise is purchased?
   (b) In which account does the value of the merchandise on hand appear?
4. Name the statement (balance sheet, income statement, or schedule of cost of goods sold) and section of the statement in which each of the following items appears. The first item is done for you as an example.

   Example:

Item	Statement	Section
(a) Cash	balance sheet	current asset

   (b) Accounts Receivable
   (c) Sales
   (d) Office Supplies
   (e) Purchases
   (f) Sales Returns and Allowances
   (g) Salaries Expense
   (h) Purchases Returns and Allowances
   (i) Delivery Expense
   (j) Transportation-in
   (k) Building
   (l) Beginning inventory
   (m) Ending inventory
   (n) Sales Discounts
   (o) Purchases Discounts
5. Indicate whether each of the following increases or decreases the cost of the merchandise:
   (a) Transportation-in
   (b) Purchase returns and allowances
   (c) Purchase discounts
6. Explain the difference between a periodic inventory system and a perpetual inventory system.
7. If your firm is using a periodic inventory system:
   (a) Which account is debited when a customer returns merchandise bought on credit? Which account is credited?

(b) Which account is debited when a cash refund is given to a customer for returned merchandise? Which account is credited?

(c) How would these transactions differ if your firm used a perpetual inventory system?

8. Does the balance in Sales Returns and Allowances increase or decrease revenue?

9. What source document is prepared when goods are returned for credit?

10. (a) Do sales discounts increase or decrease revenue?
    (b) Are sales discounts recorded as debits or credits? Why?

11. Merchandise worth $1000 was sold to R. Heidebrecht. The terms of sale were 3/10, n/30. A cheque for $970 was received from Heidebrecht within ten days. When recording the $970 cheque, is Heidebrecht's account credited for $1000 or for $970?

12. Why do businesses offer cash discounts when the final effect is a reduction in net revenue?

13. A cash discount is recorded in the books of the buyer and seller. What account would be used to record the discount in the ledger of (a) the buyer? (b) the seller?

14. What effect does a return have on the discount period offered by a business?

15. What is the difference between the Purchases account and the Office Supplies account?

16. What is the difference between the Purchases account and the Merchandise Inventory account?

17. What account is debited for each of the following items purchased by Johnson's Hardware?
    (a) 1 desk and chair for the office
    (b) 10 ladders
    (c) 1 box of computer paper
    (d) 2000 bags for the check-out counter
    (e) 150 lengths of rope for clothes lines

18. What is the difference between the Delivery Expense account and the Transportation-in account?

19. Name the increase side (debit or credit) for each of the following accounts and give a reason for your answer:

Periodic System: (a) Purchases
                                    (b) Delivery Expense
                                    (c) Transportation-in
                                    (d) Purchases Returns and Allowances
                                    (e) Sales Returns and Allowances
                                    (f) Purchases Discounts
                                    (g) Sales
                                    (h) Sales Discounts

Perpetual System: (i) Merchandise Inventory
                                    (j) Cost of Goods Sold

Exercises Part A

1. In January, Cardinal Gifts had net sales of $4800 and cost of goods sold of $2200.
   (a) What is the gross profit?
   (b) If expenses totalled $1800, what is the net income or net loss?

2. In February, Cardinal Gifts' net sales were $5600 and the cost of goods sold was $3400. Expenses totalled $1960.
   (a) What is the gross profit for February?
   (b) What is the net income or net loss for the month?

3. Cardinal Gifts' March figures were net sales $2300, cost of goods sold $1200, total expenses $1500.
   (a) What is the gross profit for March?
   (b) What is the net income or net loss?

4. Complete the following equations by supplying the missing term:
   (a) Net Sales − Cost of Goods Sold = ?
   (b) ? − Sales Returns and Allowances − Sales Discounts = Net Sales
   (c) Net Income + Operating Expenses = ?
   (d) Cost of Goods Sold + Ending Inventory = ?
   (e) Beginning Inventory + ? − Purchases Returns and Allowances − Purchases Discounts + Transportation-in = Cost of Goods Purchased

5. University Colony Variety uses a periodic inventory system. The cost accounts follow. Prepare a schedule of cost of goods sold for each of the following months.
   (a) January 1: Inventory $5000; Purchases $1000.
       January 31: Inventory $4000.
   (b) February 1: Inventory $4000; Purchases $3000.
       February 28: Inventory $3500.
   (c) March 1: Inventory $3500; Purchases $2900; Purchases Returns and Allowances $300; Purchases Discounts $100; Transportation on Purchases $190.
       March 31: Inventory $3100.
   (d) April 1: Inventory $3100; Purchases $5600; Purchases Returns and Allowances $600; Purchases Discounts $150; Transportation on Purchases $320.
       April 30: Inventory $4700.

6. University Colony Variety uses a periodic inventory system.
   (a) How would the March 31 inventory value of $3100 be determined if this were the end of the fiscal year and financial statements were being prepared?
   (b) How would the April 1 inventory total be determined?

7. Prepare the revenue section of the income statement for University Colony Variety on March 31 from the following information:

- Sales Discounts $150
- Sales $31 000
- Sales Returns and Allowances $350

8. (a) The documents on page 310 were issued by Warrendon Sports.
    (i) Identify the source documents.
    (ii) Prepare a general journal entry to record each source document. Warrendon Sports uses a periodic inventory system.

  (b) Record the following transactions in a journal for Warrendon Sports. Use the accounts Cash, Accounts Receivable, Sales, and Sales Returns and Allowances.

Mar. 1   Cash register summary:
      Cash received from sales, $1200.

    2   Sales invoices:
       No. 301, Nepean Hockey Association, $1950.
       No. 302, Laurier High School, $850.
       No. 303, S. Edgerton, $85.

    3   Cash refund slip:
       No. 29, for $75, refund for the return of a pair of children's skates.

    8   Cash register summary:
       Cash received from sales, $2120.

    9   Credit invoice:
       No. 89, for $250, hockey jackets returned by Nepean Hockey Association—wrong size.

   10   Sales invoices:
       No. 304, Kanata Tennis Club, $875.
       No. 305, H. Burger, $55.

   15   Cash receipts:
       Cheque 483 from Nepean Hockey Association, $1700.
       Cheque 111 from S. Edgerton, $85.

WARRENDON SPORTS

2579 Base Line Road
Ottawa, ON K2H 7B3
Tel: 684-1287   Fax: 684-5381

INVOICE   Order No.

Sold To   **Ship To**
Woodroffe High School   Same
2410 Georgina Drive
Ottawa, ON   K2B 7M8

Date Jan. 4, 20—   Invoice No. 26   Terms Net 30 days   Cash   Charge

Quantity	Description	Unit Price	Amount
30	Hockey Sticks	$20	$600

WARRENDON SPORTS

2579 Base Line Road
Ottawa, ON K2H 7B3
Tel: 684-1287   Fax: 684-5381

CREDIT INVOICE

Sold To   No.   18
Woodroffe High School   Date   Jan. 10, 20—
2410 Georgina Drive
Ottawa, ON   K2B 7M8

Quantity	Description	Unit Price	Amount
5	Re: Our Invoice 26—hockey sticks received in damaged condition	$20	$100

CREDIT

9. (a) On what date is the net amount to be paid for each of the following invoices? Discounts are not to be taken. Use a third column headed "Payment Date" to record your answers.

Invoice Date	Terms
March 5	EOM
March 6	n/30
March 8	n/60
March 14	15 EOM
March 17	2/10, n/30
March 19	C.O.D.
March 20	Receipt of invoice
March 25	1/10, n/30

(b) Determine the amount of the discount, the last day for obtaining the discount, and the amount to be paid for each of the following. All invoices are paid on the last day of the discount period. Record your answer in columns headed:

- Discount Date
- Amount To Be Paid
- Amount of Discount

Amount of Invoice	Terms	Date
$100	2/10, n/30	March 1
500	1/15, n/30	March 2
300	3/10, n/60	March 5
250	2/10, n/30	March 12
175	1/10, n/60	March 25

10. (a) Set up the following T-accounts:

101 Cash
110 Accounts Receivable/C. Beaulne
111 Accounts Receivable/P. Garner
112 Accounts Receivable/L. Trenholme
400 Sales
402 Sales Discounts

(b) Journalize and post the following source documents related to sales made on January 10. Use page 73 of a general journal.

Jan. 10 Sales invoices issued:
          No. 703 to C. Beaulne for $507, terms 2/10, n/30.
          No. 704 to L. Trenholme for $109, terms 2/10, n/30.
          No. 705 to P. Garner for $375, terms 2/10, n/30.
   16 Cheque received from L. Trenholme for $106.82 for Invoice 704 with a sales discount of $2.18.
   20 Cheque received from P. Garner for $367.50 for Invoice 705.
   25 Cheque received from C. Beaulne for $507 for Invoice 703.

11. (a) Journalize the following transactions for Heath's Sports. Use the accounts Cash, Accounts Payable, Purchases, Purchases Returns and Allowances, Transportation-in, Sales Returns and Allowances, and Delivery Expense.

Mar. 1 Purchase invoices:
No. 472 from Cooper Bros., $825.60 for hockey sticks.
No. 7492 from CN Express, $112.50 for transportation charges on purchases.

   2 Cheque copies:
No. 94 to Dinardo Delivery, $275, Invoice 8526 for delivery charges on sales to schools.
No. 95 to Merivale High School, $137 for return of unordered sporting goods, Invoice 246.

  10 Cheque copies:
No. 96 to Spalding Bros., $375 on account.
No. 97 to Tanyss Imports for tennis shoes, $627.50, Invoice 555.

  15 Purchase invoices:
No. 721 from Hofstra Ltd., $1639 for skis.
No. 336 from Smith Transport, $92.75 for transportation charges on purchases.
No. 8742 from Dinardo Delivery, $210.20 for delivery of goods to customers.

  16 Credit note:
No. 231 from Cooper Bros., $116 for damaged goods returned.

(b) Which inventory system is being used by Heath's Sports?

(c) Record the March 1 to 16 transactions using a perpetual inventory system. You will need to use Merchandise Inventory and Cost of Goods Sold accounts. The cost price of merchandise is 60 percent of the selling price.

12. (a) Set up the following T-accounts for Parker's Men's Wear:

101 Cash
112 Accounts Receivable/C. Baker
113 Accounts Receivable/A. Jonsson
114 Accounts Receivable/M. Yu
400 Sales
401 Sales Returns and Allowances
402 Sales Discounts

(b) Journalize and post the following source documents. Use page 94 for the general journal.

Feb. 10 Sales invoices issued:
No. 1035 to A. Jonsson for $2506, terms 2/10, n/30.
No. 1036 to C. Baker for $709, terms 2/10, n/30.
No. 1037 to M. Yu for $1750, terms 2/10, n/30.

  14 Credit Invoice 102 issued to A. Jonsson, $506 for goods returned. Goods were sold to Jonsson on February 10. It was agreed to change the discount period to date from February 14.

  17 Cheque 103 received from C. Baker, $694.82 for Invoice 1036.

  20 Cheque 46 received from M. Yu, $1715 for Invoice 1037.

  24 Cheque 74 received from A. Jonsson, $1960 for Invoice 1035, less Credit Invoice 102 for $506, less discount.

(c) Calculate the net sales for the two-week accounting period.

(d) Prepare general journal entries for the February 10 and 14 transactions using the perpetual inventory system. You will need Merchandise Inventory and Cost of Goods Sold accounts. For the purposes of this question, calculate the cost of the merchandise at 40 percent of sales.

13. Which of the following transactions should be recorded in the Purchases account for Lepp Hardware? If Purchases is not used, which account is?

(a) Purchase of advertising in the *St. Catharines Standard*

(b) Purchase of a new salesperson's car from Nemeth Motors

(c) Purchase of 12 snowblowers from John Deere for a special pre-winter sale

(d) Purchase of a new liability insurance policy

(e) Payment of three months' advance rent on the building

14. The following source documents have been received by Warrendon Sports.

(a) Identify the source documents.

(b) Prepare a general journal entry to record each source document. Use page 49. Warrendon Sports uses a periodic inventory system.

BROOMBALL MANUFACTURING

331 Marion Street
Oshawa, ON L1J 3A8
Tel: 718-3287   Fax: 718-3249

SOLD TO	SHIPPED TO	
Warrendon Sports	Same	WI-60505
2579 Base Line Road		PLEASE QUOTE THIS NUMBER
Ottawa, ON K2H 7B3		WHEN REFERRING TO OR PAYING
		THIS INVOICE

SHIP VIA	PPD.	COLL.	CUSTOMER'S ORDER NO.	TERMS		SALESPERSON	DATE MO.	DAY	YEAR
Pick-up			1214	Net 30 days		Phone	03	10	20—

NO.	DESCRIPTION	QUANTITY	UNIT	AMOUNT
25	Pairs of Broomball shoes	25	$70	$1750
			PLEASE PAY THIS AMOUNT	$1750

WILSON OFFICE SUPPLIERS

6350 Main Street
Ottawa, ON K1S 1E7
Tel: 687-1987   Fax: 687-2190

Warrendon Sports   SHIP TO   Same   INVOICE NUMBER
2579 Base Line Road   T110982
Ottawa, ON K2H 7B3

DATE	SHIP VIA	ORDER NUMBER	TERMS
Mar. 22, 20—	—	1215	n/30

QUANTITY		PRODUCT NO./DESCRIPTION	UNIT PRICE	AMOUNT
ORDERED	SHIPPED			
1	1	Pentium IV Personal Computer	$2879	$2879

THIS IS YOUR INVOICE
NO OTHER WILL BE SENT

SPORTING EQUIPMENT

347 Tachereau Blvd.
Montréal, Québec H2C 3B3
Tel: 419-8190   Fax: 419-5872

SOLD TO   Warrendon Sports   SHIPPED TO   Same   INVOICE
          2579 Base Line Road   NUMBER
          Ottawa, ON K2H 7B3   TR89-6153

Cust. Order No.	Our Order No.	Date Received	Date Shipped	Shipped Via	Invoice Date
1190	16150	Mar. 13, 20—	Apr. 4, 20—	Our Truck	Apr. 10, 20—

	Terms	F.O.B.	Salesperson
	Net 30 days		

Qty.	Description	Price	Total
50	Dolphin Clear Goggles	$12.50	$625.00

PRICES SUBJECT TO
CHANGE WITHOUT NOTICE   ORIGINAL INVOICE

OVERLAND TRANSPORT

Montréal
Ottawa
Toronto

HEAD OFFICE:
1473 Blake Road
Montréal, Québec H3J 1E4
Tel: 418-1197   Fax: 418-3862

Shipper:
Broomball Manufacturing
331 Marion Street
Oshawa, ON   L1J 3A8

Consignee:
Warrendon Sports
2579 Base Line Road
Ottawa, ON   K2H 7B3

TERMS Net 30 days   DATE   Mar. 12, 20—   Inv. No.   CK 4376

Quantity	Containers	Mass	Rate	Amount
3	Boxes	20 kg	$3.75/kg	$75.00
			Pay this amount	$75.00

CITY DELIVERY

576 Blythe Rd.
Ottawa, ON   K2A 3N6
Tel: 525-4187   Fax: 525-3897

Charge
Warrendon Sports
2579 Base Line Road
Ottawa, ON   K2H 7B3

Deliver to
Carleton Broomball League
1476 Braeside Street
Ottawa, ON   K1H 7J4

INV. NO. T-7437   TERMS Net 30 days   DATE Mar. 20, 20—

Description	Amount
5 Boxes	$55.65

CREDIT INVOICE

SPORTING EQUIPMENT

347 Tachereau Blvd.
Montréal, Québec H2C 3B3
Tel: 419-8190   Fax: 419-5872

TO Warrendon Sports   April 12, 20—
2579 Base Line Road
Ottawa, ON   K2H 7B3   **CREDIT NUMBER**   1195

WE CREDIT YOUR ACCOUNT AS SPECIFIED BELOW

Re: Invoice TR89-6153, dated April 10, 20—
6 damaged Dolphin Goggles @ $12.50 $75.00
TOTAL CREDIT DUE $75.00

Exercises Part B

15. (a) Identify which source documents in exercise 14 would be recorded differently if Warrendon Sports decided to convert their accounting system to the perpetual inventory method.

(b) Prepare the general journal entries that would be needed under this system.

16. (a) Set up the following T-accounts for Inderjit Singh Enterprises. This firm uses a perpetual inventory system.

101	Cash
120	Merchandise Inventory
202	Accounts Payable/CN Express
203	Accounts Payable/Greater Wholesalers
204	Accounts Payable/Winnipeg Manufacturers
504	Transportation on Purchases

(b) Journalize and post the following documents related to purchase invoices received on August 10. Use page 107 for the general journal.

Aug. 10 Purchase invoices:
No. 1147 from Greater Wholesalers for $3507, dated August 8, terms 3/10, n/30.
No. 8692 from CN Express for $105, dated August 9, payable on receipt of invoice.

No. 1888 from Winnipeg Manufacturers for $7017, dated August 7, terms 2/10, n/30.

11   Cheque 331 issued to CN Express for $105.

16   Credit Invoice 349 dated August 14, from Greater Wholesalers, for $215 worth of goods received in damaged condition. Discount period to begin August 14.

17   Cheque 332 for $6876.66 issued to Winnipeg Manufacturers to pay invoice dated August 7.

24   Cheque 333 for $3193.24 to Greater Wholesalers for invoice dated August 8, less credit invoice.

17. Following are the March sales figures for Gizmos and Gadgets: Sales $28 300; Sales Returns and Allowances $1300; Sales Discounts $275.

(a)   What is the net sales total for March?

(b)   Determine the cost of goods sold for March for Gizmos and Gadgets from the following:
Beginning Inventory $35 000; March purchases $17 600; Purchases Returns and Allowances $1300; Transportation-in $875; Ending inventory $37 000.

(c)   Determine the March gross profit for Gizmos and Gadgets using the answers from parts (a) and (b) of this exercise.

18. (a)   Prepare a schedule of cost of goods sold for Gizmos and Gadgets for May from the following figures:
Beginning inventory $37 900; Purchases $18 800; Purchases Returns and Allowances $800; Purchases Discounts $210; Transportation-in $975; Ending inventory $35 900.

(b)   Prepare an income statement for Gizmos and Gadgets for May using the cost of goods sold from part (a) and the following figures: Sales $38 750; Sales Returns and Allowances $950; Sales Discounts $180; Salaries $6800; Rent $1850; Delivery Expense $900; Other Expenses $2100.

UNIT 15 Provincial Sales Tax and Goods and Services Tax

What Learning You Will Demonstrate

On completion of this unit, you will be able to:

- calculate the Goods and Services Tax/Harmonized Sales Tax (GST/HST) on sales;
- calculate the amount of GST/HST that is remitted to the federal government;
- calculate the provincial sales tax (PST) on retail sales using the base price or the base price plus GST; and
- journalize transactions that involve GST and PST, or HST.

INTRODUCING SALES TAXES

In Canada, the federal and most provincial governments impose sales taxes. The companies that sell taxable items become, by law, the governments' agents for the collection of sales tax. A customer pays sales tax to a company and the company sends the money to the government(s). Manufacturers, wholesalers, and most retailers are required to register with the federal government to collect the national Goods and Services Tax or Harmonized Sales Tax (in certain Maritime provinces). Retailers are also required to register with their provincial governments to receive a provincial sales tax licence. In most provinces, retailers collect both provincial sales tax and federal Goods and Services Tax or the Harmonized Sales Tax.

The Business Number

The federal government uses a Business Number system to track its dealings with businesses involving corporate income tax, import/export, payroll deductions, and Goods and Services Tax (GST)/Harmonized Sales Tax (HST). This one number is used to record things such as income tax paid, GST/HST owed and paid, and Employment Insurance premiums and Canada Pension Plan premiums collected.

Request for a Business Number (form)

The Canada Customs and Revenue Agency registers companies and issues the Business Number. To obtain a Business Number, part A (the first page) of the Request for a Business Number form is completed (see Figure 7-15 on page 319). The second page, Part B of the form (see Figure 7-16 on page 320), is where the applicant provides the information for the GST/HST account. The government creates a GST/HST account for businesses that complete part B.

The Federal Goods and Services Tax

GST is a federal tax on the sale of most goods and services.

The federal Goods and Services Tax is a simple concept that becomes more complex in actual practice. For the purposes of this text, only the basic GST principle and introductory accounting procedures will be discussed.

REQUEST FOR A BUSINESS NUMBER (BN)

Revenue Canada / Revenu Canada

BN: [| | | | | | | | | | |]
FOR OFFICE USE ONLY

Complete this form if you have a new business and you need to apply for a Business Number (BN). If you are a sole proprietor with more than one business, your BN will apply to all your businesses. **All businesses have to complete Parts A and F.** For more information, see the pamphlet called *The Business Number and Your Revenue Canada Accounts.*
- To apply for a GST/HST account, complete Part B.
- To apply for a payroll deductions account, complete Part C.
- To apply for an import/export account, complete Part D.
- To apply for a corporate income tax account, complete Part E.

Part A - General information

A1 | Identification of business (For a corporation, enter the name and address of the head office.)

Name

Language
☐ English ☐ French

Operating, trading, or partnership name (if different from name above): If you have more than one business or if your business operates under more than one name, enter the name(s) here. If you need more space, include the information on a separate piece of paper.

Business address | Postal or zip code

Mailing address (if different from business address) | Postal or zip code

Contact person (If you choose to name a contact for your account, see our pamphlet for more information.)
First name | Last name | Language | Title | Telephone number | Fax number
☐ English ☐ French | | ( ) | ( )

Financial institution – Enter the name and address of the branch you use for your business transactions.

A2 | Client ownership type

☐ **Individual**   If so, are you: ☐ a sole proprietor? ☐ a foster parent? ☐ a domestic employer?
☐ **Partnership**
☐ **Other**   Are you incorporated?   ☐ Yes   ☐ No   (All corporations have to provide a copy of the certificate of incorporation or amalgamation.)

Check the box that best describes your type of operation.

☐ Charity ☐ Union ☐ Association ☐ Financial institution ☐ University/school ☐ Municipal government
☐ Society ☐ Hospital ☐ Non-profit ☐ Religious body ☐ Trust ☐ None of the above

Enter the following information for the sole proprietor, domestic employer, or foster parent. Also enter this information for the partner(s), corporate director(s), or officer(s) of your business. If you need more space, include the information on a separate piece of paper.

First name | Last name | Home telephone number ( ) | Home fax number ( )
Title | | Social insurance number | Work telephone number ( ) | Work fax number ( )
First name | Last name | Home telephone number ( ) | Home fax number ( )
Title | | Social insurance number | Work telephone number ( ) | Work fax number ( )

A3 | Major commercial activity

Clearly describe your major business activity.

Specify up to three main products that you mine, manufacture, or sell, or services you provide or contract. Also, please estimate the percentage of revenue that each product or service represents.
%
%
%

A4 | Requestor information (Complete this area if you are registering for a BN on behalf of a client.)

Your name (please print) | Your company's name (please print) | Year | Month | Day

RC1 E (98) | (Ce formulaire existe en français.) | 3417 | **Canada**

FIGURE 7–15 Request for a Business Number form

A5	GST/HST information		
Do you plan to sell or provide goods or services in Canada? If *no*, you **cannot** register for GST/HST. If you *export*, you may be deemed to be selling or providing goods or services in Canada. See our pamphlet for details.		Yes ☐	No ☐
Will your annual **worldwide** GST/HST taxable sales (including those of any associates) be more than $30,000, or $50,000 if you are a public service body?		Yes ☐	No ☐
Are you a non-resident who solicits orders in Canada for prescribed goods to be sent by mail or courier and whose worldwide GST/HST taxable sales will be more than $30,000? Prescribed goods include printed materials such as books, newspapers, periodicals, and magazines. If yes to either of the above questions, you **must** register for GST/HST.		Yes ☐	No ☐
Do you operate a taxi or limousine service?		Yes ☐	No ☐
Are you a non-resident who charges admission directly to audiences at activities or events in Canada?		Yes ☐	No ☐
If *yes* to either of the above, you **must** register for GST/HST, even if your worldwide GST/HST taxable sales will be $30,000 or less.			
Are all the goods or services you sell or provide exempt from GST/HST? If *yes*, you **cannot** register for GST/HST. See our pamphlet for an explanation of exempt goods and services.		Yes ☐	No ☐
Do you wish to register voluntarily? See our pamphlet for more information.		Yes ☐	No ☐

Part B – GST/HST account information

Complete sections B1 to B5 if you need a BN GST/HST account.

Do you want us to send you GST/HST information? ☐ Yes   ☐ No

B1	GST/HST account Identification (Check box ☐ if same as in Part A1 on page 1.)

Mailing address for GST/HST purposes	c/o	Account name (enter name to which we should address correspondence.)
	Address	
		Postal or zip code

Contact person (If you choose to name a contact for your account, see our pamphlet for more information.)

First name	Last name	Language
		☐ English ☐ French

Title	Telephone number ( )	Fax number ( )	

B2	Filing Information

Enter the fiscal year-end of your business. ☐☐ Month ☐☐ Day

Estimate your annual GST/HST taxable sales in Canada (including those of any associates in Canada).

☐ $30,000 or less
☐ more than $30,000 to $200,000
☐ more than $200,000 to $500,000
☐ more than $500,000 to $1,000,000
☐ more than $1,000,000 to $6,000,000
☐ more than $6,000,000

Enter the effective date of registration for GST/HST purposes.

☐☐☐☐ Year ☐☐ Month ☐☐ Day

B3	Election respecting your reporting period

If your estimated total annual GST/HST taxable sales and revenues are $500,000 or less, you will be assigned **an annual reporting period**. If your estimated total annual GST/HST sales and revenues are more than $500,000 to $6,000,000, you will be assigned **a quarterly reporting period**. If you have more than $6,000,000 in taxable sales and revenues, you **must** file monthly. If you wish to file more frequently than your assigned period, please check one of the following boxes: ☐ Quarterly ☐ Monthly
You cannot elect to file less frequently than your assigned reporting period.

B4	Type of operation

01 ☐ Government, municipality   02 ☐ Registered charity (provide your registration no.)   03 ☐ Qualifying non-profit organization   04 ☐ Listed financial institution   05 ☐ University, school board, hospital

06 ☐ Joint venture operator (not a partnership)   07 ☐ Non-resident who charges admission directly to spectators or attendees   08 ☐ Non-resident who carries on commercial activities in Canada   09 ☐ Taxi or limousine operator   99 ☐ None of the above

B5	Province or territory (Check the boxes below to indicate the provinces or territories in which you carry on commercial activities or maintain a permanent establishment.)

	Commercial activity	Permanent establishment		Commercial activity	Permanent establishment		Commercial activity	Permanent establishment		Commercial activity	Permanent establishment
Alberta	☐	☐	New Brunswick	☐	☐	Nova Scotia	☐	☐	Quebec	☐	☐
British Columbia	☐	☐	Newfoundland	☐	☐	Ontario	☐	☐	Saskatchewan	☐	☐
Manitoba	☐	☐	Northwest Territories	☐	☐	Prince Edward Island	☐	☐	Yukon Territory	☐	☐

FIGURE 7–16 GST/HST account information page

The GST is a 7 percent tax charged on most sales of services or merchandise within Canada. Manufacturers, wholesalers and retailers of merchandise, and service providers must add the GST to their selling prices.

Selling Price of Good or Service	$100
7% GST	7
Total Cost	$107

A number of items, such as basic groceries, prescription drugs, health and dental services, day-care services, residential rents, and education services, are exempt, or free, from GST.

The GST is collected by businesses that are registered with Canada Customs and Revenue Agency to collect the tax. The tax is then forwarded to the federal government.

How Does the GST Work?

A product can be bought and sold by several businesses before you, the consumer, actually purchase the item. For example, a mountain bike is purchased by a wholesaler from the manufacturer. The wholesaler sells the bike to a retailer, who in turn sells the bike to you. Each of these businesses must add 7 percent GST to the selling price. However, the federal government receives only 7 percent of the *final* sales price. How is this possible? It's possible because the business sends the federal government only the difference between GST collected and GST paid. A business collects 7 percent GST on the price of all eligible goods and services sold. Before remitting (sending) the tax collected to the federal government, the business deducts all GST paid to other businesses when purchasing goods and services. This deduction is called an input tax credit. The input tax credit ensures that the federal government is not receiving more than 7 percent GST on the final sales price of the good or service that you purchase. Let's follow the mountain bike through each step and see how the GST system actually works:

The input tax credit is the amount of GST a business pays other businesses when it buys goods or services.

Mountain Bike				
	Sale Price	GST Collected	GST Input Tax Credit	Amount Remitted
Materials Sold to Manufacturer	$100	$ 7	$ 0	$ 7
Mountain Bike Sold to Wholesaler	400	28	(7)	21
Mountain Bike Sold to Retailer	500	35	(28)	7
Mountain Bike Sold to Customer	700	49	(35)	14
Total GST Remitted to Federal Government				$49

In the example just presented, the retailer sold the mountain bike for $700 plus $49 GST. The retailer, however, sent only $14 ($49 GST minus $35 input tax credit) to the federal government. This represented the GST collected from the customer minus the GST paid on the purchase of the bike from the wholesaler. The federal government received in total 7 percent of the retail sale price, or $49, in GST from all the businesses involved in getting the product to the final consumer. In this chapter, we will discuss the basic accounting procedures used by retailers to record the federal GST, as well as provincial retail sales tax.

Provincial Retail Sales Tax (PST)

All provinces, except Alberta, impose a sales tax on retail sales. The tax is charged on the price of goods sold to consumers. In most provinces, the tax is applied only to tangible commodities, although a few services (such as telephone service) are taxed. Such items as food, drugs, children's clothes, school supplies, and farm equipment are exempt from sales tax in many provinces. PST is charged in addition to GST collected by the federal government. It can be calculated on the base price only or on the base price plus GST (see page 325).

In Ontario, exempt items include food products, children's clothes, books, and shoes valued under $30. The retail sales tax on accommodation, for example hotel and motel rooms, is 5 percent, and on liquor is 10 percent.

Each province determines the rate of sales tax to be charged, and these rates change from time to time. At the time of writing, the following rates were in effect:

Alberta	0%
British Columbia	7%
Manitoba	7%
Ontario	8%
Prince Edward Island	10%
Quebec	7.5%
Saskatchewan	6%

Nova Scotia, New Brunswick, and Newfoundland have harmonized (blended or combined) their provincial sales tax with the GST to create the Harmonized Sales Tax (HST). The HST is a 15 percent tax that combines the federal government's 7 percent GST with a uniform PST of 8 percent to provide one tax instead of two separate taxes. The HST has the same operating procedures and rules as the GST.

The Harmonized Sales Tax is a combination of the GST and provincial retail sales tax that has the same operating rules as the GST.

In those provinces not subject to HST, a retailer who sells taxable items is required by law to collect the PST. Each retailer is issued a retail sales tax vendor's permit or licence by his or her respective provincial government. In Figure 7-17 on the next page, the permit number is shown on the remittance form.

The retailer collects the tax when goods are sold to consumers, and then sends the tax to the provincial government. This is usually done each month for the previous month's collection. Figure 7-17 is the form completed in Ontario by retailers when sales tax is remitted to the provincial government.

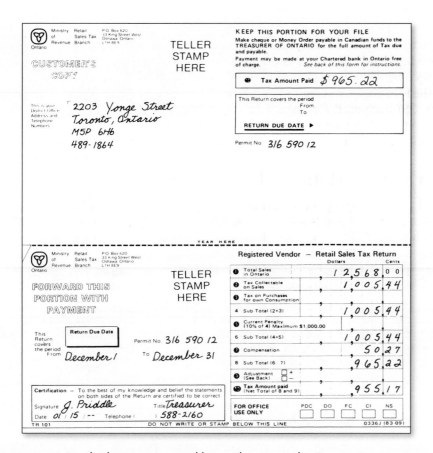

FIGURE 7-17 Retail sales tax return used by retailers to pay the Ontario Government

Provincial Sales Tax Exemptions

Figure 7-18 on the following page illustrates an invoice for a sale of paper. Notice the sales tax exempt stamp on the invoice. The buyer, Wilco Printers, uses the paper to produce items it prints, such as greeting cards. The paper becomes part of the greeting cards. PST is charged only when the cards are sold. It would be unfair to collect tax on the paper and then again on the cards. That would result in paper being taxed twice, once as paper and then a second time as part of the cards. When Wilco ordered the paper, it indicated that the paper was exempt from PST by supplying the sales tax licence number. The number has been placed on the invoice by the seller, Fine Paper Supply, to indicate the material is exempt from sales tax because this is not the final (end) sale of the paper.

FINE PAPER SUPPLY INC.
Division of Ontario Printer's Supplies Inc.
4800 Keele Street, Toronto ON M3J 2K8 (416) 555-4900
BRANCHES:

YOUR
PAPER
SOURCE

50 Talbot St., Ingersoll, ON N4A 2S4 (519) 333-4900

273 Ancaster Blvd., Ottawa, ON K1B 4S8 (613) 777-4900

Wilco Printers
1825 Valentine Road
Scarborough, ON
M1P 4A3

INVOICE DATE
Dec. 22, 20—

INVOICE NO.
04918

TERMS	PROV. SALES TAX	ORDER NO.	SLMM NO.	ACCOUNT NO.	CUSTOMER ORDER NO.
2/10, n/30	13169012	04153	72	20-5072	1209

ITEM NO.	DESCRIPTION	QUANTITY SHEETS OR UNITS	NET MASS	CODE	UNIT PRICE	CODE	AMOUNT
45984	Offset white 1 m x 1.5 m	7000	910	1	$61.60/ per 1000	3	$431.20

SALES TAX EXEMPT

Special terms for this invoice: N/30

CODE 1. KG 2. HUNDRED 3. THOUSAND 4. EACH 5. LITRE

INVOICE

CREDIT

INVOICE AMOUNT $431.20
E. & O. E.
CREDIT AMOUNT

FIGURE 7-18 Sales tax licence numbers are required for sales tax exemption.

Calculating GST and PST

When you purchased your mountain bike in the previous example, you saw that
the selling price was $700 plus $49 GST. In all provinces, except Alberta, the final
amount you will have to pay for the bike will also include PST. How much would
you finally pay in a province where the retail sales tax is 8 percent?

Calculation of GST and PST

Mountain Bike Selling Price (Base price)	$700
Goods and Services Tax (0.07 × $700)	49
	749
Provincial Sales Tax (0.08 × $700)	56
Final Price to Customer	$805

This method of calculating sales tax eliminates the payment of tax on tax since both GST and PST are calculated as a percent of the base price.

Some provinces calculate PST as a percent of the base price plus GST. Using the example above, the new figures are:

Calculation of GST and PST

Mountain Bike Selling Price (Base price)	$700.00
Goods and Services Tax (0.07 × $700)	49.00
	749.00
Provincial Sales Tax (0.08 × $749)	59.92
Final Price to Customer	$808.92

Notice that the final price to the customer is higher when this alternate method is used.

In Nova Scotia, New Brunswick, and Newfoundland, which have the HST, there is only one tax calculation.

Calculation of HST

Mountain Bike Selling Price	$700
Harmonized Sales Tax (0.15 × $700)	105
Final Price to the Customer	$805

GST and PST Payable Accounts

As a retailer, Warrendon Sports is responsible for collecting both the GST and PST from customers. The accounting system must include the accounts necessary to record both GST collected from customers and GST paid to suppliers (input tax credits) to calculate the correct amount to remit to the federal government. Remember, Warrendon will remit GST collected minus GST paid. In addition, an account is required to record the PST collected for the provincial government.

This sounds complicated, but the ledger requires only three new accounts: PST Payable, GST Payable, and GST Refundable. Why are two GST accounts necessary? You must have information on GST collected from customers and paid by your firm to suppliers.

> GST Collected   −   GST Paid   =   Net GST Owed
>
> GST Payable   −   GST Refundable   =   GST Due to Federal
>   Government

How would Warrendon Sports record the sale of the mountain bike in the previous example? The selling price was $700, the GST at 7 percent was $49, and the PST was $56 calculated on the base price. The customer paid a total of $805 for the bike. Warrendon would record the following journal entry:

Jun.	18	Cash	8 0 5 00	
		Sales		7 0 0 00
		GST Payable		4 9 00
		PST Payable		5 6 00
		Cash sale of bike.		

PST Payable

PST Payable is a liability account.

The amount of sales tax collected is owed to the provincial government. The sales tax collected during the month is credited in PST Payable (or Sales Tax Payable). This account is a liability. It increases when taxable goods are sold and taxes are collected. It decreases when the seller of taxable goods sends the tax to the provincial government.

PST Payable			PST Payable	
Jan.	3	73.43	Debit	Credit
	4	35.62	Decrease	Increase
	6	55.62		
	9	41.74	**Debit the account**	**Credit the account**
	10	31.50	**when sales tax**	**when taxable**
			is remitted to	**goods are sold**
			the government.	**and taxes are**
	31	43.65		**collected.**
		1 243.62		

At the end of the month, the amount of tax collected is calculated. In January, Warrendon collected $1243.62 in PST and must remit this amount to the Provincial Treasurer. *Note:* In some provinces, the remittance is made to the Minister of Finance. You should check the correct title for your province. When the cheque is issued, the following journal entry is made:

Feb.	15	PST Payable		1 2 4 3 62	
		Cash			1 2 4 3 62
		Cheque 299 to Provincial Treasurer for			
		January sales tax collections.			

Recording Sales Tax Commission

Several provinces pay commission to companies in return for the collection of sales tax. For example, British Columbia pays a commission of 3 percent on the first $2500 of tax collected and 1 percent of the tax collected over $2500. In Ontario, the retailer receives $20 when the tax sent to the government is between $20 and $400. On tax amounts over $400, the retailer receives 5 percent of the tax remitted (see line 7, "Compensation," in Figure 7-17 on page 323. A maximum of $1500 is available in any one year.

The commission earned by a company is usually recorded in Miscellaneous Revenue or Sales Tax Commission.

On June 15, Western Supply Ltd. of Vancouver, British Columbia, has a balance of $300 in PST Payable. This balance represents retail sales tax collected from customers in May. When Western Supply remits the tax to the provincial government, it keeps a 3 percent commission of $9 (0.03 × $300 = $9). The entry, in general journal form, to record the payment to the government and the commission earned is:

Jun.	15	PST Payable		3 0 0 00	
		Cash			2 9 1 00
		Sales Tax Commission			9 00
		To remit May sales tax and to record commission			
		earned.			

GST Payable

The amount of GST collected is also a liability. It is owed to the federal government. The amount of GST collected during the month is credited to the GST Payable account.

GST Payable

Jan.	3	93.87
	4	42.50
	6	61.75
	9	54.26
	10	38.60
	31	49.72
		1 426.10

Is this the amount of tax that is sent to the federal government? No. The retailer remits GST collected *minus* GST paid. How does Warrendon record GST paid (input tax credit) on goods or services purchased for the business?

GST Input Tax Credit

Unit 14 of this chapter introduced the new accounts used by a merchandising company. You learned that the Purchases account is used to record the cost of merchandise bought for resale. To simplify the introduction of these accounts, GST was not included in the discussion. The following example will show how the GST on the purchase of merchandise is recorded. When Warrendon Sports purchased the mountain bike from a wholesaler, it received the following cash sale slip:

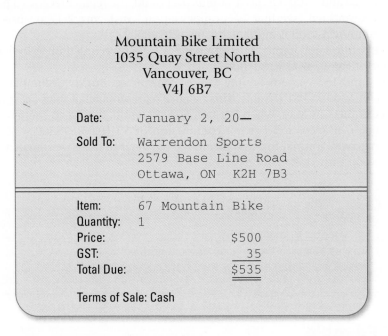

Mountain Bike Limited
1035 Quay Street North
Vancouver, BC
V4J 6B7

Date:	January 2, 20—
Sold To:	Warrendon Sports 2579 Base Line Road Ottawa, ON K2H 7B3

Item:	67 Mountain Bike	
Quantity:	1	
Price:		$500
GST:		35
Total Due:		$535

Terms of Sale: Cash

FIGURE 7-19 Cash purchase of merchandise

What is the amount recorded in the Purchases account? The $500 cost price. Why is the $35 GST not recorded as part of the cost price? As you learned earlier, the retailer deducts the GST paid to suppliers from the GST collected from the consumer before remitting the tax to the federal government. Therefore, Warrendon receives an input tax credit for the $35 GST paid to Mountain Bike Limited. How will Warrendon record the invoice shown in Figure 7-19? The journal entry will be:

Jan.	2	Purchases	5 0 0	00		
		GST Refundable	3 5	00		
		Cash			5 3 5	00
		Cash purchase of mountain bike.				

The amount of GST paid to suppliers is debited to the GST Refundable account.

GST Refundable

Jan.	1	35.00
	4	28.00
	8	42.00
	9	14.00
	11	63.00
	31	49.00
		980.63

GST Refundable is a *contra liability account* since it reduces the amount of a liability. The GST Payable balance ($1426.10) is reduced by the balance in GST Refundable ($980.63) to determine the net amount owed ($445.47). This amount is forwarded to the federal government.

GST Refundable			GST Payable		
Jan.	1	35.00	Jan.	3	93.87
	4	28.00		4	42.50
	8	42.00		6	61.75
	9	14.00		9	54.26
	11	63.00		10	38.60
	31	49.00		31	49.72
		980.63			1 426.10

Jan.	31	GST Payable	1 4 2 6 10	
		GST Refundable		9 8 0 63
		Cash		4 4 5 00
		January GST remitted, Cheque 7369.		

In the event the GST paid to suppliers exceeds the GST collected from customers, the business is able to apply for a refund from the federal government.

Recording GST for a Service Business

The GST also applies to services sold and purchased. A service business would follow the same basic accounting procedures you have just learned for a merchandising business. The business collects GST from its customers on the sale of the service, deducts GST paid to suppliers, and remits the difference to the federal government.

Accounting Procedures and the HST

Recording transactions for the HST is the same as recording transactions for the GST, except with the HST only one account is used for both the federal GST and the provincial sales tax. Here is an example:

GST Entry for Sale on Account $100, GST $7, PST $8, Invoice 0382, Bradford Ltd.

Dec.	1	Accounts Receivable		1 1 5 00	
		Sales			1 0 0 00
		PST Payable			8 00
		GST Payable			7 00
		To record Invoice 0382, Bradford Ltd.			

HST Entry for Sale on Account $100, HST $15, Invoice 0382, Bradford Ltd.

Dec.	1	Accounts Receivable		1 1 5 00	
		Sales			1 0 0 00
		HST Payable			1 5 00
		To record Invoice 0382, Bradford Ltd.			

Quick Method of Accounting

The Quick Method simplifies the procedures for paying GST/HST to the federal government. *This method is used by small businesses with annual sales of less than $200 000.* With the Quick Method, the GST/HST is collected on sales in the usual way. However, the change occurs when you calculate the amount to send to the federal government.

Quick Method Accounting Procedures for GST/HST

The Quick Method is a system for recording GST/HST that requires small business owners to collect the full GST/HST, but does not require them to keep track of input tax credits to calculate the amount of tax to remit to the federal government.

The procedures followed with the Quick Method are:

- collect the 7 percent GST (15 percent HST) on all sales;
- multiply the total amount of the sales plus GST by 5 percent, for example, to determine the GST owing to the government (10 percent for the HST); and
- send the tax owing to the government.

Quick Method Tax Rate

The 5 percent rate (10 percent for HST) shown in the example above applies to businesses such as delivery services, dry cleaners, auto repair shops, caterers, fast food outlets, travel agents, taxi drivers, photographers, and painting contractors. There are other rates for different categories of businesses. The rates and other conditions applicable to use of this method can be obtained from the Canada Customs and Revenue Agency booklet *General Information for GST/HST* or from the Agency web site.

Input Tax Credits and the Quick Method

When a business uses the Quick Method, it does not need to keep track of the GST/HST it pays or owes on purchases. The lower Quick Method rate sent to the federal government takes into account the GST/HST paid on purchases and reduces the amount of accounting record keeping that must be done.

Remitting GST/HST Using the Quick Method

Suppose that for a GST reporting period that closes at the end of February, a company made sales of $10 000 on which $700 (7 percent) GST was collected. The total sales plus GST are $10 700. When the business sends the GST to the federal government (using the Quick Method), this procedure is followed.

Amount of sales plus GST for the period, $10 700

Assume that the GST Quick Method rate is 5 percent.

Amount of GST to be sent to the government: 0.05 × $10 700 = $535

Journal entry:

Mar.	31	GST Payable		5 3 5 00	
		Cash			5 3 5 00
		To remit the February GST, Cheque 685.			

GST, PST, and Cash Discounts

A $500 sale of merchandise is made on account to J. Woodsworth. The GST at 7 percent is $35, making a total of $535. PST at 8 percent on $500 is $40. The total amount of the sale is $575. The terms of sale are 2/10, n/30.

Suppose that Woodsworth pays for the merchandise within 10 days to take advantage of the 2 percent cash discount. A question arises concerning the amount of the discount. Should it be 2 percent of the merchandise only ($500) or 2 percent of the total owing ($575)? There are arguments for both alternatives. In actual practice, it is generally accepted that the customer is allowed to take a discount of 2 percent of $575, which is $11.50 (0.02 × $575 = $11.50).

UNIT 15 CHECK YOUR READING

Questions

20. What is the GST rate?

21. Is the full amount of GST collected by a business remitted to the federal government? Explain the term *input tax credit*.

22. What is the Harmonized Sales Tax (HST)? In what provinces does it apply?

23. What types of accounts (asset, liability, revenue, or expense) are PST Payable, GST Payable, GST Refundable?
24. What does it mean if a product is *exempt from sales tax*?
25. A sale of merchandise of $200 is made with terms of net 30. GST is 7 percent and PST is 8 percent calculated on the base price. What accounts are debited and credited to record this transaction?
26. A customer buys $60 worth of merchandise on credit. GST is 7 percent and PST is 9 percent calculated on the base price. The merchandise is defective and is returned by the customer. A credit invoice is issued.
    (a) Record this sales return in general journal form for a seller who uses a Sales Returns and Allowances account.
    (b) Record the same transaction in general journal form for a seller who does not use a Sales Returns and Allowances account.
27. On November 10, your company received an invoice with terms 2/10, n/30, for $550, plus $38.50 GST, plus $44 PST.
    (a) By what date must the invoice be paid to take advantage of the discount?
    (b) Will the discount be taken on the $550 or on $632.50?
28. A service is provided for $200 cash. GST is 7 percent and PST is 11 percent calculated on the base price plus GST. What accounts are debited and credited?
29. A taxable item is sold for $478 cash. GST is 7 percent and PST is 10 percent on the base price plus GST.
    (a) Calculate the taxes and the total received from the customer.
    (b) What accounts are debited and credited to record the sale?
30. A company collected $510 in PST during March. What is the journal entry to record the cheque issued to the Provincial Treasurer to remit the PST? (Assume 4 percent commission is paid by the government.)

UNIT 15 APPLY YOUR KNOWLEDGE

Exercises Part A

19. Complete the chart shown below in your workbook.
    (a) Calculate PST on the base amount of the sale.
    (b) Calculate PST on the total of the base amount plus GST.

Amount of Sale	GST (7%)	PST (8%)	PST on Total
$ 100.00	?	?	?
7.95	?	?	?
650.00	?	?	?
4500.00	?	?	?

20. Prepare general journal entries for the following retail sales:
    (a) Sold goods for $100 to R. Shadbar, terms net 30, GST $7, PST $8. Total $115, Invoice 293.

(b) Sold goods to C. Wang for $300, GST $21, PST $24, terms 2/10, n/30, Invoice 294.

(c) Received a $115 payment from R. Shadbar to cover Invoice 293.

(d) Sold goods on account to J. Southcott for $500, HST $75, total $575. Terms net 30, Invoice 497.

(e) Sold goods for $295, HST $44.25, total $339.25. Cash Sales Slip 4663.

21. Following is a PST Payable account:

PST Payable

Apr. 5	70
12	60
19	90
30	120

(a) How much should be remitted to the provincial government for the month of April? Assume the company is located in a province that does *not* pay a commission to companies for collecting the tax.

(b) In general journal form, prepare the entry to remit the April tax to the provincial government.

22. Following are GST Payable and GST Refundable accounts:

GST Payable		GST Refundable	
May. 5	75	May 4	40
12	90	11	110
19	120	20	60
29	82	30	70

(a) How much should be remitted to the federal government for the month of May?

(b) In general journal form, prepare the entry to remit the May tax to the federal government.

23. (a) Uni Electric made taxable retail sales of $3700 during May. How much is the cheque sent to the provincial government if the retail sales tax is 8 percent and Uni Electric is allowed a commission of 5 percent for collecting the sales tax?

(b) Prepare the journal entry to record the payment.

24. (a) During June, NuEra Hardware made sales of $5000, of which $900 was paid for non-taxable items. How much is remitted to the provincial government if the PST is 6 percent and the company's commission is 3 percent?

(b) Prepare the journal entry to record the payment.

25. Record the following source documents on page 307 of a general journal:

Jun. 1 Cash register tape shows sales of $945, GST $66.15, PST $75.60.

2 Cheque received from C. Ballard for $524 to pay Invoice 803, no discount.

2 Cheque received from L. Noble to pay Invoice 799, $324 less $6.48 discount.

4 Cheque received from K. Engel, the owner, for $2500 as an additional investment in the business.

7 Bank credit memo, $9000 for a bank loan that was deposited in the company bank account.

8 Cheque received from C. Drago to pay Invoice 805, $560 less $11.20 discount.

9 Cash Sales Slips 940 to 955 for $2155 plus $150.85 GST and $172.40 PST.

26. Record the following source documents on page 193 of a general journal:

Sep. 1 Cheque received for $3000 from the owner, C. Black, as a further investment in the business.

2 Cash Sales Slips 340 to 355 for $975 plus 6 percent PST on base price and 7 percent GST.

3 Cheques received:
No. 20710 from A. Derouin, $336 on account.
No. 1472 from V. Williams to pay Invoice 6061, $437 less $8.74 discount.

5 Cheque received from A. Derouin to pay Invoice 6059, $765 less $15.30 discount.

5 Cash Sales Slips 356 to 382 for $2750 plus 6 percent PST on base price and 7 percent GST.

UNIT 16 Bank Credit Cards

What Learning You Will Demonstrate

On completion of this unit, you will be able to:

* explain the accounting procedures for bank credit cards; and
* prepare journal entries related to bank credit card transactions.

BANK CREDIT CARDS

Many merchandising enterprises accept credit cards rather than, or in addition to, extending credit to their customers. Credit card companies such as MasterCard, Visa, and American Express supply an accounts receivable service to businesses. Since MasterCard and Visa are operated by financial institutions, their cards are generally called *bank credit cards*.

Why People Use Credit Cards

Two examples follow to indicate why consumers and businesses use bank credit cards.

Cindy Hutton has just purchased a sweater from Giselle's Boutique and used her Visa card to pay for her purchase. Like many other people, Cindy uses a bank credit card to do much of her shopping. Why do people use credit cards instead of paying with cash or by cheque? Cindy prefers to shop using a credit card for the following reasons:

* She does not have to carry large amounts of cash.
* She can buy things even if she does not have cash at the time she wishes to make a purchase.
* Some businesses do not accept personal cheques and others demand several items of identification before they accept cheques.
* Her card is accepted internationally when she travels. She can obtain cash advances up to a set limit. As well, she simply finds it more convenient to use a credit card.

Figure 7-20 shows the credit card form completed by the store clerk using a point-of-sale terminal for Cindy's purchase. The form is known as a *sales draft* or *sales slip*.

Producing the Credit Card Sales Slip

Let's follow the steps in producing the credit card sales slip.

1. Cindy gives the clerk her credit card. The clerk checks the expiry date on the card to make sure it is still valid. Then, the card is passed through a scanner to authorize use of the card.

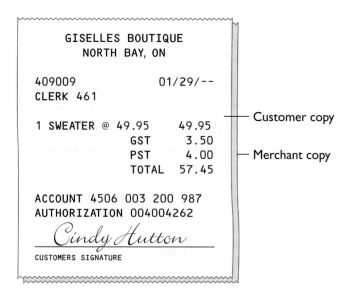

FIGURE 7-20 Credit card sales slip

2. The clerk enters the information into the point-of-sale terminal and the terminal's printer produces the credit card sales slip. The slip includes all the information found on a regular cash sales slip: the cost of the item, any GST and PST applied to the sale, and the total amount payable. The credit card slip includes an authorization number as well as a signature line.

3. Cindy is asked to sign the slip. The signature is checked against the sample signature on the back of the credit card.

4. Cindy is given a copy of the credit card sales slip, and the store keeps a copy to go in the deposit. Usually, a separate tape printout of the sale is produced that serves as a recipt for customer returns and as the source document for the accounting entry.

Cindy leaves the store with her sweater without having paid any cash for it. She will not have to pay until she receives a statement from the bank credit card company (see Figures 7-21 and 7-22 on pages 337 and 338). This is another reason why she uses a bank credit card. If she is able to pay the statement on time, she will not have to pay any interest. Depending on when a statement is issued, Visa allows up to 21 days from the date on the statement to pay, after which interest is charged. Cindy is very careful to pay her balance owing by the due date to avoid the interest charges.

Credit Card Fees

Many credit card companies impose a fee for using their credit card. The fee may be a separate charge for each transaction or a monthly or yearly fee for using the card. All credit card companies generally charge interest on balances that have not been paid within 15 to 30 days of the statement.

Figure 7-21 is the statement received from Scotiabank Visa by Cindy. It is a summary of a month's purchases and indicates that the new balance owing is $275.34. The date of the statement is 03/07/-- and the payment due date is 03/28/--. Cindy's cheque for $275.34 must reach the Visa accounts office by 03/28/-- if she is to avoid interest on the balance.

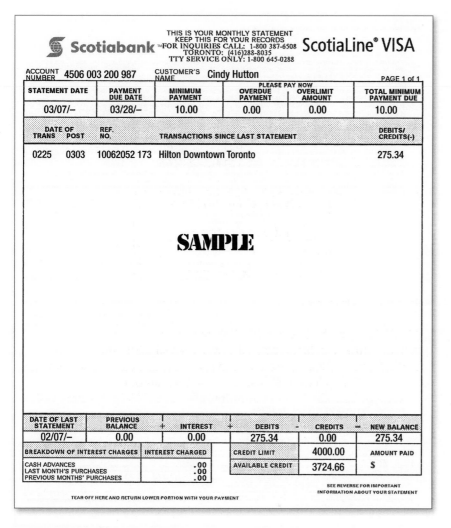

FIGURE 7-21 Monthly Visa statement

The preceding example illustrates why and how a consumer uses a bank credit card. In the next section, we will examine how and why a business uses the services of a bank credit card company such as Visa or MasterCard.

Why Businesses Use Bank Credit Cards

Giselle's Boutique uses the services provided by both Visa and MasterCard. It does so for the following reasons:

- Many people have MasterCard, Visa, or American Express credit cards and will shop at stores that accept these cards.
- The store receives its money from bank credit card sales as soon as the credit card sales slips are deposited in the bank.
- There is no risk of bad debts. The credit card company guarantees payment to the store.
- The store does not have to have an accounts receivable system to record sales to customers and does not have to worry about collecting amounts from customers.

IMPORTANT INFORMATION ABOUT YOUR SCOTIABANK STATEMENT

1. PAYMENTS

   The MINIMUM PAYMENT for VISA* cards is the greater of 2% of your new balance or $10.00 (or such other minimum payment as may be notified to you from time to time). Balances under $10.00 are to be repaid in full.

   The MINIMUM PAYMENT for ScotiaLine®, ScotiaLine VISA and ScotiaLine VISA card *for business* varies from interest only to 3% of your new balance or $50, whichever is greater and is calculated according to the option indicated in your Credit Agreement or disclosure letter (or such other payment as may be notified to you from time to time).

   FOR SCOTIA STUDENT LOANS and ScotiaLine for Students your required monthly payment is shown in the TOTAL MINIMUM PAYMENT DUE box on the front of your statement.

   Any amounts shown as OVERDUE PAYMENT or OVERLIMIT AMOUNT should be paid as soon as you receive your statement. The TOTAL MINIMUM PAYMENT DUE includes your MINIMUM PAYMENT and any amounts shown as overdue payments or amounts overlimit.

   We must receive your payment by the PAYMENT DUE DATE shown on your statement. Your payment can be made without charge at any Scotiabank branch, at any Cashstop Automated Banking Machine (ABM) using your ScotiaCard™ or Scotiabank VISA card, or through TeleScotia® Telephone Banking and Scotia OnLine® Internet Banking services using your ScotiaCard.

2. INTEREST ON DEBT

   Interest is calculated on that portion of your debt on which interest is payable up to the statement date at the annual percentage rate(s) specified on the front of your statement as previously disclosed to you.

   For VISA, ScotiaLine VISA and ScotiaLine VISA card *for business*, no interest is payable on purchases and service charges if the entire balance of the monthly statement on which the purchases and service charges first appear is paid in full by the payment due date. If payment in full is not made, purchases and service charges are subject to interest from the transaction date to the date it is repaid in full.

   Interest is payable on the outstanding balance of each VISA cash advance, or ScotiaLine/ScotiaLine for Students/ScotiaLine VISA/ScotiaLine VISA card *for business* advance and Scotia VISA or Line of Credit Cheques from the transaction date indicated on the statement to the date it is repaid in full. Interest appearing on this statement is calculated only to the statement date. Interest will continue to be charged on amounts you owe until we receive payment in full. Such interest will be reflected on your next statement.

   Interest is calculated by multiplying the daily unpaid balance of the Debt on which interest is payable by the applicable annual percentage rate(s) divided by 365. Interest is payable both before and after default or judgement.

   To pay off the full amount you owe and stop interest accumulation, ask your branch for your payout balance and pay that amount at the branch the same day. (This figure may not include insurance premiums and/or transactions not posted to your account).

3. TRANSACTION DATE AND POSTING DATE

   The date columns shown opposite an item on your statement reflect the respective dates on which the transaction occurred and was posted to your account. If the transaction date is not available, the posting date will appear in both columns. The date shown opposite a payment is the date on which it was credited to your account.

4. CREDIT BALANCE

   If you make an overpayment, the amount (indicated by a minus sign) will be applied to any future debit(s) unless you have asked us in writing to return to you the overpaid amount.

   On ScotiaGold VISA accounts, the Bank will pay you interest at the Bank's Daily Savings Account Interest rate** for each day your credit balance is $1,000 or more. The total of all daily interest paid will appear as a credit on your monthly statement.

5. TRANSACTIONS IN FOREIGN CURRENCY

   Transactions, other than VISA, ScotiaLine or ScotiaLine for Students cheques, are converted to Canadian currency at the exchange rate in effect as determined by VISA International (on our behalf) and are debited or credited to your account. This exchange rate may be different from the rate in effect on the date the transaction was made. For information purposes, the exchange rate includes an amount equal to 1.8% of the converted amount, which amount is applied to both debit and credit transactions.

   For cheques, the exchange rate used is the Bank's exchange rate in effect on the day the transaction is received by the Bank. The Bank's exchange rate may not be the same rate as the exchange rate determined above by VISA International.

6. CUSTOMER SERVICE ENQUIRIES

   If there are any errors on your statement, please contact your branch or Domestic Customer Services **within 15 days** of your statement date.
   If you wish to apply for a higher credit limit or additional cards, please contact your Scotiabank servicing branch.

7. PERSONAL IDENTIFICATION NUMBERS (PINS)

   To obtain cash advances through ABMs, visit any Scotiabank branch and select a Personal Identification Number (PIN) for use with your VISA and/or ScotiaCard™ or Cashstop card. Please select a UNIQUE PIN for each card. All authorized users requiring ABM access must individually select their own PIN(s). Once a PIN is selected, future cards mailed will include the selected PIN(s). Scotia Student loans cannot be accessed through the ABM.

8. **IF YOUR VISA CARD IS LOST OR STOLEN, PLEASE CONTACT DOMESTIC CUSTOMER SERVICES IMMEDIATELY AT THE FOLLOWING NUMBERS:**

   TORONTO AREA (416) 288-1440
   ALL OTHER AREA CODES WITHIN CANADA 1-800-387-6466
   OUTSIDE CANADA (Collect) (416) 288-1440

9. PAYMENTS AND STATEMENT ENQUIRIES MAY BE ADDRESSED TO:

   Domestic Customer Services
   P.O. Box 4100
   Postal Station "A"
   Toronto, Ontario
   M5W 1T1

PLEASE RECORD YOUR ACCOUNT NUMBER ON ALL CORRESPONDENCE AS WELL AS ON THE FRONT OF YOUR CHEQUE OR MONEY ORDER (payable to The Bank of Nova Scotia).

* VISA Int./Lic. user The Bank of Nova Scotia.
® Registered trademark of The Bank of Nova Scotia.
™ Trademarks of The Bank of Nova Scotia.
** Rates subject to change from time to time. Notice of any change will be posted in Scotiabank branches.

FIGURE 7-22 Back of Visa statement

The credit card companies provide a guaranteed, immediate collection service to companies. In return for the service, the companies pay a percentage of each sale to the bank credit card company.

Accounting Example for Bank Credit Card Transactions

In this example, we will use the Visa credit card and the Men's Wear Shop to illustrate accounting procedures for bank credit card transactions.

Merchant Deposit Summary

At the end of the day, the store accountant prepares a merchant deposit summary (Figure 7-23). This is a summary of all the credit card sales slips for the day. Figure 7-23 is the merchant summary from February 20 and represents nine Visa sales slips that total $590.80 (which includes GST and PST).

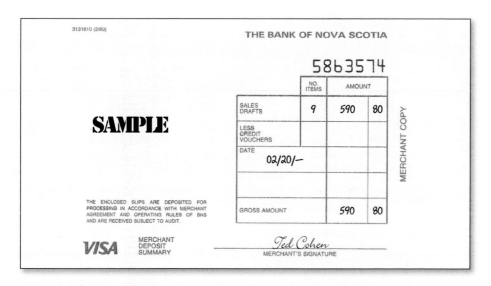

FIGURE 7-23 Visa Merchant Deposit Summary

The Visa sales slips are treated as cash and are taken to the bank and deposited at the end of the day. The bank receives the deposit and increases the balance in the account of the Men's Wear Shop.

Bank Fees

In return for providing instant cash for sales made, the bank charges the store a fee. The fee is calculated at the time of recording the deposit. The store treats this fee as an expense.

The fee charged by the bank credit card company is based on the average volume of credit card sales and the average draft size. The fee paid by the Men's Wear Shop is $2^3/4$ percent of credit card sales. This is the rate for a business with an average monthly volume of $5000 to $12 499 and an average draft size of $50 to $99.99. Figure 7-24, on page 340, provides a sample of the types of service charges paid to bank credit card companies by merchants.

Following are the transaction data and the entry made by the accountant to record the merchant deposit summary in Figure 7-23:

Feb. 20   Gross Visa sales for the day totalled $590.84, which included GST of $35.96 and PST of $41.10. The Visa discount amounted to $16.25.

The store accountant then prepares this accounting entry to record the Visa sales:

Feb.	20	Cash	5 7 4 55	
		Visa Discount Expense	1 6 25	
		GST Payable		3 5 96
		PST Payable		4 1 10
		Sales		5 1 3 74
		To record Visa credit card sales and charges.		

Although no cash has changed hands, the store has received its money—it was placed in the store's bank account by the bank.

BANK CREDIT CARD MEMBER DISCOUNT SCHEDULE				
	AVERAGE DRAFT SIZE			
Average Monthly Volume	Under $30.00	$30.00 to $49.99	$50.00 to $99.99	$100.00 and over
	%	%	%	%
$ 1 – $ 999	5½	4½	3½	3½
1 000 – 2 499	4¾	4	3½	2¾
2 500 – 4 999	4½	3¾	3	2¾
5 000 – 12 499	4½	3½	2¾	2½
12 500 – 19 999	4	3½	2½	2½
20 000 – 29 999	3¾	3	2½	2½
30 000 – 49 999	3½	2¾	2½	2
50 000 – 74 999	3½	2¾	2	2
75 000 – 149 999	3	2½	2	2
150 000 – 299 999	2½	2½	2	2
300 000 – and over	2	2	2	2

FIGURE 7-24 Sample bank credit card service charges

Merchant Statement

In the example just described, the merchant deposited the bank credit card sales slips each day and the accountant entered the Visa fee charged on the deposit each day. Increasingly, because banks use the monthly statement method of charging the fee to the merchant, businesses will make a single entry from the monthly statement to record their bank credit card costs.

The statement illustrated in Figure 7-25 was received by the Western Motor Inn in Edmonton from its bank. It is called the "merchant statement." Once a month, the statement is sent by the Visa bank to the merchant. The statement provides a summary of the Visa deposits made each day, the total deposits, and the fee charged by Visa for the month's transactions. The fee charged for the month covered in Figure 7-25 is $296.10. This accounting entry is made on the books of the Western Motor Inn to record the Visa service fee:

Jun.	28	Visa Discount Expense		2 9 6 10	
		Cash			2 9 6 10
		To record Visa discount fee for June.			

THE BANK OF NOVA SCOTIA
VISA CENTRE MERCHANT STATEMENT   **SAMPLE**

WESTERN MOTOR INN   MERCHANT NO.   589
11503 FORT RD., N.W.   STATEMENT DATE   Jun. 28, 20—
EDMONTON, AB   T5B 4G1

DATE	DEPOSIT AMOUNT	ADJUSTMENTS	CODE	REFERENCE NO.
05/29	$ 553.76			2 51301045
06/01	822.69			2 57109132
06/03	754.83			2 57109142
06/06	901.64			2 58240108
06/10	711.40			2 62300040
06/10	873.60			2 62300050
06/17	706.38			2 70223840
06/17	489.13			2 70301295
06/17	884.45			2 70301305
06/17	1,066.69			2 70301315
06/20	489.15			2 75223831
06/24	799.06			2 76246395
06/24	731.51			2 76246405
06/25	982.96			2 76246385

TOTALS $10,767.25 + $0.00= $10,767.25 NET SALES

BRANCH TRANSIT	ACCOUNT NO.	CHAIN NO.	DISCOUNT RATE	CURRENT DISCOUNT
1072	23-00214	0	2.750%	$296.10

NUMBER & AMOUNT OF SALES DRAFTS		NUMBER & AMOUNT OF CREDITS	
125	$10,767.25	0	$0.00

CARRY FORWARD AMOUNT	UNCLEARED ADJUSTMENTS	CURRENT DISCOUNT	STATEMENT TOTAL
0.00	− 0.00	+ $296.10	= $296.10

FIGURE 7-25 Merchant statement

Can you see the advantage of using the monthly statement method as compared to the daily method for recording the fee?

DEBIT CARDS

Many financial institutions have introduced debit cards, which eliminate the need to write cheques to pay for merchandise. The debit cards are part of a system that transfers funds between parties electronically rather than by paper cheques. The exchange of cash using this system is called *electronic funds transfer* (EFT). This method is already used by many employers to deposit employees' pay directly into their bank accounts while reducing the employer's account. The same type of system allows customers to present a debit card to a retailer rather than write a cheque to pay for goods purchased. The debit card is inserted into the retailer's computer terminal, which is connected to the bank. The funds to pay for the purchased goods are automatically transferred out of the customer's account into the store's account.

This system eliminates the cost of processing the paper cheque and removes the risk of bad cheques for the retailer. Implementation of this system moves us closer to the "paperless society" where there is little need to carry cash or cheques.

Generally Accepted Accounting Principles and Key Ideas

In this chapter, you learned the following key ideas:

- **A schedule of cost of goods sold** may be prepared as a supporting schedule for the income statement.
- **Costs** are recorded when incurred, whether paid for in cash or on credit.
- **Goods and Services Tax** (GST) is charged on the sale of most goods and services in Canada.
- **Provincial Sales Tax** (PST) is charged on retail sales in all provinces except Alberta.
- **Harmonized Sales Tax** (HST) combines the GST and the PST and is in effect in Newfoundland, New Brunswick, and Nova Scotia.

UNIT 16 CHECK YOUR READING

Questions

31. Why do retailers accept bank credit cards even though there is a fee charged for using this service?

32. (a) Why do consumers use bank credit cards?
   (b) What is the name of the form completed by the merchant when a sale is made to a customer who makes payment with a bank credit card?
   (c) How many copies of the form are prepared and who receives each copy?

33. Look at the Visa customer statement in Figure 7-21, page 337, and answer these questions:
    (a) What is the statement date?
    (b) What is the payment due date?
    (c) What is the new balance owing?
    (d) What is the minimum payment that must be made?
    (e) What is the credit limit for the customer?
34. The back of a Visa statement is shown in Figure 7-22, page 338. Obtain definitions for the following from the statement:
    (a) Transaction date
    (b) Payment due date
    (c) Interest calculation
    (d) Minimum payment
35. What is the name of the form completed at the end of each day that summarizes the day's bank credit card sales?
36. (a) What accounts are debited and credited by the retailer when Visa sales drafts are taken to the bank and deposited?
    (b) What accounts are debited and credited to record the fee charged by the bank?
37. What is the bank credit card fee (in percentage terms) for each of the following monthly volumes? Assume the average draft size is under $30 (refer to Figure 7-24, page 340).
    (a) $3000
    (b) $13 000
    (c) $22 000

UNIT 16 APPLY YOUR KNOWLEDGE

Exercises Part A

27. Record the following transactions on page 10 in a general journal. Use the Visa Discount Expense account to record the fee paid to Visa, and the MasterCard Discount Expense account to record the MasterCard fee.

    May 7 Cash Sales Slips 48 to 57 for $2000 (sales tax exempt), GST $140.
    7 Invoice 6, sale on account to S. Cox $548, GST 7 percent, PST 6 percent on base price.
    7 Visa credit card sales $680 (sales tax exempt), GST 7 percent.
    7 MasterCard credit card sales $890 (sales tax exempt), GST 7 percent.
    8 Visa discount fee $18.70.
    8 MasterCard discount fee $24.48.

28. Rivera Electronics offers a variety of credit terms to customers. Record the following transactions for January on page 100 in a general journal. All sales are subject to 7 percent GST and 8 percent PST calculated on the base price.

Jan. 2 Sold merchandise to J. Coon for $1600, terms 2/10, n/30, Invoice 249.

4 Sold merchandise to Lee Mazilli for $300, terms EOM, Invoice 250.

4 Paid CN Express the $75 ($70.09 plus $4.91 GST) delivery charges for the merchandise shipped to J. Coon, Cheque 201.

6 Damaged merchandise was returned by J. Coon. Credit Invoice 22 was issued today for $115 (GST $7 and $8 sales tax, $100 merchandise).

7 Received a cheque from B. Lailey for $294 in payment of Invoice 240. Since payment was received within the discount period, a $6 discount had been taken.

7 The weekly cash register tape showed cash and Visa sales of $7530, GST $527.10, PST $602.40, total $8659.50.

9 Sold merchandise to C. Corbett for $480, terms 2/10, n/30, Invoice 251.

9 Refunded $46 to a customer who made a cash purchase on January 7 (GST $2.80, $3.20 PST, and $40 merchandise). Customer provided cash register slip as proof of purchase.

10 Received Cheque 642 from L. Mako for $180 in full payment of his account.

14 Sales tax for the period was remitted to the provincial government. The tax collected totalled $3250. Rivera Electronics was entitled to a 3 percent commission for collecting the tax; Cheque 202.

16 Received Cheque 027 from J. Coon in payment of the January 2 invoice.

21 Cash and Visa sales for the week were $6090, GST $426.30, PST $487.20, total $7003.50.

22 Cheque 121 was received today from C. Corbett for the January 9 invoice, $540.96. A discount of $11.04 had been taken; however, the cheque had been received after the discount period. Therefore the discount was not granted.

30 Received Cheque 741 from L. Mazilli in full payment of the January 4 invoice.

30 The Visa merchant statement was received today. The discount fee charged for the month of January was $325.

30 GST remittance to the Receiver General: GST Payable balance $6839, GST Refundable balance $4719, Cheque 203.

Exercises Part B

29. (a) Prepare a schedule of cost of goods sold for Warrendon Sports for June from the following figures: beginning inventory $33 800, Purchases $7200, Purchases Returns and Allowances $100, Purchases Discounts $25, Transportation-in $400, ending inventory $32 100.

(b) Prepare an income statement using the cost of goods sold from part (a) and the following figures: Sales for June $14 500, Sales

Returns and Allowances $200, Sales Discounts $50, Salaries
Expense $2500, Rent Expense $2700, Delivery Expense $600,
Other Expenses $800.
(c) Prepare the current asset section of the balance sheet on June 30
using the following figures: Cash $7200, Accounts Receivable
$2700, Supplies $700. Remember that you must also use the figure for the ending inventory. Refer to part (a) of this exercise.

30. Use the information in the trial balance for Henley Outdoor
Supplies shown below.
(a) Prepare a schedule of cost of goods sold for August.
(b) Prepare an income statement for August.
(c) Prepare a classified balance sheet for August.
(d) Why does the ending inventory amount not appear on the trial balance prepared from Henley Outdoor Supplies' ledger on August 31?

Note: The August 31 inventory is $27 100.

Account	Acc. No.	Debit	Credit
Henley Outdoor Supplies			
Trial Balance			
August 31, 20—			
Cash	101	$ 5 600	
Accounts Receivable	110	2 900	
Merchandise Inventory, August 1	120	30 200	
Supplies	125	600	
Equipment	151	15 000	
Truck	152	8 000	
Furniture	153	45 000	
Accounts Payable	200		$ 2 500
PST Payable	205		400
GST Payable	206		900
GST Refundable	207	600	
Bank Loan (3 years)	210		6 500
W. Creighton, Capital	300		93 600
Sales	400		18 600
Sales Returns and Allowances	401	350	
Sales Discounts	402	50	
Purchases	500	8 300	
Purchases Returns and Allowances	501		325
Purchases Discounts	502		75
Transportation-in	503	600	
Delivery Expense	601	300	
Miscellaneous Expense	602	475	
Rent Expense	603	2 700	
Salaries Expense	604	2 100	
Visa Discount Expense	605	75	
MasterCard Discount Expense	606	50	
		$122 900	$122 900

31. Assume Henley Outdoor Supplies shown in the previous question used a perpetual inventory system.
   (a) Which accounts would no longer appear on the trial balance?
   (b) Which new account(s) would be added?
   (c) Prepare a trial balance for Henley Outdoor Supplies on August 31, 20—, as it would appear if a perpetual inventory system were used.

32. Some of the account balances of Green's Hobby Shop for the month of July are shown below.
   (a) Prepare a schedule of cost of goods sold.
   (b) Prepare an income statement.
   (c) Prepare the current asset section of the balance sheet.

Purchases Discounts	$ 25
Beginning Inventory	32 100
Purchases	9 100
Purchases Returns and Allowances	300
Transportation-in	450
Ending Inventory	30 200
Sales	18 500
Sales Returns and Allowances	350
Salaries Expense	2 900
Rent Expense	2 700
Delivery Expense	700
Other Expenses	1 400
Cash on Hand	3 500
Accounts Receivable	2 900
Supplies on Hand	500
Sales Discounts	25
Visa Discount Expense	50
MasterCard Discount Expense	75

33. Using the information in the trial balance for Waterfront Hardware on the next page,* prepare the following for the month:
   (a) Schedule of cost of goods sold
   (b) Income statement
   (c) Classified balance sheet
   (d) Why does the ending inventory amount not appear on the trial balance prepared from Waterfront Hardware's ledger on August 31?

   Note: The August 31 inventory is $27 100.

Waterfront Hardware
Trial Balance
August 31, 20—

Account	Acc. No.	Debit	Credit
Cash	101	$ 15 300	
Accounts Receivable	102	2 900	
Merchandise Inventory, August 1	120	30 200	
Supplies	125	600	
Furniture & Fixtures	150	35 000	
Equipment	151	15 000	
Truck	152	18 000	
Accounts Payable	200		$ 2 500
PST Payable	205		400
GST Payable	206		900
GST Refundable	207	300	
Bank Loan (3 years)	210		26 500
N. Jensen, Capital	300		83 000
Sales	400		18 600
Sales Returns and Allowances	401	350	
Sales Discounts	402	50	
Purchases	500	8 300	
Purchases Returns and Allowances	501		325
Purchases Discounts	502		75
Transportation-in	503	600	
Delivery Expense	601	475	
Miscellaneous Expense	602	300	
Rent Expense	603	2 700	
Salaries Expense	604	2 100	
Visa Discount Expense	605	50	
MasterCard Discount Expense	606	75	
		$132 300	$132 300

Computer Accounting

Computer Audit Trail

Integrated Accounting Software

Integrated accounting software consists of separate modules for the various accounting procedures. Most programs have modules for accounts receivable, accounts payable, and the general ledger. Some programs have additional modules such as payroll, job cost, and banking.

Journal Entries

As transactions are journalized in each module, they are assigned a *separate sequential journal entry number*. In Figure 7-26, there are two journal entries. When they were recorded, the computer *automatically* assigned a number to each journal entry. Entry J207 records a payroll transaction. It was entered in the payroll module of the program. Entry J208 is from the accounts receivable module.

Universal Construction   Account   Page 1
General Journal   Source   number
Mar. 1, 20— to Mar. 11, 20—   document

Date			Account number		Debits	Credits
03/01/--	J207	Ellis, George S.	1820	530 Wages	1331.20	—
				531 EI Expense	32.57	—
				532 CPP Expense	21.31	—
				233 EI Payable	—	55.84
				234 CPP Payable	—	42.62
				235 Income Tax Payable	—	286.91
				238 Medical Payable	—	10.00
				237 Union Payable	—	12.00
				232 Vacation Payable	—	51.20
				110 Cash	—	926.51
03/01/—	J208	Dunedin Development Corp.	1694	120 Accounts Receivable	8500.00	—
				404 Engineering Sales	—	5000.00
				402 Drafting Sales	—	3500.00

Transaction number

Explanation

FIGURE 7-26 Computer-prepared journal

Introducing the Audit Trail

If anyone wishes to check or audit the accounting records, *a complete path of information is provided by the computer journal entry*. This accounting information path is called an *audit trail*. Let's examine a typical audit trail—entry J208.

The audit trail provided by this journal entry is as follows:

- ➤ Date: The entry was recorded on January 3.
- ➤ Explanation: A credit sale was made to Dunedin Development Corporation.
- ➤ Invoice Number: The invoice number is 1694.
- ➤ Account Debited: Account 120, Accounts Receivable, was debited $8500.
- ➤ Accounts Credited: Accounts 404, Engineering Sales, and 402, Drafting Sales, were credited $5000 and $3500, respectively.

If further information is required, a person could refer to Invoice 1694. This invoice will contain a description of the exact items sold, the price, the GST and PST, the total amount, and the delivery address.

Most accounting programs have the capability of printing *all* of the journal entries in order of number and date, that is, sequentially and chronologically. Specialized entries can also be printed—for example, only accounts receivable entries. This capability is a big help in discovering errors or in tracing back transactions when a customer disagrees with the amount charged or the amount owing.

Questions

1. What is a sequential journal entry number?
2. How are sequential journal entry numbers assigned?
3. What is an audit trail?
4. What purpose is served by an audit trail?
5. What is the difference between chronological and sequential order?
6. Where would you look if you wanted to know the number of items sold, a description of the items, and the prices for transaction J208?

Computer Skills

Most employers require their employees to have computer skills. Students who take the Certified General Accountant (CGA) course will learn to use computer applications throughout their studies. The following text from a CGA-Canada web site outlines some of the technical expertise a student can expect to gain by completing the first level of the CGA designation.

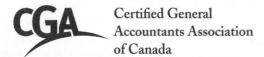

Certified General
Accountants Association
of Canada

By the time you are certified as a CGA, you will have a high level of expertise in computer and information technology. You will have:

- practical, hands-on technical knowledge of the computer as a management and financial problem-solving tool
- ability to participate in the design and control of complex information systems
- ability to manage and adapt to technological change within your organization
- steadily increasing proficiency in applying computers to problem analysis and decision making.

Once you progress beyond Level 1 of the program of professional studies, you must have access to a CGA-designated computer. The *Guide for Purchasing Computer Hardware*, published by CGA-Canada each year, outlines student purchasing considerations for the coming academic year.

The *Guide for Purchasing Computer Hardware* specifies computer components recommended by the association. The recommendations change as the technology and course requirements change from year to year. Windows is the only operating system supported in the CGA program. Similarly, Microsoft Office is a required software application for those students taking studies via the Internet or CD-ROM.

Questions:

1. Why would the ability to "adapt to technological change" within an organization be an important aspect of an accounting course of studies?
2. What is meant by "Windows is the only operating system supported"?
3. Why would the CGA program choose to only support one operating system and specific software applications like Microsoft Office?

Spreadsheet Analysis

Louise Bennett has operated her own business for five years. The results for the five years are summarized in the chart below.

	Actual Results					Projected	
	Year 1	Year 2	Year 3	Year 4	Year 5	Year 6	Year 7
Revenue	$20 000	$35 000	$59 000	$89 000	$119 000	—	—
Expenses	25 000	34 000	36 000	42 000	62 000	—	—
Net Income	—	—	—	—	—	—	—

Louise has been approached by a business associate who would like to join her firm as a partner. After lengthy negotiations, Louise has decided that there are two options available to her. They are listed below.

Option One

No change. Continue to operate the business on her own. Projected revenue and expenses if this option is chosen are:

Year 6	Revenue	$120 000
	Expenses	76 000
Year 7	Revenue	$122 000
	Expenses	84 000

Option Two

Take in a partner. This would mean sharing ownership, responsibilities, and profits. Louise would receive 70 percent of profits (or losses). The best possible results under this option are:

Year 6	Revenue	$150 000
	Expenses	96 000
Year 7	Revenue	$180 000
	Expenses	115 000

However, the worst possible results are estimated to be:

Year 6	Revenue	$125 000
	Expenses	103 000
Year 7	Revenue	$130 000
	Expenses	112 000

Questions

1. Prepare a spreadsheet that will show for the seven years:
   (a) Net income or net loss
   (b) Percentage of expenses to revenue
   (c) Percentage of net income to revenue
   (d) Louise's share of the net income, in dollars

2. Print your spreadsheet results for options one and two—best results and worst results.
3. Based on these statistics only, what would you recommend that Louise do?
4. What other non-statistical considerations do you think should be considered?
5. Based on statistics and other considerations, what is your recommendation to Louise?
6. What significant information has not been given to you?

COMPUTER ASSIGNMENTS

1. (a) Format a spreadsheet to complete exercise 9(b) on page 311.
   (b) Print your answer.

2. (a) Prepare a spreadsheet format for completing schedules of cost of goods sold.
   (b) Use the spreadsheet to complete exercise 5 on page 308, exercises 17(b) and 18(a) on page 317, and exercise 32(a) on page 346.

3. (a) Use general ledger software to record the transactions for exercise 11(a) on page 311, exercises 25 and 26 on page 334, and exercise 28 on page 343. Record them in the general journal.
   (b) Print the general journal, general ledger, and trial balance for each exercise.

4. (a) Format a spreadsheet that will calculate the GST and PST (calculated on base price) for the following invoices:

Invoice	GST	PST	Invoice Total
$100			
$798			
$539.99			
$2400			
$1667			
$23.98			
$345			

(b) Use the spreadsheet you created for 4(a) to complete exercise 19 on page 332.

www.pearsoned.ca/
principlesofaccounting

WEB EXTENSIONS

Internet Study Guide

➤ Complete the Chapter 7 review.

➤ Complete the Chapter 7 definitions.

➤ Complete the Chapter 7 online test.

Web Links

Visit the Web Links section at the Pearson Education web site to find links to debit and credit card information. Visit each site and give examples of how you can protect yourself when you use a debit or credit card.

⑪ Case Studies

Accounts Used by a Merchandising Company

A new accountant began working for Atlas Stores on July 1. During the month of July, the new accountant recorded the following group of purchase invoices:

Merchandise	$2 900
Office supplies	300
Office equipment	900
Delivery expenses	250

However, all four items were recorded as debits in the Purchases account.

(a) For each of the invoices, name the account that should have been debited.
(b) What effect will the incorrect recording of these invoices have on the:
 (i) Balance sheet?
 (ii) Schedule of cost of goods sold?
 (iii) Income statement?

Delivery Costs

Vachon Stores offers free delivery as a service to its customers. For years, a local delivery company has provided the service. Business has increased substantially and, on average, 300 deliveries per month are made. The delivery firm has just increased its charges to $20 for every delivery.

 K. Vachon, the owner, has asked the store accountant to compare the present delivery charges with the cost of buying and operating the company's own van. The accountant has determined several facts:

- A delivery van would cost $37 000.
- The van would last four years and then would be worth $10 000 as a trade-in. The accountant will calculate straight-line depreciation using a figure of $27 000 (the original cost less the salvage value).
- The driver's salary would be about $27 per hour, including all fringe benefits; the driver would work an average of 30 hours per week.
- Insurance, repairs and maintenance, licences, and fuel would average $8950 per year.

(a) What is more economical, buying the delivery equipment or using the services of the cartage firm?
(b) List factors other than costs that could affect the decision.

CASE 3 Provincial Sales Tax

Contact the department of your provincial government responsible for the provincial retail sales tax and obtain answers to the following questions. You may be able to get the answers from a regional sales tax office, or from a ministry web site.

(a) Which items are exempt from provincial retail sales tax?
(b) What is the minimum sale amount below which sales tax is not charged?
(c) What commission, if any, is paid to retailers who collect tax for the government?
(d) When must remittances be sent to the government?
(e) How is a retail sales tax licence obtained?
(f) How is the revenue from retail sales tax used by the government?
(g) Explain the retail sales tax law concerning a product (for example, a $2000 fur coat) bought in a neighbouring province and brought home to your province.
(h) List the different PST rates for each province. Why are there different rates?

CASE 4 Discounts

Henry Olsen has been an accounting clerk for Wellandvale Ltd. for 30 years. His main task is to process, record, and pay purchase invoices. In the last few years, Wellandvale's business has increased greatly.

Henry keeps invoices in two large files, one for *unpaids* and one for *paids*. About once a week, or whenever he gets around to it, Henry checks the unpaid file and issues cheques for invoices that have become due.

The controller of the company has noticed that a number of cash discounts have been lost because payments were not made within the discount period. When confronted, Henry said he was overworked and should not be blamed.

(a) What changes would you recommend in the handling of purchase invoices?
(b) Write a report to Mrs. W. Mickle, the controller, to indicate your recommendations in (a) and how you would get Henry to accept your changes.

CASE 5 Cash Discounts

Matet Porter manages Studio Sound, a stereo components specialty shop. She is in the process of negotiating a $5000 order from one of her main suppliers. The supplier has offered a 3 percent discount if payment is made within 15 days. Studio Sound does not have cash on hand to take advantage of the discount. However, the bank will lend money to Studio Sound for 30 days at an annual rate of interest of 19 percent. Matet is sure that within 30 days there will be enough cash on hand to repay the bank.

Should Matet take the 3 percent discount using money borrowed from the bank? How much will be gained or lost if the loan is taken?

⑫ Career Education Activities

1. Non-Profit Organizations

Non-profit organizations are often dedicated to helping others and providing valuable services to society. Look at the following advertisements for non-profit organizations and answer these questions:

(a) What accounting functions are performed in each of the listed jobs?
(b) What skills are mentioned as important for the candidate to be successful in these positions?
(c) List the possible advantages of working in an accounting role for a non-profit organization.

Corporate Accountant

The successful candidate will be responsible for the reporting and analysis of budgets, the investment portfolio, special event reporting, grant reporting, other balance sheet items, as well as preparation of bank reconciliation reports.

A third-level CGA or equivalent with at least three years' accounting experience is required. To be successful you require good time management skills, administrative and computer spreadsheet skills, and a desire to work in a demanding environment. The ability to work well with others, demonstrate initiative, and be part of a team are all important qualities to be successful in this position.

Send your résumé to:

Job Recruiters of Canada
1000 Bay Street, Unit 100
Toronto, ON M5B 1T6

Accounting Supervisor

Our organization is dedicated to helping children with physical disabilities lead full and rewarding lives. Our organization follows standard business procedures and reporting routines. As the accounting supervisor you will ensure the smooth operation of our financial processes. You will be responsible for the planning and support of the Ontario office. Producing monthly and year-end statements and overseeing the banking, tax submissions, financial analysis and corporate accounting functions, accounts payable, accounts receivable, and payroll are the tasks associated with this challenging position. Providing input into financial policies and procedures, and supervising a permanent staff of five will also form part of your job requirement.

We are looking for someone with a minimum five years' experience, currently working toward his or her CGA/CMA designation. Strong leadership, computing, and communication skills are essential. You are a team player with strong decision-making and problem-solving skills together with a desire to work in a helping environment.

Send your résumé to:

Job Recruiters of Canada
1000 Bay Street, Unit 100
Toronto, ON M5B 1T6

Career Profile •

Rob Hideg enjoyed his years at Sir Robert Borden High School. While at high school he took all the available business courses, including accounting, economics, and business management, but he balanced his academics with his love for soccer.

After Rob completed high school he took time off to earn some money at various part-time jobs. He was hired by Combustion Engineering to work in the accounting department and found that he enjoyed working with numbers and applying his math skills. Rob was offered an opportunity to travel to Holland on a soccer exchange but, instead, he made a career decision to stay in Canada and continue to work.

After taking some time away from school, Rob completed a financial management diploma at the local college while continuing to work part-time to help finance his studies. He used his job experiences to obtain further employment with an accounting "temp" agency. Rob worked at a variety of short-term contracts in many areas of accounting, including payroll, accounts receivable, and taxation. He began taking courses toward his CGA while working at various temporary jobs. He used his network of friends and family to find opportunities in accounting within their firms. At one point Rob worked for an engineering firm, Alstom Power, the same company that his mother worked for.

Rob continually checked want ads to look for just the right job. He saw a listing for a government-sponsored training program and completed an internship with a small local CA firm. While Rob has switched fields recently and is now working as a contractor with a cable company, he says that in the future he may complete the stock brokers course.

Rob has had an opportunity to develop a variety of skills with each job placement. He has continued to play soccer at a competitive level and he continues to improve his financial management skills.

For Discussion

(a) List the ways Rob obtained accounting experience.

(b) What are the advantages of working for a "temp" agency?

(c) Who would you include in your "network" when you look for work?

8

The Subsidiary Ledger System

What Learning You Will Demonstrate

On completion of this unit, you will be able to:

- describe the advantages of a three-ledger system;
- explain the meaning of:
  - subsidiary ledger, and
  - control account;
- describe the importance of having a division of labour; and
- demonstrate the skills necessary to verify each of the three ledgers by preparing a general ledger trial balance, a schedule of accounts payable, and a schedule of accounts receivable.

GENERAL LEDGER

As a business increases in size, the system used to record accounting information must be adapted to efficiently process an increasing amount of data. The general ledger is one of the first areas affected by the growth of the firm.

Accounts Receivable

A growing firm normally has a rapid increase in the number of customers who purchase goods or services on account. Accounts must be kept for each customer to determine the amount owed and the date payment is due. The number of accounts receivable increases from a small number for a small firm just beginning business to a very large number for a large business. How does this affect the general ledger? Look at Figure 8-1 on page 358. The dramatic increase shown for the number of accounts receivable in the general ledger makes it necessary to devise a more efficient system of ledger accounts.

Effect on the Balance Sheet

Consider the effect of this expanded number of accounts receivable on the preparation of the balance sheet. To list all of the accounts receivable individually on the balance sheet would result in a very lengthy financial statement. One of the primary objectives of financial reporting is to provide useful information to financial statement readers. The figure that statement readers are interested in is the total value of all accounts receivable, not the value of each individual account receivable. Therefore, a *total for accounts receivable* would be more useful when preparing a balance sheet.

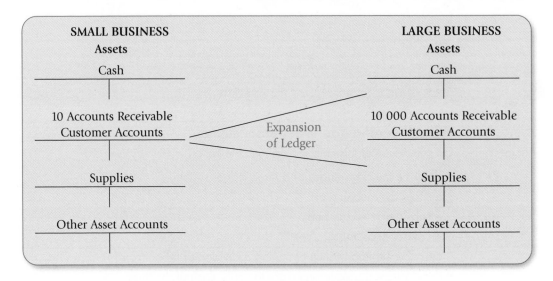

FIGURE 8-1 Partial general ledgers for small and large businesses

Accounts Payable

A similar situation develops in the accounts payable portion of the ledger as the business grows. The number of firms from which goods or services are purchased tends to increase as a business expands.

It is necessary to keep individual accounts for each of these creditors to have an accurate record of the amount owed and the payment due date for each. If this data were all recorded in the general ledger, the effect would be the same as shown previously with the accounts receivable section. There would be a large number of Accounts Payable accounts in the general ledger and a very long balance sheet. A summary figure would be more useful on the balance sheet than a large number of individual accounts.

Adapting the General Ledger

An example using T-accounts will demonstrate how the accounting system is changed to handle this increased volume of information more efficiently and also provide the required balance sheet data. A partial ledger and trial balance for Collegiate Sales are shown in Figures 8-2 and 8-3 on pages 359 and 360. A small number of accounts receivable and payable are shown to demonstrate the concept. In reality, the number of these accounts could be in the thousands but the change to the accounting system would be similar.

Figure 8-3 is the trial balance for Collegiate Sales. Each customer account is listed separately. In a large company, there could be many customer accounts. Of course, this would make the trial balance and balance sheet very lengthy.

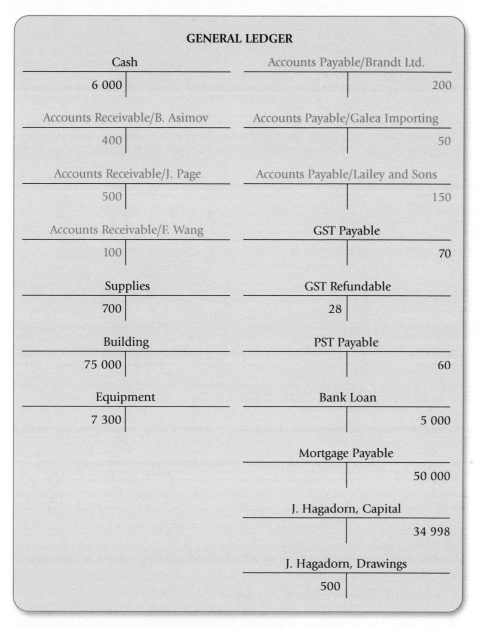

GENERAL LEDGER

Cash		Accounts Payable/Brandt Ltd.	
6 000			200

Accounts Receivable/B. Asimov		Accounts Payable/Galea Importing	
400			50

Accounts Receivable/J. Page		Accounts Payable/Lailey and Sons	
500			150

Accounts Receivable/F. Wang		GST Payable	
100			70

Supplies		GST Refundable	
700		28	

Building		PST Payable	
75 000			60

Equipment		Bank Loan	
7 300			5 000

Mortgage Payable	
	50 000

J. Hagadorn, Capital	
	34 998

J. Hagadorn, Drawings	
500	

FIGURE 8-2 Partial general ledger for Collegiate Sales

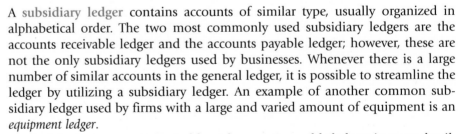

Collegiate Sales Trial Balance September 30, 20—		
Account	**Debit**	**Credit**
Cash	$ 6 000	
Accounts Receivable/B. Asimov	400	
Accounts Receivable/J. Page	500	
Accounts Receivable/F. Wang	100	
Supplies	700	
Building	75 000	
Equipment	7 300	
Accounts Payable/Brandt Ltd.		$ 200
Accounts Payable/Galea Importing		50
Accounts Payable/Lailey and Sons		150
GST Payable		70
GST Refundable	28	
PST Payable		60
Bank Loan		5 000
Mortgage Payable		50 000
J. Hagadorn, Capital		34 998
J. Hagadorn, Drawings	500	
	$90 528	$90 528

FIGURE 8-3 General ledger trial balance for Collegiate Sales

To reduce the number of accounts in the general ledger, subsidiary ledgers are set up.

SUBSIDIARY LEDGERS

A subsidiary ledger is a group of accounts of one type, usually organized in alphabetical order.

A subsidiary ledger contains accounts of similar type, usually organized in alphabetical order. The two most commonly used subsidiary ledgers are the accounts receivable ledger and the accounts payable ledger; however, these are not the only subsidiary ledgers used by businesses. Whenever there is a large number of similar accounts in the general ledger, it is possible to streamline the ledger by utilizing a subsidiary ledger. An example of another common subsidiary ledger used by firms with a large and varied amount of equipment is an *equipment ledger*.

Let's look at accounts receivable and accounts payable ledgers in more detail.

Accounts Receivable Ledger

The accounts receivable ledger is a subsidiary ledger that contains only customers' accounts in alphabetical order.

The Accounts Receivable accounts are removed from the general ledger and placed in a special accounts receivable ledger (see Figure 8-4 on page 362). Only the customer accounts (B. Asimov, J. Page, and F. Wang) are found in the accounts receivable ledger.

The customers' accounts are replaced in the general ledger by a single account called the Accounts Receivable control account. This account represents the total owing by all customers and is necessary for the general ledger to remain in balance. The balance in the Accounts Receivable control account should always equal the total of all of the individual customer accounts in the accounts receivable ledger—that is why it is called a *control account*. Notice in Figure 8-4 that the balance in the Accounts Receivable control account in the general ledger ($1000) equals the total of the accounts receivable ledger ($400 + $500 + $100).

Customer accounts are usually filed alphabetically in the accounts receivable ledger and new accounts are inserted as required.

The Accounts Receivable control account replaces the individual customer accounts in the general ledger.

Accounts Payable Ledger

A business with many creditors often removes the creditors' accounts from the general ledger and places them in alphabetical order in a subsidiary ledger called the accounts payable ledger. The creditors' accounts are replaced in the general ledger by an Accounts Payable control account (see Figure 8-4).

The total of all of the individual creditors' accounts in the accounts payable ledger ($200 + $50 + $150) should equal the balance of the Accounts Payable control account in the general ledger ($400).

The accounts payable ledger is a subsidiary ledger that contains only creditors' accounts in alphabetical order.

The Accounts Payable control account replaces the individual creditor accounts in the general ledger.

Summary

For every subsidiary ledger, there is a control account in the general ledger. The total of the accounts in the subsidiary ledger must equal the balance of the related control account in the general ledger.

VERIFYING THE ACCURACY OF THE LEDGERS

General Ledger Trial Balance

A trial balance is prepared to verify the mathematical accuracy of the *general ledger*. The procedure to prepare the trial balance is exactly the same in the three-ledger system as in the single-ledger system we used previously. The only difference is that there are now *control accounts* for accounts receivable and accounts payable rather than the individual Accounts Receivable and Accounts Payable accounts.

A trial balance is prepared to verify the mathematical accuracy of the general ledger.

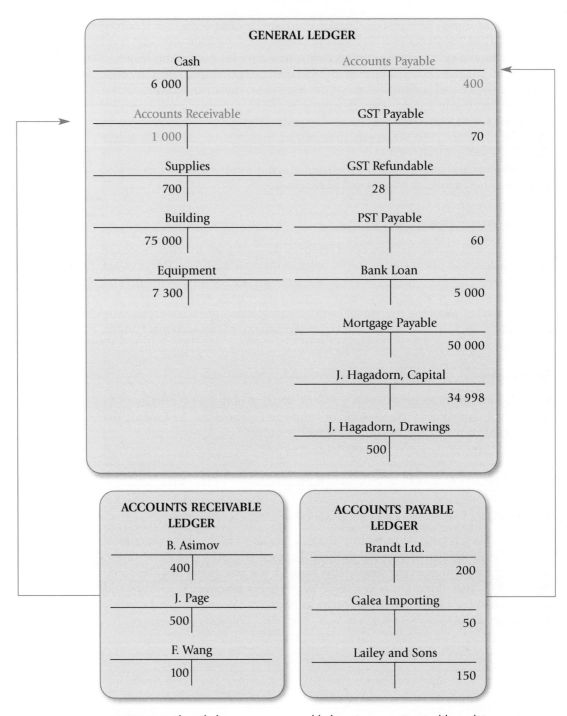

FIGURE 8-4 Three-ledger system: general ledger Accounts Receivable and Accounts Payable control accounts, accounts receivable subsidiary ledger, and accounts payable subsidiary ledger

A general ledger trial balance is shown in Figure 8-5. Notice that it contains an *Accounts Receivable control account* instead of individual customer accounts, and an *Accounts Payable control account* rather than individual creditor accounts.

Collegiate Sales Trial Balance September 30, 20—		
Account	**Debit**	**Credit**
Cash	$ 6 000	
Accounts Receivable	1 000	
Supplies	700	
Building	75 000	
Equipment	7 300	
Accounts Payable		$ 400
GST Payable		70
GST Refundable	28	
PST Payable		60
Bank Loan		5 000
Mortgage Payable		50 000
J. Hagadorn, Capital		34 998
J. Hagadorn, Drawings	500	
	$90 528	$90 528

FIGURE 8-5 General ledger trial balance

Schedule of Accounts Receivable

The schedule of accounts receivable (Figure 8-6) is prepared to verify the accuracy of the accounts receivable ledger. This schedule is a list of the customer accounts and balances. The balances are totalled and *must equal the value of the Accounts Receivable control account in the general ledger* to be correct.

A schedule of accounts receivable is prepared to prove the mathematical accuracy of the accounts receivable ledger.

What is the total of the schedule in Figure 8-6? What is the balance of the Accounts Receivable control account in Figure 8-5?

Collegiate Sales Schedule of Accounts Receivable September 30, 20—		
B. Asimov	$ 400	
J. Page	500	
F. Wang	100	Equals the Accounts
	$1 000 ←	Receivable control account in the general ledger

FIGURE 8-6 Schedule of accounts receivable

Schedule of Accounts Payable

A schedule of accounts payable is prepared to prove the mathematical accuracy of the accounts payable ledger.

A similar schedule of accounts payable is prepared from the subsidiary accounts payable ledger. This is totalled and must equal the value of the *Accounts Payable control account* in the general ledger. This verifies the correctness of the accounts payable ledger. What is the total of the schedule in Figure 8-7? What is the balance of the Accounts Payable control account in Figure 8-5?

Collegiate Sales
Schedule of Accounts Payable
September 30, 20—

Brandt Ltd.	$200	
Galea Importing	50	Equals the Accounts
Lailey and Sons	150	Payable control
	$400	account in the general ledger

FIGURE 8-7 Schedule of accounts payable

The Collegiate Sales example demonstrates a method of adapting or streamlining the accounting system to meet the needs of the business. Fraser Enterprises will be used throughout the remainder of the chapter to demonstrate how the concept is put into practice in an actual business.

ADVANTAGES OF SUBSIDIARY LEDGERS

There are two main advantages of using subsidiary ledgers in an accounting system:

- division of labour; and
- accounting control.

Division of Labour

The idea behind the division of labour is that accounting clerks can efficiently process larger amounts of accounting data when they specialize in performing one specific task.

In a small business, one employee may be able to handle all of the accounting tasks, from journalizing to preparing the financial statements. In a larger firm that must record many business transactions each day, one person cannot handle all of the accounting work. Large firms find it necessary and more efficient to implement a division of labour. The idea is to divide the work among several people, each of whom specializes in an area of accounting. Large firms identify the special accounting roles by job titles: accounts receivable clerk, accounts payable clerk, and accounting supervisor. Other companies may use other titles for these same jobs, such as junior clerk, posting clerk, senior accountant, chief accountant, or accounting manager.

Accounting Control

In a small business, the owner is involved in most of the transactions that take place. The owner can spot irregularities or errors made by employees or by other businesses with which the owner deals. A large business has a number of people involved in the handling and recording of transactions, so systems have to be put in place to replace the kind of hands-on control the owner of a small business can exert.

Accounting control refers to the accounting procedures used as a check on the reliability of the information contained in the accounting records. An example is the use of a control account to verify the total of the accounts in a subsidiary ledger. The *control account balances* in the general ledger must equal the *totals of the account balances in each of the subsidiary ledgers*. When different people are responsible for each of the ledgers, they act as a check on the accuracy of each other's work.

A good accounting system controls how information is recorded, checks the accuracy of the information, and verifies the honesty of the people involved.

UNIT 17 CHECK YOUR READING

Questions

1. In a larger business, why are the customer accounts removed from the general ledger and placed in an accounts receivable ledger?
2. What is the name of the account in the general ledger that replaces all of the individual *customer* accounts?
3. What is the name of the account in the general ledger that replaces all of the individual *creditor* accounts?
4. What is a control account? Give two examples.
5. What is a subsidiary ledger? Give two examples.
6. What are the three ledgers in a three-ledger system?
7. Give two advantages of using subsidiary ledgers.
8. From which ledger does one obtain the information required to prepare the financial statements?
9. (a) What account represents the customers in the general ledger trial balance?
   (b) What account represents the creditors in the general ledger trial balance?
10. (a) What is a schedule of accounts receivable?
    (b) What is a schedule of accounts payable?
11. (a) To what must the total of the schedule of accounts receivable be equal?
    (b) To what must the total of the schedule of accounts payable be equal?

UNIT 18 Accounting Systems

What Learning You Will Demonstrate

On completion of this unit, you will be able to complete the tasks of:

- the accounts payable clerk;
- the accounts receivable clerk; and
- the accounting supervisor.

The accounting system for a business consists of all of the activities performed to provide the information needed to make business decisions. Managers rely on information provided by the accounting system to answer questions such as the following:

- Did we make a profit?
- Should we expand our business?
- Are sales increasing or decreasing?
- Are expenses increasing or decreasing?
- How efficient are the employees?
- Which products are most profitable?

Questions such as these can be answered when there is an effective accounting system to provide data. A company must record all transactions accurately. It must provide clear financial statements to its managers. If it does not, it will lose money and risk bankruptcy.

INTRODUCING FRASER ENTERPRISES

Figure 8-8 illustrates some of the parts of an accounting system. Each part is actually a subsystem. For example, the accounts receivable system consists of a series of tasks completed for all credit sales to customers.

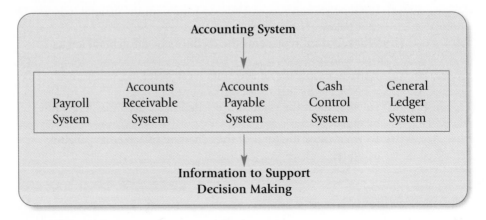

FIGURE 8-8 The accounting system provides information to management.

In this unit, part of the accounting system for a company called Fraser Enterprises will be described. The company is a wholesaler of heating and refrigeration equipment. It buys from the manufacturer and sells to companies that, in turn, sell or install the equipment. Fraser Enterprises does not charge PST on its sales. The company's head office is in Ottawa. It has branch offices in Moncton and Fredericton, New Brunswick; Halifax, Nova Scotia; and Pembroke, Sault Ste. Marie, Timmins, and Sudbury, Ontario. Among Fraser's customers are fuel oil dealers, engineering firms, and mechanical equipment firms.

Fraser Enterprises must keep track of GST.

PROCESSING DATA FOR THE ACCOUNTS PAYABLE SYSTEM

The five tasks listed below make up the accounts payable system for Fraser Enterprises:

Task 1: Process purchase invoices.
Task 2: Record purchase invoices.
Task 3: Pay creditors.
Task 4: Update creditors' accounts.
Task 5: Prepare a schedule of accounts payable.

At Fraser Enterprises, Mary Houlton, the accounts payable clerk, performs most of these tasks.

Duties of the Accounts Payable Clerk

Fraser Enterprises purchases goods and services from a number of suppliers, or creditors. Mary Houlton started as a part-time data input clerk at Fraser Enterprises, but, after a few months, she took over as accounts payable clerk in the Ottawa office. Now, she is kept busy, full-time, just handling transactions that involve accounts payable.

Figure 8-9 on page 368 is an invoice received from a creditor, Western Supply Ltd. Mary calls this a *purchase invoice* because Fraser Enterprises has purchased supplies from Western Supply Ltd. To process the invoice shown in Figure 8-9, Mary performs the accounting tasks for the accounts payable system.

A purchase invoice is a bill received from a creditor.

Task 1: Process Purchase Invoices

Mary's first responsibility is to confirm that her company, Fraser Enterprises, ordered the goods specified in the invoice and that the total amount of the invoice is correct.

In a file of purchase orders that she maintains, Mary locates Purchase Order 683, sent out about a month before by Fraser to Western Supply Ltd. She checks to see that the order price and the invoice price are the same and that there are no mathematical errors on the invoice.

Next, she must find out if the goods have actually been received. The person who receives and checks the goods completes a receiving report and sends a copy to Mary. Mary checks her file of receiving reports and locates a report that shows

The details on the purchase invoice and purchase order must match.

WSL

WESTERN SUPPLY LTD.

147 McDermot Ave.
Winnipeg, MB R3B 0R9
Tel: 474-2061   Fax: 474-3185

SOLD TO: Fraser Enterprises
125 Murray St.
Ottawa, ON K1N 5M5

DATE: Jan. 4, 20—

INVOICE NO: W-43

TERMS: Net 30 days

CUST. ORDER NO: 683

VIA: CN Express

QUANTITY	DESCRIPTION	PRICE	AMOUNT
2	Visual Card Files	$190	$380.00
10 000	Stock Cards	$5/1000	50.00
			430.00
		GST	30.10
		Total Due	$460.10

P.O. NO. 683
REC. REP. NO. 709
PRICE O.K. ✓
EXTENSIONS ✓
A.P. LEDGER ✓
JOURNAL ✓

FIGURE 8-9 Purchase invoice received from Western Supply Ltd.

the goods have been received. The three documents—the purchase order, the purchase invoice, and the receiving report—are presented to a supervisor for approval before they are recorded.

Task 2: Record Purchase Invoices

The approved invoice is returned to Mary, who records the amount owed to Western. First, Mary locates the account in the accounts payable ledger and then raises the balance by entering a credit. (Remember, a liability increases on the credit side.)

The invoice, with the purchase order and receiving report attached, is now placed in a date file until it is due to be paid—which will be within the 30-day period specified on the invoice.

Task 3: Pay Creditors

When the time approaches that the invoice is due to be paid, Mary removes the invoice from the date file. A cheque with a copy is prepared and the original cheque is sent to the creditor. Payment must be received by the creditor 30 days from the invoice date.

Task 4: Update Creditors' Accounts

Using the copy of the cheque as her source of information, Mary now decreases the balance owed to Western. It is Mary's job to maintain an accurate record of the amount owed to each creditor. She does this by recording purchases as credits and payments as debits.

Task 5: Prepare a Schedule of Accounts Payable

Mary's job is highly specialized. She works with only one type of account—accounts payable, that is, with creditor accounts. She is responsible for the accounts payable ledger, which contains only creditor accounts. Each month, Mary prepares a *schedule of accounts payable*, as shown in Figure 8-10. This schedule lists all of the accounts payable with their balances. Figure 8-10, the February schedule, is a shortened version of a schedule of accounts payable. In reality, it would contain many more creditor accounts and would be several pages in length.

Fraser Enterprises Schedule of Accounts Payable February 28, 20—	
Acme Ltd.	$ 200
Evans Co.	900
Falco Ltd.	400
Mentor Ltd.	500
	$2 000

FIGURE 8-10 Schedule of accounts payable

Mary's job as accounts payable clerk does not include journalizing the purchase invoices. This is done by the accounting supervisor, who journalizes the source documents after Mary has finished with them. Mary *posts* information *directly* into the accounts payable ledger from the invoices and cheque copies. This is known as **direct posting**. Figure 8-11 is a summary of Mary's duties.

Direct posting is the recording of information from source documents directly into the subsidiary ledger accounts.

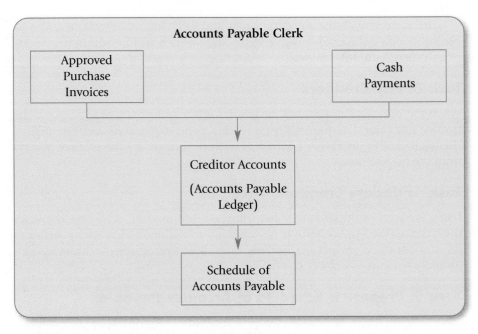

FIGURE 8-11 Duties of an accounts payable clerk

PROCESSING DATA FOR THE ACCOUNTS RECEIVABLE SYSTEM

The four tasks listed below make up the accounts receivable system for Fraser Enterprises:

Task 1: Process sales invoices.
Task 2: Record sales invoices.
Task 3: Process cash received from customers.
Task 4: Prepare a schedule of accounts receivable.

Fraser Enterprises has so many customers that Mary Houlton is unable to service accounts receivable as well as accounts payable. A second accounting clerk, George Savard, handles transactions that involve the customer accounts. His job title is accounts receivable clerk.

Duties of the Accounts Receivable Clerk

Figure 8-12 on the following page is a copy of a sales invoice sent to Meyer & Mandl. When the sale was made, an invoice was prepared in duplicate. The original copy was mailed to Meyer & Mandl. The copy shown in Figure 8-12 was sent to George. To process the invoice, George performs the accounting tasks for the accounts receivable system.

Fraser Enterprises

125 Murray St., Ottawa, ON K1N 5M5

SOLD TO: Meyer & Mandl
            27 Lakeview Terrace
            Ottawa, ON K1S 3H3

DATE: Feb. 2, 20—
INVOICE NO.: 671
CUSTOMER ORDER NO.: 43015

TERMS: Net 30 days

QUANTITY	DESCRIPTION	UNIT PRICE	TOTAL
4	Electric Heaters, Model 8-C	$19.50	$78.00
		GST	5.46
		Total Due	$83.46

ACCOUNTING COPY

FIGURE 8-12 Accounting department copy of the sales invoice sent to Meyer & Mandl

Task 1: Process Sales Invoices

George's first task is to ensure that there are no errors on the invoice. He does this by checking the extensions (quantity × unit price), the GST calculations, and the addition. George checks the extension of Invoice 671 by multiplying the quantity (4) by the unit price ($19.50). He checks the GST by multiplying the extension ($78) by 7 percent. George then checks the addition to prove that the total ($83.46) shown on the invoice is correct.

Task 2: Record Sales Invoices

Using the direct posting procedure, George locates Meyer's account in the accounts receivable ledger and increases the balance with a debit. (Remember, an account receivable is an asset and assets increase on the debit side.) George then initials the invoice and sends it, along with others he has processed, to his accounting supervisor who will journalize the credit sale.

Task 3: Process Cash Received from Customers

When cash (currency, cheques, or money orders) is received from customers, a daily cash receipts list is prepared showing the customers' names, the invoices

Cash received decreases customer account balances.

being paid, and the amounts received. The money is deposited in the bank each day. George does not actually see the money but is given a list like the one in Figure 8-13.

> **Fraser Enterprises**
> **Daily Cash Receipts**
> **February 4, 20—**
>
> | Customer | Amount |
> |---|---|
> | W. Turko, Invoice 514 | $ 50 |
> | C. Bard, Invoice 526 | 300 |
> | T. Roesler, Invoice 496 | 200 |
> | Total Deposited | $550 |

FIGURE 8-13 List of daily cash receipts

George locates the accounts of the customers shown on the cash receipts list and reduces the balances in these accounts with credits. When George has posted the invoices and daily cash receipts, he passes them on to the accounting supervisor for journalizing.

Task 4: Prepare a Schedule of Accounts Receivable

At the end of each month, George prepares a list that shows the balance owed by each customer. This list is called the *schedule of accounts receivable*. A shortened version is shown in Figure 8-14.

> **Fraser Enterprises**
> **Schedule of Accounts Receivable**
> **February 28, 20—**
>
> | | |
> |---|---|
> | C. Bard | $1 000 |
> | D. Meyer | 700 |
> | T. Roesler | 800 |
> | W. Turko | 1 000 |
> | | $3 500 |

FIGURE 8-14 Schedule of accounts receivable

As you will have noticed, George's job is also highly specialized. He deals with only one type of account—accounts receivable, that is, with customer accounts. A summary of George's duties is presented in Figure 8-15.

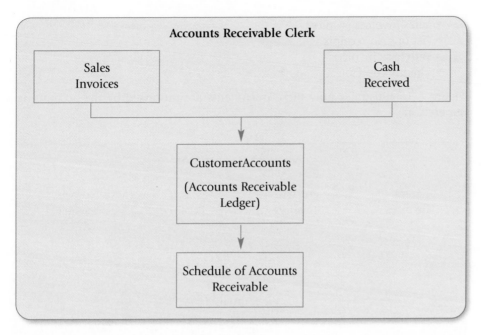

FIGURE 8-15 Duties of an accounts receivable clerk

COMPUTERIZED SYSTEM

Many firms of all sizes use computerized accounts receivable and accounts payable software to improve the efficiency of recording transactions that affect the subsidiary ledgers. This system will be more fully explained later in this unit. Although more and more businesses are using computerized systems, it is important that you fully understand the manual accounting procedures and practices that provide the foundation for these more efficient systems.

ACCOUNTING SUPERVISOR

As has been shown in the first two job descriptions, Fraser Enterprises employs two accounting clerks: the accounts payable clerk and the accounts receivable clerk. Both clerks answer to an accounting supervisor who fills a third accounting position in the department. Marni Roberts is the accounting supervisor at Fraser Enterprises. While she was going to school, Marni worked at Fraser as a part-time clerk. When she graduated from high school, she was hired as an accounts payable clerk. Several years later, Marni was promoted to the position of accounting supervisor. Her job involves the supervision of the work of the accounting clerks, the preparation of journal entries, the posting of journal entries to the general ledger, and the preparation of a general ledger trial balance.

Marni is given source documents after they have been posted directly to the accounts receivable and accounts payable ledgers by George and Mary. The source documents involved are:

- sales invoices (copies)
- list of cash receipts
- purchase invoices
- cheque copies

Figure 8-16 illustrates how these documents are processed by the accounting supervisor.

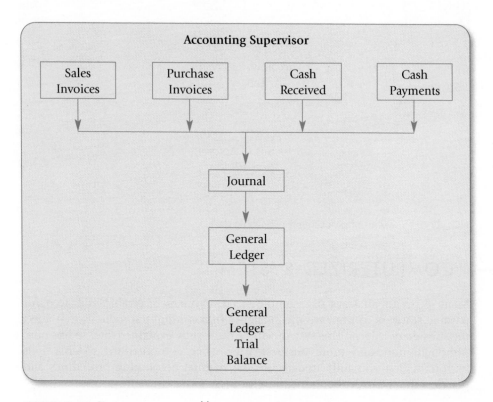

FIGURE 8-16 Documents processed by an accounting supervisor

Preparing Journal Entries

Journal entries are prepared to record the source documents (sales invoices, cash receipt lists, purchases invoices, and cheque copies) sent to Marni from George and Mary.

Sales Invoices

To journalize batch totals is to record the total of a number of source documents of one type in a single journal entry.

The journal entry to record sales invoices is shown on the next page. Notice that in this entry individual customers are not debited. Instead, the Accounts Receivable control account is debited. Also, several sales documents (Invoices 671–675) are totalled and recorded in one entry. This is known as batch journalizing.

Feb.	4	Accounts Receivable	7 8 1 10	
		Sales		7 3 0 00
		GST Payable		5 1 10
		To record Invoices 671–675.		

Batch journalizing is used to efficiently record similar transactions that are frequently repeated. Suppose a business issues 35 invoices to customers over a short period of time. For each invoice, a journal entry such as this is made by the accounting supervisor:

Feb.	1	Accounts Receivable	1 0 7 00	
		Sales		1 0 0 00
		GST Payable		7 00
		To record Invoice 101.		

However, rather than record this entry 35 separate times, i.e., once for each invoice, a total may be taken of all of the invoices and this total recorded as follows:

Feb.	1	Accounts Receivable	4 4 9 4 00	
		Sales		4 2 0 0 00
		GST Payable		2 9 4 00
		To record Invoices 101–135 for sales on account.		

Cash Receipts Lists

The entry to record the cash received from customers is shown below. Notice that in this entry the Accounts Receivable control account is credited, not the individual customer accounts.

Feb.	4	Cash	5 5 0 00	
		Accounts Receivable		5 5 0 00
		To record cash receipts for February 4.		

As with sales invoices, the accounting supervisor may batch journalize daily cash receipts. This is the entry made when cash receipts are batched:

Feb.	5	Cash	2 2 0 0 00	
		Accounts Receivable		2 2 0 0 00
		To record cash received from customers		
		February 1–5.		

Purchase Invoices

The accounting supervisor's journal entry to record invoices for Supplies ($430), Miscellaneous Expense ($170), and Equipment ($700) is shown below. Notice that in this entry several invoices are recorded. This is another example of batch journalizing. Also, Accounts Payable control is credited instead of the individual creditor accounts. *Can you explain why there are four accounts debited but only one account credited?*

Feb.	4	Supplies	4 3 0 00	
		Miscellaneous Expense	1 7 0 00	
		Equipment	7 0 0 00	
		GST Refundable	9 1 00	
		Accounts Payable		1 3 9 1 00
		To record purchase invoices from Western		
		Supply Ltd. (A39871), Nelson Ltd. (71984),		
		and Matheson Equipment (D331).		

Cheque Copies

The entry to record payments to creditors is shown below. This entry records several documents (Cheques 71–73) and is another example of batch journalizing. Accounts Payable control is debited instead of the individual creditor accounts.

Feb.	4	Accounts Payable	1 2 0 0 00	
		Cash		1 2 0 0 00
		To record Cheques 71–73.		

Posting the Journal

Marni is also responsible for posting the journal entries to the general ledger. When these entries have been posted, the Accounts Receivable control account in the general ledger has the same balance as the total of the balances of the customer accounts in the accounts receivable ledger. Remember that the sales invoices were recorded as debits in the customer accounts, and the cash amounts received were recorded as credits in the customer accounts by George, the accounts receivable clerk.

The Accounts Payable control account in the general ledger also has the same balance as the total of the balances in the creditor accounts in the accounts payable ledger. Remember that the purchase invoices and cash payments (cheque copies) were recorded by Mary, the accounts payable clerk.

All of the source documents have been recorded twice: once by the accounting supervisor and once by the accounting clerks. This is necessary if the balances of the control accounts in the general ledger are to equal the total of the accounts in the subsidiary ledgers.

Preparing Other Journal Entries

The accounting supervisor is responsible for journalizing all source documents, not just those that involve accounts receivable and accounts payable. Some examples of other journal entries made by Marni follow.

(1) A $200 cash sale was made:

Feb.	8	Cash	2 1 4 00	
		Sales		2 0 0 00
		GST Payable		1 4 00
		Cash sale.		

(2) The owner invested $5000:

Feb.	8	Cash	5 0 0 0 00	
		D. Fraser, Capital		5 0 0 0 00
		Additional investment.		

(3) Cheque 74 for $200 was issued to pay the telephone bill:

Feb.	9	Telephone Expense	1 8 6 92	
		GST Refundable	1 3 08	
		Cash		2 0 0 00
		Cheque 74.		

(4) The owner withdrew $400 for personal use:

Feb.	15	D. Fraser, Drawings	4 0 0 00	
		Cash		4 0 0 00
		Cheque 75, personal use.		

SUMMARY OF DIRECT POSTING PROCEDURE

A summary of the direct posting procedure used by Fraser Enterprises is illustrated on the next page.

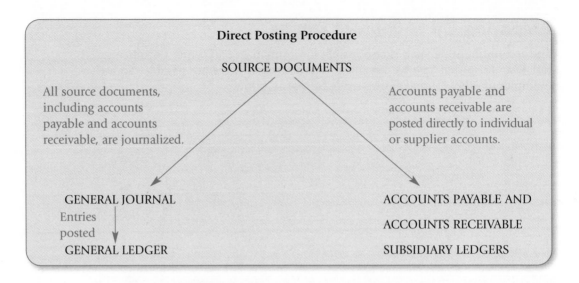

INDIRECT POSTING PROCEDURE

To do indirect posting is to record information from source documents in the general journal and then post to both the general ledger control accounts and the individual subsidiary ledger accounts.

Many businesses, especially smaller firms, want to use a subsidiary ledger system but continue to be capable of having all accounting tasks performed by one accounting clerk. These businesses use an alternative method of posting to the subsidiary ledgers. An **indirect posting** procedure allows the accounting clerk to record all source documents in the general journal and then post to both the general ledger control accounts and the individual subsidiary ledger accounts. The changes in procedure required to utilize this system are:

Transactions that change the value of Accounts Receivable or Accounts Payable must be double posted.

What is meant by double posting? Examine the journal entry below:

Feb.	4	Accounts Receivable/N. Doresco		2 2 6 00	
		Sales			2 0 0 00
		GST Payable			1 4 00
		PST Payable			1 2 00
		Invoice 2110 on account.			

Notice that the entry indicates the name of the customer as well as the fact that Accounts Receivable is affected. Why is this required?

In the indirect posting system, both the general ledger and the accounts receivable ledger are posted from the general journal. Let's examine the posting procedure:

Feb.	4	Accounts Receivable/N. Doresco	110 ✓	2 2 6 00	
		Sales	400		2 0 0 00
		GST Payable	206		1 4 00
		PST Payable	205		1 2 00
		Invoice 2110 on account.			

The posting of $226 to the Accounts Receivable control account in the general ledger is indicated by placing the account number in the P.R. column of the general journal. In addition, a posting is required to update N. Doresco's account in the accounts receivable ledger. This posting of $226 is indicated by placing a ✓ on the same line in the P.R. column. You will notice that the P.R. column has been divided with a diagonal line to accommodate two posting references for the same transaction. The remaining portion of the transaction is posted to the general ledger, as indicated by the account numbers in the P.R. column.

Why are two postings required to record the Accounts Receivable portion of the transaction? Two postings are required so that the control account and the subsidiary ledger remain in balance.

What other transactions would require double posting? Any transactions that involve the Accounts Payable control account must be double posted. The following entry illustrates this:

Mar.	27	Purchases	500	1 0 0 00	
		GST Refundable	207	7 00	
		Accounts Payable/K. El Amid	210 ✓		1 0 7 00
		Purchase Invoice 87717.			

Is a double posting required in the following entry?

Feb.	15	D. Fraser, Drawings		4 0 0 00	
		Cash			4 0 0 00
		Cheque 75, personal use.			

Since this entry does not change the value of a subsidiary ledger account, there is no need to double post any portion of the entry.

In an indirect posting system, all entries that affect the Accounts Payable or Accounts Receivable control accounts must be double posted.

SUMMARY OF INDIRECT POSTING PROCEDURE

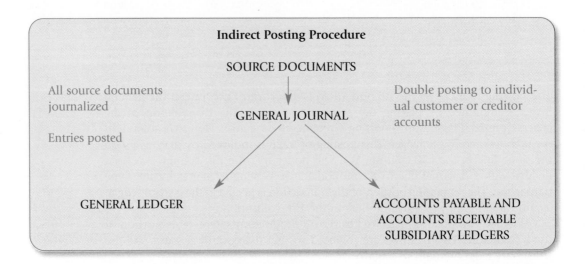

Generally Accepted Accounting Principles and Key Ideas

In this chapter, you learned the following key ideas:

- **Subsidiary ledgers** are created when a business has a large number of accounts of the same type.
- **A control account** is set up in the general ledger for every subsidiary ledger. The balance in the control account must equal the total of all of the subsidiary ledger account balances.
- **A division of labour** is required so accounting clerks can efficiently process larger amounts of accounting data when they specialize in performing one specific task.
- **The matching of purchase documents** requires that, in processing an account payable, details on the purchase order, purchase invoice, and receiving report are matched and must agree.
- **The direct posting procedure** requires that source documents be recorded directly into the subsidiary ledger accounts.
- **The indirect posting procedure** requires that source documents be recorded in the general journal and then posted to both the general ledger control accounts and the individual subsidiary ledger accounts.

UNIT 18 CHECK YOUR READING

Questions

12. What source documents does an accounts payable clerk handle?
13. (a) What documents are entered as debits in the accounts payable ledger?
    (b) What documents are entered as credits in the accounts payable ledger?
14. Explain what is meant by *direct posting*.
15. Who receives the documents after the accounts payable clerk?
16. What is the accounts receivable clerk's first task with the copies of the sales invoices?
17. Specify whether the accounts receivable clerk records:
    (a) Sales invoices as debits or credits
    (b) Cash receipts as debits or credits
18. List the source documents for which the accounting supervisor is responsible.
19. (a) What two accounts are always affected by a sales invoice?
    (b) What documents are entered as credits in the accounts payable ledger?
20. (a) What two general ledger accounts are always affected by a list of cash receipts?
    (b) Give an example of a journal entry that results from a list of cash receipts.
21. (a) What account is always credited when copies of cheques issued are journalized?
    (b) Explain why the debit is not always the same when cheque copies are journalized.
22. (a) What two general ledger accounts are always affected by copies of cheques issued on account?
    (b) Give an example of a journal entry that results from a copy of a cheque on account.
23. What is the name given to the main ledger for a company that has more than one ledger?
24. Accounts in the general ledger are numbered and organized in numerical sequence. How are the accounts in subsidiary ledgers usually organized?
25. What is the rule concerning the relationship between a subsidiary ledger and the general ledger?
26. What statement or document is prepared to prove the accuracy of the general ledger?
27. What statement or document is prepared to prove the accuracy of the accounts receivable ledger?
28. Explain the process of journalizing batch totals.
29. What are the two advantages of using subsidiary ledgers?

Exercises Part A

1. You are the accounts payable clerk for Crawford Enterprises. Your duties include recording purchase invoices in creditor accounts.
   (a) Set up the following accounts in your accounts payable ledger:

      * Corbett's Service Station
      * Grant Equipment
      * Noonan Fuels Ltd.
      * Wilson Supply Ltd.

   (b) The following purchase invoices represent purchases on account made by Crawford. Record them in the accounts payable ledger. The price shown is the final cost of the item and includes GST and PST.

   Feb. 1   Noonan Fuels Ltd., No. 6931 for fuel oil, $120.
             Wilson Supply Ltd., No. K-213 for office supplies, $75.
             Grant Equipment, No. 316 for a printer, $495.
         2   Corbett's Service Station, No. 179 for gas and oil for the company automobiles, $49.
         3   Grant Equipment, No. 391 for filing equipment, $260.
             Wilson Supply Ltd., No. K-272 for stationery, $50.
         8   Corbett's Service Station, No. 225 for car repairs, $160.
             Noonan Fuels Ltd., No. 6983 for furnace servicing, $40.
         9   Corbett's Service Station, No. 238 for gasoline, $35.
             Wilson Supply Ltd., No. K-317 for miscellaneous supplies, $24.
        15   Grant Equipment, No. 421 for a cheque protecting machine, $175.

2. Your duties as accounts payable clerk for Crawford Enterprises also include recording payments made to creditors. Record the following copies of cheques issued in the accounts payable ledger used for exercise 1.

   Feb. 10   No. 116 to Corbett's Service Station, $49 for Invoice 179.
             No. 117 to Noonan Fuels Ltd., $120 for Invoice 6931.
        15   No. 118 to Wilson Supply Ltd., $75 for Invoice K-213.
             No. 119 to Corbett's Service Station, $35 for Invoice 238.
        20   No. 120 to Grant Equipment, $200 in part payment of Invoice 316.
             No. 121 to Wilson Supply Ltd., $50 for Invoice K-272.

3. Prepare a schedule of accounts payable dated February 28 for the accounts payable ledger of Crawford Enterprises. Your schedule should total $954.

4. In this exercise, you will act as the accounts receivable clerk for Crawford Enterprises. Your duties include posting sales invoices directly into the customer accounts in the subsidiary accounts receivable ledger.

(a) Set up the following accounts in your accounts receivable ledger:

- T. Chan
- R. Mask
- W. Seth
- G. Toth

(b) The following sales invoices represent sales on account made by the company to your customers. Post them directly into the accounts receivable ledger. The price shown is the final cost of the item and includes GST and PST.

Feb. 2   R. Mask, No. 76-15, $200.
            G. Toth, No. 76-16, $300.
        3   W. Seth, No. 76-17, $500.
            T. Chan, No. 76-18, $195.
        8   T. Chan, No. 76-19, $205.
            R. Mask, No. 76-20, $125.
       10   W. Seth, No. 76-21, $95.
            G. Toth, No. 76-22, $175.
       15   T. Chan, No. 76-23, $430.
            W. Seth, No. 76-24, $155.

5. The accounts receivable clerk's job at Crawford Enterprises includes recording money received from customers. Record the following cash receipts as credits in the customer accounts used in exercise 4.

Feb. 15   T. Chan, $195 for Invoice 76-18.
           R. Mask, $200 for Invoice 76-15.
           G. Toth, $100 toward payment of Invoice 76-16.
       18 T. Chan, $205 for Invoice 76-19.
           W. Seth, $500 for Invoice 76-17.
       28 G. Toth, $375 for Invoices 76-16 and 76-22.
           W. Seth, $95 for Invoice 76-21.

6. Prepare a schedule of accounts receivable dated February 28 for the accounts receivable ledger of Crawford Enterprises. Your schedule should total $710.

7. (a) How can the total of $954 for the schedule of accounts payable (exercise 3) be checked for accuracy?
   (b) How can the total of $710 for the schedule of accounts receivable (exercise 6) be checked for accuracy?
   (c) If your totals do not agree with $954 and $710 what does this indicate?

8. In this exercise, you are the accounting clerk for Entrepreneurial Educators International, which uses the indirect posting procedure.
   (a) Set up the accounts in the general ledger from the following January 1 information:

101	Cash	$ 4 325	
110	Accounts Receivable	12 000	
120	Merchandise Inventory	22 000	
130	Office Supplies	1 275	
151	Furniture and Equipment	17 000	
200	Accounts Payable		$10 500
205	PST Payable		1 975
206	GST Payable		1 560
207	GST Refundable	1 350	
300	G. Rolanski, Capital		27 415
400	Sales		42 000
500	Purchases	20 000	
600	Rent Expense	5 500	
607	Office Expense	0	
		$83 450	$83 450

(b) The accounts receivable ledger contains the following accounts and balances on January 1. Open the ledger.

K. Lancks	$ 7 000
K. Mullane	5 000
	$12 000

(c) The accounts payable ledger contains the following accounts and balances on January 1. Open the accounts.

Dunn Ltd.	$ 2 350
Teshima Inc.	6 350
Ziraldo Corp.	1 800
	$10 500

(d) Record the entries below on page 45 of a general journal.
(e) Post the entries to the general and subsidiary ledgers using the indirect posting method.
(f) Prepare a trial balance, accounts receivable summary, and accounts payable summary on January 7.

Jan. 2 Purchase invoices:
No. 302 from Ziraldo Corp. for merchandise, $1050 plus $73.50 GST.

2 Cheque No. 252 to Teshima Inc. for $3350, partial payment of account.

2   Purchase of office supplies from Beatties Stationery, $108 plus $7 GST, Cheque No. 253.

3   Sales invoices:
K. Mullane, No. 1515, $500 plus $35 GST and $40 PST.
K. Lancks, No. 1516, $785 plus $54.95 GST and $62.80 PST.

4   Purchase invoices:
No. C475 from Dunn Ltd. for merchandise, $1650 plus $115.50 GST.
No. 15147 from Teshima Inc. for merchandise, $2300 plus $161 GST.

5   Cash sales for the week $4500, plus $315 GST and $360 PST.

6   Paid rent for the month, $2000 plus $140 GST, Cheque No. 254.

6   Cheques received from K. Lancks ($7000) and K. Mullane ($5000) in partial payment of their accounts.

9. (a) As the accounts receivable clerk for Crawford Enterprises, perform the following duties:

(i)   Set up the following accounts and balances in the accounts receivable ledger:

T. Chan	$430
R. Mask	125
W. Seth	155
G. Toth	nil

(ii)   Post the following source documents directly to the accounts receivable ledger. *Note*: All are sales PST exempt.

Mar. 2   Sales invoices:
W. Seth, No. 76-25, $355 (sale $331.78 plus $23.22 GST).
R. Mask, No. 76-26, $37 (sale $34.58 plus $2.42 GST).

3   Sales invoices:
R. Mask, No. 76-27, $670 (sale $626.17 plus $43.83 GST).
G. Toth, No. 76-28, $149 (sale $139.25 plus $9.75 GST).

4   Cash receipts:
R. Mask, $125 for Invoice 76-20.
W. Seth, $155 for Invoice 76-24.

5   Sales invoices:
T. Chan, No. 76-29, $476 (sale $444.86 plus $31.14 GST).
R. Mask, No. 76-30, $275 (sale $257.01 plus $17.99 GST).

G. Toth, No. 76-31, $850 (sale $794.39
plus $55.61 GST)

5   Cash receipts:
T. Chan, $430 for Invoice 76-23.
R. Mask, $707 for Invoices 76-26 and 76-27.
G. Toth, $149 for Invoice 76-28.

(iii)   Prepare a schedule of accounts receivable dated
March 5, 20—.

(b) As the accounting supervisor for Crawford Enterprises,
perform the following duties:

(i)   Set up the following accounts and balances in the general
ledger as at March 1:

101	Cash	$2 109
110	Accounts Receivable	710
206	GST Payable	0
400	Sales	0

(ii)   Journalize on page 35 the source documents received from
the accounts receivable clerk in part (a) of this exercise.

(iii)   Post the journal to the general ledger.

(iv)   Compare the Accounts Receivable control account with
the schedule of accounts receivable prepared in part (a).

10. (a) As the accounts payable clerk for Crawford Enterprises, perform
the following duties:

(i)   Set up the following accounts and balances dated
March 1 in the accounts payable ledger:

Corbett's Service Station	$160
Grant Equipment	730
Noonan Fuels Ltd.	40
Wilson Supply Ltd.	24

(ii)   Post the following source documents directly to the
accounts payable ledger:

Mar.   9   Purchase invoices:
Wilson Supply Ltd., No. K-597 for office forms,
$81.31, GST $5.69, total $87.
Grant Equipment, No. 480 for an office copier,
$1195.33, GST $83.67, total $1279.

10   Purchase invoices:
Corbett's Service Station, No. 447 for gas and
oil, $104.67, GST $7.33, total $112.
Noonan Fuels Ltd., No. 7340 for fuel oil,
$72.90, GST $5.10, total $78.

11 Cheque copies:
No. 122 to Corbett's Service Station, $160 for
Invoice 225.
No. 123 to Grant Equipment, $295 for the bal-
ance of Invoice 316.

13 Purchase invoices:
Corbett's Service Station, No. 470 for towing the
car and recharging the battery, $112.15, GST
$7.85, total $120.
Wilson Supply Ltd., No. K-673 for stationery,
$73.83, GST $5.17, total $79.

13 Cheque copies:
No. 124 to Grant Equipment, $435 for Invoices
391 and 421.
No. 125 to Noonan Fuels Ltd., $40 for Invoice
6983.
No. 126 to Corbett's Service Station, $112 for
Invoice 447.

(iii) Prepare a schedule of accounts payable dated March 15, 20—.

(b) As the accounting supervisor for Crawford Enterprises, perform the
following duties:

(i) Set up the following accounts and balances on March 9 in
the general ledger:

101	Cash	$5 750
103	Office Supplies	0
110	Office Equipment	0
200	Accounts Payable	954
206	GST Payable	0
207	GST Refundable	0
600	Car Expense	0
601	Heating Expense	0

(ii) Journalize on page 36 the source documents received from
the accounts payable clerk.

(iii) Post the above to the general ledger.

(iv) Compare the Accounts Payable control account with the
schedule of accounts payable prepared in part (a) of
this exercise.

Exercises Part B

11. Source documents for some of the transactions of Carlo's TV Repairs
are shown on pages 388–393. Source documents for other transactions
are listed on page 393. The accounts and balances in the three ledgers
for Carlo's TV Repairs are as follows:

Carlo's TV Repairs
Schedule of Accounts Receivable
May 3, 20—

B. Dover	$ 235.60
Drive-Inn Motor Hotel	1 356.70
L. Malyk	526.70
	$2 119.00

Carlo's TV Repairs
Trial Balance
May 3, 20—

Account	Acc. No.	Debit	Credit
Cash	101	$ 7 350.00	
Accounts Receivable	110	2 119.00	
Repair Parts	140	2 470.00	
Equipment	151	25 000.00	
Truck	155	18 000.00	
Accounts Payable	200		$ 1 945.79
GST Refundable	205	0	
GST Payable	206		0
PST Payable	207		0
C. Amato, Capital	300		52 993.21
C. Amato, Drawings	301	0	
Sales	400		0
Truck Expense	602	0	
Rent Expense	604	0	
		$54 939.00	$54 939.00

Carlo's TV Repairs
Schedule of Accounts Payable
May 3, 20—

Electronic Suppliers	$1 675.83
Melvyn's Body Repairs	0
Poulin's Service Station	269.96
	$1 945.79

In this exercise, you will perform the duties of three different employees of Carlo's TV Repairs:

- Accounts receivable clerk
- Accounts payable clerk
- Accounting supervisor

(a) Open the three ledgers and record the balances.

(b) In the accounts receivable ledger, record the appropriate source documents given on May 4 and May 5; then prepare a schedule of accounts receivable.

(c) In the accounts payable ledger, record the appropriate source documents and other transactions given on May 5; then prepare a schedule of accounts payable.

(d) Record all source documents on page 47 in the journal; post to the general ledger; and prepare a trial balance of the general ledger.

INVOICE
Carlo's TV Repairs
1750 Elgin Street, Winnipeg, Manitoba   R3E 1C3
Tel: 941-8232   Fax: 941-3987

DATE:	May 4, 20—
INV. NO:	2450
TERMS:	Net 30 days

SOLD TO:
Drive-Inn Motor Hotel
1460 River Road
Winnipeg, Manitoba
R2M 3Z8

RE: TVs in rooms 107 and 214

Labour	$112.60
Parts	189.08
	301.68
GST	21.12
PST on Parts	13.24
	$336.04

AMOUNT OF THIS INVOICE: $336.04

INVOICE
Carlo's TV Repairs
1750 Elgin Street, Winnipeg, Manitoba   R3E 1C3
Tel: 941-8232   Fax: 941-3987

DATE: May 4, 20—
INV. NO: 2451
TERMS: Net 30 days

SOLD TO:
B. Dover
141 Dynes Road
Winnipeg, Manitoba
R2J 0Z8

RE: G.E. B/W TV

Labour	$ 50.64
Parts	87.30
	137.94
GST	9.66
PST on Parts	6.11
	$153.71

AMOUNT OF THIS INVOICE: $153.71

Daily Cash Receipts
May 4, 20—

Customer	Invoice	Amount
L. Malyk	2340	$ 526.70
Drive-Inn Motor Hotel	2355	1 375.00
Cash Sales: Sales $1 084.91		
GST 75.94		
PST 75.94		1 236.79
		$3 138.49

INVOICE
Carlo's TV Repairs
1750 Elgin Street, Winnipeg, Manitoba   R3E 1C3
Tel: 941-8232   Fax: 941-3987

DATE:	May 4, 20—
INV. NO:	2452
TERMS:	Net 30 days

SOLD TO:
L. Malyk
543 Kilburn Street
Winnipeg, Manitoba
R2B 1B1

RE: Sony Colour TV

Labour	$ 74.71
Parts	175.10
	249.81
GST	17.49
PST on Parts	12.26
	$279.56

AMOUNT OF THIS INVOICE: $279.56

ELECTRONIC SUPPLIERS
Montreal
Toronto
Winnipeg
Vancouver

147 Industrial Blvd., Winnipeg, Manitoba   R2W 0J7

Tel. 475-6643
Fax   475-2843

Terms: Net 15 days

SOLD TO

Carlo's TV Repairs
1750 Elgin Street
Winnipeg, Manitoba   R3E 1C3

SHIP TO

Same

GST Registration No.	Prov. Sales Tax No.	Date Invoiced	Invoice No.
S473542119	435 70913	05/05/—	9875

Quantity	Description	Unit Price	Amount
2	X780 Speakers	$177.53	$355.06
	GST		24.85
	Pay this amount		$379.91

Melvyn's Body Repairs
4765 Borden Road, Winnipeg, Manitoba R2C 3C6
Telephone: 422-7368   Fax: 422-8734

Name:	Carlo's TV Repairs	Inv. No. 74709
Address:	1750 Elgin Street	Terms: Net 30 days
	Winnipeg, Manitoba	
	R3E 1C3	

Make:	GMC Truck	Licence: A-4597
Date:	May 5, 20—	

Quantity	Description	Unit Price	Amount
1	Fender	$950.78	$ 950.78
4	Brackets	10.75	43.00
			993.78
	Labour		587.45
			1 581.23
	GST		110.69
	Pay this amount		$1 691.92

ELECTRONIC SUPPLIERS   **CHEQUE 576**

Date	Item	Amount	Discount	Net Amount
Apr. 15	Inv. 9621	$203.76		
17	Inv. 9632	514.83		$718.59

POULIN'S SERVICE STATION   **CHEQUE 577**

Date	Item	Amount	Discount	Net Amount
Apr. 10	Inv. B-376	$ 24.50		
15	Inv. B-437	209.76		
20	Inv. B-533	35.70		$269.96

COCHRAN REALTIES   **CHEQUE 578**

Date	Item	Amount	Discount	Net Amount
Apr. 30	Rent for May	$1 168.22		
	GST	81.78		$1 250.00

Source Documents for Other Transactions:

May 5   Sales invoices:
No. 2453 to Drive-Inn Motor Hotel, $278.18 plus GST
and PST at 7 percent;
No. 2454 to L. Malyk, $50.33 plus GST and PST.

Daily cash receipts:
B. Dover, $235.60 on account.
Cash sales $1369.91, GST $95.89, PST $95.89.

Purchase invoices:
Electronic Suppliers, No. 9778, $276.30 for parts ($258.22
sale plus $18.08 GST).
Poulin's Service Station, No. B-675, $147.25 for a tune-up
on the truck ($137.62 plus $9.63 GST).

Cheque copies:
No. 579 to Melvyn's Body Repairs, $1000 on account.
No. 580 to C. Amato, the owner, $500 for personal use.

12. The accounts and balances in the three ledgers for Mullane
Consulting Services are as follows:

Mullane Consulting Services
Schedule of Accounts Receivable
February 28, 20—

Battista Ltd.	$1 250
Morgan & Co.	1 600
Quinn Inc.	185
Wong Imports	2 250
	$5 285

Mullane Consulting Services
Schedule of Accounts Payable
February 28, 20—

Dustbane Enterprises	$1 190
Matheson Office Supplies	1 195
Potter's Texaco	0
Underwood Equipment Ltd.	1 470
	$3 855

Mullane Consulting Services
Trial Balance
February 28, 20—

Account	Acc. No.	Debit	Credit
Cash	100	$ 11 000	
Accounts Receivable	101	5 285	
Office Supplies	103	500	
Equipment	113	14 000	
Automobile	114	16 000	
Accounts Payable	200		$ 3 855
GST Payable	206		0
GST Refundable	207		0
K. Mullane, Capital	300		42 930
K. Mullane, Drawings	301	0	
Fees Income	400		0
Cleaning Expense	500	0	
Car Expense	501	0	
		$46 785	$46 785

In this exercise, you are the accounting clerk for Mullane Consulting Services, which uses an indirect posting procedure.

(a) Open three ledgers and record the balances from the preceding information.
(b) Perform the accounting clerk's job by journalizing all of the source documents and posting to the ledgers. Then prepare the March 31 trial balance and appropriate schedules.

> *Note:* 8 percent PST is charged on the base price only where applicable.

Mar. 1 Sales invoices:
No. 309 to Quinn Inc., $450 plus 7 percent GST.
No. 310 to Wong Imports, $300 plus GST.
No. 311 to Battista Ltd., $200 plus GST.
No. 312 to Morgan & Co., $500 plus GST.
3 Cash receipts:
$185 from Quinn Inc., their Cheque 1743.
$600 from Morgan & Co., their Cheque 46295.
5 Purchase invoices:
Dustbane Enterprises, No. F-301, $90 plus GST for cleaning office.

Potter's Texaco, No. 498, $85 plus GST for repairs to the company automobile.

Underwood Equipment Ltd., No. 189, $300 plus GST and 8 percent PST for equipment.

8   Sales invoices:

No. 313 to Quinn Inc., $200 plus GST.

No. 314 to Morgan & Co., $450 plus GST.

10   Cheque copies:

No. 471, $90 to Dustbane Enterprises.

No. 472, $470 to Underwood Equipment Ltd.

15   Purchase invoices:

Dustbane Enterprises, No. F-396, $90 plus GST for cleaning office.

Matheson Office Supplies, No. M-201, $65 plus GST and PST for office supplies.

Potter's Texaco, No. 569, $70 plus GST for repairs to the company car and $40 for gasoline for Mullane's family car, total $114.90.

17   Cash receipts:

$1100 from Battista Ltd., their Cheque 1074.

$1000 from Morgan & Co., their Cheque 46367.

$1250 from Wong Imports, their Cheque 2649.

$2140 received from providing services to two customers for cash ($2000 plus $140 GST), Cash Receipts 147 and 148.

20   Cheque copies:

No. 473, $90.95 to Potter's Texaco on account.

No. 474, $195 to Matheson Office Supplies on account.

No. 475, $500 to K. Mullane for personal use.

24   Cash receipts:

$270 from Battista Ltd., their Cheque 1112.

$517.50 from Quinn Inc., their Cheque 1777.

$321 received from cash services ($300 sale plus $21 GST), Cash Receipt 149.

31   Cheque copies:

No. 476, $192.60 to Dustbane Enterprises.

No. 477, $114.90 to Potter's Texaco.

31   Sales invoices:

No. 315 to Battista Ltd., $500 plus GST.

No. 316 to Quinn Inc., $285 plus GST.

31   Purchase invoice:

No. 800, $50 for gas for company car, Potter's Texaco.

Computer Accounting

Web-Based Accounting

Many organizations are turning to the Internet for web-based accounting solutions. Oracle Small Business Suite (www.oraclesmallbusiness.com) offers accounting software service over the Internet.

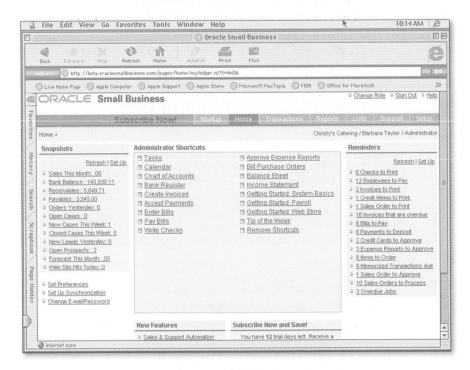

Features of Oracle Small Business Suite

Oracle Small Business Suite provides integrated online accounting software services for small and medium-sized businesses. It provides everything needed to run a business, including a general ledger, cheque writing, bank reconciliation, budgeting, accounts receivable, estimates, sales orders, online customer ordering, invoicing, inventory, job/ project tracking, expense reporting, accounts payable, purchase orders, time & billing, payroll, online employee access, and customizable reporting.

Oracle Small Business Suite offers the following to its clients:

- Employees, customers, and vendors can access up-to-the-minute data.
- Online payroll functions calculate earnings, withholdings, and deductions for employees and generate employee paychecks.
- Tax law changes and schedules are automatically updated and implemented.
- Customers connect via the Internet to view their account balances, check on payments, and pay invoices online.

- Employees can complete expense reports online for their supervisors to approve and automatically generate expense checks—all using their Internet browser.
- Sales orders are automatically recorded and customers receive copies of their sales orders via e-mail.
- Customers will automatically receive statements that include past due amounts.
- Oracle Small Business Suite will automatically calculate and track discounts for early payments.
- Oracle Small Business Suite produces over 50 reports and graphs to manage the accounting data.
- Software upgrades are done automatically; the software never becomes an "older version."

What's Needed for a Company to Use Oracle Small Business Suite?

To access the software service, companies will require a computer with an Internet connection and any Internet browser. All of the software and data are stored and backed up on the Oracle Small Business Suite computers.

What Are the Costs?

A monthly fee is charged per user. A basic fee applies for access to the majority of the accounting functions. Additional charges provide access to components such as payroll.

Questions

1. If you were the accountant for a small business and you received a visit from an Oracle Small Business Suite representative, what questions would you ask?

2. What factors would you consider in deciding whether to use this service?

3. What other information would you like to have before you make a decision?

4. What advantages might this service offer compared to a traditional in-house computer application such as QuickBooks and Peachtree Accounting?

In Chapter 4, you learned that Simply Accounting software consists of six integrated modules. There are separate groups of instructions for each of General, Payables, Receivables, Payroll, Inventory and Services, and Project. Once accounting information has been input using one module, it is combined (integrated) with information from other modules. In this example, we will examine how Simply Accounting is used to record transactions that involve accounts receivable. This includes sales to customers for cash or on credit. It also includes cash received from customers to pay amounts owed by them.

The Receivables Module

When Simply Accounting is loaded onto the computer, the main menu (home screen) is displayed on the screen. Under the heading Receivables there are three choices:

- **Customers:** shows a list of all customers and details for each, including name, address, shipping and payment terms, and sales history.
- **Sales, Orders & Quotes:** provides the invoice form shown in Figure 8-17.
- **Receipts:** presents a cash received input form on the screen.

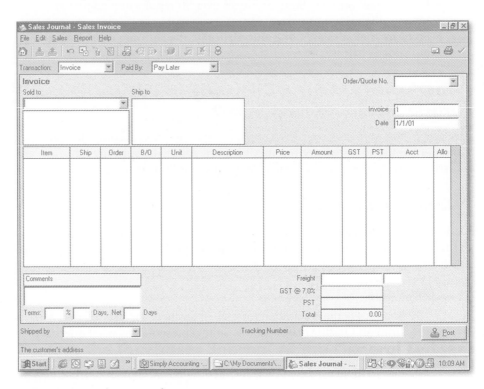

FIGURE 8-17 Sales invoice form

Recording a Credit Sale

Let's assume you wish to record credit sales to customers. First, you would select **Sales, Orders & Quotes** from the Receivables list in the main menu. The monitor will now display the sales invoice form illustrated in Figure 8-17.

To record a credit sale, the details are entered on the sales invoice form as follows:

- *Sold to*: Click on this window and select the customer from the complete list of customers.
- *Ship to*: Enter the ship to address if it is different from the customer's mailing address.

- *Invoice* and *Date*: This information is automatically provided by the software.
- *Sale details*: Enter the appropriate information in the Item, Ship, Unit, Description, Price, etc. columns. The program will automatically calculate the GST, PST, and amount items.
- From the Report menu, choose **Display Sales Journal Entry** to check your work (Figure 8-18). Notice that transaction number J337 has been allocated to the entry. The debit amount is equal to the total of the credits and the revenue (sale) has been allocated to the Renfrew Project.

Universal Construction
Sales Transaction Detail 12/20/00

(J337)		Debits	Credits	Project
1200	Accounts Receivable	532.71		
2460	PST Payable		32.71	
2510	GST Charged on Sales		32.71	
4040	Engineering Consulting—		467.29	
	Renfrew Project			467.29
		532.71	532.71	

FIGURE 8-18 Sales transaction detail

- To print the invoice, from the File menu, choose **Print**. To e-mail the invoice, choose **E-mail**.
- To complete the entry and permanently record the data, choose **Post**. This is usually only done after the details have been checked (Figure 8-18). The Post button is found in the lower right corner of the input form.

Summary

When the entry is completed by choosing **Post**, the customer's account balance will be increased in the accounts receivable ledger, the Accounts Receivable control account in the general ledger will be updated, the sale will be recorded in the Sales account, and the inventory records will be updated. The information is integrated in the Receivables, General, and Inventory modules. The program also updates the To-Do List, to remind you when the customer's payment is due.

A typical journal entry for a credit sale to a building supply company is shown in Figure 8-18.

Notice that the computer entry lists the totals of the debits and credits. This ensures that for every entry the accountant has made, debits equal credits. The accounts receivable/sales transaction data that have just been recorded will become part of the general ledger information. Therefore, the information about sales required for the income statement will be correct. The information about assets (accounts receivable) for the balance sheet will also be correct.

Simply Accounting: Accounts Payable

In the previous section, the Simply Accounting accounts receivable module was described. The accounts payable module is handled in the same way. To record a purchase on account, select **Purchases, Orders & Quotes** in the Payables list on the main menu. A purchase order input form appears on the screen. When the details are completely entered on the purchase input form, the entry is processed and the vendor's account in the payables module, the Accounts Payable control account in the general ledger, and the Inventory account are all updated.

Questions

1. What steps are followed to record a credit sale using Simply Accounting?

2. What happens when you select **Post** in the receivables module?

3. What accounts are updated when a receivables transaction has been completed?

4. What are the major differences between the manual method of recording a sale on account and the computer method?

Manual vs. Computer Accounting

In this chapter, you learned the manual accounting system tasks performed by the accounts payable clerk (Figure 8-11), the accounts receivable clerk (Figure 8-15), and the accounting supervisor (Figure 8-16). These tasks can be summarized as follows:

Manual Accounting System Tasks

In manual systems, accounting staff perform all these tasks by hand.

Step 1: Prepare source documents (sales or purchase invoices).
Step 2: Prepare journal entries to record the source documents.
Step 3: Post the entries to the customer and creditor accounts.
Step 4: Post the entries to the general ledger control accounts and to the Sales and Purchases accounts.
Step 5: Prepare schedules of accounts receivable and accounts payable and a general ledger trial balance to prove the accuracy of the ledgers.
Step 6: Prepare financial statements.

Computer Accounting Systems

Computer accounting systems utilize the concept of the database to perform accounting procedures. Data are entered and the accounting software is programmed to use the data to update accounting records and to produce reports and documents. Much of the routine work done by hand in a manual accounting system is eliminated. The steps in a computer accounting system are summarized as *data input, data processing,* and *output (reports).* The only task performed by the accountant is the data input. The other tasks are performed by the software as it processes the data according to its programming code. Here is a summary:

Computer Accounting System Tasks

Input data: Transaction data are entered into the database (e.g., customer, amount, and account number).

Process data: The software updates the accounts and uses the data to prepare pre-programmed reports on demand.

Output (reports): The software prints reports, such as the schedules of accounts receivable and payable, the trial balance, the income statement, and the balance sheet at any time.

COMPUTER ASSIGNMENTS

1. Use the accounts payable module of a computer accounting program to complete exercises 1, 2, and 3 on page 382. Do these three exercises as if they were one exercise. Print the schedule of accounts payable and the creditor accounts.

2. Use the accounts receivable module of a computer accounting program to complete exercises 4, 5, and 6 on pages 382 and 383. Do these three exercises as if they were one exercise. Print the schedule of accounts receivable and the customer accounts.

3. Complete exercise 10, on pages 386 and 387, using a computer.

4. Complete exercise 11, on pages 387 to 393, using a computer.

WEB EXTENSIONS

www.pearsoned.ca/
principlesofaccounting

Internet Study Guide

➤ Complete the Chapter 8 review.

➤ Complete the Chapter 8 definitions.

➤ Complete the Chapter 8 online test.

Web Links

Visit the Web Links section at the Pearson Education web site to find links to online accounting services. Visit each site and give examples of how these organizations could benefit small businesses.

⑪ Case Studies

CASE 1 Personal Values

George Sloan is the accounts payable clerk for Clifford Enterprises. He is considered a reliable employee. Frank Clifford, the firm's owner, lets George "run his own show" and rarely checks the work done by George.

George is responsible for matching purchase orders, receiving reports, and purchase invoices. He audits the invoices and checks them for mathematical accuracy. Invoices are then initialled by George. A cheque is prepared, attached to the invoice, and presented to Mr. Clifford. The cheques are routinely signed by Mr. Clifford. He assumes the invoice and cheque amounts are correct because "George never makes mistakes" and "George always catches overcharges made by suppliers."

One night, while having dinner with a friend, George meets Gord Chamberlain, who is a major supplier of goods to Clifford Enterprises. Gord insists on paying George's cheque and buys him an expensive bottle of wine, saying, "It's the least we can do for such a good customer."

Soon afterwards, George is invited by Chamberlain to play golf at the Hunt Club. After a game of golf and dinner, George receives an offer: In return for accepting phoney invoices from Chamberlain's company and getting them paid by Mr. Clifford, George will be paid half the amount of each cheque. Chamberlain argues that George can earn $500 a month with no risk of being caught since he has the authority to approve invoices and his work is never questioned. George realizes he could get away with this plan without being caught.

(a) If you were George, what would you do?
(b) List several alternatives open to George.
(c) What are the consequences of each alternative?

CASE 2 Balancing the Accounts Receivable Ledger

The following transactions were journalized and posted to the general ledger of P. & C. Gusen Ltd. during May:

Sales on account	$10 800
Cash received from customers	9 700
Cash sales	4 200

The schedule of accounts receivable prepared on May 31 shows a total of $5800 owed by customers.

(a) Open a T-account for the Accounts Receivable control account. The May 1 balance is $4600.

(b) Record the May transactions that involve accounts receivable to the T-account. Determine the May 31 balance in the Accounts Receivable control account.

(c) Have any errors been made that involve accounts receivable? Give reasons for your answer.

Locating Errors

CASE 3

As the accounting supervisor, you have prepared a trial balance of the general ledger at the end of the month and it balances. The accounting clerk prepares schedules of accounts receivable and accounts payable from the subsidiary ledgers and gives them to you to verify. The accounts receivable schedule balances to the control account in your trial balance, but the accounts payable schedule is $54 less than the control account.

(a) Which total is in error—the control account or the schedule of accounts payable? Why?

(b) What type of error could cause the difference?

(c) How would the error be located?

Credit Bureaus

CASE 4

A credit bureau is a business that tracks the credit history of consumers. Credit bureaus can be found in every major metropolitan area of Canada. They provide their services to credit grantors (any firm that offers credit to its customers).

When you apply for a credit card or for a loan, the lender will want to know your credit history. When deciding whether or not to lend you money, the lender may contact the local credit bureau for information. The credit bureau does not decide whether to lend you money, they simply provide information to the potential lenders who make the final decision whether credit should be given to a particular person. To obtain this information, a credit grantor must join the credit bureau and pay a membership fee.

What's Included in Your Credit File?

Depending on your province and the particular credit bureau, the file may vary, but most will include the following:
- name, address, date of birth, and number of dependants;
- social insurance number;
- your employer's name and your employment history;
- home ownership status;
- estimated salary;
- marital status and spouse's employer and position;
- credit card payment records;
- public record items, such as court judgments, and seizures and collection items; and
- credit history.

The credit history provides detailed information to the lender. The history may include:
- types of businesses where you shop;
- dates of opening charge accounts;
- previous amounts of credit granted;
- balances owing; and
- past-due amounts.

Who Pays for this Service?

The company that requests information about a consumer pays a service charge to the credit bureau. Consumers can look at their own file by visiting a credit bureau and showing proper identification. A fee is usually charged to see the content of your own credit file. If you disagree with the information contained in the credit file, you can submit a statement to challenge the information.

Where Does the Information Come from?

Most of the information on your file will have come from credit grantors. These may be banks, car dealers, mortgage companies, department stores, and public records such as bankruptcies. Figure 8-19 illustrates the basic operations of a credit bureau.

Why Are Credit Bureaus Needed?

Credit bureaus are needed to assist legitimate businesses in deciding whether or not to grant credit. Some people will purchase items on credit but rarely pay for their purchases. When the credit balance has built up they will move to a new location, making it difficult for businesses to locate them. These individuals continually obtain new charge accounts and avoid payments by skipping town. To retail stores, this type of person is known as a "skip." Credit bureaus exist because of "skips" and other people who might otherwise create bad debts for businesses. Bad debts cost all consumers money because companies implicitly factor in an amount to compensate for bad debts when they price the goods and services we all buy.

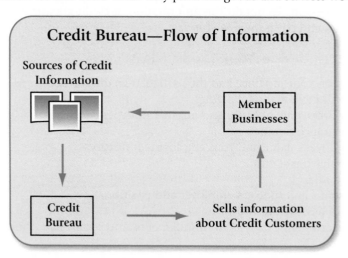

FIGURE 8-19 Operations of a credit bureau

Laws and Regulations

Provincial governments have passed laws to control agencies such as credit bureaus. These laws outline how credit reports are to be used. They outline procedures for ensuring the accuracy and confidentiality of information about a consumer.

The credit bureaus are linked by the Associated Credit Bureaus of Canada. This association has established rules and policies to govern the manner in which credit bureaus operate.

(a) What is a credit bureau?
(b) How is it financed?
(c) Who joins a credit bureau?
(d) What services does it provide?
(e) Who benefits from the services of the credit bureau?
(f) What is a credit grantor?

One-Write Systems

CASE 5

A one-write system is a manual accounting system that uses specially treated accounting forms and a pegboard or one-write board. Anything written on the top form is automatically transferred to forms placed beneath it. There is no copying from one form to another. For example, when you issue a cheque all the pertinent information, such as payee, cheque number, amount, and date, is automatically transferred to the journal page beneath. This ensures accurate recording of data and eliminates transposition errors.

A one-write system is a manual accounting system that uses specially treated accounting forms and a peg board or one-write board to hold the forms in place.

Research one-write systems either by contacting a small business organization that uses a one-write system, or by completing a search of companies that sell one-write products. Your research should include the following information:

(a) The typical size of organizations that use one-write systems
(b) The costs involved in implementing a one-write system
(c) The accounting applications available in one-write systems
(d) The advantages and disadvantages of using a one-write system
(e) The reason some companies choose a one-write system over a computerized system

⑫ Career Education Activities

1. Behaviour and Values—What Is Important to You?

Our behaviour—the things we do—is based on our personal values. Often we act spontaneously without reflecting on WHY we are doing WHAT we are doing. As well, our values change over time, as maturity and life experiences affect them.

It is worthwhile to pause occasionally to examine our personal values; to ask the question: "What are my values?" Having a clear understanding of our values can lead to self-confidence, to a clear understanding of self, and to positive self-esteem. It can also lead to improved decision making.

Thinking about careers, planning ahead, and job finding are not easy. Many decisions have to be made and often plans must be changed. It is helpful, when making such decisions and choices, to know the basis for your decisions—to know yourself and what you feel is important.

The following exercise is designed to make you think about your values and to help you to know yourself a little better. This self-knowledge can help you in the long run to make better-informed decisions about what you would like to do when career decisions have to be made—or changed.

Below is a list of beliefs and values. Make a copy of the list for yourself. Then, for each item on the list, place a check mark in one of the three columns—very important, important, or not important. Add items to your list that you consider values. You will likely find that you place check marks in all three categories.

For Discussion

(a) Select the five most important values to you. Ask yourself why they are important. Do these five values lead to action or behaviour on your part? Why or why not?
(b) Pick out three of the least important values to you.
(c) Do your values have any relationship to your ultimate career?

Belief or Value	Very Important	Important	Not Important
Cooperation, working with others			
Freedom			
Being wealthy			
Stability, calmness			
Winning			
Being at peace with self			
Adventure			
Being promoted			
Self-respect			
Helping others			
Achievement			
Material possessions (car, clothes, house)			
Personal growth and development			
Friendship			
Power over others			
Creativity			
Relaxation			
Recreation and athletics			
Pleasure, fun			
Hard work			
Physical fitness			

2. Accounts Payable Position

After completing the first eight chapters of this textbook, you now have many of the qualifications required for the position of payroll clerk. The accounting skills you are learning will also prepare you for positions such as an accounts payable clerk.

For Discussion

(a) List the accounting functions that are outlined in these two job postings.
(b) Explain why the positions require spreadsheet and word processing skills.
(c) What does it mean to be "detail-oriented"?

Payroll Clerk

Responsible for the computerized processing of payroll, record keeping, answering employee payroll inquiries, preparation of bank reconciliation statements, and benefit reporting. The successful candidate is reliable, detailed-oriented, has payroll background, and has a minimum 2 years' accounting experience. Proficiency with both spreadsheets and word processing is required.

Accounts Payable Clerk

Responsible for processing invoices, dealing with public inquiries, account reconciliation, expense analysis, and special presentations to clients. You must possess good accounting skills, have a minimum 3 years' accounts payable experience, and be proficient with Microsoft Excel.

To apply for either of these positions, please send your résumé to:

Mrs. Maria Makrakis
International Languages Program
100 Lotta Ave,
London, ON N6F 2E5

Career Profile

Shahe Avedissian operates a successful retail office supply store. The business, Laurier Office-Mart Inc., is located on Laurier Avenue in Ottawa, quite close to the University of Ottawa. Shahe felt that a business selling school and computer supplies, and offering colour and black and white photo-copying services, would do well in that location. He has been proven right, since he has built a strong relationship with the students attending the university and with the local businesses.

While at high school, Shahe took on a number of part-time jobs. These included: pizza delivery, salesperson for a retail company, inventory control clerk, and salesperson for a merchandising firm. He also did volunteer work for a local cultural society.

In his final year of high school, Shahe took classes in the morning and completed an afternoon cooperative education program. Each afternoon he worked for three hours for an accounting firm. This provided him with valuable work experience and two additional credits toward his graduation diploma.

After graduation from high school, he completed a business course at Algonquin College. His first full-time job was as an accounting clerk for a small retail business.

Shahe knew that he wanted to own and operate his own company. To realize this dream meant taking risks and working long hours. His part-time jobs taught him many business skills and the value of hard work. When an opportunity turned up that allowed him to lease a retail store he decided to go into business for himself.

To prepare to operate his own business, he continued to improve his skills by attending business seminars and accumulating his own small library of reference books. He made himself familiar with municipal regulations as well as government incentives for small business owners.

After 14 years of operating Laurier Office-Mart, Shahe has opened up a second office and a warehouse catering to commercial businesses. He is now married and has a young son. He has continued to update his computer skills and manages his own accounting records using SBT accounting software. He hires staff to do the basic inputting of records, but he likes to complete the month-to-month profit and loss statements himself so that he can stay on top of where his business is heading. He hires an accountant at year-end to prepare his corporate tax return.

For Discussion

(a) What attitudes and determination did Shahe demonstrate that allowed him to become successful?
(b) Why does Shahe like to be involved in the accounting functions for his company?

9

The Columnar Journal

What Learning You Will Demonstrate

On completion of this unit, you will be able to:

- record transactions in a columnar journal;
- prove the accuracy of a columnar journal by balancing its totals; and
- forward totals in a columnar journal.

In Chapter 8, you learned that many business enterprises use subsidiary ledgers as well as a general ledger. The use of more than one ledger provides:

- division of labour; and
- accounting control.

In the next two chapters, you will learn that companies use several different *journal systems* that provide similar and additional accounting advantages and benefits.

INTRODUCING THE COLUMNAR JOURNAL

Examine the general journal in Figure 9-1 on page 410. GST and PST have been omitted to simplify the example. These seven journal entries require 28 lines of space. Notice that recording the entries involves writing certain words and account names over and over. How many times is Cash written? Sales? Imagine how many entries that involve Cash, Sales, Purchases, and other frequently used accounts a large business would have!

The same seven transactions are shown in the columnar journal in Figure 9-2 on page 411. Only seven lines are required to record the same transactions. Examine the first entry for cash sales. Notice that there is a *special column for Cash debits,* and a *special column for Sales credits.* The words *Cash* and *Sales* do not have to be written by the accountant to record this transaction. Only the date, explanation, and amount need to be written—a considerable saving of time and space.

A columnar journal has special columns for accounts that are used often to record transactions.

The **columnar journal** is designed so that *there are special columns for accounts used often by a business.* If a transaction involves an account for which a special column is not provided, the Other Accounts columns are used. The columnar journal is also known as a *combination journal* or a *synoptic journal.*

The number of columns in a columnar journal is determined by the types of transactions a company has. Ultimately, of course, the number of columns has to be limited by the size of the journal page. However, it is not uncommon to have 13 or 14 columns in a columnar journal.

	GENERAL JOURNAL			PAGE 17
DATE	PARTICULARS	P.R.	DEBIT	CREDIT
20—				
Nov. 1	Cash		5 2 0 00	
	Sales			5 2 0 00
	Cash Sales Slips 781–799.			
1	Accounts Receivable/E. Marano		2 3 9 60	
	Sales			2 3 9 60
	Invoice B-601, n/30			
4	Cash		6 0 3 70	
	Sales			6 0 3 70
	Cash Sales Slips 800–819.			
4	Purchases		1 9 0 0 00	
	Accounts Payable/Acme Ltd.			1 9 0 0 00
	Invoice K-206, merchandise, n/30.			
5	Accounts Receivable/A. Komar		4 1 6 00	
	Sales			4 1 6 00
	Invoice B-602, n/30.			
5	Purchases		8 4 1 00	
	Cash			8 4 1 00
	Cheque 16239, merchandise.			
8	Cash		1 2 5 0 00	
	Sales			1 2 5 0 00
	Cash Sales Slips 820–839.			

FIGURE 9-1 Two-column general journal

COLUMNAR JOURNAL — PAGE 26

DATE	ACCOUNT OR EXPLANATION	REF. NO.	P.R.	CASH DEBIT	CASH CREDIT	OTHER ACCOUNTS DEBIT	OTHER ACCOUNTS CREDIT	ACCOUNTS RECEIVABLE DEBIT	ACCOUNTS RECEIVABLE CREDIT	SALES CREDIT	GST REFUND DEBIT	GST PAYABLE CREDIT	PST PAYABLE CREDIT	PURCHASES DEBIT	ACCOUNTS PAYABLE DEBIT	ACCOUNTS PAYABLE CREDIT
20—																
Feb. 1	Cash Sales Slips	781–799		5 2 0 00						5 2 0 00						
1	E. Marano, n/30	B-601						2 3 9 60		2 3 9 60						
4	Cash Sales Slips	800–819		6 0 3 70						6 0 3 70						
4	Acme Ltd., n/30	K-206												1 9 0 0 00		1 9 0 0 00
5	A. Komar, n/30	B-602						4 1 6 00		4 1 6 00						
5	Cheque	16239			8 4 1 00									8 4 1 00		
8	Cash Sales Slips	820–839		1 2 5 0 00						1 2 5 0 00						

FIGURE 9-2 Columnar journal

COLUMNAR JOURNAL — PAGE 13

DATE	ACCOUNT OR EXPLANATION	REF. NO.	P.R.	CASH DEBIT	CASH CREDIT	OTHER ACCOUNTS DEBIT	OTHER ACCOUNTS CREDIT	ACCOUNTS RECEIVABLE DEBIT	ACCOUNTS RECEIVABLE CREDIT	SALES CREDIT	GST REFUND DEBIT	GST PAYABLE CREDIT	PST PAYABLE CREDIT	PURCHASES DEBIT	ACCOUNTS PAYABLE DEBIT	ACCOUNTS PAYABLE CREDIT
20—																
Feb. 1	Cash sale	193		3 4 5 00						3 0 0 00		2 1 00	2 4 00			
3	A. Walker, n/30	175						2 3 0 00		2 0 0 00		1 4 00	1 6 00			
6	D. Dodd, n/30	176		1 0 0 00				3 6 0 00		4 0 0 00		2 8 00	3 2 00			
9	Office Supplies	135				1 5 0 00										
	Office Equipment	135			8 5 1 85	6 5 0 00					5 1 85					
13	National Wholesale	B-117									2 8 00			4 0 0 00		4 2 8 00
16	Rent Expense	171			6 4 2 00	6 0 0 00					4 2 00					
18	Telephone Expense	172			1 0 1 16	9 5 00					6 16					
20	A. Walker			2 1 6 00					2 1 6 00							
24	Butler Mfg.	173			7 4 9 00							4 9 00			7 0 0 00		
28	G. LePensée, Drawings	174			1 0 0 00	1 0 0 00										

FIGURE 9-3 Transactions recorded in a columnar journal

Another feature of the columnar journal is the provision of a Reference Number column. It is located next to the explanation section, and is used to record source document numbers such as cheque and invoice numbers.

RECORDING TRANSACTIONS IN A COLUMNAR JOURNAL

The recording of transactions in a columnar journal is illustrated by the examples given below. Read each example and examine the corresponding entry in Figure 9-3 (on page 411), which is the completed columnar journal that contains these transactions. The advantages of this journal will be evident to you.

Transaction 1: Cash Sale

Feb. 1   Sold merchandise for cash, $300 plus 7 percent GST and 8 percent PST calculated on the base price, Cash Sales Slip 193.

In general journal form, the entry would be:

Feb.	1	Cash	3 4 5 00	
		Sales		3 0 0 00
		GST Payable		2 1 00
		PST Payable		2 4 00
		Cash Sales Slip 193.		

Most transactions require only one line when recorded in a columnar journal.

Compare this with the entry in Figure 9-3. An explanation of the transaction is written in the Account or Explanation column; source document number 193 is shown in the Reference Number column; $345 is entered in the Cash debit column, $300 in the Sales credit column, $21 in the GST Payable credit column, and $24 in the PST Payable credit column. The transaction requires *only one line* and *very little writing* compared to the same entry in a general journal.

Transaction 2: Sale on Account

Feb. 3   Sales Invoice 175 to A. Walker, $200 plus 7 percent GST and 8 percent PST, terms n/30.

Again, look at the entry in Figure 9-3. The name of the customer and the terms of the sale are shown in the Account or Explanation column; invoice number 175 is recorded in the Reference Number column; $230 is entered in Accounts Receivable debit, $200 in Sales credit, $14 in GST Payable credit, and $16 in PST Payable credit.

Transaction 3: Sale with a Down Payment

Feb. 6   Sales Invoice 176 to D. Dodd, $400 plus 7 percent GST and 8 percent PST. Received $100 cash, balance of $360 to be paid in 30 days.

Although this transaction involves five accounts, the entry is done on one line in the columnar journal. In Figure 9-3, locate the debits to Cash of $100 and to Accounts Receivable of $360, and the credits to Sales of $400, to GST Payable of $28, and to PST Payable of $32.

Transaction 4: Cash Purchase of Supplies and Equipment

Feb. 9   Cheque 135 for $856 to E.T. Wilson Ltd., payment for office supplies $150, office equipment $650, and $51.85 GST.

The columnar journal does not have special columns for office supplies or office equipment. Therefore, the Other Accounts section is used. To identify which accounts change, the account titles Office Supplies and Office Equipment are written on separate lines in the *Account or Explanation* column. The amount debited is written on the same line in the Other Accounts debit column. In Figure 9-3, this transaction is recorded on two lines.

Additional Transactions

Some further transactions are listed below. Examine them and decide how you would record them in a columnar journal. Check your ideas with Figure 9-3.

Feb. 13   Received Purchase Invoice B-117 from National Wholesale, $400 plus $28 GST, on account.
16   Cheque 171 to Royal Real Estate, $600 plus $42 GST, for rent.
18   Cheque 172, $95 plus $6.16 GST, for telephone bill.
20   Received $216 from A. Walker on account.
24   Cheque 173 to Butler Mfg., $700 plus $49 GST, for cash purchase of merchandise.
28   Cheque 174 to G. LePensée, the owner, $100 for personal use.

SPECIAL SECTIONS OF THE COLUMNAR JOURNAL—SUMMARY

Account or Explanation Column

When a transaction causes a change in a customer or a creditor account, the name of the customer or creditor is shown in the Account or Explanation column.

Other Accounts Section

When a transaction includes a debit or credit for which there is not a special column in the columnar journal, the Other Accounts section is used. The account title is written in the Account or Explanation column so that the entry may be posted to that account in the general ledger.

The Other Accounts columns are used to record transactions that involve accounts for which special columns have not been provided in the columnar journal.

Reference Number Column

A Reference Number column is located next to the Account or Explanation column. This column is used to record the number of the source document from which the transaction was recorded. For a sale on account, the number of the sales invoice is recorded. For other transactions, the cheque number, purchase invoice number, or credit invoice number is shown.

BALANCING THE COLUMNAR JOURNAL

The debit totals should equal the credit totals on each page of the columnar journal.

Balancing, or cross-balancing, a columnar journal page determines if the debit totals equal the credit totals.

If transactions have been recorded properly, *the debits should equal the credits on every page of the columnar journal.* To determine this, at the bottom of each page and at the end of the month, the totals of each column are shown. This is known as *balancing* the journal. The process may also be called *cross-balancing.* If the debit column totals equal the credit column totals, that particular page of the journal is in balance. If a printing calculator is used to prove the totals, the tape may be attached to the journal as proof that the page balances. The steps to be followed in balancing a columnar journal are described below.

Steps in Balancing the Columnar Journal

The following steps are illustrated in the columnar journal in Figure 9-4:

1. Rule a single line across all money columns below the last line used.
2. Add the columns. Write the totals in pencil at the foot of each column.
3. Add the debit column totals and the credit column totals.
4. If the debit totals equal the credit totals, write the column totals in ink at the bottom of each column. Write the debit and credit totals in the Account or Explanation column.
5. Rule double lines across the date and all money columns.

LOCATING ERRORS IN THE COLUMNAR JOURNAL

If the journal totals do not balance, a recording error may have been made. Errors may be located by following this procedure:

- Start on the first line and check to see if there are equal debits and credits on each line.
- Recheck all additions.
- Then follow the steps for locating errors outlined in Chapter 4.

COLUMNAR JOURNAL PAGE 13

DATE	ACCOUNT OR EXPLANATION	REF. NO.	CASH DEBIT	CASH CREDIT	P.R.	OTHER ACCOUNTS DEBIT	OTHER ACCOUNTS CREDIT	ACCOUNTS RECEIVABLE DEBIT	ACCOUNTS RECEIVABLE CREDIT	SALES CREDIT	GST REFUND. DEBIT	GST PAYABLE CREDIT	PST PAYABLE CREDIT	PUR- CHASES DEBIT	ACCOUNTS PAYABLE DEBIT	ACCOUNTS PAYABLE CREDIT
20—																
Feb. 1	Cash sale	193	3 4 5 00							3 0 0 00		2 1 00	2 4 00			
3	A. Walker, n/30	175						2 3 0 00		2 0 0 00		1 4 00	1 6 00			
6	D. Dodd, n/30	176	1 0 0 00					3 6 0 00		4 0 0 00		2 8 00	3 2 00			
9	Office Supplies	135				1 5 0 00										
	Office Equipment	B-117		8 5 1 85		6 5 0 00					5 1 85					
13	National Wholesale										2 8 00			4 0 0 00		4 2 8 00
16	Rent Expense	171		6 4 2 00		6 0 0 00					4 2 00					
18	Telephone Expense	172		1 0 1 16		9 5 00					6 16					
20	A. Walker	173	2 1 6 00						2 1 6 00							
24	Butler Mfg.			7 4 9 00							4 9 00			7 0 0 00		
28	G. LePensée, Drawings	174		1 0 0 00		1 0 0 00										
			6 6 1 00	2 4 4 4 01		1 5 9 5 00		5 9 0 00	2 1 6 00	9 0 0 00	1 7 7 01	6 3 00	7 2 00	1 1 0 0 00		4 2 8 00
	Debits = $4123.01															
	Credits = $4123.01															

FIGURE 9-4 Balancing the columnar journal

FORWARDING PAGE TOTALS

When a page of a journal is filled, it should be balanced and the totals carried forward to the next page. The word *Forwarded* is written in the Account or Explanation column on the same line as the totals. On the next journal page, the date, including the year and the month, is written on the first line of the Date column. The word *Forwarded* is written on the first line in the Account or Explanation column and the totals are written in the money columns. For example, if column totals were being forwarded on February 14, the first line on the new journal page would appear as follows:

			COLUMNAR JOURNAL					
			CASH				OTHER ACCOUNTS	
DATE	ACCOUNT OR EXPLANATION	REF. NO.	DEBIT	CREDIT	P.R.	DEBIT	CREDIT
20—								
Feb. 14	Forwarded		6 2 1 00	2 9 1 4 01	✓	1 0 9 5 00	3 4 6 72

Totals on each page are carried forward until the end of the month.

Totals are carried forward in this manner until the end of the month. At that time, the journal is balanced and the totals for the entire month are posted to the general ledger.

UNIT 19 CHECK YOUR READING

Questions

1. How many lines does it take to record an ordinary entry in a general journal? How many lines does it generally take to record an entry in a columnar journal?
2. What are other names for a columnar journal?
3. When is an account given its own column in a columnar journal?
4. Why does it take two lines to record the February 9 entry (in Figure 9-3) in a columnar journal?
5. When is a debit or a credit amount recorded in the Other Accounts section of a columnar journal?
6. How is a columnar journal balanced?
7. How are page totals forwarded in a columnar journal?
8. What procedure is followed if a columnar journal page does not balance?

UNIT 19 APPLY YOUR KNOWLEDGE

Exercises

1. (a) Journalize the June transactions for Costello Enterprises in a columnar journal on page 13. All sales are subject to 7 percent GST and 8 percent PST calculated on the base price.

Jun. 1 Issued Cheque 76 for $800 plus $56 GST, to pay the June rent.

      1 Cash sales slips: sales $395 plus GST and PST.

      5 Sales invoices, terms n/30:
          No. 171 to M. Swords, $75 plus GST and PST.
          No. 172 to W. Kranz, $180 plus GST and PST.
          No. 173 to J. Moore, $130 plus GST and PST.

      5 Purchased merchandise for $750 plus $52.50 GST from Tanyss Trading, Invoice B-316, terms n/30.

      8 Bought office supplies for $55 plus $3.56 GST, issued Cheque 77.

   10 Cash purchase of merchandise for $200 plus $14 GST, Cheque 78.

   13 Paid $370 plus $25.90 GST to *The Star* for advertising, Cheque 79.

(b) Total, balance, and rule the journal.

2. (a) Forward the totals from page 13 in exercise 1. Continue to journalize transactions for Costello Enterprises in the columnar journal, page 14.

Jun. 15 Received cheques from customers:
          M. Swords, $86.25 for Invoice 171.
          J. Moore, $149.50 for Invoice 173.

   17 Purchased merchandise for $250 plus $17.50 GST from National Wholesale, terms 1/10, n/30.

   19 Cash sales slips: sales $500, GST $35, and PST $40.

   22 Issued Cheque 80 to Tanyss Trading for $250 on account.

   22 The owner, P. Costello, invested an additional $4000 in the business.

   23 Sales invoices, terms 2/10, n/30:
          No. 174 to M. Swords, $200 plus taxes.
          No. 175 to L. Usher, $730 plus taxes.

   25 Issued Cheque 81 for $2700 to pay the month's wages.

   26 Issued Cheque 82 to National Wholesale for invoice of June 17. Amount of cheque $264.82; amount of discount taken $2.68.

   29 Cheque received for $207 from W. Kranz.

   30 Issued Cheque 83 for $95 plus $6.65 GST to pay utilities expenses for the month.

(b) Total, balance, and rule the journal.

UNIT 20 Posting the Columnar Journal

What Learning You Will Demonstrate

On completion of this unit, you will be able to:

- record credit invoices in a columnar journal;
- post the columnar journal;
- state the advantages to using a columnar journal; and
- state the disadvantages to using a columnar journal.

METHODS OF POSTING

Direct Post to the Subsidiary Ledgers

Many businesses post to the subsidiary accounts receivable and accounts payable ledgers directly from source documents on a daily basis. The source documents are then batch journalized in the columnar journal. This method is known as *direct posting*.

Posting to all Ledgers from the Journal

If the direct posting method is not used, source documents can be entered into the columnar journal and then the individual Accounts Receivable and Accounts Payable entries are posted to the subsidiary accounts receivable and accounts payable ledgers daily. Amounts in the Other Accounts columns are posted individually to the general ledger on a monthly basis.

As illustrated in Figure 9-5 on the next page, there are three basic steps in posting to the subsidiary ledgers and the general ledger from the columnar journal.

Step 1: Post Accounts Receivable and Payable

The amounts in the Accounts Receivable and Accounts Payable columns are posted daily to the subsidiary ledgers.

Each day, the individual accounts receivable and payable are posted to the subsidiary ledgers to update the customer and creditor accounts. As each amount is posted, a check mark (✓) is placed in the Posting Reference column of the journal. A check mark is used since Accounts Receivable and Accounts Payable are kept in alphabetical order rather than numbered.

Step 2: Post the Other Accounts Section

Amounts in the Other Accounts columns are posted individually.

At the end of the month, the *amounts in the Other Accounts section are posted individually* to the general ledger. The names of the accounts to which postings are made are found in the Account or Explanation column. As the postings are made, the account numbers are shown in the Posting Reference column of the columnar journal.

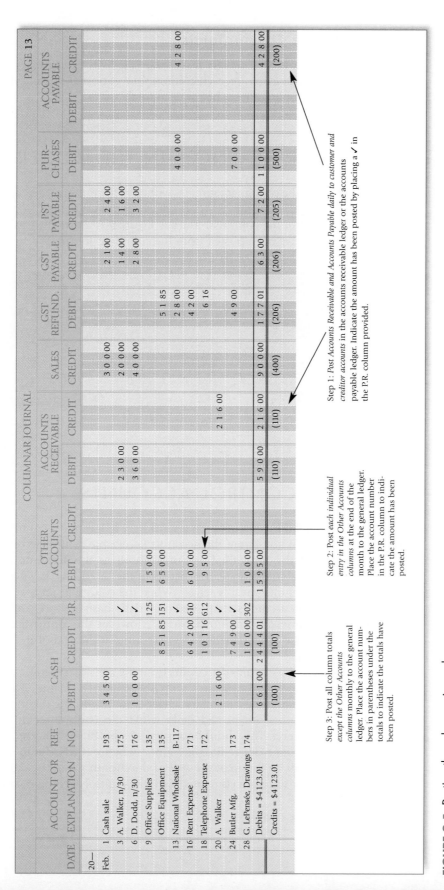

FIGURE 9-5   Posting the columnar journal

Step 3: Post the Column Totals

All column totals except the Other Accounts totals are posted to the general ledger.

At the end of the month, *all column totals except the Other Accounts column totals are posted to the general ledger*. As each column total is posted, the number of the account is written in parentheses below each total.

POSTING REFERENCES IN THE LEDGER

The page number of the columnar journal is written in the Posting Reference column of the general ledger accounts. For example, C13 indicates that a posting was made from page 13 of the columnar journal. Figure 9-6 shows the Cash account after the amounts have been posted from the columnar journal.

	GENERAL LEDGER						
ACCOUNT Cash							No. 100
DATE	PARTICULARS	P.R.	DEBIT	CREDIT	DR. CR.	BALANCE	
20—							
Feb. 1	Forwarded	✓			DR.	11 0 0 0 00	
28		C13	6 6 1 00		DR.	11 6 6 1 00	
28		C13		2 4 4 8 65	DR.	9 2 1 2 35	

FIGURE 9-6 Cash account after posting the columnar journal totals

POSTING CONTROL ACCOUNTS

In Chapter 8, the relationship between a subsidiary ledger and a control account was demonstrated. As you know, the Accounts Receivable control account equals the value of all of the individual accounts found in the accounts receivable ledger. A similar relationship exists between the Accounts Payable control account and the accounts payable ledger. When the columnar journal is posted, the subsidiary ledger accounts are posted on a daily basis to have current information in the customer and creditor accounts. However, the control accounts are posted along with the other general ledger accounts at the end of the month to save time in posting.

If you prepared a schedule of accounts from the subsidiary ledger during the month, would it necessarily balance with the control account? The control account would not equal the subsidiary ledger amounts during the month since the individual accounts are posted daily while the control account is only updated at month's end. This should not present a problem, however, since the individualized customer or creditor accounts contain current amounts at all times. Any errors will be found at the end of the month when the schedules of subsidiary ledger accounts are compared with the control account balances.

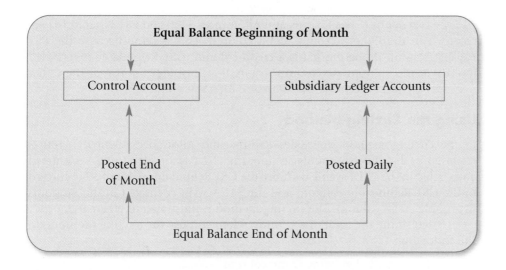

Equal Balance Beginning of Month

Control Account

Subsidiary Ledger Accounts

Posted End
of Month

Posted Daily

Equal Balance End of Month

RECORDING CREDIT INVOICES IN THE COLUMNAR JOURNAL

5

Two methods are followed to record credit invoices in the columnar journal: *circling the amount* and *using the Other Accounts section*. The following sample transactions illustrate the two methods.

Recording a Sales Return

The following transaction illustrates how a credit invoice for a sales return is recorded.

Sample Transaction

Feb. 28   D. Dodd returned $100 worth of merchandise. Credit Invoice 613 was issued for $100 plus $7 GST and $8 PST.

In general journal form, this transaction would be recorded as follows:

Feb.	28	Sales Returns and Allowances	1 0 0	00		
		GST Payable	7	00		
		PST Payable	8	00		
		Accounts Receivable/D.Dodd			1 1 5	00
		Credit Invoice 613.				

Using the "Other Accounts" Section

One method of recording a credit invoice in the columnar journal is to use the Other Accounts section.

The two debits (Sales Returns and Allowances $100 and PST Payable $8) are recorded in the Other Accounts debit column. This is done because the PST Payable column in the journal is a credit column. GST Refundable is recorded directly in the appropriate column. Figure 9-7 illustrates the use of the Other Accounts section to record a credit invoice for a sales return.

Using the Circling Method

In the circling method, the Sales Returns and Allowances debit of $100 is recorded in the Other Accounts section; the PST Payable debit of $8 is entered and circled in the PST Payable column; the GST Refundable debit of $7 is entered in the GST Refundable column; and the $115 credit is entered in the Accounts Receivable credit column. The circling method is illustrated in Figure 9-8.

To determine the total of a column when you use the circling method, do the following:

- Add the uncircled items in the column.
- Subtract the circled items.
- Enter the result as the column total.

Circled items are subtracted from the total of the uncircled items to determine column totals.

In Figure 9-8, the uncircled items in the PST Payable column total $72 ($24 + $16 + $32). The column total of $64 is arrived at by subtracting the $8 circled item from $72.

Recording a Purchase Return

The following transaction illustrates how a credit invoice for a purchase return is recorded both in general journal form and in the columnar journal (see Figure 9-9).

Sample Transaction

Feb. 28   Received Credit Invoice N-15 from National Wholesale, $53.50 plus $3.75 GST, for merchandise returned to them earlier in the month.

In general journal form, the entry is:

Feb.	28	Accounts Payable/National Wholesale		5 7 25	
		Purchases Returns and Allowances			5 3 50
		GST Refundable			3 75
		Credit Invoice N-15.			

In the columnar journal in Figure 9-9, this transaction is recorded in the Accounts Payable debit column, the Other Accounts credit column, and the GST Refundable debit column with the amount circled. The $3.75 is circled because it is a credit entry in a debit column.

COLUMNAR JOURNAL — PAGE 13

DATE	ACCOUNT OR EXPLANATION	REF. NO.	P.R.	CASH DEBIT	CASH CREDIT	OTHER ACCOUNTS DEBIT	OTHER ACCOUNTS CREDIT	ACCOUNTS RECEIVABLE DEBIT	ACCOUNTS RECEIVABLE CREDIT	SALES CREDIT	GST REFUND. DEBIT	GST PAYABLE CREDIT	PST PAYABLE CREDIT	PURCHASES DEBIT	ACCOUNTS PAYABLE DEBIT	ACCOUNTS PAYABLE CREDIT
20—																
Feb. 28	Sales Returns & Allow.	613				1 0 0 00										
	PST Payable	613				8 00										
	D. Dodd	613						1 1 5 00			7 00					

FIGURE 9-7 Using the Other Accounts section

COLUMNAR JOURNAL — PAGE 13

DATE	ACCOUNT OR EXPLANATION	REF. NO.	P.R.	CASH DEBIT	CASH CREDIT	OTHER ACCOUNTS DEBIT	OTHER ACCOUNTS CREDIT	ACCOUNTS RECEIVABLE DEBIT	ACCOUNTS RECEIVABLE CREDIT	SALES CREDIT	GST REFUND. DEBIT	GST PAYABLE CREDIT	PST PAYABLE CREDIT	PURCHASES DEBIT	ACCOUNTS PAYABLE DEBIT	ACCOUNTS PAYABLE CREDIT
20—																
Feb. 1	Cash sale	193		3 4 5 00						3 0 0 00		2 1 00	2 4 00			
3	A. Walker, n/30	175						2 3 0 00		2 0 0 00		1 4 00	1 6 00			
6	D. Dodd, n/30	176		1 0 0 00				3 6 0 00		4 0 0 00		2 8 00	3 2 00			
28	Sales Returns & Allow.					1 0 0 00			1 1 5 00		7 00		(8 00)			
	D. Dodd						1 0 0 00		1 1 5 00							
				4 4 5 00		1 0 0 00	1 0 0 00	5 9 0 00	1 1 5 00	9 0 0 00	7 00	6 3 00	6 4 00			

FIGURE 9-8 Using the circling method

COLUMNAR JOURNAL — PAGE 13

DATE	ACCOUNT OR EXPLANATION	REF. NO.	P.R.	CASH DEBIT	CASH CREDIT	OTHER ACCOUNTS DEBIT	OTHER ACCOUNTS CREDIT	ACCOUNTS RECEIVABLE DEBIT	ACCOUNTS RECEIVABLE CREDIT	SALES CREDIT	GST REFUND. DEBIT	GST PAYABLE CREDIT	PST PAYABLE CREDIT	PURCHASES DEBIT	ACCOUNTS PAYABLE DEBIT	ACCOUNTS PAYABLE CREDIT
20—																
Feb. 28	National Wholesale	N-15													5 7 25	
	Purch. Ret. & Allow.	N-15					5 3 50				(3 75)					

FIGURE 9-9 Recording a purchase return requires two lines.

ADVANTAGES OF THE COLUMNAR JOURNAL

There are two main advantages to using the columnar journal:

- Posting is reduced compared to the posting of a two-column journal.
- The special columns save time and space in recording transactions.

One of the major advantages of a columnar journal is the reduction in the amount of posting to the general ledger. The use of special columns makes it possible to post only the column totals to the accounts. For example, in Figure 9-5 there are three transactions in the Cash debit column, yet only one posting is made to debit the Cash account in the ledger. Only the total debit is posted. There are five entries in the Cash credit column, yet only one posting (the total) is required.

> The use of special columns greatly reduces the amount of posting and is an important advantage of the columnar journal compared to the two-column general journal.

DISADVANTAGES OF THE COLUMNAR JOURNAL

There are three disadvantages to using the columnar journal:

- The multicolumn journal may be cumbersome and inconvenient to use.
- The risk of error is increased by the large number of columns (i.e., the danger of putting the amounts in the wrong columns).
- The use of the columnar journal is restricted to a business with relatively few transactions that can be recorded by one person.

Generally Accepted Accounting Principles and Key Ideas

In this chapter, you learned two key ideas:

- **Columnar journals** contain special columns for accounts that are used often to record transactions.
- **The use of special columns** in a journal reduces the work involved in journalizing and posting transactions.

UNIT 20 CHECK YOUR READING

9. (a) When is the columnar journal balanced?
   (b) When is the columnar journal posted?
10. List the three basic steps followed in posting the columnar journal.
11. What columnar journal totals are not posted?

12. For which columns in the columnar journal are the entries posted individually?

13. When column totals have been posted, where are the posting references shown in the journal?

14. Give two advantages and three disadvantages of the columnar journal.

15. When a credit invoice is recorded for a sales return, which accounts are debited and credited?

16. When a credit invoice is recorded for a purchase return, which accounts are debited and credited?

17. When there is a circled item in a column, how is the total of that column determined?

18. Which method of posting should be recommended for a company that has a very large number of accounts receivable and payable—the direct posting method or posting the transactions from the columnar journal to the subsidiary ledgers? Give reasons for your answer.

UNIT 20 APPLY YOUR KNOWLEDGE

Exercises Part A

3. The trial balance for the Outdoor Life Shop is shown on page 426.

(a) Record the following source documents on page 47 of a columnar journal; then total, balance, and rule the journal.

May   1   Sales invoices issued:
No. 703 to K. Prentice, $450 plus $31.50 GST and $36 PST.
No. 704 to Sheridan College, $376 plus $26.32 GST, no PST.
No. 705 to C. Mathers, $133 plus $9.31 GST and $10.64 PST.

      2   Purchase invoices received:
No. 7436 from Northern Wholesalers, $2576 plus $180.32 GST for merchandise.
No. 2437 from CCKK TV, $378 plus $26.46 GST for TV advertising.
No. RT1768 from Robinson Trucking, $156 plus $10.92 GST for transportation of merchandise from Northern Wholesalers.

      3   List of cash receipts:
Cheque 47966 from Sheridan College, $538.
Cheque 173 from C. Mathers, $346.
Cheque 491 from L. Flynn, the owner, $2000 extra investment.

      4   Copies of cheques issued:
No. 931 for $650 for employees' weekly salaries.
No. 932 for $1270 to Northern Wholesalers on account.
No. 933 for $100 to Robinson Trucking on account.

Outdoor Life Shop
Trial Balance
April 30, 20—

Account	Acc. No.	Debit	Credit
Cash	101	$ 11 500	
Accounts Receivable	110	1 756	
Store Supplies	126	6 551	
Accounts Payable	200		$ 4 407
PST Payable	205		
GST Payable	206		
GST Refundable	207		
L. Flynn, Capital	300		15 400
Sales	400		
Purchases	500		
Transportation on Purchases	503		
Advertising Expense	600		
Salaries Expense	604		
		$19 807	$19 807

(b) Open a general ledger using the trial balance figures above.
(c) Post the journal to the general ledger on May 4.
(d) Prepare a trial balance.

4. Continue the accounting procedures for the Outdoor Life Shop.
  (a) Set up an accounts receivable ledger and an accounts payable ledger with the balances shown in the schedules below.
  (b) Post the subsidiary ledgers from the columnar journal.
  (c) Prepare a schedule of accounts receivable and a schedule of accounts payable. Check your totals with the control accounts in the general ledger for exercise 3.

Outdoor Life Shop
Schedule of Accounts Receivable
April 30, 20—

C. Mathers	$ 346
K. Prentice	735
Sheridan College	675
	$1 756

Outdoor Life Shop
Schedule of Accounts Payable
April 30, 20—

CCKK TV	$ 532
Northern Wholesalers	3 573
Robinson Trucking	302
	$4 407

5. Librock Enterprises' general journal contains the following entries:

DATE		PARTICULARS	P.R.	DEBIT	CREDIT
		GENERAL JOURNAL			PAGE 87
20—					
Mar.	1	Cash		2 2 6 00	
		Sales			2 0 0 00
		GST Payable			1 4 00
		PST Payable			1 2 00
		Cash register summary.			
	2	Accounts Receivable/H. Hume		3 3 9 00	
		Sales			3 0 0 00
		GST Payable			2 1 00
		PST Payable			1 8 00
		Invoice 301, n/30			
	3	Sales Returns and Allowances		5 0 00	
		PST Payable		3 00	
		GST Payable		3 50	
		Cash			5 6 50
		Cash Refund Slip 29.			
	8	Accounts Receivable/ Waldorf Schools		4 2 8 00	
		Sales			4 0 0 00
		GST Payable			2 8 00
		Tax-exempt sale on account, Invoice 302, n/30.			
	9	Sales Returns and Allowances		1 0 0 00	
		PST Payable		6 00	
		GST Payable		7 00	
		Accounts Receivable/H. Hume			1 1 3 00
		Credit Invoice 63.			
	10	Cash		2 2 6 00	
		Accounts Receivable/H. Hume			2 2 6 00
		Cash received on account.			

(a) How many lines are used to record the six entries in this journal (including spaces)?

(b) How many lines would be used to record the same six transactions in a columnar journal?

6. (a) Record the following transactions for Crawford Enterprises on page 26 of a columnar journal; then total, balance, and rule the journal. All sales are non-taxable (PST), terms n/30.

Mar. 2 Sales invoices:
No. 76-25 to W. Squire, $355 plus $24.85 GST.
No. 76-26 to R. Mask, $370 plus $25.90 GST.

5 Cash sales slips:
Nos. 69 to 85, for the week, total $12 970 plus $907.90 GST.

9 Purchase invoices:
No. K-297 from Wilson Supply for merchandise, $987 plus $69.09 GST, terms n/30.
No. 491 from Grant Ltd. for merchandise, $500 plus $35 GST, terms n/30.

10 Cash receipts:
Cheque 126 from R. Mask, $1250 for Invoice 76-20.
Cheque 412 from W. Squire, $1550 for Invoice 76-24.

10 Credit invoice issued:
No. CI-16 for $300 plus $21 GST to T. Campbell for goods returned (goods were sold to Campbell on February 15).

12 Cheques issued:
No. 122 to Corbett's for $1600 to pay Invoice 225.
No. 123 to Grant Ltd. for $7300 to pay Invoice 420.
No. 124 to the *Citizen* for advertising, $450 plus $31.50 GST.

12 Cash receipts:
Cheque 417 from W. Squire, $379.85 for Invoice 76-25.

15 Sales invoices:
No. 76-27 to T. Campbell, $476 plus $33.32 GST.
No. 76-28 to R. Mask, $670 plus $46.90 GST.
No. 76-29 to G. Thompson, $1490 plus $104.30 GST.

15 Credit invoice received:
No. G-280 from Grant Ltd., $200 (plus GST $14) for return of defective merchandise on Invoice 491, dated March 9.

20 Cheque issued:
No. 125 for $175 plus $12.25 GST to Roadway Transport Ltd. for transportation on purchases of merchandise.

25 Purchase invoices:
No. K-320 from Wilson Supply, $75 plus $5.25 GST for office supplies, n/30.
No. 610 from Noonan Ltd., $250 plus $17.50 GST for merchandise, n/30.

26 Bank credit memo:
Bank loan for $12 500 has been deposited by the bank in Crawford Enterprises' account.

27 Cheques issued:
No. 126 for $2000 to pay for a vacation for the P. Crawford family.
No. 127 to City Hydro, $160 plus $11.20 GST for the company's hydro bill.

31 Sales invoice:
No. 76-30 to W. Squire for $790 plus $55.30 GST.

(b) Open a general ledger and post the columnar journal. The February 28 account balances are shown in the trial balance below.

(c) Prepare a trial balance dated March 31.

Crawford Enterprises
Trial Balance
February 28, 20—

Account	Acc. No.	Debit	Credit
Cash	100	$20 000	
Accounts Receivable	110	7 100	
Office Supplies	125	8 000	
Equipment	151	60 000	
Accounts Payable	200		$ 9 540
GST Payable	206		
GST Refundable	207		
Bank Loan	210		
P. Crawford, Capital	300		85 560
P. Crawford, Drawings	301		
Sales	400		
Sales Returns and Allowances	401		
Sales Discounts	402		
Purchases	500		
Purchases Returns and Allowances	501		
Purchases Discounts	502		
Transportation on Purchases	503		
Advertising Expense	600		
Utilities Expense	605		
		$95 100	$95 100

7. Continue the accounting procedures for Crawford Enterprises.
  (a) Set up accounts receivable and accounts payable ledgers with the balances shown in the schedules below.
  (b) Post the accounts receivable and accounts payable source documents directly to the customer and credit accounts in the subsidiary ledgers.
  (c) Prepare schedules of accounts receivable and accounts payable. Check your totals with the control accounts in exercise 6.

Crawford Enterprises
Schedule of Accounts Receivable
Feburary 28, 20—

T. Campbell	$4 300
R. Mask	1 250
W. Squire	1 550
G. Thompson	0
	$7 100

Crawford Enterprises
Schedule of Accounts Payable
Feburary 28, 20—

Corbett's Service Station	$1 600
Grant Ltd.	7 300
Noonan Ltd.	400
Wilson Supply	240
	$9 540

Exercises Part B

8. Sporting Goods Retailers has the following accounts on its books. Journalize the April transactions on page 35 of a columnar journal; then total, balance, and rule the journal. All sales terms are n/20.

Account Title	Acc. No.
Cash	101
Accounts Receivable	110
Building	150
Accounts Payable	200
PST Payable	205
GST Payable	206
GST Refundable	207
Bank Loan	210
A. Nemeth, Capital	300
A. Nemeth, Drawings	301
Sales	400
Sales Returns and Allowances	401
Purchases	500
Purchases Returns and Allowances	501
Purchases Discounts	502
Salaries Expense	601
Advertising Expense	602
Bank Charges Expense	603

Apr. 2 Sales invoices:
No. C-5730 to Carver Basketball League, $276 plus $19.32 GST and $22.08 PST, total $317.40.
No. C-5731 to Action Sporting Goods, $476 plus $33.32 GST, PST exempt.

4 Cash sales slips:
Nos. 795 to 863, for the week, $5759.63 plus $403.17 GST and $287.98 PST, total $6450.78.

7 Purchase invoices:
No. 9767M from Cadieux Textiles, $896 plus $62.72 GST for merchandise, terms n/30.
No. 35-7402 from Croydon Manufacturing, $1796.43 plus $125.75 GST for merchandise, terms n/30
No. 8739 from *Daily Star*, $450 plus $31.50 GST for advertising, terms n/15.

9 Cheques issued:
No. 670, $797.53 to Croydon Manufacturing for Invoice 35-5309.
No. 671, $563.45 to Cadieux Textiles for Invoice 6391M.
No. 672, $1426.53 to the Provincial Treasurer for sales tax collected in March.

10   Credit invoice issued:
No. CR 893 to the Carver Basketball League, $33 plus
$2.31 GST and $2.64 PST, total $37.95, for defective crests
on Invoice C-5730 dated April 2.

10   Cash receipts:
Vernon Athletics, $376.50 for Invoice C-5103.
Action Sporting Goods, $593.03 for Invoice C-5117.

11   Cash sales slips:
Nos. 864 to 983, for the week, $4893.55 plus
$342.55 GST and $293.61 PST, total $5529.71.

13   Cheques issued:
No. 673, $460.50 plus $32.24 GST to CKCH Radio
for advertising.
No. 674, $650 to L. Savage for his salary.
No. 675, $500 to A. Nemeth, the owner, for personal use.

15   Sales invoices:
No. C-5732 to Vernon Athletics, $573.54 plus $40.15 GST
and $45.88 PST.
No. C-5733 to Action Sporting Goods, $635.53 plus
$44.49 GST, PST exempt.

16   Cheque issued:
No. 676, $958.72 to Cadieux Textiles to pay Invoice 9767M.

17   Credit invoice received:
No. C-890 from Croydon Manufacturing, $192.12 plus
$13.45 GST, for damaged goods on Invoice 35-7402,
dated April 7.

18   Cash sales slips:
Nos. 984 to 1117, for the week, $4695.03 plus $328.65 GST
and $375.60 sales tax, total $5399.28.

20   Cash receipts:
Carver Basketball League, $497.50 for Invoice C-5105.
Action Sporting Goods, $875.03 for Invoice C-5213.

22   Cheques issued:
No. 677 for $1716.61 to Croydon Manufacturing to pay
Invoice 35-7402, less Credit Invoice C-890.
No. 678 for $500 to the Canadian Imperial Bank of
Commerce as payment on the bank loan.

24   Sales invoices:
No. C-5734 to Action Sporting Goods, $397.55 plus
$27.83 GST, PST exempt.
No. C-5735 to Vernon Athletics, $137.35 plus $9.61 GST
and $10.99 PST, total $157.95.

25   Cash sales slips:
Nos. 1118 to 1304, for the week, $3934.15 plus $275.39 GST
and $196.71 PST, total $4406.25.

28   Bank debit memo:
From CIBC, $27.53 for bank charges.

30   Cheques issued:
No. 679 for $389 to A. Nemeth for personal use.
No. 680 for $690 to L. Savage for his salary.

9. Refer to the columnar journal completed for Sporting Goods Retailers in exercise 8 and answer the following questions:
   (a) If Sporting Goods Retailers posts to Accounts Receivable directly from the source documents, how many postings will be made to the accounts receivable ledger from the columnar journal?
   (b) What will be the balance in Accounts Payable control on April 16? Will this agree with the subsidiary ledger at this date? Why?
   (c) What is the total number of postings required to update the general ledger on April 30?
   (d) What method of posting would you recommend for a business such as Sporting Goods Retailers that has a large number of customer and creditor transactions?
   (e) If a transposition error is made in posting to a customer account in the subsidiary ledger, when will it be discovered?

 Computer Accounting

DacEasy Accounting System: Accounts Receivable Aging Report

Sage Software Inc. is a provider of business management software. One of their products, DacEasy, is a full-featured accounting software solution with integrated modules to serve small business needs. This accounting package integrates with Microsoft Office so that reports can be sent directly to Excel and/or Word. The modules include:

- General Ledger;
- Accounts Receivable;
- Accounts Payable;
- Cash;
- Inventory;
- Fixed Asset; and
- Reporting.

There are many advantages to using accounting software. One advantage is the ease of generating reports. The following is an example of how one can quickly create a report to look at the age of a company's receivables.

The November 30 Accounts Receivable Aging Detail Report for a small business is shown on the next page. An accounts receivable age analysis lists all customers, showing the balance owed by each and how long the balance has been owed. The report is partial, in that it provides details on only three customers. Note that it lists the amounts owed by categories: 1 to 30 days, 31 to 60 days, and over 61 days.

An accounts receivable age analysis is a list of all customers, showing the balance owed by each and how long the balance has been owed.

Closing Date: 11/30
Sorted by: Customer
Ranked by: Balance

Aging Detail Report
Accounts Receivable

Codes:
I: Invoice   C: Credit
D: Debit   P: Payment
F: Finance Charge   T: Discount Taken

Invoice No.	Date	Due Date	Code	Amount	61+	60/31	30/1	
C43	**Baylor Hospital**							713-555-4200
0044	01/21/00	02/15/00	I	2500.00	2500.00			
0079	02/05/00	04/05/00	I	120.00	120.00			
0294	11/12/00	12/12/00	I	496.00			496.00	
	Total			3116.00	2620.00	0	496.00	
C44	**Beneficial HMO**							214-555-1234
00234	10/17/00	12/17/00	I	4400.00				
	10/31/00		C	-900.00			3500.00	
	Total			3500.00	0	0	3500.00	
C45	**MedCare**							613-555-4444
0086	02/27/00	04/27/00	I	1300.00				
	04/27/00		P	-500.00	800.00			
0288	11/03/00	12/03/00	I	795.00			795.00	
	Total			1595.00	800.00	0	795.00	

Notice that the report is sorted by customer in alphabetical order, and the contact telephone numbers are provided to make it easy for the person involved with collections to make the necessary telephone calls. The Code column letters help to describe the source of the entries in the Amount column. The code letters are defined at the top right corner of the report.

Here is how the above Accounts Receivable Aging Detail Report is prepared using DacEasy accounting software.

Step One: Launch DacEasy. Initially, you will see the following main screen:

Step Two: From the main screen, select **Reports** and the following drop-down menu will appear.

As an alternative, you could click on the fork-lift icon to access the Report menu.

Step Three: Click on **Receivables**, and another drop-down menu appears, listing possible activities the software can carry out related to receivables. From this second menu select **Aging**, as appears below:

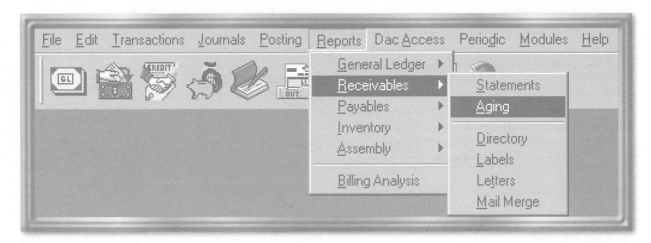

At this point, the software needs to receive direction as to how to assemble the information being requested in the accounts receivable aging report.

Step Four: Enter the required parameters for the report, as shown below.

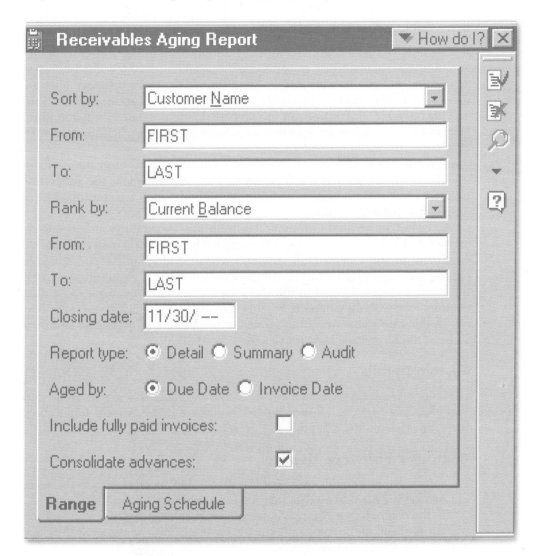

Questions:

1. What is an accounts receivable aging report?

2. What are the advantages of using accounting software to generate financial reports?

3. What are the advantages of being able to integrate accounting data with Microsoft Word and Microsoft Excel?

4. In the accounts receivable aging report shown on page 433, what do the codes I, P, and C represent? What customers and amounts owing would you be concerned about?

Canada Care Medical Corporation

Introducing Custom Software

In this text, you have learned about the Simply Accounting and QuickBooks accounting programs. They are considered *standard software* for small business accounting, because they are not designed for one particular business. They are used to perform standard accounting functions, such as accounts receivable, accounts payable, and payroll, and to prepare financial statements in a uniform format. These programs are sold by computer stores "off the shelf" and are used by a variety of small businesses.

A computer accounting program written specifically to meet the needs of one particular company is called *custom software*. An example is the accounting program used by Canada Care Medical Corporation. Computer consulting firms design this specialized software.

Canada Care Medical Corporation sells health-care products such as walkers and wheelchairs (see Figure 9-10). The company has over 8000 customers and 25 employees in the Ottawa–Hull area and operates three outlets: two stores in Ottawa and one in Hull, Quebec. All three outlets use one accounting and computer system that is located in the company's Ottawa headquarters. The outlets communicate with the computer system via modems and a high-speed ISDN line.

In this case study, we will examine the computer system used to complete some of the accounting tasks for Canada Care Medical.

System Details

The computer system includes a central file server that is linked to 20 computers in a local area network. Most of the computers are recent models. In addition, there are modems and a number of printers.

Computer Software Used

The software used with this computer was specifically designed to meet the needs of Canada Care Medical by D.E. Systems Ltd., a computer consulting firm.

In the computer's memory, a database has been created that contains information about all of the company's customers. It includes the name, address, and balance owed for each customer.

The database also contains a list of the 8000 products sold by the company, with prices for each item. It is programmed to calculate applicable PST and GST. It also keeps track of each item in inventory, how many of each has been sold, how many are on hand, and when an item needs to be reordered.

FIGURE 9-10 A Canada Care Medical Corporation store

Menu Choices

The computer system is used by a number of employees—those responsible for the accounting records, those handling sales over the counter in the store, and those handling telephone sales.

When the computer is accessed, it presents a screen menu that offers the choice of programs shown in Figure 9-11 on page 438. Each of the menu items performs specific functions. For example, choice 11 is a program that records the details of a charge sale on an invoice and then prints the invoice. Choice 14 is used to record sales in the journal. Choice 37 is selected when it is time to produce the monthly statements.

Canada Care Medical Corporation
Main Menu

Choice	Program
11	Invoice
12	Print Invoice
14	Sales Journal
15	Cancel Invoice
21	Inventory Record
23	Print Inventory List
31	Customer Records
32	Current Accounts Receivable
34	Cash Received from Customers
35	Customer List
36	Cash Payments Journal
37	Statements
38	Ministry of Health
39	Contract Sales
40	Hospital Sales
99	Good-bye

FIGURE 9-11 Menu providing the program choices

Let's examine the system to see how it completes accounts receivable tasks. The steps followed in recording a charge sale to a customer are described below.

Recording Charge Sales

When a customer enters the store and purchases goods on a charge account, these procedures are followed:

(a) Choice 11 is selected from the menu.
(b) The customer's name and initial are entered on the keyboard. The computer then retrieves the customer's file and provides the customer's address and previous balance.
(c) A blank invoice form appears on the screen. The form looks exactly like the printed copy of the invoice that will be given to the customer.
(d) The employee enters the quantity and product code on the invoice that is still on the screen. The computer automatically records the customer's name and address, the date, the invoice number, the product description, and the unit price, and then calculates the total amount of the bill (invoice). All of these details—name of customer, product description, etc.—are found by the computer in the database of information stored in its memory bank. The employee does not have to enter the detailed information or write or calculate the prices and total amount of the invoice.

(e) Choice 12 is then selected, and the computer system prints the invoice. The computer system automatically sorts all of the information about the sale and later uses it to prepare the journal entry to record the sale. The entire sequence of recording a charge sale takes less than two minutes and that includes the production and printing of the invoice.

(f) The invoice is given to the customer. Notice that the employee has only entered these data:

- menu choice;
- customer's name;
- product code (This is a number code for the item bought by the customer. All products sold have a product code.); and
- quantity purchased

The computer has done the rest. It has searched its memory and found the customer's address, the balance in the customer's account, the product description, and the price of the product. The computer has done the following things automatically:

- updated the customer's account with a debit (increase);
- calculated the amount for the item sold, calculated and added applicable taxes, determined the total of the invoice, and printed the invoice; and
- recorded the details of the sale in its memory for use later in producing the journal entry and updating the inventory by decreasing the balance on hand of the item sold.

Questions

1. What is custom software?

2. What is standard software?

3. List the steps followed in preparing a sales invoice manually.

4. List the steps followed using the Canada Care Medical computer system to prepare a sales invoice.

5. Which of the steps in the manual system are done automatically by the computer after the proper keyboard selections have been made?

COMPUTER ASSIGNMENTS

1. Figure 9-12, the income statement for Elegant Business Systems Inc., contains the combined data for the Victoria and Kelowna branch offices of the company. It provides the year-to-date, current month, and percent figures. The management of the company is interested in knowing how well each of its branch offices is doing. You have been asked to provide detailed financial information about the Victoria branch office, the Kelowna branch office, and the company as a whole.

(a) Format a spreadsheet that will provide the following:

▶ an income statement for the company as a whole, with columns
▶ for year-to-date, current month, and percent (similar to
Figure 9-12);
▶ the same information for the Victoria branch office; and
▶ the same information for the Kelowna branch office.

(b) Print copies of your spreadsheet for analysis purposes.

Elegant Business Systems Inc.
Income Statement
For the period ended September 30, 20—

Revenue	Year-to-Date	Current Month	Percent	
Sales—Victoria	$ 437 764.12	$ 53 093.13	37.93	43.28
Sales—Kelowna	669 797.98	65 481.91	58.03	53.38
Services—Victoria	25 091.35	1 925.00	2.18	1.57
Services—Kelowna	21 129.00	2 175.00	1.83	1.77
Interest Income	375.00	0.00	0.03	0.00
Total Revenue	1 154 157.45	122 675.04	100.00	100.00
Cost of Sales				
Cost of Goods Sold—Victoria	276 562.10	34 523.45	23.96	28.14
Cost of Goods Sold—Kelowna	402 803.62	57 245.65	34.90	46.66
Total Cost of Goods Sold	679 365.72	91 769.10	58.86	74.80
Gross Margin	474 791.73	30 905.94	41.14	25.19
Total Operating & Admin. Expenses	213 139.27	19 235.44	18.47	15.68
Net Income	$ 261 652.46	$ 11 670.50	22.67	9.51

FIGURE 9-12 Computer-prepared income statement

2. (a) Format a second spreadsheet that will provide an expense summary similar to the one in Figure 9-13 with columns for year-to-date, current month, and percent for the company as a whole and for each of the two branches separately.
(b) Print copies of your spreadsheet.
(c) Analyze the financial data and prepare a report for company management. Include in your report:

▶ a comparison of the revenue contributed by each branch office;
▶ a comparison of the expenses and cost of sales of each of the branch offices; and
▶ general recommendations for action to be taken by company management, including a statement that describes areas where further information or explanations are required.

Elegant Business Systems Inc.
Expense Schedule
For the period ended September 30, 20—

Expense Detail	Year-to-Date	Current Month	Percent	
Accounting & Legal	10 133.63	257.29	0.88	0.21
Advertising	44 245.88	2 742.98	3.83	2.23
Automobile	12 117.47	1 824.47	1.05	1.49
Bad Debts	893.00	0.00	0.08	0.00
Business Taxes	397.89	0.00	0.03	0.00
Company Pension Plan	9 338.00	595.00	0.81	0.48
Commissions—Victoria	6 854.98	0.00	0.59	0.00
Commissions—Kelowna	10 282.47	0.00	0.90	0.00
Cartage & Freight	10 271.95	889.95	0.89	0.72
Discounts Taken	2 342.00	0.00	0.20	0.00
Dues & Subscriptions	429.50	37.50	0.04	0.03
Equipment Rental—Victoria	1 883.63	511.89	0.16	0.42
Equipment Rental—Kelowna	2 057.60	0.00	0.18	0.00
Heat, Light, Water—Victoria	4 650.71	597.42	0.40	0.49
Heat, Light, Water—Kelowna	7 042.92	962.98	0.61	0.78
Insurance	8 766.00	927.00	0.76	0.76
Interest & Bank Charges	948.32	0.00	0.08	0.00
Maint. & Repair—Victoria	1 603.19	691.42	0.14	0.56
Maint. & Repair—Kelowna	1 367.66	0.00	0.12	0.00
Postage & Office	956.52	107.52	0.08	0.09
Rent—Victoria	4 209.38	600.00	0.37	0.49
Rent—Kelowna	6 414.07	1 000.00	0.56	0.82
Salaries—Victoria	12 961.00	1 500.00	1.12	1.22
Salaries—Kelowna	19 691.50	2 500.00	1.71	2.04
Telephone—Victoria	7 124.26	1 023.47	0.62	0.83
Telephone—Kelowna	10 386.68	1 235.49	0.90	1.01
Travel & Promotion	14 120.50	1 136.50	1.22	0.93
Employment Insurance	1 081.56	94.56	0.09	0.08
Workers' Compensation	567.00	0.00	0.05	0.00
Total All Expenses	213 139.27	19 235.44	18.47	15.68

FIGURE 9-13 Computer-prepared expense schedule

3. Format a spreadsheet that will total, balance, and print a columnar journal. Use Figure 9-2 on page 411 as a guide for the headings.
   (a) Use your formatted spreadsheet to complete the columnar journal for exercise 3(a) of this chapter.
   (b) Use your formatted spreadsheet to complete the columnar journal for Sporting Good Retailers, exercise 8.

4. (a) Use general ledger software to complete exercise 8.

(b) Compare the use of a spreadsheet to complete the columnar journal, in exercise 8, with the general ledger program's preparation of a journal. Which is the better tool for journalizing? Give reasons for your answer.

5. Outline accounting tasks that you feel are appropriate and efficient uses of a spreadsheet. Refer to computer assignments 1 to 4 when you answer this question and give reasons for your response.

www.pearsoned.ca/
principlesofaccounting

WEB EXTENSIONS

Internet Study Guide

➤ Complete the Chapter 9 review.

➤ Complete the Chapter 9 definitions.

➤ Complete the Chapter 9 online test.

Web Links

Visit the Web Links section at the Pearson Education web site to find links to accounting software applications. After you visit several sites, indicate the benefits to a small business owner of using accounting software applications.

Case Studies

Social Costs of Business Decisions

Metalco mines, refines, and ships metal products to customers in many different countries. The following chart presents a summary of operating results for the last five years and projected results for the next two years.

	Year 1	Year 2	Year 3	Year 4	Year 5	Year 6	Year 7
	Operating Results (in millions of dollars)					**Projected Results (losses)**	
Sales	500	490	480	470	460	400	390
Costs and Expenses	380	390	390	400	400	410	410
Net Income	120	100	90	70	60	(10)	(20)

This chart illustrates a decrease of $40 million in sales from Year 1 to Year 5. Costs and expenses have increased slightly. Net income has decreased dramatically from $120 million to $60 million.

World prices and the demand for Metalco's products have decreased. In the next two years, sales and net income are projected to decrease even more substantially. This forecast is based on increased competition from foreign producers in countries with very low labour costs compared to those in Canada.

Management is faced with a very difficult problem. The major company expense is wages. The company does not need about 3000 of its workers because demand is decreasing. In the last five years, unneeded people have been kept on staff because management felt a loyalty to its workers. If they had been laid off, their families would have suffered severe economic hardship.

Management must decide what to do about the next two years. If unneeded workers are not laid off, the company will definitely lose money. If unneeded workers are laid off, management will be able to decrease total expenses by about $50 million.

(a) What will be the estimated net income for Year 6 and Year 7 if unneeded workers are let go?
(b) What are the *social costs* to the community if the workers are let go?
(c) What are the *economic costs* to the community if the workers are let go?
(d) What obligation does Metalco management have to the people who have invested their savings in Metalco?
(e) What is the correct decision to make in the interest of:
   (i) the community?
   (ii) the investors?
   (iii) the company's future?
(f) Does government have the right to step in and order the company to retain all 3000 employees?
(g) If you were a member of Metalco's management team, what decision would you make? Why?

CASE 2   Decision Making

V. Iannucci worked for many years as a machinist for a large automobile manu-facturer. He lived frugally and saved money. Three years ago, he mortgaged his home, borrowed money, and invested in his own business. He now employs six persons and the business has earned a modest net income for two years.

This year, there has been a general slump in the economy. Iannucci's busi-ness has suffered, with sales decreasing 30 percent. His accountant has predicted a loss of $36 000 if three full-time workers are not laid off. Iannucci feels that his employees are almost part of his family. They have been loyal and are partly responsible for the business success of the past two years. If Iannucci does not lay off the workers, he will not be able to make his mortgage payments and will likely lose his home and perhaps his business as well.

(a) What should Iannucci do? Give two reasons why he might do that.
(b) Do you see any similarities and differences between this case and the one involving Metalco?

CASE 3   Accounting Systems

Hamilton Clothiers have been a successful clothing store for a number of years. The business has a large number of faithful customers who have charge accounts, and an accounts receivable clerk is employed full-time to handle these customer accounts. The clerk's salary is $36 000.

In the last few years, more and more customers are using credit cards such as Visa and MasterCard. An accounting clerk spends about 50 percent of his time handling these customer accounts. The table below illustrates this trend.

YEAR	TOTAL CHARGE SALES	HAMILTON CLOTHIER CHARGE ACCOUNTS	MASTERCARD & VISA CARDS
1	$120 000	$100 000	$ 20 000
2	140 000	90 000	50 000
3	145 000	75 000	70 000
4	150 000	60 000	90 000
5	170 000	50 000	120 000

The general manager feels that a change should be made in the method of handling charge sales.

(a) Prepare several alternatives for the manager's consideration. List the possible consequences of each alternative.
(b) What other information may be needed to solve this problem?

8 Career Education Activities

1. Problem-Solving Skills

Employers tend to describe good employees as having good problem-solving skills. Good judgment in making decisions is an important skill to have.

Why are some people good problem solvers? Do you know someone who can be described as having "good judgment"? Successful problem solvers have developed a model or system for making decisions, either due to knowing someone who is a good problem solver or by learning from their own experiences. Their decision-making skills improved as they matured.

Let's examine the five-step model, or method, for making decisions about problems.

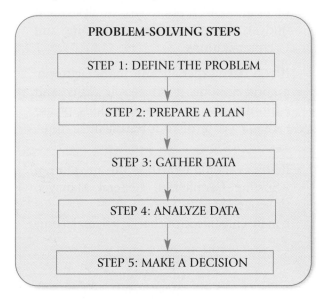

PROBLEM-SOLVING STEPS

STEP 1: DEFINE THE PROBLEM

STEP 2: PREPARE A PLAN

STEP 3: GATHER DATA

STEP 4: ANALYZE DATA

STEP 5: MAKE A DECISION

Step 1: Define the Problem

Before a decision is made, background material should be obtained and all possibilities about the nature of the problem should be investigated. An open and creative mind will lead you to ask questions such as:

• What other possibilities are there?
• Are there other hidden problems?
• Are personalities involved?
• Are personalities really the problem?

Step 2: Prepare a Plan

In this step, you must decide WHAT data are required, WHERE they can be found, and WHO is to obtain the data. In short, the tasks must be determined and deadlines set for their completion. It is critical to assign responsibility for each task and to have each person responsible make a commitment that the task will be done.

Step 3: Gather Data

At this stage, it is important to understand the nature of the problem and to ensure that only relevant and accurate information will be gathered. Judgment must be used to avoid confusing the issue with unnecessary data. It is also important to know where to go and who to ask for information in order to get data and to save time.

Step 4: Analyze Data

Information is of little use unless it is used and interpreted intelligently. Data must be understood and analyzed in relation to the problem. The use of electronic spreadsheets can greatly speed up this stage. The computer can save time, reduce mechanical errors, and provide information that might otherwise not be available.

It is important to consider this step when you prepare the plan (step 2). Often, the method of gathering and tabulating data is improved if step 4 is considered along with step 2. At this stage, it is also important to be creative and to think in terms of "What if?" and "What else?" in order to apply all possible interpretations to the data.

Step 5: Make a Decision

By this time a number of alternatives will have been identified. From these possible solutions one must be selected—the one that best solves the problem.

We often think that solutions or decisions are clear—that they are black or white, right or wrong. But, in fact, most solutions to problems differ only in degree. They improve the situation to differing extents. The trick is to use judgment to make the decision that improves the situation the most. Some problems never disappear entirely! This is why some people have problems making decisions—they want the impossible, a perfect solution. The good problem solver considers the steps listed on the previous page and creatively seeks out the best possible solution in the circumstances.

For Discussion

(a) What is meant by "solutions are not always black or white?"
(b) Suggest ways to get a person to accept responsibility for the completion of a task.
(c) What is meant by "interpreting data"?

2. Problem-Solving Assignment

Help J. Molnar to solve this problem: Molnar does not have a trade-in and requires a car for personal and job reasons. Recommend a car for Molnar to purchase using these guidelines:
• It must be new with a record of reliability.
• Maximum price is $25 000.
• Minimum options are a radio, power brakes, and power steering.
• It can be a two-door or a four-door car.

For Discussion

(a) Outline the steps Molnar should follow in making a decision.
(b) List other questions and considerations that Molnar must examine.
(c) Prepare a list of alternatives for Molnar.
(d) Make a decision as if you were Molnar.
(e) How and when will Molnar know if the correct decision has been made?

3. Position of Accountant

The general accountant position advertised here is an example of a middle-level position. The accountant reports directly to the company's general manager.

Accountant
Looking for a better job?

Coleman Candies is a fast-growing manufacturing company located in Brantford, ON. We are part of a major distribution network with revenues in excess of $5 billion.

We are looking for an accountant with a professional designation who will report directly to the general manager.

Responsibilities will include preparation of month-end reports, cost analysis, and budgets, as well as strategic planning and G/L preparations.

If you have experience in manufacturing, a good attitude, good people skills, and administrative and computer skills, please forward a copy of your résumé.

Résumés should be sent to the attention of Christine Carmichael, General Manager, Coleman Division.
e-mail: christinecarmichael@coleman.com

Coleman Candies
18 Miles Avenue
Brantford, ON

For Discussion

(a) What personal qualities are required for this position?
(b) What are the minimum education requirements?
(c) What is meant by "experience in manufacturing"?
(d) Write the covering letter and a résumé to apply for this position. Assume you have completed a professional accounting designation.

Career Profile

Mike Simpson graduated from high school and began a four-year Bachelor of Commerce degree at university. During his second year of university, Mike decided that he wanted to pursue a Chartered Accountant designation, so he took courses geared toward these professional requirements. After earning his university degree he began work with an accounting firm, KPMG. Within two years he completed his CA. In the initial years with the company he served as a junior auditor. As he gained more experience, he took on larger files and expanded his role to include a variety of accounting functions in areas such as policy, auditing, and taxation. Mike continued to take management courses and was given an opportunity to focus on knowledge-based businesses.

After 13 years, he left to join a smaller local accounting company, McIntyre and McLarty, which offered him an opportunity to become a partner in the business. He now had the final say on many issues, while acting as a business advisor and providing business financial counselling. He had spent six years with this company, when a former client presented him with a new challenge: an opportunity to become the Chief Financial Officer (CFO) with Omnimark Technologies. After spending 6 months on a contract basis with the company, he accepted the position full-time.

Mike was now responsible for the overall financial health of the organization. As CFO he handled financial reporting and investor relations, and was in charge of the administrative staff on a day-to-day basis.

One of his roles as CFO was to identify markets and create strategies for the company's future direction.

After spending time with this company, Mike decided to take on the challenge of running his own consulting business. His experience has allowed him to assist companies that are considering an initial public offering (IPO). One of his strengths is in developing business plans to show why people should consider investing in his clients' organizations and demonstrating the potential for their future success. His role allows him to liaise with potential investors to raise funds for his clients.

Mike has come a long way since he graduated from high school. His Bachelor of Commerce degree and his professional CA designation have opened many doors for him over the course of his career.

For Discussion

(a) Outline the variety of accounting functions that Mike has fulfilled over the course of his career.

(b) What opportunities did each organization offer to Mike as he progressed along his career?

The Special Journal System

What Learning You Will Demonstrate

On completion of this unit, you will be able to:

- explain the purpose of and define *purchase requisition, purchase order, purchase invoice,* and *receiving report;*
- describe the process of matching documents in order to approve purchase invoices;
- explain how outstanding invoices are filed;
- record transactions in a purchases journal;
- balance and post a purchases journal; and
- record purchase returns transactions.

INTRODUCING SPECIAL JOURNALS

In Chapters 8 and 9, which described the three-ledger system and the columnar journal, respectively, you learned about manual accounting systems and procedures that made use of the *division of labour and specialization,* and about the efficiency of journalizing in and posting from the columnar journal.

In this chapter, you will learn that *several* special columnar journals may be used by companies that have many repetitive transactions.

A large percentage of the transactions you recorded in the previous chapters fall into four major categories:

1. Purchases of goods or services on account
2. Sales of goods or services on account
3. Receipt of cash
4. Payment of cash

These four types of transactions represent the majority of financial events that happen in a business. When there are too many transactions to record in one columnar journal, several specialized columnar journals are used.

In a **special journal system**, separate journals are used for similar transactions that are repetitive. For example, a *purchases journal* is used to record all *purchases on account* (credit purchases). A *sales journal* is used to record *credit sales. Cash receipts* and *cash payments journals* are used to record *cash received* and *cash payments.* In addition, a general journal is used to record transactions that do not fit into these major categories as well as the end-of-period adjusting and closing entries.

Different people might record the transactions in each of the special journals. Thus, the five-journal system could make use of the principles of division of labour and specialization.

The following is a summary of the major categories of transactions, the source documents for these transactions, and the special journal into which each type of transaction will be journalized:

A special journal system uses separate journals for similar transactions that recur frequently.

Transactions	Common Source Documents	Journals Used
Purchases on account	Purchase invoices	Purchases journal
Sales on account	Sales invoices	Sales journal
Cash receipts	Bank credit memos Cash sales slips Cash register slips List of cheques received in the mail	Cash receipts journal
Cash payments	Bank debit memos Cheque copies or stubs	Cash payments journal
Other	Credit invoices End-of-period entries Memo—correcting entries	General journal

In this chapter, we will examine the use of each of the special journals listed above. You will find many similarities in the journalizing and posting procedures for these journals when compared to the columnar journal used in Chapter 9. This will reduce the time needed for you to become familiar with these tasks.

PURCHASING SYSTEMS

Before you examine the recording and posting procedures for a purchases journal, it is important to understand the purchasing system as a whole. Many documents and company departments are involved in a purchasing system. This is necessary to divide the work load among a number of people and to control human error and possible dishonesty. Purchasing systems differ from business to business. Warrendon Sports is used to illustrate standard procedures used by many businesses.

Ordering Goods

Figure 10-1 illustrates the steps that are usually followed when a company buys goods.

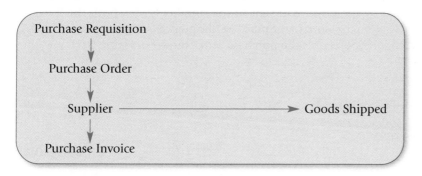

FIGURE 10-1 Steps followed in a typical purchasing system

Purchase Requisition

An employee wanting to purchase goods or services completes a request form called a purchase requisition. After it is approved by a supervisor, this form is sent to the purchasing department. Figure 10-2 is an example of a purchase requisition.

A purchase requisition is a form sent to the purchasing department requesting that goods or services be ordered.

WARRENDON SPORTS

2579 Base Line Road
Ottawa, ON K2H 7B3

PURCHASE REQUISITION		DATE July 31, 20–	
TO PURCHASING DEPARTMENT	Please Purchase the Following NO. R-72	DATE NEEDED Sep. 1, 20–	

QUANTITY	STOCK NO.	DESCRIPTION
30		Dolphin clear goggles
30		Olympian clear goggles
12		Assorted earplugs
6		Size 1-4 swim wings

REQUISITIONED BY *Anita Rizini*   APPROVED *Warren Creighton*

FIGURE 10-2 Example of a purchase requisition

Purchase Order

It is the responsibility of the purchasing department to acquire the best quality items at the best price. When a supplier has been selected, a purchase order is prepared by the buyer and sent to the supplier. When both the buyer and the seller agree on the terms of the purchase, the purchase order becomes a legal contract. Warrendon Sports uses the purchase order shown in Figure 10-3.

WARRENDON SPORTS
2579 Base Line Road
Ottawa, ON K2H 7B3

NO. 4151   PURCHASE ORDER

STORE: 2579 Base Line Road
❑ Tel: 684-1287
   Fax: 684-5381

FACTORY: 5 Melrose Ave.
❑ Tel: 729-7100
   Fax: 729-7288

DATE August 4, 20—

To: Speedquip Ltd.
Ship to: Warrendon Sports
           2579 Base Line Road,
           Ottawa, ON   K2H 7B3

Please supply the following by date specified.

REQUIRED BY September 1, 20—
SHIP BY   Parcel Post

QUANTITY	DESCRIPTION
30	Dolphin clear goggles
30	Olympian clear goggles
12	Assorted earplugs
6	Size 1-4 swim wings

Provincial Sales Tax Licence No. 41902211
GST Registration No. R119282106

Per *Warren Creighton*

FIGURE 10-3 Example of a purchase order

Figure 10-4 on the next page shows where each copy of the purchase order is sent. The original is sent to the supplier. The receiving department is sent a copy of the purchase order so that it will know that goods have been ordered and will accept *only* the goods ordered. The accounting department receives a copy of the purchase order so that it will pay only for the goods that have been ordered. The purchasing department retains a copy for its records and the final copy of the purchase order is sent to the requesting department, so that the requesting department knows that the goods have been ordered and when delivery can be expected.

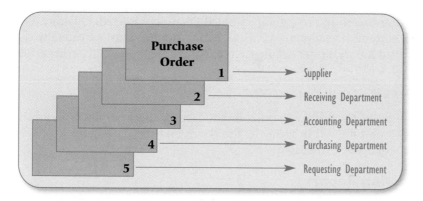

FIGURE 10-4 Distribution of purchase order and copies

Purchase Invoice

After goods have been shipped, the seller sends an *invoice* or bill to the buyer. Figure 10-5 is the invoice received by Warrendon Sports. This invoice lists the items shipped to Warrendon that were ordered on August 4 (Figure 10-3).

An invoice is a form sent by the seller to the buyer. It lists the costs of the items shipped, along with details of the shipment.

Speedquip Ltd.

992 St. Mary's Rd., Winnipeg, MB R2M 3S3
Phone: 204-256-3489   Fax: 204-256-7531

INVOICE

SOLD TO
Warrendon Sports Ltd.
2579 Base Line Road
Ottawa, ON K2H 7B3

SHIPPED TO
Same

NO. 307

DATE Sep. 1, 20—

YOUR ORDER NO. 4151

Our Order No.	Salesperson	Terms	F.O.B.	Date Shipped	Shipped Via
52876	Brown	Net 30 Days	Winnipeg	Aug. 15, 20—	Parcel Post

QUANTITY ORDERED	QUANTITY SHIPPED	STOCK NUMBER/DESCRIPTION	UNIT PRICE	AMOUNT
30	30	Dolphin clear goggles	$4.80	$144.00
30	30	Olympian clear goggles	5.10	153.00
12	12	Assorted earplugs	0.90	10.80
6	6	Size 1-5 swim wings	1.80	10.80
				318.60
		Goods and Services Tax 7%		22.30
		Total Due		$340.90
		2% added to overdue accounts		

White—Customer's Copy/Pink—Office Copy/Canary—Commission Copy/Green—Salesperson's Copy/Blue—Shipping Copy

FIGURE 10-5 Example of a purchase invoice

The information in the columns headed Quantity Ordered, Quantity Shipped, Stock Number/Description, Unit Price, and Amount must be carefully checked and is subject to further detailed controls in Warrendon's purchasing system.

Paying for Purchases

To this point, the system for ordering goods from a supplier has been shown. The steps to be followed in receiving the goods and the procedures for paying for them will now be discussed.

Receiving Report

Merchandise received from a supplier must be checked to ensure that:

- the goods received were actually ordered;
- the goods are in satisfactory condition; and
- the correct quantity and quality were shipped.

A receiving report is a form that lists and describes all goods received.

The person who receives and checks the goods completes a receiving report (Figure 10-6) and sends a copy to the purchasing department. Remember that a copy of the purchase order was initially sent to the receiving department when the goods were ordered. This purchase order copy is used to determine if the goods received were in fact ordered.

WARRENDON SPORTS

2579 Base Line Road
Ottawa, ON K2H 7B3

RECEIVING REPORT

FROM: Speedquip Ltd.

NO. R-312
DATE Sep. 5, 20—
P.O. NO. 4151

VIA   PREPAID   COLLECT

STOCK NO.	QUANTITY	DESCRIPTION	UNIT PRICE
	30	Dolphin clear goggles	
	30	Olympian clear goggles	
	12	Assorted earplugs	
	6	Size 1-4 swim wings	

CHECKED BY *R. Lee*   ENTERED IN STORES LEDGER BY *H. Kwan*

FIGURE 10-6 Example of a receiving report

Some firms do not use a receiving report. Instead, the receiver will check off each item on the purchase order when it is received. The receiver then initials the purchase order copy and sends it to the purchasing department.

Matching Process

Before an invoice is approved or recorded, a matching process occurs in which the invoice is checked and compared to the purchase order and the receiving report. This comparison is necessary to ensure that *what was ordered was received*, and *what was charged for, was ordered and received*. Usually, the matching process is the responsibility of the purchasing department. If the three documents match, the invoice is approved and sent to the accounting department.

> The matching process involves the comparison of the purchase order, the purchase invoice, and the receiving report.

Approved Invoice

The accounting department receives the invoice and supporting documents from the purchasing department and checks their mathematical accuracy. Each extension, or calculation, is checked and the amounts are added to verify the total of the invoice.

> An extension is the quantity multiplied by the unit price.

The account to be debited is indicated on the invoice. An accounting clerk then journalizes and posts the transaction. For example, the journal entry for the Speedquip invoice is:

Sep.	5	Purchases	3 1 8 60	
		GST Refundable	2 2 30	
		Accounts Payable/Speedquip Ltd.		3 4 0 90
		Invoice 307, merchandise, n/30.		

Payment on the Due Date

After journalizing, the approved invoice is placed in a date file according to the date on which payment is to be made. On that day, the invoice is taken from the file and a cheque is prepared and sent to the supplier. The payment is then journalized and posted. The journal entry to record the payment of the Speedquip invoice is:

Oct.	3	Accounts Payable/Speedquip Ltd.	3 4 0 90	
		Cash		3 4 0 90
		Invoice 307, Cheque 1977.		

Figure 10-7 illustrates the steps followed when paying an invoice.

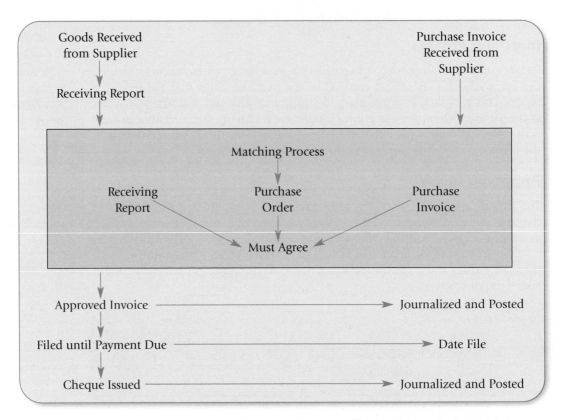

FIGURE 10-7 Typical steps followed to pay an invoice

INTRODUCING THE PURCHASES JOURNAL

A purchases journal is a special journal used to record all purchases on account.

A business that makes many purchases on account uses a purchases journal instead of a general journal to record those transactions. When invoices are received, they are approved and then recorded in the purchases journal.

Purchase Invoices ⟶ Invoices Approved ⟶ Purchases Journal

Journalizing Purchases on Account

As you know, an invoice received for items purchased on account is called a *purchase invoice*. After the purchase invoice has been approved, it is journalized. On September 5, approved invoices for the following transactions were received by the accounting department of Warrendon Sports.

Purchase Transactions

Sep. 5   Invoice 307 dated September 1 from Speedquip Ltd., $318.60 for merchandise, GST $22.30, terms n/30.

5	Invoice W184 dated September 4 from Evans and Kert, $54 for office supplies, GST $3.50, terms n/30.
5	Invoice 3871 dated September 2 from Tops Service Centre, $70 for repairs to the company automobile, GST $4.90, terms n/30.
5	Invoice B-519 dated September 1 from Ontario Hydro, $195 for the August hydro bill, GST $13.65, terms EOM.
5	Invoice 193 dated September 1 from Cooper Bros., $500 for merchandise, GST $35, terms n/30.

Figure 10-8 shows these transactions recorded in a general journal.

GENERAL JOURNAL					PAGE 17
DATE		PARTICULARS	P.R.	DEBIT	CREDIT
20—					
Sep.	5	Purchases		3 1 8 60	
		GST Refundable		2 2 30	
		Accounts Payable/Speedquip Ltd.			3 4 0 90
		Invoice 307, merchandise, n/30.			
	5	Supplies		5 4 00	
		GST Refundable		3 50	
		Accounts Payable/Evans & Kert			5 7 50
		Invoice W184, n/30.			
	5	Car Expense		7 0 00	
		GST Refundable		4 90	
		Accounts Payable/Tops Service Centre			7 4 90
		Invoice 3871, n/30.			
	5	Utilities Expense		1 9 5 00	
		GST Refundable		1 3 65	
		Accounts Payable/Ontario Hydro			2 0 8 65
		Invoice B-519, EOM.			
	5	Purchases		5 0 0 00	
		GST Refundable		3 5 00	
		Accounts Payable/Cooper Bros.			5 3 5 00
		Invoice 193, merchandise, n/30.			

FIGURE 10-8 Transactions recorded in a general journal

Figure 10-9 on page 459 shows the same invoices recorded in a purchases journal. Compare the recording of the five invoices in the general journal with the recording procedures followed in the purchases journal. *How many lines does each transaction require in the general journal and in the purchases journal? In the recording of these invoices, which journal requires less writing? Why do you think there are special*

Special columns are provided for accounts that are used frequently.

columns headed Purchases debit and Utilities Expense debit? When is the Other Accounts debit section used?

Only purchases on account appear in the purchases journal. Cash purchases are recorded in the cash payments journal.

Special Column Headings

In the purchases journal in Figure 10-9, columns are headed Purchases debit, GST Refundable debit, Accounts Payable credit, Utilities Expense debit, and Other Accounts debit. The Accounts Payable credit column is required for every transaction in the purchases journal. Merchandise is purchased frequently and that is why there are special columns for Purchases debit and GST Refundable debit in the journal. A special column is headed Utilities Expense debit because for this particular company the Utilities Expense account is involved in many transactions. Another company might use this column for Supplies or Delivery Expense or any other account used in repetitive transactions.

The Other Accounts section is used to record debits to accounts other than Purchases or Utilities Expense. Notice that the account title must be shown as well as the name of the creditor when the Other Accounts section is used.

Balancing the Purchases Journal

Since the purchases journal in Figure 10-9 has five money columns, it is quite possible to record part of an entry in the wrong column. To locate errors of this type before they are transferred to the ledger in the posting process, each page of the purchases journal is balanced. The total of the debit columns must equal the total of the credit columns. These steps should be followed when you balance a purchases journal:

1. Rule a single line across all money columns below the last line used.

2. Add the columns.

3. Where there are more than one of each, add all the debit column totals and all the credit column totals.

4. If the debit totals equal the credit totals, write the column totals at the bottom of each column. Write the debit and credit totals in the Creditor column.

5. Rule double lines across the date and all money columns.

Figure 10-10 on page 460 illustrates the balancing process after page 16 of the purchases journal has been filled. The purchases journal is balanced at the end of each page and at the end of each month.

PAGE 16

PURCHASES JOURNAL

DATE		REF. NO.	CREDITOR	TERMS	P.R.	PURCHASES DEBIT	GST REFUND. DEBIT	ACCOUNTS PAYABLE CREDIT	UTILITIES EXPENSE DEBIT	OTHER ACCOUNTS ACCOUNT	P.R.	DEBIT
20— Sep.	5	307	Speedquip Ltd.	n/30		3 1 8 60	2 2 30	3 4 0 90				
	5	W184	Evans & Kert	n/30			3 50	5 7 50		Supplies		5 4 00
	5	3871	Tops Service Centre	n/30			4 90	7 4 90		Car Expense		7 0 00
	5	B-519	Ontario Hydro	EOM			1 3 65	2 0 8 65	1 9 5 00			
	5	193	Cooper Bros.	n/30		5 0 0 00	3 5 00	5 3 5 00				

FIGURE 10-9 Transactions recorded in a purchases journal

PURCHASES JOURNAL   PAGE 16

DATE	REF. NO.	CREDITOR	TERMS	P.R.	PURCHASES DEBIT	GST REFUND. DEBIT	ACCOUNTS PAYABLE CREDIT	UTILITIES EXPENSE DEBIT	OTHER ACCOUNTS ACCOUNT	P.R.	DEBIT
20— Sep. 5	307	Speedquip Ltd.	n/30		318 60	22 30	340 90				
5	W184	Evans & Kert	n/30			3 50	57 50		Supplies		54 00
5	3871	Tops Service Centre	n/30			4 90	74 90		Car Expense		70 00
5	B-519	Ontario Hydro	EOM			13 65	208 65	195 00			
5	193	Copper Bros.	n/30		500 00	35 00	535 00				
6	419	Hall Fuel	n/30			14 00	214 00	200 00			
9	801	Coles Ltd.	n/30			70	10 70		Miscellaneous Expense		10 00
10	331	Speedquip Ltd.	n/30		200 00	14 00	214 00				
11	207	Cooper Bros.	n/30		40 00	2 80	42 80				
12	H-719	CN Express	n/15			8 05	123 05		Trans. on Purchases		115 00
16	3461	City Water Dept.	EOM			25 20	385 20	360 00			
18	219	Cooper Bros.	n/30		900 00	63 00	963 00				
20	W220	Evans & Kert	n/30			6 79	111 55		Supplies		104 76
23	231	Cooper Bros.	n/30		120 00	8 40	128 40				
27	3904	Tops Service Centre	n/30			3 15	48 15		Car Expense		45 00
30	379	Speedquip Ltd.	n/30		40 00	2 80	42 80				
		Debits = $3885.80			2 4 7 8 60	2 5 3 44	3 8 8 5 80	7 5 5 00			3 9 8 76
		Credits = $3885.80									

FIGURE 10-10 Balancing the purchases journal

Locating Errors

If the journal does not balance:

- Start on the first line and check to see if there are equal debit and credit amounts on each line.
- Recheck all addition.
- Follow the steps for locating errors given in Chapter 4.

Forwarding Totals

When a page of a journal is filled, it should be balanced and the totals carried forward to the next page. Follow the forwarding procedures described in Chapter 9.

Posting to the Ledgers

The main advantage of the purchases journal is that it reduces the recording workload since only one line is needed for most transactions. In contrast, at least three lines of writing are required when transactions are recorded directly in the general journal.

Further efficiencies are achieved in the posting process. The posting procedure is the same as for the columnar journal used in Chapter 9 and the efficiencies achieved in journalizing and posting transactions are the same. On the following pages, the steps involved in posting from the purchases journal to the accounts payable ledger and the general ledger will be described. Figure 10-11 on page 463 will illustrate the complete posting process for the purchases journal. First, however, we will briefly review the methods of posting to the subsidiary ledgers.

Methods of Posting to the Subsidiary Ledgers

As explained in the previous chapter, there are two methods commonly used to post columnar journals to the subsidiary ledgers.

Direct Posting

The direct posting method requires that source documents be posted *directly* to the subsidiary ledgers. Different people can be assigned to journalize transactions and update the subsidiary ledgers. A company with a large number of transactions involving customers and creditors would use this posting system.

Companies with a columnar purchases journal usually use this method to record source documents in the subsidiary ledgers. Purchase invoices are recorded directly into the *accounts payable ledger*. Sales invoices are recorded directly into the *accounts receivable ledger*. *Division of responsibility* is made possible since different accounting personnel can be used to perform these tasks.

Posting from the Journal

Another posting method is to enter transactions in the journal and *then* to post the entries from the journal to the ledger accounts. This method is often used by companies that may wish to use special journals but do not have enough transactions to have different people working on the journals and the ledgers. In Chapter 9, this method was demonstrated for the columnar journal. It will also be used here for the purchases journal.

Posting the Purchases Journal to the Accounts Payable Ledger

Step 1

Each day, post each entry in the Accounts Payable credit column of the purchases journal to the accounts payable ledger. In the following example, Speedquip Ltd.'s account is credited with $340.90 on September 5. P16 is written in the Posting Reference column of the account to indicate the journal and page number of the posting.

				ACCOUNTS PAYABLE LEDGER			
ACCOUNT Speedquip Ltd.							
DATE		PARTICULARS	P.R.	DEBIT	CREDIT	DR. CR.	BALANCE
20—							
Sep.	5		P16		3 4 0 90	CR.	3 4 0 90

Posting from the purchases journal to the accounts payable ledger is done daily to keep the balances in the creditors' accounts up to date.

Step 2

Place a check mark (✓) in the Posting Reference column of the purchases journal opposite each creditor (for example, Speedquip Ltd.) to indicate that the amount has been posted to the subsidiary ledger account. (See Figure 10-11 on the next page.)

Posting the Purchases Journal to the General Ledger

Step 1

At the end of the month, post the individual transactions in the Other Accounts section to the general ledger, writing the purchases journal abbreviation and page number in the Posting Reference column of the accounts (e.g., P16). Show the ledger account number in the Posting Reference column of the Other Accounts section. (See Figure 10-11.)

Step 2

At the end of the month, post the totals of each column to the appropriate account in the general ledger, again writing the purchases journal abbreviation and page number in the Posting Reference column of the accounts. The account numbers are shown in brackets under each total (see Figure 10-11). The Other Accounts total is not posted.

PURCHASES JOURNAL   PAGE 16

DATE	REF. NO.	CREDITOR	TERMS	P.R.	PURCHASES DEBIT	GST REFUND. DEBIT	ACCOUNTS PAYABLE CREDIT	UTILITIES EXPENSE DEBIT	OTHER ACCOUNTS ACCOUNT	P.R.	DEBIT
20— Sep.											
5	307	Speedquip Ltd.	n/30	✓	318 60	22 30	340 90				
5	W184	Evans & Kert	n/30	✓		3 50	57 50		Supplies	125	54 00
5	3871	Tops Service Centre	n/30	✓		4 90	74 90		Car Expense	613	70 00
5	B-519	Ontario Hydro	EOM	✓		13 65	208 65	195 00			
5	193	Copper Bros.	n/30	✓	500 00	35 00	535 00				
6	419	Hall Fuel	n/30	✓		14 00	214 00	200 00			
9	801	Coles Ltd.	n/30	✓		70	10 70		Miscellaneous Expense	614	10 00
10	331	Speedquip Ltd.	n/30	✓	200 00	14 00	214 00				
11	207	Cooper Bros.	n/30	✓	40 00	2 80	42 80				
12	H-719	CN Express	n/15	✓		8 05	123 05		Trans. on Purchases	503	115 00
16	3461	City Water Dept.	EOM	✓		25 20	385 20	360 00			
18	219	Cooper Bros.	n/30	✓	900 00	63 00	963 00				
20	W220	Evans & Kert	n/30	✓		6 79	111 55		Supplies	125	104 76
23	231	Cooper Bros.	n/30	✓	120 00	8 40	128 40				
27	3904	Tops Service Centre	n/30	✓		3 15	48 15		Car Expense	613	45 00
30	379	Speedquip Ltd.	n/30	✓	400 00	28 00	428 00				
		Debits = $3885.80			2478 60	253 44	3885 80	755 00			398 76
		Credits = $3885.80			(500)	(206)	(200)	(615)			

FIGURE 10-11 Posting the purchases journal

The following example shows the Purchases account in the general ledger after the Purchases debit column total from the purchases journal has been posted:

GENERAL LEDGER							
ACCOUNT Purchases							NO. 500
DATE	PARTICULARS	P.R.	DEBIT	CREDIT	DR. CR.	BALANCE	
20—							
Sep. 30		P16	2 4 7 8 60		DR.	2 4 7 8 60	

General Posting Procedure for Special Journals

The posting procedure described for the purchases journal is used for all of the special journals in this chapter. A summary of this procedure follows.

Step 1

Do the following:
(a) *Each day*, post all of the individual entries in the Accounts Payable or Accounts Receivable columns to the accounts in the subsidiary ledgers.
(b) Place the journal abbreviation and page number in the Posting Reference column of each account (e.g., P16, S17, CR 37, CP14, J10).
(c) Place a check mark (✓) in the first Posting Reference column in the journal beside each item to indicate that the item has been posted.

Step 2

Do the following:
(a) *At the end of the month*, post the individual items in the Other Accounts section to the relevant accounts in the general ledger.
(b) Place the journal abbreviation and page number in the Posting Reference column of each account.
(c) Place the account in the Posting Reference column of the Other Accounts section to indicate that posting of the entry is complete.

Step 3

Do the following:
(a) *At the end of the month*, post all column totals (except the Other Accounts total) to the relevant accounts in the general ledger.
(b) Place the journal abbreviation and page number in the Posting Reference column of each account.
(c) Place the account number in parentheses under the total in the journal to indicate that it has been posted.

CREDIT INVOICES

Occasionally, a buyer will return goods to the seller. This causes changes on the books of both the buyer and the seller. The source document prepared by the seller as a record of a return of goods is the credit invoice.

The seller prepares the credit invoice and sends it to the buyer. The seller decreases the amount owed by the buyer. When the buyer receives the credit invoice, the buyer decreases the amount owed to the seller.

A credit invoice is the source document prepared by a seller to record the return of goods by a customer.

Recording Credit Invoices

Credit invoices may be recorded in several ways, depending on the information required by the company and the number of credit invoices to be processed.

1. Credit invoices may be recorded in the general journal. This method will be used to complete the exercises in this chapter.
2. Credit invoices may be recorded in the purchases journal. The *circling* method can be used or *special columns* can be set up in the purchases journal for purchase returns.
3. A special account, Purchases Returns and Allowances, may be used to record returns. A Purchases Returns and Allowances account will be used to complete the exercises in this chapter.

The following sample transactions will be used to illustrate the recording of credit invoices in the buyer's books.

Transaction for a Purchase on Account

Mar. 4   Purchased merchandise on account, from Shannon Ltd., Invoice 322, terms n/30, $500 plus GST $35.

This transaction was recorded in the purchases journal in the normal way.

Transaction for a Purchase Return

Mar. 10   Returned unacceptable goods worth $100 plus $7 GST to Shannon Ltd. from merchandise purchased March 4. Shannon issued Credit Invoice C-40 for $107.

The various methods of recording this $107 credit invoice are described below.

Using the General Journal

If the general journal is used, the credit invoice is recorded as follows:

Mar.	10	Accounts Payable/Shannon Ltd.	✓200	1 0 7 00	
		Purchases Returns and Allowances	501		1 0 0 00
		GST Refundable	207		7 00
		To record Credit Invoice C-40.			

When this transaction is posted, *the $107 debit is posted to the Accounts Payable control account in the general ledger and to Shannon Ltd. in the accounts payable ledger.* A check mark (✓) is used to show the posting to the subsidiary ledger account, while account number 200 indicates that the general ledger has been posted. Both the credit of $100 to Purchases Returns and Allowances and the $7 credit to GST Refundable are posted in the general ledger.

Can you explain why the $107 debit is posted twice—once to the control account and once to Shannon's account?

Using the Purchases Journal: Special Columns

The purchases journal can have special columns added for Accounts Payable debit and Purchases Returns and Allowances credit. A company would use these two additional columns when it has many credit invoices to be recorded. Credit invoices would then be recorded as illustrated in Figure 10-12 on the next page.

Using the Purchases Journal: Circling Method

If special columns are not used, credit invoices can be recorded in the purchases journal using the circling method. Any item circled is subtracted when the columns are totalled. Circling is a method of indicating that an item is to be treated opposite to the other listed items, in this case as a debit, not as a credit. This method is illustrated for the Shannon transaction in Figure 10-13 on the next page.

ADVANTAGES OF THE PURCHASES JOURNAL

There are four advantages to using a purchases journal:

- Most entries require only one line.
- Posting is reduced.
- Explanations are eliminated.
- Division of labour and responsibilities is possible.

PURCHASES JOURNAL   PAGE 30

DATE		REF. NO.	CREDITOR	TERMS	P.R.	PURCHASES DEBIT	GST REFUND. DEBIT	ACCOUNTS PAYABLE CREDIT	PURCH. RET. & ALL. CREDITS	ACCOUNTS PAYABLE DEBIT	OTHER ACCOUNTS ACCOUNT	P.R.	DEBIT
20— Mar.	4	322	Shannon Ltd.	n/30		5 0 0 00	3 5 00	5 3 5 00					
	10	C-40	Shannon Ltd.				(7 00)		1 0 0 00	1 07 00			

FIGURE 10-12 Purchases journal with special columns for Purchases Returns and Allowances credit and Accounts Payable debit

PURCHASES JOURNAL   PAGE 16

DATE		REF. NO.	CREDITOR	TERMS	P.R.	PURCHASES DEBIT	GST REFUND. DEBIT	ACCOUNTS PAYABLE CREDIT	UTILITIES EXPENSE DEBIT	OTHER ACCOUNTS ACCOUNT	P.R.	DEBIT
20— Mar.	4	322	Shannon Ltd.	n/30		5 0 0 00	3 5 00	5 3 5 00				
	10	C-40	Shannon Ltd.			(1 0 0 00)	(7 00)	(1 07 00)				
			Totals			4 0 0 00	2 8 00	4 2 8 00				

FIGURE 10-13 Purchases journal showing the circling method. The circled amounts are subtracted when the columns are totalled.

UNIT 21 CHECK YOUR READING

Questions

1. What is a special journal system?
2. Answer the following questions about the purchase requisition shown in Figure 10-2:
   (a) Who requested the merchandise?
   (b) Who is the supervisor?
   (c) Why is it necessary to have the supervisor sign the purchase requisition?
3. What factors does the purchasing department consider before it issues the purchase order?
4. Answer the following questions about the purchase order shown in Figure 10-3:
   (a) What company was chosen to supply the goods?
   (b) Explain why each of the following receive a copy of the purchase order:
       (i)   Receiving department
       (ii)   Accounting department
       (iii) Purchasing department
       (iv)   Requesting department
5. Explain the "matching process" and indicate what three documents are matched.
6. What department is responsible for matching the documents?
7. What supporting documents are attached to the purchase invoice?
8. What type of transactions are recorded in the purchases journal?
9. Explain the steps followed in posting the purchases journal (assume direct posting is not used).
10. What is a credit invoice?
11. Which accounts are debited and credited in the general journal when you record a credit invoice for goods returned (purchase return)?

UNIT 21 APPLY YOUR KNOWLEDGE

Exercises

1. Lynn Halliwell owns Superior Electrical Services. Her firm uses a cash receipts journal (CR), cash payments journal (CP), purchases journal (P), sales journal (S), and general journal (J). Indicate which journal should be used to record each of the following transactions:

   (a) Sale of merchandise for cash.
   (b) Purchase of equipment on account.
   (c) Adjusting entry to record supplies expense for the period.
   (d) Sale of merchandise on account.
   (e) Payment of the employees' salaries for the week.
   (f) Purchase of equipment for cash.

(g) Return of merchandise by a customer for a cash refund.

(h) Receipt of a cheque from a customer to pay an outstanding account.

(i) Return of merchandise by a customer for a credit to her account.

(j) Purchase of a new printer by paying one-third in cash and the remainder on account.

2. (a) Record the following approved invoices in a purchases journal.

(b) Total, balance, and rule the journal.

Jan. 3 Purchased merchandise for $1500 from Cavers Ltd., GST $105, Invoice 554 dated December 30, terms n/30.

4 Purchased office supplies for $163 from Beatties, GST $11.41, Invoice W12 dated January 2, terms n/30.

4 Purchased merchandise for $750 from Beamer Bros., GST $52.50, Invoice 7 dated January 2, terms n/30.

5 Purchased office equipment for $750 from Grand Ltd., GST $52.50, Invoice 6-110 dated January 2, terms n/30.

3. (a) Set up the following accounts and balances for May 1 in the partial general ledger for Discount Stores:

101	Cash	$ 2 900	
110	Accounts Receivable	8 800	
125	Office Supplies	1 340	
200	Accounts Payable		$ 4 520
206	GST Payable		750
207	GST Refundable	500	
300	K. Duncan, Capital		15 970
501	Purchases	7 000	
503	Transportation on Purchases	240	
606	Truck Expense	460	
		$21 240	$21 240

(b) Set up the following accounts and balances on May 1 in the accounts payable ledger for Discount Stores:

Canadian Tire	$ 375
Graham Wholesalers	3 470
Whitman Stationers	535
Williams Trucking	140
	$4 520

(c) Enter the following approved purchase invoices on page 73 of a purchases journal for Discount Stores; then total, balance, and rule the journal.

May 4 No. 431 for merchandise from Graham Wholesalers for $576, GST $40.32.

5 No. 222 for office supplies from Whitman Stationers for $135, GST $9.45.

6 No. 1063 for gas and oil used in the truck from Canadian Tire for $35, GST $2.45.

7 No. 741 for transportation of merchandise from Williams Trucking for $47, GST $3.29.

8 No. 448 for merchandise from Graham Wholesalers for $2348, GST $164.36.

(d) Post the purchases journal to the general ledger.

(e) Prepare a trial balance for the general ledger.

(f) Post the relevant source documents directly to the accounts payable ledger.

(g) Prepare a schedule of accounts payable. Check your total with control account 200 in the general ledger.

4. (a) In a purchases journal for B & M Furniture, enter the approved purchase invoices given below. Assign page 214 to the journal. Use the partial chart of accounts given below to determine the accounts affected.

(b) Total, balance, and rule the journal.

(c) Describe how you would post this journal if all postings to the accounts in both the general ledger and accounts payable ledger are made from the purchases journal.

115	Prepaid Insurance	501	Purchases
121	Office Equipment	505	Transportation on Purchases
201	Accounts Payable	609	Delivery Expense
207	GST Refundable	639	Miscellaneous Expense

Jan. 3 Carter and Wilson, insurance agents, $3450 plus $241.50 GST for the insurance premium on the building and contents, Invoice 4975.

4 Thornhill's Service Centre, $263 plus $18.41 GST for delivery truck repairs, Invoice J-003.

4 Teak Manufacturers, $9756 plus $682.92 GST for dining room furniture, Invoice 3361.

5 McCall's Stationers, $289 plus $20.23 GST for a new filing cabinet for the office, Invoice 2828.

7 Thornhill's Service Centre, $580 plus $40.60 GST for repairs to one of the delivery trucks, Invoice J-021.

7 Rick's Towing Service, $30 plus $2.10 GST for towing a delivery truck to Thornhill's Service Centre, Invoice 24.

9 Ray's Snow Removal, $75 plus $5.25 GST for plowing the parking lot after a storm, Invoice 1492.

10   Teak Manufacturers, $7527 plus $526.89 GST for living room furniture, Invoice 3384.

11   Enders Ltd., $3651 plus $255.57 GST for the purchase of five refrigerators, Invoice E6144.

11   Hi-Way Trucking, $750 plus $52.50 GST for freight charges on the refrigerator shipment, Invoice 35722.

5. (a) In a purchases journal for the Pro-Cycle Shop, enter the approved invoices listed below. Assign page 133 to the journal. Use the following trial balance to determine the accounts affected.

Pro-Cycle Shop
Trial Balance
June 30, 20—

101	Cash	$15 000	
110	Accounts Receivable	10 000	
125	Supplies	1 500	
151	Office Equipment	30 000	
200	Accounts Payable		$ 5 000
206	GST Payable		600
207	GST Refundable	400	
300	K. Paul, Capital		60 000
301	K. Paul, Drawings	0	
500	Purchases	7 000	
503	Transportation on Purchases	500	
600	Delivery Expense	700	
601	Advertising Expense	200	
607	Repairs and Maintenance Expense	300	
		$ 65 600	$65 600

Jul.   2   Invoice 1246 for 15 bicycles from Raleigh for $2250, GST $157.50.

3   Invoice 223 for tires and tubes from Dunlop Tires for $477, GST $33.39.

4   Invoice 767 for repairs to the main entrance by Coastal Glass for $125, GST $8.75.

4   Invoice H467 for transportation of the bicycles received on July 1, $125 from Hi-Way Transport, GST $8.75.

5   Invoice 2967 for gas and oil used in the delivery truck during June, $187.50 from Craig's Service Station, GST $13.13.

8   Invoice 5655 for advertising space, $430 from the *Daily News*, GST $30.10.

(b) Total, balance, and rule the journal.

(c) Assign page 134 to the next journal page and bring the totals forward from page 133; then continue by recording the following approved invoices:

Jul.   9   Invoice 268 for repairs to the owner's (K. Paul's) cottage, $1697.02 plus GST from Denver Contractors.

9   Invoice 1279 for bicycle accessories from Bellwether for $862, GST $60.34.

10   Invoice 647 for a new computer from Jason's Ltd. for $2685, GST $187.95.

10   Invoice 4346 for 10 bicycles from NORCO for $2960, GST $207.20.

11   Invoice 2164 for paper bags, wrapping paper, and other store supplies from Carter Supplies for $167, GST $11.69.

(d) Set up a general ledger and post the purchases journal.
(e) Prepare a trial balance.
(f) Describe the procedure you would prefer to use to post the accounts payable ledger. Why do you prefer this method to other methods available?

6. The following is a partial chart of accounts for Electronics Unlimited of Vancouver.

100	Cash	501	Purchases
121	Office Equipment	502	Transportation on Purchases
201	Accounts Payable	503	Purchases Returns and Allowances
205	PST Payable	604	Delivery Expense
206	GST Payable	610	Building Repairs Expense
207	GST Refundable		

(a) On page 37 of a purchases journal, record the approved purchase invoices for Electronics Unlimited shown on the following pages.
(b) Record credit invoices in a general journal.
(c) Total, balance, and rule the purchases journal.

BANNEX LTD.

1493 Bridge Road, Toronto, ON M6A 1Z5
Phone 416-594-6655   Fax 416-594-8731

Sold to Electronics Unlimited
795 Beaver Drive
Vancouver, BC
V7N 3H6

INVOICE 17493
DATE   Feb. 3, 20—
TERMS   Net 30 days

Quantity	Description	Unit Price	Total
5	Spools of #10 copper wire	$23.50	$117.50
		GST	8.23
		Total Due	$125.73

Received March 2

Received by BK
Price O.K. ✓
Account 501
Payment O.K. CD

Sales Tax Exempt

Received March 4

White & Turner

Heating Contractors
for all your heating supplies

Fax   Telephone
793-8340 or 793-8050

497 Albion Rd., Vancouver, BC V7A 3E4

Sold to Electronics Unlimited
795 Beaver Drive
Vancouver, BC
V7N 3H6

Invoice No. 86B743
Date Feb. 4, 20—
Terms 2/10, n/30

Stock No.	Description	Quantity	Price	Amount
N-21-2	2 cm x 3 m pipes	7	$4.50	$31.50
R-63-47	Boxes #3 washers	2	0.75	1.50
			Subtotal	33.00
			GST	2.31
			Sales Tax	1.98
			Total	$37.29

Cash ❑
Charge ❑

Received by BK
Price O.K. ✓
Account 510
Payment O.K. CD

Received by	*BK*
Price O.K.	✓
Account	*501*
Payment O.K.	*CD*

EVC
Limited
1793 Pennfield Drive, Los Angeles, CA 96430-5893

Received March 5

TO: Electronics Unlimited
795 Beaver Drive
Vancouver, BC, Canada
V7N 3H6

Invoice No.	E-437073
Terms	Net 30 days F.O.B.
Your Order No.	7434
Ship Via	WCT
Date Shipped	Feb. 28, 20—
Date of Inv.	March 1

Quantity	Description	Unit Price	Amount
20	EVC 40 Speakers	$109	$2180.00
10	EVC 50 Speakers	129	1290.00
10	SP-743-H Receivers	133	1330.00
5	SP-843-H Receivers	152	760.00
	Sales Tax Exempt	Sub Total	5560.00
		GST	389.20
		Total	$5949.20

WEST COAST TRANSPORT

Vancouver
73 Commissioner Rd.
Vancouver, BC
Canada V7R 3T6
Phone (604) 937-4370
Fax (604) 937-4819

Seattle
1890 Industrial Rd.
Seattle, Washington
U.S.A. 92000-8191
Phone (206) 347-8650
Fax: (206) 347-9190

Los Angeles
734 Green Street
Los Angeles, California
U.S.A. 96300-9852
Phone (213) 474-8503
Fax: (213) 474-8888

Shipper:
EVC Limited
1793 Pennfield Drive
Los Angeles, CA 96430-5893

Consignee:
Electronics Unlimited
795 Beaver Drive
Vancouver, BC. V7N 3H6

Prepaid   Collect X

Date   March 1, 20—   Terms: Net 30   Inv. No. W.B. 74343

No. of Containers	Mass	Rate	Amount
45 boxes	300 kg	$0.40/kg	$120.00
		GST	8.40
		Total	$128.40
		Pay this Amount →	$128.40

Received by	*BK*
Price O.K.	✓
Account	*502*
Payment O.K.	*CD*

Received March 8

Same Day Delivery

LOCAL DELIVERIES

475 Dynes Road
Vancouver, BC V7E 3R1
Phone 837-4390

Invoice No.   657
Terms   Net 30
Date   March 7, 20—

Charge	Deliver to
Electronics Unlimited	Mr. K. Stafford
795 Beaver Drive	473 Elm Street
Vancouver, BC	Vancouver, BC
V7N 3H6	V6L 2L4

Description		Amount	
4 boxes	*Received March 9*		$100.00
	Received by *BK* / Price O.K. ✓ / Account 503 / Payment O.K. *CD*	GST	7.00
		Total	$107.00

Jonsson

Office Specialities Ltd.

63 Main Street, Vancouver, BC V6A 2S2   Phone 343-7512   Fax 343-1817

For all Your Office Needs

Sold to		
Electronics Unlimited	Our Invoice No.	73B4973
795 Beaver Drive	Your Order No.	7440
Vancouver, BC	Terms	2/10, n/30
V7N 3H6	Date Shipped	March 7, 20—
	Date of Invoice	March 7, 20—

Quantity	Description	Unit Price	Amount
1	Printer PX585	$465.64	$465.64
	Received by *BK* / Price O.K. ✓ / Account 121 / Payment O.K. *CD*	*Received March 9*	
		GST	32.59
		PST	27.94
		Pay this amount	$526.17

EVC
Limited
1793 Pennfield Drive, Los Angeles, CA 96430-5893

TO: Electronics Unlimited
    795 Beaver Drive
    Vancouver, BC, Canada
    V7N 3H6

Credit No. 1396
March 7, 20—

We credit your account as specified below.

Re: Inv. #E-437073, dated March 1, 20—
    1 SP-743-H Receiver $133.00
    1 SP-843-H Receiver   152.00
    Sub Total $285.00
    GST   19.95
        $304.95

Received March 9

CREDIT MEMORANDUM

UNIT 22 Sales Journal

What Learning You Will Demonstrate

On completion of this unit, you will be able to:

- record sales invoices in a sales journal;
- record credit invoices;
- total, balance, and post a sales journal;
- explain the purpose of a customer statement; and
- explain the cycle billing method of preparing statements.

In this unit, the system for processing sales of goods on account will be discussed as well as the recording and posting procedures for a sales journal.

PROCEDURES FOR SALES INVOICES

For each credit sale, a source document called a *sales invoice* is prepared. This document, commonly called a *bill*, is the seller's evidence that a transaction occurred. The sales invoice in Figure 10-14 was prepared by Warrendon Sports.

WARRENDON SPORTS

2579 Base Line Road
Ottawa, ON K2H 7B3
Tel: 684-1287   Fax: 684-5381

INVOICE   Order No.

Sold To   Ship To
High School of Commerce   Same
300 Rochester Street
Ottawa, ON   K1R 7N4

Date Oct. 15, 20—   Invoice No. 105   Terms Net 30 days   Cash   Charge

Quantity	Description	Unit Price	Amount
3	Volleyballs, vinyl specials	$19.65	$58.95
		GST (7%)	4.13
		PST (8%)	4.72
		Total Due	$67.80

GST Registration No. R119282106

FIGURE 10-14 Sales invoice

See if you can answer the following questions about the invoice in Figure 10-14:

- Who is the seller?
- Who is the buyer?
- What is the total to be paid by the customer and when must it be paid?
- How are the $58.95, $4.13, and $4.72 amounts calculated?

Four copies of the invoice are normally prepared and distributed as indicated in Figure 10-15.

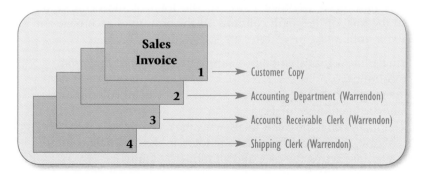

FIGURE 10-15 Distribution of sales invoice copies

INTRODUCING THE SALES JOURNAL

A sales journal is used to record sales on account.

Earlier in this chapter, you learned that a purchases journal is used to record purchases of goods and services on credit. The use of special columns saves times and effort in recording and posting purchases. For the same reasons, the sales journal is used to record *sales on account (credit sales)*.

In a sales journal, each transaction requires only one line. Figure 10-16, the sales journal for Warrendon Sports, shows some transactions where the customer is charged sales tax, while others are not taxed. This is because some are sales of non-taxable items.

					ACCOUNTS REC.	SALES	GST PAYABLE	PST PAYABLE
DATE	INV. NO.	CUSTOMER	TERMS	P.R.	DEBIT	CREDIT	CREDIT	CREDIT
20—								
Jul. 5	71	J. Hunt	n/30	✓	1 1 5 00	1 0 0 00	7 00	8 00
7	72	C. Bard	n/30	✓	3 4 5 00	3 0 0 00	2 1 00	2 4 00
8	73	M. Wong	n/30	✓	8 0 25	7 5 00	5 25	
12	74	G. Saikeley	n/30	✓	4 8 1 50	4 5 0 00	3 1 50	
13	75	K. Rice	n/30	✓	8 0 5 00	7 0 0 00	4 9 00	5 6 00
15	76	C. Bard	n/30	✓	6 9 0 00	6 0 0 00	4 2 00	4 8 00
		Debits = $2516.75			2 5 1 6 75	2 2 2 5 00	1 5 5 75	1 3 6 00
		Credits = $2516.75			(110)	(400)	(206)	(205)

FIGURE 10-16 Sales journal for Warrendon Sports showing correct balancing and posting procedures

The sales journal in Figure 10-16 has been balanced and posted. The steps involved in both of these procedures will now be described.

Balancing the Sales Journal

If transactions have been recorded correctly, the total of the debit columns should equal the total of the credit columns. At the bottom of each page and at the end of the month, these procedures are followed:

1. Rule a single line across all money columns below the last line used.
2. Add the columns.
3. Where there are more than one of each, add all the debit column totals and all the credit column totals.
4. If the debit totals equal the credit totals, write the column totals at the bottom of each column. Write the debit and credit totals in the Customer column.
5. Rule double lines across the date and all money columns.

Look again at Figure 10-16 to see an example of a sales journal that has been balanced. If the month has not ended, the totals are carried forward to the next page. At the end of the month, the totals are posted to the general ledger.

Posting the Sales Journal

The use of a sales journal means that only two steps are needed to post the entries. The amounts in the Accounts Receivable debit column are posted daily to the customer accounts in the accounts receivable ledger and the four totals are posted to the general ledger at the end of the month. The posting process is similar to that of the purchases journal:

1. *Each day*, post the entries in the Accounts Receivable debit column to the customer accounts in the accounts receivable ledger. Write the sales journal abbreviation and page number in the Posting Reference column of each account (e.g., S17). Enter a check mark (✓) in the Posting Reference column of the journal opposite each customer.
2. *At the end of the month*, post the journal totals to Accounts Receivable control, Sales, GST Payable, and PST Payable in the general ledger. Enter the sales journal abbreviation and page number in the Posting Reference column of the accounts. Write the account numbers below the totals in the sales journal (see Figure 10-16).

RECORDING CREDIT INVOICES

When sold goods are returned, a credit invoice is prepared and sent to the customer. Four methods are used to record sales returns on the books of the seller:

1. In the general journal, use the Sales Returns and Allowances account and record the credit invoices as debits in that account.
2. In the general journal, decrease the Sales account with a debit.
3. In the sales journal, record the return in the Sales Returns and Allowances debit column and decrease the GST Payable, PST Payable, and Accounts Receivable accounts using the circling method.
4. In the sales journal, use the circling method to decrease the Sales, GST Payable, PST Payable, and Accounts Receivable accounts.

The circling method is illustrated in Figure 10-17 on page 480.

If the circling method is not used and if the sales journal does not have special columns to accommodate a sales return transaction, then the transaction is recorded in the general journal. An example follows:

Jul.	21	Sales Returns and Allowances	401	5 0 00		
		GST Payable	206	3 50		
		PST Payable	205	4 00		
		Accounts Receivable/C. Bard	110✓		5 7 50	
		Credit invoice C-12 for goods returned.				

					ACCOUNTS REC.	SALES	GST PAYABLE	PST PAYABLE
DATE	INV. NO.	CUSTOMER	TERMS	P.R.	DEBIT	CREDIT	CREDIT	CREDIT
20—								
Jul. 5	71	J. Hunt	n/30	✓	1 1 5 00	1 0 0 00	7 00	8 00
7	72	C. Bard	n/30	✓	3 4 5 00	3 0 0 00	2 1 00	2 4 00
8	73	M. Wong	n/30	✓	8 0 25	7 5 00	5 25	
12	74	G. Saikeley	n/30	✓	4 8 1 50	4 5 0 00	3 1 50	
13	75	K. Rice	n/30	✓	8 0 5 00	7 0 0 00	4 9 00	5 6 00
15	76	C. Bard	n/30	✓	6 9 0 00	6 0 0 00	4 2 00	4 8 00
21	C-21	C. Bard		✓	(5 7 50)	(5 0 00)	(3 50)	(4 00)
		Debits = $2459.25			2 4 5 9 25	2 1 7 5 00	1 5 2 25	1 3 2 00
		Credits = $2459.25			(110)	(400)	(206)	(205)

SALES JOURNAL — PAGE 17

FIGURE 10-17 Circled items represent sales returns and are subtracted from uncircled items.

As you have seen previously, the $57.50 must be posted to both the Accounts Receivable control account in the general ledger and to C. Bard's account in the accounts receivable ledger to maintain the equality of the control account and the subsidiary ledger.

Each of the exercises in this chapter will state the company's accounting policy for recording credit invoices.

STATEMENT OF ACCOUNT

Suppose a company has a customer by the name of J. Clarke, and another named J. Clark. A sale of $100 to J. Clarke was incorrectly posted to J. Clark's account. In the seller's accounts receivable ledger, J. Clarke's account balance would be $100 too low and J. Clark's account balance would be $100 too high. *How would this error be discovered?*

A statement of account is a form sent to customers that shows charges, amounts credited, and the balance of an account.

To locate errors of this type, many companies send a **statement of account** to their customers (Figure 10-18). At regular periods, usually every month, a copy of the debits and credits in a customer's account is mailed to that customer. In effect, a copy of the entries made to the ledger account since the last statement is sent to the customer. The statement of account serves two purposes:

- It enables a customer to compare his or her records with those of the seller and thus to locate errors.
- It reminds a customer of the balance owing.

The statement of account may be prepared by hand or by computer.

Cycle Billing

A company that has only a few customers usually sends a statement of account to each customer at the end of the month.

A company with a large number of customers may find it impossible to prepare all of the statements at the end of the month. A more efficient method of handling

Renfrew Printing

COMMERCIAL PRINTING • BOOK PRINTING • PHOTOCOPIES • RUBBER STAMPS
173 Raglan Street South, Renfrew, ON K7V 1R2
Tel (613) 432-6449 Fax (613) 432-1147

TO   MacKillican & Associates
     252 Raglan Street S.
     Renfrew, ON K7V 1R1

MONTH OF   October 20—
AMOUNT OF
REMITTANCE $

PLEASE RETURN THIS PART WITH YOUR REMITTANCE

IN ACCOUNT
  WITH

PLEASE KEEP
THIS PART

DATE	PARTICULARS	DEBIT	CREDIT	BALANCE
Oct. 1	PREVIOUS BALANCE FORWARD			$263.20
15	5000 #10 Envelopes	$321.82		585.02

2% PER MONTH (24% PER ANNUM) INTEREST
CHARGED ON OVERDUE ACCOUNTS

PLEASE PAY LAST
AMOUNT
IN THIS COLUMN

FIGURE 10-18 Monthly statement of account sent to a customer, showing the balance forwarded from the previous month and the transactions for the current month

the preparation of the statements is to distribute the work evenly over the month. Figure 10-19 illustrates how the work may be scheduled.

In cycle billing, the records of transactions (source documents such as invoices and cash receipt lists) for someone like J. Clarke would be accumulated from the date of the last statement. These transactions would be entered in the customer's account and the statement of account would be prepared on the 6th day of each month. The statement of account for Resticon Ltd. would be prepared on the 21st day of each month.

Cycle billing is a method of spreading over the month the work of preparing and mailing statements to customers.

Cycle Billing Schedule		
Initial of Customer's Last Name	Includes Transactions up to	Day of the Month on Which Statement Is Prepared
A–E	5th	6th
F–L	13th	14th
M–R	20th	21st
S–Z	29th	30th

FIGURE 10-19 Cycle billing

SUMMARIZING THE SYSTEM FOR RECORDING SALES

Earlier in this text, you learned that a system is a series of steps followed to complete a task. In this unit, you learned the system for recording sales. Figure 10-20 summarizes that system.

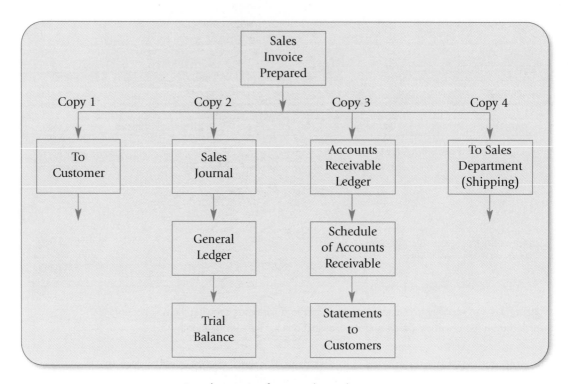

FIGURE 10-20   Complete system for recording sales

UNIT 22 CHECK YOUR READING

Questions

12. What source document is prepared for a credit sale?

13. In which special journal is a credit sale recorded?

14. There is a $100 entry circled in a sales journal's Accounts Receivable debit column. Should the $100 be posted as a debit or as a credit to the customer's account?

15. To which ledger are copies of a sales invoice posted when a company uses direct posting?

16. (a) What is a statement of account?
(b) What two purposes are served by the statement of account?

17. Explain the cycle billing method of preparing customer statements.

UNIT 22 APPLY YOUR KNOWLEDGE

Exercises

7. (a) Answer the following questions about the invoice shown below:

   (i)   Who is the seller?
   (ii)   Who is the customer?
   (iii) What is the date of the invoice?
   (iv)   What are the terms of sale?
   (v)   What is the last day for payment?
   (vi)   How was the $66 calculated?
   (vii) Why is provincial sales tax not added to the invoice?

   (b) Assuming you are the seller, record the entry for this invoice in general journal form.

---

kid bindery

132 Railside Road, Don Mills, ON M3A 1B8   Phone 416-449-5565/Fax 416-449-7516

Wilco Printers
1825 Valentine Road
Scarborough, ON M1R 3C5

Invoice 14973   Date   1/15/—
Docket no.   3100
Terms ......net 30 days
Customer's order no.

Quantity	Description	Price	Per	Total
110 000	Rectangular labels, 45 mm x 330 mm	$0.60	1000	$66.00
	Goods and Services Tax 7%			4.62
	Total Due			$70.62

Provincial
Sales Tax Exempt

GST No. S22621120
Prov. Lic. 31659012

---

8. You are employed by White Star Wholesale Ltd., which sells merchandise to retailers. There is no provincial sales tax on the sales because the retailer is not the end user of the merchandise, but resells it to the public.

(a) Record the following invoices on page 71 of a sales journal:

Jun.   3   No. 171 to Bayridge Ltd., terms n/15, amount $193.50 plus GST $13.55.

7 No. 172 to Dacon Corp., terms 1/10, n/30, amount $633.98 plus GST $44.38.

1 5 No. 173 to Frontenac Enterprises, terms 1/10, n/30, amount $247 plus GST $17.29.

22 No. 174 to Bayridge Ltd., terms n/15, amount $130 plus GST $9.10.

30 No. 175 to Fillion Co., terms n/15, amount $67.50 plus GST $4.73.

(b) Total, balance, and rule the journal.

9. Jayman Enterprises does not use a Sales Returns and Allowances account. Its accounting policy is to record returns and allowances in the sales journal using the circling method. All sales are n/30. Add 7 percent GST and 8 percent PST calculated on the base price.
(a) Record the following invoices in a sales journal:

Sep. 4 Sales Invoice 816, R. Dasai, $400.

5 Sales Invoice 817, R.T. Greer, $250.

7 Credit Invoice 67, R.T. Greer, $30.

1 1 Sales Invoice 818, M. Bianco, $775.

1 5 Sales Invoice 819, R. Ivasian, $79.

1 8 Sales Invoice 820, R. Nakheeda, $250.

1 9 Sales Invoice 821, M. Wong, $95.

21 Sales Invoice 822, R. Ingall, $150.

23 Credit Invoice 68, R. Ingall, $75.

25 Sales Invoice 823, J.R. Smoke, $350

(b) Total, balance, and rule the journal.

10. You are an accounting clerk for Michela's Fashion Boutique. Sales invoices are recorded in a sales journal and credit invoices in a general journal. A Sales Returns and Allowances account is used to record credit invoices. Terms for all sales on account are n/30. All sales are subject to GST of 7 percent and PST of 8 percent calculated on the base price plus GST.
(a) Record the sales invoices listed below on page 37 of the sales journal and the credit invoices on page 22 of the general journal. Calculate all taxes.

Nov. 2 Sales Invoice 201 to L. Ursini, amount $270.

3 Credit Invoice C-41 to L. Ursini, goods returned $30.

5 Sales Invoice 202 to M. Conway, amount $400.

9 Sales Invoice 203 to C.L. Ramsay, amount $449.50.

12 Sales Invoice 204 to E. Revell, amount $200.

13 Credit Invoice C-42 to E. Revell, goods returned $50.

15 Sales Invoice 205 to L. Ursini, amount $319.95.

16 Sales Invoice 206 to M. Conway, amount $428.75.

20 Sales Invoice 207 to E. Revell, amount $279.

22 Sales Invoice 208 to C.L. Ramsay, amount $489.

23 Sales Invoice 209 to M. Conway, amount $399.

24 Credit Invoice C-43 to M. Conway, goods returned $399.

29 Sales Invoice 210 to C.L. Ramsay, amount $140.

(b) Total, balance, and rule the sales journal.

(c) Open an accounts receivable ledger and post the source documents to the customer accounts from the journal. You require these customer accounts: M. Conway, C.L. Ramsay, E. Revell, and L. Ursini.

(d) Prepare a schedule of accounts receivable. Compare your total to the general ledger control account (see (g) below).

(e) Open general ledger accounts: Accounts Receivable 102, PST Payable 205, GST Payable 206, Sales 410, and Sales Returns and Allowances 411.

(f) Post the transactions in the general journal to the general ledger. Post the totals of the sales journal to the general ledger.

(g) Prepare a general ledger trial balance.

11. Fernwood Industries Ltd. does not use a Sales Returns and Allowances account. It is their accounting policy to record returns and allowances in the sales journal using the circling method. All sales are n/30. Add on 7 percent GST and 6 percent PST calculated on the base price.

(a) Record the following on page 19 of the sales journal.

Feb.	4	Sales Invoice 116, P. Weitz, $600.
	5	Sales Invoice 117, M.A. Rowe, $518.
	7	Credit Invoice 5, M.A. Rowe, $48.
	11	Sales Invoice 118, V.P. Remple, $687.
	15	Sales Invoice 119, C.D. Nguyen, $418.
	18	Sales Invoice 120, L.S. Chan, $800.
	19	Sales Invoice 121, C.D. Nguyen, $85.
	21	Sales Invoice 122, P.M. Garcia, $767.
	22	Sales Invoice 123, A.V. Joe, $950.
	23	Credit Invoice 6, A.V. Joe, $50.
	25	Sales Invoice 124, B.D. Wongsam, $330.
	27	Sales Invoice 125, F.O. Bhatia, $225.

(b) Total, balance, and rule the sales journal.

UNIT 23 Cash Receipts Journal

What Learning You Will Demonstrate

On completion of this unit, you will be able to:

- record cash received in the cash receipts journal; and
- balance and post the cash receipts journal.

A cash receipts journal is used to record all cash received.

In the special journal system, all money received is recorded in the cash receipts journal. The items considered to be money—i.e., cash receipts—include cheques, money orders, and currency.

INTRODUCING THE CASH RECEIPTS JOURNAL

Figure 10-21 on the next page is a cash receipts journal with seven money columns. There are *debit columns* for *Cash* and *Sales Discounts,* and *credit columns* for *Accounts Receivable, Sales, GST Payable,* and *PST Payable.* There is also an Other Accounts credit column that is used to record credits to any account for which a column is not provided.

Most transactions require only one line. However, an occasional compound transaction requires two lines. When the Other Accounts column is used, the name of the account must be shown in the Customer or Account column. Similarly, the customer's name must be shown when an entry is made in the Accounts Receivable column. Additional columns may be added to the journal if a particular account is used frequently.

The cash receipts journal is totalled and balanced at the bottom of each journal page and at the end of the month, as shown in Figure 10-21. The procedure followed in balancing and posting is the same as the procedure for the sales or purchases journals. The following points regarding posting are illustrated by Figure 10-21:

1. Accounts receivable are posted to the accounts receivable ledger daily. A check mark in the Posting Reference column indicates that an entry has been posted to the customer's account.

2. Other Accounts column entries are posted individually at the end of the month to the general ledger. A number in the Posting Reference column indicates that an entry has been posted and gives the account number.

3. Column totals are posted to the general ledger at the end of the month. A number in parentheses under a column indicates that a total has been posted and gives the account number.

CASH RECEIPTS JOURNAL   PAGE 37

DATE		REF. NO.	CUSTOMER OR ACCOUNT	P.R.	CASH DEBIT	SALES DISCOUNTS DEBIT	ACCOUNTS REC. CREDIT	SALES CREDIT	GST PAYABLE CREDIT	PST PAYABLE CREDIT	OTHER ACCOUNTS CREDIT
20—											
Nov.	14		Forwarded		3 1 1 0 60		1 9 5 5 00	1 0 0 0 00	7 5 60	8 0 00	
	14	105	H.S. of Commerce	✓	6 7 80		6 7 80				
	14	108	W. Mulvihill	✓	6 0 1 40	1 8 60	6 2 0 00				
	16	71	Cash sale		2 6 75			2 5 00	1 75		
	20	300	W. Creighton, Capital		2 0 0 0 00						2 0 0 0 00
	30	BOM	Bank interest earned	420	7 5 00						7 5 00
					5 8 8 1 55	1 8 60	2 6 4 2 80	1 0 2 5 00	7 7 35	8 0 00	2 0 7 5 00
			Debits = $5900.15		(100)	(410)	(102)	(400)	(206)	(221)	
			Credits = $5900.15								

FIGURE 10-21 Cash receipts journal after balancing and posting

RECORDING SOURCE DOCUMENTS FOR CASH RECEIPTS

Cash Receipts from Customers

Source documents for two transactions that involve cash received from customers are shown recorded in Figure 10-21. We will examine each of them.

Cheque Received for Payment on Account

A credit sale was made by Warrendon Sports to the High School of Commerce on October 15. The terms of the sale were net 30 days. This meant that a cheque should be received by Warrendon Sports by November 14, 30 days from the invoice date.

A voucher cheque is a two-part form comprised of a cheque with an attached statement describing the purpose of the payment.

The cheque received by Warrendon Sports is shown in Figure 10-22. Notice that this cheque is different from the personal cheques used by most individuals. It is called a voucher cheque and contains two parts:

- the cheque; and
- the attached statement describing the purpose of the payment.

HIGH SCHOOL OF COMMERCE **SAMPLE** CURRENT ACCOUNT
300 Rochester St.   CHEQUE NUMBER 75039
Ottawa, ON K1R 7N4   Oct. 15, 20—

PAY TO THE
ORDER OF   Warrendon Sports -------------------------------$ 67.80

SUM OF   Sixty-seven--80/100 DOLLARS

THE BANK OF NOVA SCOTIA
517 Ward Ave.
Ottawa, ON K1Z 7W5
                                          L. McKillican
                                          HIGH SCHOOL OF COMMERCE

⑦5039 ⑥1428 002 124 582 0

(Detach and retain this statement)
- -

THE ATTACHED CHEQUE IS IN PAYMENT OF ITEMS LISTED BELOW

DATE	ITEM	AMOUNT	DISCOUNT	NET AMOUNT
Oct. 15	Invoice 105	$67.80		$67.80

FIGURE 10-22 Voucher cheque

When the cheque is received, it is recorded in the cash receipts journal as shown in Figure 10-21. Cash is debited $67.80 and the customer's account is decreased with a credit of $67.80. Notice that the credit is written in the Accounts Receivable credit column and the customer's name is shown in the section next to the date. As with many transactions in special journals, the recording procedure is completed on one line.

Cheque Received for Account Payment Less Sales Discount

You have learned that sellers offer discounts to customers to encourage early payment of account balances. When sales are being made, the buyer and seller agree on payment terms. When the final details of a sale have been completed, both parties should understand clearly when and how payment is to be made. The payment terms should appear on the purchase invoice, the sales invoice, and the monthly statement. Any penalty for late payment should also be clearly outlined on the sale documents.

Cash discounts are offered to encourage early payment of customer account balances.

Figure 10-21 on page 487 shows how the receipt of a cheque for the payment of Sales Invoice No. 108 less a sales discount is recorded in the cash receipts journal. On November 14, a customer, W. Mulvihill, paid $601.40, being $620 less a cash discount of $18.60 ($620 $\times$ 0.03 = $18.60) for paying the invoice within ten days. The customer's account is credited for the full amount of the invoice, $620. The credit of $620 is recorded in the Accounts Receivable credit column. The sales discount of $18.60 is recorded in the Sales Discounts debit column. The cash received, $601.40, is recorded in the Cash debit column.

Other Cash Receipts

As well as money received from customers paying the balances in their accounts, cash is received from the following types of transactions:

- cash sales to customers;
- owner investments;
- cash refunds received for purchases returns;
- interest earned on bank accounts and other investments; and
- miscellaneous sources.

Source documents for three transactions of this type are shown recorded in Figure 10-21. Each will be examined.

Cash Sales Slip

A $25 PST-exempt cash sale is made by Warrendon on November 16. The customer pays for the item and receives Cash Sales Slip 71, which describes the transaction and serves as proof of payment. Cash sales slips are prenumbered and the number of the slip is often recorded in the Reference Number column of the journal. This transaction is shown in the cash receipts journal in Figure 10-21. Notice that for this cash sale it is not necessary to show anything in the Customer or Account column.

Cheque Received for New Investment

On November 20, W. Creighton, the owner of Warrendon Sports, uses a personal cheque to invest an additional $2000 in the business. Figure 10-21 shows the entry made to record the cheque in the cash receipts journal. Cash is debited $2000. The credit to Capital is recorded in the Other Accounts credit column because there is no Capital credit column.

Bank Credit Memo

A bank credit memo indicates an increase in a bank account.

A bank credit memo (memorandum) is a source document received from a bank when the bank adds money to a customer's account. Warrendon received a bank credit memo for $75 on November 30. It indicated that $75 interest had been earned and added by the bank to Warrendon's account. The $75 is recorded on the debit side of the Cash account (an asset increasing), and on the credit side of the Bank Interest Earned account.

Bank Interest Earned is a revenue account and has a credit balance.

Bank Interest Earned is a revenue account; therefore, interest received is recorded on the credit side of the account. This transaction is shown in T-accounts below:

Cash		Bank Interest Earned	
Nov. 30 75			Nov. 30 75

This transaction represents money received and therefore is recorded in the cash receipts journal (Figure 10-21). The $75 debit to the Cash account is placed in the Cash debit column. The $75 credit to the Bank Interest Earned account is entered in the Other Accounts credit column.

UNIT 23 CHECK YOUR READING

Questions

18. What source document is prepared for a cash sale?

19. What is a voucher cheque?

20. What is the purpose of the voucher that is attached to the voucher cheque?

21. Does a bank credit memo indicate a company's bank account has increased or decreased?

22. On November 10, your company received an invoice with terms 2/10, n/30 for $550 plus $33 PST plus $38.50 GST.

  (a) By what date must the invoice be paid to take advantage of the discount?

  (b) Will the discount be taken on the $550 or $621.50?

  (c) Calculate the amount of the cheque that must be issued to pay the invoice within the discount period.

Exercises

12. Record the following source documents in a general journal:

Aug. 23   Cash Sales Slip 314 for $25 plus $1.50 PST plus $1.75 GST.
   23   Cheque received from the owner, B. McAdam, for $2000 as an additional investment in the business.
   23   Bank credit memo from the Bank of Montreal showing that $75 in interest has been added to the bank account.
   23   Cheque received from M. Mulvihill for $196 to pay Invoice 405 for $200 less 2 percent discount allowed. Invoice date July 26. Invoice terms 2/10, n/30.
   23   Cheque received from T. Davis for $200 to pay Invoice 399, no discount.
   24   Cash Sales Slip 315 for $120 plus $7.20 PST plus $8.50 GST.

13. (a) Record the following source documents on page 191 of a cash receipts journal:

Jun.   1   Cash register tape shows sales of $2465 plus $172.55 GST and $197.20 PST.
   2   Cheque received from C. Ballard for $524 to pay Invoice 803 for $524 dated April 1. Terms: n/30.
   2   Cheque received from L. Noble for $317.52 to pay Invoice 799, $324 less 2 percent discount. Invoice dated May 30. Terms: 2/10, n/30.
   3   Bank credit memo, $125 for interest deposited into the bank account.
   4   Cheque received from K. Engel, the owner, for $2500 as an additional investment in the business.
   7   Bank credit memo, $9000 for a bank loan that was deposited in the company bank account.
   8   Cheque received from C. Drago for $548.80 to pay Invoice 805, $560 less 2 percent discount. Invoice dated June 5. Terms: 2/10, n/30.
   9   Cash Sales Slips 940 to 955 for $2155 plus $150.85 GST and $172.40 PST.
   10   Cash register tape for sales of $1890 plus $132.30 GST and $151. 20 PST.
   11   Money order received from C. Tierney for $875.14 to pay Invoice 810, $893 less 2 percent discount. Invoice dated May 20. Terms: 2/10, n/30.

(b) Total, balance, and rule the cash receipts journal.
(c) Describe how you would post this journal if this firm did not use a direct posting system for creditor accounts.

14. (a) Record the source documents listed on the next page on page 193 of a cash receipts journal.

(b) Total, balance, and rule the cash receipts journal.

(c) Set up a general ledger and an accounts receivable ledger for September 1 with the following accounts and balances; then post the cash receipts journal.

Cash	101	$1 400	
Accounts Receivable	102	3 869	
PST Payable	205		$ 350
GST Payable	206		400
C. Black, Capital	301		15 000
Sales	401		0
Sales Discounts	402	0	

**Schedule of
Accounts Receivable
September 1, 20—**

A. Derouin	$2 576
B. Jennings	346
V. Williams	947
	$3 869

Sep. 1   Cheque received for $3000 from the owner, C. Black, as a further investment in the business.

2   Cash Sales Slips 340 to 355 for $975 plus $68.25 GST and $78 PST.

3   Cheques received:
$336 from A. Derouin on account.
$428.26 from V. Williams to pay Invoice 6061 for $437. Invoice dated August 26. Terms: 2/10, n/30.

4   Bank credit memo for $346 that the bank collected from B. Jennings on account.

5   Cheque received from A. Derouin for $749.70 to pay Invoice 6059 for $765. Invoice dated August 25. Terms: 2/10, n/30.

5   Cash Sales Slips 356 to 382 for $2750 plus $192.50 GST and $220 PST.

15. (a) Record the following source documents on page 705 of a cash receipts journal.

Nov. 1   Bank credit memo, $3000 for a bank loan that was approved and deposited in the bank account.

3   Cheques received:
$344.96 from K. Bandy to pay Invoice 756 for $352 dated October 24, terms 2/10, n/30.
$463.54 from L. Kessba to pay Invoice 754 for $473 dated October 23, terms 2/10, n/30.

4   Cash register tape showing $976 in sales plus $78.08 PST
and $68.32 GST.

5   Bank credit memo, $43 for interest earned.

5   Money order received from C. Taylor for $565 to pay
Invoice 601 dated October 4, terms: EOM.

(b) Total, balance, and rule the cash receipts journal.

(c) Set up a general ledger and an accounts receivable ledger with the
following accounts and balances; then post the cash receipts journal.

Cash	101	$7 050	
Accounts Receivable	103	2 453	
PST Payable	205		$256
GST Payable	206		0
Bank Loan	207		0
Sales	401		0
Sales Discounts	402	0	
Bank Interest Earned	403		0

**Schedule of
Accounts Receivable
November 1, 20—**

K. Bandy	$ 730
L. Kessba	473
C. Taylor	1 250
	$2 453

UNIT 24 Cash Payments Journal

What Learning You Will Demonstrate

On completion of this unit, you will be able to:

• record payments, including refunds, in the cash payments
journal; and

• balance and post the cash payments journal.

So far in this chapter, special columnar journals for purchases, sales, and cash
receipts have been described. Now we will discuss how to record cash payments
in a special journal called the cash payments journal.

MAKING CASH PAYMENTS

Payment by Cheque

A basic accounting principle is that *all payments, except very small ones, should be made by cheque*. Each cheque should be authorized. Documents such as receiving reports and approved invoices should be available to support the issuing of the cheque.

Cheque Requisition

In many companies, a cheque request form is completed before a cheque is issued. This form is called a *cheque requisition*. The cheque requisition is accompanied by all of the documents related to the transaction because the person with the responsibility to authorize the issuing of a cheque may wish to trace the entire history of the transaction.

Voucher Cheque

Many firms use the voucher form of cheque shown in Figure 10-23. The cheque is prepared with three copies. Copy 1 is the cheque sent to the creditor. Copy 2 is used by the accounting department as the source document for the journal entry. Copy 3 is filed with the invoice. Notice that the cheque in Figure 10-23 requires two signatures. Many firms require two people to sign all cheques so that there is some control over the cash (see Cash Control, page 529).

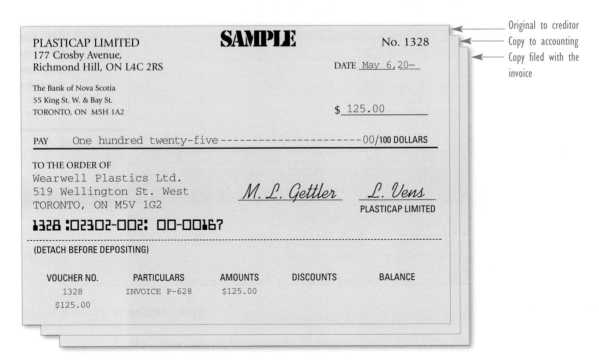

FIGURE 10-23 Voucher cheque showing distribution of copies

INTRODUCING THE CASH PAYMENTS JOURNAL

Because of the large number of payments made, many companies record their cheques in a **cash payments journal**. Special columns are provided for accounts that are used often. In the cash payments journal in Figure 10-24, special columns are headed Cash credit, Accounts Payable debit, GST Refundable debit, Purchases debit, and Purchases Discounts credit. The Other Accounts debit column is provided for those accounts that do not fit into the special columns. Source documents for various transactions that involve cash payments are shown recorded in Figure 10-24. In the following section, each will be examined.

A cash payments journal is used to record all payments.

DATE	CH. NO.	CREDITOR OR ACCOUNT	P.R.	CASH CREDIT	ACCOUNTS PAYABLE DEBIT	GST REFUNDABLE DEBIT	PURCHASES DEBIT	PURCHASES DISCOUNTS CREDIT	OTHER ACCOUNTS DEBIT
20—									
Nov. 19	326	Sporting Goods Ltd.		5 24 30	5 35 00			1 0 70	
20	DM	Bank Interest Expense		1 50 00					1 5 0 00
22	327	Sylvia Post		1 09 25					
		Sales Returns & Allow.							9 5 00
		PST Payable							7 60
		GST Payable							6 65

FIGURE 10-24 Cash payments journal

Recording Source Documents for Cash Payments

Cheque Issued for Account Payment Less Purchase Discount

On November 4, Warrendon Sports received Purchase Invoice 4918 for $500 worth of basketballs, plus $35 GST, from Sporting Goods Ltd. Terms of sale on the invoice were 2/15, n/30. The invoice was checked for accuracy, and since the order was received in good condition the invoice was passed for payment. The invoice was recorded in Warrendon's books as shown by the following T-accounts:

Purchases	Accounts Payable/ Sporting Goods Ltd.	GST Refundable
Nov. 4 500	Nov. 4 535	Nov. 4 35

The invoice was placed in the date file in a folder dated November 19. A cheque for $524.30 dated November 19 was prepared and sent to Sporting Goods Ltd. From the cheque copy, entries were made in Warrendon's books as shown by the following T-accounts:

Cash	Accounts Payable/ Sporting Goods Ltd.	Purchases Discounts
Nov.19 524.30	Nov.19 535 | Nov. 4 535	Nov.19 10.70

In general journal form, the entries shown in these two sets of T-accounts would appear as follows:

Nov.	4	Purchases		5 0 0 00	
		GST Refundable		3 5 00	
		Accounts Payable/Sporting Goods Ltd.			5 3 5 00
		Invoice 4918, terms 2/15, n/30.			
	19	Accounts Payable/Sporting Goods Ltd.		5 3 5 00	
		Cash			5 2 4 30
		Purchases Discounts			1 0 70
		Invoice 4918, less discount, Cheque 326.			

Purchases Discounts is a negative cost account.

This payment on account was recorded in a cash payments journal as illustrated in Figure 10-24.

Bank Debit Memo

A bank debit memo indicates a decrease in a bank account.

A bank debit memo indicates a decrease in a bank account. On November 20, Warrendon Sports received a bank debit memo from the Bank of Nova Scotia. The memo indicated $150 had been deducted from Warrendon's bank account for the monthly interest on their bank loan.

The $150 is an expense and must be recorded in the Bank Interest Expense account. In Figure 10-24, the debit to Bank Interest Expense is placed in the Other Accounts debit column and the credit is entered in the Cash credit column.

Cheque Issued for Refund on Cash Sale with GST and PST

On November 20, Sylvia Post purchased a pair of tennis shoes for $65 and a racquet for $95. She paid a total of $184 cash for her purchases, which included GST of $11.20 ($0.07 \times \$160 = \$11.20$) and PST of $12.80 ($\$160 \times 0.08 = \$12.80$). The seller, Warrendon Sports, recorded the sales as follows:

Nov.	20	Cash		1 8 4 00	
		Sales			1 6 0 00
		GST Payable			1 1 20
		PST Payable			1 2 80
		To record a cash sale.			

Sylvia was unhappy with the quality of the racquet and returned it on November 22. She received Cheque 327 for $109.25 as a refund. The cheque consisted of $95 plus $6.65 GST ($0.07 \times \$95 = \$6.65$) and PST of $7.60 ($\$95 \times 0.08 = \$7.60$) for a total of $109.25.

This refund cheque affected the books of Warrendon Sports as shown by the following T-accounts:

Cash				Sales Returns & Allowances		
Nov. 20	184	Nov. 22	109.25	Nov. 22	95	

PST Payable				GST Payable		
Nov. 22	7.60	Nov. 20	12.80	Nov. 22	6.65	Nov. 20	11.20

The refund cheque of $109.25 is recorded in the Cash credit column of the cash payments journal (Figure 10-24, page 495). The sale amount, $95, is debited to Sales Returns and Allowances using the Other Accounts debit column. Since Warrendon Sports refunded the $6.65 GST and the $7.60 PST to Sylvia, it no longer owes this amount to the governments. Therefore, Warrendon decreased its liabilities to the governments by debiting GST Payable $6.65 and PST Payable $7.60 in the Other Accounts debit column of the journal. Notice that the entry on November 22 in Figure 10-24 requires four lines because the journal does not have a Sales Returns and Allowances debit column, or a PST Payable debit column, or a GST Payable debit column.

Recording Transactions in a Cash Payments Journal

The transactions shown recorded in Figure 10-25 on page 498 provide examples of a number of common cash payment transactions that occur in business. See if you can trace them to the journal from the list of sample transactions.

Sample Transactions

May 1   Issued Cheque 101 for $535 to Tanyss Trading; purchased merchandise $500, GST $35, Invoice 598.

3   Issued Cheque 102 for $149 to Speedquip Ltd. for Invoice B-231 dated April 2.

8   Issued Cheque 103 for $75 to Len's Service Centre to pay for repairs to the company automobile ($70.09, GST $4.91), Invoice 4829.

12   Issued Cheque 104 for $200 to Willson's Ltd. as partial payment of account.

15   Issued Cheque 105 for $500 to *The Star*; advertising $467.29, GST $32.71, Invoice S-4829.

17   Issued Cheque 106 for $220 to Angelo's Masonry to pay for a patio at the home of the owner, B. McAdam, Invoice 333.

22   Issued Cheque 107 for $49 to Evans & Kert; purchased supplies $45.79, GST $3.21, Invoice 221.

23   Issued Cheque 108 for $127 to the Provincial Treasurer for last month's sales tax collections.

25   Issued Cheque 109 for $288.90 to Willson's Ltd; purchased merchandise $270, GST $18.90, Invoice 1433.

28   Issued Cheque 110 for $343 to Tanyss Trading in payment of Invoice 673 ($350, discount taken $7).

31 Issued Cheque 111 for $3400, monthly salaries.
31 Issued Cheque 112 for $300 to Receiver General; GST remittance.

Balancing and Posting the Cash Payments Journal

Procedures similar to those used with the other special journals are followed when balancing and posting the cash payments journal.

				CASH PAYMENTS JOURNAL					PAGE 44	
DATE	CH. NO.	CREDITOR OR ACCOUNT	P.R.	CASH CREDIT	ACCOUNTS PAYABLE DEBIT	GST REFUNDABLE DEBIT	PURCHASES DEBIT	PURCHASES DISCOUNTS CREDIT	OTHER ACCOUNTS DEBIT	
20—										
May 1	101	Tanyss Trading		5 35 00		35 00	5 00 00			
3	102	Speedquip Ltd.	✓	1 49 00	1 49 00					
8	103	Car Repairs Expense		75 00		4 91			70 09	
12	104	Willson's Ltd.	✓	2 00 00	2 00 00					
15	105	Advertising Expense		5 00 00		32 71			4 67 29	
17	106	B. McAdam, Drawings		2 20 00					2 20 00	
22	107	Supplies Expense		49 00		3 21			45 79	
23	108	Sales Tax Payable		1 27 00					1 27 00	
25	109	Willson's Ltd.		2 88 90		18 90	2 70 00			
28	110	Tanyss Trading	✓	3 43 00	3 50 00			7 00		
31	111	Salaries Payable		34 00 00					34 00 00	
31	112	GST Payable		3 00 00					3 00 00	
		Debit = $6193.90		61 86 90	6 99 00	94 73	7 70 00	7 00	46 30 17	
		Credits = $6193.90		(100)	(200)	(206)	(500)	(501)		

FIGURE 10-25 Recording transactions in a cash payments journal

1. Each page is totalled and balanced. Page totals are carried forward if the month has not ended.
2. *At the end of each month*, the journal is totalled, balanced, and ruled; it is then posted.
3. Entries in the Accounts Payable debit column are *posted daily* to the creditor accounts in the accounts payable ledger.
4. The Other Accounts debit column entries are posted individually *at the end of each month*.
5. The column totals are posted to the general ledger *at the end of each month*.
6. The Other Accounts column total is not posted.

SUMMARY OF DIRECT POSTING TO THE SUBSIDIARY LEDGERS

Figures 10-26 and 10-27 summarize the procedures followed when source documents are posted directly to the subsidiary ledgers. Figure 10-26 shows how transactions that involve customers are posted directly from the source documents to the customer accounts in the accounts receivable ledger. Transactions that involve creditors are posted directly to the accounts in the accounts payable ledger.

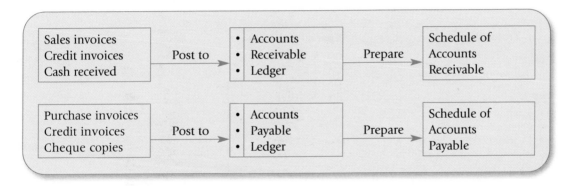

FIGURE 10-26 Direct posting to the subsidiary ledgers

The same transactions are entered in the journals and then posted to the general ledger. Figure 10-27 illustrates how this is done.

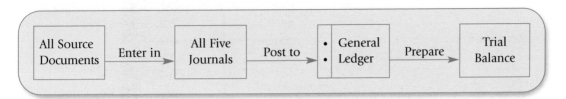

FIGURE 10-27 Posting to the general ledger

SUMMARY OF THE SPECIAL JOURNAL SYSTEM

Since many business transactions are similar, journals may be specially designed to handle the recording of transactions that occur frequently. The following special journals are used by many firms:

- **Purchases Journal:** Used for recording purchases on account.
- **Sales Journal:** Used for recording sale of merchandise on account.
- **Cash Receipts Journal:** Used for recording all cash received.
- **Cash Payments Journal:** Used for recording all payments of cash.

The special journal system is summarized in Figure 10-28.

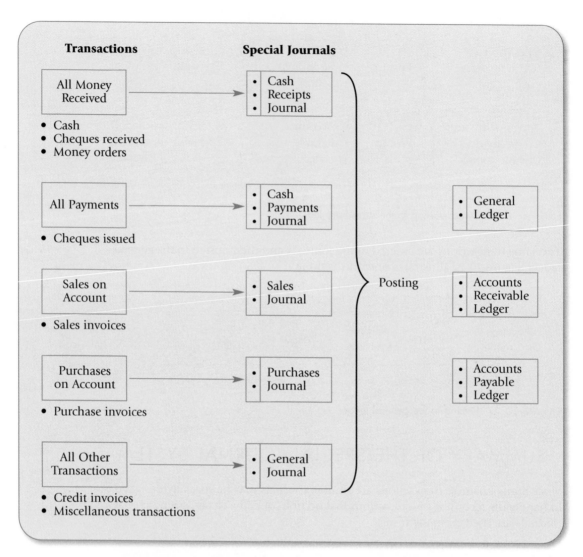

FIGURE 10-28 Special journal system

Generally Accepted Accounting Principles and Key Ideas

In this chapter, you learned the following key ideas:

- **Several special columnar journals** may be used in a manual accounting system by companies that have many repetitive transactions.
- **The five-journal system** can be beneficial in that it makes use of division of labour and specialization.
- **All payments** except very small amounts are made by cheque.
- **Most companies** require two people to sign all cheques.

UNIT 24 **CHECK YOUR READING**

Questions

23. (a) What is a cheque requisition?
(b) What is a voucher cheque?
24. Are purchase discounts recorded as debits or credits? Why?
25. Does a bank debit memo indicate the bank account has increased or decreased?
26. Should the PST Payable account be increased or decreased when a customer returns goods on which tax has been charged?
27. Is anything other than a cheque number recorded in the Cheque Number column of the cash payments journal?
28. Briefly describe the types of transactions recorded in each of the following:
(a) Sales journal
(b) Cash receipts journal
(c) Purchases journal
(d) Cash payments journal
(e) General journal
29. Superior Electrical Services uses a five-journal accounting system. Answer the following questions regarding their system:
(a) In which journal will you find the closing entries?
(b) Which journal will contain the fewest entries?
(c) If accounts payable and accounts receivable ledgers are used, explain how transactions are posted to these ledgers. (Assume a direct posting system is not used.)
(d) When are transactions usually posted to the general ledger?
(e) Which journals contain information that must be posted to the Accounts Receivable control account?

UNIT 24 **APPLY YOUR KNOWLEDGE**

Exercises

16. (a) Using the accounts below, record the following source documents on page 319 of a cash payments journal:

May 1   Cheque 1890, $530 to K. Bellamy for a week's salary.
    3   Cheque 1891, $700 to P. Meikle, the owner, for personal use.
    5   Bank debit memo, $3.50 for service charges.
    6   Cheque 1892, $833 to General Distributors for $850 less $17 discount, Invoice 2469.
    6   Cheque 1893, $73.60 to Bill's Service Centre on account.
    7   Bank debit memo, $300 for monthly payment on the bank loan.

9   Cheque 1894, $4410 to Electronic Wholesalers, for $4500 less $90 discount, Invoice 2966.

(b) Total, balance, and rule the cash payments journal.

(c) Set up a general ledger and an accounts payable ledger for May 1 with the following accounts and balances; then post the cash payments journal.

101	Cash	$18 493	
200	Accounts Payable		$ 9 458
210	Bank Loan		25 000
300	P. Meikle, Drawings	0	
502	Purchases Discounts		0
600	Salaries Expense	0	
615	Bank Charges Expense	0	

Schedule of Accounts Payable
May 1, 20—

Bill's Service Centre	$ 145
Electronic Wholesalers	7 056
General Distributors	2 257
	$9 458

17. (a) Record the following source documents on page 109 of a cash payments journal:

Dec. 3   Cheque 705, $2600 plus GST to Clark Realtors for the December rent.

3   Cheque 706, to Colonial Manufacturers for Invoice 17849 for $14 500 less 1 percent discount. Invoice dated November 23. Terms: 1/10, n/30.

4   Bank debit memo M85192 for $24.75 for bank charges.

6   Refund Cheque 707, $179.40 to C. Bartoli, a customer, for a $156 coffee table (returned today) plus $12.48 PST and $10.92 GST.

6   Cheque 708 for Invoice 11529 for $2656 to Dupuis Cabinets on account. Invoice dated November 10. Terms: n/30.

7   Cheque 709 to General Electric for Invoice B8521 for $7561 less discount. Invoice dated November 27. Terms: 2/10, n/30.

8   Cheque 710, $500 to L. Colby for personal use.

(b) Total, balance, and rule the cash payments journal.

(c) Set up a general ledger and accounts payable ledger with the following accounts and balances; then post the cash payments journal.

101	Cash	$56 793.56	
202	Accounts Payable		$35 696.67
205	PST Payable		0
206	GST Payable		0
207	GST Refundable	1 126.10	
302	L. Colby, Drawings	13 490.44	
403	Sales Returns and Allowances	2 376.49	
503	Purchases Discounts		5 976.56
600	Rent Expense	28 600.00	
613	Bank Charges Expense	1 673.55	

**Schedule of Accounts Payable
December 1, 20—**

Colonial Manufacturers	$14 500.00
Dupuis Cabinets	9 400.23
General Electric	11 796.44
	$35 696.67

Part B Supplementary Manual or Computer Exercises

Exercises 18 and 19 may be done manually or on a computer. If completed manually, the required forms are in the Study Guide and Working Papers. If completed with a computer, students may set up their own accounts or the teacher may use the CD provided by the publisher. The CD contains files for these exercises prepared with Simply Accounting software.

18. The accounting system of Brock County Kennels includes a general journal, four special journals, a general ledger, and two subsidiary ledgers. All credit sales have terms of n/30. GST of 7 percent is charged on all sales of service or merchandise. PST of 8 percent calculated on the base price is charged on pet food sales only. Grooming is performed only on a cash basis. The firm's chart of accounts appears on page 505.
   (a) Enter the March transactions given below in the five journals used by Brock County Kennels.
   (b) Total, balance, and rule the journals.
   (c) Show how the postings *would be made* by placing the ledger account numbers and check marks in the appropriate columns of the journals. Brock County Kennels does not use a direct posting system to the subsidiary ledgers.

   Mar. 1 The owner, S. Robson, deposited $2000 in the firm's bank account as a further personal investment in the business.
        3 Purchased additional grooming equipment from Jayco Supplies ($2897.20 plus $202.80 GST); paid $1000 cash

and agreed to pay the remaining $2100 EOM, Invoice 7463.

4   Signed an agreement with J. Johnson to train and exhibit her dog at a price of $250 per month plus expenses, to be billed at the end of each month.

4   Sold dog food worth $85 plus taxes to Greenlane Kennels on account, Invoice 874.

6   Received $187.25 (including GST) cash for boarding Wanda Szpilewski's dog for the past three weeks, Cash Sales Slip 1003.

7   Purchased a load of Joy Dog Food for resale, $2400 plus $168 GST, terms n/30, Invoice 89246.

7   Sold two bags of dog food for cash, $78 plus taxes, Cash Sales Slip 1004.

7   Grooming income for the week was $780 plus $54.60 GST, Cash Sales Slips 1005 to 1021.

9   Billed M. Kennedy $300 plus GST for training her dog for the past month, Invoice 875.

10   Greenlane Kennels returned one bag of feed for credit, $36 plus taxes. Credit Invoice 73 was issued today.

12   Purchased supplies for $75 plus $5.25 GST, Cheque 386.

13   Purchased dog food for use in own kennel for $700 plus $49 GST from Purina on account, Invoice A68471, terms n/30.

14   Grooming income for the week was $910 plus $63.70 GST, Cash Sales Slips 1022 to 1041.

15   Received payment from Greenlane Kennels for the purchase on March 4 less returns.

15   Sold $250 plus taxes worth of pet food to Casey's Kennel on account, Invoice 876.

15   Purchased additional fencing materials for the kennel from Lincoln Farm Supply, $450 plus $31.50 GST, on 30-day account, Invoice 64372.

16   Received Credit Invoice 612 today from Joy Dog Food for $100 worth of damaged goods (plus $7 GST), which were returned previously.

16   Billed Grousehaven Kennels $1000 plus GST for the monthly training fee, Invoice 877.

18   Billed B. Iannizzi $52 plus GST for boarding his dog for four days, Invoice 878.

19   Received $490 from P. Partington in payment of training fee previously billed on Invoice 861.

21   Grooming revenue for the week is $650 plus $45.50 GST, Cash Sales Slips 1042 to 1056.

22   Purchased dog food for resale from Beatrice Foods, $1450 plus $101.50 GST, on 30-day account, Invoice B-6134.

22   Paid the freight charges on the Beatrice shipment, $63 plus $4.41 GST, Cheque 222.

23   Paid Purina $3100 on account, Cheque 223.

24   Sold an old set of grooming clippers to P. Dolynski for $175 on account. The clippers were recorded in the Grooming Equipment account at a cost of $250.

26   Borrowed $2500 from the bank and signed a note payable.

28   Sold pet food to Brookfield Kennels, $375 plus taxes, on account, Invoice 879.

28   Grooming fees for the week, $1050 plus $73.50 GST, Cash Sales Slips 1057 to 1074.

29   Paid the monthly salary, $1275, Cheque 224.

30   Paid Jayco Supplies in full for the March purchase, Cheque 225.

30   Sold pet food to P. Partington, $83 plus taxes, on account, Invoice 880.

30   Received $321 from M. Kennedy in payment of her account.

100	Cash	301	S. Robson, Drawings
110	Accounts Receivable	302	Income Summary
120	Merchandise Inventory	410	Pet Food Sales
125	Supplies	420	Grooming Revenue
126	Feed Supply	430	Boarding Revenue
135	Prepaid Insurance	440	Training Revenue
150	Land	450	Interest Earned
160	Building	475	Sales Returns & Allow.
163	Kennel Fencing	500	Purchases
165	Furniture and Fixtures	525	Purchases Returns & Allow.
168	Grooming Equipment	550	Transportation-in
200	Accounts Payable	600	Salaries Expense
205	PST Payable	601	Taxes Expense
206	GST Payable	602	Supplies Expense
207	GST Refundable	603	Insurance Expense
210	Bank Loan	604	Interest Expense
250	Mortgage Payable	605	Feed Expense
300	S. Robson, Capital	606	Loss on Sale of Equipment

19. Studio 21 offers terms of 2/10, n/30 to credit customers. All sales are exempt from provincial sales tax. A chart of accounts (showing only those accounts necessary for this exercise) and schedules of accounts receivable and payable as of April 30 appear on page 507.

(a) Record the May transactions given below in the following journals:

- Sales journal
- Purchases journal
- Cash receipts journal
- Cash payments journal
- General journal

(b) Total, balance, and rule all special journals.

(c) Indicate how the postings *would be made* to the general ledger by placing the ledger account numbers in the appropriate places in the journals.

(d) Post to the subsidiary ledgers.

(e) Prepare schedules of accounts receivable and payable as of May 31.

The control accounts in the general ledger on this date show Accounts Receivable $4000 and Accounts Payable $7150.

May 1 Purchased merchandise from W. Hagadorn Inc. for $15 000 ($14 018.69 plus $981.31 GST), Invoice 39187, terms 2/15, n/30.

4 Issued Cheque 232 for $18 000 to W. Hagadorn Inc. for an April purchase, Invoice 38714. No discount was taken.

4 Sold merchandise to A. Akmel, $5607.48 plus GST, Invoice 275.

5 Sold merchandise, $7850 plus GST. Cash Sales Summary.

7 Received Credit Invoice C1826 from W. Hagadorn Inc. for returned merchandise valued at $1000 ($934.58 plus $65.42 GST).

9 Issued Cheque 233 for $160.50 ($150 plus $10.50 GST) to A. Wing for merchandise returned today.

10 Purchased merchandise from K. Lee & Associates for $8411.22 plus $588.78 GST. Invoice 4499 dated May 8, terms 2/10, n/30.

11 Sold merchandise to G. Alvarez for $7943.93 plus GST, Invoice 276.

13 Received payment from A. Akmel to pay account in full.

14 Issued Credit Invoice 78 to G. Alvarez for $500 ($467.29 plus $32.71 GST).

15 Sold excess equipment for $12 149.53 plus GST to Tieche Co. A cash down payment of $3000 was received, with the remainder due on a promissory note in 60 days. The equipment originally cost $12 500.

17 Received a cheque from G. Alvarez for $18 800 for an April sale.

19 Purchased a one-year liability insurance policy from Royal Insurance for $887.85 plus $62.15 GST on account, Invoice R-36429.

20 Paid K. Lee and Associates, in full Cheque 234.

22 Paid W. Hagadorn Inc. for the May 1 purchase less returns, Cheque 235.

23 Received payment from G. Alvarez for May 11 purchase.

24 Purchased new equipment for $32 710.28 plus $2289.72 GST. Paid 10 percent down (Cheque 236) and signed a promissory note with Avco Finance for the remainder.

25 Sold merchandise on account to A. Akmel, $4205.61 plus GST, Invoice 277.

26 Purchased merchandise from K. Lee and Associates, $5794.39 plus $405.61 GST. Invoice dated today, terms 2/10, n/30.

28 Paid the $2200 monthly mortgage payment, of which $1200 was interest expense, Cheque 237.

30 Issued Credit Invoice 79 to A. Akmel, $467.29 plus $32.71 GST, for goods returned today.

30 Purchased merchandise from Dupont Services, $1250 plus $87.50 GST, Cheque 239.

31 Paid the monthly office salaries, $5400, Cheque 238.

100	Cash	475	Sales Returns & Allow.
120	Accounts Receivable	480	Sales Discounts
125	Notes Receivable	500	Purchases
130	Supplies	525	Purchases Returns & Allow.
135	Prepaid Insurance	550	Purchases Discounts
160	Equipment	555	Transportation-in
200	Accounts Payable	601	Salaries Expense
206	GST Payable	602	Supplies Expense
207	GST Refundable	603	Insurance Expense
210	Notes Payable	604	Loss on Sale of Equipment
220	Mortgage Payable	605	Interest Expense
400	Sales		

Schedule of Accounts Receivable
April 30, 20—

G. Alvarez	$18 800
A. Akmel	10 750
	$29 550

Schedule of Accounts Payable
April 30, 20—

W. Hagadorn Inc.	$18 000
K. Lee & Associates	12 000
	$30 000

Computer Accounting

E-Business

Various definitions exist for e-business but most contain elements of the following: business conducted over the Internet, other computer networks, or through wireless communications. E-business has also been referred to as e-commerce. E-commerce is the exchange of goods or services between a buyer and a seller facilitated by computer networks. Internet transactions over the World Wide Web now account for several hundred billion dollars annually.

Advantages of E-Commerce

E-commerce presents many benefits to both the seller and the buyer. Sellers can reach a much larger market than would have otherwise been possible. Virtual storefronts can be established without the costs of a physical site. Purchasers can track the status of their orders online and receive product information and updates on a continual basis. In some cases the product can even be delivered online, such as digitized music, software, and e-books.

Concerns about E-Commerce

E-commerce between consumers and retailers and between businesses is becoming common. Those hesitant to become involved with e-commerce often cite concerns such as:

- not being able to actually touch the product to ensure its quality;
- fear of credit card fraud;
- fear of misuse of personal information; and
- concern that the product cannot be returned if a physical store does not exist.

Web Trust

In response to concerns about the safety of online transactions, the Canadian Institute of Chartered Accountants (C.I.C.A.) and the American Institute of Certified Public Accountants (A.I.C.P.A.) issue a Web Trust Seal of Assurance that a web site meets certain standards. The seal indicates that a site meets high standards of business practice and consumer information protection. CAs and CPAs who have been licensed by their national professional organization issue the seal of approval. The CA or CPA is responsible for ensuring and verifying compliance on an ongoing basis every few months. The seal is revoked if the web site no longer complies with the Web Trust principles.

Questions

1. In addition to the benefits noted above, what are the advantages of e-commerce to both the retailer and the consumer?
2. In addition to the concerns noted above, what are the potential disadvantages of e-commerce to both the retailer and the consumer?
3. Why would a CA or a CPA be involved in validating an Internet web site?
4. In addition to Web Trust, what roles do accountants play in the new e-commerce marketplace?

Computer Security

Computerized records are very sensitive—ask anyone who has accidentally erased information after spending two or three hours entering data. It is very easy to lose information, to misplace electronic files, to damage disks, or to have another person inadvertently delete, destroy, or inaccurately enter information. As well, computer files can contain confidential information such as the balance in a company's bank account, personal payroll information, and the amount of money owed to others. For these reasons, most accounting programs contain a security system to protect accounting records. Here is a general description of how a computer accounting security system works. Each program will contain slight variations.

Accounting Software Security

Barb Yip is an accounts receivable clerk for a business that uses a computerized accounting program. This program is an integrated accounting package similar to the ones seen in this text. Barb's program contains modules for accounts receivable, payroll, accounts payable, general ledger, and inventory control. Let's look at the security controls involved when Barb needs to use the software to record accounts receivable transactions.

Step 1

First, Barb turns on the computer and calls up the program by clicking on the program icon on her screen. Then, the text shown in Figure 10-29 appears on the computer screen.

> Accounting System
>
> System generated on DD.MM.YY.
>
> Please enter your password.

FIGURE 10-29 A typical password menu

Step 2

The program now requires Barb to enter a *password*. Barb types the assigned password, Zerox2!. If this secret password is not properly entered, access to the accounting records is denied. After Barb has entered the current password, Figure 10-30 appears on the screen.

> Accounting System—Master Menu
> [Storage Type] Configuration
>
> Would you like to:
> 1. Run the Accounts Receivable System?
> 2. Run the Accounts Payable System?
> 3. Run the General Ledger System?
> 4. Run the Inventory System?
> 5. Run the Invoicing System?
> 6. Run the Point of Sale System?
> 7. Run the Daily Sales System?
> 8. Initialize the Company Name?
> X. Exit the system?
>
> Enter number of desired action.

FIGURE 10-30 The master menu

Step 3

Barb now selects option 1 and the computer proceeds to run the accounts receivable module. Barb enters the day's accounts receivable transactions and then exits the program.

If Barb tried to select and use accounts payable, the computer would deny access to the accounts payable program. This is because a separate password, not known to Barb, is required.

Three-Level Security System

The software Barb uses contains a three-level security system that is designed to prevent unauthorized persons from using the accounting program. The three levels are:

Security Level 1

The Level 1 password allows a person to use a very limited amount of the program. It thus limits the person to only a small part of the company's accounting records. For example, the password Zerox2! allows Barb to access only the accounts receivable procedures and records. Barb does not know any other password.

Security Level 2

Madhu Chandra is the second person in the company who uses the accounting system. She knows the Level 1 password, Zerox2!, and the Level 2 password, 4Gumper&. The password 4Gumper& allows access to several other programs, including accounts payable and payroll.

Security Level 3

The third level of security is reserved for the manager and allows access to all of the accounting records, including financial statements, bank records, and all account balances. Barb and Madhu do not know the Level 3 password and therefore are restricted by the computer system to using only the programs and records in the first and second levels. Only Sheila Berg, the company manager, knows the password for Level 3. Sheila is the only person who has access to the company's entire accounting system.

Questions

1. Why are security systems necessary in computerized accounting systems?
2. Describe the three-level security system.
3. Can you see any weaknesses in the security system described above? Explain your answer.
4. Does your school's computer system have a security process? If yes, explain how it works.

Using Simply Accounting to Record Cash Payments

In this chapter, you learned how to use special journals such as the cash receipts and cash payments journals. Now we will examine how cash transactions are recorded using integrated software such as Simply Accounting.

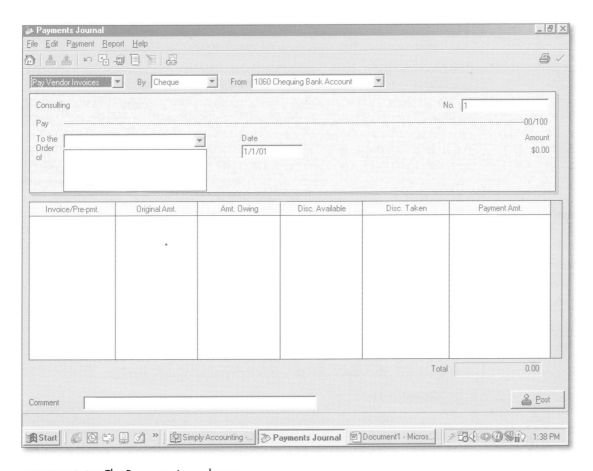

FIGURE 10-31 The Payments Journal screen

These are the steps to record payments using Simply Accounting:

1. From the main menu (Home window), select **Payments** from the Payables list. A form that resembles a cheque will appear on the screen, see Figure 10-31.
2. In the first field, select **Pay Vendor Invoices**.
3. In the By field, select the method of payment (**Cheque**, Cash).
4. In the From field, select the bank account (**1080: Regal Bank: Current**) from which the money will be taken.
5. In the To The Order Of field, select the creditor (**Jackson Construction Ltd.**) that you are paying.
6. If paying by cheque, in the No. field enter the cheque number (**300**).
7. Enter the date on which you will make the payment (**06/06/00**). This date is printed on the cheque and is also recorded as the transaction date.
8. In the Discount Taken column, enter the amount of any discount you are taking (in this case, **0.00**).
9. In the Payment amount column, enter the amount you wish to pay toward the invoice (**7953.95**).
10. Select **Display Payments Journal Entry** from the Report menu to check the transaction.

11. Click on **Post** to update the accounts and finalize the entry.
12. If you are using this option, print the cheque.

The program updates the creditor's account (debit) and decreases Cash (credit). It will also debit the Accounts Payable control account.

In an integrated accounting system, such as Simply Accounting, the posting is done automatically from the one source of information. As soon as the journal entry is made, the posting is also done. There is no need for special columns, totals, and end-of-month posting as in the manual system. Therefore, there is no need for special journal formats with special columns for often-used accounts. The computer processes the transaction data only once and the data are stored in the computer's memory to be used in the ledger, journal, trial balance, and financial statements. Perhaps the greatest advantage of using computer accounting software is the elimination of a great deal of manual accounting, including posting, totalling, and balancing.

Using Simply Accounting to Record Cash Receipts

Cash receipts are recorded in a similar manner to cash payments. Select **Receipts** and enter the customer's account number and the following information: Date, Amount, and the customer's cheque number. When the transaction is entered, the program updates the customer's account (credit) and increases Cash (debit). It will also credit the Accounts Receivable control account.

Questions

1. In the Simply Accounting system, how is an entry checked before it is finalized?
2. What are the advantages of recording cash payments using Simply Accounting compared to using a manual cash payments journal?

COMPUTER ASSIGNMENTS

1. (a) Format a spreadsheet for a sales journal. Use the headings in Figure 10-16.
   (b) Complete exercise 8 of this chapter using your spreadsheet.
   (c) Complete the journal for exercise 10 using your spreadsheet.

2. (a) Format a spreadsheet for a statement of account using the illustration in Figure 10-18 as a guide.
   (b) Use your spreadsheet to print the November statement of account for L. Ursini, exercise 10.

3. Use general ledger software to complete exercise 18. Follow these instructions:
   (a) Prepare a chart of accounts using computer numbers suggested by the software you are using.
   (b) Record the transactions manually on data entry sheets. (*Note:* If enough computers are available, your teacher may have you enter the transactions directly onto the computer.)

    (c) Enter the transactions from your data entry sheet using your
        school's computer system.

    (d) Print the journal, ledger, and trial balance.

4. Use general ledger software to complete exercise 19. Follow the
    instructions given above for exercise 18.

5. To complete this exercise you will be required to visit a company
    and obtain the following information about its accounting system
    software. Write a research report that describes the functions of its
    computer accounting program. Prepare your report using an accept-
    able reporting format. The report should include:

- a description of the company;
- the accounting software used;
- a description of the hardware—number of terminals, capacity, etc;
- the cost of the software and the hardware;
- the number of employees involved in accounting;
- accounting functions performed by the software;
- other characteristics of the software, for example, the type of menu
  system, modular design, etc;
- reports produced and the frequency of reporting; and
- other descriptive material.

WEB EXTENSIONS

www.pearsoned.ca/
principlesofaccounting

Internet Study Guide

- Complete the Chapter 10 review.
- Complete the Chapter 10 definitions.
- Complete the Chapter 10 online test.

Web Links

Visit the Web Links section at the Pearson Education web site to find
links to the C.I.C.A. site. Explain the role of the C.I.C.A. in ensuring
safe e-commerce transactions for consumers.

⑬ Case Studies

CASE 1

Designing a Journal System

The Canadian Furniture Company specializes in the production of patio furniture. It manufactures tables, chairs, umbrellas, and swings. It has experienced a substantial growth in sales in recent years.

The accounting system is being computerized by a computer consulting firm. A special journal system will be used, with a general journal and four special journals. It will be possible to customize the journals and to use whatever columns seem best.

You have been asked to make recommendations to the computer consultant who is designing the software. To date you have gathered this information:

- Each month 400 to 600 sales invoices are processed. Sales are made in these proportions: tables 30 percent, chairs 30 percent, swings 20 percent, and umbrellas 20 percent.
- PST is not charged on sales.
- GST is charged on all sales.
- Sales are made on a 2/10, n/30 basis. About 30 percent of customers take advantage of the opportunity to obtain the 2 percent cash discount. There are no cash sales.
- About 60 purchases of materials used in producing the furniture are made each month. They consist of metal bars 30 percent, plastic materials 35 percent, paint 10 percent, and miscellaneous materials 25 percent. About 40 percent of the purchases are made on a cash basis and many involve discounts.
- Each month there are about 15 purchase returns and about 25 sales returns. These are about 50 percent cash and 50 percent on account.

Prepare a recommendation for the headings to be used in the sales, purchases, cash receipts, and cash payments journals. There is no limit on the number of columns that may be used.

CASE 2

Special Journal System

McEwen Consultants uses a five-journal accounting system. On April 30, upon completion of all posting for the month, the Accounts Receivable control account had a debit balance of $142 000, and the Accounts Payable control account had a credit balance of $52 000. The May transactions recorded in the four special journals are summarized below.

- Purchases journal: Total transactions $61 000.
- Sales journal: Total transactions $106 000.
- Cash receipts journal: Accounts Receivable column total $75 200.
- Cash payments journal: Accounts Payable column total $63 900.

(a) From the above information, indicate the figures that would be posted to the Accounts Receivable and Accounts Payable control accounts.
(b) Based on this information, what would the control account balances be upon completing the May 31 posting?

Designing a Sales System

CASE 3

Superior Manufacturing produces specialized equipment. About 90 percent of its sales are made to four customers. The remaining 10 percent of sales are made to companies that make one or two purchases per year. An average of ten invoices is issued each week. As the new accountant, you have been given the task of designing a system for recording sales and handling accounts receivable.

(a) Consider each of the following systems for recording sales invoices:

• Columnar journal and accounts receivable ledger
• Ledgerless system with file folders for each customer (sales to be recorded in a sales journal)
• Ledgerless system with file folders for each customer and journalless system of recording sales in which batch totals of sales invoices are directly posted to the general ledger

(b) Give advantages and disadvantages of each of the preceding alternatives. Select one method as your choice and give your reasons.

Terms of Sale

CASE 4

You are the credit manager for a large manufacturer of sporting goods. One of your main jobs is to decide if a new customer is to be allowed to buy on credit. Depending on the customer, your firm allows one of the following terms of payment:

• C.O.D. (cash on delivery)
• net 30 days
• net 90 days

Astro Sports, a new customer, has ordered $10 000 worth of merchandise. Which term of payment would you grant to Astro Sports? Its balance sheet follows. Give reasons for your answer.

Astro Sports
Balance Sheet
October 31, 20—

Assets		Liabilities	
Cash	$ 3 000	Accounts Payable	$ 95 000
Accounts Receivable	14 000	Bank Loan	35 000
Inventory	90 000	Mortgage Payable	100 000
Building	195 000	Total Liabilities	230 000
Equipment	30 000		
		Owner's Equity	
		M. Cassidy, Capital	102 000
		Total Liabilities and	
Total Assets	$332 000	Owner's Equity	$332 000

CASE 5   ## Cash Payments

J. Ballast is the owner of Canadian Enterprises Ltd., a large company in the entertainment business. The revenue of the business is about $6 million per year. In the past several years Ballast has spent the following:
- Swimming pool built at his home: $22 000
- Renovations to his cottage: $8000
- Landscaping around his home: $2000
- Plumbing and air conditioning installed in his home: $4000.

Although each of these expenditures was of a personal nature, Ballast requested that invoices for the charges be sent to his company, Canadian Enterprises. All of the expenditures were recorded in the books of the company in various expense accounts. Payments were made from company funds. Examples of the accounting procedures used follow:

Jun.	1	Building Repairs Expense	22 0 0 0 00	
		Cash		22 0 0 0 00
		Cheque 1190 to Modern Contractors.		
	30	Maintenance Expense	2 0 0 0 00	
		Cash		2 0 0 0 00
		Cheque 1264 to Valley Landscaping.		

(a) From an accounting theory point of view, what is wrong with recording the transactions as expenses of the business?
(b) What is the effect on the company's net income and income tax?

⑭ Career Education Activities

1. Keeping Good Employees

Once you have a job, how do you keep it? How do you get promoted and continue along your desired career path?

Anne Marie Lever is a senior human resources associate for Nortel Networks. Her responsibilities include the attraction and retention of talent, leadership development, implementation of human resources initiatives, and market analysis to ensure that Nortel remains competitive with its employee packages.

Anne Marie was asked: "What type of employees excel along their career paths?" Her answer is summarized below:

Skills

Successful employees have university degrees in areas such as math, business, engineering, physics, and computer science.

Attitudes

Employees who advance are excellent team players who show initiative. They believe in their own abilities and in those of their fellow team workers. They are not threatened by others around them, but instead build on the strengths of others in the company.

Abilities

A key ability that leads to success is the ability to take initiative—to be constantly upgrading one's skills, always staying current, and always learning.

Other Characteristics

Successful employees are often good leaders who foster loyalty from their team members. They are able to communicate and build strong relationships. They have an ability to work with people in various positions throughout the organization.

Overall, Anne Marie feels that the employees who often move quickly along their career path are those who are dedicated, have good work habits, and, most importantly, have a good combination of technical and interpersonal skills

For Discussion

In small groups of three or four students, discuss the importance of the following:

(a) How does one become a good team player?
(b) How can you demonstrate good work habits?
(c) Explain the statement: "They are not threatened by others around them, but instead build on the strengths of others in the company."
(d) Once you are working full-time, what opportunities exist to stay current and upgrade your skills?

2. Getting Organized

Have you ever missed an appointment? Forgotten a deadline? Forgotten to do something important? We all have problems keeping ourselves organized. There are activities and distractions that compete for our attention and time and it is quite easy to inadvertently forget to do things that must be done.

People in the business world cannot afford to be forgetful. To be a success, a person must be on top of things, able to decide what is important, and able to meet deadlines. A well-organized person is able to keep on top of things and to do what has to be done—on time.

Leslie Sloane is considered to be one of these organized persons. One simple technique that helps Leslie is a *Things To Do Today* list such as the one shown below. Every day, Leslie determines the things that must be done and writes them in the *urgent* section of the list. Other things, which are not so vital, are written in the second part of the list. The urgent activities are treated as a challenge, and Leslie attempts to get them done every day.

THINGS TO DO TODAY
DATE

URGENT   DONE

  1. ———————————— ————

  2. ———————————— ————

  3. ———————————— ————

  4. ———————————— ————

OTHER THINGS TO DO

  5. ———————————— ————

  6. ———————————— ————

  7. ———————————— ————

  8. ———————————— ————

  9. ———————————— ————

10. ———————————— ————

For Discussion

(a) What things have you forgotten to do and thereby caused yourself embarrassment?

(b) What do you do to keep yourself organized?

(c) Name two people in your class who are considered to be organized. Ask them what organization techniques they use.

(d) Speak to two friends or relatives who have completed their education. Ask them how they keep themselves organized. Share your results with your class.

(e) How can technology help people to stay organized?

Career Profile •

Liset Stanton grew up in Lacombe, Alberta. In high school, she developed an interest in business, so she studied accounting, economics, and computer science to prepare for university. Afterwards, she entered the four-year Bachelor of Commerce program at Queen's University in Kingston. Her career goal at that time was to work as a manager or the administrator in a large business.

To help finance her degree and to gain business experience, Liset took several part-time jobs. These included being an office clerk and a teller at the local credit union. Liset believed her high school business courses helped her succeed in these part-time jobs.

As she progressed through university, Liset changed career goals, ultimately deciding to become a chartered accountant. To achieve this, she took the following courses: Principles of Economics, Financial Statement Analysis, Introduction to Finance, Taxation, Accounting Theory, Business Law, Organizational Behaviour, Introduction to Auditing, Statistics, Management Accounting, Macroeconomic Theory, Management Control Systems, and Current Issues in Financial Accounting.

Liset completed the CA program, including the Uniform Final Examination and her work experience, and attained her goal.

After working on an audit team in a large accounting firm for five years, Liset was hired by Lindquist Avey Macdonald Baskerville, a firm specializing in forensic accounting.

Subsequently, Liset transferred to the Ottawa office of Kroll Lindquist Avey, also in the field of forensic accounting.

As a forensic accountant, Liset worked with lawyers and corporate clients to prepare legal materials and reports for the courts. She dealt with fraud, damage, and civil cases that required professional accounting consultation services.

Liset balances her work life with her personal life. She bikes, swims, and participates in other sports. She also has several hobbies, including making homemade sweaters.

Forensic Accounting

Forensic accountants examine financial data for possible stock market fraud, computer crime, supplier kickbacks, bank fraud, and secret commissions and deals.

CAs who specialize in forensic accounting work can earn the special designation CA-IFA (Investigative and Forensic Accounting) from the CICA. Professional accountants can also study for a Diploma in Investigative and Forensic Accounting (D.I.F.A.), which is a two-year distance education program.

The Association of Certified Fraud Examiners (CFEs) has over 25 000 members, including auditors, accountants, attorneys, educators, and criminologists.

For Discussion

(a) How did career planning in high school help Liset?

(b) Have you set a career goal? If yes, what planning have you done to attain your goal? If no, how can you get started?

(c) What challenges are involved in changing your career goal? If you decide to change your goal, how can you get help with your decision?

(d) What activities do you participate in to relieve stress? Why would it be important for an account-ant to have outside hobbies and interests?

(e) What role would an accountant have in a court case involving fraud?

(f) Why would someone who is already a CA want to obtain additional certification?

Performance Task 3

What Learning You Will Demonstrate

You will:

- demonstrate an understanding of the recording and decision-making aspects of accounting;
- demonstrate an understanding of the basic accounting cycle procedures and principles for a merchandising business;
- record source documents manually in five journals and three ledgers of a merchandising business;
- record the source documents of a merchandising business using accounting software; and
- compare the five-journal, columnar journal, and computerized systems of accounting.

Background Information

Elizabeth Cheung, owner of Creature Comforts, has exclusive rights to distribute the products of Teak Manufacturers and of General Appliances Ltd. The store has been operating successfully for a number of years. The accounting system includes three ledgers and five journals. The journals are:

- Purchases journal
- Sales journal
- Cash receipts journal
- Cash payments journal
- General journal

The general journal is used for returns and allowances and for correcting entries.

The Task

Creature Comforts is considering a change in its accounting system from five journals to one columnar journal or to a computerized accounting system. You have been hired as a consultant to complete a comparison of the methods and to make a recommendation as to which system is more appropriate. A rationale should accompany your comparison and recommendation in the form of a memo to E. Cheung, the owner. There are four parts to this task:

I. The manual five-journal accounting system
II. The computerized accounting system
III. The columnar journal (design)
IV. Recommendations

Materials Required

- January transaction data
- Manual accounting system forms for the five-journal system
- Accounting software program and data-entry sheets

I. The Manual Five-Journal Accounting System

1. Open the five journals. Open the ledgers and record the January 10 balances. In the appropriate journals, record the January transactions provided. Prepare one batch entry for each day's cash sales.
2. Total, balance, and rule the journals. Post the journals to the subsidiary ledgers and the general ledger.
3. Prepare schedules for the subsidiary ledgers and a trial balance for the general ledger.
4. Prepare a schedule of cost of goods sold and an income statement for the two weeks ending January 17. The January 17 merchandise inventory is $257 931.12.
5. Prepare a balance sheet dated January 17, 20—.

II. The Computerized Accounting System

Complete this project using accounting software, following these instructions:

(a) Prepare a chart of accounts with appropriate computer numbers for each account.
(b) Record the transactions (manually) on data-entry sheets.
(c) Input the transactions from the data-entry sheets.
(d) Print the journal (or journals depending on the capability of your software).
(e) Print the trial balance.
(f) Prepare and print the financial statements.

III. The Columnar Journal (design)

Design a columnar journal that can be used to record transactions for Creature Comforts.

IV. Recommendations

Which system is most appropriate for the company, the manual five-journal system, the manual columnar system, or the computerized system. Write a memo to E. Cheung in which you make your recommendation. Provide an accompanying rationale.

Assessment Criteria

Examine the assessment rubric. Note the descriptions of the performance criteria and the levels of achievement.

Creature Comforts
Trial Balance
January 10, 20—

Account	Acc. No.	Debit	Credit
Cash	101	$ 27 678.50	
Accounts Receivable	110	10 617.08	
Merchandise Inventory	120	255 673.84	
Land	150	75 000.00	
Buildings	160	230 768.00	
Office Equipment	161	4 763.35	
Fixtures	162	11 342.89	
Trucks	163	24 897.88	
Accounts Payable	200		$ 14 550.06
PST Payable	205		5 369.90
GST Payable	206		4 872.10
GST Refundable	207	2 772.10	
Bank Loan	210		15 765.31
Mortgage on Building	250		103 575.35
E. Cheung, Capital	300		501 819.08
E. Cheung, Drawings	301	1 700.00	
Sales	400		13 658.73
Sales Returns and Allowances	401	146.51	
Purchases	500	9 105.82	
Purchases Returns and Allowances	501		97.33
Transportation on Purchases	502	278.85	
Salaries Expense	600	2 376.51	
Truck Repairs Expense	601	138.64	
Heating Expense	602	173.56	
Utilities Expense	603	78.53	
Bank Charges Expense	604	45.20	
Advertising Expense	605	2 150.60	
		$659 707.86	$659 707.86

<table>
<tr><td colspan="2">

Creature Comforts
Schedule of Accounts Receivable
January 10, 20—

</td></tr>
</table>

A. Bartoli	$ 4 687.35
D. Crankshaw	390.47
L. Lariviere	491.60
M. St. Amour	3 673.38
S. Walli	1 374.28
	$10 617.08

Creature Comforts
Schedule of Accounts Payable
January 10, 20—

Campbell Heating	$ 493.70
CKNH TV	767.00
General Appliances Ltd.	5 358.61
Hi-Way Transport	478.90
Teak Manufacturers	6 798.50
Welland Motors Ltd.	653.35
	$14 550.06

January Transactions

In the appropriate journals, record the transactions given below—both those shown in source documents and those listed. Prepare one batch entry for each day's cash sales. GST is 7 percent and PST is 8 percent calculated on the base price.

Jan. 13   Cash Sales Invoice 7339.

CREATURE COMFORTS

INVOICE 7339

359 Portage Ave.
Ottawa, ON
K2A 7N9

Order No. ——

Date Jan. 13, 20—

Sold D. Mitchell   Ship to Same
      19 Oakwood Ave.
      Gloucester, ON
      K2E 5B4

Terms Cash

Cash X   Charge

Quantity	Description	Unit Price	Amount
1	Washing Machine	$650.95	$ 650.95
1	Dryer	549.49	549.49
		Subtotal	1200.44
		GST (7%)	84.03
		PST (8%)	96.04
		Pay this Amount	$1380.51

Jan. 13   Other cash sales invoices:
No. 7340, $299.96 plus PST and GST.
No. 7342, $83.98 plus PST and GST.

No. 7343, $119.98 plus PST and GST.
No. 7344, $1355.74 plus PST and GST.

13   Charge Sales Invoice 7341 to L. Lariviere (on account),
     $649.90 plus PST and GST.
13   Cash received, $300 from A. Bartoli.
13   Cheque 345 issued: merchandise $445.40 plus $31.18 GST.

No. 345		
BAL.	27 678.50	
DEP.	3 135.10	
TOTAL	30 813.60	
CHEQUE	476.58	
BAL.	30 337.02	
PAY TO	Elgin Cabinets	
on account		
SUM OF $ 476.58		
DATE Jan. 13, 20—		

CREATURE COMFORTS   **SAMPLE**   NO. 345
359 Portage Ave.
Ottawa, ON K2A 7N9   January 13, 20—

PAY TO THE
ORDER OF   Elgin Cabinets $ 476.58

SUM OF   Four hundred and seventy-six----------58 /100 DOLLARS

THE BANK OF NOVA SCOTIA
Preston & Norman Branch
Ottawa, ON KIR 7V7
⑈45 70276-002⑈4351932

Jan. 14   Cheques issued:
          No. 346 to Hi-Way Transport, $359 on account.
          No. 347 to Bell Canada, $126.79 plus $8.88 GST, total $135.67.

14   Cash sales invoices:
     No. 7345, $530 plus PST and GST.
     No. 7346, $164.98 plus PST and GST.
     No. 7348, $549.98 plus PST and GST
     No. 7349, $239.98 plus PST and GST.

14   Charge sales invoices:
     No. 7347 to M. St. Amour, $574.98 plus PST and GST.
     No. 7350 to D. Crankshaw, $356.90 plus PST and GST.

14   Purchase invoices:
     No. 273 from Welland Motors Ltd. for truck repairs,
     $220.22 plus $15.41 GST; total $235.63.
     No. 4912 from Campbell Heating for fuel, $528.64
     plus $37 GST; total $565.64.

14   Correcting entry:
     On January 3 $57.53 was debited to Fixtures instead
     of Office Equipment. Make a correcting entry.

15　Credit Invoice 3470 was received from Teak
　　Manufacturers, $35 plus $2.45 GST; overcharge on
　　Invoice 110985.

15　Cash sales invoices:
　　No. 7352, $609.50 plus PST and GST.
　　No. 7353, $79.96 plus PST and GST.
　　No. 7354, $499.98 plus PST and GST.
　　No. 7355, $419.98 plus PST and GST.
　　No. 7356, $799.98 plus PST and GST.

15　Charge Sales Invoice 7351 to S. Walli, $359.98 plus
　　PST and GST.

15　Cash receipts:
　　From M. St. Amour, $350 on account.
　　From D. Crankshaw, $120 on account.

15　Purchase invoices:
　　No. 6132 from General Appliances Ltd. for merchandise,
　　$2567.56 plus $179.73 GST; total $2747.29.
　　No. 1888 from Hi-Way Transport for transportation on
　　merchandise, $467.50 plus $32.73 GST; total $500.23.

15　Cheques issued:
　　No. 348 to the Provincial Treasurer, $4265.14 for PST
　　collected in December.
　　No. 349 to Teak Manufacturers, $1567.50 on account.
　　No. 350 to CKNH TV, $450 on account.

16　Cash sales invoices:
　　No. 7357, $209.50 plus PST and GST.
　　No. 7359, $549.98 plus PST and GST.
　　No. 7361, $355 plus PST and GST.
　　No. 7362, $322 plus PST and GST.
　　No. 7363, $79.98 plus PST and GST.

16　Charge sales invoices:
　　No. 7358 to A. Bartoli, $289.98 plus PST and GST.
　　No. 7360 to M. St. Amour, $539.98 plus PST and GST.

16　Cash receipts:
　　From L. Lariviere, $250 on account.
　　From S. Walli, $95 on account.

16   Credit Invoice 175 issued:

CREATURE COMFORTS   CREDIT INVOICE 175

359 Portage Ave.
Ottawa, ON
K2A 7N9

Date Jan. 16, 20—

To: L. Lariviere
      4935 rue Champlain
      Ottawa, ON
      K1C 3P1

Quantity	Description	Unit Price	Amount
4	Chairs	$80.00	$320.00
		GST	22.40
		PST	25.60
		Total Credit	$368.00
	Overcharge on Invoice 7341		

16   Purchase invoices:
      No. 4686 from CKNH TV, $1200 plus $84 GST; total
      $1284 for advertising.
      No. 89941 from Teak Manufacturers, $1563.69 plus
      $109.46 GST; total $1673.15 for merchandise.

16   Cheques issued:
      No. 351 to Welland Motors Ltd., $450 on account.
      No. 352 to Bank of Nova Scotia, $2000 payment on the
      bank loan.
      No. 353 to Commercial Realtors, $1500 payment on
      the mortgage.

17   Bank debit memo for $54 received for bank charges.

17   Cash sales invoices:
      No. 7364, $298.98 plus PST and GST.
      No. 7365, $74.95 plus PST and GST.
      No. 7367, $599.98 plus PST and GST.
      No. 7368, $239.98 plus PST and GST.
      No. 7369, $209.98 plus PST and GST.

17   Charge Sales Invoice 7366 to D. Crankshaw, $408.96 plus PST and GST.

17   Purchase invoices:
No. 1988 From Hi-Way Transport, $367.50 plus $25.73 GST; total $393.23 for transportation of merchandise.
No. 308 from Welland Motors Ltd., $198 plus $13.86 GST; total $211.86 for truck repairs.

17   Cheques issued:
No. 354 to E. Cheung, the owner, $1450 for personal use.
No. 355 to General Appliances Ltd., $3600 on account.
No. 356 to Campbell Heating, $493.70 on account.
No. 357 to Receiver General of Canada, GST remittance $2100.

Creature Comforts: Performance Task Rubric

Assessment Criteria	Levels of Achievement			
	Level 1	Level 2	Level 3	Level 4
KNOWLEDGE AND UNDERSTANDING • understanding of recording and decision-making aspects of accounting • understanding of the debit/credit theory in recording transactions in journals and ledgers of a merchandising business	Demonstrates limited understanding of terminology, concepts, procedures, and principles.	Demonstrates some understanding of terminology, concepts, procedures, and principles.	Demonstrates considerable understanding of terminology, concepts, procedures, and principles.	Demonstrates thorough understanding of terminology, concepts, procedures, and principles.
THINKING AND INQUIRY • analysis of transactions • interpretation of the balance sheets and financial statements • forming conclusions regarding appropriateness of types of journals	Uses critical and interpretative skills with limited effectiveness. Applies few of the skills in an inquiry, or problem-solving process.	Uses critical and interpretative skills with moderate effectiveness. Applies some of the skills in an inquiry, or problem-solving process.	Uses critical and interpretative skills with considerable effectiveness. Applies most of the skills in an inquiry, or problem-solving process.	Uses critical and interpretative skills with a high degree of effectiveness. Applies all or almost all skills in an inquiry, or problem-solving process.
COMMUNICATION • completion of appropriate forms and statements • formation of memo, including recommendation and rationale	Communicates with minimal precision and clarity.	Communicates with some precision and clarity.	Communicates with considerable precision and clarity.	Communicates with complete and thorough precision and clarity.
APPLICATION • application of skills to prepare trial balance and financial statements • application of skills to record transactions in journals and ledgers	Uses skills with limited accuracy.	Uses skills with some accuracy.	Uses skills with considerable accuracy.	Uses skills with a high degree of accuracy.

11

Cash Control and Banking

What Learning You Will Demonstrate

On completion of this unit, you will be able to:

- explain the purpose and importance of the internal control system of a business;
- demonstrate why cash control is necessary;
- understand that the tasks of handling and recording cash are separated for control purposes;
- explain why cash receipts are immediately recorded by cash register or on a list;
- explain why source documents are prenumbered;
- demonstrate the skills to prepare a daily cash proof and to record shortages or overages;
- demonstrate the skills to deposit cash receipts daily;
- explain why cash payments should be made by cheque; and
- establish and maintain a petty cash fund to pay small bills.

Internal accounting control for a business refers to the method and procedures used to:

(a) protect the assets from waste, loss, theft, and fraud;
(b) ensure reliable accounting records;
(c) ensure accurate and consistent application of the firm's policies; and
(d) evaluate the performance of departments and personnel.

These components of an effective internal control system can be divided into *administrative controls* and *accounting controls*. *Administrative controls* normally relate to components (c) and (d). They increase the efficiency of the business and ensure company policies are followed. *Accounting controls* relate to components (a) and (b). They protect assets and ensure the reliability of accounting records and statements.

Internal accounting control is used to protect assets and to ensure the reliability of records and statements.

Accountants must be familiar with both administrative and accounting controls. Proper internal control ensures the accounting system is dependable and efficient and provides security for the resources of the business.

Cash includes cheques, money orders, debit card payments, bills, and coins.

In this chapter, we will discuss one portion of the accounting control system of a business—*the need for control of cash*. We will examine a number of procedures that are used to protect this important asset, as well as methods of keeping accurate cash records. It should be understood that the term *"cash"* includes cheques, money orders, debit card payments, bills, and coins.

IMPORTANCE OF CASH CONTROL

Joyce McKenzie works for Ho Electronics. One of Joyce's duties is to handle cash sales. When a customer buys merchandise for cash, a cash sales slip is completed in duplicate. One copy is given to the customer and the second is placed in the cash register with the money received from the sale. Joyce is often left alone in the store and has learned that a sale can be made, a cash sales slip given to the customer, the duplicate copy destroyed, and the money placed in Joyce's pocket instead of in the company's cash register.

This story is an example of why all companies, both large and small, require accounting systems that provide control over dishonesty and error.

Because of the ease with which cash may be lost or stolen and errors may be made in counting cash, systems are needed that give effective control over all cash received and all payments made. No two businesses operate in exactly the same way. Some have many cash sales every day while others have only a few. It is the accountant's task to design a system that suits the particular needs of a company. The system should effectively control cash, but it should not be overly complicated or expensive to operate.

In the case of Ho Electronics, the solution can be as simple as prenumbering all of the sales slips and having Joyce's supervisor check them periodically to ensure that none are missing. Cash is involved in a large portion of the transactions of a business and therefore presents opportunities for errors to occur. Cash is also an attractive target for theft and fraud. Therefore, control of cash is very important to the owner or manager of the enterprise.

CASH CONTROL PROCEDURES

A business owned and operated by one person or by a small family has little need for control procedures. However, as a company grows and employs an increasing number of people, it is often necessary to pass on to others those tasks that include financial responsibilities. This makes it necessary to control theft, fraud, and errors by people within the company. As well, control procedures can result in more efficient use of employee time. A number of established accounting procedures have been designed to provide internal control over cash. In this chapter, we will discuss the eight cash control procedures listed here:

- Procedure 1: Separation of Duties
- Procedure 2: Immediate Listing of Cash Receipts

- Procedure 3:   Daily Cash Proof
- Procedure 4:   Daily Deposit of Cash
- Procedure 5:   Payment by Cheque
- Procedure 6:   Petty Cash Procedures
- Procedure 7:   Periodic Audit
- Procedure 8:   Monthly Bank Reconciliation

Procedure 1: Separation of Duties

A key component of all control systems is the separation of employees' duties. To discourage fraud and theft as well as to ensure the accuracy of accounting data, the duties of the accounting personnel should be arranged so that one employee verifies the accuracy of another employee's work. In a cash control system, it is important that the employee responsible for preparing and depositing the cash in the bank be *different* from the employee responsible for recording the cash receipts. This provides a verification of the cash recorded and minimizes the chance of theft, since both employees would have to work together to remove cash from the company. The recording function should be divided among employees also, where possible, to provide additional verification of the accuracy of the records and protection for the asset. You have already seen this type of division of duties, where the work of the accounts receivable clerk is verified by the accounting supervisor, who compares the schedule of accounts receivable total to the control account in the general ledger. The importance of this control procedure for both cash receipts and cash payments will be demonstrated throughout this chapter.

> Different people should carry out the task of recording cash received and the task of actually handling the cash.

CONTROL OF CASH RECEIPTS

The accounting controls in Procedures 2, 3, and 4 ensure the accuracy of cash receipts.

Procedure 2: Immediate Listing of Cash Receipts

Cash receipts consist of cash received at the time of the sale, over the counter, payments made by debit card, and cheques received by mail in payment of accounts receivable.

Cash Sales

Cash registers or terminals are normally used to record cash sales as they occur. The cash register should be set up so the customer can see the amount recorded. The customer assists with the control system by preventing an error in recording a cash sale and by preventing the employee from ringing in a lower amount than that charged to the customer and then pocketing the difference. The cash register tape provides a total of the cash sales for the day. It is compared to the actual cash receipts by the manager, supervisor, or owner when preparing the daily cash proof. This allows a person other than the cashier to verify the accuracy of the cash.

> All cash should be recorded as soon as it is received.

   This procedure follows the concept of separation of duties explained previously. In addition, the immediate recording of the sale by the cash register eliminates the possibility of cash being stolen and the sale remaining unrecorded.

Computerized cash register systems provide additional accounting controls by verifying prices and updating inventory records.

Prenumbered Sales Slips

In many businesses, a prenumbered, multiple-copy sales slip is prepared for each cash sale. One copy is given to the customer and two are kept on file in the business. At the end of the day, the sales slips are totalled and compared to the cash register tape and the actual cash and debit payment slips on hand. One set of sales slips is forwarded with the cash to the person responsible for making the bank deposit. The other set and the debit payment slips are forwarded to the accounting department as source documents from which to record the cash sales for the day.

Cancelled sales slips are marked void and are kept on file.

If all documents are prenumbered, all of them must be accounted for. It is therefore impossible for the sales clerk to destroy a cash sales slip and pocket the money, since it would mean that one of the numbered slips would be destroyed. If a sales slip is spoiled or cancelled, it must be marked *void* and kept with the rest of the day's source documents. The principle of prenumbering documents is applied to many forms. For example, cheques, sales invoices, and petty cash vouchers are all prenumbered. This ensures that every document is accounted for.

Cash Received by Mail

The employee who opens the mail should prepare a list of the cheques received. One copy of this list, along with the cheques, is forwarded to the person responsible for making the daily deposit. The second copy is sent to the accounting department as a source document to record these cash receipts. In some firms, a third copy is kept on file for future reference by the employee opening the mail.

These procedures ensure a separation in duties between the employees handling the cash and the employees recording the cash receipts. This is important in order to verify the accounting records and to prevent theft.

Procedure 3: Daily Cash Proof

Each day, the owner or supervisor should balance the cash received against the source documents used to record the cash transactions. By preparing this proof daily, any major shortages or overages can be dealt with immediately. In the case of Brighton Cleaners, a daily cash proof form is completed by the owner of the business, E. Plata. This form is shown in Figure 11-1 on the next page.

Introducing the Cash Short and Over Account

The Cash Short and Over account is used to record shortages and overages of cash.

As Figure 11-1 illustrates, the cash is counted and a $150 cash float (change fund) is removed from the cash and kept for the next day's business. On June 6, the cash is short 30 cents. Since the company has lost funds, an expense must be recorded in an account called Cash Short and Over.

DAILY CASH PROOF

DATE _Jun. 6_ 20 —
TOTAL DEBIT SLIPS _$1347.50_
TOTAL CASH _____
LESS CASH FLOAT _150.00_
TOTAL DEPOSITED _$1197.50_

SALES SLIPS
NO's _706_ to _785_ _1197.80_
CASH SHORT _0.30_
or
CASH OVER _____
AUTHORIZED _E. Plata_

DAILY CASH PROOF

DATE _Jun. 7_ 20 —
TOTAL DEBIT SLIPS _$1366.73_
TOTAL CASH _____
LESS CASH FLOAT _150.00_
TOTAL DEPOSITED _$1216.73_

SALES SLIPS
NO's _786_ to _861_ _1215.73_
CASH SHORT _____
or
CASH OVER _1.00_
AUTHORIZED _E. Plata_

FIGURE 11-1 Daily cash proof showing a cash shortage

FIGURE 11-2 Daily cash proof showing a cash overage

The daily cash proof is the source document for a journal entry to record the day's sales. For June 6, the journal entry is:

Jun.	6	Cash		1 1 9 7	50		
		Cash Short and Over			30		
		Sales				1 1 9 7	80
		To record Sales Slips 706 to 785.					

The daily cash proof for the next day, June 7, is shown in Figure 11-2. Notice that the total cash deposited is $1 more than it should be according to the cash sales slips. In this entry, the overage is recorded as a credit to Cash Short and Over. The journal entry for June 7 is:

Jun.	7	Cash		1 2 16	73		
		Sales				1 2 1 5	73
		Cash Short and Over				1	00
		To record Sales Slips 786 to 861.					

These two journal entries may be summarized as follows. In the daily cash proof in Figure 11-1, the cash is *short* by 30 cents. This shortage represents a loss to the company and is charged as a debit (a decrease in owner's equity) to Cash Short and Over. If the cash is *over* (Figure 11-2), the amount is recorded in the same Cash Short and Over account. However, an overage is recorded as a credit (an increase in owner's equity).

Cash shortages are recorded as debits in Cash Short and Over.

Cash overages are recorded as credits in Cash Short and Over.

When an income statement is prepared, the Cash Short and Over account may appear in *either* the revenue or the expense section. It appears in the revenue section if the account has a *credit* balance (the overages have been greater than the shortages). It appears in the expense section if the account has a *debit* balance (the shortages have been greater than the overages).

Some companies prefer to use a separate section at the bottom of the income statement for miscellaneous items, such as cash shortages and overages. This section, called *Other Income and Expenses*, includes such items as bank interest earned, cash short and over, and gain or loss on sale of assets. The use of this section clearly indicates how much of the net income comes from the regular operations of the business and how much comes from miscellaneous sources.

Cash Short and Over Policy

A company that handles many cash transactions and prepares a daily cash proof is faced with a problem. *What should be done about shortages and overages?* There are several possibilities, including these:

- absorb all shortages and overages; or
- deduct shortages from the cashier's pay.

Many companies prefer to keep all shortage information from the cashier. The daily cash proof is prepared by someone from the accounting office. Shortages and overages are absorbed by the company and are not mentioned to the cashier, unless they are frequent and fairly large. If this occurs, the situation is discussed with the cashier. Retraining may be necessary. If errors still continue on a large scale, the cashier may be transferred or dismissed.

Procedure 4: Daily Deposit of Cash

Each day, the total cash receipts of the business (cash sales and cheques received) should be deposited in the bank. Therefore, no large amounts of money (which could be stolen) are kept on the premises. No bills should be paid out of these funds. Thus, the amount of the deposit each day will be the same as the amount recorded in the cash receipts journal by the accounting department. This allows a further verification of the records by the company's bank when the bank sends the bank statement at the end of the month. After completing the daily cash proof, Figure 11-1 on page 533, E. Plata, the owner of Brighton Cleaners, completes the deposit slip shown in Figure 11-3. The cash is deposited in the bank. A copy of the deposit slip is kept by the company.

FRASER ENTERPRISES' CASH RECEIPTS CONTROL SYSTEM

The example of Fraser Enterprises, a large wholesaler of heating and refrigeration equipment, is used to demonstrate the cash control procedures we have discussed to this point. The principle of *separation of duties* is used by Fraser Enterprises to control and record cash receipts. Each day, a list of all cash received is prepared by the mail clerk. This list shows the name of the customer, the amount received, and the invoice that is being paid. Two copies of the list are prepared. They are sent to the accounting department where the money received is recorded.

THE BANK OF NOVA SCOTIA		
CREDIT CURRENT ACCOUNTS **SAMPLE**		
NO. 91835-09	*Jun. 6, 20—*	
NAME *Brighton Cleaners*	DATE	
DEPOSITED BY *E. Plata*		
11 × 5	55	00
14 × 10	140	00
3 × 20	60	00
8 × 50	400	00
1 × 100	100	00
COIN	37	50
BONDS/COUPONS		
SUBTOTAL	792	50
CHEQUES	405	00
TOTAL	1197	50
LESS EXCHANGE		
J.W. $	1197	50
TELLER		

FIGURE 11-3 Bank deposit slip

The actual cash is taken to the bank each day by the office manager. Cheques received are stamped with a restrictive endorsement, as shown in Figure 11-4. This endorsement ensures that the cheque is deposited in the company account. It cannot be cashed by anyone. A duplicate deposit slip is prepared and one copy is kept by the bank. The second copy, signed by the bank teller, is kept by the company.

A restrictive endorsement is an instruction placed on the back of a cheque to control what happens to the funds.

DEPOSIT TO THE CREDIT
OF
FRASER ENTERPRISES
The Bank of Nova Scotia
Carlingwood & Woodroffe Branch
Ottawa, Ontario
K2A 3T3

FIGURE 11-4 Restrictive endorsement stamp on the back of a cheque

Using the List of Cash Received

When the two copies of the list of cash received are sent to the accounting department, one copy goes to the accounts receivable clerk for posting and the other copy goes to the accountant for journalizing.

Duties of the Accounts Receivable Clerk

From the list of cash received, the accounts receivable clerk posts to the customer accounts. Each account is lowered with a credit. Once a week, the accounts receivable clerk prepares a schedule of accounts receivable. This is a list that shows the amount owed by each customer and the total owed by all of the customers as a group.

Once a month, a statement is sent to each customer. The statement shows the balance, charges, and credits for cash received and it acts as a reminder of the amount owing. The statement is also used to check on the accuracy of both Fraser Enterprises' and the customer's records. The customer is sure to complain if the outstanding balance shown on the statement is too high!

Duties of the Accountant

The second copy of the list of cash receipts is sent to the accountant, who is responsible for recording cash received in the cash receipts journal. The total recorded in the cash receipts journal each day must equal the total of the daily bank deposit. The cash receipts journal is posted to the general ledger. A trial balance is prepared to prove the accuracy of the general ledger. One of the accounts on the general ledger trial balance is the *Accounts Receivable control account*. The balance in this account must equal the total of the schedule of accounts receivable prepared by the accounts receivable clerk.

Control Features

In the system just described, four people are involved in the cash receipts procedures. One person prepares the deposit and another takes the money to the bank. The duty of recording the receipt of cash is handled by two other people. This is referred to as the seperation of duties. Figure 11-5 illustrates all of the tasks that have been described.

The separation of duties shown in Figure 11-5 has several built-in control features:

The separation of duties is a key component of all accounting control systems used to discourage fraud and theft, as well as to ensure the accuracy of the accounting data.

The duties of accounting personnel should be arranged so that one employee verifies the accuracy of another employee's work.

- The entries in the cash receipts journal each day should equal the total of the day's bank deposit.
- The customer should discover any errors in the customer account when the statement is sent out.
- The total of the schedule of accounts receivable should always equal the balance of the Accounts Receivable control account in the general ledger trial balance.

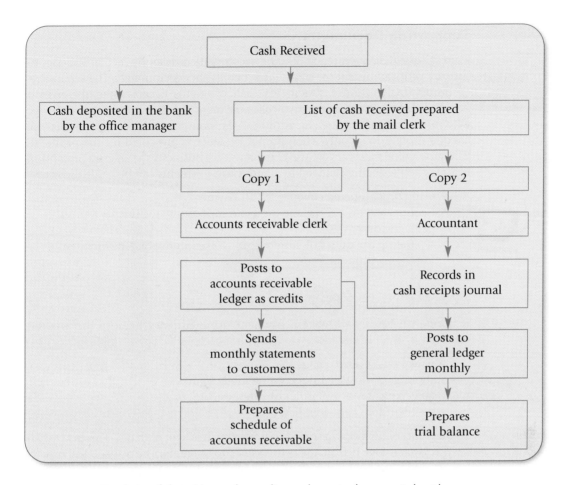

FIGURE 11-5 The duties of depositing and recording cash received are carried out by four separate people—the mail clerk, the office manager, the accounts receivable clerk, and the accountant.

The separation of duties is implemented by most large companies, but is more difficult to achieve in small businesses due to fewer employees. It is important, therefore, that the owner become involved to achieve the necessary controls.

CONTROL OF CASH PAYMENTS

Although most people think of protecting cash receipts when discussing control procedures, it is just as important to control cash payments. Procedures 5 and 6 are important parts of a cash payment control system.

Procedure 5: Payment by Cheque

All cash payments should be made by cheque. The exception is small bills paid out of petty cash, as discussed in Procedure 6. Cheques are prenumbered and spoiled cheques should be marked *void*. Therefore, all cheques can be accounted for at any time. It is important that company cheques be kept in a safe place to prevent theft.

Supporting Documents

Each cheque that is written should be accompanied by an invoice or voucher to provide verification that the payment is being made legitimately. The separation of duties in the control system for cash payments occurs when the person responsible for approving the invoice for payment is different from the employee who prepares the cheque. In addition, the company official who signs the cheque should do so only when proper evidence is presented for the payment. Cheque-signing machines are used by many large businesses as an extra precaution against cheques being changed by hand. Cash payments can be controlled by:

- using prenumbered cheques for all payments;
- issuing cheques only where there are supporting documents to justify payment; and
- separating the duties of employees involved in the cash payment function within the firm.

Procedure 6: Petty Cash Procedures

It is often necessary to make a payment using currency because the amount involved is small or because a cheque is not acceptable. For example:

- parcel post C.O.D. charge: $1.50;
- shortage of postage on incoming mail: $0.50;
- taxi charge for a rush order of supplies: $15; or
- payment for office supplies: $12.

The petty cash fund is an amount of cash used to make small payments.

To meet these situations, a small amount of cash is kept on hand. This petty cash fund is given to one person, the petty cashier, to maintain. The petty cashier usually has no connection with the accounting system of the company.

Setting up the Petty Cash Fund

To establish the petty cash fund, a cheque is issued and given to the petty cashier. The cheque is cashed and the money is usually kept in a petty cash box.

When a petty cash fund is established, this journal entry is made:

Jan.	2	Petty Cash	1 0 0 00	
		Cash		1 0 0 00
		Cheque 171 to set up a petty cash fund.		

The Petty Cash account is a current asset.

The Petty Cash account debited in this entry is found in the general ledger. It is an asset and appears in the current assets section of the balance sheet.

Making Payments

The Petty Cash voucher is a signed authorization for small payments.

The petty cashier is the only person who handles petty cash. Payments made must be authorized by a properly supporting petty cash voucher (Figure 11-6).

Petty cash vouchers are kept in the petty cash box with the remaining cash. Because they have been signed by the party receiving the cash payment, the vouchers prove that legitimate, authorized payments have been made.

Petty Cash Voucher

No. *36*

Date *Jun. 29, 20—*

Amount   *$14.95*

For   *Pens and staples*

Charge to   *Office Expense*   *$13.97*
             GST Refundable   *.98*

Approved by   *B. Mallet*

Received by   *A. Hodgson*

FIGURE 11-6 Petty cash voucher

Proving the Petty Cash

Suppose a petty cashier starts with $100 cash in the petty cash fund. At any time, the petty cash can be proven by adding the total of the cash in the box to the total of the vouchers in the box. Cash plus vouchers should always equal $100.

Replenishing the Petty Cash Fund

Replenishing petty cash means that when the petty cash fund runs low, the total currency on hand must be brought up to the original amount. The petty cashier presents the vouchers and a summary of all payments to the accountant. The vouchers prove that authorized payments have been made. The accountant then issues a cheque equal to the total of the vouchers. The petty cashier cashes the cheque and places the money in the petty cash box. This brings the petty cash fund back to its original amount. This process will now be examined in detail.

Suppose that on January 23, the petty cashier notes that there are only $12 cash left in the petty cash fund. Along with this cash are eight vouchers for payments made. Since the original amount of the fund was $100 and there are only $12 left, the payment vouchers should total $88.

The petty cashier adds the eight vouchers; they total $88. This means that there were no errors in handling the petty cash. The vouchers are then used to prepare the summary on page 540.

Replenishing the petty cash fund means bringing the total currency on hand up to the original amount.

The eight vouchers and the summary are then presented to the accountant, who checks to see that all payments are supported by numbered, signed vouchers and that all vouchers have been accounted for. Then the accountant issues a replenishing cheque for $88 to the petty cashier.

Petty Cash Summary January 2 to January 23, 20—	
K. Martin, Drawings	$ 20.00
Office Expense	23.25
Delivery Expense	17.00
Miscellaneous Expense	22.00
GST Refundable	5.75
Total Payments	88.00
Cash on hand	12.00
Total of fund	$100.00
Cheque request: $88.00	
Number of vouchers: 8	

A journal entry similar to the one that follows is made each time the petty cash fund is replenished. The accounts to be debited are determined by referring to the vouchers and the summary submitted by the petty cashier. Notice that expense accounts are debited each time the fund is replenished. *The Petty Cash account is used only when the fund is established or the size of the fund is changed.*

Jan.	23	K. Martin, Drawings	2 0 00	
		Office Expense	2 3 25	
		Delivery Expense	1 7 00	
		Miscellaneous Expense	2 2 00	
		GST Refundable	5 75	
		Cash		8 8 00
		Cheque 207 to replenish petty cash,		
		vouchers 1–8.		

The petty cashier cashes the $88 cheque, obtaining a variety of denominations of bills and coins, and places the cash in the petty cash box. The total cash is now $100 (there was a $12 cash balance before the fund was replenished).

The petty cash fund is replenished in this way whenever it runs low. In addition, the fund is also normally replenished at the end of the fiscal period whether the fund is low or not. This is necessary to provide current expense account balances for financial statement preparation.

Petty Cash Guidelines

The petty cashier is usually given a set of guidelines like the following:

- The amount of the fund is $100.
- An approved voucher is required for every payment.

- Replenish the fund when the cash level reaches $10.
- The maximum for any one payment is $15.
- Approved vouchers must be presented to the accountant when requesting a replenishing cheque.

Changing the Size of the Petty Cash Fund

At some point, the office manager may find that the petty cash fund is constantly running out of money during the month and may, therefore, want to increase the size of the fund. If the fund were to be increased to $150, the journal entry at the time of replenishing (using the previous example) would be as follows:

Jan.	23	K. Martin, Drawings		2 0 00	
		Office Expense		2 3 25	
		Delivery Expense		1 7 00	
		Miscellaneous Expense		2 2 00	
		GST Refundable		5 75	
		Petty Cash		5 0 00	
		Cash			1 3 8 00
		Cheque 207 to replenish petty cash,			
		vouchers 1–8, and to increase fund.			

Notice that this entry *does* contain a debit to Petty Cash as well as to the expense accounts. This is because the amount of the fund has been increased. How would you decrease the original fund to $75 if you found it was too large? Here is an example:

Jan.	23	K. Martin, Drawings		2 0 00	
		Office Expense		2 3 25	
		Delivery Expense		1 7 00	
		Miscellaneous Expense		2 2 00	
		GST Refundable		5 75	
		Cash			6 3 00
		Petty Cash			2 5 00
		Cheque 207 to replenish petty cash,			
		vouchers 1–8, and to decrease fund.			

In this example, the fund is replenished with only enough cash to reach the new value of $75. Petty Cash is credited since the amount of the fund is being decreased.

Questions

1. What is the purpose of an internal control system?
2. Explain the difference between administrative controls and accounting controls.
3. Why is cash control necessary?
4. What items are included when cash control is discussed?
5. What type of business must consider cash control systems?
6. What is the first principle of cash control?
7. How can the customer assist in the control of cash when an over-the-counter cash sale is made?
8. What is the purpose of prenumbering source documents?
9. What should be done with cancelled or voided cash sales slips in a prenumbered system?
10. What is a cash float?
11. The day's cash total is $583.39. The cash sales slips total $582.13. Is the cash short or over and by how much?
12. (a) Is a cash shortage recorded as a debit or a credit in the Cash Short and Over account?
    (b) How is an overage recorded?
13. The Cash Short and Over account has a debit balance of $19 at the end of a fiscal period. Is this considered a revenue or an expense? Does it increase or decrease net income?
14. Who receives the two copies of the deposit slip?
15. When all of the day's cash receipts are deposited, both the company's records and the bank's records show the cash the company has received on that day. How is this an advantage for the company?
16. Give an advantage of making all payments by cheque.
17. How is a separation of duties achieved when making payments by cheque?
18. What is the purpose of a petty cash fund?
19. How does the petty cash voucher prove that a legitimate payment was made?
20. One cash control procedure states that all payments must be made by cheque. Explain how the petty cash fund is designed so that this principle is followed.
21. What type of account is Petty Cash?
22. Some of the following practices contribute to a strong cash control system and some weaken the system. Identify each as a strength or weakness and explain your reasons.
    (a) Any cash shortage or overage in the daily cash proof is added to or removed from petty cash.
    (b) All cash receipts are deposited daily.
    (c) Cheques are issued for all cash payments other than petty cash disbursements.

(d) All payments under $175 are made through the petty cash fund.

(e) Cheques received through the mail are listed and recorded by the accounts receivable clerk.

Exercises

1. At the end of the day, the manager of a business totalled the cash on hand and prepared a deposit slip for $277.35. The cash sales slips issued during the day totalled $275.50. Prepare the daily cash proof. Is the cash short or over?

2. The change fund for Brighton Cleaners consists of:

Bills	Coins
	3 × $2
1 × $20	5 × $1
1 × $10	24 × 25¢
2 × $5	20 × 10¢
	20 × 5¢

The cash on hand for Brighton Cleaners consists of:

Bills	Coins
	18 × $2
3 × $20	39 × $1
12 × $10	40 × 25¢
20 × $5	29 × 10¢
	41 × 5¢
	26 × 1¢

The calculator tape of the day's cash sales slips for Brighton Cleaners consists of:

> Date: June 9, 20—
> Cash Sales Slips: 934-997
> Total: $316.31

(a) Remove the $60 change fund from the cash on hand and prepare a deposit slip for account no. 91835-09.

(b) Prepare the daily cash proof.

3. Prepare the journal entries to record the daily cash proofs prepared for exercises 1 and 2.

4. A petty cash fund was established with $100. At present, the petty cash box contains:

Bills	Coins	Vouchers
2 × $20	1 × $1	6 totalling $37.50
1 × $10		
2 × $5		

Have any errors been made in the handling of the petty cash?

5. Digital Direct decides to establish a petty cash fund. The office supervisor is chosen to be responsible for petty cash. The accountant issues Cheque 171 for $100 on June 1 and gives it to the supervisor to establish the fund. Record the $100 cheque in a general journal.

6. On June 19, a summary of vouchers in a petty cash box shows:

Office Expense	$35.25
G. LePensée, Drawings	25.00
Donations Expense	15.00
Miscellaneous Expense	14.50
GST Refundable	6.25
Total	$96.00

In general journal form, record the $96 cheque issued by the accountant to replenish the petty cash fund.

7. On September 7, Print-O-Matic Ltd. decided to use a petty cash fund. A cheque for $125 was issued and cashed. The $125 cash was given to the receptionist who was to act as petty cashier. The receptionist/petty cashier was told to obtain authorized vouchers for all payments. Petty cash was to be replenished when the balance in the cash box reached $25. When this happened, a summary of vouchers was to be prepared and given to the accountant.
(a) Record the $125 cheque to establish the fund on September 7.
(b) On September 19, this summary was prepared:

Delivery Expense	$ 49.90
Miscellaneous Expense	20.40
Office Expense	24.10
GST Refundable	6.60
Total	$101.00

Prepare the entry to replenish the petty cash.

(c) It was decided to increase the amount of the petty cash fund from $125 to $175. A cheque for $50 was issued. Record this cheque.

8. If only one cheque was issued in 7(b) and (c) to both replenish and increase the fund, how would the cheque be recorded in a general journal?

9. September 30 was the end of the fiscal year for Print-O-Matic. The following summary of vouchers from the petty cash fund was prepared:

Office Expense	$ 55.34
Miscellaneous Expense	15.74
Delivery Expense	21.25
S. Kerrigan, Drawings	10.00
GST Refundable	7.16
	$109.49

(a) Record the cheque issued to replenish the petty cash fund on September 30.
(b) Why was the fund replenished even though it still contained a substantial amount of cash?

UNIT 26 Checking Cash Records

What Learning You Will Demonstrate

On completion of this unit, you will be able to:

- explain the terms *audit, bank debit memo, bank credit memo, NSF cheque, cancelled cheque, outstanding cheque,* and *reconciliation statement;*
- demonstrate the skills necessary to prepare a reconciliation statement; and
- prepare journal entries that involve banking transactions.

CONCLUDING CASH CONTROL PROCEDURES

In Unit 25, we examined the first six cash control procedures. Now, in this unit, we will look at the two concluding procedures.

Procedure 7: Periodic Audit

An audit is a periodic check on the accuracy of an accounting system.

Periodically, a check or an audit is made to determine that all cash is properly accounted for. Any system, no matter how complicated or foolproof, can break down. Those involved in the system can devise ways to break the system. People can get together and contrive to defraud a company. The periodic—often unannounced—audit is designed to thwart such attempts.

An auditor, employed either by the company or by an outside accounting firm, is given the task of checking the company records. Transactions are traced from their source documents to their posting in the ledgers. Invoices and deposit slips are checked for accuracy. As you learned when studying Procedure 2, prenumbered documents should be used to record cash. However, if a check is not made to ensure that all documents and cash are accounted for, the system breaks down.

EXAMINING THE BANKING CONNECTION

Procedure 8 will involve making sure that a company's record of its money agrees with the bank's record of the company's money. This requires an understanding of the banking connection, or, in other words, an understanding of the relationship between a bank and its depositors. *What is the relationship between a company or person who deposits money and the bank? Do banks follow the same accounting rules and the same theory of debits and credits as everyone else?* The following example is a good illustration of the banking connection:

Note: GST and PST have been excluded from these transactions to simplify the examples.

Renfrew Printing makes cash sales of $1500 and deposits the $1500 in a savings account at the Bank of Nova Scotia. In the books of Renfrew Printing, the following occurs, as shown in T-account form:

Renfrew Printing's Books

Cash			Sales	
1 500				1 500

Through this transaction, Renfrew Printing has more money: its Cash account increases (debit) and its Sales account increases (credit). When the Bank of Nova Scotia receives the deposit, its books also change as shown by the following T-accounts:

Bank of Nova Scotia's Books

Cash			Renfrew Printing	
1 500				1 500

Through this transaction, the Bank of Nova Scotia has more money: its asset account Cash increases (debit). The bank owes this $1500 to Renfrew Printing; in other words, Renfrew Printing is an account payable on the bank's books. At any time, the depositor can demand the money owing and withdraw cash from the account. The bank records the debt by placing a credit of $1500 in the liability account, Renfrew Printing.

Transactions Involving the Bank's Source Documents

Some of the bank's source documents are the same as those of other companies. For example, banks receive purchase invoices and write cheques. The source document that is evidence that a depositor has withdrawn money from the bank is the *withdrawal slip*. The *deposit slip* is the source document that proves money was deposited by a depositor. Two other source documents commonly used by banks are the *bank credit memo* and the *bank debit memo*. Transactions that involve these two documents follow.

Bank Debit Memo

A bank debit memo indicates a decrease in a depositor's account. To give notice of a service charge of $22.50 for cashing cheques on Renfrew Printing's account, the Bank of Nova Scotia issues the debit memo shown in Figure 11-7 on page 548. As shown in the T-accounts below Figure 11-7, the bank deducts the $22.50 by debiting Renfrew's account. Remember, a liability decreases on the debit side.

A bank debit memo is a source document that indicates a decrease in a depositor's account.

THE BANK OF NOVA SCOTIA

SAMPLE

26189-57
Account Number

June 10, 20–
Date

DEBIT Service charge for month $22.50

Authorized by: _C.S._   Checked by: _H.G._   Entry made by: _M.G._

This slip must be initialled by an authorized signing officer.

FIGURE 11-7 A bank debit memo is the source document prepared when the bank decreases a customer's account.

Bank of Nova Scotia's Books

A depositor's account is a liability of the bank. Service charges decrease the liability of the bank.

Renfrew Printing	
22.50	1 500.00

When the depositor, Renfrew Printing, receives the debit memo, the following changes are made in its books:

Renfrew Printing's Books

Cash		Bank Charges	
1 500	22.50	22.50	

Since this transaction is a payment, it is recorded in the cash payments journal of Renfrew Printing.

Bank Credit Memo

A bank credit memo is a source document that indicates an increase in a depositor's account.

A bank credit memo indicates an increase in a depositor's account. If Renfrew Printing has a *savings account, it will earn interest* that is periodically calculated by the bank. Suppose interest amounting to $67.39 has been earned by Renfrew Printing. This means that the bank owes Renfrew more money and the bank will increase the amount in its liability account, Renfrew Printing.

Bank of Nova Scotia's Books

Renfrew Printing	
22.50	1 500.00
	67.39

A bank credit memo (Figure 11-8) is completed and serves to instruct the bank's clerk to increase the Renfrew account. A copy of the memo is sent to Renfrew to inform the company that its bank account has been increased.

THE BANK OF NOVA SCOTIA

SAMPLE

June 10, 20–
Date

CREDIT   Renfrew Printing
$67.39   Interest earned on term deposit.
Deposit to Renfrew Printing's account 26189-57.

C.Smith

FIGURE 11-8 A bank credit memo is the source document prepared when the bank increases a customer's account.

When the depositor, Renfrew Printing, receives the credit memo, it will change its accounts as follows:

Renfrew Printing's Books

Cash		Interest Earned	
1 500.00	22.50		67.39
67.39			

This transaction represents cash received and is recorded in the cash receipts journal. *After the debit and credit transactions, what is the balance in the bank's liability account, Renfrew Printing? What is the balance in Renfrew Printing's Cash account?*

    A company's Cash account should, theoretically, always have the same balance as the bank's record of the company's bank account. However, in actual practice this is rarely the situation. We will now look at Procedure 8 to see what is done to determine if the bank's records agree with the depositor's records.

Procedure 8: Monthly Bank Reconciliation

Personal Chequing Account Reconciliation

Pat and Bob Hunter are a young couple striving to make ends meet. Because they are making payments on their new home and on furniture, they have little money left over for savings. Several months ago, they received telephone calls from their insurance company and from the company holding their house mortgage. Both companies said that Pat and Bob had given them **NSF cheques**—that is,

An NSF cheque is one that cannot be paid because there are not sufficient funds in the account of the person who wrote the cheque.

the cheques had been returned by the bank with the explanation that there were *not sufficient funds* in the Hunters' account to cash the cheques.

The Hunters were quite upset because, according to their records, there was enough money in their bank account to cover the cheques. They called the bank and suggested that the bank had made an error. They were right. Somehow, the combined deposit for both their pay cheques had ended up in someone else's account! *Do banks make errors?* Of course they do! People who work in banks are human and can make mistakes just like anyone else. *Can you remember instances of banks making errors in your own or your family's bank account?* The Hunters felt good about discovering this error in their account because they kept a good record of their bank account balance. Let's look at their account records for the month of July. This will illustrate how the Hunters always check the accuracy of the bank's records by observing Procedure 8.

The Hunters have a joint personal chequing account at the Bank of Nova Scotia. They use this account to make payments for their personal expenses such as mortgage payments, utilities, and charge accounts. Every month, the bank sends them a bank statement and returns their cancelled cheques which have been cashed by the bank . At the end of July, the Hunters received the bank statement shown in Figure 11-9. According to the bank statement, the Hunters' balance

Cancelled cheques are cheques that have been cashed by the bank.

THE BANK OF NOVA SCOTIA   **SAMPLE**

Pat and Bob Hunter
675 Willow Place, Apt. 702
Ottawa, ON   ACCOUNT NUMBER
K1R 6W3   21830-42

STATEMENT OF	FROM	TO	PAGE
Personal Chequing Account	Jul. 1, 20—	Jul. 31, 20—	1

DESCRIPTION	DEBITS	CREDITS	M	D	BALANCE
Balance forward			07	01	486.79
Deposit		900.00	07	02	1,386.79
Cheque 73	12.84		07	05	1,373.95
Cheque 74	386.29		07	09	987.66
DC	499.00		07	15	488.66
Cheque 75	200.00		07	17	288.66
SC	10.90		07	29	277.76

NO. OF DEBITS	TOTAL AMOUNT OF DEBITS	NO. OF CREDITS	TOTAL AMOUNT OF CREDITS	NO. OF ENCLOSURES
5	1,109.03	1	900.00	4

FIGURE 11-9 Bank statement received by the Hunters

was $277.76. Enclosed with the bank statement were three *cancelled cheques*, numbered 73, 74, and 75 (Figure 11-10). The Hunters made one payment by bank debit card on July 15.

The cheque book provided to the Hunters by the bank included cheque record pages as shown in Figure 11-11. These provided the Hunters with a record of cheques written, deposits made, and the balance. According to their cheque record, the Hunters had a July balance of $533.48. *Which was correct—the bank statement balance of $277.76, the Hunters' balance of $533.48, or neither?*

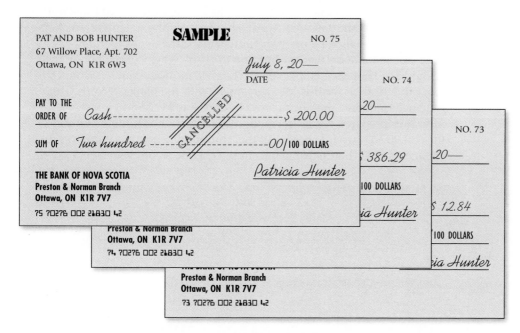

FIGURE 11-10 Cancelled cheques enclosed with bank statement

CHEQUE NO.	DATE		DESCRIPTION OF TRANSACTION	AMOUNT OF CHEQUE		✓	AMOUNT OF DEPOSIT		BALANCE	
	Jul.	1	Balance forward						486	79
		2	Deposit			✓	900	00	1 386	79
72		3	MasterCard	48	60				1 338	19
73		3	Bell Canada	12	84	✓			1 325	35
74		3	Central Mortgage Corp.	386	29	✓			939	06
DC		5	CIAG Insurance	499	00	✓			440	06
75		8	Cash	200	00	✓			240	06
76		23	The Bay	62	08				177	98
77		29	Exxon Ltd.	44	50				133	48
		31	Deposit				400	00	533	48

FIGURE 11-11 Page from the Hunters' cheque book showing their record of banking transactions

Preparing the Personal Bank Reconciliation Statement

To determine the correct balance, the Hunters did the following:

> Outstanding cheques are cheques issued but not yet cashed.

1. In their cheque record (Figure 11-11), they ticked off (✓) each of the cancelled cheques returned by the bank. The three unticked, **outstanding cheques** had been issued but had not yet been cashed by the bank. Cheques 72, 76, and 77 were outstanding.
2. They matched and ticked off the deposits on the bank statement with deposits in their cheque book record. The last deposit of $400 was not shown in the bank statement—probably because the statement was being prepared and mailed before the Hunters made the deposit.

> A reconciliation statement brings the bank's records into agreement with the depositor's records.

3. They looked for items that appeared on the bank statement but not on their records. The Hunters then prepared a **reconciliation statement** (Figure 11-12) that brought their records into agreement with the bank's records. This statement indicated that their correct balance was $522.58.
4. After they prepared the reconciliation statement, the Hunters recorded the $10.90 SC (service charge) in the Amount of Cheque column on their cheque record. Their new balance in the cheque record was then $522.58.

Pat and Bob Hunter
Bank Reconciliation Statement
July 31, 20—

Bank statement balance		$277.76
Add: Unrecorded deposit of July 31		400.00
		677.76
Less: Outstanding cheques		
No. 72	$48.60	
No. 76	62.08	
No. 77	44.50	155.18
Correct bank balance		$522.58
Cheque record balance		$533.48
Less: Service charges		10.90
Correct cheque book balance		$522.58

FIGURE 11-12 Bank reconciliation statement prepared by the Hunters

People like the Hunters wisely prepare monthly bank reconciliation statements. This ensures that their records and the bank's records agree. Reconciliation statements will bring to light errors made by the bank or by the depositor. Companies follow similar procedures.

Business Current Account Reconciliation

Fraser Enterprises has a current account with the Bank of Nova Scotia. Each month, the bank sends a statement to Fraser Enterprises and encloses cancelled cheques that were paid out of Fraser's account. The company accountant compares the bank statement balance with the balance in Fraser's Cash account.

A reconciliation statement is then prepared to bring the two into agreement. Figure 11-13 is the bank statement received by Fraser Enterprises. It shows a balance of $1999.12 on June 30. Figure 11-14 on pages 554 and 555 shows the company's cash records. The Cash account shows a balance of $3251.02 on June 30. *Which of the two balances is correct—the bank's or Fraser's? Or is neither correct?*

THE BANK OF NOVA SCOTIA   **SAMPLE**

Fraser Enterprises
125 Murray St.
Ottawa, ON
K1N 5M5

ACCOUNT NUMBER
 31924-06

STATEMENT OF	FROM	TO		PAGE
Current Account	Jun. 1, 20—	Jun. 30, 20—		1

			DATE		
DESCRIPTION	DEBITS	CREDITS	M	D	BALANCE
Balance forward			06	01	780.22
Deposit		395.00✓	06	02	1175.22
Cheque 171	75.00✓		06	05	
Deposit		1200.00✓	06	05	2300.22
Cheque 172	149.50✓		06	10	2150.72
RI	50.00		06	12	
SC	20.00		06	12	
Deposit		250.00✓	06	12	2330.72
Cheque 174	675.00✓		06	19	
Cheque 175	1500.00✓		06	19	
Deposit		1800.00✓	06	19	1955.72
Cheque 176	29.60✓		06	28	1926.12
SC	22.00		06	30	
CM		95.00	06	30	1999.12

NO. OF DEBITS	TOTAL AMOUNT OF DEBITS	NO. OF CREDITS	TOTAL AMOUNT OF CREDITS	NO. OF ENCLOSURES
8	2521.10	5	3740.00	6

FIGURE 11-13 Bank statement received by Fraser Enterprises

CASH RECEIPTS JOURNAL

PAGE 21

DATE		REF. NO.	CUSTOMER OR ACCOUNT	P.R.	CASH DEBIT	SALES DISCOUNTS DEBIT	ACCOUNTS REC. CREDIT	SALES CREDIT	GST PAYABLE CREDIT	PST PAYABLE CREDIT	OTHER ACCOUNTS CREDIT
20—											
May	31		Deposit		3 9 5 00✓						
			May Total		11 7 5 22						
Jun.	5				1 2 0 0 00✓						
	12				2 5 0 00✓						
	19				1 8 0 0 00✓						
	30				2 2 0 00						
					5 4 5 0 00						
					(101)						

Deposits made in June

CASH PAYMENTS JOURNAL   PAGE 32

DATE	CH. NO.	CREDITOR OR ACCOUNT	P.R.	CASH CREDIT	ACCOUNTS PAYABLE DEBIT	GST REFUNDABLE DEBIT	PURCHASES DEBIT	PURCHASES DISCOUNTS CREDIT	OTHER ACCOUNTS DEBIT
20—									
Jun. 1	171			7 5 00✓					
4	172			1 4 9 50✓					
11	173			5 0 00✓					
16	174			6 7 5 00✓					
17	175			1 5 0 0 00✓					
26	176			2 9 60✓					
27	177			6 8 10✓					
28	178			8 2 7 00✓					
				3 3 7 4 20✓					
				(101)					

Cheques written in June

ACCOUNT Cash   No. 101

DATE	PARTICULARS	P.R.	DEBIT	CREDIT	DR. CR.	BALANCE
20—						
May 31	Forwarded	✓			DR.	1 1 7 5 22
Jun. 30	Cash Receipts	CR21	5 4 5 0 00		DR.	6 6 2 5 22
30	Cash Payments	CP32		3 3 7 4 20	DR.	3 2 5 1 02

Cash account in the general ledger

FIGURE 11-14 Fraser Enterprises' cash records

Preparing the Business Bank Reconciliation Statement

To determine the correct balance, a bank reconciliation statement is prepared. This statement will bring the bank's balance into agreement with the company's balance to determine the true, or correct, cash balance. These procedures are followed in preparing the bank reconciliation statement:

Subtract outstanding cheques.

1. Prepare a list of the outstanding cheques. To do this, tick off in the cash payments journal all of the cancelled cheques returned by the bank (see Figure 11-14). Unticked cheques are outstanding; they have not been cashed by the bank. The cancelled cheques are also ticked off on the bank statement debits column (see Figure 11-13). The outstanding cheques (in the case of Fraser Enterprises, Nos. 173, 177, and 178) are subtracted from the bank statement balance on the reconciliation statement to bring the bank's balance into agreement with the company's balance (see Figure 11-15 on the next page).

Add outstanding deposits.

2. Compare the deposits shown in the Cash debit column of the cash receipts journal (see Figure 11-14) with those shown in the credits column of the bank statement (see Figure 11-13). Tick off the deposits on both records. Deposits not recorded on the bank statement are added to the bank statement balance on the reconciliation statement (refer to the $2200 unrecorded June 30 deposit in Figure 11-15).

Add credit memos.
Subtract debit memos.

3. Locate all unticked items on the bank statement. Add unticked items in the credits column to the company's record of the Cash balance (on the cheque book stub). In this case, CM or credit memo indicates $95 in interest must be added. Subtract the unticked items in the debits column of the bank statement from the company's record of the cash balance (on the cheque book stub). Two items must be subtracted in this example: SC (service charges) of $42 and RI of $50. RI stands for returned item and in this case is an NSF cheque. *Note:* The $20 service charge under the RI is the bank charge for the NSF cheque. For more information on NSF cheques, see page 558.

4. Journal entries to adjust the company's Cash account to reflect the unticked items on the bank statement are prepared *after* the bank reconciliation statement. Adjust both the bank's and the company's balance for any obvious errors. For example, cheque amounts could have been recorded incorrectly or arithmetic errors might have been made. If you have problems understanding whether the bank's or the company's balance should be adjusted on a bank reconciliation statement, here are a couple of rules to follow:

    (i) Adjust the balance of whoever makes a mistake (the company or the bank).
    (ii) Adjust the balance of whoever is last to know about an adjustment (e.g., an NSF cheque).

Figure 11-15 is the bank reconciliation statement prepared after completing the preceding four steps. It shows that the correct Cash account balance is $3254.02.

Fraser Enterprises
Bank Reconciliation Statement
June 30, 20—

Bank statement balance		$1999.12
Add: Unrecorded June 30 deposit		2200.00
		4199.12
Less: Outstanding cheques		
No. 173	$ 50.00	
No. 177	68.10	
No. 178	827.00	945.10
Correct bank balance		$3254.02
Cash balance per ledger		$3251.02
Add: Interest earned (CM)		95.00
		3346.02
Less: Service charges	$ 42.00	
RI (NSF cheque)	50.00	92.00
Correct cash balance		$3254.02

FIGURE 11-15 Bank reconciliation statement prepared by Fraser Enterprises

Journal Entries After Bank Reconciliation

After the reconciliation statement has been prepared, the company's Cash account balance must be brought up to date. Remember, Figure 11-14 showed that according to the company's Cash account the cash balance was $3251.02. However, the correct balance is $3254.02, as shown on the reconciliation statement. The company's Cash account is brought up to date by preparing journal entries for any unrecorded items brought to light by the reconciliation statement. A journal entry decreasing Cash is made for items such as service charges, NSF cheques, and interest charged. A journal entry increasing Cash is made for an item such as interest earned that was added by the bank.

Service Charges

The bank had deducted $42 for regular *service charges*; therefore, the company should record an expense and decrease its Cash. The following entry is made:

Jun.	30	Bank Service Charges	4 2 00	
		Cash		4 2 00
		To record bank service charges.		

The following section outlines the procedures for recording NSF cheque service charges.

NSF Cheques

An NSF cheque is usually a customer's cheque deposited by the company that cannot be cashed by the bank because there are *not sufficient funds in the customer's bank account*. Since the bank cannot collect from the writer of the cheque, it will deduct the amount of the cheque from Fraser Enterprises' account. The company will charge the amount plus the bank service charge back to its customer's account as an account receivable and will try to collect the amount. This entry is made:

Jun.	30	Accounts Receivable/G. Symons	7 0 00	
		Cash		7 0 00
		NSF cheque ($50) and bank charges ($20)		
		back to G. Symons.		

Interest Earned

Fraser Enterprises has earned $95 interest on a term deposit. Since the bank has added the $95 to Fraser Enterprises' bank account, the company must now prepare a journal entry to record the $95. The following entry is made to record the *revenue earned* and to increase the Cash account:

Jun.	30	Cash	9 5 00	
		Interest Earned		9 5 00
		To record interest earned on a term deposit.		

Interest Expense

In addition to the entries described above, it is sometimes necessary to record interest expense deducted from a company's bank account. Suppose a company has a bank loan and $120 interest is paid each month. When the bank deducts interest for the loan from the company's bank account, this entry is made on the company's books:

Jun.	30	Interest Expense	1 2 0 00	
		Cash		1 2 0 00
		To record interest on the bank loan deducted		
		by the bank.		

Generally Accepted Accounting Principles and Key Ideas

In this chapter, you learned eight cash control procedures:

- Procedure 1:   Separation of Duties
- Procedure 2:   Immediate Listing of Cash Receipts
- Procedure 3:   Daily Cash Proof
- Procedure 4:   Daily Deposit of Cash
- Procedure 5:   Payment by Cheque
- Procedure 6:   Petty Cash Procedures
- Procedure 7:   Periodic Audit
- Procedure 8:   Monthly Bank Reconciliation

UNIT 26 CHECK YOUR READING

Questions

23. Explain the role of the auditor.

24. Jan O'Dacre has a savings account with the Royal Bank. In which section of its ledger will the bank locate O'Dacre's account—the asset, liability, owner's equity, revenue, or expense section?

25. Will a debit memo increase or decrease the balance of a depositor's account?

26. Will a credit memo increase or decrease the balance of a depositor's account?

27. In which journal is a bank credit memo recorded? A bank debit memo?

28. What is an NSF cheque?

29. (a) What is a bank statement?
     (b) What is a cancelled cheque?
     (c) What is an outstanding cheque?

30. (a) Some cheques that have been issued will not appear on the bank statement. Explain how such a situation can happen.
     (b) Some deposits that have been recorded in the depositor's records may not appear on the bank statement. Explain how such a situation can happen.

31. Give examples of certain items that appear on a bank statement but not on the depositor's records.

32. A bank reconciliation statement brings into agreement two sets of records. What are they?

33. Who prepares the bank reconciliation statement, the bank or the depositor?

34. When a company prepares a bank reconciliation statement, to what is the balance on the bank statement compared?

35. What is the general journal entry to record a customer's cheque returned NSF?
36. Does cash control mean anything more than procedures used to prevent losses from fraud or theft? Explain.
37. List eight principles of cash control.
38. Which of the eight principles of cash control could be used by a small business that does not have enough employees for a complete separation of duties?

UNIT 26 APPLY YOUR KNOWLEDGE

Exercises Part A

10. Record the following transactions in a general journal for I. Noren Rowing Machines Ltd.:

Nov. 7 Cash sales slips totalled $3295 plus $230.65 GST. Cash was deposited.
7 Issued Sales Invoice 87-B to A. Michaels, terms 3/15, n/30, amount $2000, GST $140.
8 Received bank credit memo for $215 interest earned by the company.
9 Received bank debit memo for $25, plus $1.75 GST, for the annual charge for a safety deposit box.
15 Received cheque from A. Michaels, $2075.80 for Invoice 87-B less $64.20 discount. Cheque was deposited.
30 Received bank debit memo for $14.50 for service charges on current account.

11. Record the following transactions in a general journal for I. Noren Rowing Machines Ltd.:

Dec. 1 Received bank credit memo for a $10 000 loan granted and deposited in the company account, term two months, annual interest at 12 percent payable monthly.
31 Received bank debit memo for $100 deducted from the company account for interest on the loan.
Jan. 31 Received bank debit memo for $10 100 deducted from the company account ($10 000 repayment of the bank loan, $100 interest on the loan).

12. At the end of August, Pat and Bob Hunter have a balance of $1240 in their cheque record. Their bank statement balance is $1574.75. The bank statement contains a deduction of $10.60 for service charges. A comparison of the cheques issued in the Hunters' "cheque record and the cheques cashed on the statement indicates that Cheque 72 for $48.60, Cheque 86 for $250, and Cheque 89 for $46.75 are outstanding. Prepare a bank reconciliation statement dated August 31.

13. At September 30, Pat and Bob Hunter have a balance of $865.84 in their cheque record. The bank statement shows a balance of $1578.40. The bank statement contains a service charge deduction of $12.54 and a deposit made on September 15 for $400. This deposit is not recorded in the Hunters' cheque record. Cheque 92 for $48.60, Cheque 94 for $89, and Cheque 95 for $187.50 are outstanding. Prepare the September reconciliation statement.

14. (a) Prepare the April reconciliation statement for I. Finci Decorators using the following information:

Company Records:
- Cash account balance is $1990.11.
- These cheques are recorded in the cash payments journal but *not* on the bank statement:
  No. 161 $49.50   No. 170 $150   No. 176 $75
- A deposit for $400 was recorded in the cash receipts journal on April 30 but did not appear on the bank statement.

Bank Statement:
- Bank statement balance is $1839.86.
- Bank service charges of $24.75 are shown on the bank statement.

(b) In a general journal, record any entries required to bring the company records up to date.

15. (a) Prepare the May reconciliation statement for I. Finci Decorators using the following information:
- Cash account balance is $2090.51.
- Bank statement balance is $1684.51.
- These cheques were recorded in the cash payments journal but did not appear on the bank statement:
  No. 186 $75   No. 193 $297.30   No. 199 $924.60
- A deposit for $1910 dated May 31 was recorded in the cash receipts journal but did not appear on the bank statement.
- Service charges of $25.75 are shown on the bank statement.
- A cheque for $37.50 has been cashed (correctly) by the bank but was incorrectly recorded in the company's cash payments journal as $375.50. The cheque was issued for the purchase of office supplies.
- An NSF cheque for $85.15 appeared on the bank statement as a returned item. It was deducted by the bank. It had been received from J. Barkley and was recorded in the company's cash receipts journal. A bank charge of $20 was levied.

(b) In a general journal, record any entries required to bring the company records up to date.

Exercises Part B

16. Record the following selected transactions in a general journal for The Sundowner:

May   1   Established a petty cash fund by issuing Cheque 178 for $100.

        5   Cash sales slips for the week totalled $2400. Sales tax on taxable sales was $84, GST was $168. Total cash $2652.

        5   The cash proof indicated a shortage of $1.50.

        8   Issued Cheque 179 for $795 + $55.65 GST for a cash purchase of merchandise from Carswell Ltd.

     10   Issued sales invoices (all sales tax exempt, terms 2/10, n/30):
No. 818, $500 + $35 GST = $535 to Warrendon Ltd.
No. 819, $79.80 + $5.59 GST = $85.39 to Tisi and Zotta.
No. 820, $465 + $32.55 GST = $497.55 to J. Mocson & Sons.
No. 821, $720 + $50.40 GST = $770.40 to L. Gojmerac.

     12   Cash sales slips for the week totalled $1700. Sales tax was $53, GST $119. Total $1872.

     15   Replenished the petty cash. Issued Cheque 180. Summary of petty cash vouchers:
Office Expense $33
Advertising Expense   33
Postage Expense   25
GST Refundable   6

     15   Received a cheque for $83.68 from Tisi & Zotta in payment of Invoice 819 less $1.71 discount.

     16   The cash proof indicated that cash was over by $2.15.

     19   Received a bank debit memo for $83.68 plus $10 service charge. Tisi & Zotta's cheque was returned NSF.

     20   Purchased merchandise on account from Finlays Inc., $915 + $64.05 GST, terms 30 days.

     20   Received a cheque for $487.60 from J. Mocson & Sons in payment of Invoice 820 less $9.95 discount.

     29   The monthly bank reconciliation was prepared. The bank statement included a debit of $22.50 for bank service charges.

17. M. Monroe Ltd. has a current account with the Bank of Nova Scotia. The October bank statement that follows was sent to Monroe by the bank.

Bank Statement:

THE BANK OF NOVA SCOTIA

M. Monroe Ltd.
575 Goulding St.
Winnipeg, MB
R3G 2S3

ACCOUNT NUMBER
81720-00

STATEMENT OF	FROM	TO	PAGE
Current Account	Sep. 30, 20—	Oct. 31, 20—	1

DESCRIPTION	DEBITS	CREDITS	DATE M	D	BALANCE
Balance forward			09	30	2690.50
Deposit		700.00	10	01	3390.50
Deposit		200.00	10	05	3590.50
Cheque 301	200.00		10	08	3390.50
Deposit		75.00	10	10	3465.50
Cheque 303	1200.00		10	15	2265.50
Deposit		225.00	10	19	2490.50
Deposit		600.00	10	22	3090.50
Cheque 304	50.00		10	23	3040.50
Cheque 305	17.00		10	28	3023.50
SC	22.25		10	29	3001.25
RI	75.00		10	31	2926.25
DM	20.00		10	31	2906.25

NO. OF DEBITS	TOTAL AMOUNT OF DEBITS	NO. OF CREDITS	TOTAL AMOUNT OF CREDITS	NO. OF ENCLOSURES
6	1584.25	5	1800.00	5

Cheques:

The bank also sent the following four cancelled cheques—Nos. 301, 303, 304, and 305—and an NSF cheque for $75 that had been deposited by M. Monroe Ltd. The NSF cheque was from Bloom & Co. Inc., a customer. A bank debit memo for $20 (NSF charge) was also sent.

M. MONROE LTD.
575 Goulding St.
Winnipeg, MB R3G 2S3

NO. 301

Oct. 1, 20—
Date

PAY TO THE
ORDER OF Malcolm Enterprises-------CANCELLED----------$200.00

SUM OF Two hundred-----------------------00/100 DOLLARS

THE BANK OF NOVA SCOTIA
319 Graham Ave.
Winnipeg, MB R3C 2Y5

M. Monroe
M. MONROE LTD.

301 ⑆70276-002⑈817201⑆00

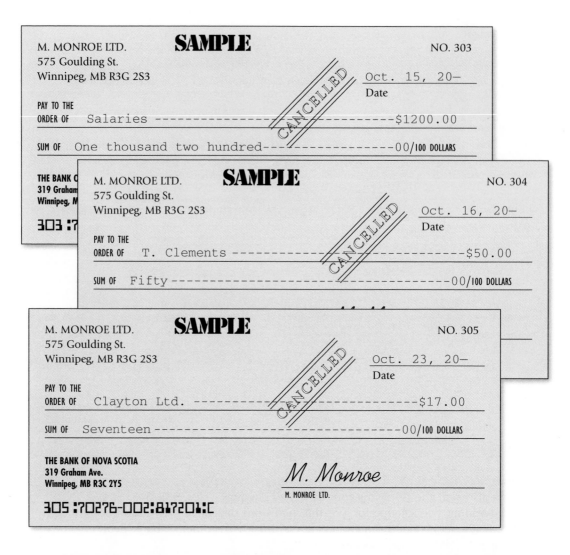

M. MONROE LTD.   **SAMPLE**   NO. 303
575 Goulding St.
Winnipeg, MB R3G 2S3   Oct. 15, 20—
                                                              Date

PAY TO THE
ORDER OF   Salaries -----------------------------------$1200.00

SUM OF   One thousand two hundred----------------00/100 DOLLARS

THE BANK O
319 Graham
Winnipeg, M

303 :7

M. MONROE LTD.   **SAMPLE**   NO. 304
575 Goulding St.
Winnipeg, MB R3G 2S3   Oct. 16, 20—
                                                              Date

PAY TO THE
ORDER OF   T. Clements -----------------------------$50.00

SUM OF   Fifty------------------------------------00/100 DOLLARS

M. MONROE LTD.   **SAMPLE**   NO. 305
575 Goulding St.
Winnipeg, MB R3G 2S3   Oct. 23, 20—
                                                              Date

PAY TO THE
ORDER OF   Clayton Ltd. -----------------------$17.00

SUM OF   Seventeen--------------------------------00/100 DOLLARS

THE BANK OF NOVA SCOTIA
319 Graham Ave.   *M. Monroe*
Winnipeg, MB R3C 2Y5   ─────────────
                                                  M. MONROE LTD.

305 :70276-002:81720l:C

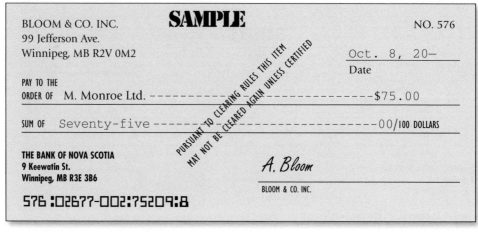

BLOOM & CO. INC.   **SAMPLE**   NO. 576
99 Jefferson Ave.
Winnipeg, MB R2V 0M2   Oct. 8, 20—
                                                             Date

PAY TO THE
ORDER OF   M. Monroe Ltd. ---------------------------$75.00

SUM OF   Seventy-five---------------------------00/100 DOLLARS

THE BANK OF NOVA SCOTIA
9 Keewatin St.   *A. Bloom*
Winnipeg, MB R3E 3B6   ─────────────
                                                  BLOOM & CO. INC.

576 :02677-002:75209:8

PAGE 14

CASH RECEIPTS JOURNAL

DATE		REF. NO.	CUSTOMER OR ACCOUNT	P.R.	CASH DEBIT	SALES DISCOUNTS DEBIT	ACCOUNTS REC. CREDIT	SALES CREDIT	GST PAYABLE CREDIT	PST PAYABLE CREDIT	OTHER ACCOUNTS CREDIT
20—											
Oct.	1		Cash Sales		7 0 0 00						
	5		J. Bentley		2 0 0 00						
	10		Bloom & Co. Inc.		7 5 00						
	19		T. Gabriel		2 2 5 00						
	22		Cash Sales		6 0 0 00						
	31		Cash Sales		4 5 0 00						
					2 2 5 0 00						
					(101)						

Company Records:
The cash records kept by M. Monroe Ltd. are illustrated below:

CASH PAYMENTS JOURNAL PAGE 17

DATE	CH. NO.	CREDITOR OR ACCOUNT	P.R.	CASH CREDIT	ACCOUNTS PAYABLE DEBIT	GST REFUNDABLE DEBIT	PURCHASES DEBIT	PURCHASES DISCOUNTS CREDIT	OTHER ACCOUNTS DEBIT
20— Jun. 1	301	Purchases		2 0 0 00					
8	302	A. Baker		1 0 0 00					
15	303	Salaries		1 2 0 0 00					
16	304	T. Clements		5 0 00					
23	305	Supplies		1 7 00					
24	306	Aster Ltd.		2 5 0 00					
30	307	Purchases		1 7 0 00					
				1 9 8 7 00					
				(101)					

ACCOUNT Cash No. 101

DATE	PARTICULARS	P.R.	DEBIT	CREDIT	DR. CR.	BALANCE
20— Oct. 1	Forwarded	✓			DR.	2 6 9 0 50
31	Cash Receipts	CR14	2 2 5 0 00		DR.	4 9 4 0 50
31	Cash Payments	CP17		1 9 8 7 00	DR.	2 9 5 3 50

Tasks Required:

(a) Prepare the bank reconciliation statement dated October 31, 20—.

(b) Prepare the necessary journal entries.

Computer Accounting

Point-of-Sale Terminals

When you studied cash control Principle 2, you learned that cash sales are recorded *as soon as they occur*. The customer assists in the control procedure by expecting to see the sale recorded, by visually checking the amounts recorded on the terminal or cash register, and by accepting a tape receipt like the one illustrated in Figure 11-16.

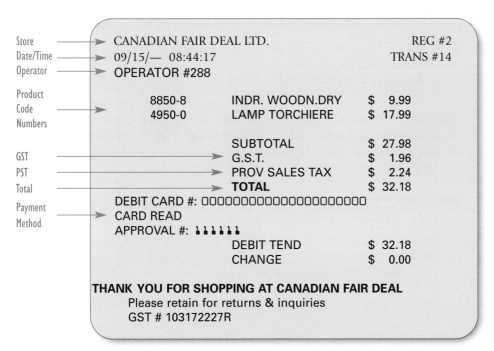

FIGURE 11-16 Customer receipt

Figure 11-16 is a customer receipt printed by a point-of-sale terminal in a Canadian Fair Deal store. A point-of-sale terminal is an electronic cash register connected to a computer.

When a sale to a customer is being recorded, the computer terminal operator enters the product code number, for example 52-4950-0, the code for the lamp. The computer accesses its database of information and prints the following:

- identification of store, terminal operator, and date;
- product code and description;
- price;
- GST;
- PST; and
- method of payment.

Linking Sales to the Computer

Each point-of-sale terminal is connected to the Canadian Fair Deal Ltd. store computer. The computer's memory contains a database of product information for all products in the store. The database includes, for every item:

- code, selling price, description;
- amount on hand;
- order quantity; and
- supplier and cost price.

As each sale is made, the customer receipt is printed; at the same time, the database is updated. Each time a product is sold, the balance of that item is decreased and the number of sales of that item is increased. At the end of each day, the computer prints an up-to-date list that shows for all items:

- volume of sales;
- new balance on hand; and
- items that need to be re-ordered.

When each operator completes a work shift, the operator turns in the cash and the sales totals for the shift. The computer prints sales information that is used to "balance the cash" to determine if errors in recording sales, making change, etc., have occurred.

Questions

1. The Canadian Fair Deal system illustrates several control principles outlined in this chapter. What are they?
2. Explain the procedure probably followed at the end of each shift to "balance the cash" for each operator.

Computer-Prepared Bank Reconciliation Statements

Throughout this chapter, you have prepared bank reconciliation statements *manually.* Here is an example of how a computer program can be used to prepare a bank reconciliation statement.

QuickBooks Integrated Accounting System

Chris Chapman is the executive assistant for a small software developer. Among her many duties are desktop publishing, dealing with vendors and customers, and performing all the accounting functions for the firm. QuickBooks software is used to do the accounting from the initial budget preparation to the financial statements. Every month Chris uses the program to prepare the monthly bank reconciliation statement.

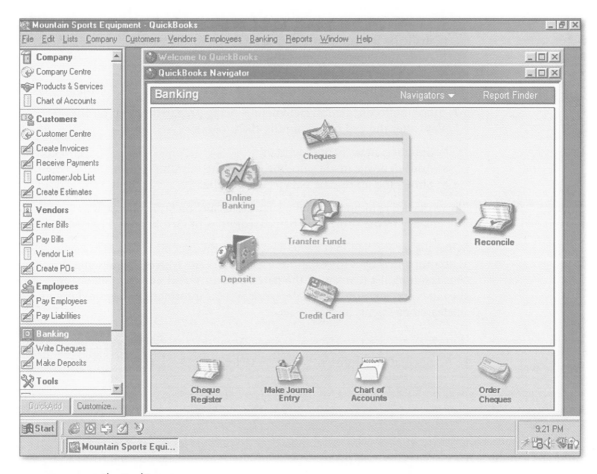

FIGURE 11-17 The Banking menu

We asked Chris how she prepares the bank reconciliation statement. She provided this series of explanations for the bank reconciliation report shown in Figure 11-18 that she prepared on October 5. It is the report for the month of September.

1. Go to the QuickBooks main menu and select **Banking** (Figure 11-17).
2. From the Banking menu, select **Reconcile**. A bank reconciliation form will appear on the screen.
3. Select the account to be reconciled and enter the ending balance from the statement received from the company's bank.
4. Enter any unrecorded bank charges or interest that appears on the bank statement.
5. Select **Reconcile**.
6. The reconciliation report appears on the screen. The program automatically performs the following steps:

➤ Shows the previous month's ending balance	$231,419.54
➤ Subtracts all the cheques and payments that have been "cleared" by the bank	84,894.77
➤ Adds all deposits recorded by the bank	43,027.18
➤ Shows a cleared balance of	189,551.95

➤ Subtracts all "uncleared" items (payments that have been
made by the company but not recorded by the bank)   33,296.41
➤ Adds any deposits made but not recorded   0
➤ Shows the new bank and Cash account balance at the
month's end $156,255.54

7. Since the reconciliation statement is being prepared several business
days after the end of the month, the program:

➤ Subtracts new cheques written   9,983.80
➤ Adds deposits made since the end of the month   9,269.72
➤ Shows the up-to-date balance on October 5 $155,541.46

The reconciled bank and accounting records balance on September 30 is $156 255.54.
The balance in the company's bank account as of October 5 is $155 541.46.

When the reconciliation statement is printed, the statement shown in Figure 11-18
is accompanied by a list of all the cleared and uncleared cheques and deposits.
This is a long list that shows the dates, amounts, and payees of all cheques and
the dates and amounts of the deposits. Similar information is printed for all the
uncleared payments and deposits.

Reconciliation Report   October 5, 20—

Bank account – General account reconciled for the period ended 30/09/—

Cleared Transactions

Previous Balance		$231,419.54
Cleared Cheques	55 items	−84,894.77
Cleared Deposits and Other Credits	4 items	43,027.18
Cleared Balance		189,551.95

Uncleared Transactions

Uncleared Cheques and Payments	31 items	−33,296.41
Uncleared Deposits and Other Credits	0 items	0.00

New Transactions

Account balance as of 30/09/— (statement closing date)		156,255.54
New Cheques and Payments	16 items	−9,983.80
New Deposits and Other Credits	2 items	9,269.72

Current Account Balance		155,541.46

FIGURE 11-18 The bank reconciliation statement

Questions

1. How is the computer printout illustrated in Figure 11-18 similar to a manually prepared bank reconciliation statement? How is it different?

2. What were the cash balances for Chris' company on

   (a) September 1?
   (b) September 30?
   (c) October 5?

3. Describe the steps and work saved by using software such as QuickBooks to prepare the bank reconciliation statement.

COMPUTER ASSIGNMENTS

1. Use general ledger software to complete exercise 16 on page 562. Print the journal.

2. Format a spreadsheet that will do a bank reconciliation statement. Use the format in Figure 11-15 on page 557. Your format should have these features:

- the bank statement balance;
- outstanding deposits (add);
- outstanding cheques (subtract);
- a three-line heading;
- the correct bank statement balance;
- the general ledger cash balance;
- bank service charges (subtract)
- NSF cheques (subtract); and
- the correct general ledger Cash balance.

3. Use the spreadsheet to complete exercises 12 and 13 on pages 560 and 561. Print the reconciliation statement.

4. Use the spreadsheet format prepared in assignment 2 above to complete exercises 14 (a) and 15 (a) on page 561.

WEB EXTENSIONS

www.pearsoned.ca/
principlesofaccounting

Internet Study Guide

- Complete the Chapter 8 review.
- Complete the Chapter 8 definitions.
- Complete the Chapter 8 online test.

Web Links

Visit the Web Links section at the Pearson Education web site to find links to entrepreneurship sites. Provide examples of the information found at these sites that would assist someone starting a small business.

Case Studies

CASE 1 Cash Control

Nick Farrell performed all of the accounting tasks for Candita Sales, a small merchandising firm. Finding himself in financial difficulty, he devised the following plan to steal money from the business.

He believed he could, at any time, remove an amount of cash from the daily deposit and replace the cash with a cheque received in the mail from a customer. He would not include the cheque in the list of cheques received for the day. To prevent the customer from complaining about an incorrect amount owing, the following general journal entry would be made by Nick for the amount of the cheque and posted to the ledger accounts affected:

Sales Returns and Allowances		1 0 0 00	
Accounts Receivable/Customer Account			1 0 0 00
To record goods returned today.			

(a) Would Candita Sales' general ledger be out of balance?
(b) Would the control account balance to the schedule of accounts receivable?
(c) Would this action be discovered or prevented by current cash control procedures? Explain.
(d) What are the weaknesses in Candita Sales' cash control system?
(e) What procedures would you implement in a small business such as Candita Sales to have effective cash control?

CASE 2 Periodic Audits

Faye Borowski worked for five years as a receptionist-secretary for Dr. P. Chau, a dentist. Her duties included billing patients, receiving cash from customers, issuing receipts, depositing money, and handling the patients' accounts. One day, Faye reduced a patient's account to zero by mistake. A month later, the patient paid $50 that was actually still owing. Faye *pocketed* the $50.

Yielding to temptation, Faye began to embezzle money regularly from Dr. Chau. When money was received from patients, she would lower the patients' accounts and prepare a bank deposit but keep some of the cash for herself. The deposit was always lower than the cash received. For example, one week she received $1900 from customers, kept $200, and deposited $1700. She lowered the customers' accounts by $1900. Over a period of 30 weeks she stole $3500. She is now awaiting trial on criminal charges! *How was she caught?*

While Faye was in Bermuda on a two-week holiday, Dr. Chau's accountant prepared the annual income statement and balance sheet. The accountant arrived at a normal profit for the year but noticed that the balance in the bank account was considerably lower than in previous years. A bank reconciliation statement was prepared but it was out by thousands of dollars. A comparison of the receipt copies issued to customers and the weekly deposit slips showed what had happened.

Faye had a surprise waiting for her on her return from Bermuda!

(a) Which principles of accounting cash control were not followed in the dentist's accounting system?
(b) Which principle resulted in the discovery of the theft?
(c) Write a short report for Dr. Chau, outlining how you would improve the system of cash control.

Internal Control

CASE 3

Lafleur Cleaners operates a drycleaning business with nine depots around the city. Customers leave their clothing at the depots. It is picked up and taken to a large, efficient cleaning plant in the centre of the city and returned the next day to the depots. Each depot is small and is operated by one person. A four-part cash sales slip is prepared for each customer's clothing. A copy accompanies the clothes to the central plant; a copy stays at the depot; a copy is given to the customer; and the fourth copy is sent to the head office's accounting department after the cleaning has been paid for. Once the customer has picked up the cleaning, it is possible for the person operating a depot to destroy all copies of the cash sales slip and to pocket the money received from the customer.

Prepare a control procedure to prevent an employee from taking company money.

Petty Cash System

CASE 4

Colton Couriers is a small five-employee business considering the implementation of a petty cash system. One of the employees asks for your advice in preparing procedures for the petty cash system. The system being considered would allow any employee to write cheques to cover costs incurred. Receipts would not be required unless the request was greater than $200.

(a) Explain to the employee any concerns you have with their suggested system.
(b) Prepare a report that recommends the procedures to be included for a proper petty cash system.
(c) Explain which accounting principles are used in your system.

Cash Short and Over Problems

CASE 5

Assume you are the owner of Brighton Cleaners. There is one person handling all transactions in your cleaning outlet. This person meets about 75 customers a day, organizes pick-ups and deliveries, prepares cash sales slips, and handles the cash. At the end of each day, you, the owner, count and deposit all of the cash and prepare a daily cash proof. The cash never seems to balance. In the past week, the results were:

Jun.	13	Short	75¢
	14	Over	5¢
	15	Short	15¢
	16	Over	99¢
	17	Short	25¢

You realize that your one clerk is responsible for these shortages and overages but also that the clerk is very busy. There is no time for a coffee break and only 40 minutes for lunch.

(a) Would you make the clerk pay for cash shortages? Why or why not?
(b) What changes do you think should be considered in the operation of this business?

CASE 6   Cash Shortages

You are an accountant for Laura's, a department store. Sales for the year are $2 million and 25 cashiers work in the store. Cashiers prepare a daily cash proof at the end of their shift. At the end of the year, you determine that there are 125 debits that account for $176 in the Cash Short and Over account. There are 91 credits that account for $49 in Cash Short and Over.

(a) Should you be concerned about the resulting $127 net debit in Cash Short and Over?
(b) What action, if any, would you recommend to the company's senior accountant?
(c) What additional information would you like to have?

CASE 7   Bank Transfer of Funds

John Southcott has been transferred by his company from Toronto to British Columbia. He has $1200 in a bank account in Toronto. Rather than withdraw the $1200 and take it with him, John asks the bank to transfer the money to a B.C. branch of the bank. When John arrives in B.C., he receives a statement from his new bank that shows a balance in his account of $12 000.

(a) Does the extra $10 800 in his account belong to John?
(b) How could such an error occur?
(c) Should John contact his bank? Why or why not?

⑩ Career Education Activities

Starting Your Own Business? Why Not!

Not everyone has the ability to start and run a business. A variety of skills and personality traits are required. This activity is designed to help you determine if owning and running a business is for you.

The first step is to develop an idea and then develop a "business plan." The plan should include:

- market research results;
- sources of financing;
- long- and short-term sales forecasts;
- startup and operating budgets;
- advertising and promotion plans;
- accounting procedures;
- government requirements; and
- legal advice.

Assistance and advice about developing a business plan and starting a business are available from local universities, provincial and federal governments, and many other sources.

How About You?

Are you cut out to be a business owner? These questions might help you decide. If you are able to answer "yes" to most questions, then perhaps you have the necessary characteristics to run a business.

1. I enjoy taking initiative and being my own boss. Y/N

2. Most people would describe me as energetic. Y/N

3. I am organized and develop personal goals. Y/N

4. I have a lot of confidence in my own abilities and skills. Y/N

5. I am prepared to take calculated risks where other people hesitate. Y/N

6. I know how to handle myself with large groups of people. Y/N

7. I have a problem-solving orientation; I like to work on difficult tasks. Y/N

8. I exercise regularly to stay in shape. Y/N

9. I have set goals for myself that are challenging, yet attainable. Y/N

10. Rather than being discouraged by failures and setbacks, I learn from them. Y/N

11. I adjust well to changing circumstances. Y/N

12. I see business opportunities all around me. Y/N

13. Personal accomplishment is more important to me than personal security. Y/N

14. I am competitive; I strive to attain self-imposed standards. Y/N

15. I am willing to change my immediate objectives, as situations dictate. Y/N

16. I am not a quitter. Y/N

17. I have the ability to find creative, innovative solutions to problems. Y/N

18. I have good "people skills"; I enjoy working with people and can motivate others to work for me. Y/N

2. Developing Your Public Relations Skills

If you're employed in any job that involves dealing with the public, it's very important to learn how to be tactful and pleasant with people. As you read the following description of an incident that happened in a bank, imagine that you are the teller involved in the story.

How to Annoy a Good Customer!

Mr. and Mrs. Doe have two accounts in a bank where they have been dealing for 12 years. One is a joint chequing account and the other a true savings account in Mrs. Doe's name. Mr. Doe's monthly paycheque is deposited directly to the chequing account by his employer and he receives a pay statement that shows the amount and date of the deposit. Each month, Mrs. Doe visits the bank to withdraw money for household expenses.

As the time for one monthly visit drew near, the Does were looking over their bank books and realized that a substantial amount had built up in their chequing account. They received no interest on this account. They decided that during Mrs. Doe's regular visit to the bank, she should transfer some of the money to her savings account.

Since it was her habit to visit the bank early in the day, Mrs. Doe always took Mr. Doe's pay statement with her in case the bank had not had time to enter the deposit yet. When her turn at the teller's wicket came, Mrs. Doe found herself facing a new teller to whom she gave her withdrawal slip and request for the transfer to her savings account. The teller disappeared for a moment, then returned and announced in a loud voice, "You don't have enough money in your account." This did not surprise Mrs. Doe too much, since she realized that the pay for the month might not have been entered in their account yet. She explained this to the teller and showed her the pay statement that had that day's date. The teller glanced at the statement and said indignantly, "Well, just because you got this today doesn't mean the money is here today. It could take a couple of days." Mrs. Doe was surprised and embarrassed and asked the teller to check it again. The teller refused.

Mrs. Doe left, very angry. She telephoned the bank manager later in the day and described what had happened.

For Discussion

(a) What do you think the bank manager might have said to Mrs. Doe? To the teller?
(b) How would you have behaved differently in the teller's position?
(c) What changes would you recommend in the bank's recording procedures?

Career Profile

André Potvin aleady knew in high school that he had an interest in personal finance. At an early age, he had begun to inquire about the stock market and how to make trades. At the age of 12, he began to make trades with the help of his father through a brokerage account in trust.

At age 18, André could legally make trades and own shares.

In high school, André took all of the available business courses, including accounting, entrepreneurship, marketing, and economics. He pursued his interest and his academics by enrolling in a business program at university, where he took courses in accounting, marketing, finance, information technology, economics, and math.

André traded throughout the four years and earned enough money to help finance his tuition. He broadened his experience by working in the shipping department at a warehouse, and also picked up contract work developing web pages for small companies. Web page development was a skill he learned on his own while attending university.

After university, André took some time to travel to Europe and develop his language skills, becoming proficient in Spanish.

After returning to Canada from Europe, André decided to become a day trader. Day trading involves buying and selling the same security (stock) on the same day. This type of trading involves considerable risk and traders are advised not to trade any amount that they cannot afford to lose.

André paid for an intensive two-week course, Direct Access Electronic Trading. After completing the course examination, André began trading on a regular basis as a day trader. He found that his business courses in accounting and finance provided him with a solid financial background

for this field of work. He continued to upgrade his skills by reading technical trading resources and speaking with other traders. André enjoyed the idea of being his own boss and being able to work his own hours, either from home or from the offices of the securities firm.

After five months of trading, André decided to pursue his interest in marketing with a small start-up organization.

For Discussion

(a) Outline the different methods André used to pay for his university program. What potential sources of revenue are available to you to finance your education?

(b) In addition to high school and university courses, what avenues did André pursue to improve his skills and knowledge?

Performance Task 4

Sandy's Personnel Agency

What Learning You Will Demonstrate

You will:

- prepare cheques and daily deposits;
- demonstrate an understanding of the basic accounting procedures for preparing a bank reconciliation statement;
- record bank reconciliation transactions in the journals and ledgers of a business;
- demonstrate an understanding that the tasks of handling and recording cash are separated for control purposes; and
- prepare cheque stubs using a computer spreadsheet.

The Task

Sandy's Personnel Agency, a firm that locates job applicants for clients who have positions to be filled, has hired you to solve a discrepancy between their records and the information received from the bank. You have also been requested to design a spreadsheet program to streamline the completion of cheque stubs.

Your teacher may require you to complete this project in groups of three or four students. The objective of the group work is to develop your teamwork skills.

Procedure

1. Cheques and Deposits (Part A)

   (a) Write cheques and prepare deposit slips for the month of June. You will require eight blank cheques, with stubs, and three current account deposit slips.
   (b) Complete the cheque stub first before you write the cheque.
   (c) Decrease the cheque stub balance each time a cheque is written. Increase the balance each time a deposit is made. Assume another employee is responsible for journalizing and posting the transactions.

2. Bank Information (Part B)

   (a) Examine the information from the bank. Why do the balances not agree? What is the correct balance?
   (b) Prepare a bank reconciliation statement. What entries would be made by the employee responsible for journalizing transactions to update Sandy's Personnel Agency's records?
   (c) Explain why the same employee does not write the cheques and record the entries. What accounting principle is involved?

3. Spreadsheet

Using a computer and spreadsheet program:
(a) Prepare a format to complete the cheque stubs.
(b) Prepare the cheque stubs for Sandy's Personnel Agency using your spreadsheet.

Materials Required

- Cheques and Deposits, Part A
- Bank Information, Part B
- Banking forms: eight cheques with stubs and three deposit slips.

Assessment Criteria

Examine the rubric. Note the descriptions of the performance criteria and the levels of achievement.

PART A

Cheques and Deposits

Jun. 1   Record the bank balance of $4350 on the first cheque stub (Cheque 21).

  1   Write Cheque 21 for $133.74 + $8.67 GST = $142.41 to Willson's Ltd. to pay for a cash purchase of office supplies.

  5   Write Cheque 22 to Bell Canada for May telephone service, $128.78 + $8.35 GST = $137.13.

  5   Prepare a deposit slip to include:

Cheques	Bills	Coins
$164.50 from Atlas Ltd.	2 × $20	$5.50
$135.72 from Murphy Gamble Ltd.	6 × $5	

  8   Issue Cheque 23 for $254.67 + $17.83 GST = $272.50 to Advertising Specialties Ltd.; desk pad sets to be used as gifts to clients.

  10   Issue Cheque 24 for $715 + $50.05 GST = $765.05 to Sherman's Real Estate; June rent.

  11   Issue Cheque 25 to Welland Hydro for $143.69 + $10.06 GST = $153.75; electricity.

  12   Prepare a deposit slip to include:

Cheques	Bills	Coins
$172.50 from Warrendon's Ltd.	9 × $20	$40.75
	15 × $10	
	3 × $5	

18 Write Cheque 26 to Echo Systems Ltd. for $23.85 + $1.67 GST = $25.52; repairs to office equipment.

26 Issue Cheque 27 to *Welland Evening Tribune* for $325.65 + $22.80 GST = $348.45; advertising.

27 Issue Cheque 28 to R. Parent Insurance Ltd. for $76.65 + $5.37 GST = $82.02; insurance of office equipment.

29 Prepare a deposit slip to include:

Cheques	Bills	Coins
$187 from Welmet Co.	5 × $20	$25
$220 from Union Carbide	6 × $10	

PART B

Bank Information

The following documents are received from the bank at the end of June: the bank statement, a bank debit memo, and a group of cancelled cheques. Notice that the ending balance on the bank statement does not agree with the balance on the last cheque stub prepared in Part A.

THE BANK OF NOVA SCOTIA **SAMPLE**

Account Number: 21840-00   Date: June 22, 20—

DEBIT   Interest charges $150.00

Authorized by: *B.V.*   Checked by: *L.D.*   Entry made by: L.S.

This slip must be initialled by an authorized signing officer.

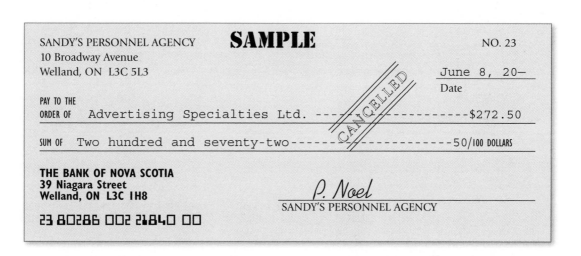

SANDY'S PERSONNEL AGENCY   **SAMPLE**   NO. 22
10 Broadway Avenue
Welland, ON L3C 5L3   June 5, 20—
                                               Date

PAY TO THE
ORDER OF Bell Canada ------------------- CANCELLED -------$137.13

SUM OF One hundred and thirty-seven------ ------------13/100 DOLLARS

THE BANK OF NOVA SCOTIA
39 Niagara Street
Welland, ON L3C 1H8   *P. Noel*
                                    SANDY'S PERSONNEL AGENCY

22 80286 002 21840 00

SANDY'S PERSONNEL AGENCY   **SAMPLE**   NO. 23
10 Broadway Avenue
Welland, ON L3C 5L3   June 8, 20—
                                               Date

PAY TO THE
ORDER OF Advertising Specialties Ltd. --- CANCELLED ----------$272.50

SUM OF Two hundred and seventy-two------ ------------50/100 DOLLARS

THE BANK OF NOVA SCOTIA
39 Niagara Street
Welland, ON L3C 1H8   *P. Noel*
                                    SANDY'S PERSONNEL AGENCY

23 80286 002 21840 00

SANDY'S PERSONNEL AGENCY   **SAMPLE**   NO. 21
10 Broadway Avenue
Welland, ON L3C 5L3   June 1, 20—
                                               Date

PAY TO THE
ORDER OF Willson's Ltd. ----------------- CANCELLED ----------$142.41

SUM OF One hundred and forty-two-------- ------------41/100 DOLLARS

THE BANK OF NOVA SCOTIA
39 Niagara Street
Welland, ON L3C 1H8   *P. Noel*
                                    SANDY'S PERSONNEL AGENCY

21 80286 002 21840 00

THE BANK OF NOVA SCOTIA **SAMPLE**

Sandy's Personnel Agency
10 Broadway Avenue
Welland, ON
L3C 5L3

ACCOUNT NUMBER
21840-00

STATEMENT OF	FROM	TO		PAGE
Current Account	Jun. 1, 20—	Jun. 30, 20—		1

			DATE		
DESCRIPTION	DEBITS	CREDITS	M	D	BALANCE
Balance Forward			06	01	4350.00
Cheque 22	137.13		06	08	4212.87
Deposit		375.75	06	08	4588.62
Cheque 23	272.50		06	12	4316.12
Cheque 21	142.41		06	14	4173.17
Deposit		558.25	06	15	4731.96
Cheque 24	765.05		06	18	3966.19
Cheque 26	25.52		06	21	3941.39
DM	150.00		06	22	3791.39
Cheque 28	82.02		06	28	3709.37
SC	22.00		06	29	3687.37

NO. OF DEBITS	TOTAL AMOUNT OF DEBITS	NO. OF CREDITS	TOTAL AMOUNT OF CREDITS	NO. OF ENCLOSURES
8	1596.63	2	934.00	7

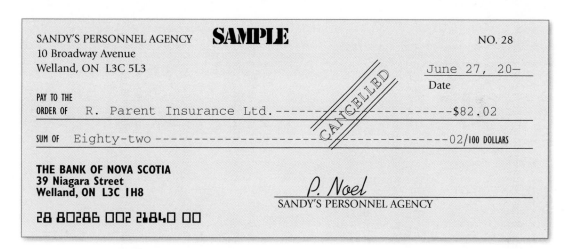

SANDY'S PERSONNEL AGENCY   **SAMPLE**   NO. 24

10 Broadway Avenue
Welland, ON L3C 5L3

June 10, 20—
Date

PAY TO THE
ORDER OF   Sherman's Real Estate ----------------CANCELLED----------------$765.05

SUM OF   Seven hundred and sixty-five--------------------05/100 DOLLARS

THE BANK OF NOVA SCOTIA
39 Niagara Street
Welland, ON L3C 1H8

P. Noel
SANDY'S PERSONNEL AGENCY

24 80286 002 21840 00

SANDY'S PERSONNEL AGENCY   **SAMPLE**   NO. 28

10 Broadway Avenue
Welland, ON L3C 5L3

June 27, 20—
Date

PAY TO THE
ORDER OF   R. Parent Insurance Ltd. ------CANCELLED----------$82.02

SUM OF   Eighty-two ----------------------------02/100 DOLLARS

THE BANK OF NOVA SCOTIA
39 Niagara Street
Welland, ON L3C 1H8

P. Noel
SANDY'S PERSONNEL AGENCY

28 80286 002 21840 00

SANDY'S PERSONNEL AGENCY   **SAMPLE**   NO. 26

10 Broadway Avenue
Welland, ON L3C 5L3

June 18, 20—
Date

PAY TO THE
ORDER OF   Echo Systems Ltd.----------------CANCELLED----------$25.52

SUM OF   Twenty-five --------------------------52/100 DOLLARS

THE BANK OF NOVA SCOTIA
39 Niagara Street
Welland, ON L3C 1H8

P. Noel
SANDY'S PERSONNEL AGENCY

26 80286 002 21840 00

Sandy's Personnel Agency: Performance Task Rubric

Assessment Criteria	Levels of Achievement			
	Level 1	Level 2	Level 3	Level 4
KNOWLEDGE AND UNDERSTANDING • understanding of the basic accounting procedures for preparing a bank reconciliation statement • understanding that the tasks of handling and recording cash are separated for control purposes	Demonstrates limited understanding of terminology, concepts, procedures, and principles.	Demonstrates some understanding of terminology, concepts, procedures, and principles.	Demonstrates considerable understanding of terminology, concepts, procedures, and principles.	Demonstrates thorough understanding of terminology, concepts, procedures, and principles.
THINKING AND INQUIRY • analysis of transactions • interpretation of the discrepancy	Uses critical and interpretative skills with limited effectiveness. Applies few of the skills in an inquiry, or problem-solving process.	Uses critical and interpretative skills with moderate effectiveness. Applies some of the skills in an inquiry, or problem-solving process.	Uses critical and interpretative skills with considerable effectiveness. Applies most of the skills in an inquiry, or problem-solving process.	Uses critical and interpretative skills with great effectiveness. Applies all, or almost all, skills in an inquiry, or problem-solving process.
COMMUNICATION • completion of appropriate forms and statements • explanation of discrepancy • preparation of spreadsheet	Communicates with minimal precision and clarity.	Communicates with some precision and clarity.	Communicates with considerable precision and clarity.	Communicates with complete and thorough precision and clarity.
APPLICATION • application of skills to prepare cheques, stubs, bank reconciliation statement • application of skills to complete the spreadsheet	Uses skills with limited accuracy.	Uses skills with some accuracy.	Uses skills with considerable accuracy.	Uses skills with a high degree of accuracy.

12

Completing the Accounting Cycle for a Merchandising Company

UNIT 27 Adjusting the Books

What Learning You Will Demonstrate

On completion of this unit, you will be able to:

- explain why adjustments are necessary;
- prepare the adjustment for bad debts using the income statement method and the balance sheet method;
- prepare entries for uncollectible accounts;
- prepare adjustments for accrued expenses;
- prepare adjustments for accrued revenue; and
- prepare adjustments for unearned revenue.

In Chapter 6, you were introduced to the accounting procedures performed at the end of the fiscal period for a service business. These included adjustments, financial statements, adjusting and closing entries, and the post-closing trial balance. A service company, Management Consultant Services, was used to explain the adjusting and closing procedures. Adjustments were prepared to record prepaid expenses, such as supplies and prepaid rent, and depreciation expense on fixed assets.

You will remember that a service company *sells a service to its customers.* A movie theatre sells entertainment. A dentist sells a dental health service. An Internet service provider sells Internet access. All of these are examples of service businesses.

A merchandising company *sells merchandise to its customers.* A clothing store sells clothes. A sporting goods store sells sports equipment.

A service company sells a service.

A merchandising company sells merchandise.

A merchandising firm must prepare adjustments for the same reason that a service company must—*so that the financial statements will be accurate.* Adjustments to prepaid expense accounts and for depreciation on fixed assets are similar to those prepared for a service company. However, additional adjustments are necessary for merchandising companies. These include adjusting the Merchandise Inventory account and recording purchases of merchandise at the end of the fiscal period.

> Bad debts are uncollectible amounts owed by customers.

Some new adjustments that apply to both service and merchandising companies will be outlined in this chapter. One adjustment is for bad debts, which are uncollectible amounts owed to the company by customers. Other adjustments at the end of the accounting period are to record amounts that have not yet been recorded.

INTRODUCING THE BAD DEBTS ADJUSTMENT

> Selling on credit is necessary for most companies.

Almost all companies and many consumers buy on credit at some time. They buy when they need or desire goods and they pay when they have cash, or according to the terms of sale. Our economy relies heavily on credit—more credit sales are made than cash sales. In many product areas, a business cannot survive if it does not offer customers the opportunity to *buy now and pay later.* Unfortunately, however, *sometimes customers do not pay*—and this can mean accounting problems for a company that makes credit sales.

Accounting Problems Caused by Bad Debts

> Bad debts expense is the loss due to uncollectible accounts.

Accounting problems arise when customers do not pay their debts and the resulting loss of revenue becomes a bad debts expense for the company. Let us take, as an example, two consecutive years in the business affairs of Sullivan Enterprises. We will consider the year 20-4 to be Year 1, and the year 20-5 to be Year 2.

Suppose that in 20-4, Sullivan Enterprises makes sales worth $320 000 and net income is $57 575. *If in the next year, 20-5,* customers default on 20-4 sales worth $2000, *the 20-4 net income of $57 575 will be incorrect.* It includes sales of $2000 for which money will never be received. A more accurate net income figure is $55 575.

In Figure 12-1, an expense of $2000, from the Bad Debts Expense account, has been included in the expense section of Sullivan Enterprises' income statement for 20-4. This results in an adjusted net income for the year of $55 575, which is more accurate than the $57 575 figure.

> The matching principle states that expenses for an accounting period should be matched with the revenue produced during the same accounting period.

The inclusion of the $2000 expense for bad debts is based on an important Generally Accepted Accounting Principle—the matching principle. *The matching principle states that expenses for an accounting period should be matched with the revenue produced during the same accounting period.* If the $2000 bad debts expense were not included, the proper total for expenses would not be matched against revenue for the 20-4 accounting period.

Figure 12-2 shows part of the balance sheet for 20-4. The Accounts Receivable figure of $53 000 includes the $2000 in credit sales that will never be paid by customers.

Sullivan Enterprises
Income Statement
For the year ended December 31, 20-4

Revenue		
Sales		$320 000
Cost of Goods Sold		
Cost of Goods Sold (per schedule)		114 000
Gross Profit		206 000
Operating Expenses		
Bad Debts	$ 2 000	
Other	148 425	
Total		150 425
Net Income		$ 55 575

FIGURE 12-1 Income statement for 20-4

When the balance sheet was prepared at the end of 20-4, the business hoped to collect all $53 000 of the accounts receivable. However, during 20-5, $2000 worth of the accounts receivable proved to be uncollectible. The $53 000 amount shown in the Accounts Receivable account in Figure 12-2 is therefore not accurate. A figure of $51 000 more correctly describes the value of Accounts Receivable.

It is the accountant's task to prepare financial statements that are as accurate as possible. For this reason, an adjustment of $2000 is required at the end of 20-4 to try to establish a more correct value for the Accounts Receivable account on the balance sheet and for the expenses on the income statement.

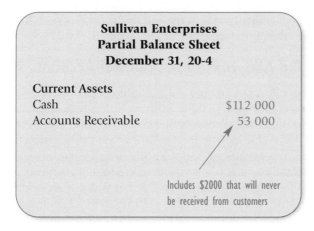

Sullivan Enterprises
Partial Balance Sheet
December 31, 20-4

Current Assets	
Cash	$112 000
Accounts Receivable	53 000

Includes $2000 that will never
be received from customers

FIGURE 12-2 Partial balance sheet for 20-4

B*ased on past experience*, the accountant for Sullivan Enterprises knows that about $2000 worth of credit sales will become uncollectible. However, which customers will not pay their bills or what the true value of the uncollectible accounts will be will not be clear until quite some time into the next accounting period, or even later. Therefore, using past experience as a guide, the accountant prepares an adjustment for bad debts to improve the accuracy of the financial statements.

Preparing the Adjustment for Bad Debts

Based on the estimated bad debts for 20-4, the accountant prepares this adjustment before preparing the 20-4 financial statements:

Dec.	31	Bad Debts Expense	2 0 0 0 00	
		Allowance for Doubtful Accounts		2 0 0 0 00
		To record the estimated bad debts for 20-4.		

The effect of this entry is shown here in T-account form:

Accounts Receivable	Allowance for Doubtful Accounts	Bad Debts Expense
Dec. 31 53 000	Dec. 31 2 000	Dec. 31 2 000
Appears on the balance sheet.	Appears on the balance sheet.	Appears on the income statement.

Examining the Bad Debts Expense Account

Bad Debts Expense appears on the income statement, as shown in Figure 12-1. At the end of the fiscal period, Bad Debts Expense is closed into the Income Summary account. During the fiscal period, there is no balance in Bad Debts Expense. It is opened with the adjustment made at the end of the fiscal period. It is then reduced to a zero balance when the closing entries are prepared.

Examining the Allowance for Doubtful Accounts Account

The partial balance sheet in Figure 12-2 contains the Accounts Receivable control account with a balance of $53 000. Sullivan Enterprises estimates that $2000 worth of the Accounts Receivable balance will become bad debts. Why is the asset Accounts Receivable not credited $2000 when the adjustment is made?

This is not done because it is not known *which* customer balances will be uncollectible. Therefore, it is not possible to credit any customer account in the accounts receivable ledger. Furthermore, it is not possible to credit the Accounts Receivable control account in the general ledger because the control account balance must always be equal to the total of the individual customer balances in the accounts receivable ledger. This is why the Allowance for Doubtful Accounts account is credited instead with the estimated uncollectible amount.

Allowance for Doubtful Accounts appears in the asset section of the balance sheet, as shown in Figure 12-3, but it is considered to be a contra account or a valuation account. As explained earlier in the text, a contra account reduces the value of the account that it describes. The Allowance for Doubtful Accounts account is used to determine a realistic valuation for the Accounts Receivable control account. The accounts used to record the accumulated depreciation on various assets are also valuation or contra accounts. Examples of such accounts are shown later in this chapter in Figure 12-13.

Sullivan Enterprises **Partial Balance Sheet** **December 31, 20-4**		
Current Assets		
Cash		$112 000
Accounts Receivable	$53 000	
Less: Allowance for Doubtful Accounts	2 000	51 000

FIGURE 12-3 Partial balance sheet with Allowance for Doubtful Accounts included

ESTIMATING BAD DEBTS EXPENSE

The two methods commonly used to estimate bad debts expense are the balance sheet method and the income statement method. Whichever method is used must be consistently followed. Both methods are described below.

Using the Income Statement Method

The **income statement method of estimating bad debts** uses a percentage of net sales. It is based on the question: "How much of this year's sales will become bad debts?" This is how it works. The accountant examines the bad debts losses in previous years. If, for instance, the losses have consistently been about 1 percent of net sales, then 1 percent is used for the adjustment. If sales are $320 000 and sales returns are $10 000, then net sales are $310 000. Since 1 percent of $310 000 is $3100, this is the amount used for the adjustment. This entry is made:

The income statement method of estimating bad debts uses a percentage of net sales as a basis for estimating bad debts expense.

Dec.	31	Bad Debts Expense	3 1 0 0 00	
		Allowance for Doubtful Accounts		3 1 0 0 00
		To record bad debts at 1 percent of net sales.		

Using the Balance Sheet Method

Many companies examine their customer accounts to estimate the uncollectible balances. This is known as the **balance sheet method of estimating bad debts** because it uses the asset Accounts Receivable as a basis for estimating bad debts expense. To determine the value of the uncollectible accounts, an accounts receivable *age analysis* (Figure 12-4) is prepared. This is a list that shows the balance owed by each customer. It also shows how long the balance has been owed.

The balance sheet method of estimating bad debts uses a percentage of accounts receivable as a basis for estimating bad debts expense.

Accounts Receivable Age Analysis
December 31, 20-4

Customer	Balance of Accounts Receivable	Current Accounts Receivable	1–30 Days Overdue	31–60 Days Overdue	61–90 Days Overdue	+90 Days Overdue
Ali	$ 400	$ 400				
Braun	200	50	$ 50	$ 100		
Clarkson	2 600	2 600				
Dervin	800				$ 800	
Elichuk	600	600				
All Others	48 400	40 000	4 800	900	800	$1 900
Total	$53 000	$43 650	$4 850	$1 000	$1 600	$1 900

FIGURE 12-4 Age analysis prepared for accounts receivable

The age analysis tells a manager which customer balances have not been paid for various time periods. The manager can then decide when to stop giving credit to a customer or when to start *collection proceedings* against a customer.

At the end of a fiscal period, the age analysis is used to determine the amount required for the bad debts expense adjustment. For each age group, the accountant estimates a percentage loss. For example, past experience might indicate that 50 percent of all debts over 90 days past due will be uncollectible. Figure 12-4 shows that $1900 is over 90 days past due. Therefore, $950 (0.50 × $1900 = $950) will probably be uncollectible. In a similar way, estimates are made for each of the age groups. Figure 12-5 shows the percentage considered uncollectible for each group and the total amount of estimated bad debts. The total of $2000 shown in Figure 12-5 is the amount required in the Allowance for Doubtful Accounts account and is used to prepare the adjustment.

Estimated Bad Debts
For the Year 20-4

Age of Accounts	Amount	Percentage Estimated to be Uncollectible	Bad Debts Estimate
Current	$43 650	1%	$ 436
1–30 days	4 850	4%	194
31–60 days	1 000	10%	100
61–90 days	1 600	20%	320
+90 days	1 900	50%	950
Total	$53 000		$2 000

FIGURE 12-5 Estimated amount of accounts receivable that will become bad debts

Accounts receivable less estimated bad debts is often referred to as *net realizable accounts receivable.*

Balance Sheet Method Steps

The following three steps are completed when you use the balance sheet method to estimate the amount of bad debts:

- **Step 1:** *Prepare an accounts receivable age analysis.* A list is prepared (Figure 12-4) that shows the balance owed by each customer. The amounts are classified according to how long they have been owed. The normal terms of payment for Sullivan Enterprises are net 30 days. This means the customer must pay the invoice amount within 30 days from the invoice date. Let's look at one customer as an example.

    In Figure 12-4, Braun owes $200. This represents *several* different sales to Braun. Of the $200 owing, $50 is current. That means $50 worth of merchandise was bought on credit and 30 days from the invoice date have *not* elapsed. However, Braun does have another $150 in the overdue columns. This means Braun has not paid the amounts within the normal terms of payment. Of this $150 owing, $50 is for an invoice between 1 to 30 days overdue. Braun also owes $100 that is 31 to 60 days overdue. In summary, Braun owes $200, which represents more than one sale or invoice. One invoice is overdue 1 to 30 days; another invoice is overdue 31 to 60 days; another invoice is current, i.e, *not* overdue.

- **Step 2:** *Estimate a percentage loss.*

- **Step 3:** *Prepare the adjusting entry.*

Previous Balance in the Allowance for Doubtful Accounts

When you use the balance sheet method to estimate bad debts, any existing balance in Allowance for Doubtful Accounts *must* be considered. For example, suppose that the balance in Allowance for Doubtful Accounts was set at $1500 the previous year, but only $1450 of receivables had to be written off. That would leave a credit balance of $50 in Allowance for Doubtful Accounts. This year the age analysis indicates an estimate for bad debts of $2000. A credit of $1950 is required to bring the balance in Allowance for Doubtful Accounts to $2000 for this period. This would be the adjusting entry:

Dec.	31	Bad Debts Expense	1 9 5 0 00	
		Allowance for Doubtful Accounts		1 9 5 0 00
		To increase the Allowance account to $2000.		
		Previous *credit* balance 50		
		Adjustment 1950		
		New balance 2000		

The result of the adjusting entry in T-account form would appear as follows:

Bad Debts Expense		Allowance for Doubtful Accounts	
Dec. 31 1 950		Balance 50	
		Dec. 31 1 950	
		New balance 2 000	
Appears on the income statement.		*Appears on the balance sheet.*	

Where does the $50 beginning balance in Allowance for Doubtful Accounts originate? It could be caused by the collection of an account previously written off or by the overestimation of bad debts for the last accounting period. Remember, the adjustment for bad debts is an *estimate* only. It is usually impossible to estimate the exact amount of the bad debts. There will generally be a credit balance in Allowance for Doubtful Accounts. When you use the balance sheet method to adjust for bad debts, the previous balance must be considered. With the income statement method, it is ignored. The reason for this is that the income statement method identifies "new" bad debts based on "new" credit sales, whereas the balance sheet method estimates "cumulative" bad debts based on all accounts receivable.

> When you use the income statement method to estimate bad debts, you ignore the previous balance in Allowance for Doubtful Accounts.

It is possible to have a temporary debit balance in Allowance for Doubtful Accounts. This occurs when the actual amount of bad debts for the period exceeds the estimate. Suppose the age analysis indicates an estimate of $2000 for bad debts, and there is an existing debit balance of $100 in Allowance for Doubtful Accounts. In this case, an adjustment of $2100 is necessary. This is the entry:

Dec.	31	Bad Debts Expense		2 1 0 0 00	
		Allowance for Doubtful Accounts			2 1 0 0 00
		To increase the Allowance account to $2000.			
		Previous *debit* balance	100		
		Adjustment, credit	2100		
		New balance, credit	2000		

WRITING OFF UNCOLLECTIBLE ACCOUNTS

Three accounts are involved in the adjustment for bad debts. They are Accounts Receivable, Allowance for Doubtful Accounts, and Bad Debts Expense. The first two accounts appear in the asset section on the balance sheet. The third, Bad Debts Expense, appears on the income statement. It is closed at the end of the fiscal period. At the beginning of the new fiscal period, these three accounts will appear in T-account form as follows:

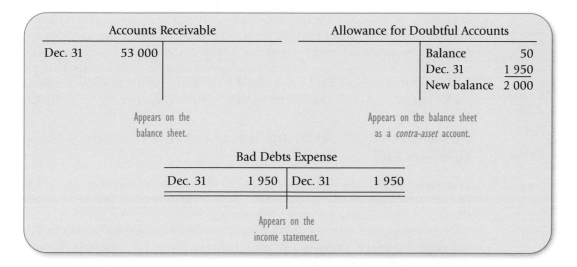

What does a company do when it determines that it will never be able to collect a debt owed by a customer? The following system is used by Sullivan Enterprises. Suppose that by March 12, it is clear that $750 owed by J. Wilson will never be collected. The following entry is made:

Mar.	12	Allowance for Doubtful Accounts	7 5 0 00	
		Accounts Receivable/J. Wilson		7 5 0 00
		To write off J. Wilson's account as uncollectible.		

The $750 credit is posted twice, once to the Accounts Receivable control account in the general ledger and also to J. Wilson's account in the accounts receivable subsidiary ledger.

Notice that in this entry, the Bad Debts Expense account is not used. The loss is written off against Allowance for Doubtful Accounts. Remember that a total of $2000 was recorded in Bad Debts Expense when the adjustment was made. To record the $750 loss in Bad Debts Expense would be wrong because the expense would be recorded twice: once in the adjustment and once in the write-off. After J. Wilson's account is written off, the T-accounts will appear as follows:

Accounts Receivable				Allowance for Doubtful Accounts			
Dec. 31	53 000	Mar. 12	750	Mar. 12	750	Dec. 31	2 000

Accounts Receivable/J. Wilson				Bad Debts Expense			
Balance	750	Mar. 12	750	Dec. 31	1 950	Dec. 31	1 950

This account now closed   No change in this account

During the year, write-off entries are made whenever it is certain that a debt is uncollectible. At the end of the year, there will probably be a balance in Allowance for Doubtful Accounts because it is almost impossible to correctly estimate a year's uncollectible accounts. When the next fiscal period ends, the balance in Allowance for Doubtful Accounts must be considered if the balance sheet method of adjusting for bad debts is used. The income statement method ignores any such balance.

Payment of an Account Receivable Previously Written Off

Sometimes an account that was assumed to be uncollectible and written off is unexpectedly collected. Such payments are termed *recovery of bad debts*. When this occurs, it is necessary to make two entries.

In the previous example, J. Wilson's account was written off on March 12. On June 1, Wilson unexpectedly pays Sullivan Enterprises the full amount ($750). Two entries are made. The first one records the debt in the customer's account again and re-establishes the amount in Allowance for Doubtful Accounts:

Jun.	1	Accounts Receivable/J. Wilson	7 5 0 00	
		Allowance for Doubtful Accounts		7 5 0 00
		To set up previously written-off account.		

The second entry records the money received and decreases the customer's account:

Jun.	1	Cash	7 5 0 00	
		Accounts Receivable/J. Wilson		7 5 0 00
		Received payment in full.		

After the entries have been posted, J. Wilson's account appears as below:

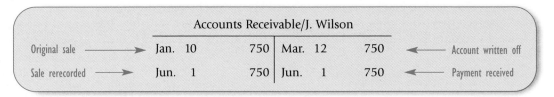

Now that we have looked at the adjustment for bad debts, we will examine two other adjustments, called *accrued expenses* and *accrued revenue*.

INTRODUCING ACCRUED EXPENSES

4

Adjusting entries are required for any expenses that are owed but not yet recorded. These are called accrued expenses. They have been *incurred but not journalized and posted to the general ledger*. Interest owed but not recorded is an example.

Accrued expenses are expenses that have been incurred but not yet recorded in the books.

Accrued Interest

Suppose $10 000 was borrowed by Sullivan Enterprises from a bank on October 1 and is to be repaid with interest in six months, on March 31. Interest of 9 percent is charged by the bank. The following entry is made when the money is borrowed:

Oct.	1	Cash	10 0 0 0 00	
		Bank Loan		10 0 0 0 00
		Borrowed $10 000 for six months at 9 percent		
		interest.		

On December 31, the end of the fiscal period, the bank is owed three months' interest. This amount is an expense and should be on the income statement. The interest for three months is $225. This amount must be shown in the Interest Expense account. The necessary adjustment is:

Dec.	31	Interest Expense	2 2 5 00	
		Interest Payable		2 2 5 00
		To record October, November, and December		
		interest ($10 000 × 0.09 × 3/12 = $225).		

After this entry has been posted, the Interest Expense, Bank Loan, and Interest Payable accounts appear as follows:

Interest Expense	Bank Loan	Interest Payable
Dec. 31 225	Oct. 1 10 000	Dec. 31 225
Appears on the income statement.	Appears on the balance sheet.	Appears on the balance sheet.

What would be wrong with the financial statements if this adjustment were not made? Which accounting principle would be violated if these expenses were not recorded at the end of the accounting period? First of all, the expenses would be too low and this would cause the net income to be $225 too high. Because net income would be overstated, the final owner's equity total would also be too high. Also, liabilities would be understated.

Such an error would result from not matching all of the expenses of a period with the revenue for that period. If the interest was not recorded until it was paid in the next accounting period, the net income in that period would be $225 too low. Can you explain why the owner's equity would be correct at the end of the second fiscal period even though the income statement was incorrect in both periods? Failure to record the expense in the first instance would result in an overstatement of net income of $225, while recording too high an expense in the second instance would result in an understatement of net income of $225. The total net income added to the owner's equity *over the two fiscal periods would be correct though both income statements would be incorrect.*

Accrued Salaries

A second example of unrecorded accrued expenses is *salaries earned but not yet paid.* The most common reason for accrued salaries is that the financial period end does not match a payday. The following is another reason for accrued salaries.

Sullivan Enterprises pays a commission to its sales staff of 10 percent of their monthly sales. The commission is paid the following month for the previous month's sales. In December, the sales staff made sales of $12 000. The commission of $1200 ($0.10 \times \$12\ 000 = \$1200$) is paid at the end of January. However, since it was earned in December, the amount of commission should be part of the financial statements prepared in December. This adjustment is necessary:

Dec.	31	Salaries Expense	1 2 0 0 00	
		Salaries Payable		1 2 0 0 00
		To record December commissions owing to sales		
		staff.		

When this entry is posted, the accounts appear as follows:

Salaries Expense			Salaries Payable	
Dec. 31	110 000		Dec. 31	1 200
31	1 200			
Balance	111 200			

If this entry were not made, by how much would the expenses be understated? By how much would the net income be overstated? By how much would the liabilities be understated?

INTRODUCING ACCRUED REVENUE

Accrued revenue is revenue earned during the fiscal period but not yet recorded in the books.

Accrued revenue is revenue that has been earned but not journalized and posted to the general ledger.

Sullivan Enterprises purchased a three-year guaranteed investment certificate for $10 000 from its bank. The certificate earns 9 percent interest, or $900 per year.

The interest (a total of $2700) will be received at the end of three years; however, $900 in interest is actually earned each year, as illustrated:

Total Interest Earned in Three Years	=	$2700	$900 Earned in Year 1 $900 Earned in Year 2 $900 Earned in Year 3

Since $900 interest is earned at the end of Year 1, that interest should be recorded as revenue and included in the income statement for Year 1. If it is not recorded, there would be a *mismatch between revenue and expenses*. Some of the revenue for the year ($900) would not be matched against the expenses for the year. To avoid that error, this adjustment is made:

Dec.	31	Interest Receivable	9 0 0 00	
		Interest Revenue		9 0 0 00
		To record one year's interest on the guaranteed investment certificate.		

INTRODUCING UNEARNED REVENUE

You have just learned the accounting procedures to record accrued revenue— revenue earned but not yet recorded. Another form of accrual is for **unearned revenue**, which is revenue that has been received but is not yet earned.

Unearned revenue is illustrated in the following example. New Star Software supplies technology support services to customers. It is preparing its financial statements on December 31. On October 1, one of New Star's customers paid $6000 for support services for six months ($1000 for each month, October, November, December, January, February, and March). This entry was made on October 1:

Unearned revenue is revenue that has been received but is not yet earned.

20—				
Oct.	1	Cash	6 0 0 0 00	
		Unearned Revenue		6 0 0 0 00
		To record revenue not yet earned.		

Unearned revenue is a *current liability*. New Star owes the customer $6000 worth of work or it must return the $6000. The $6000 is a liability until the service is provided. When the work is provided the prepayments will be recorded as revenue.

On December 31, the support services (work) have been provided for three months (October, November, and December). The value of the work, $3000, should be recorded as revenue and the liability account, *Unearned Revenue*, should be reduced by $3000 since that amount of work is no longer owed to the customer. The following adjustment is made on December 31:

20—						
Dec.	31	Unearned Revenue		3 0 0 0 00		
		Services Revenue			3 0 0 0 00	
		To adjust unearned revenue.				

After posting, the Unearned Revenue account (a current liability) appears as follows:

	Unearned Revenue	
Dec. 31	3000	Oct. 1	6000
		Bal.	3000

When the December 31 financial statements are prepared they will reflect a proper matching of revenue with expenses. The $3000 reflecting the work completed will appear in the Services Revenue account on the income statement and will increase overall revenue. The remaining $3000 of work still to be provided will remain as a current liability on the balance sheet in Unearned Revenue. Also on the balance sheet, the original $6000 that was received as a prepayment will be included as part of the Cash account balance.

SUMMARY OF ACCRUED ADJUSTMENTS

Adjusting entries are necessary for accrued revenue and for accrued expenses so that the financial statements will be accurate. This is in agreement with the matching principle. *If accrued expenses are not recorded, there will be a mismatch between expenses and revenue and the following will occur:*

- Expenses will be understated.
- Net income will be overstated.
- Liabilities will be understated.
- Owner's equity will be overstated.

If accrued revenue is not recorded, the following will occur:

- Revenue will be understated.
- Net income will be understated.
- Assets will be understated.
- Owner's equity will be understated.

If unearned revenue is not recorded, the following will occur:

- Revenue will be overstated.
- Net income will be overstated.
- Liabilities will be understated.
- Owner's equity will be overstated.

UNIT 27 CHECK YOUR READING

Questions

1. Explain the difference between a service company and a merchandising company.
2. On which financial statements do the following two accounts appear:
   (a) Bad Debts Expense?
   (b) Allowance for Doubtful Accounts?
3. (a) What is the general journal entry to record estimated bad debts?
   (b) Name the financial statement on which each account in the entry from part a would appear.
   (c) Which of the two accounts in part a are closed at the end of the fiscal period?
4. (a) Name two methods of estimating bad debts.
   (b) Which method takes into consideration the previous balance in Allowance for Doubtful Accounts?
5. What is the general journal entry to write off an uncollectible account?
6. When is an account written off as uncollectible?
7. What is the adjusting entry to record interest owed but not recorded?
8. What is the adjusting entry to record salaries owed to employees?
9. Define *accrued expenses* and give two examples.
10. Define *accrued revenue* and give two examples.
11. (a) Define *unearned revenue*.
    (b) What type of account is unearned revenue?
    (c) On which financial statement does Unearned Revenue appear?

UNIT 27 APPLY YOUR KNOWLEDGE

Exercises

1. At the end of the fiscal period, December 31, Boutique Anne Marie has a balance of $13 000 in Accounts Receivable. Allowance for Bad Debts has a zero balance. It is estimated that the bad debts will be $135.
   (a) Prepare the adjusting entry to record the estimated bad debts of $135.
   (b) Copy the T-accounts that follow. Post the adjusting entry to your own T-accounts.

Accounts Receivable	Allowance for Doubtful Accounts	Bad Debts Expense
Dec. 31 13 000		

(c) How much will appear on the income statement for Bad Debts Expense?
(d) Show how Accounts Receivable and Allowance for Doubtful Accounts will appear on the balance sheet.

2. Dave Taylor's Marina has a balance of $25 000 in Accounts Receivable. Allowance for Doubtful Accounts has a zero balance. The estimated amount for bad debts is $750.
(a) Prepare the adjusting entry to record the estimated bad debts for December 31.
(b) How much will appear in the income statement for Bad Debts Expense?
(c) Show how Accounts Receivable and Allowance for Doubtful Accounts will appear on the balance sheet.

3. The three companies in the following description all use the income statement method to estimate bad debts. For each, prepare the adjusting entry.
(a) Company A: Net sales were $100 000. Bad debts are estimated to be 1 percent of net sales.
(b) Company B: Net sales were $150 000. Bad debts are estimated to be 0.5 percent of net sales.
(c) Company C: Net sales were $225 000. Bad debts are estimated to be 0.5 percent of net sales.

4. For each of the following cases, give the adjusting entry for bad debts if the balance sheet method of estimating bad debts is being used.
(a) Estimated bad debts: $13 500; balance in Allowance for Doubtful Accounts: $175 credit.
(b) Estimated bad debts: $47 600; balance in Allowance for Doubtful Accounts: $890 debit.

5. (a) Copy the T-accounts that follow:

Accounts Receivable	Allowance for Doubtful Accounts	Bad Debts Expense
Dec. 31 146 000	Dec. 31 1 145	

(b) An age analysis shows that $2650 worth of Accounts Receivable are estimated to be uncollectible. Journalize and post the necessary adjusting entry.

6. The accounts receivable age analysis for the Gaylor Trading Company on December 31, 20-1, shows the following totals:

			Days Overdue		
Balance	**Current**	**1–30**	**31–60**	**61–90**	**+90**
$95 800	$78 600	$7 700	$2 600	$3 200	$3 700

(a) Calculate the allowance for doubtful accounts if it is estimated that the following percentages are uncollectible: Current, 3 percent; 1–30 days, 10 percent; 31–60 days, 15 percent; 61–90 days, 25 percent; over 90 days, 45 percent.

(b) Calculate the estimated value of the net realizable accounts receivable.

7. (a) Copy the T-accounts that follow:

Accounts Receivable	Allowance for Doubtful Accounts	Bad Debts Expense
Dec. 31 20 000	Dec. 31 290	

(b) Record these transactions on page 29 in a general journal and post the entries to the T-accounts:

Jan. 17 Write off L. Doresco's account of $75 as uncollectible. Doresco has gone out of business.

25 Write off C. Rosenblatt's account of $190 as uncollectible. Rosenblatt has left town and cannot be located.

30 An age analysis shows that $500 worth of the Accounts Receivable account is estimated to be uncollectible. Prepare the necessary adjusting entry. Use the balance sheet method, remembering that the balance in Allowance for Doubtful Accounts must be considered.

Feb. 28 C. Rosenblatt's cheque for $190 was received in payment of her account previously written off.

8. Journalize these transactions on page 26 in a general journal:

May 1 No entry is required. The balance in Allowance for Doubtful Accounts is $150 credit.

9 Write off J. Turner's account of $115 as uncollectible.

23 Write off E. McKurcher's account of $40 as uncollectible.

30 The age analysis indicates that $180 is required in Allowance for Doubtful Accounts. The balance sheet method is being used. Prepare the adjusting entry.

9. (a) Copy the T-Accounts that follow:

Bank Loan	Interest Payable	Interest Expense
Dec. 31 60 000		

(b) At the end of the fiscal period, $600 interest has accrued. Prepare the adjusting entry to record the $600 interest.

(c) Post the adjusting entry to the T-accounts.

10. For each of the following cases, give the adjusting entry for interest owing:

(a) Interest for 12 months of $2400, to be paid on June 30. Date of adjustment: February 28.

(b) Interest for nine months of $1873, to be paid on September 30. Date of adjustment: June 30.

(c) Interest for six months of $3768, to be paid on March 31. Date of adjustment: January 31.

11. For each of the following cases, give the adjusting entry for interest owing:

(a) Loan of $8000 for one year at 9 percent interest, to be repaid on March 31. Date of adjustment: August 31.

(b) Loan of $12 000 for six months at 8 percent interest, to be repaid on October 31. Date of adjustment: June 30.

12. (a) Copy the T-accounts that follow:

Salaries Expense		Salaries Payable	
Dec. 31 29 000			

(b) At the end of the fiscal period, $750 is owed to the employees. Prepare the adjusting entry to record the salaries owing.

(c) Post the adjusting entry to the T-accounts.

13. For each of the following cases, give the adjusting entry for salaries owing:

(a) Sales staff receive a 5 percent commission on their monthly sales. In May, they sold $26 000 worth of goods for which they are to be paid on June 30. The date of the adjustment is May 31.

(b) The total earnings of all hourly employees is $3500 per day, excluding Saturdays and Sundays. They are paid every Friday. What will the adjusting entry be if the financial statements are prepared as at the end of the work day on Wednesday?

14. At the end of the fiscal period, April 30, W. Pollock, a lawyer, had completed $6000 worth of work for clients, but had not yet prepared the invoices.

(a) Prepare the journal entry to record the information.

(b) Post the entry to T-accounts for April 30.

15. New Star Software is preparing financial statements for the end of the fiscal period December 31, 20—. On November 1, New Star received $20 000 in contract revenue. As of December 31, half of the contract work had been completed and supplied to the customer.

(a) Prepare the journal entry to record the unearned revenue ($20 000) on November 1.

(b) Record the December 31 adjustment to Unearned Revenue and Contract Revenue.

(c) After posting, what will be the December 31 balance in Unearned Revenue?

What Learning You Will Demonstrate

On completion of this unit, you will be able to:

- record the beginning and ending inventory on a work sheet for a company, using the periodic inventory system;
- record adjustments on a work sheet; and
- complete a work sheet for a merchandising company, using either the periodic or the perpetual inventory system.

In the first unit of this chapter, you learned how to prepare adjustments for bad debts, accrued expenses, and accrued revenue. These adjustments were described in general journal form. In this unit, the work sheet will be used to plan the adjustments for a merchandising company.

RECORDING ADJUSTMENTS ON THE WORK SHEET

The accountant for Sullivan Enterprises has prepared the trial balance for the fiscal period ended December 31, 20-4. It is shown on the work sheet in Figure 12-6 on page 604. The following information is used to prepare the adjustments on the work sheet:

- The age analysis indicates that a balance of $2000 is required in Allowance for Doubtful Accounts.
- Supplies worth $2000 are left at the end of the year.
- Depreciation is recorded using the declining-balance method. The equipment depreciates 20 percent and the building 5 percent per year.
- Interest of $225 is owed on the bank loan.
- Salaries of $1200 are owed to the employees.

Analysis of the Work Sheet Adjustments

Adjustment for Bad Debts

Sullivan Enterprises uses the balance sheet method to estimate bad debts. The age analysis indicates that $2000 is required in Allowance for Doubtful Accounts. Since there is already a credit balance, an adjustment of $1950 is made. Bad Debts Expense is added to the work sheet and is debited $1950. A credit of $1950 is written on line 3 opposite Allowance for Doubtful Accounts. The debit and credit amounts in the adjustments columns are coded (a). The adjustments are coded to provide easy identification of the debit and credit portions of the entry.

Sullivan Enterprises, Work Sheet
For the year ended December 31, 20-4

	ACC. NO.	TRIAL BALANCE DEBIT	TRIAL BALANCE CREDIT	ADJUSTMENTS DEBIT	ADJUSTMENTS CREDIT	INCOME STATEMENT DEBIT	INCOME STATEMENT CREDIT	BALANCE SHEET DEBIT	BALANCE SHEET CREDIT	
Cash	101	112 000 00						112 000 00		1
Accounts Receivable	110	53 000 00						53 000 00		2
Allowance for Doubtful Accounts	111		5 0 00		(a) 1 9 5 0 00				2 0 0 0 00	3
Merchandise Inventory, January 1	120	90 000 00				90 000 00	86 000 00	86 000 00		4
Supplies	125	4 5 0 0 00						2 0 0 0 00		5
Building	150	160 000 00						160 000 00		6
Accum. Depreciation—Building	151		48 2 0 0 00		(c) 5 5 9 0 00				53 7 9 0 00	7
Equipment	160	23 000 00						23 000 00		8
Accum. Depreciation—Equipment	161		10 2 0 0 00		(d) 2 5 6 0 00				12 7 6 0 00	9
Accounts Payable	200		23 4 5 0 00						23 4 5 0 00	10
PST Payable	205		2 1 3 0 00						2 1 3 0 00	11
GST Payable	206		1 8 7 0 00						1 8 7 0 00	12
GST Refundable	207	6 4 0 0 00						6 4 0 0 00		13
Bank Loan	240		10 000 00						10 000 00	14
Mortgage Payable	250		88 000 00						88 000 00	15
E. Sullivan, Capital	300		200 640 00						200 640 00	16
E. Sullivan, Drawings	301	8 000 00						8 000 00		17
Sales	400		320 000 00				320 000 00			18
Purchases	500	110 000 00				110 000 00				19
Advertising Expense	600	5 000 00				5 000 00				20
General Expense	601	4 000 00				4 000 00				21
Salaries Expense	602	120 000 00		(f) 1 2 0 0 00		121 2 0 0 00				22
Utilities Expense	603	7 4 0 0 00				7 4 0 0 00				23
Insurance Expense	604	7 0 0 0 00				7 0 0 0 00				24
		704 5 4 0 00	704 5 4 0 00							25
Bad Debts Expense	605			(a) 1 9 5 0 00		1 9 5 0 00				26
Supplies Expense	606			(b) 2 5 0 0 00		2 5 0 0 00				27
Depreciation Expense—Building	607			(c) 5 5 9 0 00		5 5 9 0 00				28
Depreciation Expense—Equipment	608			(d) 2 5 6 0 00		2 5 6 0 00				29
Interest Expense	609			(e) 2 2 5 00		2 2 5 00				30
Interest Payable	215				(e) 2 2 5 00				2 2 5 00	31
Salaries Payable	220				(f) 1 2 0 0 00				1 2 0 0 00	32
				14 0 2 5 00	14 0 2 5 00	357 4 2 5 00	406 000 00	444 640 00	396 0 6 5 00	33
Net Income						48 5 7 5 00			48 5 7 5 00	34
						406 000 00	406 000 00	444 640 00	444 640 00	35
										36

Note: (1) Adjustments coded with letters for easy identification; (2) Opening inventory extended to income statement debit column; (3) Ending inventory extended to income statement credit and balance sheet debit columns.

FIGURE 12-6 Completed work sheet for a merchandising business

Adjustment for Prepaid Expenses

As you may recall, prepaid expenses such as prepaid rent, prepaid insurance, and supplies must be adjusted on the work sheet.

An inventory of supplies shows a $2000 total for supplies on hand at the end of the year. The Supplies account on the work sheet has a $4500 balance. An adjustment of $2500 is required. Supplies Expense is added to the work sheet and is debited $2500, the amount of the supplies used. Supplies (line 5) is credited $2500. This adjustment is coded (b).

Adjustment for Depreciation

The declining-balance method of depreciating fixed assets is used by Sullivan Enterprises.

The building depreciates at the rate of 5 percent per year on the declining balance, which is now $111 800 ($160 000 − $48 200 accumulated depreciation =$111 800). Depreciation Expense—Building is added to the work sheet and debited $5590 ($111 800 × 0.05 = $5590). Accumulated Depreciation—Building is credited $5590 (line 7). The adjustment is coded (c).

The declining balance of the Equipment account is $12 800 ($23 000 − $10 200 accumulated depreciation = $12 800). The rate of depreciation is 20 percent per year. Depreciation Expense—Equipment is added to the work sheet and debited $2560 (0.20 × $12 800 = $2560). Accumulated Depreciation—Equipment is credited $2560 (line 9). This adjustment is coded (d).

Adjustment for Accrued Interest

Three months' interest is owed on the bank loan and amounts to $225 ($10 000 × 0.09 × 3/12 = $225). Both Interest Expense and Interest Payable are added to the work sheet. The $225 adjustment is coded (e).

Adjustment for Accrued Salaries

The salaries adjustment is made to record the $1200 owed to the employees. Salaries is debited $1200. Salaries Payable is added to the work sheet and is credited $1200. The adjustment is coded (f).

Adjustment for Merchandise Inventory—
Perpetual Inventory System

Under the perpetual inventory system, discussed in Chapter 7, the Merchandise Inventory account is continually adjusted as merchandise is bought and sold during the accounting period. What entry may be required to ensure the accuracy of the inventory account at the end of the accounting period? As you learned in Chapter 7, an entry may be required to record the difference between the physical inventory (counting and pricing the inventory) taken at the end of the fiscal period and the Merchandise Inventory ledger account.

The calculation to determine the inventory position on December 31 is as follows:

Merchandise Inventory (ledger balance)	$76 000
Physical Inventory (an actual account)	75 450
Inventory Shortage	$ 550

The journal entry to record the inventory shortage is:

Dec.	31	Inventory Shortage	5 5 0 00	
		Merchandise Inventory		5 5 0 00
		To adjust the balance of Merchandise Inventory		
		to equal the physical inventory.		

Inventory Shortage is an expense account and is shown on the income statement.

The entries required to adjust inventory for a firm like Sullivan Enterprises, which uses a periodic inventory system, are somewhat different.

Adjustment for Merchandise Inventory— Periodic Inventory System

The Merchandise Inventory account shows the cost of goods on hand at a specific date.

The work sheet in Figure 12-6 on page 604 contains the Merchandise Inventory account with a January balance of $90 000. This means that at the beginning of the fiscal period, the goods on hand cost $90 000. During the year, merchandise was sold and the sales transactions were recorded in the Sales account. Merchandise was purchased when it was required and recorded in the Purchases account.

At the end of the year, Merchandise Inventory must be adjusted since it contains the cost of the merchandise on hand at the beginning of the year, January 1. This figure is incorrect. It has changed because of sales and purchases of merchandise during the year. Merchandise Inventory must be adjusted so that it contains the value of the inventory on hand at the end of the year (December 31). This value is obtained by taking a physical inventory at the end of the fiscal year. This adjustment will now be examined in greater detail.

EXAMINING THE MERCHANDISE INVENTORY ADJUSTMENT

In line with the periodic inventory method, entries were not made in Sullivan Enterprises' Merchandise Inventory account during the accounting period. At the end of the accounting period, an adjustment is needed to update the balance of Merchandise Inventory. We will look first at the steps involved in making this adjustment and at the journal entries required.

Steps in Inventory Adjustment

Three steps are completed in adjusting the Merchandise Inventory account.

Step 1: Determine the Value of the Inventory

At the end of the fiscal period, a physical count, called *taking an inventory*, is made of merchandise on hand. This results in a new dollar amount of $86 000 for the Merchandise Inventory account. This is the actual value of the merchandise on hand.

Step 2: Prepare the Closing Entry for Merchandise Inventory

An entry is made to remove the beginning inventory figure. This is necessary because the beginning merchandise value *has been replaced* by the end-of-the-year inventory figure of $86 000. This entry is made to close out the beginning inventory to Income Summary:

Dec.	31	Income Summary	90 0 0 0 00	
		Merchandise Inventory		90 0 0 0 00
		To close the beginning inventory into the		
		Income Summary account.		

Step 3: Prepare the Entry to Record the Value of the Inventory

This entry is made to record the new inventory figure:

Dec.	31	Merchandise Inventory	86 0 0 0 00	
		Income Summary		86 0 0 0 00
		To record the ending inventory.		

This entry is necessary because the inventory on hand at the end of the year is an asset and must be recorded.

The Merchandise Inventory account now appears as follows:

Merchandise Inventory

Beginning inventory →	Jan. 1	90 000	Dec. 31	90 000 ← To close beginning inventory
To enter ending inventory →	Dec. 31	86 000		

The balance in Merchandise Inventory is now $86 000, the value of the ending inventory. When the financial statements are prepared, Merchandise Inventory $86 000 will appear in the current assets section of the balance sheet.

The Income Summary T-account follows. Note that it has a debit and a credit in it as a result of the inventory adjustments:

Income Summary			
Dec. 31	90 000	Dec. 31	86 000

The beginning inventory of $90 000 is on the left, or expenses and cost side, of the Income Summary account. The new inventory figure of $86 000 (the cost of goods not sold yet) is on the revenue side. The debit of $90 000 and the credit of $86 000 were recorded on the work sheet shown earlier in Figure 12-6.

Two entries that involve inventory have been described. One entry reduces Merchandise Inventory to zero by transferring *the beginning inventory to the Income Summary account. The other entry records the ending inventory in the Merchandise Inventory account.*

Recording the Inventory Adjustment on the Work Sheet

The two entries that have just been described explain how Merchandise Inventory is adjusted at the end of the accounting period. This adjustment can be organized on a work sheet before the journal entries are made. Figures 12-7, 12-8, and 12-9 illustrate, in three steps, the recording of the adjustment on a work sheet.

- **Step 1:** Transfer the beginning inventory value ($90 000) to the debit column of the income statement section. This $90 000 figure is required as part of the calculation for the cost of merchandise sold (see Figure 12-7).

- **Step 2:** Record the new inventory value ($86 000) in the credit column of the income statement section (see Figure 12-8). This is the other part of the calculation required for the cost of merchandise sold.

- **Step 3:** Record the new inventory value ($86 000) in the debit column of the balance sheet section. This records the ending inventory as an asset at cost (see Figure 12-9).

Trace the three steps described above through Figures 12-7, 12-8, and 12-9. Rather than preparing separate entries to adjust Merchandise Inventory, the account is adjusted as part of the closing entry procedure discussed in the next unit.

COMPLETING THE WORK SHEET

After the individual amounts on the trial balance section of the work sheet are transferred to either the income statement section or the balance sheet section, the columns are totalled and the net income is determined. Then, the work sheet columns are balanced and double ruled.

Look again at Figure 12-6 on page 604 to see the completed work sheet for Sullivan Enterprises. The major difference between this work sheet and that of a service company is the addition of the Purchases and Merchandise Inventory accounts. The Purchases account is transferred to the income statement section. As for the Merchandise Inventory account, the old, or beginning, inventory value is shown in the debit column of the income statement section. The new inventory value is shown in the debit column of the balance sheet section and in the credit column of the income statement section.

Sullivan Enterprises, Work Sheet
For the year ended December 31, 20-4

	ACC. NO.	ACCOUNT TITLE	TRIAL BALANCE DEBIT	TRIAL BALANCE CREDIT	ADJUSTMENTS DEBIT	ADJUSTMENTS CREDIT	INCOME STATEMENT DEBIT	INCOME STATEMENT CREDIT	BALANCE SHEET DEBIT	BALANCE SHEET CREDIT	
1	101	Cash	112 000 00						112 000 00		1
2	110	Accounts Receivable	53 000 00						53 000 00		2
3	111	Allowance for Doubtful Accounts		5 0 00		(a) 1 9 5 0 00				2 000 00	3
4	120	Merchandise Inventory, January 1	90 000 00				90 000 00				4
5	125	Supplies	4 500 00			(b) 2 5 0 0 00			2 000 00		5

FIGURE 12-7 Transfer the beginning inventory balance of $90 000 from the trial balance section to the debit column of the income statement section of the work sheet.

Sullivan Enterprises, Work Sheet
For the year ended December 31, 20-4

	ACC. NO.	ACCOUNT TITLE	TRIAL BALANCE DEBIT	TRIAL BALANCE CREDIT	ADJUSTMENTS DEBIT	ADJUSTMENTS CREDIT	INCOME STATEMENT DEBIT	INCOME STATEMENT CREDIT	BALANCE SHEET DEBIT	BALANCE SHEET CREDIT	
1	101	Cash	112 000 00						112 000 00		1
2	110	Accounts Receivable	53 000 00						53 000 00		2
3	111	Allowance for Doubtful Accounts		5 0 00		(a) 1 9 5 0 00				2 000 00	3
4	120	Merchandise Inventory, January 1	90 000 00				90 000 00	86 000 00			4
5	125	Supplies	4 500 00			(b) 2 5 0 0 00			2 000 00		5

FIGURE 12-8 Record the new inventory value of $86 000 in the credit column of the income statement section of the work sheet.

Sullivan Enterprises, Work Sheet
For the year ended December 31, 20-4

	ACC. NO.	ACCOUNT TITLE	TRIAL BALANCE DEBIT	TRIAL BALANCE CREDIT	ADJUSTMENTS DEBIT	ADJUSTMENTS CREDIT	INCOME STATEMENT DEBIT	INCOME STATEMENT CREDIT	BALANCE SHEET DEBIT	BALANCE SHEET CREDIT	
1	101	Cash	112 000 00						112 000 00		1
2	110	Accounts Receivable	53 000 00						53 000 00		2
3	111	Allowance for Doubtful Accounts		5 0 00		(a) 1 9 5 0 00				2 000 00	3
4	120	Merchandise Inventory, January 1	90 000 00				90 000 00	86 000 00	86 000 00		4
5	125	Supplies	4 500 00			(b) 2 5 0 0 00			2 000 00		5

Beginning inventory and ending inventory values are required to calculate cost of goods sold on the income statement.

Ending inventory value is required for the balance sheet.

FIGURE 12-9 Record the new inventory value of $86 000 in the debit column of the balance sheet section of the work sheet.

ALTERNATIVE WORK SHEET METHOD OF ADJUSTING MERCHANDISE INVENTORY

The method of adjusting Merchandise Inventory that you just learned for Sullivan Enterprises is commonly used by accountants. However, there are other methods that are just as acceptable. The following method treats the entries for beginning and ending inventories as adjusting entries on the work sheet, rather than preparing them as part of the closing entries discussed previously. The same data from Sullivan Enterprises will be used to illustrate this method. The work sheet in Figure 12-10 has been completed using the merchandise inventory adjustment method. *Can you identify the changes in the work sheet?* These are adjusting entries (g) and (h) to correct the value of Merchandise Inventory. *What effect do these entries have on the Merchandise Inventory and Income Summary accounts?*

Adjusting Entries

(g)	Income Summary		90 0 0 0 00	
	Merchandise Inventory			90 0 0 0 00
	To close beginning inventory to			
	Income Summary.			
(h)	Merchandise Inventory		86 0 0 0 00	
	Income Summary			86 0 0 0 00
	To record ending inventory.			

Accounts

Merchandise Inventory

Jan. 1	Beginning Inventory	90 000	Dec. 31 (g)		90 000
Dec. 31	(h)	86 000			

Income Summary

Dec. 31	(g)	90 000	Dec. 31 (h)		86 000

The two entries of the alternative merchandise inventory adjustment method have been recorded and posted. *Are the account balances the same as the previous method?* Yes. They are both acceptable methods resulting in an accurate ending inventory figure for statement preparation.

Sullivan Enterprises, Work Sheet
For the year ended December 31, 20-4

	ACCOUNT TITLE	ACC. NO.	TRIAL BALANCE DEBIT	TRIAL BALANCE CREDIT	ADJUSTMENTS DEBIT	ADJUSTMENTS CREDIT	INCOME STATEMENT DEBIT	INCOME STATEMENT CREDIT	BALANCE SHEET DEBIT	BALANCE SHEET CREDIT	
1	Cash	101	112 000 00						112 000 00		1
2	Accounts Receivable	110	53 000 00						53 000 00		2
3	Allowance for Doubtful Accounts	111		5 0 00		(a) 1 9 5 0 00				2 0 0 0 00	3
4	Merchandise Inventory, January 1	120	90 000 00		(h)86 0 0 0 00	(g)90 0 0 0 00			86 0 0 0 00		4
5	Supplies	125	4 5 0 0 00			(b) 2 5 0 0 00			2 0 0 0 00		5
6	Building	150	160 000 00						160 000 00		6
7	Accum. Depreciation—Building	151		48 2 0 0 00		(c) 5 5 9 0 00				53 7 9 0 00	7
8	Equipment	160	23 000 00						23 000 00		8
9	Accum. Depreciation—Equipment	161		10 2 0 0 00		(d) 2 5 6 0 00				12 7 6 0 00	9
10	Accounts Payable	200		23 4 5 0 00						23 4 5 0 00	10
11	PST Payable	205		2 1 3 0 00						2 1 3 0 00	11
12	GST Payable	206		1 8 7 0 00						1 8 7 0 00	12
13	GST Refundable	207	6 4 0 00						6 4 0 00		13
14	Bank Loan	240		10 0 0 0 00						10 0 0 0 00	14
15	Mortgage Payable	250		88 0 0 0 00						88 0 0 0 00	15
16	E. Sullivan, Capital	300		200 6 4 0 00						200 6 4 0 00	16
17	E. Sullivan, Drawings	301	8 0 0 0 00						8 0 0 0 00		17
18	Income Summary	302			(g)90 0 0 0 00	(h)86 0 0 0 00	90 0 0 0 00	86 0 0 0 00			18
19	Sales	400		320 0 0 0 00				320 0 0 0 00			19
20	Purchases	500	110 0 0 0 00				110 0 0 0 00				20
21	Advertising Expense	600	5 0 0 0 00				5 0 0 0 00				21
22	General Expense	601	4 0 0 0 00				4 0 0 0 00				22
23	Salaries Expense	602	120 0 0 0 00		(f) 1 2 0 0 00		121 2 0 0 00				23
24	Utilities Expense	603	7 4 0 0 00				7 4 0 0 00				24
25	Insurance Expense	604	7 0 0 0 00				7 0 0 0 00				25
26			704 5 4 0 00	704 5 4 0 00							26
27	Bad Debts Expense	605			(a) 1 9 5 0 00		1 9 5 0 00				27
28	Supplies Expense	606			(b) 2 5 0 0 00		2 5 0 0 00				28
29	Depreciation Expense—Building	607			(c) 5 5 9 0 00		5 5 9 0 00				29
30	Depreciation Expense—Equipment	608			(d) 2 5 6 0 00		2 5 6 0 00				30
31	Interest Expense	609			(e) 2 2 5 00		2 2 5 00				31
32	Interest Payable	215				(e) 2 2 5 00				2 2 5 00	32
33	Salaries Payable	220				(f) 1 2 0 0 00				1 2 0 0 00	33
34					190 0 2 5 00	190 0 2 5 00	357 4 2 5 00	406 0 0 0 00	444 6 4 0 00	396 0 6 5 00	34
35	Net Income						48 5 7 5 00			48 5 7 5 00	35
36							406 0 0 0 00	406 0 0 0 00	444 6 4 0 00	444 6 4 0 00	36
37											37

FIGURE 12-10 Completed work sheet for a merchandising business
Alternative merchandise adjustment method

The use of bar codes and optical readers makes taking a physical inventory count less "physical."

UNIT 28 CHECK YOUR READING

Questions

12. Where is the beginning inventory figure found on the work sheet?

13. Why is the inventory figure in the trial balance section of the work sheet different from the inventory figure in the balance sheet section of the work sheet?

14. How is the ending inventory determined?

15. What is the general journal entry to set up the new inventory value at the end of the fiscal period?

16. What is the general journal entry to close the beginning inventory?

17. How is the inventory adjustment shown on the work sheet?

18. What are the major differences between a work sheet for a service business and a work sheet for a merchandising business?

19. How would your answers to questions 15, 16, and 17 change if your firm used an acceptable alternate method of adjusting merchandise inventory?

UNIT 28 APPLY YOUR KNOWLEDGE

Exercises

16. The first four columns of Murray Hunt Enterprises' work sheet for the month appear on the next page. Complete the work sheet in your workbook. The December 31 inventory was determined to be $6400.

ACCOUNT TITLE	ACC. NO.	TRIAL BALANCE		ADJUSTMENTS	
		DEBIT	CREDIT	DEBIT	CREDIT
Cash	101	2 8 0 00			
Accounts Receivable	110	1 9 2 0 00			
Merchandise Inventory, December 1	120	6 8 0 0 00			
Unexpired Insurance	130	5 8 0 00			(b) 2 4 0 00
Store Equipment	160	2 3 0 0 00			
Accum. Depreciation—Store Equipment	161		6 2 0 00		(a) 2 6 0 00
Accounts Payable	200		2 8 8 0 00		
PST Payable	205		3 5 2 00		
GST Payable	206		3 0 8 00		
GST Refundable	207	2 1 0 00			
M. Hunt, Capital	300		6 6 2 0 00		
M. Hunt, Drawings	301	1 8 0 0 00			
Sales	400		52 8 0 0 00		
Sales Returns and Allowances	401	1 6 0 0 00			
Sales Discounts	402	1 2 0 0 00			
Purchases	500	36 0 0 0 00			
Purchases Returns and Allowances	501		1 6 0 0 00		
Purchases Discounts	502		8 0 0 00		
Transportation-in	508	9 0 0 00			
Advertising Expense	600	5 3 9 0 00			
Rent Expense	601	2 8 0 0 00			
Salaries Expense	602	4 2 0 0 00			
		65 9 8 0 00	65 9 8 0 00		
Depreciation Expense—Store Equipment	603			(a) 2 6 0 00	
Insurance Expense	604			(b) 2 4 0 00	
				5 0 0 00	5 0 0 00

17. From the year-end trial balance for Jeans Unlimited shown on page 614, and the following information, prepare a work sheet. Set up your own account names and numbers.

Additional Information:

- Merchandise Inventory, December 31, valued at $58 000.
- Supplies on hand, December 31, valued at $2200.
- Allowance for Doubtful Accounts must be increased to $600 using the balance sheet method.
- Store fixtures depreciate 20 percent per year using the declining-balance method.
- Interest owing but unrecorded, $750.
- Salaries owing to employees, $500.

Jeans Unlimited
Trial Balance
December 31, 20—

Account	Acc. No.	Debit	Credit
Cash	100	$ 13 530	
Accounts Receivable	102	30 000	
Allowance for Doubtful Accounts	103		$ 50
Merchandise Inventory, January 1	120	60 000	
Supplies	131	5 000	
Store Fixtures	141	15 000	
Accum. Depreciation—Store Fixtures	142		7 300
Accounts Payable	200		9 000
PST Payable	205		1 730
GST Payable	206		1 520
GST Refundable	207	470	
Bank Loan	221		8 000
L. Steeves, Capital	300		51 225
L. Steeves, Drawings	301	19 000	
Sales	400		260 000
Purchases	500	80 000	
Advertising Expense	610	8 000	
Office Expense	611	4 000	
Store Expense	612	9 000	
Rent Expense	613	14 000	
Salaries Expense	614	80 000	
Interest Expense	615	825	
		$338 825	$338 825

18. Prepare a work sheet for Vashti Ali Stores using the trial balance on the following page and the information below.

Additional Information:

- Merchandise Inventory, December 31, valued at $2400.
- Supplies on hand valued at $450.
- Insurance expired, $1200.
- The building depreciates 5 percent and the equipment 20 percent per year.
- Bad debts are recorded at 1 percent of net sales.

19. Prepare the work sheet for Jeans Unlimited in question 17 using the alternate merchandise inventory adjustment method.

20. Explain the difference between the work sheet that you prepared for Vashti Ali Stores and the one that was completed using the alternate merchandise inventory adjustment method.

Vashti Ali Stores
Trial Balance
December 31, 20—

Account	Acc. No.	Debit	Credit
Cash	100	$ 2 440	
Accounts Receivable	102	8 000	
Merchandise Inventory, January 1	120	21 000	
Supplies	121	1 700	
Prepaid Insurance	122	2 000	
Land	140	40 000	
Building	141	120 000	
Equipment	143	40 000	
Accounts Payable	200		$ 13 700
PST Payable	205		1 300
GST Payable	206		1 140
GST Refundable	207	560	
Mortgage Payable	210		50 000
P. Kanani, Capital	300		137 560
P. Kanani, Drawings	301	6 000	
Sales	400		195 000
Sales Returns and Allowances	401	1 000	
Sales Discounts	402	300	
Purchases	500	95 000	
Transportation on Purchases	501	7 000	
Purchases Returns and Allowances	502		3 300
Purchases Discounts	503		3 000
Salaries Expense—Selling	610	30 000	
Salaries Expense—Administrative	611	20 000	
Delivery Expense	612	7 000	
General Expense	613	2 000	
Property Tax Expense	614	1 000	
		$405 000	$405 000

21. Masako Ichikawa formed Ichikawa Engineering Supply on January 1, 20—. At year-end, the trial balance on page 616 was prepared. Prepare an eight-column work sheet for Ichikawa Engineering Supply using the trial balance and the additional information given. Set up any additional accounts you require. Choose appropriate account names and numbers.

Additional Information:

- Merchandise Inventory, December 31, valued at $58 000.
- Cost of insurance that expired during the year, $560.
- Supplies on hand, $840.
- The building depreciates 5 percent and the equipment 20 percent per year.

- Interest to date on the bank loan, $290.
- Salaries and wages owing at the end of the year, $875.
- Property taxes accrued but unpaid, $900.
- An Allowance for Doubtful Accounts account must be set up, with bad debts recorded at 1 percent of gross sales.

Ichikawa Engineering Supply
Trial Balance
December 31, 20—

Account Title	Acc. No.	Debit	Credit
Cash	101	$ 6 680	
Accounts Receivable	110	34 000	
Merchandise Inventory, January 1	120	72 000	
Supplies	126	2 840	
Unexpired Insurance	127	1 080	
Land	140	140 000	
Building	150	200 000	
Equipment	155	24 000	
Accounts Payable	200		$ 56 620
PST Payable	205		2 540
GST Payable	206		2 225
GST Refundable	207	1 320	
Bank Loan	210		25 000
M. Ichikawa, Capital	300		340 235
M. Ichikawa, Drawings	301	15 000	
Sales	400		389 500
Sales Returns and Allowances	401	7 000	
Sales Discounts	402	1 000	
Purchases	500	232 000	
Purchases Returns and Allowances	501		4 000
Purchases Discounts	502		1 680
Transportation-in	503	9 640	
Advertising Expense	601	11 510	
Delivery Expense	602	3 500	
Salaries and Wages Expense	603	59 230	
Property Tax Expense	604	1 000	
		$821 800	$821 800

What Learning You Will Demonstrate

On completion of this unit, you will be able to:

- prepare the following for a merchandising company that uses a periodic inventory system:
  - schedule of cost of goods sold,
  - classified income statement,
  - classified balance sheet, and
  - adjusting, closing, and reversing entries;
- outline the differences in completing the accounting cycle procedures between firms using periodic and perpetual inventory systems; and
- prepare the following for a merchandising company that uses a perpetual inventory system:
  - work sheet, and
  - income statement.

MERCHANDISING BUSINESS USING A PERIODIC INVENTORY SYSTEM

When the work sheet has been completed, financial statements are prepared. These include the schedule of cost of goods sold, the income statement, and the balance sheet. The financial statements may also include a separate statement of owner's equity. If such a statement is used, the complete equity calculation is not included in the owner's equity section of the balance sheet. Examples of this situation were shown in Chapter 5 in Figures 5-9 and 5-10, pages 179 and 180.

Preparing the Schedule of Cost of Goods Sold

The first statement prepared is the schedule of cost of goods sold. The cost information used to prepare this schedule is found in the income statement section of the work sheet. The cost information used by Sullivan Enterprises includes Merchandise Inventory—beginning and ending inventories—and Purchases. Other cost accounts that appear in the schedule of cost of goods sold of some merchandising companies are:

- Transportation on Purchases;
- Purchases Returns and Allowances; and
- Purchases Discounts.

Sullivan Enterprises uses a periodic inventory system. The schedule of cost of goods sold for 20-4 is shown in Figure 12-11.

Sullivan Enterprises
Schedule of Cost of Goods Sold
For the year ended December 31, 20-4

Merchandise Inventory, January 1	$ 90 000
Add: Purchases	110 000
Total Cost of Merchandise	200 000
Less: Merchandise Inventory, December 31	86 000
Cost of Goods Sold	$114 000

FIGURE 12-11 Schedule of cost of goods sold for Sullivan Enterprises

Preparing the Income Statement

Now that the cost of goods sold figure has been determined from the schedule of cost of goods sold, the income statement can be prepared. Figure 12-11 indicates that the goods sold during the year cost $114 000. This figure is now used on the income statement (Figure 12-12) to determine the gross profit. The items in the revenue and expenses sections of the income statement are obtained from the work sheet.

Classified Income Statement

The grouping of accounts using a standardized format is an aid to those who examine and interpret financial statements. Owners, managers, creditors, and government officials examine the financial statements of a variety of companies. Their task is made easier by the use of standard or *classified financial statements*.

The income statement shown in Figure 12-12 is a classified statement. There are three main sections in a classified income statement: revenue, cost of goods sold, and operating expenses. In some instances, two separate categories might be found in the expenses sections of merchandising companies: administrative expenses and selling expenses.

Administrative Expenses

Money spent in the general operation of a business is usually classified as an administrative expense. This would include expenses involved in the operation of the business office and all departments other than sales. Office salaries, office supplies, and building maintenance are a few examples.

Selling Expenses

Money spent for the direct purpose of selling goods is classified as a selling expense. Some examples include salespersons' salaries, advertising, deliveries, and sales supplies.

Allocating Responsibility for Expenses

Classifying expenses as administrative or selling expenses provides a detailed breakdown of where the money is being spent. It also allows the top management of a company to allocate responsibility for the spending of money. For example, if the sales manager is held responsible for all selling expenses, it is the responsibility of the sales manager to justify the money spent for all of the selling expenses. Responsibility for administrative expenses may be allocated in the same manner. An office manager may be held responsible for controlling the administrative expenses.

Sullivan Enterprises
Income Statement
For the year ended December 31, 20-4

Revenue		
Sales		$320 000
Cost of Goods Sold		
Cost of Goods Sold (per schedule)		114 000
Gross Profit		206 000
Operating Expenses		
Administrative Expenses:		
Depreciation—Building	$ 5 590	
Depreciation—Equipment	2 560	
Interest	225	
General	4 000	
Office Salaries	81 200	
Office Supplies	1 500	
Office Insurance	4 000	
Utilities	7 400	
Total Administrative Expenses		$106 475
Selling Expenses:		
Advertising	5 000	
Bad Debts	1 950	
Salespersons' Salaries	40 000	
Sales Supplies	1 000	
Sales Insurance	3 000	
Total Selling Expenses		50 950
Total Operating Expenses		157 425
Net Income		$ 48 575

FIGURE 12-12 Classified income statement for Sullivan Enterprises

Some expenses may be allocated as both selling and administrative expenses. For example, Insurance Expense may be incurred on behalf of both the office and the sales departments. Depreciation may have to be divided between the administrative and the sales sections. It is the accountant's task to determine a fair basis for allocating the expense. For example, if the office occupies 30 percent of the building, then 30 percent of the depreciation on the building would be charged as an administrative expense. If the remaining 70 percent is occupied by the sales section, then 70 percent of the depreciation on the building would be charged as a selling expense.

Preparing the Balance Sheet or Statement of Financial Position

Statement of financial position is another name for a balance sheet.

Another name for a balance sheet is a statement of financial position. The data required for a balance sheet are found in the balance sheet section of the work sheet. The balance sheet for Sullivan Enterprises is shown in Figure 12-13. Notice how Capital is updated in the equity section. The additional investments and the difference between the net income and Drawings are added to the Capital account.

Classified Balance Sheet or Statement of Financial Position

The balance sheet shown in Figure 12-13 is also a classified statement. As was said previously in regard to the income statement, it is much easier for users to examine and interpret such standard or *classified financial statements*.

Order of liquidity is the order in which current assets will be converted into cash.

As you learned in Chapter 5, Unit 10, assets are divided into two sections on a classified balance sheet—*current* and *fixed* (sometimes called Plant and Equipment or Property, Plant, and Equipment), as shown in Figure 12-13. The current assets are listed in order of liquidity; that is, in the order in which they will be converted into cash. The fixed assets that have the longest life are listed first in the fixed assets section.

Current assets are listed in order of liquidity.

Fixed assets are listed in order of longest life first.

Current Assets	**Fixed Assets**
Cash	Land
Accounts Receivable	Building
Merchandise Inventory	Equipment
Prepaid Expenses	

Liabilities are also divided into two sections—*current* and *long-term*. Current liabilities are those that will be paid within one year. *They are listed according to maturity,* that is, in the order in which they will be paid. Long-term liabilities are those that have a due date longer than one year. *They are also listed according to maturity.*

Current liabilities are listed according to maturity.

Long-term liabilities are listed according to maturity.

Current Liabilities	**Long-Term Liabilities**
Accounts Payable	Bank Loan (3 years)
Salaries Payable	Mortgage Payable (25 years)
Interest Payable	
Bank Loan (6 months)	

Sullivan Enterprises
Balance Sheet
December 31, 20-4

Assets

Current Assets			
Cash		$112 000	
Accounts Receivable	$ 53 000		
Less: Allowance for Doubtful Accounts	2 000	51 000	
Merchandise Inventory		86 000	
Supplies		2 000	
Total Current Assets			$251 000
Fixed Assets			
Building	160 000		
Less: Accumulated Depreciation	53 790	106 210	
Equipment	23 000		
Less: Accumulated Depreciation	12 760	10 240	
Total Fixed Assets			116 450
Total Assets			$367 450

Liabilities and Owner's Equity

Current Liabilities		
Accounts Payable	$ 23 450	
Salaries Payable	1 200	
PST Payable	2 130	
GST Payable	1 870	
GST Refundable	(640)	
Interest Payable	225	
Bank Loan	10 000	
Total Current Liabilities		$ 38 235
Long-Term Liabilities		
Mortgage Payable		88 000
Total Liabilities		126 235
Owner's Equity		
E. Sullivan, Capital January 1	100 640	
Add: New Investment for Year	$100 000	
Add: Net Income for Year	48 575	
Less: E. Sullivan, Drawings	(8 000)	
Increase in Capital	140 575	
E. Sullivan, Capital, December 31		241 215
Total Liabilities and Owner's Equity		$367 450

FIGURE 12-13 Classified balance sheet for Sullivan Enterprises

Preparing Journal Entries

The adjustments on the work sheet are recorded in the general journal and then posted to the general ledger.

Adjusting Entries

Adjusting journal entries are required so that the adjustments made on the work sheet become part of the permanent records. When the adjustments on the work sheet are coded with letters such as (a), (b), (c), etc., the preparation of the adjusting journal entries is made quite simple. The adjusting entries for Sullivan Enterprises are shown in the general journal in Figure 12-14. See if you can trace these entries back to the work sheet (Figure 12-6 on page 604).

Adjusting Entries

DATE		PARTICULARS	P.R.	DEBIT	CREDIT
20-4		GENERAL JOURNAL			PAGE 33
Dec.	31	Bad Debts Expense		1 9 5 0 00	
		Allowance for Doubtful Accounts			1 9 5 0 00
		To record estimated bad debts according to age analysis.			
	31	Supplies Expense		2 5 0 0 00	
		Supplies			2 5 0 0 00
		To record supplies used.			
	31	Depreciation Expense—Building		5 5 9 0 00	
		Accumulated Depreciation—Building			5 5 9 0 00
		To record depreciation at 5 percent using the declining-balance method.			
	31	Depreciation Expense—Equipment		2 5 6 0 00	
		Accumulated Depreciation—Equipment			2 5 6 0 00
		To record depreciation at 20 percent using the declining-balance method.			
	31	Interest Expense		2 2 5 00	
		Interest Payable			2 2 5 00
		To record three months' interest owed on bank loan.			
	31	Salaries Expense		1 2 0 0 00	
		Salaries Payable			1 2 0 0 00
		To record December commissions owed to sales staff.			

FIGURE 12–14 Adjusting entries in the general journal

Closing Entries

Closing entries are required to prepare the ledger for the next fiscal period and to update the owner's Capital account. The revenue, expense, and cost of goods sold accounts are closed into Income Summary. The Income Summary and Drawings accounts are closed into Capital. The four basic closing entries shown in Figure 12-15 are:

1. Close the credits from the income section of the work sheet into the Income Statement account.
2. Close the debits from the income section of the work sheet into the Income Summary account.
3. Close the Income Summary account into the Capital account.
4. Close the Drawings account into the Capital account.

Closing Entries

	GENERAL JOURNAL			PAGE 34
DATE	PARTICULARS	P.R.	DEBIT	CREDIT
20-4				
Dec. 31	Merchandise Inventory		86 0 0 0 00	
	Sales		320 0 0 0 00	
	Income Summary			406 0 0 0 00
	To record the new inventory and to close the Sales account.			
31	Income Summary		357 4 2 5 00	
	Merchandise Inventory			90 0 0 0 00
	Purchases			110 0 0 0 00
	Advertising Expense			5 0 0 0 00
	General Expense			4 0 0 0 00
	Salaries Expense			121 2 0 0 00
	Utilities Expense			7 4 0 0 00
	Insurance Expense			7 0 0 0 00
	Bad Debts Expense			1 9 5 0 00
	Supplies Expense			2 5 0 0 00
	Depreciation Expense—Building			5 5 9 0 00
	Depreciation Expense—Equipment			2 5 6 0 00
	Interest Expense			2 2 5 00
	To close the Inventory account, the cost of goods sold accounts, and the expense accounts.			
31	Income Summary		48 5 7 5 00	
	E. Sullivan, Capital			48 5 7 5 00
	To transfer the year's net income to the Capital account.			
31	E. Sullivan, Capital		8 0 0 0 00	
	E. Sullivan, Drawings			8 0 0 0 00
	To close the Drawings account.			

FIGURE 12-15 Closing entries in the general journal

Included in these entries are two that involve the adjustment for Merchandise Inventory. One entry closes the beginning inventory amount and the other records the ending inventory amount in Merchandise Inventory.

The general journal in Figure 12-15 contains the closing entries prepared from the work sheet (Figure 12-6 on page 604). Can you trace each entry back to the work sheet? What effect does the credit of $90 000 have on Merchandise Inventory? What effect does the debit of $86 000 have on Merchandise Inventory?

Posting to the Ledger

The adjusting and closing entries in the general journal are posted to the general ledger. After this is done, the revenue, expense, and cost of goods sold accounts, as well as the Drawings account, will have *zero* balances. They will be ready to receive the transactions for the new fiscal period. Merchandise Inventory will contain the new inventory figure. The Capital account will contain the new balance that reflects the operating results for the fiscal period.

Figure 12-16 below shows several general ledger accounts after the adjusting and closing entries have been posted. Notice that the Sales account is prepared for the next fiscal period. It has a zero balance and has been ruled closed. The Merchandise Inventory account has been closed and re-opened. It contains the new inventory of $86 000. The Capital account has a balance of $241 215, the same as the new Capital amount on the balance sheet in Figure 12-13.

ACCOUNT	Merchandise Inventory						No. 120
DATE		PARTICULARS	P.R.	DEBIT	CREDIT	DR. CR.	BALANCE
20-4							
Jan.	1	Beginning balance	✓	90 0 0 0 00		DR.	90 0 0 0 00
Dec.	31	To close	J34		90 0 0 0 00		0 00
	31	To record new inventory	J34	86 0 0 0 00		DR.	86 0 0 0 00

ACCOUNT	E. Sullivan, Capital						No. 300
DATE		PARTICULARS	P.R.	DEBIT	CREDIT	DR. CR.	BALANCE
20-4							
Jan.	1	Balance	✓			CR.	100 6 4 0 00
Jun.	30	New investment	J18		100 0 0 0 00	CR.	200 6 4 0 00
Dec.	31	Net income	J34		48 5 7 5 00	CR.	249 2 1 5 00
	31	Drawings	J34	8 0 0 0 00		CR.	241 2 1 5 00

ACCOUNT	E. Sullivan, Drawings						No. 301
DATE		PARTICULARS	P.R.	DEBIT	CREDIT	DR. CR.	BALANCE
20-4							
Dec.	31	Balance	✓			DR.	8 0 0 0 00
	31	To close	J34		8 0 0 0 00		0 00

ACCOUNT	Income Summary						No. 302
DATE	PARTICULARS	P.R.	DEBIT	CREDIT	DR. CR.	BALANCE	
20-4							
Dec. 31	Merch. Inventory & Sales	J34		406 0 0 0 00	CR.	406 0 0 0 00	
31	Merch. Inv., Costs and Exp.	J34	357 4 2 5 00		CR.	48 5 7 5 00	
31	Net Income to Capital	J34	48 5 7 5 00			0 00	

ACCOUNT	Sales						No. 400
DATE	PARTICULARS	P.R.	DEBIT	CREDIT	DR. CR.	BALANCE	
20-4							
Dec. 31	Balance	✓			CR.	320 0 0 0 00	
31	To close	J34	320 0 0 0 00			0 00	

FIGURE 12-16 Partial general ledger after posting of adjusting and closing entries

Alternative Merchandise Inventory Adjustment Method Closing Entries

The closing entries for Sullivan Enterprises using the alternative method of adjusting merchandise inventory are shown in Figure 12-17 on page 626.

Previous Adjustments

Remember, the following entries that adjust Merchandise Inventory have already been recorded.

Dec.	31	Income Summary	90 0 0 0 00	
		Merchandise Inventory		90 0 0 0 00
		To close beginning inventory to Income Summary.		
	31	Merchandise Inventory	86 0 0 0 00	
		Income Summary		86 0 0 0 00
		To record ending inventory.		

Closing Entries

The general journal in Figure 12-17 contains the closing entries prepared from the work sheet (Figure 12-6 on page 604). Can you trace each entry back to the work sheet?

Note that no entries are made to Merchandise Inventory. This account was updated through the adjusting entries shown above.

Both methods of recording inventory are acceptable and result in the same information being generated for the firm; however, the first method described had two advantages:

- fewer journal entries are required; and
- the entries to Income Summary are obtained directly from the income statement column totals in the work sheet.

As mentioned previously, the first method is used in this text unless the alternative method is specified.

GENERAL JOURNAL				PAGE **34**	
DATE	PARTICULARS	P.R.	DEBIT	CREDIT	
20-4					
Dec. 31	Sales		320 0 0 0 00		
	Income Summary			320 0 0 0 00	
	To close the Sales account.				
31	Income Summary		267 4 2 5 00		
	Purchases			110 0 0 0 00	
	Advertising Expense			5 0 0 0 00	
	General Expense			4 0 0 0 00	
	Salaries Expense			121 2 0 0 00	
	Utilities Expense			7 4 0 0 00	
	Insurance Expense			7 0 0 0 00	
	Bad Debts Expense			1 9 5 0 00	
	Supplies Expense			2 5 0 0 00	
	Depreciation Expense—Building			5 5 9 0 00	
	Depreciation Expense—Equipment			2 5 6 0 00	
	Interest Expense			2 2 5 00	
	To close the cost of goods sold accounts and				
	the expense accounts.				
31	Income Summary		48 5 7 5 00		
	E. Sullivan, Capital			48 5 7 5 00	
	To transfer the year's net income to the Capital account.				
31	E. Sullivan, Capital		8 0 0 0 00		
	E. Sullivan, Drawings			8 0 0 0 00	
	To close the Drawings account.				

FIGURE 12-17 Closing entries in the general journal

Preparing the Post-Closing Trial Balance

A final proof is required to ensure that the general ledger is in balance to start the new fiscal period. Figure 12-18 shows the trial post-closing balance that is prepared after the closing entries have been posted. It contains only asset, liability, and equity accounts. All of the revenue, expense, and cost of goods sold accounts have been closed and do not have to be shown on the last trial balance.

**Sullivan Enterprises
Post-Closing Trial Balance
December 31, 20-4**

Account	Acc. No.	Debit	Credit
Cash	101	$112 000	
Accounts Receivable	110	53 000	
Allowance for Doubtful Accounts	111		$ 2 000
Merchandise Inventory	120	86 000	
Supplies	125	2 000	
Building	150	160 000	
Accumulated Depreciation—Building	151		53 790
Equipment	160	23 000	
Accumulated Depreciation—Equipment	161		12 760
Accounts Payable	200		23 450
PST Payable	205		2 130
GST Payable	206		1 870
GST Refundable	207	640	
Interest Payable	215		225
Salaries Payable	220		1 200
Bank Loan	240		10 000
Mortgage Payable	250		88 000
E. Sullivan, Capital	300		241 215
		$436 640	$436 640

FIGURE 12-18 Post-closing trial balance that proves the accuracy of the recording
process in preparation for the new fiscal period

Examining Reversing Entries

Earlier in this chapter, you learned how to adjust accrued expenses. The example used was $225 in interest that was owed on a bank loan. The loan was for six months. At the end of the fiscal period, three months' interest of $225 was owed, but had not been recorded because it was not due to be paid until March 31. The following T-accounts illustrate the adjusting and closing entries made on December 31.

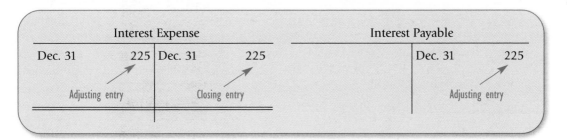

On March 31, payment was made to the bank for six months' interest of $450. This covered the full period of the loan, October 1 to March 31. When this entry was made, Interest Expense was debited $450, and Cash was credited $450 as shown here:

Interest Expense				Cash		
Dec. 31	225	Dec. 31	225		Mar. 31	450
Mar. 31	450					

But there is a dilemma here. Can you see it? How much interest on this loan had already been recorded in December?

Because of the adjusting entry, the interest for October 1 to December 31 ($225) was recorded twice—once when the adjustment was made and again when the interest was actually paid to the bank in March. A total of $675 ($225 + $450) has been recorded in the Interest Expense account. The actual amount of the interest is $450. This double recording of interest is avoided by the use of a *reversing entry*. In general, *reversing entries* are used to make adjustments to accrued revenue and accrued expense accounts to avoid double recording of those items.

On January 3, the first working day after the end of the fiscal period, this reversing entry is made:

Jan.	3	Interest Payable	2 2 5 00	
		Interest Expense		2 2 5 00
		To reverse the adjusting entry of Dec. 31.		

Reversing entries are necessary to make adjustments to accrued expense and accrued revenue accounts.

The effect of this entry is shown in the following T-accounts:

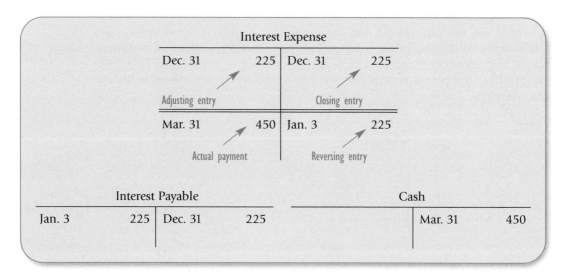

Notice that the reversing entry of January 3 has the effect of allocating half of the actual interest paid to the new fiscal period and half to the previous fiscal period. This is correct and results in *the correct matching of expenses and revenue for each fiscal period.*

Other Reversing Entries

Reversing entries are required for all accrued expense and accrued revenue adjustments. Earlier in this chapter, an adjusting entry for salaries owed ($1200) was explained. The adjusting entry is shown in these T-accounts:

Salaries Expense				Salaries Payable		
Dec. 31	1 200				Dec. 31	1 200

This entry is necessary because sales commissions are paid the month after they are earned. The closing entries result in the following:

	Salaries Expense		
Dec. 31	1 200	Dec. 31	1 200

The reversing entry shown below is made on January 3. This entry is necessary to avoid a double recording of the sales commissions.

Jan.	3	Salaries Payable	1 2 0 0 00	
		Salaries Expense		1 2 0 0 00
		To reverse the adjusting entry of Dec. 31.		

The accounts now appear as follows:

Salaries Expense					Salaries Payable			
Dec. 31	1 200	Dec. 31	1 200		Jan. 3	1 200	Dec. 31	1 200
		Jan. 3	1 200					

On January 31, the sales commissions are paid and this entry is made:

Jan.	31	Salaries Expense	1 2 0 0 00	
		Cash		1 2 0 0 00
		To pay December commissions.		

The accounts are shown below:

Salaries Expense				Cash		
Dec. 31	1 200	Dec. 31	1 200		Jan. 31	1 200
Jan. 31	1 200	Jan. 3	1 200			

Similar reversing entries are prepared on the first working day of the new fiscal period for all accrued expense and revenue adjustments.

Reversing entries could be avoided by debiting the payable account when payment is made in the new fiscal period. However, this is *not* done; with a number of accrueds and payments spread out over months, it would be easy to forget to handle the transactions correctly. To avoid errors and reliance on one person's memory, it is standard accounting practice to use reversing entries.

MERCHANDISING BUSINESS USING A PERPETUAL INVENTORY SYSTEM

The completion of the accounting cycle for a merchandising business that uses a perpetual inventory system follows the same procedure as for a periodic inventory system. However, there are some differences in the preparation of the work sheet and financial statements.

Work Sheet

A completed work sheet for New Enterprise Store, a merchandising business that uses a perpetual inventory system, is shown in Figure 12-19. It differs from the periodic system in two ways:

1. The cost of goods sold is recorded as sales are made and is found in the Cost of Goods Sold account on the work sheet. The calculation of cost of goods sold in the work sheet, or on a separate schedule, or in the income statement is not required.
2. The Merchandise Inventory account on the trial balance is an accurate ending inventory value since it has been updated continually. There is no need to adjust the value at the end of the accounting period. Any difference between the physical inventory and the ledger balance has already been adjusted.

Interim financial statements can be prepared under the perpetual inventory system.

The continuous availability of these two pieces of information enables merchandising firms to generate accurate financial statements during the accounting period as well as at the end. This improved information can be valuable to the decision-making process.

New Enterprise Store, Work Sheet
For the year ended December 31, 20-4

	ACC. NO.	ACCOUNT TITLE	TRIAL BALANCE DEBIT	TRIAL BALANCE CREDIT	ADJUSTMENTS DEBIT	ADJUSTMENTS CREDIT	INCOME STATEMENT DEBIT	INCOME STATEMENT CREDIT	BALANCE SHEET DEBIT	BALANCE SHEET CREDIT
1	100	Cash	13 420 00						13 420 00	
2	102	Accounts Receivable	30 000 00						30 000 00	
3	103	Allowance for Doubtful Accounts		5 0 00		(b) 5 5 0 00				6 0 0 00
4	120	Merchandise Inventory	58 000 00						58 000 00	
5	131	Supplies	5 000 00			(a) 2 8 0 0 00			2 200 00	
6	141	Store Fixtures	15 000 00						15 000 00	
7	142	Accum. Depreciation—Store Fixtures		7 300 00		(c) 1 5 4 0 00				8 840 00
8	200	Accounts Payable		9 000 00						9 000 00
9	205	PST Payable		1 730 00						1 730 00
10	206	GST Payable		1 520 00						1 520 00
11	207	GST Refundable	5 80 00						5 80 00	
12	221	Bank Loan		8 000 00						8 000 00
13	300	G. Lucziw, Capital		51 225 00						51 225 00
14	301	G. Lucziw, Drawings	19 000 00						19 000 00	
15	400	Sales		260 000 00				260 000 00		
16	500	Cost of Goods Sold	82 000 00				82 000 00			
17	610	Advertising Expense	8 000 00				8 000 00			
18	611	Office Expense	4 000 00				4 000 00			
19	612	Store Expense	9 000 00				9 000 00			
20	613	Rent Expense	14 000 00				14 000 00			
21	614	Salaries Expense	80 000 00		(e) 5 0 0 00		80 500 00			
22	615	Interest Expense	8 25 00		(d) 7 5 0 00		1 5 75 00			
23			338 825 00	338 825 00						
24	616	Supplies Expense			(a) 2 8 0 0 00		2 800 00			
25	617	Bad Debts Expense			(b) 5 5 0 00		5 50 00			
26	618	Depreciation Expense—Store Fixtures			(c) 1 5 4 0 00		1 5 40 00			
27	201	Interest Payable				(d) 7 5 0 00				7 50 00
28	202	Salaries Payable				(e) 5 0 0 00				5 00 00
29					6 140 00	6 140 00	203 965 00	260 000 00	138 200 00	82 165 00
30		Net Income					56 035 00			56 035 00
31							260 000 00	260 000 00	138 200 00	138 200 00
32										

FIGURE 12-19 Completed work sheet for a merchandising business that uses a perpetual inventory system

Preparing the Income Statement

The first statement prepared by New Enterprise Store from the work sheet is the income statement shown in Figure 12-20. There are two things you should notice:

- A schedule of cost of goods sold is not prepared.
- Cost of Goods Sold is shown as an expense in the income statement rather than as a separate section.

A schedule of cost of goods sold is not necessary when using a perpetual inventory system.

Cost of Goods Sold is found in the expense section of the income statement for firms using the perpetual inventory system.

The classified income statement and balance sheet would be prepared using the data from the work sheet in exactly the same way you prepared the statements for a business using the periodic inventory system.

New Enterprise Store Income Statement For the year ended December 31, 20-4		
Revenue		
Sales		$260 000
Expenses		
Cost of Goods Sold	$ 82 000	
Advertising	8 000	
Office	4 000	
Store	9 000	
Rent	14 000	
Salaries	80 500	
Interest	1 575	
Supplies	2 800	
Bad Debts	550	
Depreciation—Store Fixtures	1 540	
Total Expenses		203 965
Net Income		$ 56 035

FIGURE 12-20 Income statement for a merchandising business that uses a perpetual inventory system

Adjusting and Closing Entries

The adjusting and closing entries for a merchandising firm that uses the perpetual inventory system are prepared from the work sheet in the same manner as the entries for a periodic inventory system.

Completing the Accounting Cycle

You have now learned the final steps in the accounting cycle for a merchandising company. Figure 12-21 summarizes the complete accounting cycle and illustrates all of the tasks completed during the accounting period.

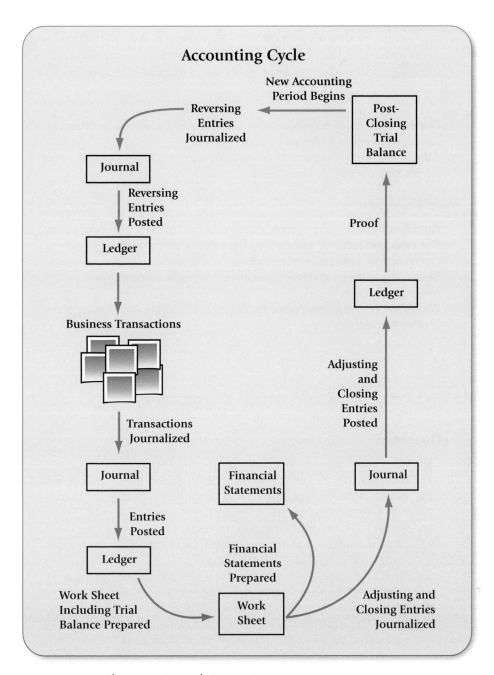

FIGURE 12-21 The accounting cycle is a continuous process.

> ## Generally Accepted Accounting Principles and Key Ideas
>
> In this chapter, you continued to learn about the matching principle, which requires that:
>
> - **The revenue** for an accounting period must be matched with the expenses for that period to determine the net income.
> - **Adjustments** must be made for accrued revenue and accrued expenses so that the matching principle can be applied.
>
> You also learned that:
>
> - **An adjustment** is made to record the estimated bad debts for each fiscal period.
> - **The two methods of estimating bad debts** are the income statement method and the balance sheet method.
> - **Reversing entries** are required for all accrued expense and accrued revenue adjustments.
> - **Classified financial statements** are an aid to persons who examine and interpret financial data.

UNIT 29 CHECK YOUR READING

Questions

20. What is the purpose of classifying financial statements?
21. What are two classes into which operating expenses may be divided?
22. What are the five separate sections on a classified balance sheet?
23. Why are reversing entries necessary?
24. Which adjusting entries require reversing entries?
25. Explain how the closing entries result in Merchandise Inventory being both closed and then re-opened.
26. Which inventory system does not require a schedule of cost of goods sold? Explain why this schedule is unnecessary.
27. Which inventory system provides the most current information to prepare monthly or weekly financial statements? Why are interim statements useful to the management of a company?

UNIT 29 APPLY YOUR KNOWLEDGE

Exercises Part A

22. (a) Prepare schedules of cost of goods sold for each of the following companies. The fiscal period is the month of May, 20—.

Company A

Beginning Merchandise Inventory	$140 000
Purchases	600 000
Transportation on Purchases	12 000
Purchases Returns and Allowances	30 000
Ending Merchandise Inventory	120 000

Company B

Beginning Merchandise Inventory	$50 000
Purchases	80 000
Transportation on Purchases	4 900
Duty	6 000
Purchases Returns and Allowances	6 000
Purchases Discounts	1 800
Ending Merchandise Inventory	52 000

Company C

Beginning Merchandise Inventory	$ 75 000
Purchases	125 000
Transportation on Purchases	5 000
Sales Discounts	4 000
Sales Returns and Allowances	5 000
Purchases Returns and Allowances	7 500
Ending Merchandise Inventory	85 000

(b) Which inventory system do Companies A, B, and C use?

23. (a) Shown on the following page is a list of expenses. Divide the list into two sections: administrative expenses and selling expenses. Insurance, Utilities, Telephone, and Depreciation—Building are all divided 75 percent to selling expenses and 25 percent to administrative expenses.

(b) What is the total of the selling expenses and the total of the administrative expenses?

(c) What is the net income if the gross profit is $44 000?

(d) What are the net sales if the cost of goods sold is $30 000?

Expenses	
Advertising	$2 000
Utilities	1 200
Salaries—Office	5 000
Delivery	6 000
Office Supplies (used)	400
Insurance	300
Depreciation—Building	2 000
Depreciation—Truck	1 000
Store Supplies (used)	800
Telephone	200

24. (a) Prepare a classified income statement for exercise 17 on pages 613 and 614. Jeans Unlimited classifies Bad Debts Expense as a selling expense and allocates Supplies Expense, Rent Expense, Depreciation Expense, and Salaries Expense 70 percent to selling expenses and 30 percent to administrative expenses.
(b) Prepare a classified balance sheet.
(c) Journalize the adjusting and closing entries.
(d) Post the adjusting and closing entries.
(e) Prepare a post-closing trial balance.

25. (a) Kyra Enterprises has a perpetual inventory system. Use the work sheet on the next page to prepare an income statement and a balance sheet.
(b) Journalize the adjusting and closing entries.

26. The following adjustments were prepared on December 31. In a general journal, prepare the reversing entries that would be made on January 3.

20-4				
Dec.	31	Interest Expense	3 5 0 00	
		Interest Payable		3 5 0 00
		To record interest owed but not yet paid.		
	31	Salaries Expense	2 1 9 5 00	
		Salaries Payable		2 1 9 5 00
		To record salaries owed to workers but not yet paid.		

27. A company pays its workers every two weeks. The next payday is January 4. Employees are owed (but have not been paid) $1800 for work in December.
(a) Prepare the adjusting entry to record salaries owing.
(b) Prepare the reversing entry.

Kyra Enterprises, Work Sheet
For the year ended December 31, 20-4

ACCOUNT TITLE	ACC. NO.	TRIAL BALANCE DEBIT	TRIAL BALANCE CREDIT	ADJUSTMENTS DEBIT	ADJUSTMENTS CREDIT	INCOME STATEMENT DEBIT	INCOME STATEMENT CREDIT	BALANCE SHEET DEBIT	BALANCE SHEET CREDIT	
Cash	100	2 8 0 00						2 8 0 00		1
Accounts Receivable	102	1 7 7 0 00						1 7 7 0 00		2
Merchandise Inventory	120	6 4 0 0 00						6 4 0 0 00		3
Unexpired Insurance	130	5 8 0 00			(b) 2 4 0 00			3 4 0 00		4
Store Equipment	140	2 3 0 0 00						2 3 0 0 00		5
Accum. Depreciation—Store Equipment	141		6 2 0 00		(a) 2 6 0 00				8 8 0 00	6
Accounts Payable	200		2 2 2 2 00						2 2 2 2 00	7
PST Payable	205		3 5 0 00						3 5 0 00	8
GST Payable	206		3 0 8 00						3 0 8 00	9
GST Refundable	207	1 5 0 00						1 5 0 00		10
L. Kyra, Capital	300		7 2 8 0 00						7 2 8 0 00	11
L. Kyra, Drawings	301	1 8 0 0 00						1 8 0 0 00		12
Sales	400		52 8 0 0 00				52 8 0 0 00			13
Sales Returns and Allowances	401	1 6 0 0 00				1 6 0 0 00				14
Sales Discounts	402	1 2 0 0 00				1 2 0 0 00				15
Cost of Goods Sold	500	34 9 0 0 00				34 9 0 0 00				16
Advertising Expense	610	5 6 0 00				5 6 0 00				17
Rent Expense	615	2 8 0 0 00				2 8 0 0 00				18
Salaries Expense	616	4 2 0 0 00				4 2 0 0 00				19
		63 5 8 0 00	63 5 8 0 00							20
Depreciation Exp.—Store Equipment	617			(a) 2 6 0 00		2 6 0 00				21
Insurance Expense	618			(b) 2 4 0 00		2 4 0 00				22
				5 0 0 00	5 0 0 00	50 8 0 0 00	52 8 0 0 00	13 0 4 0 00	11 0 4 0 00	23
Net Income						2 0 0 0 00			2 0 0 0 00	24
						52 8 0 0 00	52 8 0 0 00	13 0 4 0 00	13 0 4 0 00	25
										26

28. Prepare the necessary reversing entries for Ichikawa Engineering Supply in exercise 21 on pages 615 and 616.

29. At the end of the fiscal period, a company has earned, but not received, interest of $1200 on a long-term deposit. Prepare the adjusting and reversing entries. The accounts involved are Interest Receivable and Interest Income.

Exercises Part B

30. Alvarez Stores uses a perpetual inventory system. Use the work sheet on the next page to:
  (a) Prepare a classified income statement. When you classify the income statement, distribute Supplies Expense, Insurance Expense, and Depreciation Expense 75 percent to selling expense and 25 percent to administrative expense. Bad Debts Expense is classified as an administrative expense by Alvarez Stores.
  (b) Prepare a classified balance sheet.
  (c) Journalize and post the adjusting and closing entries.
  (d) Prepare a post-closing trial balance.

Alvarez Stores, Work Sheet
For the year ended December 31, 20—

#	ACCOUNT TITLE	ACC NO.	TRIAL BALANCE DEBIT	TRIAL BALANCE CREDIT	ADJUSTMENTS DEBIT	ADJUSTMENTS CREDIT	INCOME STATEMENT DEBIT	INCOME STATEMENT CREDIT	BALANCE SHEET DEBIT	BALANCE SHEET CREDIT
1	Cash	100	2 5 3 0 00						2 5 3 0 00	
2	Accounts Receivable	102	8 0 0 0 00						8 0 0 0 00	
3	Merchandise Inventory	120	24 0 0 0 00						24 0 0 0 00	
4	Supplies	121	1 7 0 0 00			(a) 1 2 5 0 00			4 5 0 00	
5	Prepaid Insurance	122	2 0 0 0 00			(b) 1 2 0 0 00			8 0 0 00	
6	Land	140	40 0 0 0 00						40 0 0 0 00	
7	Building	141	120 0 0 0 00						120 0 0 0 00	
8	Equipment	143	40 0 0 0 00						40 0 0 0 00	
9	Accounts Payable	200		13 7 0 0 00						13 7 0 0 00
10	PST Payable	205		1 3 0 0 00						1 3 0 0 00
11	GST Payable	206		1 1 4 0 00						1 1 4 0 00
12	GST Refundable	207	4 7 0 00						4 7 0 00	
13	Mortgage Payable	210		47 5 6 0 00						47 5 6 0 00
14	G. Alvarez, Capital	300		140 0 0 0 00						140 0 0 0 00
15	G. Alvarez, Drawings	301	6 0 0 0 00						6 0 0 0 00	
16	Sales	400		195 0 0 0 00				195 0 0 0 00		
17	Sales Returns and Allowances	401	1 0 0 0 00				1 0 0 0 00			
18	Sales Discounts	402	3 0 0 00				3 0 0 00			
19	Cost of Goods Sold	500	92 7 0 0 00				92 7 0 0 00			
20	Salaries Expense—Selling	610	30 0 0 0 00				30 0 0 0 00			
21	Salaries Expense—Administration	611	20 0 0 0 00				20 0 0 0 00			
22	Delivery Expense	612	7 0 0 0 00				7 0 0 0 00			
23	General Expense	613	2 0 0 0 00				2 0 0 0 00			
24	Property Tax Expense	614	1 0 0 0 00				1 0 0 0 00			
25			398 7 0 0 00	398 7 0 0 00						
26	Supplies Expense	615			(a) 1 2 5 0 00		1 2 5 0 00			
27	Insurance Expense	616			(b) 1 2 0 0 00		1 2 0 0 00			
28	Depreciation Expense—Building	617			(c) 6 0 0 0 00		6 0 0 0 00			
29	Accumulated Depreciation—Building	142				(c) 6 0 0 0 00				6 0 0 0 00
30	Depreciation Expense—Equipment	618			(d) 8 0 0 0 00		8 0 0 0 00			
31	Accumulated Depreciation—Equipment	144				(d) 8 0 0 0 00				8 0 0 0 00
32	Bad Debts Expense	619			(e) 1 9 3 7 00		1 9 3 7 00			
33	Allowance for Doubtful Accounts	103				(e) 1 9 3 7 00				1 9 3 7 00
34					18 3 8 7 00	18 3 8 7 00	172 3 8 7 00	195 0 0 0 00	242 2 5 0 00	219 6 3 7 00
35	Net Income						22 6 1 3 00			22 6 1 3 00
36							195 0 0 0 00	195 0 0 0 00	242 2 5 0 00	242 2 5 0 00
37										

Computer Accounting

Using a Work Sheet: Yes or No?

Most accounting programs have three stages—*input, processing,* and *output.* In the input stage, transaction information is entered (recorded) using the computer. The transaction information forms a database that is processed in a variety of ways depending on the program. Then the program produces the output (reports) required by the accountant. These stages are illustrated in Figure 12-22.

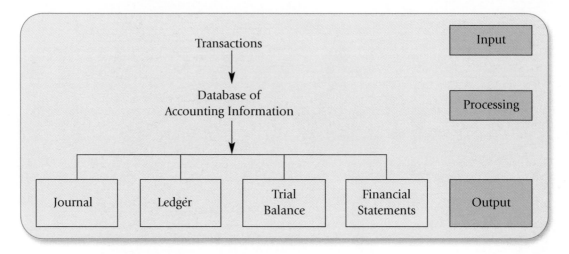

FIGURE 12-22 Three computer stages

Figure 12-22 illustrates that a variety of reports (output) can be produced. If the computer system is capable of doing this, why is a work sheet necessary?

In a manual accounting system, the work sheet is a planning and organizing device that the accountant uses to prepare the financial statements. In particular, the format of the work sheet assists the accountant in preparing the adjustments, adjusting entries, and closing entries.

In a computerized system, some accountants still prepare a work sheet *manually* for the same reasons. They feel it is easier and quicker to prepare adjustments and closing entries with the computer if the planning is *first* done on a work sheet.

What do you think? Complete assignment 2 of the following Computer Assignments before you decide.

COMPUTER ASSIGNMENTS

1. (a) Format a spreadsheet to do the following for the data in the chart on the next page:
   (i) Total the amount column.
   (ii) Calculate the bad debts estimate and total the bad debts estimate column.
   (b) Enter the data and print the spreadsheet.

<table>
<tr><td colspan="4" align="center">**Estimated Bad Debts**
For 20—</td></tr>
<tr>
<th>Age of
Accounts</th>
<th>Amount</th>
<th>Percentage
Estimated To Be
Uncollectible</th>
<th>Bad Debts
Estimate</th>
</tr>
<tr><td>Current</td><td>$149 000</td><td>1%</td><td>?</td></tr>
<tr><td>1–30 days</td><td>68 000</td><td>3%</td><td>?</td></tr>
<tr><td>31–60 days</td><td>25 000</td><td>10%</td><td>?</td></tr>
<tr><td>61–90 days</td><td>8 100</td><td>15%</td><td>?</td></tr>
<tr><td>+ 90 days</td><td>8 800</td><td>45%</td><td>?</td></tr>
<tr><td>Totals</td><td>?</td><td></td><td>?</td></tr>
</table>

2. (a) Format a spreadsheet for exercise 16 on pages 612 and 613.
   (b) Enter the data and print the work sheet.
3. Complete exercise 22(a) on pages 634 and 635, using a spreadsheet.
4. Use a spreadsheet to complete Case 2: Interpreting Accounting Data on page 644.
5. Complete Case 4: Age Analysis on page 645, using a spreadsheet for part (a).
6. BKP Electronics

BKP Electronics is a large supplier of electronic equipment with locations in Canada and the United States. The company supplies, installs, and repairs electronic products, projection devices, and sound systems. Its products are purchased by, and installed in, large theatres, performance centres, and arenas. Its employees are highly trained technologists and engineers, who design, install, and maintain the equipment, some of which is used for advertising at major events and performances.

Many of BKP Electronics' customers purchase extended warranties and service contracts for the ongoing maintenance of the equipment and systems. To protect customers against the possible failure of an electronic component, testing and monitoring procedures are built into the systems. These tests will identify any part of the system that is faulty.

The customer can send a faulty component back to the company for repair. If the product is under warranty, the repair is done at no charge to the customer. If the component is not under warranty, the customer covers the costs of the materials, labour, testing, and shipping.

Obviously, in this type of business, keeping track of job costs—be they labour or parts—is critical for the current and future financial health of the firm. An electronic form is used to calculate the costs associated with each repair. A printout is sent to the accounting department where an invoice is prepared and sent to the customer.

(a) Prepare a spreadsheet similar to the form shown on the next page. Format the spreadsheet to do the following:

   (i) Calculate labour costs for testing, assembly, and quality control.

   (ii) Calculate the parts cost.

   (iii) Add the shipping cost.

   (iv) Add the customs brokerage charges for foreign customers.

   (v) Calculate and add the GST and PST.

   (vi) Show the total cost of the repair.

(b) Use the spreadsheet you have prepared to calculate the charges for the following repairs. PST of 8 percent is charged on parts and GST of 7 percent is charged on both parts and labour.

   (i) Performing Arts Centre. Model ALP-6, Purchase Order 9087210. Tested and repaired a transceiver module, installed a fuse ($1.95, part no. Q-165) and an integrated circuit ($3.75, part no. I.C.377). Labour includes 2 hours testing, ½ hour assembly, and ¼ hour quality control. Shipping charges are $29.

   (ii) Glendale Properties. Model EXT-A, Purchase Order 01-92. Tested and repaired an interface unit, installed a relay ($27, part no. E006) and a transistor ($1.23, part no. Q0021). Labour includes 1 hour testing, ¼ hour assembly, and ¼ hour quality control. Shipping charges are $7, and the customs brokerage fee is $83.

www.pearsoned.ca/
principlesofaccounting

WEB EXTENSIONS

Internet Study Guide

❧ Complete the Chapter 12 review.

❧ Complete the Chapter 12 definitions.

❧ Complete the Chapter 12 online test.

Web Links

Visit the Web Links section at the Pearson Education web site to find links to goal setting. Use the information provided to outline the importance of setting goals.

Repair and Overhaul Pricing Form

Customer: _____   Date: _____

Model & No.: _____   Purchase Order: _____

Repair Description

Labour Charges

	Hours	Rate per Hour	Total
Testing	_____	$100.00	_____
Assembly	_____	$ 80.00	_____
Quality Control	_____	$ 85.00	_____

Total Labour Costs

Material Charges

Part No.	Quantity	Price	Total
_____	_____	_____	_____
_____	_____	_____	_____
_____	_____	_____	_____
_____	_____	_____	_____
_____	_____	_____	_____

Total Material Costs

Cost Summary:

Labour	_____
Material	_____
GST	_____
PST	_____
Shipping	_____
Customs Brokerage Fee	_____

Total   _____

14 Case Studies

CASE 1 Taking Inventory

At the end of the last fiscal period, employees for Trans-Canada Distributors counted all merchandise on hand. However, a complete section of the warehouse was missed when the inventory was taken. The cost of the merchandise that was not included in the ending inventory figure was $7500.

(a) What effect has this error on the income statement and on the balance sheet this year?
(b) If the error went undiscovered, would the net income in the second year be too high or too low?
(c) Over the two-year period, what is the total error in the net income (assuming the second year's inventory is done correctly)?
(d) Is the owner's equity total correct or incorrect in the second-year balance sheet? Explain your answer.

CASE 2 Interpreting Accounting Data

The following table presents the net sales and the *actual* bad debts for five years. For each of these years, calculate the percentage of bad debts in relation to sales. Then project (or estimate) the percentage of sales that will become bad debts for Year 6.

Year	Net Sales	Actual Bad Debts	Bad Debts Percentage
1	$250 000	$2 000	?
2	400 000	6 000	?
3	425 000	4 000	?
4	470 000	9 000	?
5	450 000	8 000	?

CASE 3 Bad Debts

A company does not adjust its accounts receivable by estimating bad debts at the end of the fiscal period. It uses a method called *direct write-off*. With this method, accounts receivable are written off when they are determined to be uncollectible. For example, on January 31, 20-2, a debt of $1500 was determined to be uncollectible because the customer, P. Kully, had declared bankruptcy. The sale of $1500 had been made in the previous fiscal period.

This entry was made on January 31, 20-2:

Jan.	31	Bad Debts Expense	1 5 0 0 00	
		Accounts Receivable/P. Kully		1 5 0 0 00
		To write off account of bankrupt customer.		

(a) How does the fact that an adjustment for estimated bad debts was not made in 20-1 affect the financial statements for that year?
(b) How does the write-off entry affect the financial statements of 20-2?

Age Analysis

CASE 4

Canada Imports has a very small accounting department. The employees in accounting prepare an age analysis and send it to the sales department, which is also responsible for granting credit and collecting overdue accounts. Canada Imports is often required to borrow from its bank to pay its creditors. Part of an age analysis for Canada Imports follows.

Canada Imports
Partial Age Analysis
December 31, 20—

Customer	Balance	Current	1–30 Days Overdue	31–60 Days Overdue	61–90 Days Overdue	+90 Days Overdue
A. Adobe	$ 400	$ 400				
K. Anan	700		$ 100	$ 300		$ 300
J. Artois	120				$ 120	
M. Aziz	220	120		100		
Others	42 000	19 000	11 000	2 000	5 100	4 900
Totals	$43 440	$19 520	$11 100	$2 400	$5 220	$5 200

(a) Calculate the percentage of the balance column total represented by the total of each column of the age analysis.
(b) Prepare recommendations for the management of Canada Imports regarding their credit and collection procedures.

CASE 5

Accounting Analysis

You are considering buying Knockout Sporting Goods. The income statements for the last three years include the following key figures:

	Year 3	Year 2	Year 1
Net Sales*	$530 000	$525 000	$500 000
Cost of Goods Sold	296 800	299 250	300 000
Gross Profit	$233 200	$225 750	$200 000
Gross Profit Percentage	44%	43%	40%

* *Note:* Operating expenses are 30 percent of net sales each year.

The current owner informs you that the statements indicate that the business is becoming more profitable each year and that it would be an ideal time for you to purchase Knockout Sporting Goods. He explains that not only is the total gross profit increasing, but also the gross profit percentage (gross profit expressed as a percent of sales) is increasing.

You hire an accountant to examine the books of Knockout Sporting Goods before you make a final decision. She finds the following previously undetected errors:

- Inventory was too low by $15 000 at the end of Year 1.
- Inventory was too high by $24 500 at the end of Year 3. All of the remaining records of the firm were found to be accurate.

(a) Prepare a revised three-year schedule of gross profit.
(b) Recalculate the gross profit percentage for each year.
(c) Compare the statement trends before and after the correction.
(d) Would you be willing to pay as much for this firm now as you would have before the audit? Explain.
(e) Would you still consider purchasing the business? Why?

⑮ Career Education Activities

1. Setting Goals and Planning Your Future

In each chapter of this text, there is a description of a particular career. These careers range from students doing co-operative education tasks or having part-time jobs to accounting clerks beginning their careers; accountants working on their CGA, CA, or CMA professional accounting designations; and graduate professional accountants filling senior positions in business. At the end of this chapter, you will read about Celia Hector, an assistant bank manager.

Have you thought about your career? This is what the Career Profile sections have been trying to get you to do. Have you thought about the stages you might progress through in your career? Have you begun to investigate the many careers open to you—not only those directly involving accounting? To facilitate your planning, complete the following questions.

Right Now

On a sheet of paper, write down the current year and answer these questions.

(a) With whom do you live?
(b) Who provides your clothes, food, and shelter?
(c) Who are your three closest friends or relatives?
(d) To whom do you go to discuss your problems?
(e) Where do you obtain your spending money?
(f) What job(s), full-time or part-time, might you have in the next year or so?
(g) What do you do with your spare time? (How much time do you spend studying? How much time do you spend on personal entertainment, such as TV, music, visits with friends, surfing the net, etc.)?

Five Years from Now

Now write down the date five years from now and answer these questions.

(h) Five years from now, will you still be going to a school? If the answer is yes, what type of school?
(i) With whom will you be living?
(j) Who will provide your clothes, food, and shelter?
(k) Who will be your closest friends?
(l) To whom will you go to discuss problems?
(m) Will you be working (full-time or part-time)?
(n) What type of job will you have?
(o) What will you be doing with your time outside of school or your job?
(p) Where will you obtain your money?

Ten Years from Now

Now write down the date ten years from now and answer these questions.

(q) Where will you be living ten years from now?
(r) With whom will you be living?
(s) Will you be single or married? Will you have children?
(t) Will you have completed your education?
(u) Will you be studying part-time?
(v) Who will provide your clothes, food, shelter, and spending money?
(w) What will your hobbies and interests be?
(x) Who will be your closest friends?
(y) With whom will you discuss your problems?

To look into the future and to predict what you will be doing is difficult. *It is necessary* to set goals to plan for the future. However, it is necessary to do this in a way that doesn't produce anxiety and worry. It should be done with the realization that goals will change, interests will change, opportunities will occur unexpectedly, there will be personal successes and failures, and failure to reach a goal is not the end of the world.

By having you look into the future, these questions will have helped you to realize that planning is necessary for personal and professional fulfilment. Realistic goal-setting and planning can help to assure that each person reaches the fullest individual development.

2. Pricing Analyst Position

Many companies advertise financial-related positions that do not require a professional accounting designation. These may be entry-level or senior management positions. Read the advertisement that follows and answer the questions that accompany it.

For Discussion

(a) What qualifications do you currently have related to this position?
(b) What is meant by "competitive salary and comprehensive benefits"?
(c) Why would a company ask you to submit your salary requirements?

Pricing Analyst

Looking for a new career?

You will create and maintain price lists and manage all internal aspects of price changes to ensure accurate computer price files.

You will ensure prompt processing of all quotation requests and recommend pricing strategies.

The qualified candidate will have a college diploma in business administration and 2+ years of related pricing/marketing experience.

Requires strong computer skills in both Microsoft Word and Microsoft Excel. Must possess solid analytical, communication, and decision-making skills plus an ability to perform multiple tasks with speed and accuracy. Must work well with others in a fast-paced team environment.

We offer a competitive salary and comprehensive benefits. For immediate consideration, please fax your résumé and salary requirements to (514) 888-6262.

Human Resources
Montreal Packaging
125 Beliveau Drive
Montreal, Quebec
www.montpackaging.com

Career Profile •

Celia Hector has proved that you can start at an entry-level job and work up to a management position.

Celia grew up in Saint John, New Brunswick, and attended St. Vincent's High School.

After graduation, she decided to go directly to work as a teller in a bank in Saint John. Since then, Celia has taken courses, moved a number of times, and had a variety of jobs in the banking field, including: accounting clerk, auditor, bank accountant, senior operations officer, and assistant bank manager.

Celia has qualified for increasingly responsible positions through experience and by taking a variety of courses. Most of these were taken at night and included accounting and business communications courses offered by the Institute of Canadian Bankers. The courses provided Celia with the theory and knowledge required for advancement in banking. Another helpful course was a University of British Columbia psychology course.

Celia's current job title is Assistant Manager of Operations. She is responsible for the daily operations of the bank; personnel administration; marketing; and organizing, reviewing, and delegating the work in the bank. This includes handling the problems that occur each day in any office. When asked what skills are required in her position, Celia said that the most important are self-motivation, a willingness to accept responsibility and handle problems, and the ability to enjoy working closely with other people.

Celia feels it is important to have realistic goals and to work toward them in a planned way. Her own goals are to become an assistant operations manager in a large bank, and then to work in personnel administration in the bank's general office.

To relax, Celia participates in curling, skiing, reading, and social activities with friends.

For Discussion

(a) What skills are required for Celia's current position?

(b) Interview a bank employee and determine the following:
   - What does an auditor do in a bank?
   - What is personnel administration?
   - What does "marketing" mean?
   - What skills and education are required for an entry-level job in a bank?

(c) What short-term goals (less than two years) have you set for yourself?

(d) What are your long-term goals?

(e) Interview someone who has worked for about ten years. Ask what training programs and courses this person has taken since leaving school.

Performance Task 5

ElectronicWorld.com

> **NOTE TO THE TEACHER:**
> *Performance Task 5 may be done manually and/or using a computer. If a computer is used, a template containing the chart of accounts is available on a CD in the Teacher's Manual. The template is prepared for use with Simply Accounting software. If the project is to be done manually, the required forms are in the Study Guide and Working Papers.*

What Learning You Will Demonstrate

On completion of this task, you will demonstrate the ability to:

- record transactions for a merchandising company using a columnar journal, three ledgers, and the periodic inventory system;
- prepare adjustments for prepaid expenses, accrued expenses, accrued revenue, and depreciation;
- prepare the financial statements for a merchandising company that uses a periodic inventory system; and
- prepare adjusting, closing, and reversing entries.

Background

Performance Task 5 takes you through the accounting cycle for ElectronicWorld.com, a merchandising company. The company sells electronic equipment such as DVD players, CD players, TVs, and computer hardware. The company uses a manual accounting system comprised of a columnar journal and a three-ledger system (general ledger, accounts payable ledger, and accounts receivable ledger). It uses a periodic inventory system.

The Task

You have been retained by M. Lemieux, the manager of ElectronicWorld.com, to make recommendations in a report regarding an accounting system and principles of control that you think should be used. In your report you should compare the manual and computerized systems as part of the rationale for your recommendations. There are three parts to this task:

- Part I.   The Manual Accounting System
- Part II.   The Computerized Accounting System
- Part III. Accounting System Report

Procedure

Part I.   The Manual Accounting System

1. Record May transactions in the subsidiary ledgers.
   (a) Post sales invoices, cash received, and credit invoices issued directly into the customer accounts in the accounts receivable ledger. Open accounts as required.
   (b) Post purchase invoices, cheques issued, and credit invoices received directly into the accounts payable ledger. Open accounts as required.
   (c) On May 31 prepare schedules for each of the subsidiary ledgers.

2. Record May transactions in the columnar journal. You will note that ElectronicWorld.com records GST collected as well as the input tax credits; therefore, GST Refundable DR and GST Payable CR columns are included in journal.
   (a) Total, balance, and rule the columnar journal.
   (b) Post the columnar journal to the general ledger.
   (c) Prepare a general ledger trial balance.

3. Prepare financial statements using the following information:
   • Equipment depreciates 30 percent per year.
   • One month of the 12-month insurance policy has expired.
   • At the end of the month, there are $85 worth of supplies on hand.
   • The ending merchandise inventory is $1150.

4. Journalize the adjusting and closing entries in a general journal and post to the general ledger. Prepare a post-closing trial balance.

Part II.   The Computerized Accounting System

1. Record the May transactions.

2. Print the journal, the general ledger, and the trial balance.

3. Record the adjusting entries.

4. Print the financials statements and the ledgers.

5. Record the closing entries.

6. Print the general ledger and the post-closing trial balance.

Part III. The Accounting System Report

Compare the manual and computerized accounting methods and make recommendations regarding an accounting system for M. Lemieux. Two employees are involved in the accounting system: a clerk who posts the receivables and payables, and an accountant who journalizes and updates the general ledger. Prepare a report that recommends the principles of control to be implemented and the type of system that you think should be used by ElectronicWorld.com.

Materials Required

- Background information and chart of accounts
- May transactions
- Manual accounting system forms
- Computer software and template

Assessment

Examine the assessment rubric. Note the descriptions of the performance criteria and the levels of achievement.

The Chart of Accounts

General Ledger Accounts			
100	Cash	400	Sales
101	Petty Cash	401	Sales Returns and Allowances
110	Accounts Receivable	402	Sales Discounts
120	Merchandise Inventory	500	Purchases
125	Office Supplies	501	Purchases Returns and Allowances
126	Prepaid Insurance	502	Purchases Discounts
150	Equipment	503	Transportation on Purchases
151	Accum. Deprec.—Equipment	600	Advertising Expense
200	Accounts Payable	601	Delivery Expense
205	PST Payable	602	Accounting Fees Expense
206	GST Payable	603	Miscellaneous Expense
207	GST Refundable	604	Rent Expense
210	Salaries Payable	605	Salaries Expense
300	M. Lemieux, Capital	606	Telephone Expense
301	M. Lemieux, Drawings	607	Utilities Expense
302	Income Summary		

May Transactions

May 1 M. Lemieux invested $50 000 to start ElectronicWorld.com.

2 Cheque copies:
No. 1 to J. Kisel, CA, $1500 plus 7 percent GST for organizing an accounting system.
No. 2 to Dot Personnel, $1000 plus GST for hiring services (Miscellaneous Expense).
No. 3 to Maxwell Realty Ltd., $2000 plus GST for May rent.

No. 4 to Lambton Mfg. Ltd., $3500 plus GST for a cash purchase of merchandise.
No. 5 to *Daily Express*, $450 plus GST for advertising.

3　Purchase invoices:
No. T-5986 from Technology International Inc., $1700 plus $119 GST for merchandise, terms n/60.
No. 9324 from Willson's Ltd., $270 plus $17.50 GST, for letterhead, business forms, and miscellaneous office supplies, terms net 30 days.
No. 4438 from Halton Interiors, $9720 plus $630 GST, for office equipment and furnishings, terms: three equal payments, May 15, May 30, and June 30.
No. SM7955 from Synchrotech Mfg. Ltd., $2000 plus $140 GST for merchandise, terms 2/10, n/30.

4　Cash sales:
Cash Sales Slips 1 to 4, $3250 plus GST and 8 percent PST.

5　Sales invoices (terms 2/10, n/30 for all sales on account):
No. 1, $200 plus GST and PST, to J. Barnes.
No. 2, $300 plus GST and PST, to M. Charters.
No. 3, $1200 plus GST and PST, to A. Falcone.
No. 4, $140 plus GST and PST, to L. Parrish.

8　Purchase invoices:
No. 4987321 from Bell Canada, $90 plus $6.30 GST for installation services.
No. H4836 from CP, $120 plus $8.40 GST for transportation of merchandise purchased.
No. 3952 from Jenkins Enterprises, $2900 plus $203 GST for merchandise, terms 3/10, n/60.

9　Credit invoices received:
No. C-8924 from Technology International Inc., $120 for defective merchandise, plus $8.40 GST, total credit $128.40.
No. C-5558 from Halton Interiors, $250 allowance off the price of scratched furnishings plus $17.50 GST and $20 PST, total credit $287.50.

10　Cash sales:
Cash Sales Slips 5 to 8, $2400 plus GST and PST.

11　Credit invoice issued:
No. C-1 to M. Charters, for $100 worth of merchandise returned plus $8 PST and $7 GST, total $115.

12   Sales invoices:
No. 5 to L. Becker, $1200 plus GST and PST.
No. 6 to T. Gabriel, $5000 plus GST and PST.
No. 7 to M. Charters, $2200 plus GST and PST.

12   Cheque copies:
No. 6 to Bell Canada, $96.30 on account.
No. 7 to CP, $128.40 on account.
No. 8 to Halton Interiors, $3450 on account.
No. 9 to Synchrotech Mfg., $2097.20 for invoice of May 3 less 2 percent discount.

15   Purchase invoice:
No. SM8347 from Synchrotech Mfg. for merchandise, $275 plus $19.25 GST, terms 2/10, n/30.

15   Cheque copies:
No. 10, $1200 for a 12-month comprehensive business insurance policy effective May 1 to Metropolitan Life.
No. 11, $100 to establish a petty cash fund.

15   Cash received from customers:
Cheque 123 from J. Barnes, $225.40 for May 5 invoice less 2 percent cash discount.
Cheque 446 from L. Parrish, $157.78 for May 5 invoice less 2 percent cash discount.

16   Sales invoices:
No. 8 to. L. Becker, $4000 plus GST and PST.
No. 9 to T. Gabriel, $650 plus GST and PST.
No. 10 to M. Braganolo, $940 plus GST and PST.
No. 11 to N. Lumsden, $895 plus GST and PST.

18   Cheque copies:
No. 12 for $126 plus GST to pay for an invoice received today for delivery services from Mac's Delivery Service, terms cash.
No. 13 for $500 to M. Lemieux for personal use.
No. 14 for $3009.91 to Jenkins Enterprises for May 8 invoice less 3 percent discount.

19   Cash sales:
Cash Sales Slips 9 to 15, $3170 plus GST and PST.

22   Purchase invoices:
No. H5981 from CP, $79 for transportation on purchase of merchandise plus $5.53 GST.
No. 9947 from Willson's Ltd., $49.68 for office supplies and $3.22 GST.

24　Cheque copy:
　　No. 15 for $288.36 to Synchrotech Mfg. Ltd.
　　for May 15 invoice less 2 percent discount.

24　Credit invoice issued:
　　No. C-2 to N. Lumsden, $45 plus GST and PST, for
　　defective merchandise.

25　Cheque copy:
　　No. 16 for $98.20 to replenish petty cash.
　　Summary of petty cash vouchers:
　　Office Supplies $37.80; Miscellaneous Expenses $35.64;
　　M. Lemieux, Drawings $20; GST $4.76.

25　Sales invoices:
　　No. 12 to J. Barnes, $798 plus GST and PST.
　　No. 13 to T. Gabriel, $240 plus GST and PST.

30　Cheque copies:
　　No. 17 for $3450 to Halton Interiors on account.
　　No. 18 for $1200 to M. Lemieux for personal use.

30　Purchase invoices:
　　No. 4988412 from Bell Canada, $42.12 plus $2.73 GST.
　　No. D4941 from City Light and Power, $185 plus $12.95
　　GST for hydro.
　　No. 8348 from *Daily Express*, $870 plus $60.90 GST for
　　newspaper advertising.

ElectronicWorld.com: Performance Task Rubric

Levels of Achievement

Assessment Criteria	Level 1	Level 2	Level 3	Level 4
KNOWLEDGE AND UNDERSTANDING • understanding the recording and decision-making aspects of accounting • understanding the principles of control • understanding financial statements for a merchandising company using a periodic inventory system	Demonstrates limited understanding of terminology, concepts, procedures, and principles.	Demonstrates some understanding of terminology, concepts, procedures, and principles.	Demonstrates considerable understanding of terminology, concepts, procedures, and principles.	Demonstrates thorough understanding of terminology, concepts, procedures, and principles.
THINKING AND INQUIRY • analysis of transactions • comparison of systems • formation of conclusions regarding systems and control	Uses critical and interpretative skills with limited effectiveness. Applies few of the skills in an inquiry, or problem-solving process.	Uses critical and interpretative skills with moderate effectiveness. Applies some of the skills in an inquiry, or problem-solving process.	Uses critical and interpretative skills with considerable effectiveness. Applies most of the skills in an inquiry, or problem-solving process.	Uses critical and interpretative skills with a high degree of effectiveness. Applies all or almost all skills in an inquiry, or problem-solving process.
COMMUNICATION • completion of appropriate forms and statements • formation of written reports making comparisons and recommendations	Communicates with minimal precision and clarity.	Communicates with some precision and clarity.	Communicates with considerable precision and clarity.	Communicates with complete and thorough precision and clarity.
APPLICATION • application of skills to record transactions using a columnar journal, three-ledger, and periodic inventory systems • application of skills to prepare adjustments for prepaid expenses, accrued expenses, accrued revenue, and depreciation	Uses skills with limited accuracy.	Uses skills with some accuracy.	Uses skills with considerable accuracy.	Uses skills with a high degree of accuracy.

Introduction to Financial Analysis

UNIT 30 Interpreting Accounting Data

What Learning You Will Demonstrate

On completion of this unit, you will be able to:

- analyze a company's liquidity, solvency, and return on investment by using comparative financial statements, trend analysis, and common-size statements;
- prepare condensed financial statements for comparison purposes;
- analyze financial statements to determine developing trends; and
- highlight financial data by using condensed financial statement analysis.

Throughout this book, it has been stressed that *accounting provides information for decision making.* A good accounting system supplies data that enable the management of a company to make informed decisions. For example, sales figures can be provided for each month. The sales for each month can then be compared with sales for the same month in the previous year. Similar comparisons can be made for expenses, assets, and liabilities. Such comparisons indicate trends both favourable and unfavourable. Management is able to take action when unfavourable trends begin to develop and is able to take advantage of favourable trends. Examples of information provided to management for decision-making purposes has been provided in case studies throughout this book. The analysis of accounting statements and records is an important part of the senior accountant's job.

It was also stressed earlier in this book that accounting data are used for decision making by persons outside the company. Bankers and large creditors may wish to analyze a number of the financial statements of a business to determine the company's ability to repay debts. Potential investors are interested in the trends in net income, growth potential, and net worth to decide whether the firm represents a good investment. Labour unions are interested in whether employees are paid fairly in relation to company profitability.

As you can see, the accounting information found on the financial statements of an enterprise is used for decision making by a variety of users, both inside and outside the business. To assist with the interpretation of financial information, a number of common techniques of analysis are used. These techniques are described in this chapter.

ACCOUNTING ANALYSIS

The figures on any one set of financial statements are not especially revealing by themselves. They gain significance when compared to other statements. They also become important when they are expressed in a manner that indicates developing trends. A thorough financial statement analysis includes the following six components:

1. Analysis of Comparative Financial Statements
2. Condensed Statement Analysis
3. Trend Analysis
4. Ratio Analysis
5. Comparison with Similar Businesses
6. Analysis of Non-Financial Factors

The first three components are outlined in this unit. The remaining three components are described in the next unit.

ANALYSIS OF COMPARATIVE FINANCIAL STATEMENTS

Comparative financial statements illustrate changes over several years.

The changes in a firm's financial data can be seen by comparing the financial statements of two or more years. The changes that occur over this period provide information regarding the growth of the firm, its profitability, and other important trends. Comparative financial statements provide two or more years' financial data, with the dollar change from year to year indicated beside each item.

The comparative financial statements for McEwan Enterprises are shown in Figures 13-1 and 13-2 on pages 659 and 660. These statements will be used to demonstrate several components of financial analysis.

Analyzing Exceptions

When analyzing the comparative financial statements, management or interested outsiders look for items that exhibit unusual or *exceptional changes* (very high increases or decreases in account balances). These items are then examined further to determine *why* the changes took place. Management uses this information to correct weaknesses or to reinforce or expand good management practices. Outsiders try to determine the strengths or weaknesses of the firm to assist them in making decisions about extending credit or investing in the business.

An analysis of the comparative financial statements of McEwan Enterprises shows several exceptional items:

McEwan Enterprises
Comparative Income Statement
For the years ended December 31, 20-2, 20-1

	20-2	20-1	Increase (+) Decrease (−)
Revenue			
Sales	$612 200	$493 600	+ $118 600
Sales Returns and Allowances	13 000	13 600	− 600
Net Sales	599 200	480 000	+ 119 200
Cost of Goods Sold			
Inventory, January 1	40 000	32 900	+ 7 100
Net Purchases	441 500	335 100	+ 106 400
Cost of Goods for Sale	481 500	368 000	+ 113 500
Inventory, December 31	64 300	40 000	+ 24 300
Cost of Goods Sold	417 200	328 000	+ 89 200
Gross Profit	182 000	152 000	+ 30 000
Operating Expenses			
Advertising	27 200	18 000	+ 9 200
Salaries	61 075	45 725	+ 15 350
Truck	7 900	4 800	+ 3 100
Depreciation—Building	10 000	10 000	
Depreciation—Office Equipment	4 000	4 000	
Depreciation—Truck	19 500	24 700	− 5 200
Telephone	1 050	950	+ 100
Utilities	3 450	2 850	+ 600
Insurance	3 100	1 600	+ 1 500
Interest and Bank Charges	7 900	8 400	− 500
General	425	375	+ 50
Total Expenses	145 600	121 400	+ 24 200
Net Income	$ 36 400	$ 30 600	+ $ 5 800

FIGURE 13-1 Comparative income statement for McEwan Enterprises

1. According to Figure 13-1, sales have increased $118 600, which appears to be very favourable. However, some, or all, of this increase may have resulted from an inflationary rise in prices rather than from an increase in items sold. This factor should be considered by the analyst before drawing any conclusions about the change in sales.

2. The fact that sales returns have remained constant, while sales have increased, indicates efficient management in this area.

3. Advertising has increased by $9200. With sales increasing by such a large amount, it appears the increased expenditure on advertising was a good investment. Management may want to investigate whether further increases in this area will result in additional large sales increases.

McEwan Enterprises
Comparative Balance Sheet
December 31, 20-2, 20-1

	20-2	20-1	Increase (+) Decrease (−)
Assets			
Current Assets			
Cash	$ 36 200	$ 25 880	+ $10 320
Marketable Securities	68 000	94 020	− 26 020
Accounts Receivable	46 000	48 000	− 2 000
Merchandise Inventory	64 300	40 000	+ 24 300
Prepaid Expenses	5 500	5 300	+ 200
Total Current Assets	220 000	213 200	+ 6 800
Plant and Equipment			
Land	50 000	59 700	− 9 700
Buildings	140 000	150 000	− 10 000
Office Equipment	16 000	20 000	− 4 000
Truck	29 800	49 300	− 19 500
Total Plant and Equipment	235 800	279 000	− 43 200
Total Assets	$455 800	$492 200	− $36 400
Liabilities and Owner's Equity			
Current Liabilities			
Accounts Payable	$ 54 000	$ 61 200	− $ 7 200
Bank Loan	30 000	36 000	− 6 000
Total Current Liabilities	84 000	97 200	− 13 200
Long-Term Liabilities			
Mortgage	40 000	80 000	− 40 000
Total Liabilities	124 000	177 200	− 53 200
Owner's Equity			
J. McEwan, Capital	331 800	315 000	+ 16 800
Total Liabilities and Owner's Equity	$455 800	$492 200	− $36 400

FIGURE 13-2 Comparative balance sheet for McEwan Enterprises

4. Salaries have increased by $15 350. This may have been the result of hiring additional staff to handle the increased sales, but management should make sure it did not result from excessive overtime or unnecessary hiring.
5. Insurance costs have nearly doubled. This may be the result of increased prices or additional necessary coverage, but management may want to review the firm's insurance coverage to ensure that no unnecessary policies are in force.

6. The fact that sales increased $118 600, while net income only increased $5800, is of concern. The large increase in cost of goods sold and a smaller increase in operating expenses have resulted in a small increase in net income.

7. According to the comparative balance sheet, Figure 13-2, the marketable securities (government bonds or shares in corporations that can be easily converted to cash) have *decreased* $26 020. This has been offset, however, by *increases* in the Cash and Merchandise Inventory accounts. The increase in the amount of cash may not be a good thing; normally, more interest is earned by marketable securities than by bank accounts. The reason for the increase in cash and the decrease in marketable securities requires further investigation by management.

8. The large increase in inventory, $24 300 (Figure 13-2), combined with a dramatic increase in net purchases, $106 400 (Figure 13-1), may indicate the beginning of some problems. If the change is the result of bulk purchasing at a special price, the increases may be justified. However, the changes may indicate that too much inventory is being kept on hand, that unsaleable merchandise is being kept in inventory, or that overbuying or dramatic price increases are occurring.

9. The fact that the accounts receivable have remained essentially the same, while sales have increased substantially, probably indicates good control of collection policies. Management may, however, wish to review these policies to ensure they are not too strict, thereby losing potential customers.

10. The mortgage has been reduced by one-half, thereby improving the long-term debt-paying ability of the firm.

Better management of the exceptional items discussed previously is necessary to improve the profitability of the firm.

CONDENSED STATEMENT ANALYSIS

Financial statements can be presented in *condensed format* to highlight information. This technique provides *selected statement amounts shown as a percentage of a base figure*. Single totals are provided for key items such as operating expenses and net sales. These key figures on the condensed statements indicate any important trends that require further investigation.

Condensed statements provide single totals for key items on the statements.

Condensed Income Statements

The income statement for Cosentino Enterprises will be used to illustrate condensed income statements. The condensed, comparative income statement in Figure 13-3 on page 662 shows only the key income statement figures. Notice that the data are listed with the most recent years shown first.

An analysis of the figures shows that, in dollar terms, sales are growing and gross profit is increasing slightly. However, net income is decreasing. The cause of the downward trend is the increase in expenses and the large increase in the cost of goods sold. Users will find it helpful to compare these changes in *percentage terms* as well as in dollars.

Cosentino Enterprises
Condensed Income Statement
For the years 20-4, 20-3, 20-2, 20-1
(in thousands of dollars)

	20-4	20-3	20-2	20-1
Net Sales	$141	$132	$125	$101
Cost of Goods Sold	85	78	72	50
Gross Profit	56	54	53	51
Operating Expenses	47	43	40	35
Net Income	$ 9	$ 11	$ 13	$ 16

FIGURE 13-3 Condensed income statement showing the key amounts for each year

Converting to Percentages

The key figures are converted to a percentage of a base figure—in this example, net sales—to obtain information that may be hidden by large dollar amounts. Two steps are followed when you convert to percentages:

- **Step 1:** The value of 100 percent is given to net sales, since this is the base figure used in the income statement.

- **Step 2:** All other figures are converted to a percentage of net sales.

Figure 13-4 shows the condensed comparative income statement of Cosentino Enterprises, both with dollar values and *with each key figure expressed as a percentage of net sales.*

Cosentino Enterprises
Condensed Income Statement
For the years 20-4, 20-3, 20-2, 20-1
(in thousands of dollars)

	20-4		20-3		20-2		20-1	
Net Sales	$141	100.0%	$132	100.0%	$125	100.0%	$101	100.0%
Cost of Goods Sold	85	60.3%	78	59.1%	72	57.6%	50	49.5%
Gross Profit	56	39.7%	54	40.9%	53	42.4%	51	50.5%
Operating Expenses	47	33.3%	43	32.6%	40	32.0%	35	34.7%
Net Income	$ 9	6.4%	$ 11	8.3%	$ 13	10.4%	$ 16	15.8%

FIGURE 13-4 Condensed comparative income statement showing dollar amounts and percentages

The calculations of the percentages in Figure 13-4, for year 20-4, are shown below.

$$\text{(a)} \quad \frac{\text{Cost of Goods Sold}}{\text{Net Sales}} \times 100\% = \frac{85}{141} \times 100\% = 60.3\%$$

(b) $\dfrac{\text{Gross Profit}}{\text{Net Sales}} \times 100\% = \dfrac{56}{141} \times 100\% = 39.7\%$

(c) $\dfrac{\text{Operating Expenses}}{\text{Net Sales}} \times 100\% = \dfrac{47}{141} \times 100\% = 33.3\%$

(d) $\dfrac{\text{Net Income}}{\text{Net Sales}} \times 100\% = \dfrac{56}{141} \times 100\% = 39.7\%$

A *horizontal analysis* is now possible by comparing the changes in percentages, from *year to year*. It reveals that the major reason for the decrease in net income is the increase in cost of goods sold from 49.5 percent of sales in 20-1 to 60.3 percent in 20-4, thus producing the decrease in gross profit. Operating expenses have remained at a relatively stable percentage of net sales (slightly lower) even though the dollar value has increased. This information becomes more evident when you examine percentage changes rather than dollar values.

Condensed Balance Sheets

Condensed balance sheets (Figure 13-5) may also be prepared. Totals are shown for key items, including current assets, fixed assets, current liabilities, long-term liabilities, and owner's equity. These totals can be converted to percentages of a base figure. In this example, total assets is the base figure used as 100 percent. All other figures on the balance sheet are then calculated as a percentage of the base figure.

Figure 13-5 shows a condensed, comparative balance sheet for Fraser Enterprises. Examine Figure 13-5. Which items have changed significantly? Can you give reasons or explanations for the significant changes?

Condensed balance sheets use total assets as the base figure.

Fraser Enterprises
Condensed Balance Sheet
December 31, 20-4, 20-3

	20-4		20-3	
	Assets			
Current Assets	$151 000	56.5%	$147 000	54.7%
Fixed Assets	116 450	43.5%	121 770	45.3%
Total Assets	$267 450	100.0%	$268 770	100.0%
	Liabilities and Owner's Equity			
Current Liabilities	$ 34 875	13.0%	$ 38 950	14.4%
Long-Term Liabilities	88 000	32.9%	91 000	33.9%
Total Liabilities	122 875	45.9%	129 950	48.3%
Owner's Equity	144 575	54.1%	138 820	51.7%
Total Liabilities and Owner's Equity	$267 450	100.0%	$268 770	100.0%

FIGURE 13-5 Condensed comparative balance sheet

Common-Size Statements

Common-size statements highlight key items by presenting them as percentages of a major item or total. This form of calculation is called vertical analysis. Common-size statements, such as the one shown for Cosentino Enterprises in Figure 13-6, contain these percentages alone, without the corresponding dollar figures. As you can see, all key items are expressed as a percentage of net sales. Common-size percentages may also be used to analyze balance sheet data.

Cosentino Enterprises
Common-Size Income Statement
(percentage of net sales)
For the years 20-4, 20-3, 20-2, 20-1

	20-4	20-3	20-2	20-1
Net Sales	100.0%	100.0%	100.0%	100.0%
Cost of Goods Sold	60.3%	59.1%	57.6%	49.5%
Gross Profit	39.7%	40.9%	42.4%	50.5%
Operating Expenses	33.3%	32.6%	32.0%	34.7%
Net Income	6.4%	8.3%	10.4%	15.8%

FIGURE 13-6 Common-size income statement showing percentages

TREND ANALYSIS

Those persons involved in analyzing and interpreting accounting data generally do not examine one set of financial statements in isolation. It is common practice to examine several years' data. Some analysts prepare comparative figures for ten years. This points out developing trends and is a help in forecasting what will happen in the future. An analysis of trends can be done by examining the percentage changes shown on the condensed financial statements.

Percentage Changes from a Base Year

It is helpful to compare the changes in terms of percentages and to relate these changes to a base year. A *base year* is one common year to which all other years are compared. In Figure 13-7, figures for the years 20-2, 20-3, and 20-4 are compared to base year 20-1. The results for 20-1 are considered to be 100 percent. Results for the three following years are stated as a percentage of the base year figures. Amounts used to calculate the percentages have been obtained from Figure 13-3 on page 662.

Cosentino Enterprises
Percentage Changes
Base Year 20-1

	20-4	20-3	20-2	20-1
Net Sales	140%	131%	124%	100%
Cost of Goods Sold	170%	156%	144%	100%
Gross Profit	110%	106%	104%	100%
Operating Expenses	134%	123%	114%	100%
Net Income	56%	69%	81%	100%

FIGURE 13-7 Percentage changes from a base year

This type of horizontal analysis highlights the change in the percentage increase or decrease, from year to year, of each of the key figures. As you can see, net sales have increased 40 percent (from 100 percent to 140 percent), but cost of goods sold has increased 70 percent (from 100 percent to 170 percent), accounting for most of the decrease in net income. From this trend analysis we can conclude:

1. Sales have experienced a steady growth over the past three years after a dramatic increase in 20-2.
2. Cost of goods sold has increased at a faster rate than net sales for the past four years, resulting in a decline in gross profit. Sales increased 40 percent but cost of goods sold increased 70 percent. This trend should be followed up internally to discover the cause and to attempt to improve the situation. If this trend continues, it could result in non-profitable operation of the enterprise.
3. Operating expenses have been controlled reasonably well by the firm, since they have increased at a rate less than that of net sales each year. This has had a positive effect on net income. Sales have increased 40 percent but operating expenses have increased only 34 percent.

The analysis of condensed, comparative statements for Cosentino Enterprises has provided information on trends in the company that are of interest to any of the users of the financial statements. This analysis has provided a picture of the financial position and performance over a number of years. From this information, conclusions can be drawn regarding the strengths and weaknesses of the enterprise to date; and perhaps an informed forecast can be made using this trend analysis of past performance. Remember that the components of analysis should be used together. An examination of the statements of other firms in the same business may indicate all firms are faced with rising costs and lower profits. It is important to obtain as much relevant information as possible through your analysis before making any final decisions. It is also important to realize that profits do not always increase and that there are often external causes of poor performance, such as a general slump in the economy.

UNIT 30 CHECK YOUR READING

Questions

1. Why are financial statements analyzed?
2. Name three groups who are interested in the information provided by financial statement analysis.
3. List the six basic components of financial statement analysis.
4. What is meant by the term *comparative financial statement*?
5. How do you determine whether or not a change in an item is exceptional?
6. When an exceptional item is discovered, what action should be taken?
7. How is a condensed financial statement prepared?
8. What is meant by *horizontal analysis of condensed comparative statements*?
9. What is the base figure for a condensed income statement?
10. What is a common-size financial statement? How is it prepared?
11. What is the base figure for a condensed balance sheet?
12. Why is trend analysis useful to financial statement users?

UNIT 30 APPLY YOUR KNOWLEDGE

Exercises Part A

1. The following is the comparative balance sheet for Lailey Sports for 20-1 and 20-2. Calculate the amount of change for each item on the statement. Indicate an increase by placing a + sign before the amount and a decrease by placing a − sign before the amount.

Lailey Sports
Comparative Balance Sheet
December 31, 20-2, 20-1

	20-2	20-1	Increase (+) Decrease (−)
Assets			
Current Assets			
Cash	$ 6 300	$ 13 720	?
Accounts Receivable	38 360	44 380	?
Merchandise Inventory	41 350	39 670	?
Prepaid Expenses	5 330	5 270	?
Total Current Assets	91 340	103 040	?
Plant and Equipment			
Land	79 800	79 800	?
Building	178 500	150 500	?
Store Equipment	53 500	49 000	?
Delivery Equipment	51 360	43 260	?
Total Plant and Equipment	363 160	322 560	?
Total Assets	$454 500	$425 600	?
Liabilities and Owner's Equity			
Current Liabilities			
Accounts Payable	$ 19 890	$ 18 630	?
Bank Loan	32 000	25 000	?
Total Current Liabilities	51 890	43 630	?
Owner's Equity			
B. Lailey, Capital	402 610	381 970	?
Total Liabilities and Owner's Equity	$454 500	$425 600	?

2. The following is the comparative income statement for Gledhill Products for 20-4 and 20-5. Calculate the amount of change for each item on the statement. Indicate an increase by placing a + sign before the amount and a decrease by placing a − sign before the amount.

Gledhill Products **Comparative Income Statement** **For the years ended December 31, 20-5, 20-4**			
	20-5	**20-4**	**Increase (+)** **Decrease (−)**
Revenue			
Sales	$289 450	$302 480	?
Sales Returns and Allowances	12 775	13 040	?
Net Sales	276 675	289 440	?
Cost of Goods Sold			
Inventory, January 1	25 375	20 060	?
Net Purchases	120 730	113 380	?
Cost of Goods for Sale	146 105	133 440	?
Inventory, December 31	28 065	25 375	?
Cost of Goods Sold	118 040	108 065	?
Gross Profit	158 635	181 375	?
Operating Expenses			
Salaries	32 035	31 471	?
Depreciation—Building	1 525	1 660	?
Depreciation—Equipment	1 450	1 580	?
Depreciation—Automobile	4 600	5 770	?
Bad Debts	1 975	460	?
Insurance	325	320	?
Supplies	3 000	2 500	?
Telephone	360	250	?
Utilities	4 200	3 500	?
Automobile	7 770	7 630	?
Delivery	4 150	3 890	?
Miscellaneous	2 600	2 450	?
Total Expenses	63 990	61 481	?
Net Income	$ 94 645	$119 894	?

3. The following is the comparative balance sheet for J. Palmer Enterprises for 20-8 and 20-9. Calculate the amount of change for each item on the statement. Indicate an increase by placing a + sign before the amount and a decrease by placing a − sign before the amount.

J. Palmer Enterprises
Comparative Balance Sheet
December 31, 20-9, 20-8

	20-9	20-8	Increase (+) Decrease (−)
Assets			
Current Assets			
Cash	$ 72 000	$ 44 500	?
Marketable Securities	33 000	25 000	?
Accounts Receivable	170 000	130 000	?
Merchandise Inventory	230 000	240 000	?
Prepaid Expenses	5 000	3 000	?
Total Current Assets	510 000	442 500	?
Plant and Equipment			
Land	225 000	225 000	?
Building	675 000	560 000	?
Equipment	95 000	115 000	?
Delivery Equipment	80 000	72 500	?
Total Plant and Equipment	1 075 000	972 500	?
Total Assets	$1 585 000	$1 415 000	?
Liabilities and Owner's Equity			
Current Liabilities			
Accounts Payable	$ 350 000	$ 285 000	?
Bank Loan	50 000	55 000	?
Total Current Liabilities	400 000	340 000	?
Long-Term Liabilities			
Mortgage	450 000	400 000	?
Total Liabilities	850 000	740 000	?
Owner's Equity			
J. Palmer, Capital	735 000	675 000	?
Total Liabilities and Owner's Equity	$1 585 000	$1 415 000	?

4. Analyze the following comparative income statement for J. Palmer Enterprises and determine the main factor(s) that caused a decrease in the net income between 20-8 and 20-9.

J. Palmer Enterprises
Comparative Income Statement
For the years ended December 31, 20-9, 20-8

	20-9	20-8
Revenue		
Sales	$1 530 000	$1 320 800
Sales Returns and Allowances	30 000	20 800
Net Sales	1 500 000	1 300 000
Cost of Goods Sold		
Inventory, January 1	240 000	200 000
Net Purchases	1 030 000	892 500
Cost of Goods for Sale	1 270 000	1 092 500
Inventory, December 31	220 000	240 000
Cost of Goods Sold	1 050 000	852 500
Gross Profit	450 000	447 500
Operating Expenses		
Advertising	15 300	15 000
Salaries	116 400	110 950
Bad Debts	1 600	1 350
Bank Charges and Interest	47 200	43 100
Delivery	19 500	19 000
Depreciation—Building	33 750	28 000
Depreciation—Equipment	17 800	19 500
Depreciation—Delivery Equipment	12 500	14 600
Utilities	16 450	16 250
Other	10 500	13 550
Total Expenses	291 000	281 300
Net Income	$ 159 000	$ 166 200

5. The condensed income statement for Ramsay Enterprises appears below.
   (a) What trends are developing?
   (b) Suggest action management might take.

Ramsay Enterprises
Condensed Income Statement
For the years 20-5, 20-4, 20-3, 20-2, 20-1
(in thousands of dollars)

	20-5	20-4	20-3	20-2	20-1
Revenue	$122	$125	$130	$140	$120
Expenses	87	82	77	72	67
Net Income	$ 35	$ 43	$ 53	$ 68	$ 53

6. Present Ramsay Enterprises' data in exercise 5 in percentages. Use 20-1 as the base year (100 percent).

7. (a) Prepare percentages to compare the dollar figures for years 20-2, 20-3, 20-4, and 20-5 to the base year, 20-1, for the following condensed income statement:

Susan Toth Sales Co.
Condensed Income Statement
For the years 20-5, 20-4, 20-3, 20-2, 20-1
(in thousands of dollars)

	20-5	20-4	20-3	20-2	20-1
Net Sales	$375	$330	$292	$243	$225
Cost of Goods Sold	220	201	181	180	175
Gross Profit	155	129	111	63	50
Operating Expenses	118	99	87	77	75
Net Income or (Net Loss)	$ 37	$ 30	$ 24	$(14)	$(25)

   (b) Prepare a line graph to show sales and net income for the years 20-1 to 20-5.
   (c) Describe the trends that are developing.

8. (a) Complete the percentage columns for the following condensed balance sheet.

(b) List the exceptional changes.

(c) Give possible reasons for the changes.

Kennedy Company
Condensed Balance Sheet
June 30, 20-8, 20-7

	20-8	Percentage	20-7	Percentage
Assets				
Current Assets	$225 750	?	$248 675	?
Plant and Equipment	173 075	?	182 000	?
Total Assets	$398 825	100.0%	$430 675	100.0%
Liabilities and Owner's Equity				
Current Liabilities	$ 73 500	?	$ 85 000	?
Long-Term Liabilities	35 000	?	50 000	?
Total Liabilities	108 500	?	135 000	?
Owner's Equity	290 325	?	295 675	?
Total Liabilities and Owner's Equity	$398 825	100.0%	$430 675	100.0%

9. (a) Complete the percentage columns for the following condensed income statement for Morley Motors.

(b) List and prepare possible explanations for the changes.

(c) Recommend action to be taken by company management.

Morley Motors
Condensed Income Statement
For the years ended April 30, 20-1, 20-0

	20-1	Percentage	20-0	Percentage
Revenue				
Net Sales	$637 500	100.0%	$765 000	100.0%
Cost of Goods Sold	357 000	?	450 500	?
Gross Profit	280 500	?	314 500	?
Operating Expenses				
Selling	89 250	?	119 850	?
Administrative	80 750	?	107 100	?
Total Operating Expenses	170 000	?	226 950	?
Net Income	$110 500	?	$ 87 550	?

Exercises Part B

10. Prepare a condensed balance sheet for Lailey Sports from the information provided in exercise 1.

11. (a) Prepare a condensed income statement for Gledhill Products from the information provided in exercise 2.

(b) Mr. Gledhill asks you to examine the statements to determine why his net income is decreasing. List the items that you believe led to this decrease. What action would you recommend to Mr. Gledhill?

12. (a) Prepare condensed financial statements for J. Palmer Enterprises from the information provided in exercises 3 and 4.

(b) Which exceptional items would you consider to be the most significant if you were analyzing these statements to determine whether you should buy the business from Mrs. Palmer?

(c) After completing your analysis, would you still be interested in purchasing the firm? Give reasons for your decision.

13. (a) Using the following condensed income statement information for Grimwood Printers, prepare a percentage trend analysis schedule.

Grimwood Printers
Condensed Income Statement
For the years ended July 31, 20-9, 20-8, 20-7, 20-6, 20-5

	20-9	20-8	20-7	20-6	20-5
Net Sales	$334 100	$327 500	$324 500	$315 100	$312 000
Cost of Goods Sold	193 800	186 700	183 300	173 300	169 000
Gross Profit	140 300	140 800	141 200	141 800	143 000
Operating Expenses	80 000	79 000	78 600	79 100	78 000
Net Income	$ 60 300	$ 61 800	$ 62 600	$ 62 700	$ 65 000

(b) What trends are indicated by each line of your analysis schedule?

(c) What factor is the major cause of the decline in net income?

UNIT 31 Additional Methods of Analyzing Data

What Learning You Will Demonstrate

On completion of this unit, you will be able to:

- explain the importance of current assets and current liabilities when interpreting a balance sheet;
- use ratios and percentage analyses to evaluate the liquidity, the borrowing power, and the profitability of a business;
- explain and calculate working capital, current ratio, quick ratio, turnover ratios, and rate of return on net sales and on owner's equity;
- demonstrate the importance of industry comparisons and non-financial factors to the analysis of financial statements; and
- evaluate a company's ability to meet its financial obligations, using financial analysis.

In Unit 30, three of the six components of financial analysis were described. They were:

1. Analysis of Comparative Financial Statements
2. Condensed Statement Analysis
3. Trend Analysis

In this unit, three additional analysis components will be outlined. They are:

4. Ratio Analysis
5. Comparison with Similar Businesses
6. Analysis of Non-Financial Factors

RATIO ANALYSIS

There are a large number of ratios that can be used to analyze financial statements. Remember, the purpose of the analysis is to provide relevant information for decision making. Ratios should only be calculated if they will provide useful information. This book will provide an introduction to a number of basic ratios that can be used to assist in the analysis of a firm's liquidity, borrowing capacity, and profitability. These three major categories are of interest to users of financial statements, both inside and outside the business.

Analysis of Liquidity

Liquidity ratios indicate the ability to pay debts.

Liquidity ratios indicate the ability of the business to pay current liabilities without having to borrow funds or sell assets. This information is of interest to bankers and creditors who are considering the ability of a possible debtor to repay short-term loans or credit accounts. It is also important to the management of the firm who will use this information to assist in the efficient management of current assets. The following ratios and values are commonly used to analyze liquidity:

- Working Capital
- Current Ratio
- Quick Ratio
- Turnover Ratios:
  - Merchandise Turnover
  - Accounts Receivable Collection Period

Working Capital

A company must be able to pay its current liabilities as they become due. The working capital figure is an indication of the ability to pay short-term debts.

Working capital is the difference between the total current assets and the total current liabilities:

$$\text{Working Capital} = \text{Current Assets} - \text{Current Liabilities}$$

Although this figure is not expressed as a ratio, it provides important information regarding the liquidity of the firm. The working capital equals the amount of *cash or near cash* items on hand after providing for the payment of the current liabilities. The condensed balance sheet for Levesque Sales is shown in Figure 13-8. The working capital for the business is calculated below:

$$
\begin{aligned}
\text{Working Capital} &= \text{Current Assets} - \text{Current Liabilities} \\
&= \quad \$170\,000 \quad - \quad \$60\,000 \\
&= \quad \$110\,000
\end{aligned}
$$

Working capital is the difference between total current assets and total current liabilities.

Levesque Sales
Condensed Balance Sheet
December 31, 20—

Assets

Current Assets		
Cash	$10 000	
Accounts Receivable	70 000	
Merchandise Inventory	80 000	
Prepaid Expenses	10 000	
Total Current Assets		$170 000
Fixed Assets		300 000
Total Assets		$470 000

Liabilities and Owner's Equity

Current Liabilities	$60 000
Long-Term Liabilities	200 000
Total Liabilities	260 000
Owner's Equity	210 000
Total Liabilities and Owner's Equity	$470 000

FIGURE 13-8 Condensed balance sheet for Levesque Sales

Levesque Sales' working capital is $110 000. A potential lender would be satisfied with this total because it indicates that there is sufficient cash to repay a short-term debt. However, this person might also want to consider working capital value over the past few years to see if there are any significant trends.

Current Ratio

The current ratio is the relationship between current assets and current liabilities.

Another method of measuring a company's ability to pay its current debts is to calculate the *current ratio*. The current ratio is determined by dividing the total current assets by the total current liabilities. As our example for this, we will use the Levesque Sales' condensed balance sheet (see Figure 13-8).

The current ratio for Levesque Sales is 2.8 : 1. This was obtained by dividing the current assets ($170 000) by the current liabilities ($60 000) and expressing the result as a ratio. *But what is the significance of a current ratio of 2.8 : 1?* Basically it means that the company has 2.8 dollars' worth of current assets for each dollar of current liabilities. This indicates that the company should be able to generate enough cash from its current assets to pay its current debts when they become due.

A general rule is that a current ratio of 2 : 1 is satisfactory and suggests that a company can pay its debts. A low ratio such as 1 : 1 would clearly be unfavourable in the eyes of creditors. But even a very high ratio, for example, 6 : 1, may not necessarily be good. It could, for instance, indicate poor management, with perhaps too much money tied up in inventory or in overdue accounts receivable caused by customers not paying their debts on time.

The current ratio is of special interest to creditors and to potential lenders such as banks. From their point of view, a favourable current ratio is a positive factor in granting credit or loans. It means they feel the borrower is in a good position to repay debts and is also a good credit risk.

Other factors to consider along with the current ratio are (a) the nature of the company's business, (b) the composition and type of its current assets, and (c) the turnover ratio of some of its current assets, such as inventory turnover and accounts receivable turnover. These factors indicate a need for another measure called the quick ratio.

Quick Ratio

The quick ratio compares the current assets that are very easily converted to cash with the current liabilities.

The quick ratio compares the current assets that are very easily converted to cash with the current liabilities. Examples of current assets used for this ratio are cash, accounts receivable, and marketable securities. Marketable securities are items that can be readily converted to cash—for example, government bonds and publicly traded shares in other companies.

In Figure 13-8, the assets that are easily converted to cash are Cash ($10 000) and Accounts Receivable ($70 000), which make a total of $80 000. The current liabilities are $60 000. The quick ratio is obtained by this calculation:

$$\text{Quick Ratio} \quad = \quad \frac{80\ 000}{60\ 000} \quad = \quad 1.3 : 1$$

A quick ratio of 1 : 1 is generally considered a satisfactory rule of thumb.

The quick ratio and the current ratio, when considered together, provide a good indication of a company's ability to pay its debts. These ratios are used by creditors as factors in deciding if credit or loans should be granted to a company. The terms "acid test" and "cash ratio" are sometimes used instead of quick ratio.

Turnover Ratios

The *merchandise turnover and accounts receivable collection ratios* are used by short-term lenders to estimate the time required by the business to convert these assets to cash. This information supplements the previous ratio analysis. The condensed income statement for Levesque Sales shown in Figure 13-9 provides the additional information necessary for the turnover ratio calculations.

Levesque Sales
Condensed Income Statement
For the year ended December 31, 20—

Net Sales	$1 260 000
Cost of Goods Sold	756 000
Gross Profit	504 000
Operating Expenses	315 000
Net Income	$ 189 000

FIGURE 13-9 Condensed income statement for Levesque Sales

Merchandise Turnover

The **merchandise turnover** is the number of times the average inventory is sold during an accounting period. A high turnover is generally a good sign. To calculate merchandise turnover, divide the cost of goods sold by the average inventory.
The merchandise turnover for Levesque Sales is:

$$\text{Merchandise Turnover} = \frac{\text{Cost of Goods Sold}}{\text{Average Inventory}}$$

$$= \frac{756\ 000}{80\ 000}$$

$$= 9.45$$

The merchandise turnover is the number of times a company's average inventory is sold during an accounting period.

This means the average inventory was sold 9.45 times during the the year. In this example, $80 000 is the average of the beginning and ending inventories for the year.

Accounts Receivable Collection Period

The **accounts receivable collection period** is the number of days required to collect an average account receivable. An acceptable collection period extends up to approximately 45 days for most businesses that offer 30-day credit terms. A period longer than this may indicate poor collection procedures or a number of accounts included in the accounts receivable that will be hard to collect. This could reduce the cash available to the firm in the future. Too short a collection period may indicate credit policies are so strict that potential good customers are turned away.
If the terms are 2/10, n/30 the collection period should be shorter. This is because many customers will take advantage of the discount offered and pay within 10 days.

The accounts receivable collection period is the time it takes to collect accounts receivable.

Levesque Sales' credit sales generally average 50 percent of total net sales in a fiscal period. The accounts receivable turnover period is calculated below:

$$\frac{\text{Accounts Receivable}}{\text{Collection Period}} = \frac{\text{Average Accounts Receivable}}{\text{Net Sales on Credit}} \times 365$$

$$= \frac{70\ 000}{630\ 000} \times 365$$

$$= 40.6 \text{ days}$$

Levesque Sales collects accounts receivable on the average in 40.6 days. This is within the acceptable limit for most firms; however, management will want to check credit procedures to make sure the period does not increase.

Analysis of Borrowing Capacity

Several other ratios are used to measure a company's ability to pay debts. These include the equity ratio and the debt ratio.

Equity Ratio and Debt Ratio

The equity ratio is the relationship between owner's equity and total assets.

The debt ratio is the relationship between total debts and total assets.

The money to purchase company assets comes from the liabilities or from the owner. The equity ratio describes the relationship between owner's equity and total assets. The debt ratio describes the relationship between total debts and total assets. These ratios are methods of comparing the amount of funds to purchase assets supplied by the creditors to the amount supplied by the owner.

In Figure 13-8 on page 675, the total assets are $470 000. The owner's Capital is $210 000. The *equity ratio* is obtained by this calculation:

$$\text{Equity Ratio} = \frac{\text{Owner's Equity}}{\text{Total Assets}} \times 100\% = \frac{210\ 000}{470\ 000} \times 100\% = 45\%$$

In the Levesque Sales balance sheet, the total liabilities, or debts, are $260 000 and total assets are $470 000. The debt ratio is determined by this calculation:

$$\text{Debt Ratio} = \frac{\text{Total Debts}}{\text{Total Assets}} \times 100\% = \frac{260\ 000}{470\ 000} \times 100\% = 55\%$$

The two ratios, equity and debt, when considered together indicate that 55 percent of the assets are financed through debt and 45 percent by the owner. Generally, the owner of a business favours a *low* equity ratio and a higher debt ratio. This is especially true if earnings are satisfactory and interest on the debt is relatively low. However, if the company must pay high interest on its debt, the situation is unfavourable because the company must pay out interest and there could be a problem earning enough income to pay the interest.

From a creditor's point of view, the *higher* the equity ratio, the better. A high equity ratio, for example 70 percent, indicates that the owner is personally financing the assets to a great extent. The company should be in a fairly good position to repay its debts because its debt ratio is low. Also, the company should be able to afford to pay its interest on borrowed funds.

Further Ratio Considerations

Comparative Ratios

When analyzing ratios, it may be beneficial to calculate them for more than one year to determine whether the ratios show historical improvement or worsening of financial performance.

Analysis of Profitability

The success of a business is judged by its profitability. Net income in dollars is one expression of the profitability of the firm for one year. The profitability trend can be seen by examining the comparative financial statements explained earlier in the chapter. However, this gross dollar amount may not easily reflect important changes in the profitability of the firm.

Rate of Return on Net Sales

The rate of return on net sales, or the net profit percentage, that was discussed in the section on condensed financial statements is a valuable indicator of profitability. The following example demonstrates how the dollar amount of net income does not necessarily show the complete picture of the success of the business. Figure 13-10 provides the comparative financial information for Page and Associates. An analysis of this information shows that the dollar amounts of net sales and net income are increasing each year, indicating a successful and increasingly profitable business. However, when the net income percentage is calculated, you can see that the actual rate of return on net sales is decreasing steadily. It has decreased from 10.0 percent to 9.0 percent.

Page and Associates
Selected Income Statement Data
For the years ended December 31, 20-3, 20-2, 20-1

	20-3	20-2	20-1
Net Sales	$1 000 000	$900 000	$750 000
Net Income	90 000	87 000	75 000
Net Income Percentage	9.0%	9.7%	10.0%

FIGURE 13-10 Selected income statement data for Page and Associates

Rate of Return on Average Owner's Equity

It is important to remember that the owner of the firm could use the money invested in this business to invest in other ways. The net income of the business is the amount of money earned on the capital the owner has invested in the business. The rate of return on average owner's equity is calculated using the following formula. First the average owner's equity is calculated:

$$\text{Average Owner's Equity} = \frac{\text{Beginning Owner's Equity} + \text{Ending Owner's Equity}}{2}$$

Then the rate of return on the equity is determined:

$$\text{Rate of Return} = \frac{\text{Net Income}}{\text{Average Owner's Equity}} \times 100\% = 45\%$$

You are given the information that the beginning owner's equity figure in 20-3 for Page and Associates is $850 000; the ending figure is $890 000. The rate of return on average owner's equity for 20-3 is calculated as follows:

$$\text{Average Owner's Equity} = \frac{850\ 000 + 890\ 000}{2}$$

$$= 870\ 000$$

$$\text{Rate of Return} = \frac{90\ 000}{870\ 000} \times 100\%$$

$$= 10.34\%$$

The percentage, or rate of return, should be as high as, or higher than, the rate of return the owner could receive from other forms of investment such as the stock market, bonds, bank term deposits, or another business. This form of analysis is obviously of interest to potential investors as well as to the owners of an enterprise.

Summary of Measurements for Analysis

The various measurements for finanical analysis are summarized in Figure 13-11.

COMPARISON WITH SIMILAR BUSINESSES

Many of the ratios and percentages we have discussed become more useful when they are compared with data from similar enterprises in the same type of business. Information is available from various sources within an industry, such as accountants who are familiar with the industry, Statistics Canada, financial newspapers, and specific industry magazines.

Comparing the net income percentage for a firm that is being analyzed with the industry average gives further information on the success of the firm. Most ratios and percentages will provide additional relevant information when compared to industry averages if this information is available. It is beyond the scope of this text to expand on this type of analysis, but you should be aware of its importance in completing a thorough financial analysis.

ANALYSIS OF NON-FINANCIAL FACTORS

All of the information about a firm is not necessarily reflected by the components of financial analysis described throughout this chapter. In many cases, non-financial factors have a strong impact on an enterprise and influence decisions made by investors, creditors, and management.

Ratio/Percentage or Other Measure	Method of Calculation	Importance
Working Capital	Current Assets − Current Liabilities	Is a measure of short-term debt-paying ability
Current Ratio	$\dfrac{\text{Current Assets}}{\text{Current Liabilities}}$	Is a measure of short-term debt-paying ability
Quick Ratio	$\dfrac{\text{Cash} + \text{A/R} + \text{Marketable Securities}}{\text{Current Liabilities}}$	Is a measure of short-term liquidity and debt-paying ability
Merchandise Turnover	$\dfrac{\text{Cost of Goods Sold}}{\text{Average Inventory}}$	Indicates how often the entire inventory is sold
Accounts Receivable Collection Period	$\dfrac{\text{Average Accounts Receivable}}{\text{Net Sales on Credit}} \times 365$	Indicates the effectiveness of the firm's collection policies and procedures
Equity Ratio	$\dfrac{\text{Owner's Equity}}{\text{Total Assets}} \times 100\%$	Indicates the percentage of assets financed by the owner's equity
Debt Ratio	$\dfrac{\text{Total Debts}}{\text{Total Assets}} \times 100\%$	Indicates the percentage of assets financed through debt
Rate of Return on Net Sales	$\dfrac{\text{Net Income}}{\text{Net Sales}} \times 100\%$	Indicates the profitability of the business by expressing net income as a percentage of net sales
Rate of Return on Average Owner's Equity	(1) $\dfrac{\text{Beginning Equity} + \text{Ending Equity}}{2} = \text{Average Equity}$ (2) $\dfrac{\text{Net Income}}{\text{Average Owner's Equity}} \times 100\%$	Indicates the success of the owner's investment in the firm by expressing the percentage return on the owner's investment

FIGURE 13-11 Summary of measurements for analysis

A firm with poor ratios and performance over several years may have just hired a dynamic new person to run the firm, or have just discovered a new product. Such factors may positively influence decisions made regarding lending money or investing in the business. Another firm may have the patent running out on its product, or have just lost a key executive to a rival firm; and these factors may have a negative effect on future performance.

Where possible, these *non-financial factors* should be considered to provide a complete analysis. It is not easy to obtain this type of information but it should be sought by the analyst whenever possible.

COMBINING THE COMPONENTS

As you can see, it is important to combine the information that results from using *all* of the components of analysis. Individual components provide useful data; but only when all of the information is combined will a complete picture of the financial performance and position of the enterprise be evident.

Generally Accepted Accounting Principles and Key Ideas

In this chapter, you learned four key ideas:

- **The analysis of accounting statements and records** is an important part of the senior accountant's job.
- **Comparative and condensed financial statements** are used for analysis purposes.
- **Ratios, trends, and percentage analysis** are tools used for analytical purposes.
- **Industry comparisons and non-financial factors** are part of financial analysis.

UNIT 31 CHECK YOUR READING

Questions

13. What three main categories of information do ratios provide?
14. What information is provided by liquidity ratios?
15. Why would financial statement users outside the firm be interested in liquidity ratios?
16. List the four liquidity ratios.
17. Which of the liquidity ratios is not actually a ratio?
18. Explain how the four liquidity ratios are calculated and the significance of each to the analyst.

19. (a) Which category of information is analyzed using equity and debt ratios?
    (b) How are these ratios calculated?
    (c) What is the significance of a high debt ratio?
20. (a) Name the two percentage measurements used as an indicator of profitability.
    (b) How are they calculated?
21. How can an examination of previous years' ratios and percentages assist the analyst?
22. Why is it beneficial to compare the data from the company being analyzed with those of other companies in the same industry?
23. How can a knowledge of non-financial factors regarding the business you are analyzing improve your analysis?

UNIT 31 APPLY YOUR KNOWLEDGE

Exercises Part A

14. (a) A firm's total current assets are $250 000 and its current liabilities are $190 000. What is the current ratio?
    (b) What is an acceptable current ratio for most businesses? Can a very high current ratio be a disadvantage to a firm? Why?
    (c) Calculate the working capital.
    (d) Explain a circumstance in which you could have a strong working capital position yet be in need of cash to pay current liabilities.
    (e) Calculate the quick ratio using the appropriate data from the following: Cash $6000; Accounts Receivable $90 000; Government Bonds $20 000; Building $200 000; Current Liabilities $100 000.
    (f) Determine the merchandise turnover from the following data: Ending Inventory $8000; Beginning Inventory $9000; Cost of Goods Sold $75 600.
    (g) Accounts receivable average $65 000 and net sales on credit total $610 000. How long is the accounts receivable collection period?
    (h) Why is it important to keep the accounts receivable collection period as short as possible?
    (i) Calculate the equity ratio and the debt ratio from the following: Total Assets $490 000; Total Liabilities $300 000; Owner's Equity $190 000.
    (j) Why would a potential investor be interested in the equity and debt ratios?

15. (a) The following is the condensed balance sheet for the P. Scobie Company. Calculate the working capital, current ratio, quick ratio, debt ratio, and equity ratio for the company.

P. Scobie Company
Condensed Balance Sheet
December 31, 20—

Assets

Current Assets

Cash	$ 85 000	
Accounts Receivable	350 000	
Merchandise Inventory	400 000	
Prepaid Expenses	80 000	
Total Current Assets		$ 915 000
Fixed Assets		1 300 000
		$2 215 000

Liabilities and Owner's Equity

Current Liabilities	$ 400 000
Long-Term Liabilities	900 000
Total Liabilities	1 300 000
Owner's Equity	915 000
Total Liabilities and Owner's Equity	$2 215 000

(b) Comment on the liquidity and borrowing capacity of the company.

16. (a) Use the following condensed income statement and the condensed balance sheet in exercise 15 to calculate the turnover, ratios, the rate of return on net sales, and the rate of return on average owner's equity. (*Note*: All sales were credit sales; the January 1 balance in owner's equity was $1 050 000 and the accounts receivable balance was $525 000; and average inventory is $180,000.)

P. Scobie Company
Condensed Income Statement
For the year ended December 31, 20—

Net Sales	$3 500 000
Cost of Goods Sold	1 680 000
Gross Profit	1 820 000
Operating Expenses	1 540 000
Net Income	$ 280 000

(b) Do the turnover ratios provide any further useful information for your analysis of liquidity in 15(b)? Explain.

Exercises Part B

17. The income statement for J. Palmer Enterprises is shown below and the balance sheet is shown on the next page. All sales are on credit. As of January 1, the balance in J. Palmer, Capital was $675 000 and the balance in Accounts Receivable was $130 000. Calculate the following:
  (a) Working capital
  (b) Current ratio
  (c) Quick ratio
  (d) Merchandise turnover
  (e) Accounts receivable collection period
  (f) Equity ratio
  (g) Debt ratio
  (h) Rate of return on net sales
  (i) Rate of return on average owner's equity

J. Palmer Enterprises
Income Statement
For the year ended December 31, 20-1

Revenue	
Sales	$1 530 000
Sales Returns and Allowances	30 000
Net Sales	1 500 000
Cost of Goods Sold	
Inventory, January 1	240 000
Net Purchases	1 030 000
Cost of Goods for Sale	1 270 000
Inventory, December 31	220 000
Cost of Goods Sold	1 050 000
Gross Profit	450 000
Operating Expenses	
Advertising	15 300
Salaries	116 400
Bad Debts	1 600
Bank Charges and Interest	47 200
Delivery	19 500
Depreciation—Building	33 750
Depreciation—Equipment	17 800
Depreciation—Delivery Equipment	12 500
Utilities	16 450
Other	10 500
Total Expenses	291 000
Net Income	$ 159 000

J. Palmer Enterprises
Balance Sheet
December 31, 20-1

Assets

Current Assets

Cash	$	72 500
Marketable Securities		32 500
Accounts Receivable		170 000
Merchandise Inventory		230 000
Prepaid Expenses		5 000
Total Current Assets		510 000

Plant and Equipment

Land	225 000
Building	675 000
Equipment	95 000
Delivery Equipment	80 000
Total Plant and Equipment	1 075 000
Total Assets	$1 585 000

Liabilities and Owner's Equity

Current Liabilities

Accounts Payable	$	350 000
Bank Loan		50 000
Total Current Liabilities		400 000

Long-Term Liabilities

Mortgage	450 000
Total Liabilities	850 000

Owner's Equity

J. Palmer, Capital	735 000
Total Liabilities and Owner's Equity	$1 585 000

18. You are the credit manager of a potential supplier of J. Palmer Enterprises. The sales manager has requested that we extend credit to J. Palmer Enterprises to purchase $25 000 worth of merchandise. Prepare written comments on the appropriate ratios and percentages involving J. Palmer Enterprises that you prepared in 17(a) to (i). Include a recommendation voicing approval or disapproval of the sales manager's request.

19. The comparative balance sheet and income statement for McEwan Enterprises are shown on pages 687 and 688. All sales are credit sales. As of January 1, 20-1, the balance in J. McEwan, Capital was $305 000 and the balance in Accounts Receivable was $45 000. Calculate the following for the years 20-1 and 20-2:
(a) Working capital
(b) Current ratio

(c) Quick ratio
(d) Merchandise turnover
(e) Accounts receivable collection period
(f) Equity ratio
(g) Debt ratio
(h) Rate of return on net sales
(i) Rate of return on average owner's equity

McEwan Enterprises
Comparative Balance Sheet
December 31, 20-2, 20-1

	20-2	20-1
Assets		
Current Assets		
Cash	$ 36 200	$ 25 880
Marketable Securities	68 000	94 020
Accounts Receivable	46 000	48 000
Merchandise Inventory	64 300	40 000
Prepaid Expenses	5 500	5 300
Total Current Assets	220 000	213 200
Plant and Equipment		
Land	50 000	59 700
Buildings	140 000	150 000
Office Equipment	16 000	20 000
Trucks	29 800	49 300
Total Plant and Equipment	235 800	279 000
Total Assets	$455 800	$492 200
Liabilities and Owner's Equity		
Current Liabilities		
Accounts Payable	$ 54 000	$ 61 200
Bank Loan	30 000	36 000
Total Current Liabilities	84 000	97 200
Long-Term Liabilities		
Mortgage	40 000	80 000
Total Liabilities	124 000	177 200
Owner's Equity		
J. McEwan, Capital	331 800	315 000
Total Liabilities and Owner's Equity	$455 800	$492 200

McEwan Enterprises
Comparative Income Statement
For the years ended December 31, 20-2, 20-1

	20-2	20-1
Revenue		
Sales	$612 200	$493 600
Sales Returns and Allowances	13 000	13 600
Net Sales	599 200	480 000
Cost of Goods Sold		
Inventory, January 1	40 000	32 900
Net Purchases	441 500	335 100
Cost of Goods for Sale	481 500	368 000
Inventory, December 31	64 300	40 000
Cost of Goods Sold	417 200	328 000
Gross Profit	182 000	152 000
Operating Expenses		
Advertising	27 200	18 000
Salaries	61 075	45 725
Truck	7 900	4 800
Depreciation—Building	10 000	10 000
Depreciation—Office Equipment	4 000	4 000
Depreciation—Trucks	19 500	24 700
Telephone	1 050	950
Utilities	3 450	2 850
Insurance	3 100	1 600
Interest and Bank Charges	7 900	8 400
General	425	375
Total Expenses	145 600	121 400
Net Income	$ 36 400	$ 30 600

20. (a) If you were considering buying McEwan Enterprises, which of the measurements in 19(a) to (i) would be of most interest to you?

    (b) Would you consider an opportunity to purchase McEwan Enterprises for $350 000? What additional information would you wish to obtain before you make a final decision?

21. Following is a list of accounts and balances for Wincott Tours:

Cash	$202 500
Marketable Securities	135 000
Accounts Receivable (Net)	418 500
Merchandise Inventory	216 000
Prepaid Expenses	27 000
Accounts Payable	303 750
Accrued Liabilities	20 250

The following transactions occurred during the year:
(a) Paid accounts payable, $24 000.
(b) Purchased merchandise on account, $40 500.
(c) Collected accounts receivable, $81 000.
(d) Borrowed cash on a short-term bank note, $135 000.
(e) Wrote off uncollectible accounts, $7100.
(f) Purchased new equipment on credit, $216 000.
(g) Bought additional marketable securities for cash, $47 250.
    (i)   Calculate the amount of current assets, quick (liquid) assets, and current liabilities at the beginning of the period.
    (ii)   Compute the current ratio, quick ratio, and working capital at the beginning of the period.
    (iii)   Indicate the effect of each of the transactions during the period on these ratios. Use the same headings as those shown in the chart below, where transaction (a) is done for you as an example.

Transaction	Current Ratio	Quick Ratio	Working Capital
(a)	Increase	Increase	No Change

22. Partial data from the financial statements of Schmidt Stores and High Stores for the year just ended are shown below. Calculate the following for both companies:
(a) Net income
(b) Accounts receivable collection period
(c) Merchandise turnover

	Schmidt	High
Total liabilities	$ 440 000	$ 220 000
Total assets	1 760 000	880 000
Sales (all on credit)	3 520 000	2 640 000
Beginning inventory	509 000	320 000
Ending inventory	528 000	308 000
Average receivables	440 000	220 000
Gross profit as a percentage of sales	40%	30%
Operating expenses as a percentage of sales	38%	26%
Net income as a percentage of sales	2%	4%

UNIT 32 Budgets

What Learning You Will Demonstrate

On completion of this unit, you will be able to:

- explain the factors that influence budgetary forecasts;
- describe a budgeted income statement;
- describe a budgeted balance sheet; and
- compare budget and actual financial results.

What Is a Budget?

A budget is a financial plan for a specific accounting period.

In very simple terms, a budget is a financial plan for a specific accounting period. A budget can be prepared for an individual, for a family, or for any type of organization or business. For our purposes, we will define *a budget as a plan that outlines an organization's financial and operational goals*. In this section, we will examine some of the basics of budgeting for businesses, and the budgeted income statement and budgeted balance sheet.

Purpose of Budgets

Budgets are a planning and control tool for companies. They assist management in making financial and operating decisions on an ongoing basis. Budgets can help to make decisions such as the number of staff needed if the company goals are to be met and how much must be spent on advertising and marketing to reach company sales targets. They also help with other decisions related to the future operations of the business.

After the budgets have been prepared and approved, actual results are compared to the budget and differences are determined. The managers responsible must explain these differences.

Types of Budgets

A master budget is an overall budget for a company.

A capital budget is a plan that estimates the equipment and building items to be purchased during the period.

A sales budget is an estimate of the goods to be sold and the total revenue to be realized from sales.

There are a number of different types of business budgets, starting with the master budget, which is the overall budget for a company. The master budget includes a number of other budgets, such as the *sales or revenue budget*, the *expense budget*, and the *capital budget*. A plan that estimates the equipment and building items to be purchased during the period is called a capital budget. A sales budget is an estimate of the goods to be sold and the total revenue to be realized from sales. The components and nature of the master budget depend on the size, complexity, and management requirements of a business.

The Budget Process

The management of a company decides how much planning it will require of its managers. This in turn dictates the nature of the master budget and the number of other budgets that will make up the master budget. The budget process generally includes these steps:

- management determines the budget(s) to be prepared;
- company priorities and goals are set;
- deadlines and the approval process are developed;
- responsibility for preparation of each budget is allocated;
- the revenue and expense budgets are prepared;
- the capital budget is prepared;
- other budgets are prepared as required;
- the budgeted income statement is prepared;
- the budgeted balance sheet is prepared;
- the management committee considers and approves (or alters) the budgets; and
- the final master budget is approved.

In this process there can be many changes to individual budgets as managers compete for their share of the overall budget. It is a challenge for each department or division to get its budget and plans approved by the management committee.

Factors that Influence Budgetary Forecasts

Each main division or department of a company prepares a budget for its area, beginning with the budget for the previous period and adjusting it for the company's current priorities. For example, the sales department may realize that a product is "getting older" and has reached its revenue peak. In the budget, the sales for this product will be decreased for the next budget period. As well, the marketing and advertising costs may also be decreased. If a new product is to be introduced, this will increase estimates for revenue, production costs, and marketing costs for the product.

Other Factors Influencing Forecasts

Many factors influence budget estimates, including:

- general economic conditions;
- availability of resources, funding, materials, and staff;
- estimated future costs of funding, materials, and salaries;
- company goals;
- staff capabilities; and
- competition and government influences.

Can you think of any other factors?

The Budgeted Income Statement

A budgeted income statement is an estimate of the revenue, expenses, and net income for the financial period. One of the final steps in the budget process is the preparation of the budgeted income statement. Generally, a large number of accounts are incorporated into the statement through the use of subsidiary ledger control accounts or summary accounts. This makes the consideration of the income statement manageable; however, the details in the individual accounts are necessary and must be justified by each person responsible. Figure 13-12 is a sample of a budgeted income statement for New Star Software, a software development company.

A budgeted income statement is an estimate of the revenue, expenses, and net income for the financial period.

New Star Software
Budgeted Income Statement
For the three months ended March 31, 20—

Sales		$400 000 (note 1)
Cost of Goods Sold		80 000 (note 2)
Gross Profit		320 000
Operation Expenses		
Production Development	$100 000 (note 3)	
Marketing	80 000 (note 4)	
Administrative	50 000 (note 5)	
Total Operating Expenses		230 000
Net Income before Income Taxes		90 000
Income Taxes (25%)		22 500
Net Income		$ 67 500

FIGURE 13-12 A budgeted income statement

In Figure 13-12, *note 1* appears beside the sales figure and *note 2* beside the cost of goods sold figure. These refer to supporting notes that provide the detail justifying the dollar figure. For example, *note 1* would be a summary of revenue to be generated by each product that the company sells, including the number of units and the price.

At least monthly during the financial period, most companies will compare their actual results to the budgeted figures (Figure 13-14). Decisions may be made to alter plans as a result of the comparison.

The Budgeted Balance Sheet

A budgeted balance sheet shows the estimated assets, liabilities, and equity at the end of the period.

A budgeted balance sheet is a projected (estimated) balance sheet for the end of the financial period. Figure 13-13 is the budgeted balance sheet for New Star. It shows the *estimated* assets, liabilities, and equity at the end of March.

Comparing Budget and Actual Results

The accounting program used by New Star is capable of printing a variety of reports. For the budget, the software can show and print a report that compares the budget vs. the actual results for any identified period. It can produce the report monthly, quarterly, yearly, etc. Figures 13-12 and 13-13 are the *budgeted* income statement and the *budgeted* balance sheet New Star prepared in January. They are *estimates* made for planning and control purposes. How close did the company come to its plan?

Figure 13-14 is a report produced by the software at the end of the three months. It shows the budgeted income statement, the actual results, the dollar amounts over or under the budget, and the percent over or under the budgeted figures. These amounts are called variances. *How well did New Star do compared to its plans? Can you see the value of this report?*

New Star Software
Budgeted Balance Sheet
As at March 31, 20—

Current Assets		
Cash	$ 95 000	
Accounts Receivable	200 000	
Inventory	35 000	
Total Current Assets		$330 000
Fixed Assets		
Fixed Assets	400 000	
Accumulated Depreciation	80 000	
Total Fixed Assets		320 000
Total Assets		$650 000
Liabilities		
Accounts Payable	$ 50 000	
Income Tax Payable	25 000	
Total Liabilities		$ 75 000
Equity		
Common Stock	275 000	
Retained Earnings	300 000	
Total Equity		575 000
Total Liabilities and Equity		$650 000

FIGURE 13-13 A budgeted balance sheet

New Star Software
Income Statement
Budget vs. Actual
For the three months ended March 31, 20—

	Actual	Budget	$ Over	% Budget
Sales	$410 000	$400 000	$10 000	2.5%
Cost of Goods Sold	82 000	80 000	2 000	2.5%
Gross Profit	328 000	320 000	8 000	2.5%
Product Development Expenses	102 000	100 000	2 000	2.0%
Marketing Expenses	75 000	80 000	(5 000)	(6.3)%
Administrative Expenses	45 000	50 000	(5 000)	(10.0)%
Total Operating Expenses	222 000	230 000	(8 000)	(3.5)%
Net Income before Income Taxes	106 000	90 000	16 000	17.8%
Income Taxes (25%)	26 500	22 500	4 000	17.8%
Net Income	$ 79 500	$ 67 500	$12 000	17.8%

FIGURE 13-14 A budget vs. actual income statement

CHECK YOUR READING

Questions

24. What is a budget?

25. What is a budgeted income statement?

26. What is a budgeted balance sheet?

27. What is the purpose of budgets?

28. List five factors that influence budget forecasts.

29. What purpose is served by budget vs. actual reports? Of what value is the information provided?

APPLY YOUR KNOWLEDGE

Exercises

23. Figure 13-15 is New Star's revenue budget for the month of May.

    (a) Complete the $ Over and the % Budget columns.

    (b) Comment on the revenue results for May.

New Star Software Revenue Budget Budget vs. Actual For the month ended May 31, 20—				
	Actual	**Budget**	**$ Over**	**% Budget**
Revenue				
Sales, Product A	$25 000	$23 000		
Sales, Product B	11 000	16 000		
Sales, Product C	19 000	20 000		
Contract Revenue	10 000	10 000		
Technical Support Revenue	5 000	7 000		
Total Revenue	$70 000	$76 000		

FIGURE 13-15 A budget vs. actual revenue budget

24. Figure 13-16 is New Star's software development budget for the month of May.

    (a) Complete the $ Over and the % Budget columns.

    (b) Comment on the software development cost results for May.

New Star Software
Software Development Budget
Budget vs. Actual
For the month ended May 31, 20—

	Actual	Budget	$ Over	% Budget
Graphic Artwork	$18 000	$15 000		
Programming	25 000	20 000		
Supplies, Services, Licences	7 000	6 000		
Other Development Costs	2 000	2 000		
Total Software Development	$52 000	$43 000		

FIGURE 13-16 The budget vs. actual software development budget for May

25. A budget vs. actual income statement for the three months ended
    March 31 is shown in Figure 13-14.
    (a) Was the net income more or less than planned?
    (b) What were the significant differences in actual results compared to
        the budget?

26. The budget vs. actual income statement for the month of April is
    shown in Figure 13-17. Assume you are the vice-president of opera-
    tions for New Star. Examine the statement. List four conclusions you
    might come to regarding company operations for the month of April.

New Star Software
Income Statement
Budget vs. Actual
For the month ended April 30, 20—

	Actual	Budget	$ Over	% Budget
Sales	$100 000	$130 000	$(30 000)	(23.1)%
Cost of Goods Sold	25 000	30 000	(5 000)	(16.7)%
Gross Profit	75 000	100 000	(25 000)	(25.0)%
Product Development Expenses	60 000	40 000	20 000	50.0%
Marketing Expenses	19 000	20 000	(1 000)	(5.0)%
Administrative Expenses	15 000	15 000		
Total Operating Expenses	94 000	75 000	19 000	25.3%
Net Income before Income Taxes	(19 000)	25 000	(44 000)	(176.0)%
Income Taxes (25%)	(4 750)*	6 250	(11 000)	(176.0)%
Net Income	$(14 250)	$ 18 750	$(33 000)	(176.0)%

* decrease in the amount of income tax owing for the year

FIGURE 13-17 A budget vs. actual income statement for April

Computer Accounting

Analyzing Accounting Data

Pat Lunney is the manager of Chatelaine, a retail store that specializes in clothing fashions. Each month, Pat receives marketing and financial information from Statistics Canada about companies in the same retail business.

Using Statistics Canada information, Pat has prepared a comparison of several account balances, matching the results of Pat's company with averages for all other companies. The comparison follows:

Account	Pat's Company (in $000s)	Industry Average (in $000s)
Cash	$ 7	$ 15
Accounts Receivable	250	150
Merchandise Inventory	300	195
Accounts Payable	90	45
Bank Loan	40	10
Sales	800	800
Cost of Goods Sold	400	400
Interest Charges Expense	5	1
Warehouse Expense	60	35
Bad Debts Expense	5	2
Salaries Expenses	250	200
Other Expenses	10	10
Net Income	?	?

Questions

1. Use a spreadsheet to determine the net income for the industry and for Pat's company.
2. Use a spreadsheet to calculate a "percentage of industry average" chart for Pat. The chart should show, for each item, the percentage that the figure for Pat's company is of the industry average figure. For example, Pat's Cash balance is 46.7 percent of the industry figure. Your spreadsheet should have the following headings:

Account	Pat's Company (in $000s)	Industry Average (in $000s)	Percentage of Industry Average

3. Print your spreadsheet.
4. Prepare recommendations for improving the financial position of Pat's company.

COMPUTER ASSIGNMENTS

1. Format a spreadsheet that can be used to complete exercises 1, 2, and 3 of this chapter.

2. Use a spreadsheet to complete exercise 7(a). Print the condensed income statement.

3. Locate a business that uses a computer to do its accounting. Consider your doctor, optometrist, dentist, a local store, or a large business or organization. Ask for a demonstration of how the computer program is used to do one or more of the following:
   - prepare invoices;
   - update the customer accounts;
   - record sales and cash received;
   - prepare the customer statements; and/or
   - prepare the monthly bank reconciliation statement.

   After you have seen the demonstration, prepare a written report that outlines the computer system. Include:

   - samples of the screen menus;
   - a description of the hardware, the operating system, and network capabilities;
   - a description of the software used, including a list of the modules
   - that make up the program; and
   - a list and samples of the accounting forms and reports produced.

4. Format a spreadsheet that will be used to produce the budget in Figure 13-14 on page 693.

5. Format a spreadsheet that will be used to produce the budget in Figure 13-17 on page 695.

WEB EXTENSIONS

www.pearsoned.ca/
principlesofaccounting

Internet Study Guide

- Complete the Chapter 13 review.
- Complete the Chapter 13 definitions.
- Complete the Chapter 13 online test.

Web Links

Visit the Web Links section at the Pearson Education web site to find links to company annual reports. Outline why this type of online data is important to accountants. What are the advantages of online annual reports compared to print versions?

(12) Case Studies

CASE 1 Interpreting Accounting Data

You are a loan manager and have received an application for a loan from J. Traskle Ltd. From the financial statements provided by J. Traskle, the following data have been calculated. Considering the data provided, would you grant the loan? Give reasons for your answer.

	20-7	20-6	20-5	20-4	20-3
Current Ratio	2 : 1	2 : 1	2 : 1	2.7 : 1	3 : 1
Quick Ratio	1 : 1	1 : 1	0.7 : 1	0.9 : 1	1 : 1
Debt Ratio	48%	49%	50%	55%	45%
Equity Ratio	52%	51%	50%	45%	55%

CASE 2 Industry Comparisons

Big Top Carnivals operates travelling carnival shows. Following are selected income statement data for the business and a summary for the industry obtained from trade magazines.

(a) Prepare a percentage of sales statement for Big Top Carnivals from the data provided.
(b) Point out the significant differences between the results of Big Top Carnivals and the industry average.
(c) What are some possible reasons and solutions for these exceptional items?

	Big Top Carnivals	Industry Average
Revenue		
Net Sales	$3 400 000	100%
Cost of Goods Sold	2 142 000	58%
Gross Profit	1 258 000	42%
Operating Expenses		
Selling	510 000	10%
General and Administrative	544 000	15%
Total Operating Expenses	1 054 000	25%
Net Income	$ 204 000	9%
Return on Owner's Equity	10%	18%

Financial Statement Ratios

CASE 3

The following are the partial condensed financial statements for Ironside and Associates. Use the additional information provided to calculate the data missing from the statements.

Ironside and Associates
Condensed Balance Sheet
December 31, 20—
(in thousands of dollars)

Assets

Current Assets	
Cash	?
Accounts Receivable	?
Merchandise Inventory	?
Total Current Assets	?
Plant and Equipment	300
Total Assets	?

Liabilities and Owner's Equity

Current Liabilities	?
Long-Term Liabilities	?
Total Liabilities	?
Owner's Equity	240
Total Liabilities and Owner's Equity	

Ironside and Associates
Condensed Income Statement
For the year ended December 31, 20—
(in thousands of dollars)

Net Sales	?
Cost of Goods Sold	?
Gross Profit (25% of Net Sales)	250
Operating Expenses	?
Net Income (8% of Net Sales)	?

Additional Information:

- The equity ratio is 40 percent.
- The debt ratio is 60 percent.
- The current ratio is 2 to 1.

- The quick ratio is 1 to 1.
- The accounts receivable collection period is 42 days. (Assume that all sales are credit sales. Round your answer to the nearest whole number.)

CASE 4 Comparative Financial Data

You are the loan manager for a bank. One of your duties is to analyze the financial reports of companies that come to your bank for loans. Two companies have come to you for a loan. They have presented you with the financial information that is summarized below.

BALANCE SHEET
COMPARATIVE DATA

	Company A	Company B
Cash	$ 19 000	$ 26 000
Accounts Receivable	51 000	78 000
Inventory	54 000	92 000
Equipment	290 000	300 000
Total	?	?
Current Liabilities	70 000	100 000
Long-Term Loan	110 000	121 000
Capital	234 000	275 000
Total Liabilities and Capital	?	?

INCOME STATEMENT
COMPARATIVE DATA

	Company A	Company B
Sales	$545 000	$739 000
Cost of Goods Sold	299 000	475 000
Gross Margin	?	?
Expenses	205 000	232 000
Net Income	?	?

(a) For each of the companies, calculate the current ratio, working capital, quick ratio, equity ratio, and debt ratio.

(b) For each of the companies, calculate the gross margin, net income, rate of return on sales, and gross margin as a percentage of sales.

(c) In your position as loan manager, you can grant a loan to only one of the two companies. Based on an analysis of the information, to which of the two companies would you give the loan? Give reasons for your answer.

Career Education Activities

1. Taking a Personal Inventory

This activity will help you to learn about yourself, your interests, and your work values through the following chart on job values.

For Discussion

(a) How important is each value to you? Either respond mentally to each item or write your answers in your notebook.

(b) Prepare a list of the three items you value the most, and a list of the three items you value the least. Compare your list with that of a classmate. Discuss the reasons for your choices.

(c) Prepare a list of three jobs that might contain many of the values you rank as very important. Compare and discuss lists with a classmate.

Job Value	Very Important	Important	Not Important
• Being with people			
• Regular hours			
• Working alone			
• Working as part of a team			
• Supervising other people			
• Large salary			
• Quality of the office			
• Fringe benefits			
• Working for a large company			
• Working for a small company			
• Working for myself			
• Working with people			
• Working with data			
• Working with equipment			
• Opportunity for advancement			
• Long holidays			
• Challenging work			
• Physical work			
• Work requiring special skills			

2. Practising Your Analytical Skills

An accountant performs a variety of roles, including analyzer of data and decision maker. In this example, you will be the analyzer and decision maker. You are presented with a problem and data to support the alternatives. Your function is to make a recommendation to your supervisor based on the results of your analysis.

Statement of the Problem

Your company has outgrown its current model of a general accountant handling all of the accounting functions. It is considering either moving to a computerized payroll system or outsourcing the payroll function to an Internet-based accounting firm. Your task is to consider the data presented and to make a recommendation to your supervisor.

Data Gathered

The computerized payroll system requires the company to hire a payroll clerk. Moving to a computerized payroll system also includes the purchase of a new computer, a printer, a backup tape storage system, and a payroll accounting software package. The costs associated with this option are as follows:

Computer Hardware	$ 8 000	one-time cost (anticipated five-year life)
Software	3 000	one-time cost (anticipated five-year life)
Training	2 000	one-time cost
Service and Support	1 000	annual fee
Supplies (forms, etc.)	1 000	annual cost
Payroll Clerk	40 000	annual cost

The outsourcing to an online Internet-based accounting firm would result in the following costs:

Setup and Training	$5 000	one-time fee
Monthly Service Fee	1 000	monthly fee

The costs of the computer hardware and software can be spread over the five-year life of the equipment and software. Costs such as CPP, employment insurance, health insurance premiums, vacation pay, and training, combined, will average 12 percent of the salary for each new employee.

For Discussion

(a) What is the annual cost of each system averaged over a five-year period?
(b) What are the advantages and disadvantages of each system?
(c) What additional information would you like to have to make the decision?
(d) Have any costs been left out of the cost summaries?
(e) What system would you recommend: the computer system or the online accounting services firm? Explain your decision.

3. Position Requiring Analytical Skills

The position of operational auditor described in the accompanying advertisement requires some of the analytical skills described in this chapter.

For Discussion

(a) What are the personal skills required for this position?
(b) What are the educational requirements?
(c) What is an auditor?

Operational Auditor

The City of Woodstock requires an individual with initiative and proven analytical and problem-solving skills to perform audits and other management functions such as cost–benefit studies, financial investigations, and project planning.

Applicants will be finalists or graduates of the CGA, CMA, or CA program and have at least 2 years' experience auditing. The ability to work as part of a team and communicate with staff at all levels in the organization is essential.

We offer a starting salary in the $38 000– $47 000 range and an excellent benefits package.

Please send your résumé to:
Sherry West, Director of Staffing
City of Woodstock
39C Cameron Street, Woodstock, ON

An Equal Opportunity Employer

Career Profile

Don Fretz has continued his education on the job after completing high school. Let's examine his career path.

Don attended Merriton High School, where he took a combination of academic and business courses. The business courses included keyboarding and accounting. After graduating, Don went directly into the workforce. His first job with a chartered accounting firm lasted for four years. During that time, he completed three years of the CGA program, governed by the Certified General Accountants' Association, as a part-time student.

Don then worked for five years as the controller for a real estate development company. A controller is responsible for the accounting and finances of a business.

Budget Control Officer is Don's current job title at a board of education. Don has four main responsibilities:

1. maintaining the general ledger and supervising all entries to the ledger;
2. controlling cash and cash management;
3. preparing financial reports; and
4. assisting in preparing the annual budget.

Don's employer has a computerized accounting system with programs specially designed for the accounting function. It was necessary for Don to learn to use the system on the job.

Higher education and advanced accounting skills, including the ability to prepare and interpret financial reports, are required for Don's current job. Equally important are personal skills such as the ability to learn new systems and procedures, and the ability to get along with people.

Don is presently enrolled in the bachelor of business administration program at Brock University. He feels that a university degree in business will provide him with broader career opportunities. He recommends that students consider post-secondary education, even if it is begun later in life after obtaining work experience. Don has completed two years of his university business program and continues to take courses in the evening.

Don's future career goal is to work in government accounting and to work toward the position of manager of financial services. Don and his wife have two children. Don's hobbies include sports (baseball, hockey, and bowling), and his favourite personal pastime is Trivial Pursuit.

For Discussion

(a) Prepare a diagram that outlines Don's career path from high school graduation to the present. Include work experience and education.

(b) Based on the information given, estimate how many years Don has been involved in part-time education while working in accounting.

(c) Don suggests that the ability to learn is an important skill. Give examples of this skill from Don's career profile.

(d) Interview a person who works in accounting and obtain answers to the following questions:
  (i)   What is your job title and what do you do?
  (ii) What is a controller?
  (iii) What is an annual budget?
  (iv) What does "to interpret financial reports" mean?
  (v)   What financial reports, other than an income statement and a balance sheet, are prepared in your organization?

Performance Task 6

Financial Statement Analysis

What Learning You Will Demonstrate

You will:

- work with other students to prepare a written report analyzing the financial statements of a company;
- present a seminar to your class explaining the findings of your research;
- demonstrate the ability to use ratios and percentage analyses to examine the liquidity, the borrowing power, and the profitability of a business;
- demonstrate the ability to explain and calculate working capital, current ratio, quick ratio, turnover ratios, and rate of return on net sales and on owner's equity; and
- explain the importance of industry comparisons and non-financial factors to the analysis of financial statements.

Background Information

By law, Canadian corporations must prepare annual financial statements and send copies to the owners of the company—the shareholders. The statements are included as part of the annual report sent to the shareholders. Included in most annual reports are a message from the president, an income statement, a balance sheet, a statement of changes in shareholders' equity, five- or ten-year summaries of financial results, a product summary, a description of future plans, and general information about the company.

The Task

A symposium is being held to review the status of Canadian corporations. You are a member of a team invited to make a presentation at the symposium.

Parameters of the Presentation

You have been provided a 30-minute time slot at the symposium.

Your team should research a Canadian corporation and prepare a written report that contains the following information:

- the name of the company;
- the names of the president and two directors;
- the location of the head office;
- a list of the products sold or services performed;

- the date of the financial statements;
- the name of the auditors of the financial statements;
- the method used to depreciate the fixed assets;
- a trend analysis for the past five years that shows both the dollar change and the percentage change for working capital, net sales revenue, and net income;
- a list of other companies owned in whole or in part;
- a comparative statement of earnings (income statement) that shows the net change for two years;
- a comparative balance sheet that shows the net change for two years;
- a percentage income statement for this year and last year; and
- a list of key ratios for this year and last year, including a statement about what each ratio means and how it has changed.

Your report will form the basis of your presentation, but your team should be prepared to answer general questions related to the company and to indicate why you would, or would not, invest in it.

Procedure

1. As a team, review the background information and the requirements of the task.
2. Meet as a team to prepare an overall plan with deadlines.
3. Obtain the annual report for a company. It may be obtained by writing to the secretary of a corporation or to financial publications such as the *Financial Post*, the *Financial Times*, or the *Report on Business* and obtaining names of corporations that provide reports to the public. Reports may also be obtained from friends who are shareholders of companies, or from the reference or business sections of public libraries. Internet sites are another source of financial reports. Try doing an Internet search or visit either www.prars.com or www.annualreportservice.com. These sites provide online annual reports.
4. Prepare your report.
5. Plan and rehearse your presentation.

Materials Required

- Financial report for a company

Assessment

Examine the assessment rubric. Note the descriptions of the performance criteria and the levels of achievement.

Financial Statement Analysis: Performance Task Rubric

Levels of Achievement

Assessment Criteria	Level 1	Level 2	Level 3	Level 4
KNOWLEDGE AND UNDERSTANDING • understanding of recording and decision-making aspects of accounting • understanding of the debit/credit theory in recording transactions in the journals and ledgers of a service business	Demonstrates limited understanding of terminology, concepts, procedures, and principles.	Demonstrates some understanding of terminology, concepts, procedures, and principles.	Demonstrates considerable understanding of terminology, concepts, procedures, and principles.	Demonstrates a thorough understanding of terminology, concepts, procedures, and principles.
THINKING AND INQUIRY • analysis of transactions • interpretation of the balance sheets • assessment of financial status • forming conclusions regarding profitability	Uses critical and interpretative skills with limited effectiveness. Applies few of the skills in an inquiry, or problem-solving process.	Uses critical and interpretative skills with moderate effectiveness. Applies some of the skills in an inquiry, or problem-solving process.	Uses critical and interpretative skills with considerable effectiveness. Applies most of the skills in an inquiry, or problem-solving process.	Uses critical and interpretative skills with a high degree of effectiveness. Applies all or almost all skills in an inquiry, or problem-solving process.
COMMUNICATION • completion of appropriate forms and statements • formation of a written report using appropriate procedures and principles • presentation to owners	Communicates with minimal precision and clarity.	Communicates with some precision and clarity.	Communicates with considerable precision and clarity.	Communicates with complete and thorough precision and clarity.
APPLICATION • application of skills to prepare trial balances and financial statements	Uses skills with limited accuracy.	Uses skills with some accuracy.	Uses skills with considerable accuracy.	Uses skills with a high degree of accuracy.

Payroll Accounting

UNIT 33 Paying Employees

What Learning You Will Demonstrate

On completion of this unit, you will be able to:

- identify three compulsory deductions;
- identify five voluntary deductions;
- calculate a net claim code for income tax deduction purposes;
- explain the purpose served by the social insurance number;
- outline the benefits and services provided by Canada Pension Plan, employment insurance, health insurance, credit unions, registered pension plans, group insurance, and extended health insurance;
- calculate net earnings;
- identify five pay periods used by businesses;
- identify six payment methods used by employers; and
- define *payroll, compulsory deductions, voluntary deductions, T1 form, gross earnings, statement of earnings,* and *net earnings.*

All companies pay their employees a wage or a salary and have a payroll accounting procedure as part of their accounting system. The word **payroll** means a list (*roll*) of employees and the money (*pay*) to be paid to them. Thus you can see the origin of the phrase "being on the payroll."

The accounting procedures used by a company to prepare the payroll depend on the number of employees, the type of equipment available, the complexity of the payroll, and the number of people available in the accounting department.

Payroll procedures may be performed manually, using a one-write system, or using a computer system. Some companies prefer to buy a payroll service from an accounting firm or from a bank. Such businesses do the payroll work for other companies and charge a fee for the service.

> A payroll is a list of employees and the amount of money to be paid to them.

EMPLOYMENT LAWS

Companies are required by law to keep certain payroll records, to prepare payroll reports, and to provide each employee with a statement of earnings and deductions. There are both federal and provincial laws that govern the payment of employees. One of these is the *Employment Standards Act*.

Provincial Laws

All provinces have an *Employment Standards Act*. These provincial laws govern:

- minimum wages;
- hours of work;
- statutory holidays;
- vacation pay;
- overtime; and
- many other employment practices.

Provincial ministries of labour or departments of labour administer these Acts. One of their tasks is to investigate employee complaints of unfair treatment.

These laws ensure that all employees receive fair treatment. For example, all employees must receive the following statutory holidays: New Year's Day, Good Friday, Victoria Day, Canada Day, Labour Day, Thanksgiving, and Christmas. The Acts also set out the payroll records that must be kept and give provincial government auditors the authority to inspect company records.

Federal Laws

A number of federal laws impose payroll requirements on employers and affect the pay received by all employees. These laws include the *Income Tax Act*, the *Canada Pension Act*, and the *Employment Insurance Act*. The example of M. Lostracco, used in this chapter, will illustrate how all workers are affected by the federal laws.

EARNINGS

A statement of earnings and deductions is provided to all employees and shows how net earnings are determined.

M. Lostracco is an employee of Western Systems, a computer consulting firm located in Vancouver. Lostracco earns a salary of $1400 per week as a supervisor. However, the pay cheque received by Lostracco for one week's pay is for $920.74. The cheque is shown in Figure 14-1. Notice that it also includes a statement of earnings and deductions that shows how net earnings are determined by listing the gross earnings and payroll deductions.

If Lostracco earns $1400 and receives only $920.74, what happens to the difference of $479.26? Does the company keep it? No. The $479.26 deducted from Lostracco's cheque by the employer is passed on to other agencies for Lostracco. For example, $393.75 is sent to the federal government to pay Lostracco's personal income tax; $33.60 is paid out for employment insurance; and $51.91 is paid out for the Canada Pension Plan.

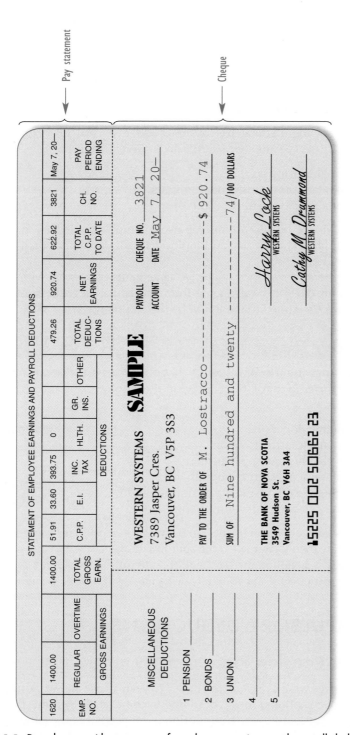

FIGURE 14-1 Pay cheque with statement of employee earnings and payroll deductions

DEDUCTIONS

Deductions are amounts subtracted from an employee's gross earnings.

The items deducted from an employee's gross earnings are called payroll deductions. Some deductions are *compulsory*—they apply to all workers. Others are voluntary on the part of the employee.

Compulsory Deductions

Compulsory payroll deductions include income tax, Canada Pension Plan, and employment insurance.

Employers are required by law to make three payroll deductions for their employees. These compulsory payroll deductions include:

- personal income tax;
- employment insurance premiums; and
- Canada Pension Plan contributions.

In some provinces, health insurance is also a compulsory deduction. In Ontario, however, employers must pay an Employer Health Tax rather than deduct premiums from employees.

Employers may also have collective agreements (contracts) with unions that require union dues to be deducted from the employees' earnings. The union dues are then forwarded to the union by the company.

Voluntary Deductions

Voluntary payroll deductions are made from gross earnings by the employer at the request of the employee.

There are a large number of voluntary payroll deductions that an employee may ask the employer to make. Depending on the employer and the situation, these may include:

- charitable donations;
- payments to a credit union;
- group life insurance payments;
- purchase of government bonds;
- extended health insurance premiums; and
- private pension plan contributions.

These deductions are made by the company *only if an employee requests that they be made*. They are then forwarded to the appropriate agency by the company. In effect, the company is handling the payment of some of the employee's personal bills. Each of the compulsory and voluntary deductions will now be examined in detail.

COMPULSORY DEDUCTIONS

Canada Pension Plan

Every employee who is over 18 and under 70 years of age and working in Canada (with minor exceptions) must contribute to the Canada Pension Plan (C.P.P.). Currently, the amount of the contribution is 4.3 percent of the employee's salary (to a maximum salary of $38 300). Anyone who has contributed to the plan will receive a pension at age 65. A reduced amount is available to those who request a pension between ages 60–65. There is a disability pension available if necessary, and, in the event of death, the contributor's dependants receive a one-time death benefit plus survivor benefits.

Federal legislation requires that the employer also make C.P.P. contributions on behalf of each employee. The employer contributes an amount equal to the employee's contribution (4.3 percent). Thus, both the employee and the employer pay for the employee's future pension. Once a month, the company sends all of the employee's deductions along with the employer's share to the federal government. In effect, the business acts as a collection agent for the government and also helps to finance the C.P.P. benefits for the employee.

The province of Quebec has organized the Quebec Pension Plan, which is operated in much the same way as the C.P.P.

Employment Insurance

Employment insurance (E.I.) is designed to provide income to those workers who become unemployed through no fault of their own. Most workers in Canada must contribute to the E.I. fund. Benefits are received only when a person becomes unemployed. This means that those workers fortunate enough never to be unemployed will contribute to the E.I. fund but will not receive payments from it.

With minor exceptions, all full-time employees are required to make E.I. payments. The employer makes payroll deductions from the employee's earnings and forwards the money to the federal government.

The employer must also contribute 1.4 times the amount deducted for each employee. For example, since Lostracco's E.I. premium is $33.60 (see the E.I. table in Figure 14-5 on page 721), the employer must contribute $47.04 (1.4 × $33.60) on behalf of Lostracco.

Employment Insurance and the Record of Employment

A form called the *Record of Employment* must be completed by the employer and given to an employee who leaves employment. This form is used to decide if a person is eligible for E.I. benefits, the amount of the benefits, and how long the person can collect benefits. In effect, it is the employee's proof that contributions have been made and that the employee is entitled to receive E.I. benefits. The Record of Employment must be issued by the employer within five days of the stoppage in employment.

Personal Income Tax

The *Income Tax Act* requires employers to deduct an amount for income tax from each employee's earnings each payday. Once a month, the employer must send the amounts deducted to the federal government. Through these deductions, workers pay their income tax on a regular basis.

Each year by April 30, Canadians must complete a personal income tax return. This form, called the T1, is used to determine the amount of income tax for which each person is responsible. The total amount payable is compared to the amount the employee has already paid through payroll deductions each payday. The result may be a refund (money back) for the employee if the payroll deductions have been too large, or an extra amount owing if the payroll deductions have been too low.

The amount of tax payable is determined in two steps.

A T1 is the income tax return completed each year by taxpayers.

Step 1: Calculation of Taxable Income

The amount of taxable income is determined by the amount of income earned minus allowable deductions. Allowable deductions include payments made for items such as registered pension plan (R.P.P.) contributions, child care expenses, and union dues.

Income − (R.P.P. Contributions +Child Care Expenses + Union Dues) = Taxable Income

Step 2: Calculation of Income Tax

The amount of tax payable is determined by subtracting non-refundable tax credits from the amount of tax owing on taxable income. Non-refundable tax credits for items such as dependants, C.P.P. or E.I. contributions, and tuition reduce the amount of federal income tax payable. They are called non-refundable because, if these credits are more than your federal income tax, the difference is not refunded to you.

To determine an employee's credits, the employer is required to have each employee complete a *Personal Tax Credit Return* (*TD1* form) when credits change. The TD1 form is used to determine a person's tax credits that affect the amount of income tax to be paid. Tax credits are amounts of income on which income tax is not paid. Therefore, a person with a number of tax credits (e.g., for dependent children) pays less income tax than a person with few tax credits. Figure 14-2 shows the federal TD1 form completed by M. Lostracco. You will notice that the employee lists all personal credits to arrive at a net claim code. For Lostracco, the net claim code is 1. This code is used by the employer to determine the tax deduction to be made each payday.

A TD1 form shows an employee's claim for non-refundable tax credits. It must be completed by all employees yearly or when credits change.

Tax on Income (TONI)

As of January 2001, the TONI method of calculating provincial income tax came into effect in all Canadian provinces. With the TONI method, provincial tax is calculated by applying provincial tax rates to the taxable income amount. Prior to adopting the TONI method of calculation, the provincial income tax was calculated as a percentage of the basic federal tax.

Employers remit both federal and provincial income tax deductions to the federal government.

Under the TONI method, a *federal TD1 form* is used to determine the claim code and a set of federal tax deduction tables is used to determine the *federal income tax deduction*. A *provincial TD1 form* is used to determine the *claim code* and a set of provincial tax deduction tables is used to determine the *provincial income tax deduction*. The two income tax deductions are added together each payday and deducted from the employee's pay. The employer sends the two taxes to the federal government.

Figure 14-2 is the federal TD1 form. Figure 14-3 on page 716 shows a portion of the back of the TD1 form with the different net claim codes for the two tax jurisdictions.

2001 PERSONAL TAX CREDITS RETURN TD1

Canada Customs and Revenue Agency Agence des douanes et du revenu du Canada

Complete this TD1 form if you have a new employer or payer and you will receive salary, wages, commissions, pensions, Employment Insurance benefits, or any other remuneration. Be sure to sign and date it on the back page and give it to your employer or payer who will use it to determine the amount of your payroll tax deductions.

If you do not complete a TD1 form, your new employer or payer will deduct taxes after allowing the basic personal amount **only**.

You **do not** have to complete a new TD1 form every year unless there is a change in your personal tax credit amounts. Complete a new TD1 form no later than seven days after the change.

You can get the forms and publications mentioned on this form from our Internet site at **www.ccra-adrc.gc.ca** or by calling 1-800-959-2221.

Last name	First name and initial(s)	Date of birth (YYYY/MM/DD)	Employee number
LOSTRACCO	MARY WO		1620

Address including postal code	For non-residents only — Country of permanent residence	Social insurance number
19 QUEENS QUAY VANCOUVER B.C. V5 6A4		452 638 529

1. Basic personal amount – Every resident of Canada can claim this amount. If you will have more than one employer or payer in 2001, see the section called "Income from other employers or payers" on the back page. If you are a non-resident, see the section called "Non-residents" on the back page. **$7,412**

2. Age amount – If you will be 65 or older on December 31, 2001, and your net income for the year will be $26,941 or less, enter $3,619. If your net income will be between $26,941 and $51,068 and you want to calculate a partial claim, get the *Worksheet for the 2001 Personal Tax Credits Return* (TD1-WS) and complete the appropriate section.

3. Pension income amount – If you will receive regular pension payments from a pension plan or fund (excluding Canada or Quebec Pension Plans (CPP/QPP), Old Age Security and guaranteed income supplements), enter $1,000 or your estimated annual pension income, whichever is less.

4a. Tuition and education amounts (full-time) – If you are a student enrolled full-time at a university, college, or educational institution certified by Human Resources Development Canada, enter the total of the tuition fees you will pay, if more than $100 per institution, plus $400 for each month that you will be enrolled full-time.

4b. Tuition and education amounts (part-time) – If you are a student enrolled part-time at a university, college, or educational institution certified by Human Resources Development Canada, enter the total of the tuition fees you will pay, if more than $100 per institution, plus $120 for each month that you will be enrolled part-time.

5. Disability amount – If you will claim the disability amount on your income tax return by using Form T2201, *Disability Tax Credit Certificate*, enter $6,000.

6. Spousal amount – If you are supporting your spouse or common-law partner who lives with you, and his or her net income for the year will be $629 or less, enter $6,294. If his or her net income for the year will be between $629 and $6,923 and you want to calculate a partial claim, get the *Worksheet for the 2001 Personal Tax Credits Return* (TD1-WS) and complete the appropriate section.

7. Equivalent-to-spouse amount – If you do not have a spouse or common-law partner and you support a dependent relative who lives with you, and his or her net income for the year will be $629 or less, enter $6,294. If his or her net income for the year will be between $629 and $6,923 and you want to calculate a partial claim, get the *Worksheet for the 2001 Personal Tax Credits Return* (TD1-WS) and complete the appropriate section.

8. Caregiver amount – If you are taking care of a dependant who lives with you, whose net income for the year will be $11,953 or less, and who is either your or your spouse's or common-law partner's:
- parent or grandparent age 65 or older, **or**
- relative age 18 or older who is dependent on you because of an infirmity,

enter $3,500. If the dependant's net income for the year will be between $11,953 and $15,453 and you want to calculate a partial claim, get the *Worksheet for the 2001 Personal Tax Credits Return* (TD1-WS) and complete the appropriate section.

9. Amount for infirm dependant age 18 or older – If you are supporting an infirm dependant age 18 or older who is your or your spouse's or common-law partner's relative, who lives in Canada, and his or her net income for the year will be $4,966 or less, enter $3,500. You cannot claim an amount for a dependant claimed on line 8. If the dependant's net income for the year will be between $4,966 and $8,466 and you want to calculate a partial claim, get the *Worksheet for the 2001 Personal Tax Credits Return* (TD1-WS) and complete the appropriate section.

10. Amounts transferred from your spouse or common-law partner – If your spouse or common-law partner will not use all of his or her age amount, pension income amount, tuition and education amounts (maximum $5,000), or disability amount on his or her income tax return, enter the unused part.

11. Amounts transferred from your dependant – If your dependant will not use all of his or her tuition and education amounts (maximum $5,000) or disability amount on his or her income tax return, enter the unused part.

12. TOTAL CLAIM AMOUNT – Add lines 1 through line 11. Your employer or payer will use this amount to determine the amount of your payroll tax deductions. **$ 7412**

Form continues on the back ——

TD1 E (01) (Ce formulaire existe en français.) Canada

FIGURE 14-2 Personal tax credit return—federal TD1 form (side 1)

Claim codes

For 2001, the claim amounts that correspond to the federal claim codes will not be the same as the claim amounts that correspond to the provincial claim codes. Therefore, there is a federal claim codes chart (see Chart 1 on page A-12) and a provincial claim codes chart (see Chart 2 on page 12).

The claim code amounts will not appear on either the federal or the provincial TD1 forms.

Codes de demande

Pour 2001, les montants des déductions correspondant aux codes de demande fédéraux ne sont pas identiques aux montants correspondant aux codes provinciaux. Par conséquent, il existe un tableau des codes de demande fédéraux (voir le tableau 1 de la page A-12) et un tableau des codes de demande provinciaux (voir le tableau 2 de la page 12).

Le montant des codes de demande ne figure pas sur les formulaires TD1 fédéraux et provinciaux.

Chart 1 – Tableau 1
Federal claim codes – Codes de demande fédéraux

Total claim amount ($) Montant total de la demande ($)			Claim code Code de demande	Total claim amount ($) Montant total de la demande ($)			Claim code Code de demande
No claim amount/Nul			0	15,632.01	–	17,276.00	7
Minimum	–	7,412.00	1	17,276.01	–	18,920.00	8
7,412.01	–	9,056.00	2	18,920.01	–	20,564.00	9
9,056.01	–	10,700.00	3	20,564.01	–	22,208.00	10
10,700.01	–	12,344.00	4	22,208.01	and over/et plus		X
12,344.01	–	13,988.00	5	Manual calculation is required by the employer Calcul manuel est requis par l'employeur			
13,988.01	–	15,632.00	6	No withholding/Aucune retenue			E

Chart 2 – Tableau 2
British Columbia claim codes – Codes de demande de la Colombie-Britannique

Total claim amount ($) Montant total de la demande ($)			Claim code Code de demande	Total claim amount ($) Montant total de la demande ($)			Claim code Code de demande
No claim amount/Nul			0	17,000.01	–	18,800.00	7
Minimum	–	8,000.00	1	18,800.01	–	20,600.00	8
8,000.01	–	9,800.00	2	20,600.01	–	22,400.00	9
9,800.01	–	11,600.00	3	22,400.01	–	24,200.00	10
11,600.01	–	13,400.00	4	24,200.01	and over/et plus		X
13,400.01	–	15,200.00	5	Manual calculation is required by the employer Calcul manuel est requis par l'employeur			
15,200.01	–	17,000.00	6	No withholding/Aucune retenue			E

Claim code "0"

If the federal claim code is "0" because the employee is a non-resident, the provincial claim code must also be "0."

Code de demande « 0 »

Si le code de demande fédéral est « 0 » parce que l'employé est un non-résident, le code de demande provincial doit aussi être « 0 ».

A-12 BC

FIGURE 14-3 Personal tax credit return—federal TD1 form (side 2)

VOLUNTARY DEDUCTIONS

Group Life Insurance

Many companies provide a group life insurance plan for their employees. Because of the large number of people joining the plan, the insurance companies provide a group discount rate. The amount paid by each employee is determined by the amount of insurance requested and the age of the employee. For example, an employee who decides to purchase $50 000 worth of life insurance for a premium of 26 cents per $1000 per month, would pay $13. The $13 is deducted from earnings by the employer and sent to the insurance company for the employee.

Credit Union

A *credit union* is a non-profit banking organization operated by the employees of a company or by an organization. A credit union is similar to a banking institution. It receives deposits from members and gives interest on the deposits. Funds contributed by the members are lent to other members who pay interest on money borrowed. The expenses of a credit union are low because it is operated by its own members, facilities are often provided by the employer, and bad debts on loans are rare since loans are only made to the members, who are all employed workers. Credit unions provide many banking services, including:

- loans;
- chequing accounts;
- savings accounts;
- mortgages; and
- registered retirement savings plans.

Deposits to the credit union, or payments on loans granted by the credit union, may be made via payroll deductions. The employer deducts the appropriate amounts from the employees' earnings and transfers them to the credit union for the employees.

Health Insurance

In Canada, there is *universal health coverage*. This means that everyone is able to obtain health insurance. Each province operates its own health plan. The benefits provided by provincial health insurance plans include payment of:

- doctors' fees for required services; and
- hospital expenses.

The cost to the public for this insurance varies from province to province. Many companies pay part or all of the health insurance premium as a fringe benefit for their employees. Often this is part of a contract negotiated with a union. The portion of the monthly premium paid by the company is an expense of operating the business and is recorded in an account called Health Insurance Expense or Payroll Expense. In Ontario, the public does not pay directly for health insurance. Employers pay an Employer Health Tax, which will be explained later in this chapter.

In provinces where employees pay part or all of the premium, it is deducted from earnings by the employer and sent to the provincial health plan organization.

Extended Health Insurance Plans

Provincial health plans do not pay for all health services. Many employees like to have additional health insurance, which is provided by insurance companies. The premiums for additional health insurance are deducted from the employees' earnings by the employer and sent to the appropriate insurance organization.

Extended health plans provide benefits not covered by provincial plans, such as:

- prescription drugs;
- special medical services and supplies;
- semi-private or private hospital accommodation; and
- home care nursing.

Registered Pension Plans

At some companies, employees can voluntarily join the company's private pension plan. This type of plan provides retirement pension benefits to the employees in addition to the C.P.P. benefits they will receive.

While working, the employee contributes to the private pension plan through payroll deductions. The employer sends the money deducted to the pension administrator. Usually, the employer makes a matching contribution on behalf of the employee.

Private pension plans are usually registered with the federal government. Contributions made to a registered pension plan (R.P.P.) are an eligible income tax deduction. Each year when completing their personal income tax returns (T1), employees are allowed to deduct the payments made to an R.P.P. This lowers the amount of income tax to be paid by the worker.

A registered pension plan is a private pension plan registered with the federal government. Contributions to an R.P.P. are tax deductible.

GOVERNMENT REQUIREMENTS

To receive C.P.P. and E.I. benefits, a person must have contributed to the plans. The contributions are recorded using each person's social insurance number (S.I.N.).

Social Insurance Number

The recording of contributions is much more efficiently done by S.I.N. than by name. Can you imagine how many *Jack Chins, Mary Smiths,* or *Maurice Leblancs* there are in Canada? By assigning numbers to each person, the possibilities of error due to similarities in names is eliminated. Canada Customs and Revenue Agency also uses the S.I.N. to handle the tax records of Canadians.

Books and Records

Every person operating a business in Canada is required by law to keep records and accounts for income tax, C.P.P., and E.I. purposes. The records must contain enough information to determine the correct payroll deductions. On request, the records must be made available to officers of Canada Customs and Revenue Agency. Normally, the records must be kept for a minimum of six years, and written permission of the Minister of National Revenue is required before records are destroyed.

CALCULATING NET EARNINGS

Gross earnings are the total earnings of an employee before deductions. The **net earnings** for an employee are determined as follows:

Gross Earnings   –   Deductions   =   Net Earnings

In M. Lostracco's case:

$1400   – $479.26   = $920.74

The deductions of $479.26 include:

Canada Pension Plan	$ 51.91
Employment Insurance	33.60
Income Tax	393.75
Total Deductions	$479.26

Gross earnings are the total earnings of an employee before deductions.

Net earnings is the balance remaining after deductions have been subtracted from gross earnings.

Let's examine the calculation of each of these deductions.

Canada Pension Plan Deduction

Lostracco's employer consults the Canada Customs and Revenue Agency's *Payroll Deduction Tables* to get the C.P.P. deduction. Figure 14-4 on page 720 is a page from this booklet. It indicates that the C.P.P. contribution required on gross weekly earnings of $1400 is $51.91.

Note: Taking 4.3 percent of an employee's earnings will not give the same figures as the C.P.P. chart. The reason is that there is a basic yearly exemption (currently $3500).

Employment Insurance Deduction

The same booklet contains a section on E.I. Figure 14-5 on page 721 indicates that the E.I. premium deduction required on gross weekly earnings of $1400 is $33.60. Notice, however, that maximum premium deductions are noted at the bottom of each page. In this table, the yearly maximum premium payable by a worker is $936. When this amount has been reached, no further deductions are made for the rest of the year.

Canada Pension Plan Contributions
Weekly (52 pay periods a year)

Cotisations au Régime de pensions du Canada
Hebdomadaire (52 périodes de paie par année)

Pay Rémunération From - De	To - À	CPP RPC	Pay Rémunération From - De	To - À	CPP RPC	Pay Rémunération From - De	To - À	CPP RPC	Pay Rémunération From - De	To - À	CPP RPC
1053.33	1063.32	38.65	1773.33	1783.32	66.73	2493.33	2503.32	94.81	3213.33	3223.32	122.89
1063.33	1073.32	39.04	1783.33	1793.32	67.12	2503.33	2513.32	95.20	3223.33	3233.32	123.28
1073.33	1083.32	39.43	1793.33	1803.32	67.51	2513.33	2523.32	95.59	3233.33	3243.32	123.67
1083.33	1093.32	39.82	1803.33	1813.32	67.90	2523.33	2533.32	95.98	3243.33	3253.32	124.06
1093.33	1103.32	40.21	1813.33	1823.32	68.29	2533.33	2543.32	96.37	3253.33	3263.32	124.45
1103.33	1113.32	40.60	1823.33	1833.32	68.68	2543.33	2553.32	96.76	3263.33	3273.32	124.84
1113.33	1123.32	40.99	1833.33	1843.32	69.07	2553.33	2563.32	97.15	3273.33	3283.32	125.23
1123.33	1133.32	41.38	1843.33	1853.32	69.46	2563.33	2573.32	97.54	3283.33	3293.32	125.62
1133.33	1143.32	41.77	1853.33	1863.32	69.85	2573.33	2583.32	97.93	3293.33	3303.32	126.01
1143.33	1153.32	42.16	1863.33	1873.32	70.24	2583.33	2593.32	98.32	3303.33	3313.32	126.40
1153.33	1163.32	42.55	1873.33	1883.32	70.63	2593.33	2603.32	98.71	3313.33	3323.32	126.79
1163.33	1173.32	42.94	1883.33	1893.32	71.02	2603.33	2613.32	99.10	3323.33	3333.32	127.18
1173.33	1183.32	43.33	1893.33	1903.32	71.41	2613.33	2623.32	99.49	3333.33	3343.32	127.57
1183.33	1193.32	43.72	1903.33	1913.32	71.80	2623.33	2633.32	99.88	3343.33	3353.32	127.96
1193.33	1203.32	44.11	1913.33	1923.32	72.19	2633.33	2643.32	100.27	3353.33	3363.32	128.35
1203.33	1213.32	44.50	1923.33	1933.32	72.58	2643.33	2653.32	100.66	3363.33	3373.32	128.74
1213.33	1223.32	44.89	1933.33	1943.32	72.97	2653.33	2663.32	101.05	3373.33	3383.32	129.13
1223.33	1233.32	45.28	1943.33	1953.32	73.36	2663.33	2673.32	101.44	3383.33	3393.32	129.52
1233.33	1243.32	45.67	1953.33	1963.32	73.75	2673.33	2683.32	101.83	3393.33	3403.32	129.91
1243.33	1253.32	46.06	1963.33	1973.32	74.14	2683.33	2693.32	102.22	3403.33	3413.32	130.30
1253.33	1263.32	46.45	1973.33	1983.32	74.53	2693.33	2703.32	102.61	3413.33	3423.32	130.69
1263.33	1273.32	46.84	1983.33	1993.32	74.92	2703.33	2713.32	103.00	3423.33	3433.32	131.08
1273.33	1283.32	47.23	1993.33	2003.32	75.31	2713.33	2723.32	103.39	3433.33	3443.32	131.47
1283.33	1293.32	47.62	2003.33	2013.32	75.70	2723.33	2733.32	103.78	3443.33	3453.32	131.86
1293.33	1303.32	48.01	2013.33	2023.32	76.09	2733.33	2743.32	104.17	3453.33	3463.32	132.25
1303.33	1313.32	48.40	2023.33	2033.32	76.48	2743.33	2753.32	104.56	3463.33	3473.32	132.64
1313.33	1323.32	48.79	2033.33	2043.32	76.87	2753.33	2763.32	104.95	3473.33	3483.32	133.03
1323.33	1333.32	49.18	2043.33	2053.32	77.26	2763.33	2773.32	105.34	3483.33	3493.32	133.42
1333.33	1343.32	49.57	2053.33	2063.32	77.65	2773.33	2783.32	105.73	3493.33	3503.32	133.81
1343.33	1353.32	49.96	2063.33	2073.32	78.04	2783.33	2793.32	106.12	3503.33	3513.32	134.20
1353.33	1363.32	50.35	2073.33	2083.32	78.43	2793.33	2803.32	106.51	3513.33	3523.32	134.59
1363.33	1373.32	50.74	2083.33	2093.32	78.82	2803.33	2813.32	106.90	3523.33	3533.32	134.98
1373.33	1383.32	51.13	2093.33	2103.32	79.21	2813.33	2823.32	107.29	3533.33	3543.32	135.37
1383.33	1393.32	51.52	2103.33	2113.32	79.60	2823.33	2833.32	107.68	3543.33	3553.32	135.76
1393.33	1403.32	51.91	2113.33	2123.32	79.99	2833.33	2843.32	108.07	3553.33	3563.32	136.15
1403.33	1413.32	52.30	2123.33	2133.32	80.38	2843.33	2853.32	108.46	3563.33	3573.32	136.54
1413.33	1423.32	52.69	2133.33	2143.32	80.77	2853.33	2863.32	108.85	3573.33	3583.32	136.93
1423.33	1433.32	53.08	2143.33	2153.32	81.16	2863.33	2873.32	109.24	3583.33	3593.32	137.32
1433.33	1443.32	53.47	2153.33	2163.32	81.55	2873.33	2883.32	109.63	3593.33	3603.32	137.71
1443.33	1453.32	53.86	2163.33	2173.32	81.94	2883.33	2893.32	110.02	3603.33	3613.32	138.10
1453.33	1463.32	54.25	2173.33	2183.32	82.33	2893.33	2903.32	110.41	3613.33	3623.32	138.49
1463.33	1473.32	54.64	2183.33	2193.32	82.72	2903.33	2913.32	110.80	3623.33	3633.32	138.88
1473.33	1483.32	55.03	2193.33	2203.32	83.11	2913.33	2923.32	111.19	3633.33	3643.32	139.27
1483.33	1493.32	55.42	2203.33	2213.32	83.50	2923.33	2933.32	111.58	3643.33	3653.32	139.66
1493.33	1503.32	55.81	2213.33	2223.32	83.89	2933.33	2943.32	111.97	3653.33	3663.32	140.05
1503.33	1513.32	56.20	2223.33	2233.32	84.28	2943.33	2953.32	112.36	3663.33	3673.32	140.44
1513.33	1523.32	56.59	2233.33	2243.32	84.67	2953.33	2963.32	112.75	3673.33	3683.32	140.83
1523.33	1533.32	56.98	2243.33	2253.32	85.06	2963.33	2973.32	113.14	3683.33	3693.32	141.22
1533.33	1543.32	57.37	2253.33	2263.32	85.45	2973.33	2983.32	113.53	3693.33	3703.32	141.61
1543.33	1553.32	57.76	2263.33	2273.32	85.84	2983.33	2993.32	113.92	3703.33	3713.32	142.00
1553.33	1563.32	58.15	2273.33	2283.32	86.23	2993.33	3003.32	114.31	3713.33	3723.32	142.39
1563.33	1573.32	58.54	2283.33	2293.32	86.62	3003.33	3013.32	114.70	3723.33	3733.32	142.78
1573.33	1583.32	58.93	2293.33	2303.32	87.01	3013.33	3023.32	115.09	3733.33	3743.32	143.17
1583.33	1593.32	59.32	2303.33	2313.32	87.40	3023.33	3033.32	115.48	3743.33	3753.32	143.56
1593.33	1603.32	59.71	2313.33	2323.32	87.79	3033.33	3043.32	115.87	3753.33	3763.32	143.95
1603.33	1613.32	60.10	2323.33	2333.32	88.18	3043.33	3053.32	116.26	3763.33	3773.32	144.34
1613.33	1623.32	60.49	2333.33	2343.32	88.57	3053.33	3063.32	116.65	3773.33	3783.32	144.73
1623.33	1633.32	60.88	2343.33	2353.32	88.96	3063.33	3073.32	117.04	3783.33	3793.32	145.12
1633.33	1643.32	61.27	2353.33	2363.32	89.35	3073.33	3083.32	117.43	3793.33	3803.32	145.51
1643.33	1653.32	61.66	2363.33	2373.32	89.74	3083.33	3093.32	117.82	3803.33	3813.32	145.90
1653.33	1663.32	62.05	2373.33	2383.32	90.13	3093.33	3103.32	118.21	3813.33	3823.32	146.29
1663.33	1673.32	62.44	2383.33	2393.32	90.52	3103.33	3113.32	118.60	3823.33	3833.32	146.68
1673.33	1683.32	62.83	2393.33	2403.32	90.91	3113.33	3123.32	118.99	3833.33	3843.32*	147.07
1683.33	1693.32	63.22	2403.33	2413.32	91.30	3123.33	3133.32	119.38			
1693.33	1703.32	63.61	2413.33	2423.32	91.69	3133.33	3143.32	119.77			
1703.33	1713.32	64.00	2423.33	2433.32	92.08	3143.33	3153.32	120.16			
1713.33	1723.32	64.39	2433.33	2443.32	92.47	3153.33	3163.32	120.55			
1723.33	1733.32	64.78	2443.33	2453.32	92.86	3163.33	3173.32	120.94			
1733.33	1743.32	65.17	2453.33	2463.32	93.25	3173.33	3183.32	121.33			
1743.33	1753.32	65.56	2463.33	2473.32	93.64	3183.33	3193.32	121.72			
1753.33	1763.32	65.95	2473.33	2483.32	94.03	3193.33	3203.32	122.11			
1763.33	1773.32	66.34	2483.33	2493.32	94.42	3203.33	3213.32	122.50			

* If the earnings are above this amount, follow the calculation method shown in publication T4001, *Payroll Deductions - Basic Information*

* Si la rémunération dépasse ce montant, consultez la méthode de calcul qui se trouve dans la publication T4001, *Renseignements de base sur les retenues sur la paie.*

B-10 Employee's maximum CPP contribution for the year 2000 is $1329.90   La cotisation maximale de l'employé au RPC pour l'année 2000 est de 1329,90 $

FIGURE 14-4 C.P.P. contributions table

Employment Insurance Premiums — Cotisations à l'assurance-emploi

Insurable Earnings Rémunération assurable		EI premium Cotisation d'AE	Insurable Earnings Rémunération assurable		EI premium Cotisation d'AE	Insurable Earnings Rémunération assurable		EI premium Cotisation d'AE	Insurable Earnings Rémunération assurable		EI premium Cotisation d'AE
From - De	To - À		From - De	To - À		From - De	To - À		From - De	To - À	
1320.21 -	1320.62	31.69	1350.21 -	1350.62	32.41	1380.21 -	1380.62	33.13	1410.21 -	1410.62	33.85
1320.63 -	1321.04	31.70	1350.63 -	1351.04	32.42	1380.63 -	1381.04	33.14	1410.63 -	1411.04	33.86
1321.05 -	1321.45	31.71	1351.05 -	1351.45	32.43	1381.05 -	1381.45	33.15	1411.05 -	1411.45	33.87
1321.46 -	1321.87	31.72	1351.46 -	1351.87	32.44	1381.46 -	1381.87	33.16	1411.46 -	1411.87	33.88
1321.88 -	1322.29	31.73	1351.88 -	1352.29	32.45	1381.88 -	1382.29	33.17	1411.88 -	1412.29	33.89
1322.30 -	1322.70	31.74	1352.30 -	1352.70	32.46	1382.30 -	1382.70	33.18	1412.30 -	1412.70	33.90
1322.71 -	1323.12	31.75	1352.71 -	1353.12	32.47	1382.71 -	1383.12	33.19	1412.71 -	1413.12	33.91
1323.13 -	1323.54	31.76	1353.13 -	1353.54	32.48	1383.13 -	1383.54	33.20	1413.13 -	1413.54	33.92
1323.55 -	1323.95	31.77	1353.55 -	1353.95	32.49	1383.55 -	1383.95	33.21	1413.55 -	1413.95	33.93
1323.96 -	1324.37	31.78	1353.96 -	1354.37	32.50	1383.96 -	1384.37	33.22	1413.96 -	1414.37	33.94
1324.38 -	1324.79	31.79	1354.38 -	1354.79	32.51	1384.38 -	1384.79	33.23	1414.38 -	1414.79	33.95
1324.80 -	1325.20	31.80	1354.80 -	1355.20	32.52	1384.80 -	1385.20	33.24	1414.80 -	1415.20	33.96
1325.21 -	1325.62	31.81	1355.21 -	1355.62	32.53	1385.21 -	1385.62	33.25	1415.21 -	1415.62	33.97
1325.63 -	1326.04	31.82	1355.63 -	1356.04	32.54	1385.63 -	1386.04	33.26	1415.63 -	1416.04	33.98
1326.05 -	1326.45	31.83	1356.05 -	1356.45	32.55	1386.05 -	1386.45	33.27	1416.05 -	1416.45	33.99
1326.46 -	1326.87	31.84	1356.46 -	1356.87	32.56	1386.46 -	1386.87	33.28	1416.46 -	1416.87	34.00
1326.88 -	1327.29	31.85	1356.88 -	1357.29	32.57	1386.88 -	1387.29	33.29	1416.88 -	1417.29	34.01
1327.30 -	1327.70	31.86	1357.30 -	1357.70	32.58	1387.30 -	1387.70	33.30	1417.30 -	1417.70	34.02
1327.71 -	1328.12	31.87	1357.71 -	1358.12	32.59	1387.71 -	1388.12	33.31	1417.71 -	1418.12	34.03
1328.13 -	1328.54	31.88	1358.13 -	1358.54	32.60	1388.13 -	1388.54	33.32	1418.13 -	1418.54	34.04
1328.55 -	1328.95	31.89	1358.55 -	1358.95	32.61	1388.55 -	1388.95	33.33	1418.55 -	1418.95	34.05
1328.96 -	1329.37	31.90	1358.96 -	1359.37	32.62	1388.96 -	1389.37	33.34	1418.96 -	1419.37	34.06
1329.38 -	1329.79	31.91	1359.38 -	1359.79	32.63	1389.38 -	1389.79	33.35	1419.38 -	1419.79	34.07
1329.80 -	1330.20	31.92	1359.80 -	1360.20	32.64	1389.80 -	1390.20	33.36	1419.80 -	1420.20	34.08
1330.21 -	1330.62	31.93	1360.21 -	1360.62	32.65	1390.21 -	1390.62	33.37	1420.21 -	1420.62	34.09
1330.63 -	1331.04	31.94	1360.63 -	1361.04	32.66	1390.63 -	1391.04	33.38	1420.63 -	1421.04	34.10
1331.05 -	1331.45	31.95	1361.05 -	1361.45	32.67	1391.05 -	1391.45	33.39	1421.05 -	1421.45	34.11
1331.46 -	1331.87	31.96	1361.46 -	1361.87	32.68	1391.46 -	1391.87	33.40	1421.46 -	1421.87	34.12
1331.88 -	1332.29	31.97	1361.88 -	1362.29	32.69	1391.88 -	1392.29	33.41	1421.88 -	1422.29	34.13
1332.30 -	1332.70	31.98	1362.30 -	1362.70	32.70	1392.30 -	1392.70	33.42	1422.30 -	1422.70	34.14
1332.71 -	1333.12	31.99	1362.71 -	1363.12	32.71	1392.71 -	1393.12	33.43	1422.71 -	1423.12	34.15
1333.13 -	1333.54	32.00	1363.13 -	1363.54	32.72	1393.13 -	1393.54	33.44	1423.13 -	1423.54	34.16
1333.55 -	1333.95	32.01	1363.55 -	1363.95	32.73	1393.55 -	1393.95	33.45	1423.55 -	1423.95	34.17
1333.96 -	1334.37	32.02	1363.96 -	1364.37	32.74	1393.96 -	1394.37	33.46	1423.96 -	1424.37	34.18
1334.38 -	1334.79	32.03	1364.38 -	1364.79	32.75	1394.38 -	1394.79	33.47	1424.38 -	1424.79	34.19
1334.80 -	1335.20	32.04	1364.80 -	1365.20	32.76	1394.80 -	1395.20	33.48	1424.80 -	1425.20	34.20
1335.21 -	1335.62	32.05	1365.21 -	1365.62	32.77	1395.21 -	1395.62	33.49	1425.21 -	1425.62	34.21
1335.63 -	1336.04	32.06	1365.63 -	1366.04	32.78	1395.63 -	1396.04	33.50	1425.63 -	1426.04	34.22
1336.05 -	1336.45	32.07	1366.05 -	1366.45	32.79	1396.05 -	1396.45	33.51	1426.05 -	1426.45	34.23
1336.46 -	1336.87	32.08	1366.46 -	1366.87	32.80	1396.46 -	1396.87	33.52	1426.46 -	1426.87	34.24
1336.88 -	1337.29	32.09	1366.88 -	1367.29	32.81	1396.88 -	1397.29	33.53	1426.88 -	1427.29	34.25
1337.30 -	1337.70	32.10	1367.30 -	1367.70	32.82	1397.30 -	1397.70	33.54	1427.30 -	1427.70	34.26
1337.71 -	1338.12	32.11	1367.71 -	1368.12	32.83	1397.71 -	1398.12	33.55	1427.71 -	1428.12	34.27
1338.13 -	1338.54	32.12	1368.13 -	1368.54	32.84	1398.13 -	1398.54	33.56	1428.13 -	1428.54	34.28
1338.55 -	1338.95	32.13	1368.55 -	1368.95	32.85	1398.55 -	1398.95	33.57	1428.55 -	1428.95	34.29
1338.96 -	1339.37	32.14	1368.96 -	1369.37	32.86	1398.96 -	1399.37	33.58	1428.96 -	1429.37	34.30
1339.38 -	1339.79	32.15	1369.38 -	1369.79	32.87	1399.38 -	1399.79	33.59	1429.38 -	1429.79	34.31
1339.80 -	1340.20	32.16	1369.80 -	1370.20	32.88	1399.80 -	1400.20	33.60	1429.80 -	1430.20	34.32
1340.21 -	1340.62	32.17	1370.21 -	1370.62	32.89	1400.21 -	1400.62	33.61	1430.21 -	1430.62	34.33
1340.63 -	1341.04	32.18	1370.63 -	1371.04	32.90	1400.63 -	1401.04	33.62	1430.63 -	1431.04	34.34
1341.05 -	1341.45	32.19	1371.05 -	1371.45	32.91	1401.05 -	1401.45	33.63	1431.05 -	1431.45	34.35
1341.46 -	1341.87	32.20	1371.46 -	1371.87	32.92	1401.46 -	1401.87	33.64	1431.46 -	1431.87	34.36
1341.88 -	1342.29	32.21	1371.88 -	1372.29	32.93	1401.88 -	1402.29	33.65	1431.88 -	1432.29	34.37
1342.30 -	1342.70	32.22	1372.30 -	1372.70	32.94	1402.30 -	1402.70	33.66	1432.30 -	1432.70	34.38
1342.71 -	1343.12	32.23	1372.71 -	1373.12	32.95	1402.71 -	1403.12	33.67	1432.71 -	1433.12	34.39
1343.13 -	1343.54	32.24	1373.13 -	1373.54	32.96	1403.13 -	1403.54	33.68	1433.13 -	1433.54	34.40
1343.55 -	1343.95	32.25	1373.55 -	1373.95	32.97	1403.55 -	1403.95	33.69	1433.55 -	1433.95	34.41
1343.96 -	1344.37	32.26	1373.96 -	1374.37	32.98	1403.96 -	1404.37	33.70	1433.96 -	1434.37	34.42
1344.38 -	1344.79	32.27	1374.38 -	1374.79	32.99	1404.38 -	1404.79	33.71	1434.38 -	1434.79	34.43
1344.80 -	1345.20	32.28	1374.80 -	1375.20	33.00	1404.80 -	1405.20	33.72	1434.80 -	1435.20	34.44
1345.21 -	1345.62	32.29	1375.21 -	1375.62	33.01	1405.21 -	1405.62	33.73	1435.21 -	1435.62	34.45
1345.63 -	1346.04	32.30	1375.63 -	1376.04	33.02	1405.63 -	1406.04	33.74	1435.63 -	1436.04	34.46
1346.05 -	1346.45	32.31	1376.05 -	1376.45	33.03	1406.05 -	1406.45	33.75	1436.05 -	1436.45	34.47
1346.46 -	1346.87	32.32	1376.46 -	1376.87	33.04	1406.46 -	1406.87	33.76	1436.46 -	1436.87	34.48
1346.88 -	1347.29	32.33	1376.88 -	1377.29	33.05	1406.88 -	1407.29	33.77	1436.88 -	1437.29	34.49
1347.30 -	1347.70	32.34	1377.30 -	1377.70	33.06	1407.30 -	1407.70	33.78	1437.30 -	1437.70	34.50
1347.71 -	1348.12	32.35	1377.71 -	1378.12	33.07	1407.71 -	1408.12	33.79	1437.71 -	1438.12	34.51
1348.13 -	1348.54	32.36	1378.13 -	1378.54	33.08	1408.13 -	1408.54	33.80	1438.13 -	1438.54	34.52
1348.55 -	1348.95	32.37	1378.55 -	1378.95	33.09	1408.55 -	1408.95	33.81	1438.55 -	1438.95	34.53
1348.96 -	1349.37	32.38	1378.96 -	1379.37	33.10	1408.96 -	1409.37	33.82	1438.96 -	1439.37	34.54
1349.38 -	1349.79	32.39	1379.38 -	1379.79	33.11	1409.38 -	1409.79	33.83	1439.38 -	1439.79	34.55
1349.80 -	1350.20	32.40	1379.80 -	1380.20	33.12	1409.80 -	1410.20	33.84	1439.80 -	1440.20	34.56

C-12 Yearly maximum insurable earnings are $39,000   Le maximum annuel de la rémunération assurable est de 39 000 $
Yearly maximum employee premiums are $936   Le cotisation maximal annuelle de l'employé est de 936 $

FIGURE 14-5 E.I. premiums table

Income Tax Deduction

Lostracco's income tax deduction for the week is determined by referring to the *Payroll Deduction Tables* and using the TD1 form. This is done for both the provincial and federal income tax amounts. Figures 14-6A and 14-6B on pages 723 and 724 are used to determine the provincial and federal deductions. The two deductions total $393.75.

When an employee contributes to an R.P.P. or pays union dues, for example, the contribution reduces taxable earnings. To find the **taxable earnings** for employees who have these deductions, the calculation is:

> Taxable earnings are the earnings that remain after non-taxable deductions. Taxable earnings are used to determine the amount of income tax that will be deducted.

Taxable Earnings = Gross Earnings − (Registered Pension Plan Contributions + Union Dues + Other Authorized Deductions [Alimony Payments, Living Away from Home Deductions, Child Care, etc.])

Would Lostracco's income tax deduction change if she had paid union dues or made an R.P.P. contribution during the pay period? Yes, it would, since the income tax deduction is based on taxable earnings.

Example:

Gross Earnings	−	R.P.P.	−	Union Dues	=	Taxable Earnings
$1400	−	$84	−	$30	=	$1286

Figures 14-6A and 14-6B indicate the income tax deduction for taxable earnings of $1286 at net claim code 1 is $341.35 ($120.70 provincial plus $220.65 federal). Therefore, Lostracco's tax deduction is reduced as a result of having these additional income tax deductions.

Net Earnings

Lostracco's cheque, Figure 14-1, was for net earnings of $920.74. This figure was arrived at as follows:

Gross Earnings	−	Deductions	=	Net Earnings
$1400	−	$479.26	=	$920.74

PAYROLL ACCOUNTING PROCEDURES

M. Lostracco is paid a salary of $1400 for a work period of one week. It is common, however, to see several other pay periods used as well.

Pay Periods

Payrolls are prepared for different time periods, such as:

- *daily*: for short-term jobs that may last for only a day or two;
- *weekly*: every week, or 52 times a year;
- *bi-weekly*: every two weeks, or 26 times a year;
- *semi-monthly*: twice a month, or 24 times a year; and
- *monthly*: every month, or 12 times a year.

British Columbia
Provincial tax deductions only
Effective January 1, 2001
Weekly (52 pay periods a year)

Colombie-Britannique
Retenues d'impôt provincial seulement
En vigueur le 1er janvier 2001
Hebdomadaire (52 périodes de paie par année)

Pay / Rémunération		Provincial claim codes/Codes de demande provinciaux										
From De	Less than Moins de	0	1	2	3	4	5	6	7	8	9	10
							Deduct from each pay Retenez sur chaque paie						
929. -	941	86.90	74.00	72.55	69.65	66.70	63.80	60.90	58.00	55.10	52.20	49.25
941. -	953	88.35	75.40	73.95	71.05	68.15	65.25	62.35	59.40	56.50	53.60	50.70
953. -	965	89.75	76.85	75.40	72.50	69.55	66.65	63.75	60.85	57.95	55.05	52.15
965. -	977	91.20	78.25	76.80	73.90	71.00	68.10	65.20	62.30	59.35	56.45	53.55
977. -	989	92.60	79.70	78.25	75.35	72.45	69.50	66.60	63.70	60.80	57.90	55.00
989. -	1001	94.05	81.15	79.65	76.75	73.85	70.95	68.05	65.15	62.25	59.30	56.40
1001. -	1013	95.50	82.55	81.10	78.20	75.30	72.40	69.45	66.55	63.65	60.75	57.85
1013. -	1025	96.90	84.00	82.55	79.60	76.70	73.80	70.90	68.00	65.10	62.20	59.25
1025. -	1037	98.35	85.40	83.95	81.05	78.15	75.25	72.35	69.40	66.50	63.60	60.70
1037. -	1049	99.75	86.85	85.40	82.50	79.55	76.65	73.75	70.85	67.95	65.05	62.10
1049. -	1061	101.20	88.25	86.80	83.90	81.00	78.10	75.20	72.30	69.35	66.45	63.55
1061. -	1073	102.60	89.70	88.25	85.35	82.45	79.50	76.60	73.70	70.80	67.90	65.00
1073. -	1085	104.05	91.10	89.65	86.75	83.85	80.95	78.05	75.15	72.20	69.30	66.40
1085. -	1097	105.45	92.55	91.10	88.20	85.30	82.35	79.45	76.55	73.65	70.75	67.85
1097. -	1109	106.90	94.00	92.55	89.60	86.70	83.80	80.90	78.00	75.10	72.15	69.25
1109. -	1121	108.35	95.40	93.95	91.05	88.15	85.25	82.30	79.40	76.50	73.60	70.70
1121. -	1133	109.75	96.85	95.40	92.45	89.55	86.65	83.75	80.85	77.95	75.05	72.10
1133. -	1145	111.20	98.25	96.80	93.90	91.00	88.10	85.20	82.25	79.35	76.45	73.55
1145. -	1157	112.60	99.70	98.25	95.35	92.40	89.50	86.60	83.70	80.80	77.90	75.00
1157. -	1169	114.05	101.10	99.65	96.75	93.85	90.95	88.05	85.15	82.20	79.30	76.40
1169. -	1181	115.60	102.70	101.20	98.30	95.40	92.50	89.60	86.70	83.80	80.85	77.95
1181. -	1193	117.60	104.70	103.25	100.30	97.40	94.50	91.60	88.70	85.80	82.85	79.95
1193. -	1205	119.60	106.70	105.25	102.35	99.40	96.50	93.60	90.70	87.80	84.90	81.95
1205. -	1217	121.60	108.70	107.25	104.35	101.40	98.50	95.60	92.70	89.80	86.90	84.00
1217. -	1229	123.60	110.70	109.25	106.35	103.45	100.50	97.60	94.70	91.80	88.90	86.00
1229. -	1241	125.60	112.70	111.25	108.35	105.45	102.50	99.60	96.70	93.80	90.90	88.00
1241. -	1253	127.65	114.70	113.25	110.35	107.45	104.55	101.60	98.70	95.80	92.90	90.00
1253. -	1265	129.65	116.70	115.25	112.35	109.45	106.55	103.60	100.70	97.80	94.90	92.00
1265. -	1277	131.65	118.70	117.25	114.35	111.45	108.55	105.65	102.70	99.80	96.90	94.00
1277. -	1289	133.65	120.70	119.25	116.35	113.45	110.55	107.65	104.70	101.80	98.90	96.00
1289. -	1301	135.65	122.70	121.25	118.35	115.45	112.55	109.65	106.75	103.80	100.90	98.00
1301. -	1313	137.65	124.70	123.25	120.35	117.45	114.55	111.65	108.75	105.80	102.90	100.00
1313. -	1325	139.65	126.75	125.25	122.35	119.45	116.55	113.65	110.75	107.85	104.90	102.00
1325. -	1337	141.65	128.75	127.30	124.35	121.45	118.55	115.65	112.75	109.85	106.90	104.00
1337. -	1349	143.65	130.75	129.30	126.35	123.45	120.55	117.65	114.75	111.85	108.95	106.00
1349. -	1361	145.85	132.90	131.45	128.55	125.65	122.75	119.85	116.90	114.00	111.10	108.20
1361. -	1373	148.10	135.15	133.70	130.80	127.90	125.00	122.05	119.15	116.25	113.35	110.45
1373. -	1385	150.35	137.40	135.95	133.05	130.15	127.25	124.30	121.40	118.50	115.60	112.70
1385. -	1397	152.55	139.65	138.20	135.30	132.40	129.45	126.55	123.65	120.75	117.85	114.95
1397. -	1409	154.80	141.90	140.45	137.55	134.60	131.70	128.80	125.90	123.00	120.10	117.20
1409. -	1421	157.05	144.15	142.70	139.75	136.85	133.95	131.05	128.15	125.25	122.35	119.40
1421. -	1433	159.30	146.40	144.95	142.00	139.10	136.20	133.30	130.40	127.50	124.55	121.65
1433. -	1445	161.55	148.60	147.15	144.25	141.35	138.45	135.55	132.65	129.70	126.80	123.90
1445. -	1457	163.80	150.85	149.40	146.50	143.60	140.70	137.80	134.90	131.95	129.05	126.15
1457. -	1469	166.05	153.10	151.65	148.75	145.85	142.95	140.05	137.10	134.20	131.30	128.40
1469. -	1481	168.30	155.35	153.90	151.00	148.10	145.20	142.25	139.35	136.45	133.55	130.65
1481. -	1493	170.50	157.60	156.15	153.25	150.35	147.40	144.50	141.60	138.70	135.80	132.90
1493. -	1505	172.75	159.85	158.40	155.50	152.55	149.65	146.75	143.85	140.95	138.05	135.15
1505. -	1517	175.00	162.10	160.65	157.75	154.80	151.90	149.00	146.10	143.20	140.30	137.35
1517. -	1529	177.25	164.35	162.90	159.95	157.05	154.15	151.25	148.35	145.45	142.50	139.60
1529. -	1541	179.50	166.60	165.10	162.20	159.30	156.40	153.50	150.60	147.70	144.75	141.85
1541. -	1553	181.75	168.80	167.35	164.45	161.55	158.65	155.75	152.85	149.90	147.00	144.10
1553. -	1565	184.00	171.05	169.60	166.70	163.80	160.90	158.00	155.05	152.15	149.25	146.35
1565. -	1577	186.25	173.30	171.85	168.95	166.05	163.15	160.20	157.30	154.40	151.50	148.60
1577. -	1589	188.45	175.55	174.10	171.20	168.30	165.35	162.45	159.55	156.65	153.75	150.85

This table is available on diskette (TOD).   E-4   Vous pouvez obtenir cette table sur disquette (TSD).

FIGURE 14-6A Provincial tax deduction table for BC

British Columbia
Federal tax deductions only
Effective January 1, 2001
Weekly (52 pay periods a year)

Colombie-Britannique
Retenues d'impôt fédéral seulement
En vigueur le 1ᵉʳ janvier 2001
Hebdomadaire (52 périodes de paie par année)

Pay — Rémunération		Federal claim codes/Codes de demande fédéraux										
From De	Less than Moins de	0	1	2	3	4	5	6	7	8	9	10
						Deduct from each pay / Retenez sur chaque paie						
917. -	929	160.25	137.45	134.95	129.90	124.80	119.75	114.70	109.65	104.60	99.55	94.45
929. -	941	162.90	140.10	137.60	132.50	127.45	122.40	117.35	112.30	107.25	102.15	97.10
941. -	953	165.55	142.75	140.20	135.15	130.10	125.05	120.00	114.95	109.85	104.80	99.75
953. -	965	168.20	145.40	142.85	137.80	132.75	127.70	122.65	117.55	112.50	107.45	102.40
965. -	977	170.85	148.05	145.50	140.45	135.40	130.30	125.25	120.20	115.15	110.10	105.05
977. -	989	173.50	150.65	148.15	143.10	138.00	132.95	127.90	122.85	117.80	112.75	107.65
989. -	1001	176.10	153.30	150.80	145.70	140.65	135.60	130.55	125.50	120.45	115.35	110.30
1001. -	1013	178.75	155.95	153.40	148.35	143.30	138.25	133.20	128.15	123.05	118.00	112.95
1013. -	1025	181.40	158.60	156.05	151.00	145.95	140.90	135.85	130.75	125.70	120.65	115.60
1025. -	1037	184.05	161.25	158.70	153.65	148.60	143.50	138.45	133.40	128.35	123.30	118.25
1037. -	1049	186.65	163.85	161.35	156.30	151.20	146.15	141.10	136.05	131.00	125.95	120.85
1049. -	1061	189.30	166.50	164.00	158.90	153.85	148.80	143.75	138.70	133.65	128.55	123.50
1061. -	1073	191.95	169.15	166.60	161.55	156.50	151.45	146.40	141.35	136.25	131.20	126.15
1073. -	1085	194.60	171.80	169.25	164.20	159.15	154.10	149.05	143.95	138.90	133.85	128.80
1085. -	1097	197.25	174.45	171.90	166.85	161.80	156.70	151.65	146.60	141.55	136.50	131.45
1097. -	1109	199.85	177.05	174.55	169.50	164.40	159.35	154.30	149.25	144.20	139.15	134.05
1109. -	1121	202.50	179.70	177.20	172.10	167.05	162.00	156.95	151.90	146.85	141.75	136.70
1121. -	1133	205.15	182.35	179.80	174.75	169.70	164.65	159.60	154.55	149.45	144.40	139.35
1133. -	1145	207.80	185.00	182.45	177.40	172.35	167.30	162.25	157.15	152.10	147.05	142.00
1145. -	1157	210.45	187.65	185.10	180.05	175.00	169.90	164.85	159.80	154.75	149.70	144.65
1157. -	1169	213.05	190.25	187.75	182.70	177.60	172.55	167.50	162.45	157.40	152.35	147.25
1169. -	1181	215.70	192.90	190.40	185.30	180.25	175.20	170.15	165.10	160.05	154.95	149.90
1181. -	1193	218.50	195.70	193.15	188.10	183.05	178.00	172.95	167.90	162.80	157.75	152.70
1193. -	1205	221.65	198.80	196.30	191.25	186.20	181.10	176.05	171.00	165.95	160.90	155.80
1205. -	1217	224.75	201.95	199.40	194.35	189.30	184.25	179.20	174.10	169.05	164.00	158.95
1217. -	1229	227.85	205.05	202.55	197.45	192.40	187.35	182.30	177.25	172.20	167.10	162.05
1229. -	1241	231.00	208.20	205.65	200.60	195.55	190.50	185.40	180.35	175.30	170.25	165.20
1241. -	1253	234.10	211.30	208.75	203.70	198.65	193.60	188.55	183.50	178.40	173.35	168.30
1253. -	1265	237.25	214.40	211.90	206.85	201.80	196.70	191.65	186.60	181.55	176.50	171.40
1265. -	1277	240.35	217.55	215.00	209.95	204.90	199.85	194.80	189.70	184.65	179.60	174.55
1277. -	1289	243.45	220.65	218.15	213.05	208.00	202.95	197.90	192.85	187.80	182.70	177.65
1289. -	1301	246.60	223.80	221.25	216.20	211.15	206.10	201.00	195.95	190.90	185.85	180.80
1301. -	1313	249.70	226.90	224.35	219.30	214.25	209.20	204.15	199.10	194.00	188.95	183.90
1313. -	1325	252.85	230.00	227.50	222.45	217.40	212.30	207.25	202.20	197.15	192.10	187.00
1325. -	1337	255.95	233.15	230.60	225.55	220.50	215.45	210.40	205.30	200.25	195.20	190.15
1337. -	1349	259.05	236.25	233.75	228.65	223.60	218.55	213.50	208.45	203.40	198.30	193.25
1349. -	1361	262.20	239.40	236.85	231.80	226.75	221.70	216.60	211.55	206.50	201.45	196.40
1361. -	1373	265.30	242.50	239.95	234.90	229.85	224.80	219.75	214.70	209.60	204.55	199.50
1373. -	1385	268.45	245.60	243.10	238.05	233.00	227.90	222.85	217.80	212.75	207.70	202.60
1385. -	1397	271.55	248.75	246.20	241.15	236.10	231.05	226.00	220.90	215.85	210.80	205.75
1397. -	1409	274.65	251.85	249.35	244.25	239.20	234.15	229.10	224.05	219.00	213.90	208.85
1409. -	1421	277.80	255.00	252.45	247.40	242.35	237.30	232.20	227.15	222.10	217.05	212.00
1421. -	1433	280.90	258.10	255.55	250.50	245.45	240.40	235.35	230.30	225.20	220.15	215.10
1433. -	1445	284.05	261.20	258.70	253.65	248.60	243.50	238.45	233.40	228.35	223.30	218.20
1445. -	1457	287.15	264.35	261.80	256.75	251.70	246.65	241.60	236.50	231.45	226.40	221.35
1457. -	1469	290.25	267.45	264.95	259.85	254.80	249.75	244.70	239.65	234.60	229.50	224.45
1469. -	1481	293.40	270.60	268.05	263.00	257.95	252.90	247.80	242.75	237.70	232.65	227.60
1481. -	1493	296.50	273.70	271.15	266.10	261.05	256.00	250.95	245.90	240.80	235.75	230.70
1493. -	1505	299.65	276.80	274.30	269.25	264.20	259.10	254.05	249.00	243.95	238.90	233.80
1505. -	1517	302.75	279.95	277.40	272.35	267.30	262.25	257.20	252.10	247.05	242.00	236.95
1517. -	1529	305.85	283.05	280.55	275.45	270.40	265.35	260.30	255.25	250.20	245.10	240.05
1529. -	1541	309.00	286.20	283.65	278.60	273.55	268.50	263.40	258.35	253.30	248.25	243.20
1541. -	1553	312.10	289.30	286.75	281.70	276.65	271.60	266.55	261.50	256.40	251.35	246.30
1553. -	1565	315.25	292.40	289.90	284.85	279.80	274.70	269.65	264.60	259.55	254.50	249.40
1565. -	1577	318.35	295.55	293.00	287.95	282.90	277.85	272.80	267.70	262.65	257.60	252.55

This table is available on diskette (TOD).   D-4   Vous pouvez obtenir cette table sur disquette (TSD).

FIGURE 14-6B Federal tax deduction table for BC

Payment Plans

A variety of payment plans are used by companies. M. Lostracco is paid on a salary basis.

Salary

To be paid a salary means the employee's earnings are a set amount for a stated period of time. Examples of salaries are $1400 per week, $5000 per month, or $72 000 per year. A common practice is to hire on a yearly basis and then pay the worker according to one of the pay periods described above.

Hourly Rate

In this plan, workers are paid an hourly rate for each hour worked. An employee paid at the rate of $12 per hour who works 40 hours a week would earn $480 (before deductions!).

Commission

Sales personnel are often paid on a commission basis. Their earnings are based on a percentage of the sales they make. The gross earnings for a person who gets a 4 percent commission and has sales of $10 000 are $400 ($10 000 × 0.04 = $400).

Commission is a method of payment to workers based on a percentage of the sales they make.

Combination of Salary and Commission

It is more common to see a combination of a set minimum salary plus a commission on sales. An employee might receive a base salary of $200 per week plus a 2 percent commission on sales. If the week's sales are $10 000, the employee receives a total of $400 ($200 + 0.02 × $10 000 = $400).

Piece Rate

Some manufacturing companies, in the garment industry for example, use the piece rate method. To provide an incentive to workers, piece rate payment is based on the number of units the worker produces. If an employee is paid $1.75 per unit and completes 250 units, the earnings are $437.50.

Piece rate is a method of payment that is based on the number of units a worker produces.

Overtime

Provincial laws require that extra pay be given after a certain number of hours have been worked in a week. For example, if 40 hours were the maximum number of hours at regular pay, an employee who worked more than that would receive extra pay for the time worked over 40 hours.

Suppose a person earns $9 per hour for the first 40 hours worked each week, plus time and one-half for overtime. The overtime hours are paid at the rate of $13.50 per hour, (the regular hourly rate of $9 plus one-half, $4.50). If the person works 48 hours in the week, a total of $468 would be earned. The earnings are calculated as follows:

$$
\begin{array}{rcl}
\$\ 9.00\ \times\ 40\ =\ \$360 \\
13.50\ \times\ \ 8\ =\ \underline{\ \ 108} \\
\$468
\end{array}
$$

Overtime regulations are set by the provincial governments and by agreements between the employer and the employees.

UNIT 33 CHECK YOUR READING

Questions

1. What does *payroll* mean?
2. List three federal laws that affect payroll accounting procedures.
3. (a) What are the two parts of M. Lostracco's cheque in Figure 14-1?
   (b) What is the purpose of the statement of earnings?
4. What are the compulsory deductions in your province?
5. List five voluntary deductions.
6. (a) Who must contribute to the Canada Pension Plan?
   (b) What percentage of gross earnings must be contributed to C.P.P. by employees?
   (c) If all of the employees of a company together made C.P.P. contributions of $327.10 in the week, what must the company also contribute?
7. (a) Who must pay E.I. premiums?
   (b) If all of the employees of a company together paid E.I. premiums of $297.46, what is the amount of the premium paid by the company?
8. (a) What is a TD1 form?
   (b) Explain why Lostracco's net claim code is 1.
   (c) What is a non-refundable tax credit?
9. Refer to Figure 14-1 to answers these questions.
   (a) What are the gross earnings?
   (b) What are the net earnings?
   (c) What are the deductions?
   (d) What is Lostracco's take-home pay?
   (e) For which deductions must the employer also make a contribution? How much is the employer's contribution?
10. What purpose is served by the S.I.N.?
11. Describe five commonly used pay periods.
12. Describe four of the six payment methods.
13. What benefits or services are provided by the following:
    (a) Provincial health insurance
    (b) Extended health insurance
    (c) Canada Pension Plan

(d) Employment insurance
(e) Group life insurance
(f) Credit unions
(g) Registered pension plans

UNIT 33 APPLY YOUR KNOWLEDGE

Exercises

Note: Where necessary, use either current payroll deduction booklets or the tables given on pages 731–737 to complete the exercises in this chapter.

1. (a) Calculate each week's gross earnings for Renato DiCarlo, a salesperson who earns a 6 percent commission on weekly sales.

Week	Sales
1	$12 152.60
2	13 420.33
3	12 366.29
4	14 986.50

   (b) Calculate the total sales and commission for the four weeks.

2. What are Nancy Koosman's gross earnings if she receives a 4.5 percent commission and had sales of $15 570 during the week?

3. Motoko Haslam is paid a basic salary of $220 plus 2.5 percent commission on sales. The sales made for four weeks are shown below.

Week	Sales
1	$11 680
2	13 493
3	18 514
4	9 400

   (a) Calculate gross earnings for each week.
   (b) Calculate total earnings for the month.
   (c) If Motoko had received a straight commission of 5 percent of sales, what would the month's commission be?
   (d) Which method would you prefer—salary and commission or commission only? Why?

4. Ulla Eckhardt works for a firm that produces electronic components. She is paid according to the number of components she assembles. Calculate Ulla's gross earnings for each day of the week if she is paid $1.79 for each assembly.

Day	No. of Components
Monday	70
Tuesday	74
Wednesday	81
Thursday	87
Friday	75

5. Determine the gross earnings for each of the following employees:

Name	Hourly Rate	Hours
C. Giuliani	$12.60	40
C. Murphy	9.00	39
D. Ota	14.50	40
R. Takacs	13.85	38

6. If each employee in exercise 5 works five hours of overtime in addition to the regular hours, and is paid time and one-half for each hour of overtime, what are the gross earnings for each?

7. Charmaine Hooper, a welder, is paid on a piece-rate basis. She receives $3.95 for each sheet metal part produced. What are her earnings for each day and for the week?

Day	Number Produced
Monday	46
Tuesday	55
Wednesday	61
Thursday	49
Friday	38

8. Lois Belincki is paid at the rate of $12/h and time and one-half for overtime. Any work over eight hours in one day is considered overtime. Calculate her week's gross earnings if she worked the following hours:

Day	Hours
Monday	8.00
Tuesday	7.50
Wednesday	10.00
Thursday	7.75
Friday	8.00

9. During the month of August, Veronica Drepko's gross earnings were as follows:

Week	Gross Earnings
1	$796.75
2	807.53
3	785.34
4	793.53

Calculate the C.P.P. and E.I. premiums for the month of August.

10. (a) Charles Toth contributes $24 per week to the company pension plan and $10 per week to union dues. Calculate his taxable earnings in July if his gross earnings for the four weeks were as follows:

Week	Gross Earnings
1	$898.75
2	925.64
3	919.26
4	907.49

(b) Toth's net claim code for income tax deduction purposes is 8. Calculate the income tax deduction for each week in July.

(c) Calculate the C.P.P. and E.I. premiums that Toth pays each week.

(d) As well as the deductions you calculated in parts (a), (b), and (c), Toth also has the following weekly deduction: group life insurance for $30 000 at a premium of 15¢ per $1000. In the fourth week, he chose to buy a Canada Savings Bond at $25 per week. Calculate his total deductions and his net earnings for the four weeks.

11. Grace Trumball contributes $11.25 per week to her company's pension plan. She also has the following weekly deductions: Group life insurance of $25 000 at a cost of 17¢ per $1000 and union dues of $5.55. Her net claim code for tax purposes is 1. Her gross earnings in July were as follows:

Week	Gross Earnings
1	$747.50
2	799.56
3	758.61
4	702.66

(a) Calculate the taxable earnings and income tax payable.
(b) Calculate the C.P.P. and E.I. premiums.
(c) Calculate net earnings.

12. Use the TD1 form shown in Figures 14-2 and 14-3 on pages 715 and 716 to determine the net claim code for each of the following:
(a) Richard Rancourt has one dependant, 21 years old. The dependant attends college for eight months of the year, earns $6000 per year, and pays tuition fees of $3000.
(b) Sarah Taber has a dependent spouse who has no income.
(c) Gerald Ouellette has a spouse who earns $600 working part-time.
(d) Leslie Phelan is a single parent with two dependent children ages 3 and 6.
(e) Pat Brophy is a college student for eight months of the year and pays tuition of $3000.
(f) B. Falconer is 66 years old, has a dependent spouse, and receives a $15 000 pension.

13. Refer to exercise 12. Use this year's TD1 form to determine the net claim code for each person.

Canada Pension Plan Contributions
Weekly (52 pay periods a year)

Cotisations au Régime de pensions du Canada
Hebdomadaire (52 périodes de paie par année)

Pay Rémunération From - De	To - À	CPP RPC	Pay Rémunération From - De	To - À	CPP RPC	Pay Rémunération From - De	To - À	CPP RPC	Pay Rémunération From - De	To - À	CPP RPC
669.98 -	670.20	25.92	686.72 -	686.95	26.64	703.47 -	703.69	27.36	720.21 -	720.43	28.08
670.21 -	670.43	25.93	686.96 -	687.18	26.65	703.70 -	703.92	27.37	720.44 -	720.67	28.09
670.44 -	670.67	25.94	687.19 -	687.41	26.66	703.93 -	704.16	27.38	720.68 -	720.90	28.10
670.68 -	670.90	25.95	687.42 -	687.64	26.67	704.17 -	704.39	27.39	720.91 -	721.13	28.11
670.91 -	671.13	25.96	687.65 -	687.88	26.68	704.40 -	704.62	27.40	721.14 -	721.37	28.12
671.14 -	671.37	25.97	687.89 -	688.11	26.69	704.63 -	704.85	27.41	721.38 -	721.60	28.13
671.38 -	671.60	25.98	688.12 -	688.34	26.70	704.86 -	705.09	27.42	721.61 -	721.83	28.14
671.61 -	671.83	25.99	688.35 -	688.57	26.71	705.10 -	705.32	27.43	721.84 -	722.06	28.15
671.84 -	672.06	26.00	688.58 -	688.81	26.72	705.33 -	705.55	27.44	722.07 -	722.30	28.16
672.07 -	672.30	26.01	688.82 -	689.04	26.73	705.56 -	705.78	27.45	722.31 -	722.53	28.17
672.31 -	672.53	26.02	689.05 -	689.27	26.74	705.79 -	706.02	27.46	722.54 -	722.76	28.18
672.54 -	672.76	26.03	689.28 -	689.50	26.75	706.03 -	706.25	27.47	722.77 -	722.99	28.19
672.77 -	672.99	26.04	689.51 -	689.74	26.76	706.26 -	706.48	27.48	723.00 -	723.23	28.20
673.00 -	673.23	26.05	689.75 -	689.97	26.77	706.49 -	706.71	27.49	723.24 -	723.46	28.21
673.24 -	673.46	26.06	689.98 -	690.20	26.78	706.72 -	706.95	27.50	723.47 -	723.69	28.22
673.47 -	673.69	26.07	690.21 -	690.43	26.79	706.96 -	707.18	27.51	723.70 -	723.92	28.23
673.70 -	673.92	26.08	690.44 -	690.67	26.80	707.19 -	707.41	27.52	723.93 -	724.16	28.24
673.93 -	674.16	26.09	690.68 -	690.90	26.81	707.42 -	707.64	27.53	724.17 -	724.39	28.25
674.17 -	674.39	26.10	690.91 -	691.13	26.82	707.65 -	707.88	27.54	724.40 -	724.62	28.26
674.40 -	674.62	26.11	691.14 -	691.37	26.83	707.89 -	708.11	27.55	724.63 -	724.85	28.27
674.63 -	674.85	26.12	691.38 -	691.60	26.84	708.12 -	708.34	27.56	724.86 -	725.09	28.28
674.86 -	675.09	26.13	691.61 -	691.83	26.85	708.35 -	708.57	27.57	725.10 -	725.32	28.29
675.10 -	675.32	26.14	691.84 -	692.06	26.86	708.58 -	708.81	27.58	725.33 -	725.55	28.30
675.33 -	675.55	26.15	692.07 -	692.30	26.87	708.82 -	709.04	27.59	725.56 -	725.78	28.31
675.56 -	675.78	26.16	692.31 -	692.53	26.88	709.05 -	709.27	27.60	725.79 -	726.02	28.32
675.79 -	676.02	26.17	692.54 -	692.76	26.89	709.28 -	709.50	27.61	726.03 -	726.25	28.33
676.03 -	676.25	26.18	692.77 -	692.99	26.90	709.51 -	709.74	27.62	726.26 -	726.48	28.34
676.26 -	676.48	26.19	693.00 -	693.23	26.91	709.75 -	709.97	27.63	726.49 -	726.71	28.35
676.49 -	676.71	26.20	693.24 -	693.46	26.92	709.98 -	710.20	27.64	726.72 -	726.95	28.36
676.72 -	676.95	26.21	693.47 -	693.69	26.93	710.21 -	710.43	27.65	726.96 -	727.18	28.37
676.96 -	677.18	26.22	693.70 -	693.92	26.94	710.44 -	710.67	27.66	727.19 -	727.41	28.38
677.19 -	677.41	26.23	693.93 -	694.16	26.95	710.68 -	710.90	27.67	727.42 -	727.64	28.39
677.42 -	677.64	26.24	694.17 -	694.39	26.96	710.91 -	711.13	27.68	727.65 -	727.88	28.40
677.65 -	677.88	26.25	694.40 -	694.62	26.97	711.14 -	711.37	27.69	727.89 -	728.11	28.41
677.89 -	678.11	26.26	694.63 -	694.85	26.98	711.38 -	711.60	27.70	728.12 -	728.34	28.42
678.12 -	678.34	26.27	694.86 -	695.09	26.99	711.61 -	711.83	27.71	728.35 -	728.57	28.43
678.35 -	678.57	26.28	695.10 -	695.32	27.00	711.84 -	712.06	27.72	728.58 -	728.81	28.44
678.58 -	678.81	26.29	695.33 -	695.55	27.01	712.07 -	712.30	27.73	728.82 -	729.04	28.45
678.82 -	679.04	26.30	695.56 -	695.78	27.02	712.31 -	712.53	27.74	729.05 -	729.27	28.46
679.05 -	679.27	26.31	695.79 -	696.02	27.03	712.54 -	712.76	27.75	729.28 -	729.50	28.47
679.28 -	679.50	26.32	696.03 -	696.25	27.04	712.77 -	712.99	27.76	729.51 -	729.74	28.48
679.51 -	679.74	26.33	696.26 -	696.48	27.05	713.00 -	713.23	27.77	729.75 -	729.97	28.49
679.75 -	679.97	26.34	696.49 -	696.71	27.06	713.24 -	713.46	27.78	729.98 -	730.20	28.50
679.98 -	680.20	26.35	696.72 -	696.95	27.07	713.47 -	713.69	27.79	730.21 -	730.43	28.51
680.21 -	680.43	26.36	696.96 -	697.18	27.08	713.70 -	713.92	27.80	730.44 -	730.67	28.52
680.44 -	680.67	26.37	697.19 -	697.41	27.09	713.93 -	714.16	27.81	730.68 -	730.90	28.53
680.68 -	680.90	26.38	697.42 -	697.64	27.10	714.17 -	714.39	27.82	730.91 -	731.13	28.54
680.91 -	681.13	26.39	697.65 -	697.88	27.11	714.40 -	714.62	27.83	731.14 -	731.37	28.55
681.14 -	681.37	26.40	697.89 -	698.11	27.12	714.63 -	714.85	27.84	731.38 -	731.60	28.56
681.38 -	681.60	26.41	698.12 -	698.34	27.13	714.86 -	715.09	27.85	731.61 -	731.83	28.57
681.61 -	681.83	26.42	698.35 -	698.57	27.14	715.10 -	715.32	27.86	731.84 -	732.06	28.58
681.84 -	682.06	26.43	698.58 -	698.81	27.15	715.33 -	715.55	27.87	732.07 -	732.30	28.59
682.07 -	682.30	26.44	698.82 -	699.04	27.16	715.56 -	715.78	27.88	732.31 -	732.53	28.60
682.31 -	682.53	26.45	699.05 -	699.27	27.17	715.79 -	716.02	27.89	732.54 -	732.76	28.61
682.54 -	682.76	26.46	699.28 -	699.50	27.18	716.03 -	716.25	27.90	732.77 -	732.99	28.62
682.77 -	682.99	26.47	699.51 -	699.74	27.19	716.26 -	716.48	27.91	733.00 -	733.23	28.63
683.00 -	683.23	26.48	699.75 -	699.97	27.20	716.49 -	716.71	27.92	733.24 -	733.46	28.64
683.24 -	683.46	26.49	699.98 -	700.20	27.21	716.72 -	716.95	27.93	733.47 -	733.69	28.65
683.47 -	683.69	26.50	700.21 -	700.43	27.22	716.96 -	717.18	27.94	733.70 -	733.92	28.66
683.70 -	683.92	26.51	700.44 -	700.67	27.23	717.19 -	717.41	27.95	733.93 -	734.16	28.67
683.93 -	684.16	26.52	700.68 -	700.90	27.24	717.42 -	717.64	27.96	734.17 -	734.39	28.68
684.17 -	684.39	26.53	700.91 -	701.13	27.25	717.65 -	717.88	27.97	734.40 -	734.62	28.69
684.40 -	684.62	26.54	701.14 -	701.37	27.26	717.89 -	718.11	27.98	734.63 -	734.85	28.70
684.63 -	684.85	26.55	701.38 -	701.60	27.27	718.12 -	718.34	27.99	734.86 -	735.09	28.71
684.86 -	685.09	26.56	701.61 -	701.83	27.28	718.35 -	718.57	28.00	735.10 -	735.32	28.72
685.10 -	685.32	26.57	701.84 -	702.06	27.29	718.58 -	718.81	28.01	735.33 -	735.55	28.73
685.33 -	685.55	26.58	702.07 -	702.30	27.30	718.82 -	719.04	28.02	735.56 -	735.78	28.74
685.56 -	685.78	26.59	702.31 -	702.53	27.31	719.05 -	719.27	28.03	735.79 -	736.02	28.75
685.79 -	686.02	26.60	702.54 -	702.76	27.32	719.28 -	719.50	28.04	736.03 -	736.25	28.76
686.03 -	686.25	26.61	702.77 -	702.99	27.33	719.51 -	719.74	28.05	736.26 -	736.48	28.77
686.26 -	686.48	26.62	703.00 -	703.23	27.34	719.75 -	719.97	28.06	736.49 -	736.71	28.78
686.49 -	686.71	26.63	703.24 -	703.46	27.35	719.98 -	720.20	28.07	736.72 -	746.71	29.00

B-10 Employee's maximum CPP contribution for the year 2001 is $1496.40   La cotisation maximale de l'employé au RPC pour l'année 2001 est de 1496,40 $

Extracts from C.P.P. tables

Canada Pension Plan Contributions
Weekly (52 pay periods a year)

Cotisations au Régime de pensions du Canada
Hebdomadaire (52 périodes de paie par année)

Pay Rémunération		CPP RPC	Pay Rémunération		CPP RPC	Pay Rémunération		CPP RPC	Pay Rémunération		CPP RPC
From - De	To - À		From - De	To - À		From - De	To - À		From - De	To - À	
746.72	756.71	29.43	1466.72	1476.71	60.39	2186.72	2196.71	91.35	2906.72	2916.71	122.31
756.72	766.71	29.86	1476.72	1486.71	60.82	2196.72	2206.71	91.78	2916.72	2926.71	122.74
766.72	776.71	30.29	1486.72	1496.71	61.25	2206.72	2216.71	92.21	2926.72	2936.71	123.17
776.72	786.71	30.72	1496.72	1506.71	61.68	2216.72	2226.71	92.64	2936.72	2946.71	123.60
786.72	796.71	31.15	1506.72	1516.71	62.11	2226.72	2236.71	93.07	2946.72	2956.71	124.03
796.72	806.71	31.58	1516.72	1526.71	62.54	2236.72	2246.71	93.50	2956.72	2966.71	124.46
806.72	816.71	32.01	1526.72	1536.71	62.97	2246.72	2256.71	93.93	2966.72	2976.71	124.89
816.72	826.71	32.44	1536.72	1546.71	63.40	2256.72	2266.71	94.36	2976.72	2986.71	125.32
826.72	836.71	32.87	1546.72	1556.71	63.83	2266.72	2276.71	94.79	2986.72	2996.71	125.75
836.72	846.71	33.30	1556.72	1566.71	64.26	2276.72	2286.71	95.22	2996.72	3006.71	126.18
846.72	856.71	33.73	1566.72	1576.71	64.69	2286.72	2296.71	95.65	3006.72	3016.71	126.61
856.72	866.71	34.16	1576.72	1586.71	65.12	2296.72	2306.71	96.08	3016.72	3026.71	127.04
866.72	876.71	34.59	1586.72	1596.71	65.55	2306.72	2316.71	96.51	3026.72	3036.71	127.47
876.72	886.71	35.02	1596.72	1606.71	65.98	2316.72	2326.71	96.94	3036.72	3046.71	127.90
886.72	896.71	35.45	1606.72	1616.71	66.41	2326.72	2336.71	97.37	3046.72	3056.71	128.33
896.72	906.71	35.88	1616.72	1626.71	66.84	2336.72	2346.71	97.80	3056.72	3066.71	128.76
906.72	916.71	36.31	1626.72	1636.71	67.27	2346.72	2356.71	98.23	3066.72	3076.71	129.19
916.72	926.71	36.74	1636.72	1646.71	67.70	2356.72	2366.71	98.66	3076.72	3086.71	129.62
926.72	936.71	37.17	1646.72	1656.71	68.13	2366.72	2376.71	99.09	3086.72	3096.71	130.05
936.72	946.71	37.60	1656.72	1666.71	68.56	2376.72	2386.71	99.52	3096.72	3106.71	130.48
946.72	956.71	38.03	1666.72	1676.71	68.99	2386.72	2396.71	99.95	3106.72	3116.71	130.91
956.72	966.71	38.46	1676.72	1686.71	69.42	2396.72	2406.71	100.38	3116.72	3126.71	131.34
966.72	976.71	38.89	1686.72	1696.71	69.85	2406.72	2416.71	100.81	3126.72	3136.71	131.77
976.72	986.71	39.32	1696.72	1706.71	70.28	2416.72	2426.71	101.24	3136.72	3146.71	132.20
986.72	996.71	39.75	1706.72	1716.71	70.71	2426.72	2436.71	101.67	3146.72	3156.71	132.63
996.72	1006.71	40.18	1716.72	1726.71	71.14	2436.72	2446.71	102.10	3156.72	3166.71	133.06
1006.72	1016.71	40.61	1726.72	1736.71	71.57	2446.72	2456.71	102.53	3166.72	3176.71	133.49
1016.72	1026.71	41.04	1736.72	1746.71	72.00	2456.72	2466.71	102.96	3176.72	3186.71	133.92
1026.72	1036.71	41.47	1746.72	1756.71	72.43	2466.72	2476.71	103.39	3186.72	3196.71	134.35
1036.72	1046.71	41.90	1756.72	1766.71	72.86	2476.72	2486.71	103.82	3196.72	3206.71	134.78
1046.72	1056.71	42.33	1766.72	1776.71	73.29	2486.72	2496.71	104.25	3206.72	3216.71	135.21
1056.72	1066.71	42.76	1776.72	1786.71	73.72	2496.72	2506.71	104.68	3216.72	3226.71	135.64
1066.72	1076.71	43.19	1786.72	1796.71	74.15	2506.72	2516.71	105.11	3226.72	3236.71	136.07
1076.72	1086.71	43.62	1796.72	1806.71	74.58	2516.72	2526.71	105.54	3236.72	3246.71	136.50
1086.72	1096.71	44.05	1806.72	1816.71	75.01	2526.72	2536.71	105.97	3246.72	3256.71	136.93
1096.72	1106.71	44.48	1816.72	1826.71	75.44	2536.72	2546.71	106.40	3256.72	3266.71	137.36
1106.72	1116.71	44.91	1826.72	1836.71	75.87	2546.72	2556.71	106.83	3266.72	3276.71	137.79
1116.72	1126.71	45.34	1836.72	1846.71	76.30	2556.72	2566.71	107.26	3276.72	3286.71	138.22
1126.72	1136.71	45.77	1846.72	1856.71	76.73	2566.72	2576.71	107.69	3286.72	3296.71	138.65
1136.72	1146.71	46.20	1856.72	1866.71	77.16	2576.72	2586.71	108.12	3296.72	3306.71	139.08
1146.72	1156.71	46.63	1866.72	1876.71	77.59	2586.72	2596.71	108.55	3306.72	3316.71	139.51
1156.72	1166.71	47.06	1876.72	1886.71	78.02	2596.72	2606.71	108.98	3316.72	3326.71	139.94
1166.72	1176.71	47.49	1886.72	1896.71	78.45	2606.72	2616.71	109.41	3326.72	3336.71	140.37
1176.72	1186.71	47.92	1896.72	1906.71	78.88	2616.72	2626.71	109.84	3336.72	3346.71	140.80
1186.72	1196.71	48.35	1906.72	1916.71	79.31	2626.72	2636.71	110.27	3346.72	3356.71	141.23
1196.72	1206.71	48.78	1916.72	1926.71	79.74	2636.72	2646.71	110.70	3356.72	3366.71	141.66
1206.72	1216.71	49.21	1926.72	1936.71	80.17	2646.72	2656.71	111.13	3366.72	3376.71	142.09
1216.72	1226.71	49.64	1936.72	1946.71	80.60	2656.72	2666.71	111.56	3376.72	3386.71	142.52
1226.72	1236.71	50.07	1946.72	1956.71	81.03	2666.72	2676.71	111.99	3386.72	3396.71	142.95
1236.72	1246.71	50.50	1956.72	1966.71	81.46	2676.72	2686.71	112.42	3396.72	3406.71	143.38
1246.72	1256.71	50.93	1966.72	1976.71	81.89	2686.72	2696.71	112.85	3406.72	3416.71	143.81
1256.72	1266.71	51.36	1976.72	1986.71	82.32	2696.72	2706.71	113.28	3416.72	3426.71	144.24
1266.72	1276.71	51.79	1986.72	1996.71	82.75	2706.72	2716.71	113.71	3426.72	3436.71	144.67
1276.72	1286.71	52.22	1996.72	2006.71	83.18	2716.72	2726.71	114.14	3436.72	3446.71	145.10
1286.72	1296.71	52.65	2006.72	2016.71	83.61	2726.72	2736.71	114.57	3446.72	3456.71	145.53
1296.72	1306.71	53.08	2016.72	2026.71	84.04	2736.72	2746.71	115.00	3456.72	3466.71	145.96
1306.72	1316.71	53.51	2026.72	2036.71	84.47	2746.72	2756.71	115.43	3466.72	3476.71	146.39
1316.72	1326.71	53.94	2036.72	2046.71	84.90	2756.72	2766.71	115.86	3476.72	3486.71	146.82
1326.72	1336.71	54.37	2046.72	2056.71	85.33	2766.72	2776.71	116.29	3486.72	3496.71	147.25
1336.72	1346.71	54.80	2056.72	2066.71	85.76	2776.72	2786.71	116.72	3496.72	3506.71	147.68
1346.72	1356.71	55.23	2066.72	2076.71	86.19	2786.72	2796.71	117.15	3506.72	3516.71	148.11
1356.72	1366.71	55.66	2076.72	2086.71	86.62	2796.72	2806.71	117.58	3516.72	3526.71	148.54
1366.72	1376.71	56.09	2086.72	2096.71	87.05	2806.72	2816.71	118.01	3526.72	3536.71	148.97
1376.72	1386.71	56.52	2096.72	2106.71	87.48	2816.72	2826.71	118.44	3536.72	3546.71	149.40
1386.72	1396.71	56.95	2106.72	2116.71	87.91	2826.72	2836.71	118.87	3546.72	3556.71	149.83
1396.72	1406.71	57.38	2116.72	2126.71	88.34	2836.72	2846.71	119.30	3556.72	3566.71	150.26
1406.72	1416.71	57.81	2126.72	2136.71	88.77	2846.72	2856.71	119.73	3566.72	3576.71	150.69
1416.72	1426.71	58.24	2136.72	2146.71	89.20	2856.72	2866.71	120.16	3576.72	3586.71	151.12
1426.72	1436.71	58.67	2146.72	2156.71	89.63	2866.72	2876.71	120.59	3586.72	3596.71	151.55
1436.72	1446.71	59.10	2156.72	2166.71	90.06	2876.72	2886.71	121.02	3596.72	3606.71	151.98
1446.72	1456.71	59.53	2166.72	2176.71	90.49	2886.72	2896.71	121.45	3606.72	3616.71	152.41
1456.72	1466.71	59.96	2176.72	2186.71	90.92	2896.72	2906.71	121.88	3616.72	3626.71 *	152.84

Employee's maximum CPP contribution for the year 2001 is $1496.40
* If the earnings are above this amount, follow the calculation method shown in publication T4001, *Payroll Deductions - Basic Information*.

La cotisation maximale de l'employé au RPC pour l'année 2001 est de 1496,40 $ **B-11**
* Si la rémunération dépasse ce montant, consultez la méthode de calcul qui se trouve dans la publication T4001, *Renseignements de base sur les retenues sur la paie*.

Extracts from C.P.P. tables

Employment Insurance Premiums   Cotisations à l'assurance-emploi

Insurable Earnings Rémunération assurable		EI premium Cotisation d'AE	Insurable Earnings Rémunération assurable		EI premium Cotisation d'AE	Insurable Earnings Rémunération assurable		EI premium Cotisation d'AE	Insurable Earnings Rémunération assurable		EI premium Cotisation d'AE
From - De	To - À		From - De	To - À		From - De	To - À		From - De	To - À	
640.23 -	640.66	14.41	672.23 -	672.66	15.13	704.23 -	704.66	15.85	736.23 -	736.66	16.57
640.67 -	641.11	14.42	672.67 -	673.11	15.14	704.67 -	705.11	15.86	736.67 -	737.11	16.58
641.12 -	641.55	14.43	673.12 -	673.55	15.15	705.12 -	705.55	15.87	737.12 -	737.55	16.59
641.56 -	641.99	14.44	673.56 -	673.99	15.16	705.56 -	705.99	15.88	737.56 -	737.99	16.60
642.00 -	642.44	14.45	674.00 -	674.44	15.17	706.00 -	706.44	15.89	738.00 -	738.44	16.61
642.45 -	642.88	14.46	674.45 -	674.88	15.18	706.45 -	706.88	15.90	738.45 -	738.88	16.62
642.89 -	643.33	14.47	674.89 -	675.33	15.19	706.89 -	707.33	15.91	738.89 -	739.33	16.63
643.34 -	643.77	14.48	675.34 -	675.77	15.20	707.34 -	707.77	15.92	739.34 -	739.77	16.64
643.78 -	644.22	14.49	675.78 -	676.22	15.21	707.78 -	708.22	15.93	739.78 -	740.22	16.65
644.23 -	644.66	14.50	676.23 -	676.66	15.22	708.23 -	708.66	15.94	740.23 -	740.66	16.66
644.67 -	645.11	14.51	676.67 -	677.11	15.23	708.67 -	709.11	15.95	740.67 -	741.11	16.67
645.12 -	645.55	14.52	677.12 -	677.55	15.24	709.12 -	709.55	15.96	741.12 -	741.55	16.68
645.56 -	645.99	14.53	677.56 -	677.99	15.25	709.56 -	709.99	15.97	741.56 -	741.99	16.69
646.00 -	646.44	14.54	678.00 -	678.44	15.26	710.00 -	710.44	15.98	742.00 -	742.44	16.70
646.45 -	646.88	14.55	678.45 -	678.88	15.27	710.45 -	710.88	15.99	742.45 -	742.88	16.71
646.89 -	647.33	14.56	678.89 -	679.33	15.28	710.89 -	711.33	16.00	742.89 -	743.33	16.72
647.34 -	647.77	14.57	679.34 -	679.77	15.29	711.34 -	711.77	16.01	743.34 -	743.77	16.73
647.78 -	648.22	14.58	679.78 -	680.22	15.30	711.78 -	712.22	16.02	743.78 -	744.22	16.74
648.23 -	648.66	14.59	680.23 -	680.66	15.31	712.23 -	712.66	16.03	744.23 -	744.66	16.75
648.67 -	649.11	14.60	680.67 -	681.11	15.32	712.67 -	713.11	16.04	744.67 -	745.11	16.76
649.12 -	649.55	14.61	681.12 -	681.55	15.33	713.12 -	713.55	16.05	745.12 -	745.55	16.77
649.56 -	649.99	14.62	681.56 -	681.99	15.34	713.56 -	713.99	16.06	745.56 -	745.99	16.78
650.00 -	650.44	14.63	682.00 -	682.44	15.35	714.00 -	714.44	16.07	746.00 -	746.44	16.79
650.45 -	650.88	14.64	682.45 -	682.88	15.36	714.45 -	714.88	16.08	746.45 -	746.88	16.80
650.89 -	651.33	14.65	682.89 -	683.33	15.37	714.89 -	715.33	16.09	746.89 -	747.33	16.81
651.34 -	651.77	14.66	683.34 -	683.77	15.38	715.34 -	715.77	16.10	747.34 -	747.77	16.82
651.78 -	652.22	14.67	683.78 -	684.22	15.39	715.78 -	716.22	16.11	747.78 -	748.22	16.83
652.23 -	652.66	14.68	684.23 -	684.66	15.40	716.23 -	716.66	16.12	748.23 -	748.66	16.84
652.67 -	653.11	14.69	684.67 -	685.11	15.41	716.67 -	717.11	16.13	748.67 -	749.11	16.85
653.12 -	653.55	14.70	685.12 -	685.55	15.42	717.12 -	717.55	16.14	749.12 -	749.55	16.86
653.56 -	653.99	14.71	685.56 -	685.99	15.43	717.56 -	717.99	16.15	749.56 -	749.99	16.87
654.00 -	654.44	14.72	686.00 -	686.44	15.44	718.00 -	718.44	16.16	750.00 -	750.44	16.88
654.45 -	654.88	14.73	686.45 -	686.88	15.45	718.45 -	718.88	16.17	750.45 -	750.88	16.89
654.89 -	655.33	14.74	686.89 -	687.33	15.46	718.89 -	719.33	16.18	750.89 -	751.33	16.90
655.34 -	655.77	14.75	687.34 -	687.77	15.47	719.34 -	719.77	16.19	751.34 -	751.77	16.91
655.78 -	656.22	14.76	687.78 -	688.22	15.48	719.78 -	720.22	16.20	751.78 -	752.22	16.92
656.23 -	656.66	14.77	688.23 -	688.66	15.49	720.23 -	720.66	16.21	752.23 -	752.66	16.93
656.67 -	657.11	14.78	688.67 -	689.11	15.50	720.67 -	721.11	16.22	752.67 -	753.11	16.94
657.12 -	657.55	14.79	689.12 -	689.55	15.51	721.12 -	721.55	16.23	753.12 -	753.55	16.95
657.56 -	657.99	14.80	689.56 -	689.99	15.52	721.56 -	721.99	16.24	753.56 -	753.99	16.96
658.00 -	658.44	14.81	690.00 -	690.44	15.53	722.00 -	722.44	16.25	754.00 -	754.44	16.97
658.45 -	658.88	14.82	690.45 -	690.88	15.54	722.45 -	722.88	16.26	754.45 -	754.88	16.98
658.89 -	659.33	14.83	690.89 -	691.33	15.55	722.89 -	723.33	16.27	754.89 -	755.33	16.99
659.34 -	659.77	14.84	691.34 -	691.77	15.56	723.34 -	723.77	16.28	755.34 -	755.77	17.00
659.78 -	660.22	14.85	691.78 -	692.22	15.57	723.78 -	724.22	16.29	755.78 -	756.22	17.01
660.23 -	660.66	14.86	692.23 -	692.66	15.58	724.23 -	724.66	16.30	756.23 -	756.66	17.02
660.67 -	661.11	14.87	692.67 -	693.11	15.59	724.67 -	725.11	16.31	756.67 -	757.11	17.03
661.12 -	661.55	14.88	693.12 -	693.55	15.60	725.12 -	725.55	16.32	757.12 -	757.55	17.04
661.56 -	661.99	14.89	693.56 -	693.99	15.61	725.56 -	725.99	16.33	757.56 -	757.99	17.05
662.00 -	662.44	14.90	694.00 -	694.44	15.62	726.00 -	726.44	16.34	758.00 -	758.44	17.06
662.45 -	662.88	14.91	694.45 -	694.88	15.63	726.45 -	726.88	16.35	758.45 -	758.88	17.07
662.89 -	663.33	14.92	694.89 -	695.33	15.64	726.89 -	727.33	16.36	758.89 -	759.33	17.08
663.34 -	663.77	14.93	695.34 -	695.77	15.65	727.34 -	727.77	16.37	759.34 -	759.77	17.09
663.78 -	664.22	14.94	695.78 -	696.22	15.66	727.78 -	728.22	16.38	759.78 -	760.22	17.10
664.23 -	664.66	14.95	696.23 -	696.66	15.67	728.23 -	728.66	16.39	760.23 -	760.66	17.11
664.67 -	665.11	14.96	696.67 -	697.11	15.68	728.67 -	729.11	16.40	760.67 -	761.11	17.12
665.12 -	665.55	14.97	697.12 -	697.55	15.69	729.12 -	729.55	16.41	761.12 -	761.55	17.13
665.56 -	665.99	14.98	697.56 -	697.99	15.70	729.56 -	729.99	16.42	761.56 -	761.99	17.14
666.00 -	666.44	14.99	698.00 -	698.44	15.71	730.00 -	730.44	16.43	762.00 -	762.44	17.15
666.45 -	666.88	15.00	698.45 -	698.88	15.72	730.45 -	730.88	16.44	762.45 -	762.88	17.16
666.89 -	667.33	15.01	698.89 -	699.33	15.73	730.89 -	731.33	16.45	762.89 -	763.33	17.17
667.34 -	667.77	15.02	699.34 -	699.77	15.74	731.34 -	731.77	16.46	763.34 -	763.77	17.18
667.78 -	668.22	15.03	699.78 -	700.22	15.75	731.78 -	732.22	16.47	763.78 -	764.22	17.19
668.23 -	668.66	15.04	700.23 -	700.66	15.76	732.23 -	732.66	16.48	764.23 -	764.66	17.20
668.67 -	669.11	15.05	700.67 -	701.11	15.77	732.67 -	733.11	16.49	764.67 -	765.11	17.21
669.12 -	669.55	15.06	701.12 -	701.55	15.78	733.12 -	733.55	16.50	765.12 -	765.55	17.22
669.56 -	669.99	15.07	701.56 -	701.99	15.79	733.56 -	733.99	16.51	765.56 -	765.99	17.23
670.00 -	670.44	15.08	702.00 -	702.44	15.80	734.00 -	734.44	16.52	766.00 -	766.44	17.24
670.45 -	670.88	15.09	702.45 -	702.88	15.81	734.45 -	734.88	16.53	766.45 -	766.88	17.25
670.89 -	671.33	15.10	702.89 -	703.33	15.82	734.89 -	735.33	16.54	766.89 -	767.33	17.26
671.34 -	671.77	15.11	703.34 -	703.77	15.83	735.34 -	735.77	16.55	767.34 -	767.77	17.27
671.78 -	672.22	15.12	703.78 -	704.22	15.84	735.78 -	736.22	16.56	767.78 -	768.22	17.28

C-6 Yearly maximum insurable earnings are $39,000   Le maximum annuel de la rémunération assurable est de 39 000 $
Yearly maximum employee premiums are $877.50   La cotisation maximale annuelle de l'employé est de 877.50 $

Extracts from E.I. tables

Employment Insurance Premiums / Cotisations à l'assurance-emploi

Insurable Earnings Rémunération assurable		EI premium Cotisation d'AE	Insurable Earnings Rémunération assurable		EI premium Cotisation d'AE	Insurable Earnings Rémunération assurable		EI premium Cotisation d'AE	Insurable Earnings Rémunération assurable		EI premium Cotisation d'AE
From - De	To - À		From - De	To - À		From - De	To - À		From - De	To - À	
768.23	768.66	17.29	800.23	800.66	18.01	832.23	832.66	18.73	864.23	864.66	19.45
768.67	769.11	17.30	800.67	801.11	18.02	832.67	833.11	18.74	864.67	865.11	19.46
769.12	769.55	17.31	801.12	801.55	18.03	833.12	833.55	18.75	865.12	865.55	19.47
769.56	769.99	17.32	801.56	801.99	18.04	833.56	833.99	18.76	865.56	865.99	19.48
770.00	770.44	17.33	802.00	802.44	18.05	834.00	834.44	18.77	866.00	866.44	19.49
770.45	770.88	17.34	802.45	802.88	18.06	834.45	834.88	18.78	866.45	866.88	19.50
770.89	771.33	17.35	802.89	803.33	18.07	834.89	835.33	18.79	866.89	867.33	19.51
771.34	771.77	17.36	803.34	803.77	18.08	835.34	835.77	18.80	867.34	867.77	19.52
771.78	772.22	17.37	803.78	804.22	18.09	835.78	836.22	18.81	867.78	868.22	19.53
772.23	772.66	17.38	804.23	804.66	18.10	836.23	836.66	18.82	868.23	868.66	19.54
772.67	773.11	17.39	804.67	805.11	18.11	836.67	837.11	18.83	868.67	869.11	19.55
773.12	773.55	17.40	805.12	805.55	18.12	837.12	837.55	18.84	869.12	869.55	19.56
773.56	773.99	17.41	805.56	805.99	18.13	837.56	837.99	18.85	869.56	869.99	19.57
774.00	774.44	17.42	806.00	806.44	18.14	838.00	838.44	18.86	870.00	870.44	19.58
774.45	774.88	17.43	806.45	806.88	18.15	838.45	838.88	18.87	870.45	870.88	19.59
774.89	775.33	17.44	806.89	807.33	18.16	838.89	839.33	18.88	870.89	871.33	19.60
775.34	775.77	17.45	807.34	807.77	18.17	839.34	839.77	18.89	871.34	871.77	19.61
775.78	776.22	17.46	807.78	808.22	18.18	839.78	840.22	18.90	871.78	872.22	19.62
776.23	776.66	17.47	808.23	808.66	18.19	840.23	840.66	18.91	872.23	872.66	19.63
776.67	777.11	17.48	808.67	809.11	18.20	840.67	841.11	18.92	872.67	873.11	19.64
777.12	777.55	17.49	809.12	809.55	18.21	841.12	841.55	18.93	873.12	873.55	19.65
777.56	777.99	17.50	809.56	809.99	18.22	841.56	841.99	18.94	873.56	873.99	19.66
778.00	778.44	17.51	810.00	810.44	18.23	842.00	842.44	18.95	874.00	874.44	19.67
778.45	778.88	17.52	810.45	810.88	18.24	842.45	842.88	18.96	874.45	874.88	19.68
778.89	779.33	17.53	810.89	811.33	18.25	842.89	843.33	18.97	874.89	875.33	19.69
779.34	779.77	17.54	811.34	811.77	18.26	843.34	843.77	18.98	875.34	875.77	19.70
779.78	780.22	17.55	811.78	812.22	18.27	843.78	844.22	18.99	875.78	876.22	19.71
780.23	780.66	17.56	812.23	812.66	18.28	844.23	844.66	19.00	876.23	876.66	19.72
780.67	781.11	17.57	812.67	813.11	18.29	844.67	845.11	19.01	876.67	877.11	19.73
781.12	781.55	17.58	813.12	813.55	18.30	845.12	845.55	19.02	877.12	877.55	19.74
781.56	781.99	17.59	813.56	813.99	18.31	845.56	845.99	19.03	877.56	877.99	19.75
782.00	782.44	17.60	814.00	814.44	18.32	846.00	846.44	19.04	878.00	878.44	19.76
782.45	782.88	17.61	814.45	814.88	18.33	846.45	846.88	19.05	878.45	878.88	19.77
782.89	783.33	17.62	814.89	815.33	18.34	846.89	847.33	19.06	878.89	879.33	19.78
783.34	783.77	17.63	815.34	815.77	18.35	847.34	847.77	19.07	879.34	879.77	19.79
783.78	784.22	17.64	815.78	816.22	18.36	847.78	848.22	19.08	879.78	880.22	19.80
784.23	784.66	17.65	816.23	816.66	18.37	848.23	848.66	19.09	880.23	880.66	19.81
784.67	785.11	17.66	816.67	817.11	18.38	848.67	849.11	19.10	880.67	881.11	19.82
785.12	785.55	17.67	817.12	817.55	18.39	849.12	849.55	19.11	881.12	881.55	19.83
785.56	785.99	17.68	817.56	817.99	18.40	849.56	849.99	19.12	881.56	881.99	19.84
786.00	786.44	17.69	818.00	818.44	18.41	850.00	850.44	19.13	882.00	882.44	19.85
786.45	786.88	17.70	818.45	818.88	18.42	850.45	850.88	19.14	882.45	882.88	19.86
786.89	787.33	17.71	818.89	819.33	18.43	850.89	851.33	19.15	882.89	883.33	19.87
787.34	787.77	17.72	819.34	819.77	18.44	851.34	851.77	19.16	883.34	883.77	19.88
787.78	788.22	17.73	819.78	820.22	18.45	851.78	852.22	19.17	883.78	884.22	19.89
788.23	788.66	17.74	820.23	820.66	18.46	852.23	852.66	19.18	884.23	884.66	19.90
788.67	789.11	17.75	820.67	821.11	18.47	852.67	853.11	19.19	884.67	885.11	19.91
789.12	789.55	17.76	821.12	821.55	18.48	853.12	853.55	19.20	885.12	885.55	19.92
789.56	789.99	17.77	821.56	821.99	18.49	853.56	853.99	19.21	885.56	885.99	19.93
790.00	790.44	17.78	822.00	822.44	18.50	854.00	854.44	19.22	886.00	886.44	19.94
790.45	790.88	17.79	822.45	822.88	18.51	854.45	854.88	19.23	886.45	886.88	19.95
790.89	791.33	17.80	822.89	823.33	18.52	854.89	855.33	19.24	886.89	887.33	19.96
791.34	791.77	17.81	823.34	823.77	18.53	855.34	855.77	19.25	887.34	887.77	19.97
791.78	792.22	17.82	823.78	824.22	18.54	855.78	856.22	19.26	887.78	888.22	19.98
792.23	792.66	17.83	824.23	824.66	18.55	856.23	856.66	19.27	888.23	888.66	19.99
792.67	793.11	17.84	824.67	825.11	18.56	856.67	857.11	19.28	888.67	889.11	20.00
793.12	793.55	17.85	825.12	825.55	18.57	857.12	857.55	19.29	889.12	889.55	20.01
793.56	793.99	17.86	825.56	825.99	18.58	857.56	857.99	19.30	889.56	889.99	20.02
794.00	794.44	17.87	826.00	826.44	18.59	858.00	858.44	19.31	890.00	890.44	20.03
794.45	794.88	17.88	826.45	826.88	18.60	858.45	858.88	19.32	890.45	890.88	20.04
794.89	795.33	17.89	826.89	827.33	18.61	858.89	859.33	19.33	890.89	891.33	20.05
795.34	795.77	17.90	827.34	827.77	18.62	859.34	859.77	19.34	891.34	891.77	20.06
795.78	796.22	17.91	827.78	828.22	18.63	859.78	860.22	19.35	891.78	892.22	20.07
796.23	796.66	17.92	828.23	828.66	18.64	860.23	860.66	19.36	892.23	892.66	20.08
796.67	797.11	17.93	828.67	829.11	18.65	860.67	861.11	19.37	892.67	893.11	20.09
797.12	797.55	17.94	829.12	829.55	18.66	861.12	861.55	19.38	893.12	893.55	20.10
797.56	797.99	17.95	829.56	829.99	18.67	861.56	861.99	19.39	893.56	893.99	20.11
798.00	798.44	17.96	830.00	830.44	18.68	862.00	862.44	19.40	894.00	894.44	20.12
798.45	798.88	17.97	830.45	830.88	18.69	862.45	862.88	19.41	894.45	894.88	20.13
798.89	799.33	17.98	830.89	831.33	18.70	862.89	863.33	19.42	894.89	895.33	20.14
799.34	799.77	17.99	831.34	831.77	18.71	863.34	863.77	19.43	895.34	895.77	20.15
799.78	800.22	18.00	831.78	832.22	18.72	863.78	864.22	19.44	895.78	896.22	20.16

Yearly maximum insurable earnings are $39,000
Yearly maximum employee premiums are $877.50

Le maximum annuel de la rémunération assurable est de 39 000 $
La cotisation maximale annuelle de l'employé est de 877.50 $ **C-7**

Extracts from E.I. tables

Employment Insurance Premiums   Cotisations à l'assurance-emploi

Insurable Earnings Rémunération assurable		EI premium Cotisation d'AE	Insurable Earnings Rémunération assurable		EI premium Cotisation d'AE	Insurable Earnings Rémunération assurable		EI premium Cotisation d'AE	Insurable Earnings Rémunération assurable		EI premium Cotisation d'AE
From - De	To - À		From - De	To - À		From - De	To - À		From - De	To - À	
896.23	896.66	20.17	928.23	928.66	20.89	960.23	960.66	21.61	992.23	992.66	22.33
896.67	897.11	20.18	928.67	929.11	20.90	960.67	961.11	21.62	992.67	993.11	22.34
897.12	897.55	20.19	929.12	929.55	20.91	961.12	961.55	21.63	993.12	993.55	22.35
897.56	897.99	20.20	929.56	929.99	20.92	961.56	961.99	21.64	993.56	993.99	22.36
898.00	898.44	20.21	930.00	930.44	20.93	962.00	962.44	21.65	994.00	994.44	22.37
898.45	898.88	20.22	930.45	930.88	20.94	962.45	962.88	21.66	994.45	994.88	22.38
898.89	899.33	20.23	930.89	931.33	20.95	962.89	963.33	21.67	994.89	995.33	22.39
899.34	899.77	20.24	931.34	931.77	20.96	963.34	963.77	21.68	995.34	995.77	22.40
899.78	900.22	20.25	931.78	932.22	20.97	963.78	964.22	21.69	995.78	996.22	22.41
900.23	900.66	20.26	932.23	932.66	20.98	964.23	964.66	21.70	996.23	996.66	22.42
900.67	901.11	20.27	932.67	933.11	20.99	964.67	965.11	21.71	996.67	997.11	22.43
901.12	901.55	20.28	933.12	933.55	21.00	965.12	965.55	21.72	997.12	997.55	22.44
901.56	901.99	20.29	933.56	933.99	21.01	965.56	965.99	21.73	997.56	997.99	22.45
902.00	902.44	20.30	934.00	934.44	21.02	966.00	966.44	21.74	998.00	998.44	22.46
902.45	902.88	20.31	934.45	934.88	21.03	966.45	966.88	21.75	998.45	998.88	22.47
902.89	903.33	20.32	934.89	935.33	21.04	966.89	967.33	21.76	998.89	999.33	22.48
903.34	903.77	20.33	935.34	935.77	21.05	967.34	967.77	21.77	999.34	999.77	22.49
903.78	904.22	20.34	935.78	936.22	21.06	967.78	968.22	21.78	999.78	1000.22	22.50
904.23	904.66	20.35	936.23	936.66	21.07	968.23	968.66	21.79	1000.23	1000.66	22.51
904.67	905.11	20.36	936.67	937.11	21.08	968.67	969.11	21.80	1000.67	1001.11	22.52
905.12	905.55	20.37	937.12	937.55	21.09	969.12	969.55	21.81	1001.12	1001.55	22.53
905.56	905.99	20.38	937.56	937.99	21.10	969.56	969.99	21.82	1001.56	1001.99	22.54
906.00	906.44	20.39	938.00	938.44	21.11	970.00	970.44	21.83	1002.00	1002.44	22.55
906.45	906.88	20.40	938.45	938.88	21.12	970.45	970.88	21.84	1002.45	1002.88	22.56
906.89	907.33	20.41	938.89	939.33	21.13	970.89	971.33	21.85	1002.89	1003.33	22.57
907.34	907.77	20.42	939.34	939.77	21.14	971.34	971.77	21.86	1003.34	1003.77	22.58
907.78	908.22	20.43	939.78	940.22	21.15	971.78	972.22	21.87	1003.78	1004.22	22.59
908.23	908.66	20.44	940.23	940.66	21.16	972.23	972.66	21.88	1004.23	1004.66	22.60
908.67	909.11	20.45	940.67	941.11	21.17	972.67	973.11	21.89	1004.67	1005.11	22.61
909.12	909.55	20.46	941.12	941.55	21.18	973.12	973.55	21.90	1005.12	1005.55	22.62
909.56	909.99	20.47	941.56	941.99	21.19	973.56	973.99	21.91	1005.56	1005.99	22.63
910.00	910.44	20.48	942.00	942.44	21.20	974.00	974.44	21.92	1006.00	1006.44	22.64
910.45	910.88	20.49	942.45	942.88	21.21	974.45	974.88	21.93	1006.45	1006.88	22.65
910.89	911.33	20.50	942.89	943.33	21.22	974.89	975.33	21.94	1006.89	1007.33	22.66
911.34	911.77	20.51	943.34	943.77	21.23	975.34	975.77	21.95	1007.34	1007.77	22.67
911.78	912.22	20.52	943.78	944.22	21.24	975.78	976.22	21.96	1007.78	1008.22	22.68
912.23	912.66	20.53	944.23	944.66	21.25	976.23	976.66	21.97	1008.23	1008.66	22.69
912.67	913.11	20.54	944.67	945.11	21.26	976.67	977.11	21.98	1008.67	1009.11	22.70
913.12	913.55	20.55	945.12	945.55	21.27	977.12	977.55	21.99	1009.12	1009.55	22.71
913.56	913.99	20.56	945.56	945.99	21.28	977.56	977.99	22.00	1009.56	1009.99	22.72
914.00	914.44	20.57	946.00	946.44	21.29	978.00	978.44	22.01	1010.00	1010.44	22.73
914.45	914.88	20.58	946.45	946.88	21.30	978.45	978.88	22.02	1010.45	1010.88	22.74
914.89	915.33	20.59	946.89	947.33	21.31	978.89	979.33	22.03	1010.89	1011.33	22.75
915.34	915.77	20.60	947.34	947.77	21.32	979.34	979.77	22.04	1011.34	1011.77	22.76
915.78	916.22	20.61	947.78	948.22	21.33	979.78	980.22	22.05	1011.78	1012.22	22.77
916.23	916.66	20.62	948.23	948.66	21.34	980.23	980.66	22.06	1012.23	1012.66	22.78
916.67	917.11	20.63	948.67	949.11	21.35	980.67	981.11	22.07	1012.67	1013.11	22.79
917.12	917.55	20.64	949.12	949.55	21.36	981.12	981.55	22.08	1013.12	1013.55	22.80
917.56	917.99	20.65	949.56	949.99	21.37	981.56	981.99	22.09	1013.56	1013.99	22.81
918.00	918.44	20.66	950.00	950.44	21.38	982.00	982.44	22.10	1014.00	1014.44	22.82
918.45	918.88	20.67	950.45	950.88	21.39	982.45	982.88	22.11	1014.45	1014.88	22.83
918.89	919.33	20.68	950.89	951.33	21.40	982.89	983.33	22.12	1014.89	1015.33	22.84
919.34	919.77	20.69	951.34	951.77	21.41	983.34	983.77	22.13	1015.34	1015.77	22.85
919.78	920.22	20.70	951.78	952.22	21.42	983.78	984.22	22.14	1015.78	1016.22	22.86
920.23	920.66	20.71	952.23	952.66	21.43	984.23	984.66	22.15	1016.23	1016.66	22.87
920.67	921.11	20.72	952.67	953.11	21.44	984.67	985.11	22.16	1016.67	1017.11	22.88
921.12	921.55	20.73	953.12	953.55	21.45	985.12	985.55	22.17	1017.12	1017.55	22.89
921.56	921.99	20.74	953.56	953.99	21.46	985.56	985.99	22.18	1017.56	1017.99	22.90
922.00	922.44	20.75	954.00	954.44	21.47	986.00	986.44	22.19	1018.00	1018.44	22.91
922.45	922.88	20.76	954.45	954.88	21.48	986.45	986.88	22.20	1018.45	1018.88	22.92
922.89	923.33	20.77	954.89	955.33	21.49	986.89	987.33	22.21	1018.89	1019.33	22.93
923.34	923.77	20.78	955.34	955.77	21.50	987.34	987.77	22.22	1019.34	1019.77	22.94
923.78	924.22	20.79	955.78	956.22	21.51	987.78	988.22	22.23	1019.78	1020.22	22.95
924.23	924.66	20.80	956.23	956.66	21.52	988.23	988.66	22.24	1020.23	1020.66	22.96
924.67	925.11	20.81	956.67	957.11	21.53	988.67	989.11	22.25	1020.67	1021.11	22.97
925.12	925.55	20.82	957.12	957.55	21.54	989.12	989.55	22.26	1021.12	1021.55	22.98
925.56	925.99	20.83	957.56	957.99	21.55	989.56	989.99	22.27	1021.56	1021.99	22.99
926.00	926.44	20.84	958.00	958.44	21.56	990.00	990.44	22.28	1022.00	1022.44	23.00
926.45	926.88	20.85	958.45	958.88	21.57	990.45	990.88	22.29	1022.45	1022.88	23.01
926.89	927.33	20.86	958.89	959.33	21.58	990.89	991.33	22.30	1022.89	1023.33	23.02
927.34	927.77	20.87	959.34	959.77	21.59	991.34	991.77	22.31	1023.34	1023.77	23.03
927.78	928.22	20.88	959.78	960.22	21.60	991.78	992.22	22.32	1023.78	1024.22	23.04

C-8 Yearly maximum insurable earnings are $39,000   Le maximum annuel de la rémunération assurable est de 39 000 $
Yearly maximum employee premiums are $877.50   La cotisation maximale annuelle de l'employé est de 877.50 $

Extracts from E.I. tables

Ontario
Federal tax deductions only
Effective January 1, 2001
Weekly (52 pay periods a year)

Ontario
Retenues d'impôt fédéral seulement
En vigueur le 1er janvier 2001
Hebdomadaire (52 périodes de paie par année)

Pay / Rémunération		Federal claim codes/Codes de demande fédéraux										
From De	Less than Moins de	0	1	2	3	4	5	6	7	8	9	10
					Deduct from each pay / Retenez sur chaque paie							
477. -	485	72.40	49.60	47.05	42.00	36.95	31.85	26.80	21.75	16.70	11.65	6.60
485. -	493	73.60	50.75	48.25	43.20	38.15	33.05	28.00	22.95	17.90	12.85	7.75
493. -	501	74.75	51.95	49.45	44.40	39.30	34.25	29.20	24.15	19.10	14.05	8.95
501. -	509	75.95	53.15	50.65	45.60	40.50	35.45	30.40	25.35	20.30	15.20	10.15
509. -	517	77.15	54.35	51.85	46.75	41.70	36.65	31.60	26.55	21.50	16.40	11.35
517. -	525	78.35	55.55	53.05	47.95	42.90	37.85	32.80	27.75	22.70	17.60	12.55
525. -	533	79.55	56.75	54.20	49.15	44.10	39.05	34.00	28.95	23.85	18.80	13.75
533. -	541	80.75	57.95	55.40	50.35	45.30	40.25	35.20	30.15	25.05	20.00	14.95
541. -	549	81.95	59.15	56.60	51.55	46.50	41.45	36.40	31.30	26.25	21.20	16.15
549. -	557	83.15	60.35	57.80	52.75	47.70	42.65	37.60	32.50	27.45	22.40	17.35
557. -	565	84.35	61.55	59.00	53.95	48.90	43.85	38.75	33.70	28.65	23.60	18.55
565. -	573	85.55	62.75	60.20	55.15	50.10	45.05	39.95	34.90	29.85	24.80	19.75
573. -	581	86.75	63.95	61.40	56.35	51.30	46.25	41.15	36.10	31.05	26.00	20.95
581. -	589	87.95	65.15	62.60	57.55	52.50	47.40	42.35	37.30	32.25	27.20	22.15
589. -	597	89.25	66.40	63.90	58.85	53.80	48.70	43.65	38.60	33.55	28.50	23.40
597. -	605	90.90	68.10	65.55	60.50	55.45	50.40	45.35	40.30	35.20	30.15	25.10
605. -	613	92.60	69.75	67.25	62.20	57.15	52.05	47.00	41.95	36.90	31.85	26.75
613. -	621	94.25	71.45	68.90	63.85	58.80	53.75	48.70	43.65	38.55	33.50	28.45
621. -	629	95.95	73.15	70.60	65.55	60.50	55.40	50.35	45.30	40.25	35.20	30.15
629. -	637	97.60	74.80	72.25	67.20	62.15	57.10	52.05	47.00	41.90	36.85	31.80
637. -	645	99.30	76.50	73.95	68.90	63.85	58.75	53.70	48.65	43.60	38.55	33.50
645. -	653	100.98	78.15	75.65	70.55	65.50	60.45	55.40	50.35	45.25	40.20	35.15
653. -	661	102.65	79.85	77.30	72.25	67.20	62.15	57.05	52.00	46.95	41.90	36.85
661. -	669	104.30	81.50	79.00	73.90	68.85	63.80	58.75	53.70	48.65	43.55	38.50
669. -	677	106.00	83.20	80.65	75.60	70.55	65.50	60.40	55.35	50.30	45.25	40.20
677. -	685	107.65	84.85	82.35	77.25	72.20	67.15	62.10	57.05	52.00	46.90	41.85
685. -	693	109.35	86.55	84.00	78.95	73.90	68.85	63.75	58.70	53.65	48.60	43.55
693. -	701	111.00	88.20	85.70	80.60	75.55	70.50	65.45	60.40	55.35	50.25	45.20
701. -	709	112.70	89.90	87.35	82.30	77.25	72.20	67.10	62.05	57.00	51.95	46.90
709. -	717	114.35	91.55	89.05	84.00	78.90	73.85	68.80	63.75	58.70	53.60	48.55
717. -	725	116.05	93.25	90.70	85.65	80.60	75.55	70.50	65.40	60.35	55.30	50.25
725. -	733	117.70	94.90	92.40	87.35	82.25	77.20	72.15	67.10	62.05	57.00	51.90
733. -	741	119.40	96.60	94.05	89.00	83.95	78.90	73.85	68.75	63.70	58.65	53.60
741. -	749	121.15	98.35	95.80	90.75	85.70	80.60	75.55	70.50	65.45	60.40	55.35
749. -	757	122.85	100.05	97.55	92.50	87.40	82.35	77.30	72.25	67.20	62.15	57.05
757. -	765	124.65	101.85	99.30	94.25	89.20	84.10	79.05	74.00	68.95	63.90	58.85
765. -	773	126.40	103.60	101.05	96.00	90.95	85.90	80.85	75.75	70.70	65.65	60.60
773. -	781	128.15	105.35	102.80	97.75	92.70	87.65	82.60	77.55	72.45	67.40	62.35
781. -	789	129.90	107.10	104.60	99.50	94.45	89.40	84.35	79.30	74.25	69.15	64.10
789. -	797	131.65	108.85	106.35	101.30	96.20	91.15	86.10	81.05	76.00	70.95	65.85
797. -	805	133.45	110.65	108.10	103.05	98.00	92.90	87.85	82.80	77.75	72.70	67.65
805. -	813	135.20	112.40	109.85	104.80	99.75	94.70	89.65	84.55	79.50	74.45	69.40
813. -	821	136.95	114.15	111.60	106.55	101.50	96.45	91.40	86.35	81.25	76.20	71.15
821. -	829	138.70	115.90	113.40	108.30	103.25	98.20	93.15	88.10	83.05	77.95	72.90
829. -	837	140.45	117.65	115.15	110.10	105.00	99.95	94.90	89.85	84.80	79.75	74.65
837. -	845	142.25	119.45	116.90	111.85	106.80	101.70	96.65	91.60	86.55	81.50	76.45
845. -	853	144.00	121.20	118.65	113.60	108.55	103.50	98.45	93.35	88.30	83.25	78.20
853. -	861	145.75	122.95	120.40	115.35	110.30	105.25	100.20	95.15	90.05	85.00	79.95
861. -	869	147.50	124.70	122.20	117.10	112.05	107.00	101.95	96.90	91.85	86.75	81.70
869. -	877	149.25	126.45	123.95	118.90	113.80	108.75	103.70	98.65	93.60	88.55	83.45
877. -	885	151.05	128.25	125.70	120.65	115.60	110.50	105.45	100.40	95.35	90.30	85.25
885. -	893	152.80	130.00	127.45	122.40	117.35	112.30	107.25	102.15	97.10	92.05	87.00
893. -	901	154.55	131.75	129.20	124.15	119.10	114.05	109.00	103.95	98.85	93.80	88.75
901. -	909	156.30	133.50	131.00	125.90	120.85	115.80	110.75	105.70	100.65	95.55	90.50
909. -	917	158.05	135.25	132.75	127.70	122.60	117.55	112.50	107.45	102.40	97.35	92.25

This table is available on diskette (TOD).   D-3   Vous pouvez obtenir cette table sur disquette (TSD).

Extracts from Ontario federal tax deduction tables

Ontario
Provincial tax deductions only
Effective January 1, 2001
Weekly (52 pay periods a year)

Ontario
Retenues d'impôt provincial seulement
En vigueur le 1er janvier 2001
Hebdomadaire (52 périodes de paie par année)

Pay / Rémunération From De — Less than Moins de	0	1	2	3	4	5	6	7	8	9	10
					Deduct from each pay / Retenez sur chaque paie						
529. - 537	31.05	22.20	21.25	19.35	17.45	15.55	13.60	11.70	9.80	7.90	6.00
537. - 545	31.50	22.65	21.70	19.80	17.90	16.00	14.10	12.20	10.25	8.35	6.45
545. - 553	32.00	23.15	22.20	20.25	18.35	16.45	14.55	12.65	10.75	8.85	6.90
553. - 561	32.45	23.60	22.65	20.75	18.85	16.90	15.00	13.10	11.20	9.30	7.40
561. - 569	32.90	24.05	23.10	21.20	19.30	17.40	15.50	13.55	11.65	9.75	7.85
569. - 577	33.40	24.50	23.55	21.65	19.75	17.85	15.95	14.05	12.10	10.20	8.30
577. - 585	33.85	25.00	24.05	22.15	20.20	18.30	16.40	14.50	12.60	10.70	8.75
585. - 593	34.30	25.45	24.50	22.60	20.70	18.75	16.85	14.95	13.05	11.15	9.25
593. - 601	34.90	26.05	25.10	23.20	21.30	19.35	17.45	15.55	13.65	11.75	9.85
601. - 609	35.60	26.75	25.80	23.90	22.00	20.05	18.15	16.25	14.35	12.45	10.55
609. - 617	36.30	27.45	26.50	24.60	22.70	20.80	18.85	16.95	15.05	13.15	11.25
617. - 625	37.00	28.15	27.20	25.30	23.40	21.50	19.60	17.65	15.75	13.85	11.95
625. - 633	37.75	28.85	27.90	26.00	24.10	22.20	20.30	18.40	16.45	14.55	12.65
633. - 641	38.45	29.60	28.60	26.70	24.80	22.90	21.00	19.10	17.20	15.25	13.35
641. - 649	39.15	30.30	29.35	27.40	25.50	23.60	21.70	19.80	17.90	16.00	14.05
649. - 657	39.85	31.00	30.05	28.15	26.20	24.30	22.40	20.50	18.60	16.70	14.80
657. - 665	40.55	31.70	30.75	28.85	26.95	25.00	23.10	21.20	19.30	17.40	15.50
665. - 673	41.25	32.40	31.45	29.55	27.65	25.75	23.80	21.90	20.00	18.10	16.20
673. - 681	41.95	33.10	32.15	30.25	28.35	26.45	24.55	22.60	20.70	18.80	16.90
681. - 689	42.65	33.80	32.85	30.95	29.05	27.15	25.25	23.35	21.40	19.50	17.60
689. - 697	43.40	34.55	33.55	31.65	29.75	27.85	25.95	24.05	22.15	20.20	18.30
697. - 705	44.10	35.25	34.30	32.35	30.45	28.55	26.65	24.75	22.85	20.90	19.00
705. - 713	44.80	35.95	35.00	33.10	31.15	29.25	27.35	25.45	23.55	21.65	19.70
713. - 721	45.50	36.65	35.70	33.80	31.90	29.95	28.05	26.15	24.25	22.35	20.45
721. - 729	46.20	37.35	36.40	34.50	32.60	30.65	28.75	26.85	24.95	23.05	21.15
729. - 737	46.90	38.05	37.10	35.20	33.30	31.40	29.45	27.55	25.65	23.75	21.85
737. - 745	47.65	38.80	37.80	35.90	34.00	32.10	30.20	28.30	26.40	24.45	22.55
745. - 753	48.35	39.50	38.55	36.65	34.75	32.85	30.90	29.00	27.10	25.20	23.30
753. - 761	49.10	40.25	39.30	37.40	35.45	33.55	31.65	29.75	27.85	25.95	24.05
761. - 769	49.85	41.00	40.05	38.10	36.20	34.30	32.40	30.50	28.60	26.65	24.75
769. - 777	50.60	41.70	40.75	38.85	36.95	35.05	33.15	31.25	29.30	27.40	25.50
777. - 785	51.30	42.45	41.50	39.60	37.70	35.80	33.90	31.95	30.05	28.15	26.25
785. - 793	52.05	43.20	42.25	40.35	38.45	36.50	34.60	32.70	30.80	28.90	27.00
793. - 801	52.80	43.95	43.00	41.10	39.15	37.25	35.35	33.45	31.55	29.65	27.70
801. - 809	53.55	44.70	43.70	41.80	39.90	38.00	36.10	34.20	32.30	30.35	28.45
809. - 817	54.25	45.40	44.45	42.55	40.65	38.75	36.85	34.95	33.00	31.10	29.20
817. - 825	55.00	46.15	45.20	43.30	41.40	39.50	37.55	35.65	33.75	31.85	29.95
825. - 833	55.75	46.90	45.95	44.05	42.15	40.20	38.30	36.40	34.50	32.60	30.70
833. - 841	56.50	47.65	46.70	44.75	42.85	40.95	39.05	37.15	35.25	33.35	31.40
841. - 849	57.25	48.35	47.40	45.50	43.60	41.70	39.80	37.90	35.95	34.05	32.15
849. - 857	57.95	49.10	48.15	46.25	44.35	42.45	40.55	38.60	36.70	34.80	32.90
857. - 865	58.70	49.85	48.90	47.00	45.10	43.20	41.25	39.35	37.45	35.55	33.65
865. - 873	59.45	50.60	49.65	47.75	45.80	43.90	42.00	40.10	38.20	36.30	34.40
873. - 881	60.20	51.35	50.40	48.45	46.55	44.65	42.75	40.85	38.95	37.00	35.10
881. - 889	60.90	52.05	51.10	49.20	47.30	45.40	43.50	41.60	39.65	37.75	35.85
889. - 897	61.65	52.80	51.85	49.95	48.05	46.15	44.20	42.30	40.40	38.50	36.60
897. - 905	62.40	53.55	52.60	50.70	48.80	46.85	44.95	43.05	41.15	39.25	37.35
905. - 913	63.15	54.30	53.35	51.45	49.50	47.60	45.70	43.80	41.90	40.00	38.05
913. - 921	63.90	55.05	54.05	52.15	50.25	48.35	46.45	44.55	42.65	40.70	38.80
921. - 929	64.60	55.75	54.80	52.90	51.00	49.10	47.20	45.25	43.35	41.45	39.55
929. - 937	65.35	56.50	55.55	53.65	51.75	49.85	47.90	46.00	44.10	42.20	40.30
937. - 945	66.10	57.25	56.30	54.40	52.50	50.55	48.65	46.75	44.85	42.95	41.05
945. - 953	66.85	58.00	57.05	55.10	53.20	51.30	49.40	47.50	45.60	43.70	41.75
953. - 961	67.60	58.70	57.75	55.85	53.95	52.05	50.15	48.25	46.30	44.40	42.50
961. - 969	68.30	59.45	58.50	56.60	54.70	52.80	50.90	48.95	47.05	45.15	43.25

This table is available on diskette (TOD).   E-3   **Vous pouvez obtenir cette table sur disquette (TSD).**

Extracts from Ontario provincial tax deduction tables

UNIT 34 Payroll Records and Journal Entries

What Learning You Will Demonstrate

On completion of this unit, you will be able to:

- complete and prove the accuracy of a payroll register;
- explain the purpose of the employee's earnings record;
- record the four basic types of payroll entries in the general journal; and
- define *payroll journal, T4, employee's earnings record, PD7A,* and *workers' compensation*.

IMPLEMENTING PAYROLL PROCEDURES

Various forms and procedures are used for payroll. We will begin this unit by examining them.

Using the Payroll Journal

To determine the amount to be paid to employees (net earnings), a number of calculations are necessary. The deductions of each employee must be listed, totalled, and subtracted from gross earnings. These calculations are performed on an accounting form called a *payroll journal,* sometimes also called a payroll register.

> A payroll journal is the form used to record gross earnings, deductions, and net earnings for all of a firm's workers.

A **payroll journal** records the payroll details for all employees for each pay period. It shows the gross earnings, deductions, and net earnings. It is a form that helps the payroll accountant organize the calculation of the payroll. An example is shown in Figure 14-7. Notice how the totals of the payroll journal are balanced as a form of mathematical proof of accuracy. Two separate proofs are prepared to avoid errors. They are:

1. Gross Earnings   −   Total Deductions   = Net Earnings
2. Gross Earnings   − Individual Deduction Totals = Net Earnings

Using the Employee's Earnings Record

By April 30 each year, Canadians must file their income tax returns with the federal government. To complete an income tax return, an employee must know how much he or she earned and the amounts of the payroll deductions withheld by the employer throughout the year. To provide this information, the federal government requires all employers to give their employees a Statement of Remuneration Paid form, which is commonly called a T4 slip. The employer must provide the T4 slip to employees by February 28 for the previous calendar year. An example of a T4 slip is shown in Figure 14-8 on page 740.

> A T4 slip provides an employee with the total earnings and deductions for the year.

COMPANY NAME __WESTERN SYSTEMS__

PAY PERIOD ENDING __MAY 7, 20—__   PAYROLL JOURNAL   PAGE 19

EMP. NO.	NAME OF EMPLOYEE	NET CLAIM CODE	GROSS EARNINGS	NON-TAXABLES R.P.P.*	NON-TAXABLES UNION DUES	TAXABLE EARNINGS	INCOME TAX	OTHER DEDUCTIONS C.P.P.	OTHER DEDUCTIONS E.I.	OTHER DEDUCTIONS HEALTH INS.	OTHER DEDUCTIONS GROUP INS.	TOTAL DEDUCTIONS	NET EARNINGS
1618	Barlow, J.	7	1800 00			1800 00	529 95	66 60	43 20			639 75	1160 25
1619	Heidebretch, I.	2	1200 00			1200 00	297 40	44 40	28 80			370 60	829 40
1620	Lostracco, M.	1	1400 00			1400 00	393 75	51 91	33 60			479 26	920 74
1621	Mullane, K.	1	900 00			900 00	196 30	33 30	21 60			251 20	648 80
1622	Mustin, P.	7	1100 00			1100 00	224 30	40 70	26 40			291 40	808 60
1623	Renner, A.	8	1000 00			1000 00	181 05	37 00	24 00			242 05	757 95
			7400 00			7400 00	1822 75	273 91	177 60			2274 26	5125 74

* The term *Registered Pension Plan* (R.P.P.) identifies deductions payable to a pension plan provided by the employer.

Proof 1

Gross Earnings	$7400.00
Less: Total Deductions	2274.26
Net Earnings	$5125.74

Proof 2

Gross Earnings		$7400.00
Less: C.P.P.	$ 273.91	
E.I.	177.60	
Income Tax	1822.75	2274.26
Net Earnings		$5125.74

FIGURE 14-7 Completed payroll journal for Western Systems

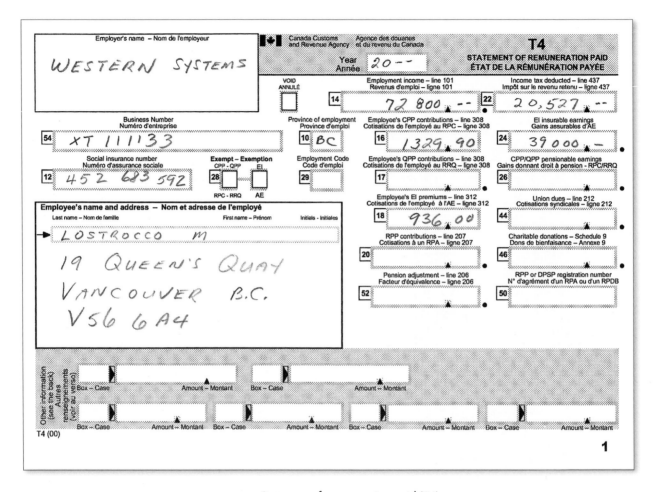

FIGURE 14-8 Statement of remuneration paid (T4)

The T4 slip in Figure 14-8 shows the employee's gross earnings and all deductions that will affect the personal income tax calculations. To prepare the T4 slip, an employer must keep cumulative totals of the employee's earnings and deductions. The totals are kept on a form called an **employee's earnings record**.

The employee's earnings record provides all of the information required for the preparation of the T4 slip. Figure 14-9 shows the earnings record for M. Lostracco. Notice which figures are transferred at year end from this form to the T-4 slip in Figure 14-8.

At the present time, every worker in Canada is required to pay 4.3 percent of gross earnings, to a maximum of $1496.40 yearly, to the Canada Pension Plan. Many employees will have paid their total year's premium of $1496.40 before the end of the year. For this reason, a special column is used on the earnings record to accumulate the C.P.P. premiums. When the total reaches $1496.40 for the year, the employee will no longer have the C.P.P. deduction made. At the year's end, the earnings record is totalled and balanced.

An employee's earnings record contains all of the payroll information for an employee for one year.

EMPLOYEE'S EARNINGS RECORD FOR THE YEAR 20—

NAME	Lostracco, M.	
ADDRESS	19 Queen's Quay	
	Vancouver, B.C. V5K 6A4	
TELEPHONE	825-6621	

DEPARTMENT	Data Processing
POSITION	Supervisor
SOCIAL INS. NO.	452-638-529
SALARY	$1400/week

DATE EMPLOYED	06/01/—
TERMINATION DATE	
NO. OF DEPENDANTS	0
NET CLAIM CODE	1

EMP. NO.	REGULAR OVERTIME	GROSS EARNINGS	DEDUCTIONS					TOTAL DEDUCTIONS	NET EARNINGS	TOTAL C.P.P. TO DATE	CH. NO.	PAY PERIOD ENDING
			C.P.P.	E.I.	INC. TAX	GR. INS.	OTHER					
1620	18 200 00 18 200 00	18 200 00	3 70 24	3 74 40	4 49 1 50			5 23 6 14	12 96 3 86	3 70 24		Jan–July 2
	1 400 00	1 400 00	51 91	33 60	3 94 75			4 80 26	9 19 74	4 22 2 15	3949	July 9
	1 400 00	1 400 00	51 91	33 60	3 94 75			4 80 26	9 19 74	4 74 06	3974	16
	1 400 00	1 400 00	51 91	33 60	3 94 75			4 80 26	9 19 74	5 25 97	3999	23
	1 400 00	1 400 00	51 91	33 60	3 94 75			4 80 26	9 19 74	5 77 88	4024	30
	1 400 00	1 400 00	51 91	33 60	3 94 75			4 80 26	9 19 74	6 29 79	4049	Aug. 7

FIGURE 14-9 Employee's earnings record

Paying Employees

Generally, employers use one of three methods to pay employees:

1. cash;
2. cheque; or
3. bank, credit union, or trust company direct deposit.

Paying by Cash

Although this method is not preferred by employers, it is sometimes necessary to pay by cash because of agreements with employees or in remote areas where banks are not readily available.

Paying by Cheque

Many companies prefer to pay by cheque. To simplify the end-of-month bank reconciliations, a separate bank account is opened for payroll. Each month, a cheque is written on the regular bank account. The amount of this cheque is exactly the total required to pay all of the employees. This cheque is deposited in the special payroll bank account. The entry to record this cheque is:

May	7	Salaries Payable	5 1 2 5 74	
		Cash		5 1 2 5 74
		To transfer funds to the payroll bank account for		
		the May 7 payroll.		

Next, cheques are issued to each employee. These cheques have the statement of earnings attached and are usually identified as payroll cheques by "payroll account" printed on the cheque face. When workers cash their cheques, the bank will pay them from the company's special payroll account. If all of the workers cash their cheques, the special payroll account balance will be reduced to zero.

Paying by Direct Deposit

Many companies and employees prefer the direct deposit method. In this case, a bank provides a payroll service to companies. The employer gives the bank a list of employees, showing the amount earned by each. In return for a fee, the bank pays the employees by depositing the money in their accounts in various banks, credit unions, or trust companies.

The direct deposit method frees the employer from having to prepare pay cheques or having to handle cash when paying employees. Employees like this system because money is placed directly in their accounts. No matter which method is used, provincial labour laws require that each employee receive a statement (like the one shown at the beginning of the chapter in Figure 14-1) that outlines their gross earnings, deductions, and net pay. Why do you think this law was passed?

Remitting Deductions

Once a month, the employer must remit the deductions taken from the employees' wages and salaries to the proper agencies. Income tax, C.P.P., and E.I. deductions must be sent to the Receiver General of Canada by the 15th of the following month. Canada Customs and Revenue Agency supplies companies with the official remittance form, PD7A, that is used to send in the deductions. Other deductions, such as union dues, life insurance premiums, etc., must also be remitted to the appropriate agencies.

Form PD7A is the official remittance form for payroll deductions to be sent to Canada Customs and Revenue Agency.

RECORDING THE PAYROLL

Up to this point, we have described the procedures for determining and keeping track of the earnings and deductions for employees. Now we will examine the recording of the payroll information in the accounting system.

Payroll involves expenses, liabilities, and payment of funds. Therefore, journal entries must be made to record these items so that the accounts and financial statements will be accurate. There are four steps for making payroll entries in the general journal. They are:

- **Step 1:** Make an entry to Salaries Expense and to the individual payroll liability accounts for each pay period. The figures for this entry are taken from the payroll journal.

- **Step 2:** Make an entry to record the payment to workers for each pay period.

- **Step 3:** Make entries to record the employer's share of C.P.P. and E.I. premiums for each pay period.

- **Step 4:** Make entries to remit the payroll deductions to the government and other agencies. These entries are made once a month.

All of these entries will now be examined.

Step 1: Record the Salaries Expense and Payroll Liabilities

The first entry involves recording the total *salaries expense* (gross earnings) and the amounts owed to the employees, the government, and other agencies, such as insurance companies.

All of the figures for the entry come from the payroll journal of Western Systems, Figure 14-7 on page 739.

May	7	Salaries Expense	7 4 0 0 00	
		C.P.P. Payable		2 7 3 91
		E.I. Payable		1 7 7 60
		Income Tax Payable		1 8 2 2 75
		Salaries Payable		5 1 2 5 74
		To record the May 7 payroll.		

This first entry records the deductions held back from the employees as liabilities on the books of the employer. As you will see, the first three payable amounts must be paid out once a month, and until paid are debts owed by the employer. The first entry also records the figures for a liability account called *Salaries Payable*. This is the amount owed to the workers (net earnings from the payroll journal) and is a liability until the workers are paid.

Step 2: Record the Payment to Employees

The second entry is made when the employees are paid. In the previous entry, a credit was entered in Salaries Payable to record the liability to the employees. When the employees are paid, this liability is cancelled.

May	7	Salaries Payable	5 1 2 5 74	
		Cash		5 1 2 5 74
		Payment of May 7 payroll.		

Step 3: Record the Employer's Payroll Expenses

As you learned earlier, the employer is required to contribute to the C.P.P. and E.I. funds on behalf of employees. *For C.P.P., the employer must contribute an amount equal to that contributed by employees. For E.I., the employer's contribution is 1.4 times the employees' premiums.*

In the case of Western Systems (Figure 14-7), the employees' C.P.P. contribution is $273.91; therefore, the employer's contribution is $273.91. The employees' E.I. contribution is $177.60; therefore, the employer's E.I. contribution is $248.64 ($1.4 \times \$177.60$).

The company records its contribution to C.P.P. as a debit to C.P.P. Expense. The company's contribution to E.I. is debited to E.I. Expense. The entries for Western Systems are as follows:

May	7	C.P.P. Expense	2 7 3 91	
		C.P.P. Payable		2 7 3 91
		To record the employer's contribution to C.P.P.		
	7	E.I. Expense	2 4 8 64	
		E.I. Payable		2 4 8 64
		To record the employer's contribution to E.I.		

The entries just described to record and pay the payroll and to record the employer's payroll expenses are made each pay period and posted to the general ledger. The partial ledger for Western Systems in Figure 14-10 shows the entries in the accounts relating to payroll after four pay periods have been posted in May. Notice that C.P.P. Payable and E.I. Payable include entries for both the employees' and employer's contributions.

GENERAL LEDGER

	Cash		101
May 1 39 000.00	May 7	5 125.74	
	14	5 125.74	
	21	5 125.74	
	28	5 125.74	

	C.P.P. Payable		220
	May 7	273.91	
	7	273.91	
	14	273.91	
	14	273.91	
	21	273.91	
	21	273.91	
	28	273.91	
	28	273.91	
		2 191.28	

	E.I. Payable		221
	May 7	177.60	
	7	248.64	
	14	177.60	
	14	248.64	
	21	177.60	
	21	248.64	
	28	177.60	
	28	248.64	
		1 704.96	

	Income Tax Payable		222
	May 7	1 822.75	
	14	1 822.75	
	21	1 822.75	
	28	1 822.75	
		7 291.00	

	Salaries Payable		224
May 7	5 125.74	May 7	5 125.74
14	5 125.74	14	5 125.74
21	5 125.74	21	5 125.74
28	5 125.74	28	5 125.74
	20 502.96		20 502.96

	Salaries Expense		620
May 7	7 400.00		
14	7 400.00		
21	7 400.00		
28	7 400.00		
	29 600.00		

	C.P.P. Expense		621
May 7	273.91		
14	273.91		
21	273.91		
28	273.91		
	1 095.64		

	E.I. Expense		622
May 7	248.64		
14	248.64		
21	248.64		
28	248.64		
	994.56		

FIGURE 14-10 Partial general ledger showing the May payroll entries for Western Systems recorded in the payroll accounts

Employer Health Tax

In several provinces, employers must pay an Employer Health Tax (E.H.T.) calculated on total gross payroll. This tax replaces employee contributions to provincial health care plans.

Employer Health Tax Rates

The rate of E.H.T. is determined by the total annual gross earnings of employees during the year. The chart in Figure 14-11 shows the earnings categories and applicable rates for Ontario.

Quebec calculates its E.H.T., known as the Health Services Fund, at between 2.7 percent and 4.26 percent, depending on the size of the gross payroll, while the Manitoba E.H.T., known as the Health and Post-Secondary Education Tax Levy, is based on the following schedule:

Gross Payroll	Rate
$1 000 000 or less	0%
$1 000 001 to $2 000 000	4.3%
$2 000 001 and over	2.15%

Tax Rates

APPLICATION   The amount of tax payable is a percentage of the total annual remuneration paid by employers during a calendar year. The tax is calculated by multiplying the total amount of remuneration paid in a year by the tax rate applicable to that amount of remuneration.

The tax rate on total remuneration is graduated, ranging from 0.98 percent to 1.95 percent, with the highest rate applying in those cases where total annual remuneration paid by the employer exceeds $400 000.

RATES   Ranges of remuneration and applicable tax rates are outlined below:

TOTAL ONTARIO ANNUAL REMUNERATION	RATE	
up to and including $200 000	0.98	percent
$200 001, up to and including $230 000	1.101	percent
$230 001, up to and including $260 000	1.223	percent
$260 001, up to and including $290 000	1.344	percent
$290 001, up to and including $320 000	1.465	percent
$320 001, up to and including $350 000	1.586	percent
$350 001, up to and including $380 000	1.708	percent
$380 001, up to and including $400 000	1.829	percent
over $400 000	1.95	percent

FIGURE 14-11 Employer Health Tax rates for Ontario

Employer Health Tax Calculation

For the moment, we will leave the example of Western Systems, which is not subject to E.H.T., and move to the province of Ontario. Ontario's E.H.T. is calculated by multiplying the appropriate rate, found in Figure 14-11, by the total gross earnings for the period. The sample company is Blackburn Hardware, whose gross earnings are $3700 per week. Blackburn has an annual payroll of under $200 000 ($3700 × 52 weeks = $192 400). Can you find the appropriate E.H.T. rate in Figure 14-11? Blackburn's rate is 0.98 percent; therefore, the E.H.T. owing is $36.26 ($3700 × 0.0098) for this pay period. The following entry is made to record the E.H.T. for the pay period.

May	28	Employer Health Tax Expense		3 6 26	
		Employer Health Tax Payable			3 6 26
		To record accrued E.H.T. for May 28 payroll.			

Step 4: Record the Payment of Payroll Deductions

We will now return to the example of Western Systems. Once a month, the employer's contributions and deductions withheld from employees are forwarded to the appropriate agencies. The payment is recorded with the entries illustrated below. The entries are made on the 15th of the following month and record the remittance of the deductions for all of the pay periods of the previous month. The amounts are obtained from the ledger accounts shown in Figure 14-10 on page 746.

The first entry shown records the payment of money to the federal government. The amounts include both the employee and employer contributions to C.P.P. and E.I., and the employees' income tax deductions:

Jun.	15	C.P.P. Payable		2 1 9 1 28	
		E.I. Payable		1 7 0 4 96	
		Income Tax Payable		7 2 9 1 00	
		Cash			11 1 8 7 24
		To record the payment of the May payroll			
		deductions to the Receiver General.			

Other payroll liabilities are also paid once a month. Similar entries are made for union dues, life insurance, health care plans in provinces that require employee contributions, and other payroll liabilities, if applicable.

Figure 14-12 on the following page illustrates the ledger accounts for Western Systems after the June 15 entries have been posted. The debts owed to the federal and provincial governments have been paid and these liability accounts are reduced to zero.

GENERAL LEDGER

	Cash			101		Salaries Payable			224
May	1	39 000.00	May	7	5 125.74	May	7	5 125.74	May	7	5 125.74
				14	5 125.74		14	5 125.74		14	5 125.74
				21	5 125.74		21	5 125.74		21	5 125.74
				28	5 125.74		28	5 125.74		28	5 125.74
			Jun.	15	11 187.24			20 502.96			20 502.96

	C.P.P. Payable			220
Jun.	15	2 191.28	May	7	273.91
				7	273.91
				14	273.91
				14	273.91
				21	273.91
				21	273.91
				28	273.91
				28	273.91
		2 191.28			2 191.28

	Salaries Expense		620
May	7	7 400.00	
	14	7 400.00	
	21	7 400.00	
	28	7 400.00	
		29 600.00	

	C.P.P. Expense		621
May	7	273.91	
	14	273.91	
	21	273.91	
	28	273.91	
		1 095.64	

	E.I. Payable			221
Jun.	15	1704.96	May	7	177.60
				7	248.64
				14	177.60
				14	248.64
				21	177.60
				21	248.64
				28	177.60
				28	248.64
		1 704.96			1 704.96

	E.I. Expense		622
May	7	248.64	
	14	248.64	
	21	248.64	
	28	248.64	
		994.56	

	Income Tax Payable			222
Jun.	15	7 291.00	May	7	1 822.75
				14	1 822.75
				21	1 822.75
				28	1 822.75
		7 291.00			7 291.00

FIGURE 14-12 Partial general ledger for Western Systems after the June 15 entries have been posted

There is one other sample entry that you need to see, Blackburn Hardware's monthly payment to the Provincial Treasurer for the E.H.T.:

Jun.	15	Employer Health Tax Payable		1 4 5 04	
		Cash			1 4 5 04
		To record the payment of Employer Health Tax			
		to the Provincial Treasurer.			

SOME CONCLUDING POINTS ABOUT PAYROLL

Workers' Compensation

All provinces provide an insurance plan for the protection of workers who suffer personal injuries or occupational diseases related to their jobs. Compensation is paid to injured workers from a fund administered by a provincial Workers' Compensation Board. Employers supply the money for the fund. The amount paid by an employer varies according to the type of business and its accident record.

In return for providing money to the fund, the employer is relieved of liability for injuries suffered by workers. The amount of compensation received by an injured worker is based on the average salary earned while working. The employer's payment to the fund is an expense of operating the business. When premiums are paid, this entry is made:

Jun.	30	Workers' Compensation Expense		1 5 0 00	
		Cash			1 5 0 00
		To pay semi-annual premium to Workers'			
		Compensation Board.			

Payroll Ledger Accounts

Payroll accounting involves a number of expense accounts. For example, Wages Expense is the account used for earnings of hourly rated workers. Salaries Expense is used for the earnings of salaried employees.

Several expense accounts are used to record employer's contributions required by various laws. These include C.P.P. Expense, E.I. Expense, and Workers' Compensation Expense. Rather than use these individual accounts, some companies prefer to use one account called Payroll Expense. This account is used for all payments such as the employer's share of C.P.P., E.I., E.H.T., and other insurances. A sample entry using the Payroll Expense account follows:

Jun.	30	Payroll Expense		3 6 9 00	
		C.P.P. Payable			8 5 00
		E.I. Payable			9 9 00
		Workers' Compensation Payable			5 0 00
		Group Insurance Payable			4 5 00
		Employer Health Tax Payable			9 0 00
		To record the employer's payroll expenses.			

SUMMARY OF PROCEDURES

Figure 14-13 illustrates the payroll accounting procedures covered in this chapter.

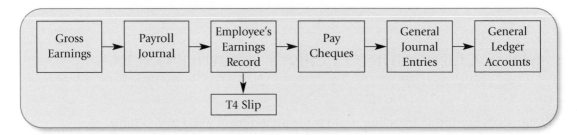

FIGURE 14-13 Summary of payroll procedures

Generally Accepted Accounting Principles and Key Ideas

In this chapter, you learned the following key ideas:

- **Every employee must receive a statement of earnings** each payday.
- **There are three compulsory payroll deductions that all employers must make:** C.P.P., E.I., and income tax.
- **All employees must complete a TDI form** each year or when credits change.
- **Employers must keep appropriate payroll records** and books; these must be retained for a minimum of six years.
- **Employers must provide a T4 slip** to employees by February 28 each year.
- **Employers must remit the previous month's government payroll deductions to the federal government** by the 15th of the following month.

UNIT 34 CHECK YOUR READING

Questions

14. Explain how a payroll journal is proven to be mathematically correct.

15. Danuta has just completed a payroll journal and the totals balance; yet there is an error in the journal. How can this happen?

16. Which payroll deductions are remitted to the federal government?

17. When must the employer remit payroll deductions to the federal government?

18. To whom is the cheque made payable when deductions are remitted to the federal government?

19. What form is completed when a remittance is made to the federal government?
20. What is the purpose of the employee's earnings record?
21. Describe the four basic types of payroll entries in the general journal.
22. (a) What insurance compensates workers injured on the job?
(b) Who pays the premiums for this insurance?
23. What single expense account may be used instead of C.P.P. Expense, E.I. Expense, and Workers' Compensation Expense?
24. How is Ontario's E.H.T. calculated?

UNIT 34 APPLY YOUR KNOWLEDGE

Exercises Part A

Note: Where necessary, use either current payroll deduction booklets or the tables given on pages 731–737 to complete the exercises in this chapter.

14. D. Houston Ltd. has six employees on the payroll.

Emp. No.	Name	Net Claim Code	Gross Earnings	Co. Pension
103	Jaswinder Singh	9	$700	$27.50
104	Bill Strahan	1	730	27.50
105	Linda Lo	10	695	27.50
106	Lesley Durvan	1	728	27.50
107	Stan Trudeau	9	695	27.50
108	Tracey St. James	1	695	27.50

(a) Record the information above in a payroll journal.
(b) Determine the taxable earnings and the income tax deduction for each employee.
(c) Determine the C.P.P. and E.I. deductions for each employee.
(d) Calculate the net earnings for each employee.
(e) Balance the payroll journal.

15. The payroll information for Maingot Manufacturers for the week ended May 7 is shown below. Every employee also pays union dues of $6.55 weekly and has $30 000 worth of group life insurance for which 12¢ per $1000 is contributed weekly.

Emp. No.	Name	Net Claim Code	Gross Earnings
101	P. Dagenais	4	$700
102	L. Rasmussen	8	710
103	C. Hayashi	1	690
104	T. Chan	6	700
105	F. Brammel	9	800
106	C. Lazzari	1	850

(a) Record the payroll in a payroll journal, determining the C.P.P. contributions, E.I. premiums, and income tax deductions.
(b) Total and prove the payroll journal.

16. The payroll information for Western Distributors for the week ended June 15 follows:

Emp. No.	Name	Net Claim Code	Gross Earnings	Co. Pension
201	T. Fong	1	$809.60	$20.00
202	A. Hjelt	9	702.25	15.00
203	A. Covington	10	685.05	12.50
204	C. Amato	1	822.00	20.00
205	P. Surat	1	899.70	25.00
206	S. Betterworth	7	784.80	17.50

Every employee also pays union dues of $9 weekly and has $35 000 worth of group life insurance for which 15¢ per $1000 is contributed weekly.
(a) Record the payroll in a payroll journal, determining C.P.P., E.I., and income tax.
(b) Total and prove the payroll journal.

17. A payroll journal for the pay period ended July 7 showed the following totals: gross earnings, $5783.20; C.P.P. contributions, $104.09; E.I. premiums, $62.70; federal income tax, $983.14; health insurance, $132; union dues, $142.50; net earnings, $4358.77. Prepare journal entries on page 23 to record:
(a) The payroll
(b) The payment to the employees
(c) The employer's share of the C.P.P. contributions and E.I. premiums

18. A payroll journal for the pay period ended May 14 showed the following totals: gross earnings, $46 793.55; C.P.P. contributions, $842.28; E.I. premiums, $495; registered pension plan, $1544.19; income tax, $7954.90; union dues, $1325.25; group insurance, $797.53; net earnings, $33 834.40. The Employer Health Tax is $912.47. Prepare journal entries on page 10 to record:
   (a) The payroll
   (b) The payment to the employees
   (c) The employer's share of the C.P.P. contributions, E.I. premiums, and Employer Health Tax

19. Refer to the completed payroll journal for exercise 14, D. Houston Ltd.
   (a) Prepare the journal entry on page 8 to record the payroll on May 24.
   (b) Prepare the entry to pay the employees.
   (c) Prepare the entry to record the company's share of C.P.P. and E.I.
   (d) Prepare the entry to record the Employer Health Tax of $87.80.

Exercises Part B

20. Delmonte Manufacturing pays its salaried employees once a month. The payroll journal at the end of May for these employees is shown on page 754. Prepare journal entries on page 27 to record:
   (a) The payroll at the end of May
   (b) The employer's share of the C.P.P. and E.I. premiums
   (c) The cheques to pay the employees
   (d) The remittance to the Receiver General on June 15
   (e) The remittance to Metropolitan Life for the group insurance and pension
   (f) The remittance to the Provincial Treasurer for the Employer Health Tax if the rate is 1.223 percent

21. Refer to the completed payroll journal for exercise 16, Western Distributors.
   (a) Prepare the journal entry to record the payroll.
   (b) Prepare the entry to pay the employees.
   (c) Prepare the entry to record the company's share of C.P.P. and E.I.

COMPANY NAME DELMONTE MANUFACTURING
PAY PERIOD ENDING MAY 31, 20—

PAYROLL JOURNAL

PAGE 307

EMP. NO.	NAME OF EMPLOYEE	NET CLAIM CODE	GROSS EARNINGS	NON-TAXABLES		TAXABLE EARNINGS	INCOME TAX	OTHER DEDUCTIONS					TOTAL DEDUCTIONS	NET EARNINGS
				R.P.P.	UNION DUES			C.P.P.	E.I.	HEALTH INS.	GROUP INS.	OTHER		
65	O'Connell, P.	9	4 025 00	125 69		3 899 31	812 60	83 38	74 88		33 61		1 130 16	2 894 84
66	Dooner, C.	1	2 875 00	77 20		2 797 80	642 10	58 08	64 69		22 93		865 00	2 010 00
67	Greenspoon, L.	1	3 115 00	110 58		3 004 42	725 90	63 36	70 09		31 50		1 001 43	2 113 57
68	Ritcher, F.	10	3 897 00	118 72		3 778 28	759 60	80 52	74 88		35 90		1 069 62	2 827 38
69	Lapchinski, C.	9	4 250 00	136 70		4 113 30	931 85	88 44	74 88		29 88		1 261 75	2 988 25
70	Karklins, A.	1	4 250 00	136 70		4 113 30	1 185 60	88 44	74 88		29 88		1 515 50	2 734 50
			22 412 00	705 59		21 706 41	5 057 65	462 22	434 30		183 70		6 843 46	15 568 54

Proof 1

Gross Earnings		$22 412.00
Less: Total Deductions		6 843.46
Net Earnings		$15 568.54

Proof 2

Gross Earnings			$22 412.00
Less: R.P.P.	$ 705.59		
Income Tax	5 057.65		
C.P.P.	462.22		
U.I.	434.30		
Group Insurance	183.70	6 843.46	
Net Earnings			$15 568.54

Computer Accounting

Computerized Payroll Accounting

Not all companies with computerized accounting systems complete their payroll using a computer. There are several reasons for this.

Each year, there are many changes in payroll accounting. The federal government changes the amounts to be deducted for C.P.P., E.I., and income tax and issues new deduction booklets. Wages and salary rates often change. Premiums change for voluntary deductions, such as group insurance, life insurance, and health insurance. All of these changes, including the thousands of items in the deduction tables, must be incorporated into the payroll software. This can mean expensive reprogramming of the computer system. Also, to do a payroll using a computer, the software must include all of the voluntary and compulsory payroll deductions. This takes up a great deal of the computer's storage capacity or requires the purchase of additional memory for the computer.

Some firms that produce payroll software have overcome these problems by providing an annual update for the software package. This update includes the change in deductions from the year's new government deduction booklets. However, many companies prefer to have their payrolls done by a bank, trust company, or professional accounting service. The company provides payroll details for each employee, such as:

- name;
- gross earnings;
- S.I.N.; and
- deductions to be made.

The accounting service then determines the deductions, calculates the net earnings, prepares payroll cheques (or bank deposits), updates the payroll records, and provides a summary to the company. Using the summary, the company prepares the journal entries to update the ledger accounts.

Computerized Payroll Deductions

Employers may use a computer to calculate the payroll deductions for C.P.P., E.I., and income tax. Rather than using the deduction tables provided by the government (such as the ones shown in this chapter), a deduction formula is included as part of the payroll software for a computer.

The formulas for both C.P.P. and E.I. include the percentage of gross earnings to be deducted from each employee's earnings, the year's maximum contribution, the year's maximum pensionable and insurable earnings, and the employee's contributions to C.P.P. and E.I. to date. Each payday, the formulas are applied to the employee's earnings and automatically the C.P.P. and E.I. deductions are determined by the computer. This eliminates the time-consuming task of looking up each employee's deductions in the table of deductions booklet. A formula may also be used to calculate the amount of each employee's deduction for income tax.

The Simply Accounting Payroll Module

In this section, we will explain how payroll is processed using Simply Accounting. The program contains the deduction tables for C.P.P., E.I., and income tax, and will automatically calculate the amount to be deducted from each employee for the three compulsory deductions. Other deductions that are made each payday can be entered into the program and they also will be deducted automatically.

These are the steps followed in paying an employee:

1. Select **Paycheques** from the Payroll module. The payroll input form shown below will appear on the screen.

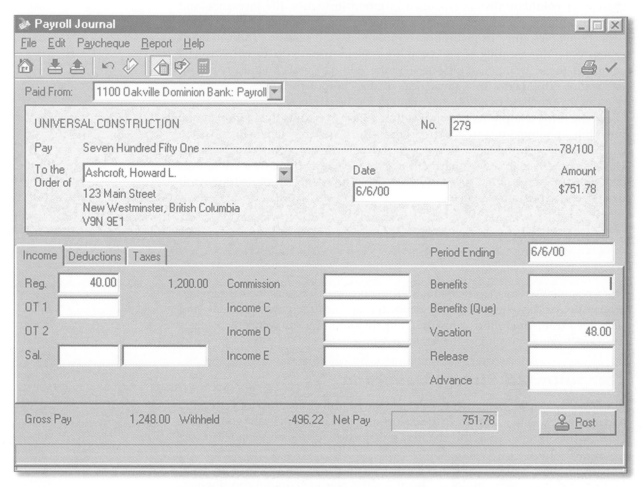

FIGURE 14-13   The Simply Accounting payroll input form

2. In the "To the Order of" section, select the name of the employee to be paid. The employee's address will automatically appear on the cheque.
3. Enter the payroll details: cheque number, date, regular hours worked, etc. by using the Tab key to move from field to field.
4. The computer program will calculate the employee's deductions for C.P.P., E.I., and income tax using the tables stored in its database. It will also

calculate the employer's share of C.P.P., E.I., and workers' compensation and record these as expenses, and it will calculate the employee's net pay.

5. From the Report menu, select **Display Payroll Journal Entry** to review the payroll transaction. The following will appear on the screen:

6/6/00 (J343)	Debits	Credits	Project
5300 Wages	1,248.00	-	
5310 EI Expense	41.93	-	
5320 CPP Expense	46.05	-	
5330 WCB Expense	53.04	-	
1100 Oakville Dominion Bank: Payroll	-	751.78	
2310 EI Payable	-	71.88	
2320 CPP Payable	-	92.10	
2330 Income Tax Payable	-	329.82	
2350 WCB Payable	-	53.04	
2400 RRSP Payable	-	62.40	
2420 Union Payable	-	16.00	
2440 Medical Payable	-	12.00	
	1,389.02	1,389.02	

FIGURE 14-14   Payroll journal entry using Simply Accounting

Notice that the computer program has also calculated the total amounts (both employer's and employee's shares) to be credited to C.P.P. Payable, E.I. Payable, Income Tax Payable, Workers' Compensation Payable, RRSP Payable, Union Payable, and Medical Payable, and it has credited the payroll bank account for the employee's net pay. Then close the journal entry screen.

6. At the top right corner of the screen, click on the printer icon to print the employee's pay cheque.

7. Click on the **Post** button at the bottom right corner of the screen to post the transaction.

Each year (for a small fee), the producers of Simply Accounting (and similar programs) provide updated tables of deductions for C.P.P., E.I., income tax, and workers' compensation.

COMPUTER ASSIGNMENTS

1. Preparing a payroll involves many mathematical calculations for each payday. A number of calculations do not change, but some will change depending upon the pay period. The necessity of these calculations makes the payroll procedure an ideal type of process for a computerized accounting or spreadsheet application. Payroll details for Nguyen Enterprises for four payroll periods appear on pages 759 and 760.
   (a) Format a spreadsheet that will complete, balance, and print the payroll journal for each month.
   (b) Print the four payroll journals.

2. Refer to the January, February, March, and April spreadsheets that you created in question number 1.
   (a) Format a spreadsheet that will print these journal entries each month:
      (i) The entry to record payroll
      (ii) The entry to pay the employees
      (iii) The entries to record the employer's C.P.P. and E.I. contributions
   (b) Print the entries for each month.
   (c) Create a spreadsheet that combines the federal and provincial income tax as one total tax deduction for each pay period.

www.pearsoned.ca/
principlesofaccounting

WEB EXTENSIONS

Internet Study Guide

➤ Complete the Chapter 14 review.

➤ Complete the Chapter 14 definitions.

➤ Complete the Chapter 14 online test.

Web Links

Visit the Web Links section at the Pearson Education web site to find links to the Canada Customs and Revenue Agency web site. Outline why this information would be important to an accountant.

January Payroll Data:

- Company Name: Nguyen Enterprises
- Journal Title: Payroll Journal
- Payroll Date: January 31, 20—

Employee Name	Employee Number	Salary	C.P.P.	E.I.	Federal Income Tax	Provincial Income Tax	Health Insurance	Other Deductions	Tax Code
J. Gallotta	00824	3 0 0 0 00	1 1 6 46	6 7 50	4 7 7 05	1 8 6 75	2 7 00	1 5 00	0
R. Nguyen	00825	5 0 0 0 00	2 0 2 32	6 7 50	8 0 5 25	3 3 7 85	5 4 00	1 5 00	2
G. Peterson	00826	3 0 0 0 00	1 1 6 46	6 7 50	2 7 9 55	1 1 1 15	2 7 00	1 0 00	6
M. Lever	00827	4 0 0 0 00	1 5 9 32	6 7 50	5 4 4 05	2 2 1 05	5 4 00	1 5 00	4
S. Fracke	00828	2 9 7 5 00	1 1 5 38	6 7 50	3 1 6 30	1 2 7 70	2 7 00	1 0 00	4

February Payroll Data:

- Payroll Date: February 28, 20—
- The only changes in February are in the Other Deductions column.

Employee Name	Employee Number	Salary	C.P.P.	E.I.	Federal Income Tax	Provincial Income Tax	Health Insurance	Other Deductions	Tax Code
J. Gallotta	00824	3 0 0 0 00	1 1 6 46	6 7 50	4 7 7 05	1 8 6 75	2 7 00	3 0 00	0
R. Nguyen	00825	5 0 0 0 00	2 0 2 32	6 7 50	8 0 5 25	3 3 7 85	5 4 00	3 0 00	2
G. Peterson	00826	3 0 0 0 00	1 1 6 46	6 7 50	2 7 9 55	1 1 1 15	2 7 00	2 0 00	6
M. Lever	00827	4 0 0 0 00	1 5 9 32	6 7 50	5 4 4 05	2 2 1 05	5 4 00	3 0 00	4
S. Fracke	00828	2 9 7 5 00	1 1 5 38	6 7 50	3 1 6 30	1 2 7 70	2 7 00	2 0 00	4

March Payroll Data:

- Payroll Date: March 31, 20—
- The March payroll data are the same as the January payroll data.

Employee Name	Employee Number	Salary	C.P.P.	E.I.	Federal Income Tax	Provincial Income Tax	Health Insurance	Other Deductions	Tax Code
J. Gallotta	00824	3 000 00	1 1 6 46	6 7 50	4 7 7 05	1 8 6 75	2 7 00	1 5 00	0
R. Nguyen	00825	5 000 00	2 0 2 32	6 7 50	8 0 5 25	3 3 7 85	5 4 00	1 5 00	2
G. Peterson	00826	3 000 00	1 1 6 46	6 7 50	2 7 9 55	1 1 1 15	2 7 00	1 0 00	6
M. Lever	00827	4 000 00	1 5 9 32	6 7 50	5 4 4 05	2 2 1 05	5 4 00	1 5 00	4
S. Fracke	00828	2 975 00	1 1 5 38	6 7 50	3 1 6 30	1 2 7 70	2 7 00	1 0 00	4

April Payroll Data:

- Payroll Date: April 30, 20—
- The only changes in April payroll data are in the Other Deductions column.

Employee Name	Employee Number	Salary	C.P.P.	E.I.	Federal Income Tax	Provincial Income Tax	Health Insurance	Other Deductions	Tax Code
J. Gallotta	00824	3 000 00	1 1 6 46	6 7 50	4 7 7 05	1 8 6 75	2 7 00	4 5 00	0
R. Nguyen	00825	5 000 00	2 0 2 32	6 7 50	8 0 5 25	3 3 7 85	5 4 00	1 4 5 00	2
G. Peterson	00826	3 000 00	1 1 6 46	6 7 50	2 7 9 55	1 1 1 15	2 7 00	2 5 00	6
M. Lever	00827	4 000 00	1 5 9 32	6 7 50	5 4 4 05	2 2 1 05	5 4 00	4 5 00	4
S. Fracke	00828	2 975 00	1 1 5 38	6 7 50	3 1 6 30	1 2 7 70	2 7 00	2 5 00	4

7 Case Studies

Personal Values

Canada's E.I. system was designed to support the active pursuit of employment. The goal of the system is to encourage people to return to the job market.

The money in the system comes from the federal government, from employers, and from employees. Employees pay 2.25 percent of their wages up to a maximum of $878 per year in E.I. premiums. Employers contribute 1.4 times the employee contribution. As an example, for every $100 contributed by employees, the employer would submit $140. Each employee pays premiums based on the first dollar earned up to a yearly maximum of $39 000.

Earnings subject to E.I. premiums include wages, salaries, paid leaves, and some payments in kind to employees. A meal given to a restaurant employee as a benefit is considered a payment in kind.

The E.I. system can be costly to operate each year. Costs increase as a result of:

(a) improved benefits paid to the unemployed;
(b) rising unemployment; and
(c) claimants cheating the system.

Read each of the following scenarios:

1. Maria is an employee at her friend Trudy's small firm. They have an agreement that Trudy will not deduct E.I. premiums from Maria's earnings. This saves Maria about $900 per year and it saves Trudy about $1260 per year. *Besides being illegal, what risk is Maria taking?*

2. Felicity has worked for several years and has never been unemployed. She decides to take a six-month trip. After deliberately getting laid off from her job, Felicity completes the required E.I. forms and begins the process to receive benefits. She has her friend John complete E.I. forms in her absence to indicate that she is actively seeking employment. John also forges Felicity's name on the government cheques and deposits them in Felicity's bank account.

3. Brian and Anne-Marie both work and earn good salaries. Each year one of them deliberately becomes unemployed to receive E.I. benefits and then goes back to work. Although they are able to find employment, they feel they deserve the money because they have contributed premiums for so many years. An employer, Sandra, figures out what they are doing but does not report them because she does not want to get involved in a court case that might hurt the reputation of her business.

4. Bill has worked for 25 years at a number of low-level jobs and has never had an E.I. claim. As Bill approaches retirement, he feels it is not fair that, after contributing so much, he has never benefited from the E.I. system. He works out a scheme to be laid off prior to retirement so that he can make an E.I. claim and then, when the funds run out, retire.

Discuss each of the scenarios with two members of your class. Answer the following questions:

(a) Rank each of the people (Maria, Trudy, Felicity, John, Brian, Anne-Marie, Sandra, and Bill) according to their honesty. Give each a number from one to eight, with one being for the most dishonest.

(b) Is each person guilty of doing something wrong? If not, indicate which person has not done anything wrong.

(c) For each scenario, what could the government do to prevent this type of abuse?

(d) For each scenario, what would you suggest as a consequence for each of the individuals that you feel has committed an illegal act?

CASE 2 Canada Pension Plan and Employment Insurance

The Canada Pension Plan came into effect in 1966 to provide financial assistance to Canadians when they retired from the workforce. Every individual in Canada who works is entitled to C.P.P. benefits when they retire. The employer is responsible for deducting C.P.P. contributions from the employee and for matching the contribution.

The E.I. program gives financial assistance to people who are unemployed, while also providing assistance for job training.

Work with a partner to determine the following:

(a) Which federal agency is responsible for C.P.P.?

(b) What is the maximum employee contribution for the year?

(c) What is the maximum employer contribution for the year?

(d) What is the year's basic exemption for C.P.P.? (Individuals who earn less than this amount do not need to contribute to C.P.P.)

(e) Which federal agency is responsible for E.I.?

(f) What is the maximum annual E.I. premium per employee?

CASE 3 Business Ethics

Wellington's is a large department store that employs many students part-time. Minimum wage laws specify the number of hours of work per week above which a student must be paid the general worker's rate. There is about a 10 percent difference between the general rate and the student rate. Wellington's offers several fringe benefits to its full-time employees. These include a free life insurance policy, 50 percent of the cost of a medical plan, and 20 days' annual sick leave. Part-time employees do not receive fringe benefits. Management of the store behaves as follows:

- The owner of the store encourages the use of many part-time students because the minimum rate for students is lower and because they do not receive fringe benefits.
- The personnel manager occasionally, but deliberately, contravenes the minimum wage law by not paying overtime as required. The owner is not aware of this.
- The manager of the sporting goods department has hired his son-in-law as a salesperson and often offers him overtime work. No one else in the department works overtime.

(a) Who do you think is the most ethical person in the store? Who is the least ethical? Rank the following from 1 to 4 in terms of ethics, with 4 being the least ethical:
   (i)   The owner
   (ii)   The personnel manager
   (iii) The sporting goods manager
   (iv)   The son-in-law
(b) What is your definition of *ethical*?
(c) Suppose you worked for Wellington's and felt that you were not being treated fairly according to several of your province's employment standard laws.
   (i)   What would you do? List your alternatives.
   (ii)   What are the possible consequences of each alternative?

Employment Standards Act

CASE 4

The Employment Standards Act is the law that contains the basic rules about working and about employing workers. It provides for rights for both workers and employers.

Contact the provincial government department that administers your province's Minimum Wage Act and Employment Standards Act.

Answer the following questions relating to these Acts:

(a) Does the Employment Standards Act cover all employees in your province? If not, indicate which groups are not covered.
(b) What is the current minimum wage for students?
(c) Is everyone entitled to the same minimum wage? Provide examples.
(d) How is the public notified about changes to the minimum wage?
(e) What is meant by the "3-hour rule" in Ontario?
(f) What is the name of the provincial government department that is responsible for minimum wages?

CASE 5 Coping With Change

One of the skills that many employers look for in an employee is their ability to deal with change. Throughout your career you will have to deal with change. These changes may be in the form of societal changes, government changes, law and regulation changes, assignment changes, and personal changes.

Depending upon the nature of the change, the employee and/or the employer must be prepared to deal with the change.

From 2001 onward, all provincial personal income tax is determined by the tax on income (TONI) method. In previous years, the basic provincial income tax was calculated as a percentage of the federal income tax. Now, all provincial income tax rates are applied to annual income.

The change requires two tax deduction tables: federal and provincial. This also results in different federal and provincial claim codes for employees. Nonetheless, employers continue to report combined federal and provincial tax deductions on payroll remittance forms. They also continue to show combined tax deductions on statements of earnings and only file one T4 slip per employee.

These changes were announced by the federal and provincial governments in radio and television releases, advertisements in newspapers, direct mailings, and documents placed on their web sites.

(a) How did the changes described above affect the average employee?
(b) How did the changes affect the employer?
(c) How can employers stay informed about federal changes that may affect their business operations, including payroll processes?
(d) How do you stay informed about societal changes?
(e) What can you do to become more informed about ongoing changes at the provincial and federal levels?
(f) Indicate where you can find detailed information about federal and provincial tax changes.

⑧ Career Education Activities

1. Personal Decision Making

Marion has worked for a large insurance company for seven years, and has received a number of promotions and pay raises. Although highly regarded by her employers, she has only limited opportunities for advancement with her present company.

After applying to a number of firms, Marion has received two management-level offers. Both companies are progressive and growing, and appear able to supply the type of future she is seeking.

Company A offers the following:

1. Salary: $44 000
2. Fringe benefits:
   - free life insurance, long-term disability insurance, and extended health care insurance
   - a company pension that is partly paid by the company (the employee pays approximately $500 a year)

Company B offers the following:

1. Salary: $47 000
2. Bonus: $3000 if employee work goals are successfully met
3. A number of benefits are paid by the workers:
   - life insurance $400 per year
   - disability insurance $500 per year
   - extended health insurance $400 per year
   - provincial medical insurance $564 per year
   - company pension $1700 per year

For Discussion

(a) What factors not given in this description should be considered before a decision is made?
(b) Which position would you accept if you were Marion? Give reasons for your answer.

2. Being a Well-Rounded Employee

It is not enough to understand accounting theory and to be able to do accounting. Employers require other skills and personal characteristics as well as the ability to do routine accounting tasks. Read the employment advertisement for a payroll administrator and answer the questions that follow.

Payroll Administrator

If you are an organizer who can use initiative and show good judgment, the Board of Education invites you to apply for a full-time, permanent position in our Payroll Department.

You will use our computer software to prepare the academic payroll for the board. You will use your sound knowledge of Canada Customs and Revenue Agency regulations to help develop and improve systems and procedures, and answer empolyee inquiries.

You will be responsible for online data entry and report generation.

You have graduated from secondary school, have taken some post-secondary accounting courses, and have worked for at least three years on a computerized payroll system at an intermediate level.

We offer you a salary ranging from $34 000 to $40 000 and a complete benefits package.

Please submit your résumé to:
The Board
Box 100, Daly Street
Vancouver, British Columbia

"An equal opportunity employer"

For Discussion

(a) What personal skills are required for this job?
(b) What accounting skills and knowledge are required?
(c) What educational background is required?
(d) How does a person apply for the job?
(e) Explain the following:
   (i) *initiative;*
   (ii) *tact;*
   (iii) *judgment;* and
   (iv) *organizer.*

Career Profile

Karen Power enjoyed science courses during high school, so she decided to study science at university. Part way through her first year she knew she had to make a difficult choice. She was interested in business and was questioning her decision to pursue a science degree, so she decided to take some time off after her first year of university.

When Karen returned to her studies she began a Bachelor of Commerce program. She found that she especially enjoyed the financial components in her classes.

She completed her degree and was hired by Deloitte & Touche, a leading accounting, tax, and consulting firm. The firm sponsored the completion of her professional CA designation. While obtaining her CA designation Karen worked on auditing. This involved visiting technology companies and analyzing their financial statements. After she passed the Universal Final Exam she began to specialize in the tax division at Deloitte & Touche. She took an in-depth two-year tax course offered by the Canadian Institute of Chartered Accountants. Her employer covered the costs of this course. Karen worked full-time for the next four years on corporate tax, personal tax, and expatriate tax (taxes applicable to Canadians who live in other countries).

Her schedule and expertise allowed her to take time off as she began to raise a family of four boys with her husband Bill. They were able to balance work schedules, while ensuring that they spent quality time with their young children.

Karen left Deloitte & Touche to join the federal government at Canada Customs and Revenue Agency. As a Senior Ruling Officer she works with corporate re-organizations. Her role is to interpret complex income tax provisions when large companies go through mergers or acquisitions. Her main clients are now CA firms and law firms.

This new experience is another stepping-stone in Karen's career path, as she becomes an expert in taxation. For many accountants becoming an expert in an area such as taxation leads to partnerships in accounting firms. Karen is currently happy with her work–life balance, and she takes advantage of income-averaging provisions so that she can take more time off to spend with her family while her children are young.

Karen has found that her CA designation allowed her to move into the government sector at a high level of pay and provided her with a variety of business opportunities to explore.

For Discussion

(a) What issues would Karen have dealt with in deciding whether to stay in the science program or switch to the business program? Would you be able to make a similar switch? Why or why not?

(b) How has Karen managed to improve her skills after completing her degree?

(c) How important is work–life balance to you? What steps can you take to balance a career with a family?

(d) Karen may one day become a partner in an accounting firm. Outline the steps that she has taken to provide herself with this type of opportunity.

Performance Task 7

PrimaVOX Call Centre

What Learning You Will Demonstrate
You will:

- demonstrate the ability to perform the duties of a payroll accountant;
- complete the payroll register for a company; and
- journalize and post payroll entries.

The Business

PrimaVOX operates a telemarketing call centre. Its employees call homes and businesses to telemarket (sell by telephone) products and services for other companies and organizations. Its clients include charities, rug-cleaning services, magazine publishers, sports teams, and restaurants.

The Task

You have the opportunity to obtain full-time summer employment with PrimaVOX Call Centre. You are requested to demonstrate your skills by performing the duties of a payroll accountant responsible for hourly rated workers. You will complete the payroll for four weeks in February, then journalize and post the entries to record the payroll. Your accurate, timely completion of this task determines whether you will be hired.

Procedure

1. (a) Complete the time cards and calculate the gross earnings for the week of February 6. The time card for B. M. Logan is done as an example on page 771.
   (b) Complete the February 6 payroll in the payroll journal.
   (c) Total and prove the payroll journal.
2. Prepare general journal entries to record:
   (a) The payroll for February 6
   (b) The employer's share of C.P.P. contributions, E.I. premiums, and E.H.T. (the rate is 1.223 percent)
   (c) The transfer of funds to the employees' bank accounts
3. Post the general journal entries to the general ledger. The accounts required are:
   101   Cash (balance $15 000)
   210   Wages Payable
   211   C.P.P. Payable
   212   E.I. Payable
   213   E.H.T. Payable
   214   Income Tax Payable
   215   R.P.P. Payable

216   Group Insurance Payable
217   Union Dues Payable
610   Wages Expense
611   C.P.P. Expense
612   E.I. Expense
613   E.H.T. Expense

4. For the week ended February 13, the gross earnings for the four employees are:

101	J. L. Carter	$704.00
102	P. S. Stelmach	728.00
103	A. A. Humphreys	688.00
104	B. M. Logan	692.30

(a) Complete the payroll journal for the week.
(b) Total and prove the payroll journal.
(c) Prepare general journal entries to record the payroll, the employer's share of C.P.P. contributions and E.I. premiums, the E.H.T., and the transfer of funds to the employees' bank accounts.
(d) Post the general journal entries.

5. For the week ended February 20, the gross earnings for the four employees are:

101	J. L. Carter	$734.60
102	P. S. Stelmach	728.00
103	A. A. Humphreys	755.30
104	B. M. Logan	688.00

(a) Complete the payroll journal for the week.
(b) Total and prove the payroll journal.
(c) Prepare general journal entries to record the payroll, the employer's share of C.P.P. contributions and E.I. premiums, the E.H.T., and the transfer of funds to the employees' bank accounts.
(d) Post the general journal entries.

6. For the week ended February 27, the gross earnings for the four employees are:

101	J. L. Carter	$756.80
102	P. S. Stelmach	755.30
103	A. A. Humphreys	739.60
104	B. M. Logan	726.70

(a) Complete the payroll journal for the week.
(b) Total and prove the payroll journal.
(c) Prepare general journal entries to record the payroll, the employer's share of C.P.P. contributions and E.I. premiums, the E.H.T., and the transfer of funds to the employees' bank accounts.
(d) Post the general journal entries.

7. Prepare the journal entries that would be made on March 15 to remit the February payroll deductions. Post these entries to the general ledger and total the accounts.

Materials Required

- Payroll information, Part A
- Time cards, Part B
- Payroll journal, general journal, and general ledger
- Payroll deduction tables

Assessment

Examine the assessment rubric. Note the descriptions of the performance criteria and the levels of achievement.

Evaluation

Will you be hired?

PART A

Payroll Information

Every employee pays weekly group insurance premiums of $0.20 per $1000 of insurance. Other weekly information is given in the following table:

Emp. No.	Name	Net Claim Code	Co. Pension	Union Dues	Group Insurance
101	J. L. Carter	1	$6.70	$5.50	$35 000
102	P. S. Stelmack	9	4.78	5.50	45 000
103	A. A. Humphreys	10	4.80	5.50	60 000
104	B. M. Logan	1	4.78	5.50	30 000

Payroll Rules

In calculating the hours worked, the following rules apply:

- Any time worked on Saturday or Sunday is paid at time and one-half.
- Time worked after 5:00 p.m. is overtime, paid at time and one-half. Record overtime in the Extra (in, out) columns of the time cards.
- Regular work hours are 8:00 a.m. to 12:00 noon and 1:00 p.m. to 5:00 p.m. Employees lose 15 minutes' pay if they are 2 to 15 minutes late, and 30 minutes' pay if they are 16 to 30 minutes late. The completed time card for B. M. Logan, Employee No. 104, illustrates how these rules are applied.

PART B

Time Cards

NO. 101 NAME J. L. Carter Regular Hours Overtime Hours				Pay Period Ending Feb. 6, 20— Regular Rate $17.60 Overtime Rate $26.40 Total Earnings		
	MORN	NOON	NOON	NIGHT	EXTRA		
	IN	OUT	IN	OUT	IN	OUT	HOURS
M	07:58	12:01	13:00	17:00			
T	08:00	12:01	13:00	17:00			
W	07:56	12:04	13:00	17:01	18:00	21:00	
T	07:59	12:03	12:55	17:01			
F	07:58	12:02	12:56	17:02			
S							
S							

NO. 102 NAME P. S. Stelmack Regular Hours Overtime Hours				Pay Period Ending Feb. 6, 20— Regular Rate $18.20 Overtime Rate $27.30 Total Earnings		
	MORN	NOON	NOON	NIGHT	EXTRA		
	IN	OUT	IN	OUT	IN	OUT	HOURS
M	07:59	12:01	12:59	17:01			
T	07:58	12:02	12:58	17:00	18:00	21:00	
W	08:02	12:01	13:02	17:02			
T	08:03	12:03	13:05	17:03			
F	07:59	12:01	13:00	17:05			
S							
S							

NO. 103
NAME A. A. Humphreys
Regular Hours
Overtime Hours

Pay Period Ending Feb. 6, 20—

Regular Rate $17.20
Overtime Rate $25.80
Total Earnings

	MORN	NOON	NOON	NIGHT	EXTRA		
	IN	OUT	IN	OUT	IN	OUT	HOURS
M			12:50	17:01			
T	07:59	12:00	12:51	17:02			
W	07:58	12:01	12:57	17:00	17:59	21:02	
T	07:57	12:04	12:55	17:05			
F	07:56	12:05	12:50	17:04			
S							
S							

NO. 104
NAME B. M. Logan
Regular Hours 35.75
Overtime Hours   3.0

Pay Period Ending Feb. 6, 20—

Regular Rate $17.20
Overtime Rate $25.80
Total Earnings $692.30

	MORN	NOON	NOON	NIGHT	EXTRA		
	IN	OUT	IN	OUT	IN	OUT	HOURS
M			12:52	17:02			4.0
T	08:00	12:00	13:04	17:02			7.75
W	07:55	12:02	13:00	17:01			8.0
T	07:58	12:01	12:59	17:00	18:00	21:01	8.0/3.0
F	07:58	12:02	12:59	17:01			8.0
S						Regular	35.75
S						O.T.	3.0

PrimaVOX Call Centre: Performance Task Rubric

Assessment Criteria	Levels of Achievement			
	Level 1	Level 2	Level 3	Level 4
KNOWLEDGE AND UNDERSTANDING • understanding of payroll records and procedures	Demonstrates limited understanding of terminology, concepts, procedures, and principles.	Demonstrates some understanding of terminology, concepts, procedures, and principles.	Demonstrates consider-able understanding of terminology, concepts, procedures, and principles.	Demonstrates thorough understanding of terminology, concepts, procedures, and principles.
THINKING AND INQUIRY • analysis of payroll information	Uses critical and interpretative skills with limited effectiveness.	Uses critical and interpretative skills with moderate effectiveness.	Uses critical and interpretative skills with considerable effectiveness.	Uses critical and interpretative skills with a high degree of effectiveness.
COMMUNICATION • completion of appropriate forms and statements	Communicates with minimal precision and clarity.	Communicates with some precision and clarity.	Communicates with considerable precision and clarity.	Communicates with complete and thorough precision and clarity.
APPLICATION • application of skills to prepare payroll register and to journalize and post entries	Uses skills with limited accuracy.	Uses skills with some accuracy.	Uses skills with considerable accuracy.	Uses skills with a high degree of accuracy.

15

Sole Proprietorships, Partnerships, Corporations, and Manufacturing Companies

UNIT 35 Sole Proprietorships and Partnerships

What Learning You Will Demonstrate

On completion of this unit, you will be able to:

- describe the advantages and disadvantages of a sole proprietorship and a partnership;

- compare the responsibilities of owners, shareholders, and partners in relation to the debt obligations of a business;

- summarize the nature of a partnership and each partner's responsibilities;

- evaluate the advantages and disadvantages of a limited partnership and a general partnership;

- explain each partner's share of equity by preparing a statement of changes in partners' equity; and

- demonstrate how profits and losses are shared by partners (fixed ratio, pro rata, and salaries).

In the first part of this book, most of the accounting theory involved businesses owned by one person. For example, Chapter 4 described the journal and ledger system used by K. Schmidt, the owner of Rainbow Painting Contractors. That business, which is owned by one person, is known as a *sole proprietorship*. Two other types of ownership are the *partnership* and the *corporation*.

In this unit we will review the advantages and disadvantages of sole proprietorships. Then we will outline the types of partnerships, their advantages and disadvantages, and some partnership accounting procedures.

SOLE PROPRIETORSHIPS

A sole proprietorship is a business owned by one person.

In a sole proprietorship, the proprietor has unlimited personal responsibility for the debts and legal obligations.

A **sole proprietorship** is a business owned by one person, who is legally responsible for all its debts and legal obligations. Many small businesses are sole proprietorships. These include small stores, restaurants, and many service businesses such as barbershops, T.V. repair firms, and hairstylists. In a sole proprietorship, the owner is personally liable for the debts of the company. This means that the owner's personal property is at risk if the business is in financial difficulty.

Advantages of Sole Proprietorships

- Pride of ownership
- Simplified decision-making
- Ease of formation and dissolution
- All net income to owner
- Freedom of action
- Personal satisfaction
- Privacy
- Possible tax savings

Disadvantages of Sole Proprietorship

- Unlimited personal liability
- Lack of continuity
- Limited capital
- Limited talent pool
- Heavy personal responsibilities

Taxation and the Sole Proprietorship

A sole proprietorship does not pay income tax on its net income. The owner must add the net income of the business to his or her personal income and then pay personal income tax on the total. There can be a tax advantage with this form of ownership when the combined net income is quite low. However, when net income becomes fairly high, there may be a tax advantage in switching to a corporate form of ownership.

PARTNERSHIPS

Two or more persons may find it worthwhile to combine their talents and money to form a partnership. Partnerships are frequently formed by doctors, lawyers, dentists, accountants, and small retail and service businesses. Some of the characteristics of the partnership are similar to those of the sole proprietorship. The net income or net loss belongs to the owners and they have unlimited personal liability for the debts of the business. Also, the net income of the business becomes the personal income of the individual partners for income tax purposes.

A partnership is a business owned by two or more persons.

Advantages of Partnerships

The partnership form of ownership overcomes some of the disadvantages of the sole proprietorship. In a partnership, two or more persons are available to share the work and the responsibilities. Between them, they may possess many of the skills and talents required to operate a business successfully. The partners each contribute personal savings and borrowing capacities to the business. In addition, the partners may complement each other and be able to combine to operate an efficient business.

Disadvantages of Partnerships

Both partners are responsible for the entire debts of the business. Unlimited personal liability is a disadvantage of a partnership just as it is for a sole proprietorship. When two people work closely together day in and day out and are responsible for the success of a business, there is a good possibility of personality conflict. Partners must be able to work with each other. If they cannot get along, it could be difficult to get out of the partnership unless they mutually agree to dissolve it. If one partner dies, the partnership may have to be dissolved to settle the estate of the deceased partner.

In a partnership, the partners have unlimited personal liability for the debts of the business.

The sharing of net income could be another disadvantage. In a sole proprietorship all net income belongs to the one owner. In a partnership, the partners must share the net income of the business. Disagreements may occur when a partner is not satisfied with his or her share. Sometimes a partner may feel that the other partners are not contributing enough effort to the business.

Advantages of Partnerships

- Ease of formation
- Low startup costs
- Additional sources of investment capital
- Shared work and responsibilities
- Broader management base

Disadvantages of Partnership

- Unlimited liability
- Lack of continuity
- Divided authority
- Difficult to find suitable partners
- Potential for conflict between partners

Limited Partnerships

One of the disadvantages of partnerships is unlimited personal liability. The *limited partnership* is a form of partnership without this disadvantage. A limited partnership has two types of partners—general partners and limited partners. At least one of the partners, the general partner(s), must assume unlimited liability for the debts of the partnership. The other partners have no personal liability except for their investment. Usually, the general partners manage the limited partnership. The other partners invest in the business but have little or no part in running it.

General Partnerships

Partnerships in which all partners have unlimited liability are called general partnerships.

Accounting Procedures for Partnerships

Two or more persons may agree orally or in writing to establish a partnership. Each of the provinces has a Partnership Act, which establishes rules and regulations for partnerships. It is a general practice to prepare a written contract of partnership. This partnership agreement outlines the rights and responsibilities of each of the parties concerned.

Partnerships and Income Taxes

As a business, a partnership does not pay income taxes on its net income. Each partner is taxed on his or her share of the partnership's income, in addition to any income received from other sources.

Ledger Accounts of a Partnership

The accounts in the ledger of a partnership are the same as those of a sole proprietorship, except that there is one Drawings account and one Capital account for *each* partner.

Drawings Accounts

The Drawings account of each partner is used in the same way in a partnership as in a sole proprietorship. Drawings is debited whenever a partner withdraws assets from the business. Typical transactions that involve Drawings accounts are:

- payment of salaries to partners;
- withdrawal of assets or cash by a partner; and
- payments of a personal nature for a partner using partnership funds.

It should be emphasized that salaries paid to partners during the year *must* be recorded in the Drawings accounts. They cannot be treated as a company expense and debited to Salaries Expense. One of the difficulties encountered by accountants is to decide if a transaction involves a legitimate business expense or should be treated as a personal withdrawal and recorded in the owner's Drawings account. Personal expenses charged to the business have the effect of lowering the net income of the business and, in the long run, the income taxes paid by the owners. By charging expenses to the business, owners can obtain free fringe benefits illegally.

Closing the Partnership Books

In a sole proprietorship, revenue and expense accounts are closed into the Income Summary account. The balance in Income Summary would be the net income or the net loss. This balance is then transferred to the owner's Capital account. The owner's Drawings account is then closed into the Capital account.

   The books of a partnership are closed in a similar way but with one difference. The balance in Income Summary is closed into each partner's Capital account according to the partnership agreement for dividing net income and net loss.

Dividing Net Income

Partners may make any agreement they wish for the division of the partnership's net income or net loss. One of the most important clauses of the partnership contract is the one stating how these will be shared. Four factors considered by partners are:

The partnership agreement states how net income or net losses are to be shared.

- payment for amount of work performed;
- return on capital;
- amount of capital invested; and
- individual skills, talent, and reputation.

Payment for Amount of Work Performed

Suppose one partner is very actively engaged in running the business, while another contributes money but does not work in the business. It seems fair that the working partner should be paid for the work performed. In some partnerships both partners work in the business, but one has a more responsible position or puts in more hours of work than the other. In preparing the partnership agreement, the partners may consider the amount of work performed in deciding how to share net income or net loss.

Return on Capital

If a partner invested money in government bonds, term deposits, or mortgages, interest would be earned on that money. Likewise, if a partner invests in a partnership, it seems reasonable to pay interest on the money invested. This is especially so when one partner invests more funds in the partnership than the other(s).

Amount of Capital Invested

If partners contribute an equal amount of money, work, time, and skills to a partnership, it seems fair to distribute net income equally to the partners. However, if one of the partners contributes more money, that partner could expect to receive a greater share. Suppose one partner contributes $50 000 and another partner contributes $100 000. The second partner could demand a greater share of net income because of the larger investment.

Individual Skills, Talent, and Reputation

Sometimes partners use factors such as individual skills, talent, and reputation to decide how to share net income or net losses. It can be argued that if a net income is earned it is because of the personal contributions of the partners.

Methods of Dividing Net Income or Net Loss

Among the many methods used to divide net income and net loss are:

- fixed ratio;
- capital ratio;
- salaries, and remaining net income (or net loss) to partners in a fixed ratio; and
- interest on capital, salaries, and remaining net income (or net loss) to partners in a fixed ratio.

Fixed Ratio

On forming their partnership, R. Ullmann and B. McArthur agreed to divide net income and net loss equally. Thus, 50 percent of net income will belong to Ullmann and 50 percent to McArthur. They felt that a 1 : 1 ratio was fair since both contributed the same amount of capital, both would work full-time in the business, and both had special skills to offer to the new business. At year-end, net income is $90 000. According to the partnership agreement, this amount is divided equally. When the books are closed, the division is made by the following entry:

Dec.	31	Income Summary	90 0 0 0 00	
		R. Ullmann, Capital		45 0 0 0 00
		B. McArthur, Capital		45 0 0 0 00
		To divide the net income equally between partners, per partnership agreement.		

Capital Ratio

The capital ratio method is used when the success of the business depends to some extent on the contribution of capital. In some businesses, such as automobile dealerships, substantial investments in equipment, buildings, and merchandise are required. The capital ratio method recognizes the importance of capital to the business and divides the net income or net loss accordingly.

J. Ibarra and D. Amato have invested $200 000 and $400 000, respectively, in their partnership. They agree to share net income and net loss in the ratio of their beginning capital. The ratio is determined as follows:

	Beginning Capital	Percentage of Total
J. Ibarra	$200 000	33.3%
D. Amato	400 000	66.7%
Total	$600 000	100.0%

Ibarra receives 33.3 percent of any net income and Amato receives 66.7 percent. They share net losses in the same way, that is, in the ratio of 33.3 : 66.7. Suppose there is net income of $100 000. The division of the net income would be calculated as follows:

		Share of Net Income
J. Ibarra	0.333 × $100 000 =	$ 33 330
D. Amato	0.667 × $100 000 =	66 700
	Total	$100 000

The entry to record the division of net income is:

Dec.	31	Income Summary	100 0 0 0 00	
		J. Ibarra, Capital		33 3 0 0 00
		D. Amato, Capital		66 7 0 0 00
		To divide the net income equally between partners, per partnership agreement.		

Salaries and Remaining Profits in a Fixed Ratio

In their partnership agreement, F. Chari and B. Yew agreed to the following:

- A salary of $50 000 is to be paid to Chari and $60 000 is to be paid to Yew per year.
- Any remaining net income after salaries is to be shared equally.

At the end of the year, there is a net income of $150 000. A special report called a *statement of distribution of net income* is prepared, as shown in Figure 15-1.

Chari & Yew Security Services **Statement of Distribution of Net Income**			
Net Income To Be Divided			$150 000
	Chari	**Yew**	**Totals**
Salaries	$50 000	$60 000	$110 000
Remaining Income Shared Equally	20 000	20 000	40 000
Totals	$70 000	$80 000	$150 000

FIGURE 15-1 Statement of distribution of net income for two partners, F. Chari and B. Yew

Interest, Salaries, and Fixed Ratio

In forming their partnership, W. Gordon and W. Mugabe agreed on the following division of net income and net loss:

- Each partner is to receive a $50 000 salary per year.
- Each partner is to be credited from net income annually with 12 percent interest on the beginning capital. Gordon invested $75 000 and Mugabe invested $125 000.
- Any remaining net income or net loss after interest and salaries is to be divided equally.

In the last fiscal year, the partnership earned net income of $150 000. The statement of distribution of net income was prepared to divide the net income.

Gordon & Mugabe Company
Statement of Distribution of Net Income

	Gordon	Mugabe	Totals
Net Income To Be Divided			$150 000
Salaries	$50 000	$50 000	$100 000
12% Interest on Beginning Capital	9 000	15 000	24 000
Remaining Income Shared Equally	13 000	13 000	26 000
Totals	$72 000	$78 000	$150 000

FIGURE 15-2 Statement of distribution of net income to W. Gordon and W. Mugabe

Dividing Net Loss and Insufficient Net Income

In each of the situations discussed to this point, there was a net income large enough to give each partner what was owed according to the partnership agreement.

However, businesses often suffer losses or do not earn enough net income to pay the partners according to the agreement. Two examples of such situations follow.

J. Ibarra and D. Amato agreed to share net income and net loss in the ratio of their beginning capital balances. This ratio was 33.3 : 66.7. This means that if there is a net loss, Ibarra absorbs 33.3 percent of the net loss and Amato absorbs 66.7 percent. Suppose the partnership suffers a net loss of $30 000. The division of the net loss would be calculated as follows:

		Share of Net Loss
J. Ibarra	0.333 × $30 000 =	$ 9 990
D. Amato	0.667 × $30 000 =	20 010
	Total	$30 000

The entry to record this division of the net loss is:

Dec.	31	J. Ibarra, Capital	9 9 9 0 00	
		D. Amato, Capital	20 0 1 0 00	
		Income Summary		30 0 0 0 00
		To close the Income Summary account		
		and to divide the net loss between the		
		partners, per partnership agreement.		

Partners' Salaries

Journal entries that involve partners' salaries occur in two ways. During the year, a debit entry is made to the individual Drawings accounts each time salaries are paid to the partners and whenever personal withdrawals are made. Another entry is made to the Capital accounts at the end of the year when the net income or net loss is divided between the partners. For example, suppose Creaco and Costanza invest $18 000 each and become partners in a web page design business. Their partnership agreement states that they are to receive salaries and to share equally any remaining net income or net loss after salaries. Each receives a salary of $60 000 per year. Once a month, each partner receives a cheque for $5000. By the end of the year, each partner will have received cash payments (salary) of $60 000.

Suppose the partnership earned net income of $150 000 for the year. According to the partnership agreement, the partners share this $150 000 by:

- receiving salaries of $60 000 each (total $120 000); and
- sharing the remainder ($30 000) equally.

When the salaries are paid to the partners each month, this entry is made:

Jul.	31	Creaco, Drawings	5 0 0 0 00	
		Costanza, Drawings	5 0 0 0 00	
		Cash		10 0 0 0 00
		Paid partners' salaries.		

After the end of the year, Drawings are closed to Income Summary. Then, the remaining profit is distributed to the partners and this entry is made:

Jan.	15	Income Summary	30 0 0 0 00	
		Creaco, Capital		15 0 0 0 00
		Costanza, Capital		15 0 0 0 00
		To distribute the remaining profit		
		($30 000) to the partners.		

Financial Statements

In a partnership, the following four financial statements may be prepared:

- the income statement;
- the statement of distribution of net income;
- the balance sheet; and
- the statement of changes in partners' equity.

Income Statement

The income statement of a partnership is very similar to that of a sole proprietorship. However, a section may be added to the bottom to show the division of the net income or net loss.

Statement of Distribution of Net Income

If the division of the net income or net loss is not shown as a note to the income statement, a *statement of distribution of net income* is prepared (see Figure 15-2 on page 780). This more formal report may be especially practical when there are salaries, interest, and a remainder of net income or loss to be divided.

Balance Sheet

There are at least two people in every partnership. For every partner there is a Capital account, which appears in the equity section of the balance sheet.

Statement of Changes in Partners' Equity

Partners are usually interested in seeing the changes in their Capital accounts from year to year. A *statement of changes in partners' equity* provides this information (see Figure 15-3). This information could be placed in the equity section of the balance sheet if it does not make the balance sheet unduly long.

The statement of changes in partners' equity shows additional investments in the business during the year, all withdrawals, and each partner's share of the net income or net loss.

Peresh & Pham Company
Statement of Changes in Partners' Equity
For the year ended December 31, 20—

	Peresh	Pham	Totals
Capital, January 1	$ 75 000	$100 000	$175 000
Add: Additional Investment	1 5 000	15 000	30 000
Share of Net Income	72 000	78 000	150 000
Totals	162 000	193 000	355 000
Less: Withdrawals	60 000	60 000	120 000
Total Capital, December 31	$102 000	$133 000	$235 000

FIGURE 15-3 Statement of changes in partners' equity for Peresh & Pham Company

UNIT 35 CHECK YOUR READING

Questions

1. Explain what the following mean:
   (a) *Sole proprietorship*
   (b) *Partnership*
   (c) *Limited partnership*
2. Explain the term *unlimited personal liability*.
3. If a sole proprietorship does not pay income tax on its net income, how does the net income get taxed?
4. How many persons may form a partnership?
5. Give three advantages and three disadvantages of sole proprietorships and partnerships.
6. List the three main items you think should be included in a partnership agreement.
7. Explain how income tax is paid on the income of a partnership.
8. Which account is used to record the payment of salaries to partners?
9. What accounts are debited and credited when a partner withdraws merchandise from the business for personal use?
10. In closing partnership books at the end of a fiscal period, into which accounts are the following closed?
    (a) The balance of the Income Summary account
    (b) The revenue and expense totals
    (c) The Drawings account
11. Y. Chow and K. Wong use the ratio of beginning capital balances as their method of dividing net income. Chow's capital balance is $75 000 and Wong's is $60 000. In what ratio is the net income divided?
12. Name the four financial statements that may be prepared for a partnership.

UNIT 35 APPLY YOUR KNOWLEDGE

Exercises

1. (a) Prepare general journal entries to record these transactions for R. Ullmann and B. McArthur:

   May 10 McArthur withdrew $150 cash for personal use.
       12 Ullmann took home merchandise worth $75, GST Refundable $5.25.
       31 Paid salaries of $1000 to each partner.

   Jun. 15 Paid $75 for golf lessons for Ullmann's daughter.
       30 Paid partners' salaries, $1000 each.

   Jul. 25 Ullmann invested an additional $5000 in the business.

(b) After closing the expense and revenue accounts, there is a $19 000 credit balance in the Income Summary account. This net income is to be divided equally between Ullmann and McArthur. Prepare the general journal entry to close Income Summary and to divide the net income between the partners.

(c) Ullmann's Drawings account has a debit balance of $6000 and McArthur's has a debit balance of $8000. Prepare the general journal entry to close the Drawings accounts.

(d) The next year, the firm of Ullmann & McArthur Services incurs a net loss of $7000. This is represented by a debit balance in the Income Summary account. Prepare the general journal entry to close Income Summary and to divide the net loss equally.

2. (a) M. Stewart and K. Steiner divide net income and net loss according to the ratio of their beginning capital balances. Stewart has a capital balance of $50 000 and Steiner has $75 000. What ratio is used?

(b) Use the ratio from part (a) to calculate how much is received by each partner if the net income is $46 000.

(c) If Stewart and Steiner incurred a net loss of $30 000, how much of the net loss would be shared by each partner?

3. J. Ibarra and D. Amato divide net income from their partnership in the ratio of their capital. The ratio is 33.3 : 66.7.

(a) The net income or net loss for each of three years follows. For each year, determine how much of the net income or net loss is allocated to Ibarra and how much is allocated to Amato.

Year I	Net income	$10 000
Year II	Net loss	16 000
Year III	Net income	60 000

(b) Prepare general journal entries to close the Income Summary account and to divide the net income or net loss each year.

4. F. Chari and B. Yew divide net income and net loss on the following basis:
   • Chari's salary is $42 000 and Yew's salary is $50 000.
   • Any remaining net income or net loss after salaries is shared equally.

(a) Prepare a statement of distribution of net income for each of these years:

Year I	Net income	$ 95 000
Year II	Net income	100 000
Year III	Net income	120 000

(b) Prepare general journal entries to distribute the net income each year.

5. W. Gordon and W. Mugabe share the net income of their partnership in the following manner:

- Salaries are $50 000 each.
- Interest on beginning capital is 12 percent. Gordon's capital is $75 000, while Mugabe's is $125 000.
- The remaining net income or net loss after salaries and interest is shared equally.

(a) Prepare a statement of distribution of net income for each of these years:

Year I	Net income	$110 000
Year II	Net income	130 000
Year III	Net loss	10 000

(b) Prepare general journal entries to distribute the net income or net loss each year.

6. Prepare a statement of changes in partners' equity for J. Klemba and T. Swords on December 31, using this information:
- January 1 capital balances: Klemba $30 000; Swords $40 000
- Additional investment: Klemba $5000
- Withdrawals: Klemba $18 000; Swords $21 000
- Share of net income: Klemba $18 000; Swords $21 000

7. Prepare a December 31 statement of changes in partners' equity for P. Doyle and M. Durivage, using this information:
- January 1 capital balances: Doyle $20 000; Durivage $15 000
- Additional investment: $7000 each
- Withdrawals: Doyle $12 000; Durivage $11 000
- Share of net income: Doyle $20 000; Durivage $16 000

UNIT 36 The Corporation

What Learning You Will Demonstrate

On completion of this unit, you will be able to:

- describe the advantages and disadvantages of a corporation;
- describe the principles of unlimited liability and limited liability;
- outline the differences between a private and a public corporation;
- prepare a statement of retained earnings; and
- distinguish the accounting elements particular to a corporation.

THE CORPORATION

What Is a Corporation?

A corporation has a legal existence of its own.

A corporation has a legal existence of its own. It is separate from its owners, so it has the right to sue and can be sued by others.

Advantages of the Corporate Form of Ownership

Limited liability of the owners is an important advantage of the corporate form of ownership. However, there are several other advantages too. A corporation has access to more capital and it may sell shares if it requires more financing. Also, corporations probably will be able to borrow more funds than partners or proprietors. And finally, a corporation does not cease to exist if an owner dies or wishes to get out of the business. The owner may sell the shares that represent the portion of the business that he or she owns and the business will continue to operate.

Limited Liability

The sole proprietorship and partnership forms of ownership have several disadvantages. One of these is illustrated by the following example:

> *John Bowers operated a very successful business as a sole proprietorship for 15 years. Through hard work and good management, John's company earned substantial net income for him. Over the years, John invested the money earned by his business by purchasing a cottage, two expensive cars, and several apartment buildings, which he rented out.*

> *However, his business suddenly became unprofitable as new products and competitors caused several large losses in consecutive years. John's business was unable to pay a number of debts on time and, as a result, the business was forced into bankruptcy. To pay off his creditors, John was ordered by the court to sell his cottage and the apartment buildings. John had to do so despite the fact that the properties belonged to him, personally, not to his business.*

The owner of a sole proprietorship is personally responsible for its debts.

> *John was personally liable for all the business debts. He lost his business investment and most of his personal assets.*

The case of John Bowers illustrates a major disadvantage of partnerships and sole proprietorships: unlimited liability. It also indirectly points out one of the advantages of forming a corporation: limited liability.

In the corporate form of ownership, an investor risks his or her investment in the business, but not personal assets. Limited liability is an important advantage of the corporate form of ownership. Because of this characteristic, the term *limited company* is often used instead of *corporation*.

In a corporation, the owners' liability is limited to their investment in the corporation.

Disadvantages of the Corporate Form of Ownership

A corporation is more complicated to form than a partnership or a sole proprietorship. This is due to the legal requirements imposed by governments. A lawyer is generally required and startup costs can be high. Shareholders elect a board of directors and the directors hire managers to operate the business. The decision-making process can get complicated when persons with many shares wish to be involved in the business operations. Also, employees of a corporation may not be as dedicated, loyal, or industrious as the owners of a sole proprietorship or a partnership. As a result, it may cost a corporation more to operate.

Advantages of Corporations

- Limited liability
- Specialized management
- Transferrable ownership
- Continuous business existence
- Separate legal entity
- Possible tax advantage (i.e., lower small business tax)
- Easier access to capital

Disadvantages of Corporations

- More legal requirements; closely regulated
- Most expensive form to organize
- Extensive record keeping required
- Double taxation of dividends

Forming a Corporation

A corporation is formed by applying to a provincial government or to the federal government for a certificate of incorporation. The application, signed by one or more persons, must include the following information:

- the name and address of the corporation;
- the types and number of shares to be authorized for issue;
- the number of directors; and
- the nature of the business to be conducted.

Generally, a corporation that will do business in only one province will apply to that province for incorporation. A business that will operate in more than one province usually applies to the federal government for incorporation.

Corporation Name

Have you ever wondered why so many businesses use Limited or Ltd. in their names? The reason for this is that the corporation laws require the words *Limited, Limitée, Incorporated,* or *Incorporée* to be part of the name. The short forms *Ltd., Ltée., Corp.,* or *Inc.* may also be used. Other requirements for the corporation name are:

- the proposed name must differ from that of any other Canadian business;
- the name must be acceptable to the public; and
- the name must be clearly displayed in all contracts, invoices, and other negotiable transactions involving the corporation.

After the application has been accepted by the government and the incorporation fee paid, the limited company or corporation comes into existence. The persons who applied for incorporation receive a *charter* or *certificate of incorporation* if issued by the federal government, or a similar form depending on the province involved.

Once a business is incorporated, a meeting of shareholders is held to elect a board of directors of the corporation. The directors, being responsible for the operation of the corporation, then hire people to manage the business. Shares are sold or exchanged for assets and the company is in business.

> A board of directors is a group of persons, elected by the shareholders, who are responsible for the operation of the corporation.

Types of Business Corporations

There are two types of business corporations:

- private corporations; and
- public corporations.

Private Corporations

Private business corporations are limited in the number of shareholders they may have and in the way they raise capital. They may not have more than 50 shareholders and must obtain funds privately. Corporate shares and bonds may not be sold to the public. Many small sole proprietorships and partnerships are transformed into private corporations for the owners to take advantage of the limited liability feature of corporations. The owners still control and own the business, yet protect their personal assets.

Public Corporations

Public business corporations can have any number of shareholders. They can also sell shares and bonds to the public.

Share Certificates

> A share certificate is a form issued by a corporation indicating the number of shares owned.

Shares represent ownership: anyone who invests in a corporation buys a portion, or a share, of the corporation. A share certificate is a form issued by a corporation showing the number of shares owned. The person purchasing the shares is called a shareholder. The terms *stock* and *stockholder* are sometimes used in place of *share* and *shareholder*.

Accounting Procedures for Corporations

Shareholders' Equity Accounts

The books and accounts of corporations are similar to those of sole proprietorships and partnerships, except for differences in the equity section. The equity accounts in a sole proprietorship or partnership are the owner's *Capital* and *Drawings accounts*. The comparable accounts in a corporation are the *Share Capital account* and the *Retained Earnings account*.

The equity section of a corporate balance sheet is shown in Figure 15-4. In the corporate form of ownership there are no *Drawings* accounts. The shareholders of a corporation may not withdraw assets. They may, however, receive a portion of the corporate net income in the form of *dividends*.

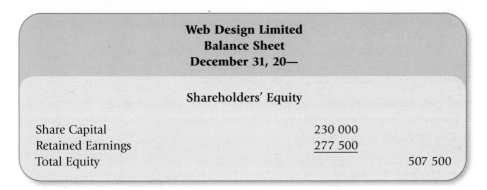

Web Design Limited
Balance Sheet
December 31, 20—

Shareholders' Equity

Share Capital	230 000	
Retained Earnings	277 500	
Total Equity		507 500

FIGURE 15-4 The shareholders' equity section of a corporate balance sheet

Note that in this simplified balance sheet, there are two new accounts in the equity section. *Share Capital* is a record of money received from the sale of shares. Retained Earnings contains the balance of net income earned by the corporation after dividends have been paid.

Corporate Net Income

The net income of a corporation increases the shareholders' equity. The decision about what happens to the net income is made by the board of directors. The board has several alternatives:

- distribute all of the net income to the shareholders;
- leave all of the net income in the corporation; or
- a combination of the above—leave part of the net income in the business and distribute part to the shareholders.

Shareholders do not participate directly in deciding what is done with corporate net income. However, if they are not satisfied with the decision of the board of directors, they can make their displeasure known at the annual shareholders' meeting. Every business corporation must hold a meeting of shareholders each year. At this meeting, the board of directors is elected by the shareholders. If enough shareholders are displeased with the operation of the corporation, some or all of the directors may be replaced. Elections are based on a majority vote of shareholders, with one vote allowed for each share owned.

Dividends

Generally speaking, the owners of a sole proprietorship or partnership may withdraw money from their business as they wish. The Drawings account is a record of such withdrawals.

There is no opportunity for shareholders in a corporation to withdraw cash in the way that proprietors or partners do. Because of the limited liability feature of corporations, creditors must be protected from the possibility of corporate owners withdrawing the assets and leaving no funds for the payment of corporate debts. Were that to occur, the creditors would lose their investment since shareholders are not personally liable for the corporation's debts.

Dividends are the portion of a corporation's net income paid to the shareholders.

The portion of a corporation's net income distributed to shareholders is called a dividend. Corporate law allows dividends to be paid to owners, or shareholders, only out of accumulated net income. The accumulated net income is recorded in Retained Earnings. This account appears in the shareholders' equity section of the balance sheet (see Figure 15-5). If there is a positive balance (i.e., a credit balance) in this account, dividends may be declared.

Closing the Books of a Corporation

The closing phase of the accounting cycle for corporations is very similar to the closing phase for partnerships and sole proprietorships. The steps in closing the books include:

1. Close revenue and expense accounts into Income Summary.
2. Close the Income Summary balance (which is the net income or net loss) into Retained Earnings.

The Retained Earnings account is an equity account that contains the balance of undistributed net income.

There is no change in the Share Capital account. The Retained Earnings balance represents the accumulated net income (credit balance) or net loss (debit balance) of the corporation. It presents a historical picture of the company's profitability.

If dividends are to be paid, Retained Earnings must have a credit balance. Dividends may be paid in a year when the corporation has sustained a loss, as long as the net income from previous years still leaves a credit balance in Retained Earnings.

Distributing Dividends

Dividends are paid out of retained earnings.

On June 15, the board of directors made a decision to pay a dividend on each of the outstanding shares of Web Design Limited. The dividend would be $2 per share to all owners on record as of June 25. The dividend cheques would be issued on July 10. This entry is made on June 15 to establish a liability on the corporate books:

Jun.	15	Retained Earnings	20 0 0 0 00	
		Dividends Payable		20 0 0 0 00
		Declared a $2 dividend on the 10 000		
		outstanding shares.		

This entry decreases shareholders' equity because some of the accumulated net income will be taken out of the business. The debit to Retained Earnings reduces the equity. This entry also establishes a current liability, *Dividends Payable*.

On July 10, cheques are issued to the shareholders of record on June 25. The entry to record the payment is:

Jul.	10	Dividends Payable	20 0 0 0 00	
		Cash		20 0 0 0 00
		Issued dividend cheques to shareholders.		

Figure 15-5 shows the shareholders' equity section of Web Design's balance sheet after several years of profitable operation.

Shareholders' Equity		
Share Capital:		
Authorized 20 000 shares		
Issued 10 000 shares	450 000	
Retained Earnings	277 500	
Total Equity		727 500

FIGURE 15-5 Shareholders' equity portion of Web Design's balance sheet

The balance of $277 500 in Retained Earnings indicates that a net income has been earned and that not all of the net income was distributed in the form of dividends.

Statement of Retained Earnings

The shareholders' equity section shown in Figure 15-5 indicates a Retained Earnings balance of $277 500 at the end of the fiscal period. However, it does not show the beginning balance or changes during the year. A supporting schedule called a statement of retained earnings provides a complete description of the changes in the Retained Earnings account (see Figure 15-6).

The statement of retained earnings provides a complete description of changes in the Retained Earnings account.

Web Design Limited	
Statement of Retained Earnings	
December 31, 20—	
Retained Earnings, January 1, 20—	$230 000
Add: Net Income for the Year	67 500
Total	297 500
Less: Dividends	20 000
Retained Earnings, December 31, 20—	$277 500

FIGURE 15-6 Statement of retained earnings showing changes to the Retained Earnings account

The statement of retained earnings shows the beginning balance, the net income added, the dividends paid, and the ending balance in Retained Earnings. A statement of retained earnings is prepared in addition to the income statement and the balance sheet.

Corporate Income Tax

A corporation has a legal existence of its own and is a taxpayer. A corporation pays income tax on its net income to the federal government (38 percent at time of writing) and to the provinces in which it earns income (10 percent to 13 percent, depending on the province). A special federal income tax rate is available to small Canadian-owned corporations. This, if applicable, results in a small Canadian business paying income tax at a rate of 12 percent on the first $200 000 of taxable income. Special accounting procedures must be followed if the reduced rate is to be obtained.

Corporate income tax rules and procedures are complex. The income tax form completed each year is called the T2. Details on corporate income tax can be obtained from booklet T 4012, *The T2 Guide to Corporate Income Tax*. The Canada Customs and Revenue Agency web site (www.ccra-adrc.gc.ca) is also a source of information.

Three provinces, Ontario, Alberta, and Quebec, require corporations to complete a separate provincial income tax return. For other provinces, a joint federal–provincial return is completed.

The income tax paid by a corporation is an expense of operating the business and appears as a deduction on the income statement, as shown in Figure 15-7.

Web Design Limited		
Income Statement		
For the year ending December 31, 20—		
Revenue		
Sales		$350 000
Expenses		
Selling	$200 000	
Administrative	70 000	270 000
Operating Income		80 000
Other Income		
Investments		10 000
Net Income before Income Taxes		90 000
Income Taxes		22 500
Net Income after Income Taxes		$ 67 500

FIGURE 15-7 Income statement

Web Design Limited had a net income of $90 000 *before* income taxes. From the information on the income statement, there was a net income of $67 500 *after* taxes. This $67 500 is the increase in shareholders' equity as a result of the year's activity and appears on the statement of retained earnings, as shown in Figure 15-6. Figure 15-6 also shows that $20 000 in dividends was distributed to the shareholders during the year.

The Stock Market

The stock market is a place where shares in a corporation are bought and sold after they have been issued. It is a place where a shareholder who wishes to sell shares may find a buyer willing to purchase the shares. Large public corporations such as Ford Motor Company of Canada, Inco, and Nortel Networks know it is important to make it easy for the public to buy and sell their shares. One reason for this is that these corporations may wish to expand their operations. Expansion requires financing, which can be obtained by issuing more shares.

To facilitate this process, large public corporations list their companies on a *stock exchange*, where shares are bought and sold. To be listed on a stock exchange, a corporation must follow detailed regulations and must provide the public with much information concerning the operation of the company. In Canada, there are stock exchanges in Calgary, Toronto, and Montreal. *Stockbrokers* act as agents for those who wish to buy and sell shares. The brokers will arrange a sale or a purchase in return for a commission. As well as handling sales of shares between buyers and sellers, stockbrokers sell large blocks of new shares for corporations in need of funds.

UNIT 36 CHECK YOUR READING

Questions

13. Give three advantages and disadvantages of the corporate form of ownership.

14. Explain what is meant by *a corporation has a legal existence of its own.*

15. (a) Why do creditors need to know whether the company applying for credit is a corporation?

 (b) Why must the name of the corporation be clearly displayed in all contracts, invoices, and other transactions?

16. Web Design Limited is a corporation, not a partnership. How does the public know this?

17. What is the board of directors?

18. What is the difference between a private and a public business corporation?

19. What form indicates that a person owns part of a corporation?

20. Name the two main equity accounts in the shareholders' equity section of a corporation's balance sheet.

21. What information does the Retained Earnings account provide?

22. What are the three options for distributing the net income of a corporation?

23. Who decides what will be done with the net income of a corporation?

24. What is the portion of a corporation's net income that is paid to the shareholders called?

25. What account is used to record the accumulated net income of a business?

26. Into which account are the revenue and expense accounts of a corporation closed?

27. Into which account is the Income Summary balance closed?

28. What does the balance in the Retained Earnings account represent?

29. (a) What effect do dividends declared have on the Retained Earnings account?

(b) What effect does net income have on the Retained Earnings account?

(c) What effect does a net loss have on the Retained Earnings account?

UNIT 36 APPLY YOUR KNOWLEDGE

Exercises

8. PC Parts Limited had a net income after income taxes of $100 000 for the year ended December 31, 20—. Income taxes paid were $25 000. Dividends totalling $30 000 were declared by the board of directors on November 15 and paid on December 1. The balance in the Share Capital account on January 1 was $500 000 and the balance in the Retained Earnings account was $70 000.
(a) Prepare the journal entries to record the declaration and the payment of the dividends.
(b) Prepare a statement of retained earnings.

9. Prepare the shareholders' equity section of a balance sheet from the following:
• A total of 500 000 shares were issued with a total value of $300 000.
• The Retained Earnings balance is $65 000.

10. Prepare a statement of retained earnings and the shareholders' equity section of the balance sheet dated April 30, 20—, for Brookfield Products Ltd.
• shares issued, 2630 valued at $263 000
• Retained Earnings, beginning balance April 1, $75 000
• net income, $60 000

11. The trial balance for Ashford Co. Ltd. follows.
(a) What is the net income before income taxes?
(b) What is the net income after income taxes? Use a 25 percent tax rate.
(c) Prepare a statement of retained earnings using this information:
• dividends paid, $80 000
• beginning balance for Retained Earnings, $210 000
• net income after taxes, $375 000

Ashford Co. Ltd.
Trial Balance
May 31, 20—

	Debits	Credits
Cash	$ 20 000	
Other Assets	940 000	
Liabilities		$ 30 000
Share Capital		300 000
Retained Earnings		130 000
Sales		2 000 000
Selling Expense	1 100 000	
Administrative Expense	300 000	
Other Expenses	100 000	
	$2 460 000	$2 460 000

UNIT 37 The Manufacturing Company

What Learning You Will Demonstrate

On completion of this unit, you will be able to:

- describe the difference between service, merchandising, and manufacturing companies;
- distinguish the accounting elements particular to a manufacturing company; and
- prepare a manufacturing statement.

TYPES OF BUSINESS OPERATIONS

Service Companies

All companies sell something, be it a product or a service. A *service company* sells a service such as Internet access, a repair service, business consulting, or entertainment. Service companies offer services to their customers. They do not sell products such as mouthwash or tires; they sell services.

To calculate the net income for a service business, expenses are subtracted from revenue. This calculation is illustrated by the equation:

$$\text{Revenue} \ - \ \text{Expenses} \ = \ \text{Net Income}$$

Merchandising Companies

A *merchandising company* sells a tangible product such as clothes, appliances, furniture, or sports equipment. However it does not make the product; it purchases the product from a manufacturer. A merchandising company must buy and pay for the merchandise it sells, as well as pay the expenses of operating the business. The following two equations illustrate how net income is calculated for a merchandising company:

| Revenue | − | Cost of Goods Sold | = | Gross Profit |
| Gross Profit | − | Expenses | = | Net Income |

Net income occurs when revenue from sales exceeds both the cost of goods sold and the operating expenses.

Manufacturing Companies

A manufacturing company makes a product.

A manufacturing company makes a product. In this section, we will examine the elements particular to a manufacturing business.

   The equations that illustrate how net income is calculated for a manufacturing company are the same as for a merchandising company:

| Revenue | − | Cost of Goods Sold | = | Gross Profit |
| Gross Profit | − | Expenses | = | Net Income |

**Cost of Goods Sold
Manufacturing Company**

Beginning Finished Goods Inventory	$350 000
Cost of Goods Manufactured (see manufacturing statement)	75 000
Goods Available for Sale	425 000
Ending Finished Goods Inventory	60 000
Cost of Goods Sold	365 000

FIGURE 15-8 Calculating the cost of goods sold for a manufacturing company

However, there are differences in the procedures for determining the cost of goods sold. Figure 15-8 illustrates a condensed cost of goods sold section for a manufacturing company. A key element in determining the cost of goods sold for a merchandising business is the schedule of cost of goods sold (see page 280). The comparable statement for a manufacturing company is the manufacturing statement. Notice the following differences.

Merchandising Company	Manufacturing Company
Beginning merchandise inventory	Beginning finished goods inventory
Cost of goods purchased	Cost of goods manufactured
Ending merchandise inventory	Ending finished goods inventory
Schedule of cost of goods sold	Manufacturing statement
Cost of goods sold	Cost of goods sold

The Manufacturing Statement

The manufacturing statement is a supporting schedule or statement that shows the cost of goods manufactured during a period. The cost of goods manufactured is used in the cost of goods sold section of the manufacturing company's income statement. There are three major components in the manufacturing statement: direct materials, direct labour, and overhead. Figure 15-9 is a sample manufacturing statement for a maker of computer components.

The manufacturing statement is a supporting schedule or statement that shows the cost of goods manufactured during a period.

PC Parts Limited
Manufacturing Statement
For the Year Ending December 31, 20—

Direct Materials		
Materials Inventory, January 1, 20—		$ 25 000
Purchases of Materials	$175 000	
Transportation on Materials	16 000	
Cost of Materials Purchased		191 000
Materials Available for Use		216 000
Materials Inventory, December 31, 20—		30 000
Total Materials Used		186 000
Direct Labour		200 000
Overhead		
Indirect Labour	20 000	
Factory Utilities	12 000	
Factory Equipment Repairs	5 000	
Factory Supplies	6 000	
Factory Building Depreciation	30 000	
Factory Taxes	20 000	
Total Factory Overhead Cost		93 000
Cost of Goods Manufactured		$479 000

FIGURE 15-9 Manufacturing statement

Accounting Elements Particular to a Manufacturing Company

The manufacturing statement and the cost of goods sold calculations require several new accounts. These accounts are used to determine the revenue, the costs, and the expenses unique to a manufacturing company. The major difference between a service company and a manufacturing company is the use of cost accounts, which are for direct labour, direct materials, and overhead. These are the key cost elements used to determine the cost of the goods produced by the company.

Direct Materials, Direct Labour, and Overhead

Direct materials become part of the finished product. For an armchair, direct materials include wood, fasteners, and upholstery. The total cost of these types of items comprises the cost of materials.

Direct labour is the cost of all employees who work to change raw materials into finished products.

All production costs other than direct materials and direct labour are overhead costs. These include factory expenses such as heat, water, electricity, maintenance, and cleaning, building costs such as property insurance and property taxes, and indirect materials such fuel for equipment and cleaning supplies.

Subsidiary Ledgers

A manufacturing company may also use subsidiary ledgers and control accounts for accounts receivable and accounts payable. In addition, it may use separate ledgers and control accounts for direct materials, overhead, and direct labour.

Direct materials are items that become part of the finished product.

Direct labour is the cost of all employees who work directly on changing the raw materials into finished products.

Overhead costs include all production costs other than materials and direct labour.

Generally Accepted Accounting Principles and Key Ideas

In this chapter, you have learned the following key ideas:

- A **sole proprietorship** is a business owned by one person who has unlimited responsibility for its debts and legal obligations.
- A **partnership** is a business owned by two or more persons who have unlimited responsibility for its debts and legal obligations.
- A **corporation** has a legal existence of its own.
- A **manufacturing company** makes a product.
- The **manufacturing statement** is a supporting schedule or statement that shows the cost of goods manufactured during a fiscal period.
- **Direct materials** are cost items that become part of the finished product.
- **Direct labour** is the cost of all employees who work directly on changing the raw materials into finished products.
- **Overhead costs** include all production costs other than direct materials and direct labour.

UNIT 37 **CHECK YOUR READING**

Questions

30. Describe the differences among service, merchandising, and manufacturing companies.

31. Prepare equations that provide the net income for a service company, a merchandising company, and a manufacturing company.

32. What is a manufacturing statement?

33. Explain and give examples of direct materials, overhead, and direct labour.

34. Describe the main differences between the cost of goods sold for a merchandising company and for a manufacturing company.

35. What is the difference between direct materials and indirect materials?

UNIT 37 **APPLY YOUR KNOWLEDGE**

Exercises

12. What is the cost of goods sold for each of these manufacturing companies?
Company A
Cost of goods manufactured, $315 000; beginning finished goods inventory, $20 000; ending finished goods inventory, $150 000
Company B
Cost of goods manufactured, $765 000; beginning finished goods inventory, $120 000; ending finished goods inventory, $100 000
Company C
Cost of goods manufactured, $85 000; beginning finished goods inventory, $20 000; ending finished goods inventory, $15 000

13. Calculate the total overhead, direct materials, and direct labour from the following information:
Production line salaries, $30 000; factory cleaning supplies, $500; product raw materials, $20 000; janitor salaries, $5000; factory taxes, $3000; machinery repairs, $700; office computer equipment, $2000

14. Prepare a manufacturing statement for Online GameToy Company for the year ended December 31, 20—, using the following information: Factory building depreciation, $10 000; materials inventory January 1, 20—, $25 000; indirect labour, $20 000; purchases of materials, $125 000; direct labour, $200 000; factory supplies, $6000; factory equipment repairs, $5000; transportation on materials, $6000; factory utilities, $12 000; materials inventory December 31, 20—, $30 000; factory taxes, $20 000

15. Prepare a manufacturing statement for Diane Clothing Company for the year ended December 31, 20—, using the following information: Factory rent, $10 000; materials inventory January 1, 20—, $35 000; indirect labour, $120 000; purchases of materials, $125 000; direct labour, $200 000; factory supplies, $6000; office salaries, $10 000; factory equipment repairs, $5000; transportation on materials, $7000; factory utilities, $4000; materials inventory December 31, 20—, $40 000; factory taxes, $10 000; sales commissions, $38 000

16. Calculate the net income for Peg Manufacturing Company for the year ended December 31, 20—, using the following information: Cost of goods manufactured, $280 000; sales, $600 000; finished goods inventory January 1, 20—, $30 000; selling expenses, $120 000; administrative expenses, $90 000; finished goods inventory December 31, 20—, $40 000

17. Calculate the net income for Western Manufacturing Company for the year ended December 31, 20—, using the following information: Cost of goods manufactured, $490 000; sales, $700 000; finished goods inventory January 1, 20—, $30 000; selling expenses, $100 000; administrative expenses, $110 000; finished goods inventory December 31, 20—, $140 000

 # Computer Accounting

Wireless Technology

The computer's widespread use has brought with it the need for hardware, software, and networking (the linking and sharing of computer files). The provision of this infrastructure is a multibillion-dollar industry. The initial infrastructure was based on a physical, "wired" environment. Now that the wires have been placed, many corporations are seeking to increase their network flexibility and access speed by moving to wireless technologies. Billions of dollars are now being spent to create wireless networks and services.

Connecting to the wireless web will allow companies to access financial and other information any place and at any time. Information can flow to all company employees at the same time without concern for a physical hookup to the company intranet. Integration with voice recognition systems allows increased usability for employees. Information can be accessed from your office, from a client's office, from home, and from virtually any location served by a wireless provider.

Wireless technology may not be for all companies, at least not yet. The quality of services and transmission varies and companies need to be prepared to deal with lost signals and spotty coverage, depending upon their physical location. Service is not available for all types of peripheral devices either. And wireless service may be an added cost to some businesses that have just recently invested in physical infrastructures.

Questions

1. What type of businesses would benefit from wireless technologies?

2. Your Chief Financial Officer (CFO) asks you for an analysis of the advantages and disadvantages of moving your accounting firm to a wireless platform. What would you include in your report? What other types of information would you want prior to answering the CFO's question?

3. What security questions would you want answered prior to moving your accounting functions to a wireless service provider?

Domain Names

Domain names refer to the easy to remember addresses on the Internet, such as Microsoft.com or Nortel.com. These names must be registered to become active. The registered name is associated with a computer on the Internet, so that others can find your site or particular information. The names actually represent a series of numbers, such as 209.57.60.205. Domain names that end with .com, .net, or .org can be registered with any one of many registrars—organizations given the authority by government to process and control Internet addresses. ICANN is a Canadian non-profit corporation that oversees the registration process for domain names.

The domain name contact information is public information. This information is made public so that a contact exists for the clarification of trademark and other laws. If a disagreement exists over who should be entitled to a domain name, the courts will decide who is legally entitled to the name. Domain names can be registered in one-year increments.

Traditionally, names ending in .net are used by network companies, .org by non-profit organizations, .com by business structures such as sole proprietorships, partnerships, and corporations, .edu by educational institutions, and .gov by government agencies. Two-letter domain names, such as .ca or .uk, refer to countries or geographical designations (Canada and the United Kingdom).

The price for registering a domain name will vary from registrar to registrar; some even offer free domain name registration if you agree to subscribe to their other services, such as hosting your web site on their computers. Most prices range from $15 to $50 per year to register a domain name.

Questions

1. Would one type of business structure benefit more than another from having a registered domain name? Why or why not?

2. You and your friend have both started your own companies. Your friend is an artist who makes sculptures and you take care of pets for people who are on holiday. Explain the benefits to each company of having a registered domain name.

3. Your accounting firm specializes in tax preparation and consulting. The firm is incorporated but does not have a registered domain name. Your annual revenue is $3.4 million. You receive an e-mail from the owners of taxpreparationservice.com and tax.com, both offering to sell you their domain names for $50 000. Would you buy either name? If yes, which name would you purchase and why? What other information would help you decide?

COMPUTER ASSIGNMENTS

1. (a) Format a spreadsheet to compare the advantages and disadvantages of each of the three business structures described in this chapter: sole proprietorship, partnership, and corporation.
   (b) Use a word-processing program to create a table to complete the comparison as described in assignment 1a.
   (c) Explain which application was better suited to complete the comparison, the spreadsheet program or the word processor.

2. Format a spreadsheet that calculates the capital ratios based on each of the following partner contributions:
   Partner A contributes $300 000.
   Partner B is considering investing one of the following amounts:
   (a) $100 000   (b) $200 000   (c) $300 000   (d) $400 000

3. Use general ledger software to record the transactions for exercise 1(a) on page 783.

4. Format a spreadsheet to complete exercise 4(a) on page 784 based on the distribution of net income provided.

5. Format a spreadsheet to complete the cost of goods sold section for manufacturing companies listed in exercise 12 on page 799.

www.pearsoned.ca/
principlesofaccounting

WEB EXTENSIONS

Internet Study Guide

➤ Complete the Chapter 15 review.

➤ Complete the Chapter 15 definitions.

➤ Complete the Chapter 15 online test.

Web Links

Visit the Web Links section at the Pearson Education web site to find links to employability skills web sites. Outline those skills that you currently possess.

16 Case Studies

Ownership Profiles

CASE 1

John Tardelli had a successful career as a professional soccer player in Italy and returned to Canada to open a soccer store. John financed the store with a portion of his substantial savings. After three years of operation, the Soccer Shop is moderately successful but is facing tough competition from the "big box" sports stores. John plans to compete with the larger stores by expanding to a total of five stores across the city. He feels that, by expanding, he will benefit from buying larger quantities of merchandise at lower prices. The greater volume of sales will also allow him to lower prices at each of the stores. John plans to use his remaining savings and a small bank loan to finance the expansion project.

The Soccer Shop is currently organized as a sole proprietorship. If the Soccer Shop expands to five locations, what type of business structure would you suggest? Give reasons for your recommendation.

Liability Levels

CASE 2

Sandra Kavanaugh was injured in an automobile accident. While she was proceeding through an intersection her car was hit by a minivan running a red light. The driver of the minivan, owned by General Courier, was clearly at fault. Several witnesses saw the accident and prepared statements for Sandra.

Sandra estimated her financial losses resulting from the accident to be close to $60 000. These included the value of her vehicle, $14 000, lost wages totalling $3000, and an estimated amount for personal expenses and personal suffering. Sandra intends to notify John E. Baylor, the owner of General Courier (a sole proprietorship), of the lawsuit since it was his business vehicle that caused the accident.

Do you think that Sandra will be successful in her lawsuit against John E. Baylor? If Sandra is successful, will John E. Baylor be responsible for coming up with the funds to settle the lawsuit?

Corporate Names

CASE 3

Ivan B. Mahoney is a high school student with an interest in the Internet. He decides to register an Internet domain name so that he can start his own programming company. He finds that the URL www.ibm.on.ca is available. His plan is to register ibm.on.ca for use on the Internet and then to legally incorporate the name as IBM.ON.CA Inc. Do you think the government will accept this name? Why or why not?

CASE 4

Dividing Net Income

A friend asks you to enter into a partnership this summer running a small business. Your friend is a very talented artist and you have a great deal of computer skill. Your friend's idea is to create a CD-ROM of local graphical images that could be sold to local businesses. Your friend only has $1000 of the estimated $5000 required to purchase the equipment needed to produce and market the CD-ROMs.

If you provide the remaining $4000 and the computer expertise, what method would you recommend for dividing any net income or net loss that may result at the end of the summer? Give reasons for your decision.

CASE 5

Corporate Entity

Cory Crawford's small computer company became so successful that he decided to apply for a certificate of incorporation. He paid all the necessary fees, a board of directors was elected, and shares were sold. Unfortunately, as the company flourished Cory became quite ill and later died of natural causes. At the time of his death, Cory owned 5 percent of all outstanding shares in the company. Cory's wife was overcome with grief and blamed the business for contributing to her husband's early death. She demanded that the board of directors sell all the company assets and shut the company down.

Will Cory's wife be able to shut down the company? Explain why or why not.

17 C a r e e r   E d u c a t i o n   A c t i v i t i e s

Selecting Your "Dream Company"

As you have seen in the Career Profiles throughout this textbook, most people who pursue a career in accounting end up working for a variety of companies and performing a range of activities in finance, accounting, or general business management. As you gain experience and skills, you become more marketable within your company and to other companies.

Read the employment advertisement below for a position that may bring with it a salary greater than U.S.$100 000 per year.

For Discussion

(a) Why do you think this company has been described as one of the "100 Best Companies to Work For in America" by *Fortune* magazine?

(b) What accounting skills are required for this position?

(c) Describe the "non-accounting" functions that are outlined in the advertisement.

(d) Create an advertisement for your own "dream job." Include location, salary, skills required, industry, benefits, and other items that would make this the job that rewards years of service in the accounting industry.

Job Title	**Senior Manager**
Education Required	**Masters Degree**
Experience	**Minimum 10 years**
Industry	**Public Accounting**
Location	**San Francisco, California**

One of the world's leading accounting and consulting firms seeks a senior manager. The firm serves multifunctional companies and large public institutions. Among our clients are more than 1000 companies with sales or assets in excess of $1 billion. Based in San Francisco, we employ more than 100 000 people in over 110 countries.

Our firm has been recognized as one of the "100 Best Companies to Work For in America" by *Fortune* magazine this year. The firm offers tremendous opportunities for talented individuals with the desire and motivation to succeed. Our commitment to staff will enable you to realize your potential, while it promotes a balanced life and provides you with responsibility and challenges. You will discover we strive to consistently exceed the expectations of our clients.

You will have the opportunity to work with a team of professionals, delivering creative and innovative solutions to our clients through a dynamic process developed from within the organization. Professionals at all levels take pride in generating and developing solutions that are shared throughout the firm.

We are an equal opportunity firm. We recruit, compensate, and promote without regard to race, religion, creed, color, marital status, or disability.

This position requires 10+ years of accounting experience and familiarity with the consulting process, in addition to the professionalism necessary for the effective analysis and resolution of problems, and communication of new solutions for our clients. The successful candidate will be an expert communicator who is comfortable with a variety of multimedia presentation tools.

As a senior manager, you will have responsibility for a multimillion-dollar budget. You will supervise the firm's multinational consulting division. In addition, you will be responsible for the development and motivation of staff, and provide leadership, direction, and career guidance.

We offer excellent benefits, including extended holidays and relocation assistance.

Career Profile •

Scott Carmichael of Brantford, Ontario, didn't discover that he had an interest in business until his final year of high school, when he took accounting and economics courses. After high school he took part-time jobs, including becoming a waiter, to help pay for a three-year small business management course at Conestoga College in Kitchener. This program included courses in accounting, marketing, psychology, organizational behaviour, economics, and resource development.

During his second year of college, Scott began a small lawn cutting service, College Care. He looked at this as a way to make some extra money while attending school. His focus on client service and retention helped him develop a larger customer base each year. At the end of his college program, he decided to register the company as "A Cut Above" and he officially became a small business owner.

As a small business owner, he handled all aspects of the business, including marketing, advertising, human resources, maintenance and repair, and bookkeeping. As the company expanded, Scott required an accounting software package to keep track of the company finances. He trained himself in an accounting application called Mind Your Own Business (MYOB).

Scott enjoys being his own boss and setting his own hours. He enjoys not having to answer to anyone but himself. However, he has also found that running his own business requires great discipline and involves long hours with no guaranteed income. His selected business is seasonal, meaning that he has to budget his money to pay bills during the winter season. Running a small business means that Scott has no guaranteed retirement plan and no benefits. If he becomes sick, he makes no money. To compensate for some of the risks associated with the business, Scott has started a snow removal service during the winter. Many of his summer clients continue on for the winter service. He employs four part-time employees during the busy periods.

Scott has also become involved with the family business, Brant Bagging Inc., which manufactures bag-filling machines. He handles the basic bookkeeping functions for the company, including invoicing and GST remittances. The company contracts out the other major accounting functions.

Overall, Scott enjoys being in control of his own destiny and, although his goals are taking longer to achieve than he first planned, he is on his way to making them come true.

For Discussion

(a) What are the reasons that Scott likes being a small business owner?

(b) What are the disadvantages that come with a small business such as the one started by Scott?

(c) What type of accounting functions did Scott's college course prepare him for?

(d) What was meant by "he has also found that running his own business requires great discipline"?

(e) How important are security and benefits to you? What characteristics do you feel are needed for someone to become a successful sole proprietor?

account: a form in which changes caused by transactions are recorded

account form balance sheet: a balance sheet that lists the assets on the left side and the liabilities and owner's equity on the right side

accounting cycle: the set of accounting procedures performed in each accounting period

accounting period: the period of time covered by the financial statements; may be a week, a month, a quarter, a year, or any other regular period of time; also known as the "fiscal period"

Accounts Payable: the account that shows the total amount owed to creditors for the purchase of goods or services by the business

Accounts Payable control: the account that replaces the individual creditor accounts in the general ledger

accounts payable ledger: a subsidiary ledger that contains only creditor accounts in alphabetical order

Accounts Receivable: the account that shows the total amount due from customers

accounts receivable age analysis: a list of all customers, showing the balance owed by each and how long the balance has been owed

accounts receivable collection period: the time it takes to collect accounts receivable

Accounts Receivable control: the account that replaces the individual customer accounts in the general ledger

accounts receivable ledger: a subsidiary ledger that contains only customer accounts in alphabetical order

accrual basis of accounting: the system under which revenue is recorded when earned and expenses are recorded when incurred

accrued expenses: expenses that are owed but not yet recorded in the books

accrued revenue: revenue that has been earned but not yet recorded in the books

accrued salaries: salaries earned but not yet paid

adjustments: accounting changes recorded to ensure that all accounts have correct balances before the financial statements are prepared

Administrative Expense: the account used to record money spent in the general operation of a business

assets: items of value owned by a business or person

audit: a periodic, systematic check of accounting records and procedures by an accountant

bad debts: uncollectible amounts owed by customers

bad debts expense: the loss due to uncollectible accounts

balance-column ledger account: a type of ledger account that provides a running balance on each line

balance sheet: a formal financial statement that lists assets, liabilities, and personal equity (net worth) at a specific date; also called a "statement of financial position"

balance sheet equation: the basic equation underlying double-entry accounting that provides the financial position of a person or a business in this form: Assets = Liabilities + Owner's Equity

balance sheet method of estimating bad debts: a method that uses a percentage of accounts receivable as a basis for estimating bad debts expense

bank credit memo: a source document sent by a bank to indicate that money has been added to a customer's account

bank debit memo: a source document sent by a bank to indicate that money has been withdrawn from a customer's account

batch journalizing: recording the total of a number of source documents of one type in a single journal entry; see also *journalizing*

board of directors: a group of persons who are responsible for the operation of a corporation; elected by shareholders

book value: the cost of an asset minus the accumulated depreciation; determined by subtracting the accumulated depreciation from the cost of the asset

budget: a financial plan for a specific accounting period; see also *capital budget, master budget,* and *sales budget*

budgeted balance sheet: an estimate of the assets, liabilities, and owners' equity at the end of the period

budgeted income statement: an estimate of the revenue, expenses, and net income or net loss for the financial period

business entity principle: says that each business is considered a separate unit or entity, and the financial data for the business must be kept separate from the owner's personal financial data

business transaction: an exchange of things of value

cancelled cheques: cheques that have been cashed by the bank

capital budget: a plan that estimates the equipment and building items to be purchased during the period

capital cost allowance: the income tax term for *depreciation*

cash basis of accounting: a system that recognizes revenue and expenses on a cash basis, not an accrual basis; expenses are recorded only when cash is paid and revenue is recorded only when cash is received.

cash payments journal: a multi-column journal used in a special journal system to record all payments made

cash receipts journal: a multicolumn journal used in a special journal system to record all money received

cash sales slip: a source document used to record a cash sale

Cash Short and Over: the account used to record shortages and overages of cash

chart of accounts: a list of all account names and numbers in the general ledger

classified balance sheet: a balance sheet that lists items in special categories, such as current assets and fixed assets

classified income statement: an income statement with main sections for revenue, cost of goods sold, operating expenses, administrative expenses, and selling expenses

closing the books: the process by which revenue and expense accounts are reduced to zero at the end of each accounting period, so they are ready to accumulate data for the next accounting period

columnar journal: an alternative journal form designed with special columns for entries to accounts used often and an Other Accounts column for entries to accounts for which a special column is not provided; also known as a "combination journal" or "synoptic journal"

commission: a method of payment to workers based on a percentage of the sales they make

common-size statements: financial statements that show key items in terms of percentages, without dollar values

comparative financial statements: statements that illustrate changes to financial data over several years

compound entry: an entry that has more than one debit or more than one credit

compulsory payroll deductions: mandatory deductions taken by an employer from an employee's gross earnings, e.g., income tax, CPP, and EI; deductions that are governed by provincial or federal legislation and must be forwarded to the appropriate government agency by the company

condensed statements: financial statements that provide single totals for key items

conservatism, principle of: says that, where there are acceptable alternatives, the accountant must select the one that will result in lower net income and net assets

contra account: an account whose balance reduces the value of the account it describes; used to arrive at the book value of assets; examples are Accumulated Depreciation—Building, and Allowance for Bad Debts (used to determine a realistic valuation for Accounts Receivable); also known as a "valuation account"

control account: a general ledger account, the balance of which equals the total of the account balances in a particular subsidiary ledger; for every subsidiary ledger, there is a control account in the general ledger.

corporation: a business that has a legal existence of its own, so the owners' liability is limited to their investment in the corporation

cost principle: says that assets must be shown on the balance sheet using the cost of their acquisition or construction

credit: the accounting term used for the right side of the account

credit invoice: a source document issued by the seller to indicate the amount of credit allowed to a customer for returned or defective goods

credit union: a non-profit organization similar to a bank that is operated by the employees of a company or organization

creditor: a person or business that has extended credit or loaned money

current assets: cash or other assets that are converted into cash in the ordinary course of business, usually within one year

current liabilities: liabilities due to be paid within a year

current ratio: an expression of the relationship between current assets and current liabilities; obtained by dividing total current assets by total current liabilities and expressing the result as a ratio

cycle billing: a method of spreading the preparation and mailing of a large number of monthly statements evenly over a month; used by companies with large numbers of customers

data entry sheet: a sheet on which to list the information to be entered into a computerized accounting system, i.e., the accounts to be debited and credited, the amount, and the explanation of the transaction

debit: the accounting term used for the left side of the account

debit cards: encoded cards provided by financial institutions and used by their account holders to withdraw cash from their accounts or to transfer funds to other parties electronically rather than by paper cheque; see also *electronic funds transfer*

debt ratio: an expression of the relationship between total debts and total assets

declining-balance depreciation: a method that allocates a greater amount of depreciation to the first years of an asset's life; used for income tax purposes

deductions: amounts subtracted from an employee's gross earnings; see also *compulsory payroll deductions*, and *voluntary payroll deductions*.

Delivery Expense: the account used to record the cost of delivering merchandise to customers

depreciation: the allocation of the cost of a fixed asset to the fiscal periods in which it is used; "capital cost allowance" is the income tax term for depreciation. See also *declining-balance depreciation* and *straight-line depreciation*

direct materials: items that become part of the finished product

direct labour: the cost of all employees who work directly on changing raw materials into finished products

direct posting: the recording of information from source documents directly into the subsidiary ledger accounts

dividends: the portion of a corporation's net income paid to its shareholders out of retained earnings

division of labour: the idea that accounting clerks can efficiently process larger amounts of accounting data when they specialize in performing one specific task

double-entry accounting: a system of financial record keeping in which debit entries must equal credit entries for each transaction

Drawings: an equity account used to record the withdrawal of assets by the owner

electronic funds transfer (EFT): a system of cash exchange in which *debit cards* are used to access bank account balances using a secure network system

employee's earnings record: a form used to record all the payroll information for an employee for one year

endorsement: the signature on the back of a cheque of the person or company depositing the cheque; see also *restrictive endorsement*

equities: claims against assets

equity ratio: an expression of the relationship between owner's equity and total assets

expenses: the costs incurred to generate revenue; separate expense accounts are used for each major type of expense.

extension: the quantity multiplied by the price

fiscal period: see *accounting period*

fixed assets: assets that have a long life (over one year); also may be termed "capital assets" or "plant and equipment"

general journal: a book of original entry that provides a chronological record of all transactions, including the accounts debited and credited; where transactions are first recorded

general partnership: a partnership in which all partners have unlimited liability

Generally Accepted Accounting Principles (GAAP): standard accounting rules and guidelines

Goods and Services Tax (GST): a 7 percent federal tax charged on most sales of services or merchandise within Canada; must be added to the selling price by manufacturers, wholesalers, and retailers of merchandise, and by service providers

gross earnings: the total earnings of an employee before *deductions*

Harmonized Sales Tax (HST): a combination of the federal GST and provincial retail sales tax that has the same operating rules as the GST

income statement: a formal financial statement that summarizes revenue and expenses to determine the *net income* or *net loss* for a stated period of time

income statement method of estimating bad debts: uses past experience as a basis to calculate the percentage of sales estimated to be bad debts

indirect posting: the recording of source documents in the general journal, then the posting of entries to both the general ledger control accounts and the individual subsidiary ledger accounts

input tax credit: the amount of GST or HST a business pays when it buys goods or services

internal accounting control: used to protect assets and to ensure the reliability of the records and statements

journal: a chronological (in order of date) record of all of a company's transactions; see also *general journal, columnar journal, sales journal, purchases journal, cash payments journal,* and *cash receipts journal*

journalizing: recording transactions in a journal

ledger: a group of accounts that may be in the form of a book containing pages for each account in a manual accounting system, or may be stored on disk or tape for computerized accounting systems

liabilities: the debts of a business or a person

limited partnership: a form of business organization that has two types of partners: general partners and limited partners; limited partners have limited personal liability. See *general partnership*

liquidity order: the order in which assets can be converted to cash

liquidity ratios: indicators of a firm's ability to pay current liabilities without having to borrow funds or sell assets

long-term liabilities: liabilities not due to be paid for at least a year

manufacturing company: a business that converts raw materials into saleable products

manufacturing statement: a supporting schedule or statement that shows the cost of goods manufactured during a period

master budget: an overall budget for a company

matching principle: says that expenses for an accounting period should be matched with the revenue generated during the same period to derive an accurate net income for that period

matching process for purchase documents: the comparison of details on the purchase order, purchase invoice, and receiving report to see they all agree before an invoice is paid

materiality, principle of: says that information that could affect the decisions of users of financial statements should be included when financial statements are prepared

maturity date: the date when liabilities are due to be paid; liabilities are listed on the balance sheet according to their maturity date.

merchandise: goods bought for resale, e.g., clothes, bicycles

Merchandise Inventory: the account that records the value of merchandise on hand for sale to customers

merchandise turnover: the number of times a company's average inventory is sold during an accounting period:

$$\frac{\text{Cost of Goods Sold}}{\text{Average Inventory}} = \frac{\text{Merchandise}}{\text{Turnover}}$$

merchandising company: a business that sells merchandise to customers; either a wholesaler or a retailer

net earnings: the balance remaining after *compulsory payroll deductions* and *voluntary payroll deductions* have been subtracted from *gross earnings*

net income: the difference between revenue and expenses when revenue is greater than expenses; increases owners' equity

net loss: the difference between revenue and expenses when expenses are greater than revenue; decreases owners' equity

NSF cheque: a cheque that cannot be cashed by the bank because there are not sufficient funds in the customer's bank account

objectivity, principle of: says that accounting records should be based on the objective evidence provided by source documents to support the values used in recording transactions

one-write system: a manual accounting system consisting of a one-write board that aligns and holds in place specially treated accounting forms so that anything written on the top form (e.g., information from a sales invoice) is transferred automatically to forms placed underneath (e.g., a customer's account and a journal), hence the term "one-write system"

opening entry: the journal entry to record the assets, liabilities, and owner's equity when a business first begins operations

order of liquidity: the order in which current assets will be converted into cash; current assets are listed in order of liquidity.

outstanding cheques: cheques issued but not cashed

overhead costs: all production costs other than materials and direct labour

owner's equity: the owner's claim against the assets of the company

partnership: a business owned by two or more persons

partnership agreement: a document that outlines the rights and responsibilities of the partners, and states how net incomes or net losses are to be shared

payroll: a list of employees and the amount of money to be paid to them

payroll journal: the form used to record gross earnings, deductions, and net earnings for all employees; also known as a "payroll register"

PD7A: the official remittance form for payroll deductions sent to Canada Customs and Revenue Agency (CCRA)

periodic inventory method: a system of inventory valuation that uses a physical count of inventory at the end of the fiscal period; *Purchases, Purchases Returns and Allowances*, and Purchases Discounts accounts are used to record the value of merchandise inventory acquired during the period.

permanent accounts: asset, liability, and owner's Capital accounts; see also *temporary accounts*

perpetual inventory method: a system of inventory valuation that requires a continuous record be kept of all merchandise on hand, with changes in inventory value to be recorded directly in the Merchandise Inventory account

personal net worth: the difference between the cost of items owned and debts owed; also referred to as "personal equity"

petty cash fund: an amount of cash used to make small payments

petty cash voucher: a signed authorization for small cash payments

physical inventory: a count of all goods on hand

piece rate: a method of paying workers based on the number of units the worker produces

point-of-sale terminal: an electronic cash register linked to a computer by a secure network

post-closing trial balance: a trial balance that is prepared after closing entries have been posted; contains only asset, liability, and capital accounts

posting: the transfer of information from a journal to the general ledger and any subsidiary ledgers

prepaid expenses: expense payments made in advance

profit: the increase in owner's equity resulting from the successful operation of a business

proprietorship: a business owned by one person; also known as a "sole proprietorship"

purchase invoice: a source document received for each purchase on credit; a bill

purchase order: a source document used to order goods from a supplier

purchase requisition: a form sent to the purchasing department requesting that goods or services be ordered

Purchases: the account used to record the cost of merchandise purchased for resale

purchases journal: a special journal used to record purchases on account

Purchases Returns and Allowances: the account used by the buyer to record the return of goods; often called a "contra cost account"

Quick Method: requires small businesses to collect the full GST/HST, but does not require them to keep track of *input tax credits* to calculate the amount to remit to the federal government; multiply sales plus GST/HST by a specified percentage (e.g., 5 percent for GST or 10 percent for HST) and remit that amount.

quick ratio: the ratio of the current assets easily converted to cash to the current liabilities

receiving report: a form that lists and describes all goods received

reconciliation statement: brings the bank's records into agreement with the depositor's records

registered pension plan (R.P.P.): a private pension plan registered with the federal government, contributions to the plan being an eligible income tax deduction

replenishing petty cash: bringing the total currency in the petty cash fund up to the original amount

restrictive endorsement: an instruction on the back of a cheque to control what happens to the funds, e.g., "For Deposit Only"

Retained Earnings: an equity account showing the balance of undistributed net income in a corporation

revenue: amounts earned by the business from the sale of goods or services during routine operations

sales budget: an estimate of the goods to be sold and the total revenue to be realized from sales

sales discount: a discount offered to a customer to encourage early payment of account balances

sales invoice: a source document prepared for each credit sale

sales journal: a special journal used to record sales on account (credit sales)

Sales Returns and Allowances: the account used by the seller to record merchandise returned by a customer; a contra revenue account

schedule: a supporting statement that details an item on a main statement

schedule of accounts payable: proves the mathematical accuracy of the accounts payable ledger; its total must equal the balance of the Accounts Payable control account.

schedule of accounts receivable: proves the mathematical accuracy of the accounts receivable ledger; its total must equal the balance of the Accounts Receivable control account.

separation of duties: a key component of all accounting control systems, used to discourage fraud and theft as well as to ensure the accuracy of accounting data; one employee verifies the accuracy of another employee's work.

service company: a business that sells a service, e.g., Internet access

share certificate: a form issued by a corporation indicating the number of shares owned

shareholder: an owner of shares in a corporation

source document: the original document showing that a transaction has occurred

special journal system: uses separate multicolumn journals for similar transactions that recur frequently

statement of account: a form sent to customers that shows charges, amounts credited, and the balance owing

statement of earnings and deductions: provides employees with information about their earnings and deductions for a pay period

statement of owner's equity: an outline of the changes in owner's equity for the accounting period

statement of retained earnings: a complete description of changes in the Retained Earnings account

straight-line depreciation: allocates the same amount of depreciation to each fiscal period

subsidiary ledger: a group of accounts of one type usually organized in alphabetical order

T1: the personal income tax return completed by Canadians

T4 slip: a form that provides information on an employee's total earnings and deductions for the year

TD1 form: completed by an employee to allow the employer to determine the income tax to be deducted each pay period; shows non-refundable tax credits

taxable earnings: the earnings that remain after non-taxable deductions; used to determine the income tax deduction

temporary accounts: revenue and expense accounts; see also *permanent accounts*

time-period principle: the definition and consistent use of the same accounting period

Transportation-in: the account used to record the transportation charges on merchandise purchased

trial balance: a list of ledger account balances; total debits must equal total credits; proves mathematical accuracy of ledger

unearned revenue: revenue received but not yet earned

valuation account: see *contra account*

vertical analysis: the presentation of key items on a financial statement as a percentage of a major item, e.g., Advertising Expense as a percentage of Sales

voluntary payroll deductions: deductions taken from gross earnings at the employee's request and forwarded to the appropriate agency, e.g., union dues, supplementary medical premiums

voucher cheque: a two-part cheque with an attached statement describing payment details

work sheet: a device that organizes accounting data for preparation of financial statements

working capital: total current assets minus total current liabilities

I N D E X

CREDITS

PHOTOS
p. 1 EyeWire; p. 4 © SuperStock; p. 35 Bob Carroll/*Windsor Star*; p. 66 PhotoDisc; p.97 IBM Canada; p. 108 PhotoEdit/David Young-Wolff; p.166 Courtesy of Elaine Pitcher; p. 200 Courtesy of David Galotta; p. 270 Courtesy of Mary Lou Mulvey; p. 278 PhotoDisc; p. 408 Courtesy of Shahe Avedissian; p. 447 Courtesy of Mike Simpson; p. 519 Courtesy of Liset Stanton; p. 577 PhotoDisc; p. 612 © SuperStock; p. 649 PhotoDisc; p. 704 PhotoDisc; p. 766 Courtesy of Karen Power.

TEXT AND SCREEN CAPTURES
p. 96 Logo courtesy of Canadian Tire Corporation. Text courtesy of Mr. Ken MacEachern of Canadian Tire Store in Ottawa; pp. 154–156 Courtesy of AccPac International; p. 165 Ontario Ministry of Finance; pp. 186–187 Reprinted with permission from Microsoft Corporation; p. 187 Courtesy of DacEasy International; p. 260 Courtesy of DacEasy International; pp. 319–320 © 2001 Her Majesty the Queen in Right of Canada. Represented by the Minister of National Revenue. All Rights Reserved; p. 323 Ontario Government Ministry of Revenue, Sales Tax Branch; pp. 337–339 Courtesy of the Scotiabank; p. 341 Courtesy of the Scotiabank; p. 349 Courtesy of CGA, Vancouver, BC; p. 396 Courtesy of Oracle Small Business; p. 398 Courtesy of AccPac International; pp. 433–435 Courtesy of DacEasy International; p. 437 Courtesy of Canada Care Medical; p. 488 Courtesy of the ScotiaBank; p. 494 Courtesy of the Scotiabank; p. 511 Courtesy of Accpac International; p. 524 Courtesy of the Scotiabank; p. 535 Courtesy of the Scotiabank; Courtesy of the Scotiabank; p. 553 Courtesy of the Scotiabank; pp. 563–564 Courtesy of the Scotiabank; pp. 569–570 Courtesy of Intuit Canada Ltd.; pp. 580–583 Courtesy of the Scotiabank; p. 711 Courtesy of the Scotiabank; pp. 715–716 © 2001 Her Majesty the Queen in Right of Canada; Represented by the Minister of National Revenue. All Rights Reserved; p. 720–721 © 2001 Her Majesty the Queen in Right of Canada. Represented by the Minister of National Revenue. All Rights Reserved; pp. 723–724 © 2001 Her Majesty the Queen in Right of Canada. Represented by the Minister of National Revenue. All Rights Reserved; pp. 731–737 © 2001 Her Majesty the Queen in Right of Canada. Represented by the Minister of National Revenue. All Rights Reserved; pp. 740 & 746 © 2001 Her Majesty the Queen in Right of Canada. Represented by the Minister of National Revenue of Canada. All Rights Reserved; pp. 756–757 Courtesy of AccPak International.